Relevance of Duties in the Contemporary World

Raman Mittal · Kshitij Kumar Singh
Editors

Relevance of Duties in the Contemporary World

With Special Emphasis on Gandhian Thought

Springer

Editors
Raman Mittal
Campus Law Centre, Faculty of Law
University of Delhi
Delhi, India

Kshitij Kumar Singh
Campus Law Centre, Faculty of Law
University of Delhi
Delhi, India

ISBN 978-981-19-1835-3 ISBN 978-981-19-1836-0 (eBook)
https://doi.org/10.1007/978-981-19-1836-0

This Springer imprint is published by the registered company Springer Nature Singapore Pte Ltd.
The registered company address is: 152 Beach Road, #21-01/04 Gateway East, Singapore 189721, Singapore

Preface

Rights and duties complement each other and deserve equal protection, enforcement and recognition. However, modern legal practices adopt a right-centric approach in most countries. As a result, duties have remained obscured within the legal systems of the world. Even in academic literature, duties find less space than rights, and a coherent relationship between rights and duties is missing in contemporary practices. Historically, a country's sociocultural and political set-up has constantly influenced protection and promotion of rights and duties. Right-based revolutions, particularly human rights revolutions, empowered vulnerable groups to raise their voice for their rights and impacted countries' policy decisions. The realisation of duties by citizens and the state helps enforce rights as well. Critics think that a duty-based regime might dilute the relevance of rights and give the state power to suppress them. However, it is the coherence between rights and duties that best protects both because of the inherent complementary relationship between rights and duties—my right is other's duty and vice versa.

The book reflects the relevance of duties in the contemporary world with a particular focus on Gandhian thoughts. It provides an insight into the philosophy of duties, analysing the east-west jurisprudence on duty and how various jurisdictions approach the right–duty relationships based on socio-economic, cultural and political influences. A duty-based jurisprudence becomes more relevant in the testing times of COVID-19 and helps significantly in finding solutions to contemporary problems such as racial tension and the refugee problem. The book discusses the duties of citizens and the State provided under the Indian Constitution, focusing on fundamental duties. However, duty-based jurisprudence in India and the Gandhian philosophy goes beyond fundamental duties and trigger a sense of duty and responsibility in spheres such as intellectual property (IP). The book is divided into four parts, presenting four significant aspects of duties.

The first part concentrates on the jurisprudence of duties from the perspectives of East and West to bring forth and analyse the commonalities and differences. It also explains Gandhi's contribution to the conceptualisation of duties with his cardinal principles such as *swaraj*, *satyagrah*, *sarvodaya* and others.

In Chapter 1, the authors examine the relevance of duties in East-West jurisprudence by analysing countries' sociopolitical and cultural set-up and a more pervasive wave of globalisation and liberalisation. It emphasises the significance of the Gandhian concept of duty to help find solutions to contemporary problems and a need to establish a coherent relationship between rights and duties by paying equal heed to both. It recognises the need to appreciate the different approaches to the duties of citizens and the State. In Chapter 2, the author compares Gandhi's deontology of justice with that of Kant and Hegel and emphasises that the former advocates for a broader or wholesome approach to justice, transcending its normative boundaries and delving into the sociocultural ethos, moving above the methodological individualism and relying on duty or action. Chapter 3 analyses the interrelationship between two competing and contrasting concepts, individual and community interests, from the perspective of East and West, and explains how Gandhian thought over the same acts as a guiding force to harmonise these interests and bridge the gap between the two.

In Chapter 4, the authors explain the interdependence of rights and duties with the help of fundamental duties embodied in the Constitution of India. Considering duties as the building blocks of rights, the authors stress a constant realisation of duties for adequate protection and enforcement of rights by contextualising Gandhian thought that duties are the precursor to rights. Chapter 5 focuses on 'following duties to secure rights' from a Gandhian perspective. It explains how duties and rights emerged from the notion of *'dharm'* by analysing the right–duty interrelationship based on jurisprudence, governance and policy. Taking the discourse forward, Chapter 6 reiterates the importance of duties in securing rights by comparing and contrasting Gandhian thought of duty with western scholars. The author also connects contemporary pressing issues such as environmental damage, public property and disharmony among people with the non-performance of duties. Chapter 7 examines the emergence of individualism against communalism, discusses its historical roots and explores the possibilities of convergence of the two in the Gandhian thoughts of *swaraj* and *sarvodaya.*

Part II focuses on the duties in the contemporary world (including the COVID-affected world) and contains chapters that reflect the current policies and politics of duties, examining the significance of duties in making the world a better place to live.

In Chapter 8, the author examines the right–duty relationship in the USA in the year 2020, plagued with racial tensions, the coronavirus and the issue of free and fair elections. The author contextualises Gandhian views on rights, duties and responsibilities and their possible application in the USA. Chapter 9 connects Gandhi's political philosophy based on *sarvodaya* (progress of all), *satyagrah* (truth force) and *dharm* (duty) with the problems of refugees in India. It explains how his philosophy and experience with refugees during the partition in the 1940s can guide the future refugee policy in India and help interpret the rights of refugees. Against the narrow understanding of Gandhi's idea of *swaraj* limited to colonial context, the authors in Chapter 10 explore an alternate regime of 'rights' and 'state' relevant to the contemporary situation in India using Gandhi's thoughts on *swaraj*, duties, rights and *dharm*. Chapter 11 analyses Gandhi's views on rights and duties, which see rights through the lens of duties and prioritise duties over rights. The authors examine the viability of using duties for social change in contemporary India. The author in Chapter 12 critically analyses the relevance of Gandhian deontological prescription of individual-centric development based on duties and Kant's categorical imperative of duty in the COVID-19 pandemic period. Finally, the author explores the possibility of making public health more robust with distributive healthcare justice.

Part III undertakes an analysis of 'Duties under the Indian Constitution', exploring the relevance of duties and Gandhian philosophy, especially in the context of Fundamental Duties and Directive Principles of State Policy. It also examines the relevance of Gandhian philosophy in the context of prison reforms, restorative justice, environmental jurisprudence and gender perspective on women.

Chapter 13 reflects the reciprocal relationship between certain obligations ordained in Part-IV Directive Principles of State Policy and Fundamental Duties under Part-IV A of the Indian Constitution. The authors established the correlation between Gandhian interpretation of *dharm* with *rajdharm* (duty of the king or the State) and *swadharm* (duty of an individual). They argued that coherence between these forms a theoretical premise where fundamental duties and DPSP converge to constitute a welfare state and egalitarian society. Emphasising the connection between the Gandhian concept of duty and the Indian Constitution, Chapter 14 analyses the jurisprudential basis of duty, right–duty correlation and reflection of Gandhian philosophy on fundamental duties. Continuing further, Chapter 15 correlates the duties in the Constitution with the Gandhian philosophy of *swaraj*, *sarvodaya*, *swadharm* and *satyagrah* and examines its relevance in modern times. Chapter 16 discusses the dichotomy between 'secularism and secularisation' constructed through the Gandhian philosophy of the secular state. The author decodes Gandhi's thoughts on secularism in the light of his two contrasting approaches: first, religion and spirituality; second, secularisation, multiculturalism and diversity of Indian society.

The authors of Chapter 17 conceptualise Gandhi's views on education and examine how it has been followed in the Indian education system through constitutional, legislative and judicial initiatives and National Education Policy 2020. Chapter 18 focuses on the Gandhian philosophy of prison reform and the concept of open prisons. The authors stress reinforcing duties essential for democracy by developing a sense of civic responsibility. The authors of Chapter 19 explore the gap between the theoretical and practical aspects of restorative justice in crime prevention in India. They argue that the alignment of restorative justice with Gandhian principles and teachings can bridge this gap. Chapter 20 examines the relevance of Gandhian philosophy and principles centred on basic needs, respect for nature and natural resources in addressing environmental issues in India. It also explains the scope of the fundamental duty of citizens to protect the environment recognised under the Indian Constitution. In continuation, the author of Chapter 21 throws light upon the development of environmental jurisprudence in India through the constitutional, legislative and judicial approaches and Gandhian philosophy. It focuses on fundamental duty contained in Article 51(A)(g) and the directive principles of state policy contained in Article 48A dealing with protecting the environment. Chapter 22 analyses Gandhi's views on the rights and duties of women in the light of Article 51A(e) of the Constitution, which enunciates to renounce practices derogatory to the dignity of women.

Part IV explores the duties, obligations and responsibilities in the intellectual property rights (IPR) regime and contextualises the relevance of Gandhian philosophy on trusteeship and property in the IP context. It explains how Indian jurisprudence on IPR developed through legislation and judicial decisions, and Gandhian philosophy contributes to exploring the duty-based approach in the global IPR regime.

Chapter 23 explains the paradox between Bhagavad Gita's inconsequential approach to duty and right-based legal systems such as those associated with intellectual property rights that focus on consequences. The author maintains that reconciling these paradoxical pairs needs an understanding of the right-based legal system in terms of duties and connects Gandhi's interpretation of Geeta that echoes this prescription. Finally, the author explores to what extent 'make without take' is applicable in the modern economy. In Chapter 24, the author exhumes explores and examines the dormant aspect of IPR. He connects the right holders' IPRs with the duty to share, focusing on the duty at the licencing stage. He explores the duties of all the stakeholders in the IP domain, including the creator, user, licensee and the State. In Chapter 25, the authors analyse the nature of the IP regime, which according to authors, tilts more towards the public interest. They argue that such a regime favours those entities and individuals that need access to essential goods such as medicines, seeds and goods. They also analyse the influence of Gandhi's teachings on the Indian IP system. In Chapter 26, the author explores the scope and relevance of duties, obligations and responsibilities under the patent system based on patent policy generally and in the context of the COVID-19 pandemic. The author undertakes an analysis of the property vs. policy debate relating to patents to appreciate the difference between patents and other properties. The author contextualises Gandhi's perspective on trusteeship while exploring the broader goals of patent policy. The author emphasises that an appreciation of duties and obligations in the patent system may produce a more pragmatic result.

We sincerely acknowledge the contribution of all the contributing authors of the book, Springer Nature, Ms. Nupoor Singh, Ms. Jayarani Premkumar, Ms. Jayanthi Jayarani and the whole publishing unit of Springer Nature for their constant support. We hope the book will trigger great interest among the readers to deliberate on the numerous dimensions of duties and help building up coherence in the right–duty relationship.

New Delhi
18 September 2022

Raman Mittal
Kshitij Kumar Singh

Contents

About the Editors

Raman Mittal is a Professor at Campus Law Centre, Faculty of Law, University of Delhi. He holds LL.M. and Ph.D. from Panjab University, Chandigarh together with M.S.S. from International Space University, France. His research interests include Intellectual Property, Contract and International Laws. He has published extensively in national and international journals and has also authored many books. Prof. Mittal has visited various national and international legal institutions in the capacity of visiting faculty; the prominent being University of Oxford, Max Planck Institute of Intellectual Property and Competition Law, Munich and University of Washington, Seattle. Prof. Mittal has advised the Ministry of Human Resource Development, Government of India in treaty negotiations and has been a member of the Drafting Committee that was tasked with the drafting of Copyright Rules, 2013.

Kshitij Kumar Singh is an Assistant Professor at Campus Law Centre, Faculty of Law, University of Delhi. He earned his LL.M. and Ph.D. degrees from Banaras Hindu University and received Canadian Commonwealth Scholarship Asia-Pacific 2010. As a Visiting Researcher, he visited the Faculty of Law, University of Western Ontario, Canada, in 2009 and 2010. His primary area of interest is the intersection of law and biotechnology, particularly ethical, legal and policy issues relating to biomedical technology. He published his first book, *Biotechnology and Intellectual Property Rights: Legal and Social Implications*, with Springer in 2015, followed by the book as an editor and author, *Policy Issues in GM Crops: A Global Perspective*, with Academic Press, Elsevier (2020). Currently, he is working on a book project, *Legal and Policy Framework of Precision Medicine*, with Prof. Shubha Ghosh, Syracuse University College of Law, New York. He has also published numerous articles, reviews and book chapters on various aspects of intellectual property law and biotechnology law with esteemed publishers including Oxford, Edward Elgar, Cambridge, Elsevier and Springer Nature.

He has been invited as a resource person and speaker in national and international workshops, conferences, seminars and government consultative groups (notably, University of Utah, Texas A&M University, Indian Patent Office, RGNIIPM, ONGC, RIS, DIPP and DPIIT, Ministry of Commerce and Industry). On 18th December

2021, he was conferred with the "International Teaching Excellence Award 2021 in Intellectual Property Law" by the Center for Professional Advancement (A Unit of IMRF registered with Government of India NITI Aayog). Recently he has been invited as the Visiting Researcher by the Centre for Advanced Studies of Biomedical Innovation Law (CeBIL), University of Copenhagen, Denmark (The visit is funded by the Novo Nordisk Foundation).

Part I
Jurisprudence of Duties

Chapter 1
Relevance of Duty Through the Lens of Gandhi and East–West Jurisprudence

Kshitij Kumar Singh and Subham Kumar Jain

1 Introduction

In the right-duty discourse, the discussion on duties has been disproportionate to rights for a long time. Though scholars insist that duties are inalienable part of rights, the focus has been predominantly on rights that have an explicit exposition in the law given the implicit nature of duties. Many scholars believe that a duty-based approach to the contemporary problems may assist in the better enforcement of rights conforming to the ethos and values of society. Approaches to duties vary from one continent to another and from one country to another, based on social, political and cultural setups. Scholars vary in their approaches; many scholars pay more heed to rights than duties, considering duties as correlative of rights; others like Kant and Duguit emphasise duties, based on categorical imperative and social solidarity theories. As a part of Hindu tradition, in India, *dharm* treats rights and duties as an integral concept. The old scriptures, such as Bhagavad Gita, emphasise the performance of duties without expecting results (non-consequential approach to duty). However, despite being defined as a duty-driven society, the original draft of the Constitution of India did not contain any provision relating to the duties of citizens though it contained a dedicated chapter on the fundamental rights of citizens and non-citizens. Therefore, confusion persists as to the non-inclusion of duties of citizens in the original draft of Indian Constitution. It raises the question, whether it was due to the perception that every right has an implicit duty and there was no need to mention it or give more weight to rights?

For instance based on the political setup, in socialist countries, duties were put up in a hierarchal order. Allegedly, the State was pushing the citizens to follow their

K. K. Singh (✉)
Assistant Professor, Campus Law Centre, Faculty of Law, University of Delhi, Delhi, India
e-mail: ksingh@clc.du.ac.in

S. K. Jain
Advocate, High Court of Delhi, Delhi, India

R. Mittal and K. K. Singh (eds.), *Relevance of Duties in the Contemporary World*,
https://doi.org/10.1007/978-981-19-1836-0_1

duties rather than claiming their rights. Many revolutions were also based on rights to challenge this kind of setup, and they had been successful in establishing democracies. However, the question arises: after establishing democracies through these revolutions, and with a constant focus on rights rather than duties, whether governments have successfully sustained good governance and ensured democratic values? Gandhi led many revolutions and campaigns arguing for rights, yet he emphasised on methods rather than ends, which indicates a distinct approach not devoid of duties. Instead, Gandhi considered duties as the source of rights, and to him, right is nothing but a well-performed duty. The waves of globalisation, liberalisation and growing consumerism have set a new set of duties that constituted the universal norm. It has made phenomenal impact on the rigid relativism approaches to duty. Article 29 of the Universal Declaration of Human Rights, 1948, recognises duties at the international level, yet it does not provide significant space for it. Though an international declaration dedicated to duties came in 1998 in the form of the Declaration of Human Duties and Responsibilities, it has not been able to produce the desired result due to numerous reasons, including a constant focus on rights and general avoidance of duties. The flagrant disregard to duties and continued erosion in social values has led us to rethink about the role of duties in ensuring the protection and enforcement of rights and creating a just society.

Against this backdrop, the present chapter examines the East–West (particularly Indian and Western) jurisprudence on duties, flagging the commonalities and differences. It also analyses the influence of globalisation and liberalisation on the unification of values around the world, setting universal duties. Finally, it explores the State's role in effectuating duties contextualised by Gandhian thought. Rather than making strict jurisprudential analyses of the principles and theories of right-duty relationship, the chapter aims at setting the background for further discussion on the topic by highlighting relativism, universalism and the impact of duty-based regime on the relationship between citizens and the State.

2 Absence of Duties in the Current Discourse

The absence of duties in the current discourse reflects our unbalanced understanding of moral and political discourse over time, which once gave obligations their due. Scholars have shown great enthusiasm writing the history of rights but such enthusiasm has been lacking in writing the history of duties.[1] Since the performance of duty guarantees the enforcement of rights, the omission of duties from the current discourse may have serious consequences for the protection of rights itself. Samuel Moyen emphasises that the history of duties provides a valuable starting point as we attend to urgent purposes today.[2] In the Western ethical theory, duties have been at

[1] Samuel Moyen, "Rights vs, Duties" Boston Review, May 16, 2016 available at https://bostonreview.net/articles/samuel-moyn-rights-duties/ (last visited 10 December, 2021).

[2] Ibid.

the centre stage. The works like Cicero' text book on practical ethics—*DeOfficiis* (translated *as On Duties*), Kant's theory of Categorical Imperative of Duty having a moral foundation and emphasis on the freedom of people to choose their ends; the legally created duties such as in tort law, German moralist Samuel Pufendorf's treatise On the Duty of Man and Citizen (in 1670s, before the declarations of the rights of man and citizen), reflect the significance of duties.[3]

The shift from duty to right-centric approach in the West was a reaction against the obligations within stark hierarchies created by the hegemony of ethical schools, religious traditions and political authorities. It led enlightened political thinkers to assert supremacy of rights and escape the confinement of duty, which at that time seems to be a right move. It was a significant advancement in human history that liberated individuals from God's enforcers, tradition's weight and the State's prerogatives. However, it raised a relevant question, "after individual freedoms had been proclaimed and won what would happen to the earlier public emphasis on duties? Would it simply disappear?"[4] Samuel Moyen maintains that though the Atlantic revolutions were right-centric as a reaction against the State oppression, they were not devoid of duties. Rather, "the revolutions were subsequently domesticated through an appeal to duties."[5]

Liberals backed duties because they based their political commitments within "historic and sociological frameworks that made individual freedom a collective achievement that depended on ongoing collective commitments and necessary common actions."[6] Many liberals elaborated on the older republican idea that "citizenship in a community of free people affords privileges but also incurs responsibilities."[7] *The Duties of Man* by Giuseppe Mazzini influenced Gandhi, which the latter endorsed as text that endorsed his own thought. Against prioritising the hedonistic calculus of Bentham, maximum happiness to maximum number of people, Mazzini opined:

> With the theory of happiness as the primary aim of existence, we shall only produce egoistic men. We have therefore to find a principle … which shall guide men toward their own improvement, teach them constancy and self-sacrifice, and unite them with their fellow men …. And this principle is Duty.[8]

Leon Duguit opined that "there is only one right, and that is to do our duty" based on his work on social solidarity and social interdependence. It could be considered an overstatement, yet the situation demands "to renovate rather than reject an emphasis on duties in light of global interdependence."[9] However, in the second

---

[3] Ibid.

[4] Ibid.

[5] Ibid. (e.g., responding to the French Declaration of the Rights of Man and Citizen 1789, the conservatives' "Declaration of the Rights and Duties of Man and citizen" 1795 stated: "The maintenance of society requires that those who compose it should both know and fulfill their duties.").

[6] Ibid.

[7] Ibid.

[8] Ibid.

[9] Ibid.

half of twentieth century, liberals lost this touch of emphasising duties.[10] Samuel concludes that duty encompasses a range of values and rejecting it entirely means rejecting "a public vocabulary which might protect socioeconomic equality, global justice, or environmental welfare."[11]

3 Varying Approaches to Duty and Factors Influencing Them

Different approaches to duty persist in different countries, influenced by their cultural and political setup and many other factors. In any community, everyone owes certain duties, which ensures the free and full development of his personality.[12] A range of factors influencing the concept of duty are political ideology (liberal and conservative) and leadership, state system and their tradition (e.g. former, USSR, Japan and Germany being the countries more duty oriented), religion, cultural diversity and pluralistic society. On an individual level, one's character, one's particular place in life like in family job and one's moral expectation for oneself contribute to her approach to duty. Right and duty have generally been regarded as the obverse and reverse of the same coin, and as complementary to each other, however, the nature of the complementarity has not received much attention. The path of duty presupposes a twofold obligation; it can be an obligation towards oneself and the community. While right starts with self-assertion, duty starts with the idea of self-discipline. Self-discipline under duties goes even to the extent of total subordination of self to the dictates of a higher authority. Here, higher authority indicates the authority of the social norm or individual conscience, "the Inner Voice."[13] The right activists may contend the total subordination of the self to the dictates of a higher authority as if it is well in tune with the realisation of rights.

4 Duties as Correlative to Rights in the East–West Jurisprudence—The Doctrine of Correlativity

It is widely accepted norm that rights "correlate" with duties. It entails that rights imply duties ("even if not all duties imply rights") and that claims of individual rights need not be recognised unless backed by the proof that corresponding obligations

[10] Ibid.

[11] Ibid.

[12] Article 29 (1) of Universal Declaration of Human Rights.

[13] G. N. Sarma, 'Gandhi's Concept of Duty', 41 *The Indian Journal of Political Science* 2 (June 1980), 214–231.

are performed: "[t]he doctrine of correlativity forms part of the view that rights must be understood in terms of duty or obligation."[14]

While discussing the abstract concept of duty, most Western liberal theorists have endeavoured to distinguish between what one ought to do, what one should do and what one is obligated to do when considering the abstract concept of responsibility. AR White, for instance speaks of what one should do, based on what is proper, fitting, or "due" under the circumstances. Duty is viewed as something that has to be done because of who one is, whereas what one should do is guided by notions of moral good. One owes duties because of one's status, for example a parent or a worker owes responsibility. On the other hand, one's "obligation" is something that one is forced to undertake due to legal, economic, prudential or moral concerns; there is no choice involved. Raz also works on the premise that one's duty is narrower than what one "ought" to do. Duty for Raz is what is morally required. Hart too distinguishes between obligations and duties: obligations may be voluntarily incurred and arising out of the character of obligatory actions, whereas duties arise out of the relationship between the parties and are not voluntarily incurred.[15]

In discussing the relationship between rights and duties, while few Western liberal theorists accept some correlation, the majority reject a total correspondence.[16] Instead, both obligations and rights are viewed as having areas of independent opinion. For duties, this area is primarily conceived as the areas of obligations of a moral or legal kind. In contrast, it is the area of freedom of rights.[17] Except White, most theorists have not disavowed all correlativity between rights and duties. Instead, in particular situations, they see a connection because they find a link in specific cases where both the right and duty arising out of the same circumstance, for example in a debt situation, the duty to pay correlates with the right to receive.[18] Some chose a more limited level of correlation—Raz, for instance regards a "right as a ground for another's obligation," while acknowledging that duties exist without rights as a ground. Most theorists, on the other hand, argue that rights do not simply grow out of obligations and that some obligations do not have equivalent rights. Duties, in particular, are seen as a domain of activity that only partially coincides with "rights."[19]

While discussing the lack of complete correlation between rights and duties, modern liberal theorists argue that the objects/beneficiaries of some duties are without legal power to enforce such claims. Regarding freestanding "duties," White points to the duty on a judge to pass a sentence or a policeman's duty to report offenders as

---

[14] David Lyons, 'The Correlativity of Rights and Duties', 4 *Noûs* 1 (February 1970), 45–55.

[15] R. B. Brandt, 'The Concepts of Obligation and Duty', 73 *Mind* 291 (July 1964), Oxford University Press, 374–393.

[16] David Lyons, 'Rights, Claimants and Beneficiaries', *Rights*, 1979, at 58.

[17] Ibid.

[18] Jack Donnelly, 'How are Rights and Duties Correlative', 16 *Journal of Value Inquiry* (1982), 287–294 at 292.

[19] Annemarie Devereux, 'Should 'Duties' Play A Larger Role In Human Rights? A Critique of Western Liberal and African Human Rights Jurisprudence', 18 *University of New South Wales Law Journal* 2 (1995) at 464.

not implying "rights" of the prisoner/offenders to fulfilment of the "duty." Similarly, he regards the duty to do something for someone as not being mirrored by the right of the recipient to that something, for example the duty of an employee to serve the employer's customers. Hart refers to "duties" that have no corresponding rights. In his terms, many "duties" such as those owed to babies, animals or family members have no corresponding person who has either the ability to choose whether or not to receive the benefit or the ability to enforce that benefit. Interestingly, the conception of duties which appears in White's and Hart's arguments encompasses both "moral rights" and "positivist"-type duties, for example duty to pay taxes or stop at the traffic signal. Implicit in their arguments is that duties encompass a wider field than rights.

Concerning the correlation of duties to rights, rights having correlative duties have been distinguished from rights having no correlative duties. A prime example given of the latter category is when two persons come across a stray pound note: each has a right to pick up the pound, but neither has a duty, for example to let the other person pick it up. Hart defines "liberties" as a category of rights in which an individual is under no obligation to abstain from a certain action. Similarly, most theorists identify a category of rights often called "liberties" or "Hohfeldian privileges" which do not have particular corresponding duties, for example the right to publish material which exists without there being any corresponding duty on another to assist in publication. Rejecting the argument that someone's right to do something correlates with the duty of another not to interfere, White, for instance cites the case where someone may have a right to teach or heal but the subject is under no duty to be taught or healed.[20]

However, the scheme of rights embodies freedoms, permitting action without requiring action from the actor or those around him or her. The scheme of rights seems to provide for more than a duty-based system. Western jurisprudence reflects that a rights-based system is superior to a duty-based system even if the systems are correlative. However, scholars do not attempt to address any shortcomings as to the reach of rights in terms of not necessarily covering all the subject matters covered by duties. These scholars consider rights inherently superior because of their rhetorical strength, their concentration on the ability and power of the right holder, their enforceability, their impact and their ability to be controlled by the right holder. It is common for theorists to assert that rights are more "enforceable," whereas the duties, being perceived as a matter for the conscience only, are less enforceable.

On the contrary, in India, the concept of *dharm* as a vital component of Hindu tradition found prominence in defining the right-duty relationship well before the modern period. The influences at work in contemporary India have produced various social modifications and intellectual reformulation.[21] The centrality of *dharm* to modern "Indian thinkers was represented by Aurobindo Ghose when he interpreted his tradition by stressing the value of *dharm* or duty as being at the heart of it."[22] The following passage from the writings of Sri Aurobindo demarcates the distinction

[20] Alan R. White, *Rights* (1984), Oxford: Clarendon Press.

[21] Austin B. Creel, 'Dharma as an Ethical Category Relating to Freedom and Responsibility', 22 *Philosophy East and West* 2 (April 1972), 155–168.

[22] Dennis Dalton's article on 'Gandhi on freedom, rights and responsibility'.

between Indian and European perspectives on right and duty, and on the antithesis of community and the individual:

> It has been said that democracy is based on the right of man; it has been replied that it should rather take its stand on the duties of man; but both rights and duties are European ideas. [*Dharm*] is the Indian conception in which rights and duties lose the artificial antagonism created by a view of the world which makes selfishness the root of action, and regain their deep and eternal unity. [*Dharm*] is the basis of democracy which Asia must recognize, for in this lies the distinction between the soul of Asia and the soul of Europe.[23]

Gandhi identifies *dharm* as a duty. He viewed individualism differently as compared to the Western approach to individualism: "Whereas Western individualism emerged in modern urban society and is bound up with the doctrine of natural rights, Gandhi's individualism derived from the concept of [*dharm*] or natural obligations…."[24] Performance of the duties of an individual in society helps society become self-sufficient and stable. "The duties of an individual contribute not only to the growth and prosperity of society but also to maintaining social order. It brings justice and peace to society."[25] According to Gandhi, *dharm* should be understood as the "quality of soul." This understanding will assist individuals in realising two primary things about their life. First, "what are their fundamental duties" and second, "how should they put up with others?" The former hints at preserving one's traditions and customs, while the latter deals with the intelligence and will of a person.[26] Gandhi "gave the word at least two essential meanings, both serving his twin principles of *satya* (truth) and *ahimsa* (nonviolence)." In the opinion of Iyer, "there was no [*dharm*] higher than truth"[27] and "no [*dharm*] higher than the supreme duty of nonviolence."[28]

The rhetoric that Western societies are right-based and eastern/Asian societies have been duty and responsibility oriented puts up a dichotomy and conflict. The contemporary scholars from the East and the West seem to be very open in accommodating the approaches from each other and critical to the prior existing regimes in their respective countries. For instance challenging the right-based arguments of the West, in a paper on Thai prostitution concerning the relationship of rights and duties, Emmerson demands "alongside the sex worker's rights, her and her client's responsibilities, to each other and to themselves, should also be taken into account."[29] However, "Yasuaki Onuma" of the University of Tokyo criticised "the simplistic

---

[23] Sarma, *supra* note 13.

[24] Raghavan N. Iyer, *The Moral and Political Thought of Mahatma Gandhi*, Oxford University Press, 1973, 115.

[25] Satya Sundar Sethy, 'Reinterpreting Gandhi's Notion of "Dharma": An Entanglement of Duty, Religion, and Ethics', 37 *Gandhi Marg* 2, 293–312.

[26] Ibid.

[27] Mahabharat, Adiparvan, ch. xi, 13.

[28] Shantiparvan, ch. CLXII, 24.

[29] Carnegie Council for Ethics in International Affairs, "Balancing Rights, Duties, and Underlying Values" in *Human Rights Dialogue* 1.7 (Winter 1996): "New Issues in East Asian Human Rights" December 5, 1996 available at https://www.carnegiecouncil.org/publications/archive/dialogue/1_07/articles/542 (last visited 12 December 2021).

abandonment of rights and resort to the 'opposite' notion of duty." He argued that in the Eastern and the Western traditions, the concept of an individual exists, but "not in an isolated manner." Rather, the individual "coexists with a concept of collectivity." Onuma considers "the exclusive emphasis placed on responsibility and duty by many Asian or African leaders is wrong-headed."[30]

Xia Yong of China, however, portrays rights and duties in a different light, raising concern about "the transformation of the traditional notion of 'sacred duty' into individual right." Reminding the situation in Ancient China, he maintains:

> there was not any legitimacy for seeking individual interests and advantage by taking part in public affairs.... Political participation was a sacred individual duty to be fulfilled for the people, for the country, and for self-realization, rather than a right.[31]

Prior to the arrival of rights language from the West, the idea of collective rights overshadowed the individual rights and created an individual creative duty. Sacred duty has since been used to legitimise contemporary Chinese regime.[32]

Other contemporary scholars in the East emphasise duties and other social virtues, along with rights. For example Chandra Muzzafar of Just World in Malaysia considers that "the human rights discourse may need to develop a holistic understanding of the individual, the family, and the community, and the explicit values that can invigorate not only rights and responsibilities, but also roles and relationships."[33] In the current COVID-19 period, the discourse on duties, obligations and responsibilities is increasingly relevant.[34]

5 Impact of Globalisation, Liberalisation, Consumerism and Relativism on Duty

The waves of globalisation and liberalisation have opened the gates of the countries worldwide and made the world a truly global village. The world is so connected that specific values have become universalised, creating universal duties, for example the duty to protect the environment. These duties have a universal appeal beyond the East–West distinction based on shared values and concerns. It has challenged the general belief that only the politics, culture, religion and personal preferences of a country essentially influence duties in that country. People were exposed to diverse cultures, traditions and societies as the trend of globalisation, liberalisation and consumerism began. People belonging to one society have adopted and assimilated the values prevalent in the other societies, leading to universalisation, homogenisation and uniformity. It has diluted the traits of relativism.

With the introduction of international human rights treaties and declarations, international law enjoins various duties. The theory that every right has a corresponding

[30] Ibid.

[31] Ibid.

[32] Ibid.

[33] Ibid.

[34] Ibid.

duty ensures the respect, protection and accomplishment. Since these treaties cast a duty on states to protect these rights through a national scheme, rights protection goes even further.[35] However, the human rights revolution disseminated the relevance and importance of rights that all humans everywhere have rights but fails to familiarise the notion that rights are protected by the fulfilment of duties.[36]

Though Article 29 of the UDHR recognises that "Everyone has duties to the community in which alone the free and full development of his personality is possible,"[37] but it does not enumerate duties, providing very little space to the discussion about duty. It might be because the drafters felt that duties are implicit in the rights prescribed under the declaration. But, it was also since the attention was more on rights rather than duties. In a significant move, UNESCO in coordination with UN High Commissioner of Human Rights came up with the Declaration of Human Duties and Responsibilities (DHDR) in 1998 on the eve of 50th anniversary of the UDHR in Valencia. The preamble of the DHDR categorically provides: "the effective enjoyment and implementation of human rights and fundamental freedoms are inextricably linked to the assumption of duties and responsibilities implicit on those rights…"[38] The declaration also highlights the concerns about new technologies and responsibilities attached thereto. The declaration contains 12 chapters and 42 articles broadly in the same line of the UDHR. The framework of duties and responsibilities was further extended to UN Millennium Declaration, the Statute of Rome, the Global Compact, the Earth Charter, the Kyoto Protocols and UNESCO declarations and conventions. All these international instruments emphasise shared responsibility. DHDR comprehensively proposes implicit system of duties and responsibilities contained in human right systems, particularly those enshrined in UDHR and subsequent international human rights instruments. Article 1 defines and distinguishes duties and responsibilities, and Article 41 includes a disclaimer in the form of a non-derogation clause, which ensures the utmost respect to human rights contained in human rights instruments.[39] Despite the elaborated content of DHDR followed by the other human rights declarations and treaties connected with the global concerns, there has been a lack

---

[35] Moyen, *supra* note 1.

[36] Ibid.

[37] Article 29 of the UDHR 1948.

[38] Preamble of the DHDR, available at https://globalization.icaap.org/content/v2.2/declare.html (last visited on 10 December 2021).

[39] Article 1 of the DHDR: "For the purposes of this Declaration, unless the context indicates otherwise:

(a) "duty" means an ethical or moral obligation;

(b) "responsibility" means an obligation that is legally "binding under existing international law."

Article 41 (1) of the UDHR provides: "Nothing in this Declaration shall be interpreted as impairing or restricting the rights contained in the Universal Declaration of Human Rights and other international and regional human rights instruments, nor shall any derogation from or restriction of any human right or fundamental freedom existing in any international human rights instrument or domestic law be admitted on the pretext that the present Declaration does not recognise such rights or that it recognises them to a lesser extent."

of political will to bring these duties forward. The current crises, such as the global pandemic, necessitates to focusing on duties, obligations and responsibilities.

6 Duties of Citizens and the State: Reflections from India

6.1 Fundamental Duties and the Original Constitution

The Supreme Court of India in *Ramlila Maidan Incident* case emphasised the relevance of duties as the correlative of rights:

> As difficult as it is to anticipate the right to any freedom or liberty without any reasonable restriction, equally difficult it is to imagine the existence of a right not coupled with a duty. The duty may be a direct or indirect consequence of a fair assertion of the right. Part III of the Constitution of India, although confers rights, still duties and restrictions are inherent thereunder.[40]

One of the pertinent questions in the context of duty is, despite being a duty-based society by tradition, why the framers of Indian Constitution did not include fundamental duties in a distinct chapter similar to fundamental rights? Justice Lahoti looked into the probable reasons for the non-inclusion of fundamental duties in the original draft of the Indian Constitution. He points out three reasons for the same: first, "the framers believed in the core values of society of which fundamental duties were a part and they took it for granted that it will be followed by the citizens as an inalienable value"; second, it might be the preamble, which imbibes these values; third, they might believe that all the fundamental rights contained in Part III have inbuilt obligations therein. It was left to the interpreters to read them "so as to spell out and understand the duties flowing therefrom."[41]

6.2 Why Does India Need Fundamental Duties?

Suppose, the abovementioned reasons justify the non-inclusion of distinct chapter on fundamental duties in the Indian Constitution; then, why has the said chapter been added to the Constitution through 42nd Constitutional Amendment in 1976? Though the Constitution's drafters were confident that the values constituting fundamental duties implicit in the preamble and other parts of the Constitution would be respected by the citizens, however, "with the lapse of time, degradation of values, particularly

[40] *Ramlila Maidan Incident vs. Home Secretary, Union of India (UOI) and Ors.* (2012) 5 SCC 1 (para 21).

[41] National Commission to Review the Working of the Constitution: A Consultation Paper on Effectuation of Fundamental Duties of Citizens (July 6, 2001), available at https://legalaffairs.gov.in/sites/default/files/(V)Effectuation%20of%20Fundamental%20Duties%20of%20Citizens.pdf (last visited on 12 December 2021).

values in public life became blatantly evident and the nation felt the need to amend the Constitution and incorporate these values specifically as the Fundamental Duties of every citizen."[42] Again, the ultimate reason and timing of the inclusion of the chapter on fundamental duties have remained contentious, given the political climate during emergency, nevertheless, the chapter found its relevance in the new government too, formed by Janata party as they kept it intact.

Despite including a chapter on fundamental duties in the Constitution of India, the effectuation of these duties has remained unsatisfactory. Commenting on the relevance of the Article 51-A on fundamental duties and its non-effectuation after many years since its inception, Justice Rangnath Mishra wrote a letter to the then Chief Justice of India:

> This article has the potential to regenerate and reconstruct the nation. It has been on the statute book for the last 24 years. It commands that – "it shall be the duty of every citizen of India" – but it is an irony that more than 99 per cent of the citizens of India do not even know about the existence of this article in the Constitution, much less its provisions.[43]

He alluded to the relevance of a duty-based society: "If society becomes duty based, everyone in India should turn attention on performance of duties and through such performance ensure and be entitled to the rights of a citizen."[44] Is there a duty of State to educate the citizens about their fundamental duties? On this question, he maintained: ".... it is the obligation of the State to educate the citizens in the matter of Fundamental Duties so that a right balance between Rights and Duties may emerge."[45]

The "Consultation Paper on Effectuation of Fundamental Duties of Citizens" highlights that "there has been some rather disproportionate emphasis on the rights of citizens as against their duties even though the traditions and temper of Indian thought through the ages laid greater emphasis on duties."[46] Gandhi also believed that duties are the source of rights and rights are nothing but the well-performed duties. It resonates Harold Laski's opinion, "rights are related to functions and are given only in return for some duties to be performed."[47] Rights are conferred on individual citizens not only for their own development but also for social good. The Universal Declaration of Human Rights put it: "Everyone has duties to the community in which alone the free and full development of the personality is possible."[48]

---

[42] Ibid.

[43] Ibid.

[44] Ibid.

[45] Ibid.

[46] Ibid.

[47] Harold J. Laski, "Authority in the Modern State", Batoche Books, Kitchener, 2000.

[48] Article 29 (1) of the UDHR.

6.3 Whether State's Push for citizen's Duties Is Justified?

As propounded by Mahatma Gandhi, the very performance of duty secures our rights; therefore, we need to adopt a calibrated approach "to strike a balance between rights and duties" because an extra emphasis on rights cast a duty only on states and does not cast corresponding duties on citizens. While extra push on duties by the State absolves the State from taking positive action towards a cause, it also shifts the burden of the citizens to correct the things for themselves. The nation-building process requires active assistance from both the citizens and the State, and a balanced approach of rights and duties can enhance the nation-building process. It has been beautifully summarised:

> Ideally, a proper balance and harmony can be achieved if the State – high functionaries of the Government and the leadership generally – cease to lecture the citizens on their duties and devote their energies and attention to protecting their rights, and the citizens themselves lay greater emphasis on discharging their responsibilities and duties instead of all the time demanding fulfillment of their rights.[49]

Nevertheless, it does not mean that State shall remain passive/indifferent to generating awareness and a sense of realisation of duties among citizens; however, it must not do it at the cost of their rights. On the contrary, State must ensure the adequate protection and enforcement of their rights. Therefore, State needs to maintain a delicate balance between securing the rights of the citizens and making them aware of their duties through education and awareness programmes.

6.4 Whether Enforcement or Sanction Is Necessary for the Implementation of Fundamental Duties?

While through legislative efforts (i.e. through enactments), a few of the fundamental duties have been provided legal sanction, the others cannot be practically enforced through legal sanctions.[50] The implementation of the duties falling in the second category does not warrant legal sanction and enforcement but need aspiration of citizens to practice.[51] When courts in India are required to examine the reasonableness of legislative limits "on the exercise of freedom," the fundamental duties enshrined in Article 51-A are taken into account. Article 51-A requires a person to follow the law, protect public property and refrain from violence. It also requires the individual to defend and safeguard the country's sovereignty, unity and integrity.

---

[49] *Supra* note 41.

[50] Ibid.; (For example: Fundamental Duties contained in clauses (b), (e), (f), (h) and (j) of Article 51 (A) of the Indian Constitution; clause (e), "to value and preserve the rich heritage of our composite culture vide clause (f), to develop scientific temper, humanism and the spirit of inquiry vide clause (h), to strive towards excellence vide clause (j) are also the noble ideals which inspired our national struggle for freedom").

[51] Ibid.

Fundamental duties under Article 51-A were included to supplement the State's responsibilities outlined in Part IV of the constitution in the form of the State's Directive Policy. Therefore, all these duties are of constitutional significance and deserve utmost respect.[52]

7 Gandhian Thought on Duty and His Focus on Methods

Gandhi led to numerous rights-based movements, and it might create a paradox that how his lifelong fight for rights could find relevance in the context of duties. This paradox is wiped away when we holistically take his philosophy. While fighting for right, he did not detach duty from right, but he thought that duties are the precursor to rights and rights are nothing but well-performed duties. He maintained that the true source of right is duty, and to make the rights meaningful, the performance of duty is a must.[53]

Gandhi had shown his concern and worry about the predominance of rights over duties way back in 1909 in Hind Swaraj: "the farce of everybody wanting and insisting on... rights, nobody thinking of... duty." Responding to the request made by Julian Huxley, the then Director-General of UNESCO, to contribute an essay to a collection of human rights, Gandhi expressed his concern about the dominance of right and emphasised the importance of duty:

> I learned from my illiterate but wise mother that all rights to be deserved and preserved come from my duty well done. Thus the very right to live accrues to us when we do the duty of citizenship of the world. From this one fundamental statement, perhaps it is easy enough to define duties of man and women and correlate every right to some corresponding duty to be first performed. Every other right can be shown to be a usurpation hardly worth fighting for.[54]

For Gandhi, duty derives the idea of dispassionate action which the Bhagavad Gita reflects: "Unless one's action is performed with a degree of detachment one would not be free from the anxiety of its future consequences." He contends "if we are sure of the 'purity' of the means we employ, we shall be led on by the faith, before which any fear and trembling melt away."[55]

Gandhi advocated an alternative view of human rights, one in which individuals earn their rights via a process of maturing into a sense of fairness. For Gandhi, gaining the capacity to give all people their due was the very minimum of justice. Gandhi seems to believe that one method to give others their due was to defer to everyone equally, whether the other was a relative, a friend or an unjust opposing person or state. *Satyagrah* was Gandhi's way of gaining rights by carrying out one's

---

[52] *Sachidananda Pandey v. State of west Bengal & Ors*, 1987 AIR 1109, 1987 SCR (2) 223.

[53] Mahatma Gandhi, Young India, 8-1-'25.

[54] Mame Omar Diop, Satya Bhushan and Varada Mohan Nikalje Ahmisa (Non-Violence), Gandhi and Global Citizenship Education (GCED).

[55] Harijan, February 20, 1937; CW, Vol 64, 317.

responsibility of combating injustice while deferring to the unjust. Justice could not be ensured in the public domain by establishing institutions to establish general responsibility and abstract equality before the law.[56]

Gandhi, in his opposition to the 1948 Universal Declaration of Human Rights, seemed to be arguing primarily against the notion of an unconditional individual entitlement to responsible or just behaviour from others when he suggested that the rights of an individual are conditional on his or her previous performance of duty:

> I would say that there is nothing like a right. For one who has no duties there are no rights either. In other words, all rights emanate from duties—if there is no duty, there is no right either. When I do my duty, it brings some result and that is my right...[57]

Gandhi seemed to be arguing that an individual has no unconditional rights. The right to responsible behaviour from others must be earned by doing justice to all others with whom he or she comes into contact or conflict. Every individual must earn the right to responsible behaviour from others by developing the human capacity for, at the very least, a minimal sense of justice while negotiating a relationship with them.

8 Gandhi-led Movements: Reflection of Rights and Duties

The idea of duty may be taken to be the core of Gandhi's teaching and philosophy. This suggestion will, on the face of it, appear contradictory to the fact that: (i) Gandhi waged battles for rights in Africa and in India, and (ii) he confronted the might of Imperial Britain to gain freedom for India and the people of India—not freedom for the country alone but for each one of the people of the country. It meant for him not only national self-determination but self-direction for the individual. The various campaigns of *satyagrah* that he waged in India and his confrontations with the government had the single aim of winning rights for individuals in different contexts. It is well known that Gandhi had pronounced that "the individual is the one supreme consideration" and that the increase of state power "does the greatest harm to mankind by destroying individuality which lies at the root of all progress."[58] The contradiction arises because while Gandhi was ostensibly fighting for rights at different levels—national, social and individual, he emphasised the idea of duty as primary. It is true that no philosopher has stressed right to the exclusion of duty or vice versa. In suggesting that the idea of duty is central to Gandhi's thought, "what is meant is that the emphasis here is more on duty than on right or rather that it is on duty as the source of right."[59]

The Gandhian movement of self-transformation, which it is claimed marked the transition from man to mahatma, was related to a sense of the violation of the basic

---

[56] Skaria, 2011 at 206.

[57] Collected Works of Mahatma Gandhi (CWMG), Vol 90, No. 81, Page 91.

[58] Nirmal Kumar Bose, *Selections from Gandhi*, 1950, Ahmedabad: Navajivan Trust.

[59] Sarma, *supra* note 13.

human rights of the self.[60] This moment, often noted by commentators, was the incident at Pietermaritzburg Railway Station in South Africa where Gandhi was physically thrown out of a first-class railway compartment despite possessing a valid ticket. In his autobiography, he related his thoughts that night:

> I began to think of my duty. Should I fight for my rights or go back to India…. I should try, if possible, to root out the disease and suffer hardships in the process. Redress for wrongs I should seek only to the extent that would be necessary for the removal of the colour prejudice.[61]

The importance of rights was therefore evident to Gandhi as early as the 1893 incident; indeed, it appears that Gandhi thought in terms of human moral rights at that time. One may note the following comment from Gandhi: "It is true that the Indians in South Africa are not poor and hungry. But man cannot live by bread alone. Money has no value before human rights. And the South African Government does not give these rights to Indians there."[62] It can therefore be argued that Gandhi's opposition to human rights discourse concerned the fact that he did not accept the philosophical presuppositions of the early liberal conception of human rights as set forth in the 1948 Declaration, rather than a failure to understand the importance of rights to human dignity. In this context, it should be noted that it was not the human rights specified in the declaration that Gandhi likely opposed; this will become clearer when we consider the kind of rights for which Gandhi led *satyagrah.* It further becomes evident from consideration of the resolution on Fundamental Rights and Economic Changes passed in the 1931 session of the Indian National Congress.

9 Conclusion

In an increasingly interdependent world, duties become as relevant as ever. The inclusion of duties in the current discourse can produce pragmatic results for society. However, the underlying forces behind rights and duties are different. Rights begin with self-assertion, duties start with self-discipline, and regard to rights may be encouraged through self-discipline. The correlativity of rights and duties has been endorsed by scholars, though the degree of the same varies (some receive a more limited level of correlation, while some take it entirely). In Western jurisprudence, there is the assertion that even if the systems are correlative, a rights-based system is superior to a duty-based system. In India, the concept of dharm treats rights and duties as an integral concept; however, in the modern period, the focus has been shifted to rights. The literature on duties was abundant in the previous ages, and the growing absence of literature on duties in the present age seems to dilute the

---

[60] Bindu Puri, 'The Rights of Man: A Gandhian Intervention', *Human Rights: Indian and the West*, 2015, Oxford Scholarship Online (A. Peetush & J. Drydyk, eds.).

[61] Mahatma Gandhi, *The Story of My Experiments With Truth*, first published in 1927, Navjivan Trust, Ahmedabad.

[62] Collected Works of Mahatma Gandhi (CWMG), Volume 90, No. 45, Page 49.

importance of duties. However, there was not the total absence of duties in human rights revolutions, and these revolutions have been domesticated through an appeal of duties. Nevertheless, the focus had been more on rights than on duties.

Given the general perception that every right has a corresponding duty, international human rights instruments have cast numerous duties on individuals and states; however, these instruments disseminated primarily the language of rights rather than the language of duties. A dedicated declaration—the Declaration of Human Duties and Responsibilities (DHDR)—could not make a significant impact due to the lack of political will of the parties. The impression that Western societies are right-centric and Asian societies are duty-centric does not find much ground in the current times. Due to the process of globalisation and liberalisation, scholars are open to accommodate the concerns of each other regarding duty-based and right-based regimes. The waves of globalisation and liberalisation bring a sense of global responsibility; the values have been transcended from one country to another and constituted a unified appeal to approach global issues such as environment and global health with global solidarity. A more holistic view by understanding the individual, family and society and their interdependence needs to be included in human rights discourse.

The duties of the State and the citizens to be approached differently as an extra push to citizens' duties by the State may give the impression that State is absolving its duty to citizens to protect their rights. Citizens also need to realise their duties to society and nation, and this realisation could be promoted by the State by education, awareness and sensitisation. However, in doing so, the State must be cautious that the rights of the citizens must not be compromised. Though Gandhi-led revolutions give an indication of right-based approach, to Gandhi, duties were at the core of these revolutions. His emphasis on individuals as the supreme consideration reflects his focus on self-direction for the individuals. Gandhi considered means more important than ends, and he emphasised the performance of duties for the attainment of rights (freedoms and liberties). Gandhian thought on duty has a universal appeal as it seems a more pragmatic approach. Rather than comparing the value of rights and duties, he adopted an approach where he considers duty as the precursor of rights, which imposes a moral obligation on individuals to perform their duties and ensures better implementation of rights. In the present context, when racial disparities (and other forms of discrimination) and a global pandemic are pervasive, Gandhian thought provides a pathway to deal with these concerns with a duty-based approach.

References

Bose N Selections from Gandhi. Navajivan, Ahmedabad

Brandt RB (1964) The concepts of obligation and duty. Oxford University Press, pp 374–393

Brown J (2000) Gandhi and human rights: in search of true humanity. In: Parel A (ed) Gandhi, freedom, and self-rule. Vistaar Publications, New Delhi, pp 87–101

Carnegie Council for Ethics in International Affairs (196) Balancing Rights, Duties, and Underlying Values in *Human Rights Dialogue* 1.7 (Winter 1996): "New Issues in East Asian Human Rights"

December 5, 1996 available at. https://www.carnegiecouncil.org/publications/archive/dialogue/1_07/articles/542
Collected Works of Mahatma Gandhi (CWMG), Vol 1–97. (n.d.). Retrieved from GandhiServe Foundation
Creel AB (1972) Dharma as an ethical category relating to freedom and responsibility. Philos East and West 22(2):155–168
Dalton D Gandhi on freedom, rights and responsibility
Devereux A Should duties play a larger role in Human Rights ? A critique of Western Liberal and African Human Rights Jurisprudence. UNSW Law J 18(2)
Dhavan SS Secularism in Indian jurisprudence
Fung SK, E (1988). The Human Rights Issue in China, 1929–1931. Cambridge University Press, pp 431–457
Gandhi M (1909) Hind Swaraj
Gandhi M (1968) The selected works of Mahatma Gandhi, vol 1: an autobiography. Navajivan Trust, Ahmedabad
Gewirth A (1988) Rights and duties. Oxford University Press
Jha M Morality, legality, and human rights: Gandhi And Ambedkar in a rights framework
Koul RL, Koul M (n.d.) Jurisprudential aspects of fundamental duties and their enforceability: a study
Lyons D (1970) The correlativity of rights and duties. Noûs 4(1), 45–55
Mattarelli S (2008) Duties and rights in the thought of Giuseppe. J Mod Ital Stud
Moyen S (2016) Rights vs duties. Boston Rev, available at https://bostonreview.net/articles/samuel-moyn-rights-duties/ (last visited 10 December, 2021)
Moyn S Opinion reclaiming the language of duty in an age of human rights.
National Commission to Review the Working of the Constitution: A Consultation Paper on Effectuation of Fundamental Duties of Citizens (2001) available at https://legalaffairs.gov.in/sites/default/files/(V)Effectuation%20of%20Fundamental%20Duties%20of%20Citizens.pdf (last visited on 12 December 2021)
Parel AJ (ed) (1997) Gandhi: Hind Swaraj and other writing. Cambridge University Press
Peetush A, Drydyk J (eds) (2015). *Human Rights: India and the West.* Oxford University Press
Puri B (2015) The rights of man: a Gandhian intervention. In: Peetush A, Drydyk J (eds) Human Rights: Indian and the West
Sarma GN (1980) Gandhi's concept of duty. The Indian J Polit Sci 41(2):214–231
Sethy SS (2015) Reinterpreting Gandhi's Notion of "Dharma": an entanglement of duty, religion, and ethics. Gandhi Marg 37(2)

Chapter 2
The Idea of Justice in Gandhian Philosophy

Mritunjay Kumar

Morality is the basis of things and truth is the substance of all morality.
—M. K. Gandhi (M.K. Gandhi, 'An Autobiography or The Story of My Experiments with Truth: A Critical Edition' (trans: Desai Mahadev), Navajivan Publishing House, Ahmedabad, p 98 (1927, 2018))

1 Introduction

Justice is an all-encompassing concept; it has diversified streams in theology, ethics, logic, aesthetics, and law. It is often enunciated in a language of compassion and empathy, a framework of right and wrong, a site for truth and falsification, a talkative subject of all diversified cultures, an aspirational ideal for the societies across the globe, a practical precondition for the possibility of society and organized culture. From the pre-Greek cultures to the age of post-modernity, there has been a unique continuity in relation to the quest of conceiving and understanding justice with multiple understandings and diverse interpretations. In Europe, from the post-enlightenment period onwards, the process of 'scientific rationalization'[1] displaced the concept of justice from the space of ethics and aesthetics and placed it under the epistemic and practical domain of reason.

[1] Alvares Claude, 'Science, Colonialism and Violence', In: Nandy Ashish (ed) Science, Hegemony and Violence: A Requiem for Modernity, Oxford University Press, Oxford, pp 75–82 (1988); (One example of the Scientific Rationality could be given in context of Hiroshima, which was chosen as a site for the scientific experiment).

Assistant Professor of Law, Himachal Pradesh National Law University, Shimla

M. Kumar (✉)
Assistant Professor of Law, Himachal Pradesh National Law University, Shimla, India
e-mail: mritunjaykumar@hpnlu.ac.in

R. Mittal and K. K. Singh (eds.), *Relevance of Duties in the Contemporary World*,
https://doi.org/10.1007/978-981-19-1836-0_2

In the process of rationalization, the diversified principles of justice were reduced to the 'logic of justification'.[2] From the period of European renaissance onwards, the language of justice witnessed its complete transformation, from the theological, ethical, and aesthetical concepts to a rationalized object of calculation, classification, verification, and articulation. The essence of humanity, like emotion, passion, love, sympathy, and empathy, evolved through various religious, social, and customary traditions, was condemned as weakness to overcome. The quest of beauty, harmony, and truth was the primary drive in ancient civilizations, but it was taken over by the self-love or the self-interest[3] of the rational-calculative beings. In the ancient and medieval periods, across the various societies, justice was conceived and understood as a practising reality, a set of customary practices, the discovery and adaptation with natural wisdom and natural laws, the diverse ways of living naturally in harmony with the world. In the kingdom of reason, the quest to elevate human beings in a godly manner, as a mystifying transcendental subject, as the master and the 'paragon'[4] of the universe, as the inventor of a new science, transformed the diverse outlooks of life and nature. The anthropomorphic gaze has changed each and everything. The genesis and growth of environmental jurisprudence have been accomplished by the modern jurists in parallel with the catastrophic destruction of ecology. The discursive practices of new science, in the leadership of Bacon, Newton, and Descartes, accomplished a dichotomous relationship in a vertical hierarchy between human nature and nature's nature. Human nature was considered as rationale unlike the rest of animal kingdom. Since then, the human species has been dialectically competing against so called inert and valueless nature's nature.[5] In the traditional societies, among the indigenous people, social practices were inclined towards the discovery of natural laws and adaptabilities to its circumstances and conditions. With the emergence of 'scientific rationality', the spirit of discovery was discarded in favour of 'instrumental rationality',[6] whereas the new spirit of age, a blend of scientism and commercialism, is inclined towards the invention of fictitious realities, to decimate the ethical and aesthetical modes of existence under the ecology of all too deceptive 'mass culture'.[7] 'Instrumental rationality' has produced a widespread culture

---

[2] Ch. Perelman, Justice and Justification. Natural Law Forum, p 5 (1965); (Explaining that 'to admit the possibility of a rational or reasoned justification is at the same time to recognize the practical use of reason....To reason is not merely to verify and to demonstrate, but also to deliberate, to criticize, and to *justify*; to give reasons for and against; in a word, to argue').

[3] Smith Adam, An Inquiry into The Nature and Causes of The Wealth of Nations (ed: Cannan Edwin), ElecBook Classics, London, p. 30 (1776, 1977); ("It is not from the benevolence of the butcher, the brewer, or the baker that we expect our dinner, but from their regard to their own interest").

[4] Shakespeare William, Hamlet (ed: Lamb Sidney). Hungry Minds, New York, p 85 (1599, 2000).

[5] Newton Isaac, Optiks. William and John Innys, London, pp 339–340 (1704, 1721).

[6] Horkheimer Max, Eclipse of Reason. Bloomsbury, London, p 13 (1947, 2013). *See* Sechter 2010, p 187.

[7] T.W. Adorno, 'The Culture Industry: Selected Essays on Mass Culture', (ed: J.M. Bernstein). Routledge, New York, pp. 1, 61 (2001).

of machination. And the 'technology of utilitarianism'[8] has displaced a value-based life based upon sentimental solidarity.

Mahatma Gandhi, a philosopher and moral scientist, belonged to culturally rich traditions of the East. He had an 'un-alienated perspective' with respect to nature and society. His thoughts were integral to the great lineage of ideas and practices begining with the Neo-Platonism to the Romanticism.[9]. He was aware about the development of modernity and its after-effects, like the industrial revolution and mass culture, occurred in the European societies, which, in the name of progress, desacralized and defiled the lively nature, and produced a strange ontology of 'methodological individualism'.[10] He did not want to see India as an urbanized and industrialized society,[11] centralized towards all around productions of goods as well as 'useful truths'. Gandhian philosophy, in a way, was a moral voice of resistance against all around brooding culture of 'alienation',[12] which is central to the Hegelian and Marxist philosophy and praxis. In this essay, the author has tried to establish a framework to understand the Gandhian ideas in context of the wider thematic expression of justice, which was quite opposite to the modern paradigm of thought and articulation. In the first section, the introductory remark has been made with respect to the theme of essay. In the second section, the concept of *Kartavya* will be explained in brief. The third section will be consisting of an analysis about the holistic perspective towards

---

[8] Foucault Michel, The Birth of Biopolitics: Lectures at The College De France (ed: Senellart Michel). Palgrave Macmillan, New York, p 41 (1978); ('Utilitarianism is a technology of government').

[9] Bilgrami Akeel, Gandhi and the Political Enlightenment, In: Asian Art Museum (06 Dec 2014) Available at: https://youtu.be/KrcV_TZOdk0. (last accessed 05 June 2020).

[10] Morrison Wayne, 'Jurisprudence: From the Greeks to Post-Modernism', Routledge, New York & London, p 107 (1997, 2005); (Explaining that 'the Hobbesian legacy offers social theories built upon methodological individualism, or taking as the basic building block individuals, rather than some collectivity...Individuals are deemed to be independent from each other and there is no natural social order'). *See also* Arrow Kenneth, Methodological Individualism and Social Knowledge, *84 American Economy Review* 2:3 (1994); (Analysing that 'the starting point for the individualist paradigm is the simple fact that all social interactions are after all interactions among individuals'). In contrast to the concept of methodological individualism, Gandhi developed the idea of trusteeship; *See* Parekh Bhikhu, 'Gandhi's Political Philosophy: A Critical Examination. Macmillan Academic', London, p 138 (1989).

[11] Parekh, *Id.*, at 43, 53; (Explaining that 'in Gandhi's view every civilisation had its own distinctive natural and social basis. Modern civilisation was born and could only survive in the cities, and was naturally carried all over the world by the commercial classes. Indian civilisation had, by contrast, been cradled and nurtured in the villages, and only the rural masses were its natural custodians').

[12] Marx Karl, 'Economic and Philosophic Manuscripts' (trans: Milligan Martin), Dover Publication, New York, p 71 (1844, 1988); Alienation and commodity fetishism are the two central theses of the Marxist critique of industrialization. Alienation is a process in which people are estranged from their own nature. (Expounding that 'Labor produces not only commodities: it produces itself and the worker as a commodity...This fact expresses merely the object which labor produces labor's product-confronts it as something alien, as a power independent of the producer. The product of labor is labor which has been congealed in an object, which has become material: it is the objectification of labor. Labor's realization is its objectification....this realization of labor appears as loss of reality for the workers; objectification as loss of the object and object-bondage; appropriation as estrangement, as alienation').

life developed by Gandhi, in order to explain the Gandhian vision for a community life and the realization of the 'social solidarity'.[13] In the fourth section, the conclusion and summation will be outlined.

2 Kartavya

Duty or *Kartavya* was not an original concept in Gandhian thought and practice. In fact, it is deeply rooted in the tradition of ancient Hindu cultures. *Karm* was a well-known metaphysical concept, found in the *Vedas* and *Purva Mimamasa.*[14] Krishna in *Gita* argued for *Nishkam Karma*, a detached performance of duty.[15] One of the meanings, attributed to *Dharm*, is *Kartavya.*[16] *Rajadharm*, a key concept in ancient Hindu jurisprudence, was practised as a *kartavya* of the king for his subjects. The two great epics in Hindu cultures, *Ramayan* and *Mahabharat,* reflect a deontological moral reasoning in norms and practices, deeply entrenched in the cultures of contemporary societies. The foundation of society was visualized, in the ancient India, at the archetypical relationship of *dharm* and *kartavya.* It does not mean that 'individual' was absent from the philosophical meditations in the ancient Hindu cultures, rather the social configuration was too vibrant and structurally strong that the spirit of individualism could not bloom. In fact, society is impossible to be conceived or organized through a predominant genre of individualistic imagination. Individualism and society cannot coexist at the same time. Both ways are opposite to each-other. For instance, the ancient societies in India were primarily the village communities, idyllic and self-sufficient.[17] And modernity thrives on individualized-anarchism. Gandhi, a moral scientist, understood the ramifications of modern culture as well as functioning and malfunctioning of industrialized and consumerized society. That may be a reason why he never hesitated to visit the past and its traditions, to learn and unlearn about the functioning of socio-political institutions. He was open to receive the ideas from all the diversified cultures of the globe, but he remained steady and

---

[13] N. Jayapalan, 'Comprehensive History of Political Thought', Atlantic Publishers and Distributors, New Delhi, p 351 (2001).

[14] Radhakrishnan Sarvepalli, Indian Philosophy, Vol 1. George Allen & Unwin, London, p 109 (1927, 1940); ('Turning to the ethics of *the Rig-Veda,* we find that the conception of *Rta* is of great significance. It is the anticipation of the law of karm, one of the distinguishing characteristics of Indian thought').

[15] K. Parmar Arjunsinh, Critical Perspectives on the Mahabharata. Sarup & Sons, New Delhi, p. 111 (2002).

[16] Sarkar Benoy Kumar, The Theory of Property, Law, and Social Order in Hindu Political Philosophy, *30 International Journal of Ethics (3)*: 311–325 (1920). Available at: http://www.jstor.org/stable/2377667. (last accessed 25 June, 2020).

[17] Sugirtharajah Sharada, Imagining Hinduism: A Postcolonial Perspective. Routledge, London & New York, p 55 (2004).

cautious in accepting them all.[18] Gandhi was a great learner of ideas, not necessarily in cognitive sense, rather he was meditative as a moral agent, unlearnt a great deal to discover, uncover and recover the eternal truths and applied them in his life-practices. He reinvented some of the important concepts, like *satyagrah*, *asahyog*, and *ahimsa*, and practised them with dedication and conviction. Gandhian deontology emerged in the anticipation of a scattered, dehumanized, disembodied and abstract society, which has come true in the age of post-modernity. In fact, the post-modern culture has brought an idiosyncratic state of being in form of solitary and defaced individuals, submerged in the boredom of existence, without having any faith, rationality, or care about meaning in life and about life. Gandhi foresaw the existential vacuum the modernity was offering to, with its materialistic-scientism and commercialized outlook, from external/internal nature to the human's relationships. He was deeply sceptical about the emergence of rights, a political and legal doxa, especially in context of individualism, since it was impossible to expunge cruelty by violent means. Right cannot be realized by a compassionate attitude towards fellow citizens rather its enforcement is a pre-condition for convergence into its realization. In fact, a compassionate society does not require the category of right, since its members are committed towards each-other in a fraternal mode of existence. He criticized the modern alienated culture and brought to forefront the deontological ethics, learnt as a meticulous student of *Gita*. Gandhian deontology emerged in the context of anxiety from which the modern institutions were suffering and there was a traditional background of knowledge, though de-legitimized by colonial-epistemic practices, germane for the harmonious reconstruction of the institutions and its practices. Traditions are generally labelled as historical evils by the modernists; however, they distort the truth by their prejudicial and preconceived surmises. It is, in fact, difficult to deny that history has witnessed many radical evils. But to overlook or condemn, everything that happened in the past, will be a gross injustice to the historical reality. History is judged from the value which is also transient and becoming an event of history. Every historical event was once lived vigorously, but now it becomes a temporal site for contests about its authenticity. Its lessons may be learnt, so that misjudgements or errors of past could not be committed again. There is something eternal about humans' existence or humans' problems, for which, history proves to be a great teacher and guide. Gandhi was well aware about the history of India as well as Europe and wanted to protect Indian society from an alienated culture developed in the West. Deontological philosophy and duty based socio-political as well as legal cultures, apart from a Kantian tradition, have not been popularly accepted in the tradition of West, reason being, they are committed towards a 'corporatized right-oriented' 'rule of market-facilitator disembodied law', supported by so called progressive constitutionalism, thriving at the foundation of moral and epistemic violence. The

[18] Gandhi Rajmohan, 'Gandhi: The Man, His People, and the Empire', University of California Press, Berkeley, p 241 (2007). *See* Gandhi 1921; ('I do not want my house to be walled in on sides and my windows to be stuffed. I want the cultures of all the lands to be blown about my house as freely as possible. But I refuse to be blown off my feet by any').

primacy of duty or responsibility is considered as an outdated and irrelevant legal-moral concept for a claim based violent and aggressive society. Nonetheless, the legal categories of duty and obligation are well-known and accepted under the schema of Hohfeld's jural categorization of correlatives and opposites. But the culture of right has reduced its significance to nothingness or at subservient position. In social and moral philosophy, the category of duty was investigated by the German philosopher Immanuel Kant and sociological jurist Leon Duguit. But the Kantian categorical moral reasoning was overshadowed by the Benthamite school of thought with their consequentialist moral reasoning. Ancient Indian literatures, such as Ramayan and Mahabharat, provide discourses on such conflicting zones between deontological and instrumentalist moral arguments. For example, Krishn counselled to Arjun in *Mahabharat* to follow his dharm (duty), irrespective of the consequences. Arjuna, the master warrior, was puzzled in the battlefield and unwilling to harm his own families, teachers, and relatives. Instead, he chose to question the utility and consequences of his actions or duties. His arguments were utilitarian or consequentialist, in a sense that, he was concerned about the consequences of his actions than being categorically aligned with deontological moral reasoning, until Krishna convinced him about his *Dharm* and *Kartavya.*[19] Kantian deontology was developed in the rejection of teleological and utilitarian moral reasoning. Immanuel Kant conceived the metaphysics of morals as categorical moral reasoning and universalized the binding moral principles for the humanity. The binding principles of duty were expounded by Kant, such as, one should never act in such a way that one treats humanity as a means only, but always an end in itself (Kant 1797, 1998)[20] or 'act only in accordance with that maxim through which you can at the same time will that it becomes a universal law' (Kant 1797, 1998).[21] These principles were conceptualized at the premise of a division between autonomous and heteronomous modes of existence, while prior is exclusively a capability inherent, as per Kant, in a human being, to transcend the limitations of causality and necessity as a moral subject, and the latter mode of existence is naturally existing in the vibration and cacophony of life from which the human species cannot be separated.[22] This division entailed a rationalized and moralized conception of man, which was subsequently predicted by Michel Foucault that 'man is invention of recent date. And one, perhaps, nearing its end'; his statement reflected the emergence of a new epoch, known as "Post-Humanism" (Foucault 1987),[23] just like Nietzsche's suspicious gaze against the belief of supernatural God and institutionalized religions, such as Christianity, resulted into freedom or liberation from transcendental source of morality or sanction. This division was questioned by many

[19] Mookherjee Braja Dulal, 'The Essence of Bhagavad Gita', Academic Publishers, Kolkata, p 91 (2002); ('Better one's own imperfect duty than well-performed duty of another; better death in doing one's own duty; duty of another person is dangerous').

[20] Kant Immanuel, 'Groundwork of the Metaphysics of Morals' (eds: Ameriks Karl & M. Clarke Desmond). Cambridge University Press, Cambridge, 31–43 at 36 (1797, 1998).

[21] Kant, *Id.*, at 31.

[22] Kant, *Id.*, at 41, 43.

[23] Foucault Michel, 'The Order of Things: An Archaeology of the Human Sciences', Routledge Classics, London & New York, pp 54, 387 (1966, 2005).

philosophers, including Jacques Derrida, who, in *The animal therefore (I am)*, raised some of the structural questions about the strange ontology of rationality, culminated intocondemnations of the animal kingdom as sensuous and irrational world. Ironically, the ambitious journey of humankind has reached on the verge annihilation of the life from the planet Earth, about which probably the so called irrational animal world might not be even aware of. The essentialized features of Kantian deontological moral reasoning may be understood as the imposing force, resulted into horrible justifications for imperialism and colonialism, such as, the white man's burden to civilize the immature-irrational societies as per the parameter of modern rationality, emerged from the narcissistic outlook towards nature and societies, which ensured the brooding omnipresence of colonialism and imperialism throughout the world. The Kantian moral reasoning ensured formalization and universalization of social and moral values so much so that substantive rationalities along with their pluralistic characteristics were negated by the colonial powers in the process of colonization. Same problem arises in international law. In the name of humanitarian laws, the sovereign affairs of a nation-state are often not respected. The well-established sovereign power, which is legitimate as per the democratic principle and setup, is not respected. It is a general tendency in the international relationship that the 'responsibility to protect',[24] a principle of international law, is often misused by the developed nation-states, to selectively intervene in the sovereign affairs of the so-called developing nation-states, even if, the non-intervention in the internal matters of sovereignty is normatively guaranteed by the Charter of the United Nations. Which moral or legal principle of the international law allows the intervention in the internal matter of the sovereignty? No pre-emptory norm, except the necessity of self-defence, allows a self-justificatory adventurism.[25] Kantian deontology provides a much wider scope to moralize a contemptible action or an intolerable offence with high-pretentious moral claims, like one was advanced by the colonizers with impunity.[26] The superimposition of duty or to universalize a moral principle is a coercive action, often dismissing the inner experiences of a moral agent. Gandhi, on the contrary, did not preach or universalize *Dharm* or *Kartvya.* He believed in *moral exemplarity*, which may or may not be noticed and followed by the fellow members of the society. But to choose for all, what is appropriate for an individual, was not acceptable to Gandhi. Especially, in a smaller unit of the village community, learning, unlearning, and co-learning from each other's conducts were possible. In an urban landscape of industrialized societies, city-dwellers appear to be a plaything of statistics, a headline of the

---

[24] Havel Vaclav & M. Tutu Desmond, Introduction, In: The Responsibility to Protect: The Promise of Stopping Mass Atrocities in our Time (eds: Genser Jared & Cotler Irwin), Oxford University Press, Oxford, p XXV.

[25] Article 51, The Charter of the United Nations, 1945 ('Nothing in the present Charter shall impair the inherent right of individual or collective self-defence if an armed attack occurs against a Member of the United Nations, until the Security Council has taken measures necessary to maintain international peace and security').

[26] Rich Jennifer, An Introduction to Critical Theory. Humanities-Ebooks, Tirril, p 66 (2007); ('...the notion of the White Man's Burden was a convenient excuse for the economic and social colonization of the Orient').

newspapers; in such a condition, thinking with compassion about neighbourours or practising selfless duty is hardly possible. People from the urban space acquire a professional identity and their bond is limited around the nucleus of utility; on the contrary, the rural landscape provides the opportunities and scopes to live a vibrant social life. The Gandhian vision for India as a 'village republic'[27] was conceived in historical context, since he was aware about the dark sides of modern culture and experienced the soul of India in Indian villages. In the urban landscape, the atomization of human being or the sense of truth and beauty is formulated in the complex language of commerce and law, inseparably made for each other. For that purpose, the invention, nurturance, and the enforcement of rights are inevitable. What, in fact, the language of right, whether it is human right, natural right, or legal right, does? It could not be understood in the traditional language of morals and ethics, rather it creates a new reality, independent from the social or natural norm. What, in fact, an identity signifies? Probably, limitation! Identity is always already a limited framework. To identify with something or someone creates a boundary between what is and what is not. In fact, 'what is' does not remain the same and 'what is not' is always a potentiality in Aristotlean sense. 'What is' and 'what is not' remain perpetually at tension with each-other, converge and often mitigate the line of demarcation. Right presupposes a web-net of identities for the possibility of its enforcement and realization, and in the process of enchantment of rights, the notions of identity are not kept 'under erasure',[28] to use the nomenclature of Jacques Derrida. Right is, though, conceived as positive as well as negative concepts; however, right, in a negative sense, is conceived predominantly in the legal and political habitude of the modern world. In fact, right commands or demands but never fulfills any positive responsibility. On the contrary, duty is a positive concept; its bearer is required to pursue some positive acts, to fulfil the responsibility in a constructive manner. Duty is a creative concept, which instils love and compassion for the self and for the society at large, if it is pursued with volition. Gandhi emphasized on duty, because, without it no society is possible. The sense of duty as a social or moral concept is the fundamental aspect of love, sympathy, and compassion. The legal and political conceptions of right came into fruition from mutual suspicion. Historically, it was invented to restrict the authority of sovereign-power, so as to protect the autonomy of citizens and subjects. One may trace a great lineage of 'suspicion jurisprudence',[29] which has been instrumental in the origin and development of the political and legal conceptions of right.

---

[27] Dasa Ratana, Gandhi in twenty-first century, Sarup & Sons, New Delhi, p 22 (2002); ('Gandhiji dreamed about an India whose each village would be republic. The decision making process would start from below. No one in this village republic will be illiterate and no one would be unemployed, the village republic should be self-sufficient in economy').

[28] Spivak Gayatri Chakravorty, Preface to the English Edition, 'In: Jacques Derrida's Of Grammatology' (trans: Spivak Gayatri Chakravorty), the John Hopkins University Press, Baltimore & London, p XVI (1998).

[29] 'Suspicion jurisprudence' is fundamentally related to the idea of self-centred welfare and non-cooperation with others. There is a general understanding among neoliberal economists that the role of collective identity or society should be suspected in the welfare on individual. According to Friedman Milton, 'Capitalism and Freedom', Fortieth Anniversary Edition, the University of

Since the ancient Greece, the social aspect of the human being was recognized and accepted as the fundamental human nature.[30] Likewise, the ancient civilization in India was primarily based on a duty-oriented society. Duty was, primarily, conceived to regulate the human's behaviours, conducts, and other social transactions. Gandhi was inspired by the ancient traditions, particularly, from its social aspects, which were instrumental in shaping his deontological thinking; from there, he discovered the significant concept of self-rule or *swaraj*. In the western jurisprudence, the legal category of right has been over-emphasized for its role in ensuring freedom and emancipation. Freedom in context of right is conceived as a negative category, whereas the state is supposed to be neutral. The state neutrality ensures the sustenance of *status quo*, in a sense that, those, who are historically and socially marginalized, remain so, and the rule of the society is written by its elites, who have been at a dominant position since long time. The positive conception of freedom in form of right is disliked by so called liberals, since it gives ample scope for the state to behave like a father. The much celebrated work of Isaiah Berlin on liberty preferred the concept of negative liberty over the positive one, for the reason that positive liberty promotes a totalitarian tendency.[31] Berlin's point of view is shared by many liberal-political thinkers. For them, individual autonomy is profoundly important. The demand of freedom or autonomy appears to be hollow, when most of the citizens are suffering to get the basic needs. The gap between 'haves' and 'have nots' creates a deep mistrust in the society, which is impossible to be overcome simply by shallow remedies provided by the rhetorical rights, enunciated in the law. Gandhi, on the contrary, belonged to 'the folks and spiritual tradition'[32] of Asiatic societies, inspired by the Vedanta and Buddhist philosophies, anticipated the malaise, which may have caused the irreparable damage to India, from which, European societies were already suffering. And he was trying to resist such forces, which had tendency to objectify nature and reify human's relationship. As a learner, he was open for any novel idea, irrespective of its sources. He learnt many great lessons from

Chicago Press, Chicago & London, p 12 (1962, 2009); ('As liberals, we take freedom of the individual, or perhaps the family, as our ultimate goal in judging social arrangements….in a society freedom has nothing to say about what an individual does with his freedom').

[30] Aristotle, Politics (trans: Jowett Benjamin), Dover Publications, New York, p 28 (400 B.C., 2000); ('Hence it is evident that the state is a creation of nature, and that man is by nature a political animal. And he who by nature and not by mere accident is without a state, is either a bad man or above humanity…').

[31] Berlin Isaiah, Freedom and Its Betrayal (ed: Hardy Henry), Princeton University Press, Princeton, p 224 (2002, 2014); ('This is liberty in the positive sense of self-direction, and the perversions of the meaning of the word which occur when fallacious analogies are made between reason, which directs the lower emotions in the individual, and the governing elite, which has a similar right to despotic rule over the lower members of a society - these very fallacies are intelligible only on the assumption that one of the central meanings of the word liberty is self-direction, whether by a man over himself or by a group over its members. This alone makes it possible for men to call for leaders and claim that this in some sense liberates them').

[32] Bilgrami Akeel, Gandhi and the Mentality of Modernity, Dialogue of Civilizations Research Institute (2014) Available at: https://youtu.be/Pv9m6L_mptU. (last accessed 10 June 2020) Available at: https://youtu.be/Pv9m6L_mptU (last visited 10 June, 2020).

the Sanatan religion of India, Christianity, Buddhism, Jainism, etc., and used those ethos in his daily practices. Gandhi never hesitated to experiment with moral ideas into the domain of social and political life. His thoughts and practices had integrity and sincerity. As a philosopher, his ideas appeared to be an integral part of an alternative paradigm of ideas, known as the romantic tradition,[33] emanated from the diverse western cultures since antiquity, but he remained committed to preserve and nurture the social and moral values prevalent in pre-modern Indian societies. Village community of pre-modern India was a duty based society. And the king was ordinarily hesitant to interfere in the governance and administration of justice. The consciousness of right and its enforcement were quite alien to those cultures. That was the reason why Gandhi believed in deontological ethics. *Kartavya*, for Gandhi, was the first step towards the realization of truth. He had insight about the demanding nature of *adhikar*, which is incomplete and futile without the performance of *kartavya*. Gandhi had a unique sense of integrity regarding spirituality and politics, both are usually considered as opposite to each other, but he managed to transform these two aspects in such a fine way that it is difficult to draw a clear line between these two different spheres in his thoughts and conducts.[34] His understanding about *kartavya* (duty) was not exclusively social, political, or spiritual category. He successfully avoided such categorization and reinvented many moral and spiritual ideas in order to practice them in social and political activism. Gandhi brought down moral values from other worldly, transcendental sphere, and made them a practical affair. His commitment towards poor, sick, and the downtrodden people was not influenced by any instrumental conception of duty in jural sense, rather it was inspired by *Sevadharm*, a duty to serve the fellow beings. His *sadhana*, in that sense, was inclined towards truth, love, and compassion. It is not the case that Gandhi did not like freedom or equality, but he was in disagreement with the modern paradigm of thought, which was responsible for all around alienated culture. Freedom in modern paradigm has been predominantly conceived in context of accumulating huge properties, and to achieve that, the everlasting competition and struggle to become excellent have been fundamentally normalized. In Gandhian thoughts and imaginations, progress is an absurd idea in a competitive sense. It thrives on violence and fear. With an inventive attitude, Gandhi established a moral paradigm to alleviate suffering of every common human being and every creature. *Kartvya*, a leap towards self-rule, a creative inner legislation, was the *leitmotif* of Gandhian deontology, which revised the western conception of coercive obligation for the spiritual realization of truth, beauty, love, and harmony. He embraced the suffering for the common good and well-being. This vision was extraordinarily courageous in comparison with the modern culture of claim–counterclaim. The Gandhian deontology was not only a crucial step towards social solidarity, but also a stepping stone to establish a holistic perspective towards life.

---

[33] Bilgrami, *supra* note 10 at 191.

[34] Parekh, *supra* note 11 at 100; ('Gandhi thought that if political life could be spiritualized, it would have a profoundly transformative effect on the rest of society').

3 Holistic Perspective Towards Life

Mahatma Gandhi was a *moral exemplar*,[35] a practitioner of truth, and a deeply committed activist, who had a holistic perspective towards nature and society. He was, of course, not against science as such; rather he appreciated its experimentalist approach.[36] Though, Gandhi was sceptical about its materialized and commercialized outlook with respect to nature.[37] The western thought, since the eighteenth century onwards, circumscribed around the 'instrumentalist conception of nature and society'.[38] For the modern scientists, nature was just an opportunity to master and control over it.[39] It was radically different from an adaptive or a holistic approach, usually prevalent in the ancient and medieval ages across the various cultures, including the Greco-Roman,[40] Christian,[41] Chinese,[42] and ancient Hindu cultures.[43] In the modern age, however, the master mentality is apparently visible in the thoughts and praxes of the human species.[44] It is practised as a guiding philosophy for the sustenance and nurturance of materialistic science. The modernity, in the process of industrialization and commercialization, has produced a homogenous culture of insatiability, fear, insecurity, violence, and incompatible relationship between the human species and nature. This outlook did not appear as a chance development, rather it was strategically pursued. 'Anthropocentrism',[45] a much celebrated concept, is able to connote the existential sin of the human species, which is still being committed in the process of damaging the ecology and endangering the lives of other species. In spite of all the warnings issued by various bodies of the United Nations,[46] the developed

---

[35] Bilgrami, *supra* note 10 at 104.

[36] Parekh, *supra* note 11 at 67; ('...he experimented with whatever religious ideas appealed to him, rigorously tested their truth in the crucible of daily life and explored their existential potential and limits').

[37] Bilgrami, *supra* note 10 at 155–156; ('Gandhi, as I said, believed that the fault-line which set us this path is the desacralization of nature that came from the outlook of modern science').

[38] Newton, *supra* note 6; *See* Bilgrami, *supra* note 10 at 142; (Instrumentalist conception functions at the premise of treating something or someone merely as a means to other end. Nature, in instrumental sense, was conceptualized and treated like a 'valueless' and 'inert object', nothing more than an opportunity to be exploited). *See also* Heidegger 1977, p 17; (Nature, in that sense, to invoke Heidegger's nomenclature, is 'standing-reserve').

[39] Bilgrami, *supra* note 10 at 161.

[40] Plato, Timaeus (trans: Jowett Benjamin), Dover Publication, New York, p 11 (360 B.C., 2003).

[41] Evans Laurence, Nature's Holism, toExel Press, Lincoln, pp 1–2 (1999).

[42] Evans, *Id*.

[43] Ahuja Ram, 'Society in India: Concepts, Theories, and Changing Trends', Rawat Publications, p 16 (1999).

[44] There are endless discourses on power or desire of powers in the modern and postmodern thoughts, from Francis Bacon to Nietzsche and Karl Marx to Michel Foucault; Bacon and Montagu 1859, pp 369, 372; *See* Nietzsche 1901, 2019, p 30; Clegg 2013, p 76; and Newman 2005, p 51.

[45] Davies Jeremy, 'The Birth of Anthropocene', University of California Press, California, pp 52, 55 (2016).

[46] Meetings Coverage and Press Releases of the United Nations, 2019 Available at: https://www.un.org/press.en/2019/ga12131.doc.htm (last visited 12 June 2020).

and the developing nations are not acting with urgency to address the existential crisis, like climate change. The master mentality, adopted by the human species, has been thoroughly cruel against all the animals; ironically, the animal kingdom is condemned as irrational and instinctive, because they do not have well-developed languages and the capacities to think and rationalize, as presumed through anthropomorphic lens. It is a matter of fact that the human species is responsible for this predicament. There are various studies and the conceptual understandings on this issue, but the structural questions have remained unanswered. It has something to do with the materialistic conception of science and its relationship with nature. The modern scientists, like Galileo, Bacon, and Newton, treated nature like a 'stupid'[47] thing devoid of any sense, feeling, perception, and values. The instrumentalist conception of science is a radical departure from the Aristotelian cosmology. The instrumental science has a 'commodified'[48] and 'fetishized'[49] perspective towards everything, from plants, animals, rivers, oceans to air, water, soil, etc. This outlook of science has been instrumental in the origin and growth of all around machination and the industrial revolution. And in fact, these developments have 'alienated'[50] the so-called rational beings from their own nature. The land enclosure movement in England was the first step towards the industrial revolution, which culminated into the organized industry, in fact, displaced the traditional cultures.[51] In the final ideological contest between the traditional French-Physiocrats and the Utilitarians, in relation to the organization and the use of land, the latter won the contest.[52] The industrial revolution in England and subsequently in the whole Europe had impoverished the 'humanism of nature and the naturalness of man',[53] to refer Karl Marx (Bilgrami 2014). Nature was deprived, at least through anthropomorphic gaze, from its values and desires, and these values

[47] Bilgrami, *supra* note 10 at 296.

[48] Marx Karl, Das Kapital, Vol 1, Swan Sonnenschein, Lowrey, & Co., London, pp 1–44 (1867).

[49] Marx, Ibid.

[50] Marx, *supra* note 13.

[51] Polanayi 1944, 2001, p 79; ('We recall our parallel between the ravages of the enclosures in English history and the social catastrophe which followed the Industrial Revolution. Improvements, we said, are, as a rule, bought at the price of social dislocation').

[52] Polanayi, *Id.*, at 117; ('Natural is that which is in accordance with the principles embodied in the mind of man…Nature in the physical sense was consciously excluded by Smith from the problem of wealth…Not the natural, but only the human factors enter. This exclusion of the biological and geographical factor in the very beginning of his book was deliberate. The fallacies of the Physiocrats served him as a warning; their predilection for agriculture tempted them to confuse physical nature with man's nature, and induced them to argue that the soil alone was truly creative. Nothing was further from the mind of Smith than such a glorification of Physis. Political economy should be a human science; it should deal with that which was natural to man, not to Nature'. In that way, the science of political economy, developed by Utilitarians like Adam Smith and Jeremy Bentham, triumphed over the traditional Physiocrats; who invested their intellectual depths in protection of land from the exploitation of self-regulating free market).

[53] Bilgrami, *supra* note 10 at 158.

were considered as a projected reality of the human species what Adam Smith neologized as 'moral sentiments'.[54] On the contrary, Mahatma Gandhi had a sacred conception of nature. He rejected the materialistic culture of modernity and its dehumanized outlook. His philosophy was diametrically opposite to the instrumentalism or the utilitarianism. He found that greed is the fundamental cause of colonialism, imperialism, economic exploitation, slavery, and degradation of ecology; otherwise, the Earth is sufficiently capable enough to take care of its habitants.[55] Gandhi was well aware about the transformations, which took place in the epoch of modernity, from the concept of nature to the concept of natural resources, the concept of human beings to the concept of citizens, the concept of people to the concept of populations, and the knowledge to live by to the expertise to rule by.[56] He was a devoted student of the Indian spiritual traditions and the Bhakti movements and had firm belief about nature's spiritual dimension. This was a widely accepted view under the philosophical tradition of Neo-Platonism,[57] Pantheism, and in other tribal communities, but the triumph of modernity was not possible with a sacred conception of nature. So, the imaginative leap of the modern paradigm became possible only after the exile of sacred from nature. The 'de-sacralization of nature'[58] or the 'disenchantment of the world'[59] has progressed, nowadays, towards the existential crisis; absurdity and 'anomie'.[60] The human beings are treated, nowadays, as resources, a means, to achieve other ends, and the purpose of education has been channelized into the direction of resource development programme. Because, the newly established industries are demanding the disciplined and cheap labourers, which are supplied after the vocational trainings, so as to normalize and cultivate in them the skills in the larger goal of efficiency of the business.[61] The abstraction of the concept of citizenship from the concept of human being inevitably followed after the emergence of nation-state in Europe, on the basis of common cultural identity,[62] and the

[54] Bilgrami, *Id.*, at 185; (David Hume and Adam Smith emphasized that nature has no value in itself; rather it is found in the human's desires and in the moral sentiments of the humans).

[55] Parekh, *supra* note 11 at 35.

[56] Bilgrami, *supra* note 10 at 133.

[57] Bilgrami, *Id.*, at 134.

[58] Bilgrami, Ibid.

[59] Weber Max, The Vocation Lectures (eds: Owen David &. Strong Tracy B., trans: Livingstone Rodney) (2004). Hackett Publishing Co., Indianapolis & Cambridge, pp 12-13; ('Thus the growing process of intellectualization and rationalization does not imply a growing understanding of the conditions under which we live….It means that in principle, then, we are not ruled by mysterious, unpredictable forces, but that, on the contrary, we can in principle control everything by means of calculation. That in turn means the disenchantment of the world').

[60] Merton Robert King & Merton Robert, Social Theory and Social Structure, The Free Press, New York, p 185 (1949, 1968).

[61] Chomsky Noam, Class Warfare: Interviews with David Barsamian. Pluto Press, London, pp 19–23, 27–31 (1996); ('There are huge efforts that do go into making people, to borrow Adam Smith's phrase, as stupid and ignorant as it is possible for a human being to be. A lot of the educational system is designed for that, if you think about it, it is designed for obedience and passivity').

[62] Bilgrami, *supra* note 10 at 146.

whole dynamics of politics revolved around the dichotomy of 'friend-enemy',[63] or 'external enemy'.[64] In that sense, the secularization was the need of hour in Europe, so as to blur the distinction among the various religious identities. Over the period of time, all the scattered powers of the people were centralized into the nation-states. The autonomous choice of self-governance, morality, and other socio-customary practices was displaced by the authority of official law, and the population became the subject matter of state's policy and law.[65] In the process of centralization, the nation-state was required to have a pervasive system of bureaucracy, consisting of the experts, belonging to the diversified disciplines. The professionalization of vocations was the inevitable culmination from an egoistic pursuit of the mastery over nature and to govern effectively and efficiently over the individual and socio-political lives of the human's community. In that sense, being in the world was no longer a goal to live by, rather the human's desire was elevated to become the master of the universe. The professionalization of various occupations brought a detached outlook towards nature and society. For example, the legal profession was developed in a formal way without having any significant participation of the people whose conflicts are addressed by it, and the structure of formal law has remained too technical and linguistically alien for the common people. The whole process of the professionalization has undoubtedly benefitted the professionals, but it has remained closed from the perspective of accessibility for a common person, for whom, it is supposed to have been brought into existence. The *panchayat* systems worked efficiently until the traditional institutions were displaced by the official courts in the colonial period. The conflicts were resolved within the community itself after a sensitive deliberation, negotiation, and compromise. The medical profession, likewise, was functioning in a quite similar way. In the ancient and medieval periods, many civilizations, including the Hindu and Chinese, were concerned with the physical and mental health; for this purpose, the traditional healers and doctors were integrally connected to the social roots.

Gandhi had the history before him, and he compared a distinct paradigm of modernity with a traditional one, which was inclined towards the adaptation within the community and in the larger framework of nature. The materialized outlook of modernity has significantly transformed the ways of life into the hallucinated competition of greed, which has destroyed the community life and robbed the vitality of nature. The

[63] Tracy B Strong, Introduction to the English Edition of Carl Schmitt's Political Theology: Four Chapters on the Concept of Sovereignty (ed: Schwab George), The University of Chicago Press, Chicago, p XVI (1922, 2005).

[64] Bilgrami, *supra* note 10 at 147.

[65] Foucault, *supra* note 9 at 317; (Michel Foucault in his lectures explained these governmental practices as Biopolitics, in his words, '...biopolitics, by which I meant the attempt, starting from the eighteenth century, to rationalize the problems posed to governmental practice by phenomenon characteristic of a set of living beings forming a population: health, hygiene, birthrate, life expectancy, race....We know the increasing importance of these problems since the nineteenth century, and the political and economic issues they have raised up to the present'). *See* Bilgrami 2014. Available at: https://youtu.be/KrcV_TZOdk0 (last visited 05 June, 2020); (Gandhi realized this phenomenon much before the elaborate works of Michel Foucault were published).

everlasting mining the minerals, the polluted air, water, and soil, the melting glaciers, and the innumerable catastrophes like floods, droughts, and pandemics are all related to the ambitious egoism of the human species. The exile of holy and sacred from nature has proved to be too unbearable for the sustenance of life. Gandhi anticipated that the future of humanity is not secure in the modern outlook of mastering nature. The Gandhian universe was a moral one, consisting of the spirit of cooperation, love, and uncompromising thrust for the truth and non-violence. He was able to find the spiritual affection in everyone and everything.

His spiritual or moral worldview was not an original one; rather it was cultivated by him with open eyes and welcoming heart. The development of Gandhian philosophy had no abstract genesis; rather it was cultivated by him in his daily practices as a moral scientist. In the modern universe of specialization and compartmentalization of justice, Gandhi was far more holistic towards the ideas of justice. He was averse to the idea that one can be truthful in the personal life, but not so in the professional one.[66] The 'integrity'[67] in Gandhian ideas is not often visible in any other leader of his contemporary age. He was one of the truest devotees of justice, not only in the social or the political life, but also in the moral or the spiritual life. His transformative ontology on suffering was the truthful service for the humanity, like what Buddha did.

4 Conclusion

The idealized projection of the principles of justice, whether it is categorized as a moral, legal, or a political concept, remains elusive. Gandhi perceived it not merely as an ideal to be conceptualized, rather a practical and moral possibility to be realized in the daily practices. He was able to concretize the metaphysical ideals, like truth and non-violence, with an inventive strategy of *Satyagrah.* Gandhi was deeply compassionate to alleviate suffering of every poor and downtrodden person. As a moral scientist, he did not hesitate to experiment with the moral ideals. He was, in fact, a critical traditionalist, who was aware about the modernity and its consequences, which caused the alienation, suffering, and mass impoverishment of the people across the globe. He was not willing to borrow the principles of modernity in the name of shallow progressivism; rather the ancient Indian and romantic traditions

---

[66] Kripalani J.B. Gandhian Revaluation of Values. Gandhi Marg 1 (1): 5–12 (1979). Available at: https://www.gandhiheritageportal.org/journals-by-others/gandhi-marg-in-english. (last accessed 02 June, 2020 (1979). Available at: https://www.gandhiheritageportal.org/journals-by-others/gandhi-marg-in-english (last visited 02 June 2020); ('The soldier does not hesitate to kill in battle those who are not his personal enemies and those who have done him no wrong, though in his social and personal life and conduct he is a harmless person....They are oblivious of the fact that by their public and professional behavior they are violating the moral law. This is because we do not consider life as an integrated whole. We have devised different moral codes for different aspects of our life. For Gandhi, life, as we have said, is one').

[67] Bilgrami, *supra* note 10 at 121.

of the west appealed him more than anything else. However, he was not a revivalist in a dogmatic sense; rather he chose to test the traditional practices at the touchstone of reason and experience. His suspicion against the modernity emerged from the past experiences, particularly from the European history. Gandhi witnessed the two World Wars in his lifetime, the invention and use of nuclear weapon in Hiroshima and Nagasaki, the terror of Nazi regime in Germany, colonialism, imperialism, and cruel and inhuman treatments of the colonial subjects, emergence of urbanized slums, destruction of ecology, meaninglessness and absurdity in the psychic experiences of modern man, etc. The western civilization has invested the huge intellectual energies in the development of epistemology and the possibility of knowledge since the birth of Cartesian philosophy, in the end, knowledge has remained elitist and far away from the truth. In fact, it was conceptualized as a plaything and amusement for the instrumentality. Gandhi, on the contrary, was deeply committed to the cause of truth in a moral sense. He opposed the widespread practices of conceiving knowledge in the cognitive and instrumental sense and emphasized upon the moral and spiritual growth of human beings.

In the postmodern age, truth is no longer valuable; particularly, the use, overuse, and misuse of social media have established a paradigm of 'post-truth'. The 'simulated'[68] ecology is making true the 'manufacturing of consent'[69] to refer Noam Chomsky, which cannot be, however, considered as a new phenomenon; however, the intensity of such practices has almost challenged the possibility of public participation in a fair and reasonable manner in choosing the representatives or in the formulation of policies for the common welfare. The cognitive truth has created a 'liar paradox',[70] whereas the knowledge is not practised in ethical sense, rather it is selectively used as an opportunity for the professional success or in the benefit of trade and business. The legal profession in India, for example, is dedicated towards the 'error of facts' rather than the truth, and the professionals are mostly dedicated to their own professional or monetary growth. Gandhi visualized the role of truth in the process of justice-administration. He, as a moral crusader against the violence and oppression, chose to resist peacefully against the oppressor for justice and peace. The Gandhian vision for justice was not limited to the humankind only; rather he had the 'ethic of care'[71] for every creature. Gandhi was not enthusiastic about the glory of right without the performance of obligation. Duty was considered by him as a positive act, meaningful for the social life and peace. Gandhian *swaraj* was visualized as the self-controlled or the self-ruled freedom without any assertiveness of claim and counterclaim. He was a great defender of freedom, not merely in negative sense, championed by the liberal thinkers, like John Stuart Mill, John Locke,

---

[68] Baudrillard Jean, 'Simulacara and Simulation' (trans: Glaser Sheila Faria), the University of Michigan Press, Michigan, p 1 (1981, 1994).

[69] Herman Edward S. & Chomsky Noam, Manufacturing Consent: The Political Economy of the Mass Media, Pantheon Books, New York, p IX (1988).

[70] J. Beall, Liar Paradox, Stanford Encyclopedia of Philosophy (2011) Available at: https://plato.stanford.edu/entries/liar-paradox/. (last accessed 05 June 2020).

[71] West Robin, Caring For Justice. New York University Press, New York & London, p 69 (1997).

Jefferson, or Isaiah Berlin, etc., rather his meditations on freedom were positive and constructive for the collective welfare of society as a whole. In the postmodern age, when the world is not at consensus to deal against some of the existential issues, like the development and climate change, the refugee crisis, the increasing threats of nuclear armaments and biological weapons, etc., the Gandhian philosophy is relevant as much as ever before. The integrity in Gandhian philosophy successfully resisted every instrumentalist or material perspective of justice in the colonial time; his philosophy of justice, based on the principles and praxes of truth, non-violence, love, compassion, moral obligation and *satyagrah*, etc., might be a guiding ray of hope for the humanity in contemporary time.

References

Adorno TW (2001) the culture industry: selected essays on mass culture. In: Bernstein JM (ed) Routledge, New York, pp 1, 61

Ahuja R (1999) Society in India: concepts, theories, and changing trends. Rawat Publications, p 16

Claude A (1988) Science, colonialism and violence. In: Ashish N (ed) Science, hegemony and violence: a requiem for modernity. Oxford University Press, Oxford, pp 75–82

Aristotle (400 B.C., 2000) Politics (trans: Benjamin J). Dover Publications, New York, p 28

Weber Max (2004) The vocation lectures. In: David O, Strong Tracy B (eds) (trans: Rodney L). Hackett Publishing Co., Indianapolis & Cambridge, pp 12–13

Kenneth A (1994) Methodological individualism and social knowledge. American Economy Review 84(2):3

Article 51 (1945) The Charter of the United Nations

Bacon F, Basil M (1859) The Works of Francis Bacon, Lord Chancellor of England, vol 3. Parry & Mcmillan, pp 369, 372

Jean B (1981, 1994) Simulacara and simulation (trans: Sheila Faria G). The University of Michigan Press, Michigan, p 1

Beall J (2011) Liar Paradox, Stanford Encyclopedia of Philosophy. Available at: https://plato.stanford.edu/entries/liar-paradox/. Accessed 05 Jun 2020

Isaiah B (2002, 2014) Freedom and Its Betrayal. In: Henry H (ed). Princeton University Press, Princeton, p 224

Akeel B (2014a) Gandhi and the political enlightenment. In: Asian Art Museum. Available at: https://youtu.be/KrcV_TZOdk0. Accessed 05 Jun 2020

Bilgrami A (2014b) Gandhi and the mentality of modernity. Dialogue of Civilizations Research Institute. Available at: https://youtu.be/Pv9m6L_mptU. Accessed 10 Jun 2020

Bilgrami A (2014b) Secularism, identity, and disenchantment. Harvard University Press, Cambridge, p 175

Chomsky N (1996) Class Warfare: Interviews with David Barsamian. Pluto Press, London, pp 19–23, 27–31

Clegg S (2013) The theory of power and organization. Routledge, London & New York, p 76

Dasa R (2002) Gandhi in 21st Century. Sarup & Sons, New Delhi, p 22

Davies J (2016) The Birth of Anthropocene. University of California Press, California, pp 52, 55

Laurence E (1999) Nature's Holism. To Exel Press, Lincoln, pp 1–2

Foucault M (1966, 2005) The order of things: an archaeology of the human sciences. Routledge Classics, London & New York, pp 54, 387

Foucault M (1978) The birth of biopolitics: lectures at The College De France (ed: Senellart Michel). Palgrave Macmillan, New York, p 41

Friedman M (1962, 2009) Capitalism and Freedom: Fortieth Anniversary Edition. The University of Chicago Press, Chicago & London, p 12
Gandhi MK (1921) Young India
Gandhi MK (1927, 2018) An autobiography or the story of my experiments with truth: a critical edition (trans: Mahadev D). Navajivan Publishing House, Ahmedabad, p 98
Gandhi R (2007) Gandhi: the man, his people, and the Empire. University of California Press, Berkeley, p 241
Havel V, Tutu Desmond M (2012) Introduction. In: The responsibility to protect: the promise of stopping mass atrocities in our time. In: Jared G, Irwin C (eds). Oxford University Press, Oxford, p XXV
Heidegger M (1977) The question concerning technology and other essays (trans: William L). Garland Publishing, New York & London, pp 5, 18
Herman Edward S, Noam C (1988) Manufacturing consent: The political economy of the mass media. Pantheon Books, New York, p IX
Horkheimer M (1947, 2013) Eclipse of reason. Bloomsbury, London, p 13
Jayapalan N (2001) Comprehensive history of political thought. Atlantic Publishers and Distributors, New Delhi, p 351
Kant I (1797, 1998) Groundwork of the metaphysics of morals. In: Karl A, Clarke Desmond M (eds). Cambridge University Press, Cambridge, pp 31–43
Kripalani JB (1979) Gandhian revaluation of values. Gandhi Marg 1 (1): 5–12. Available at: https://www.gandhiheritageportal.org/journals-by-others/gandhi-marg-in-english. Accessed 02 Jun 2020
Marx K (1844, 1988) Economic and philosophic manuscripts (trans: Martin M). Dover Publication, New York, p 71
Marx K (1867) Das Kapital, vol 1, Swan Sonnenschein, Lowrey, & Co., London, pp 1–44
Meetings Coverage and Press Releases of the United Nations (2019) 73rd Session of general assembly on climate change and sustainable development: only 11 years left to prevent irreversible damage from climate change, speakers warn during general assembly high-level meeting. In: United Nations. Available at: https://www.un.org/press.en/2019/ga12131.doc.htm. Accessed 12 Jun 2020
Merton RK, Robert M (1949, 1968) Social Theory and Social Structure. The Free Press, New York, p 185
Mookherjee BD (2002) The essence of Bhagavad Gita. Academic Publishers, Kolkata, p 91
Morrison W (1997, 2005) Jurisprudence: from the Greeks to Post-Modernism. Routledge, New York & London, p 107
Newman S (2005) Power and politics in poststructuralist thought: new theories of the political. Routledge, London & New York, p 51
Newton I (1704, 1721) Optiks. William and John Innys, London, pp 339–340
Nietzsche F (1901, 2019) The Will to Power (trans: Ludovici Anthony M). Dover Publications, New York, p 30
Parekh B (1989) Gandhi's political philosophy: a critical examination. Macmillan Academic, London, p 138
Parmar Arjunsinh K (2002) Critical perspectives on the Mahabharata. Sarup & Sons, New Delhi, p 111
Perelman Ch (1965) Justice and justification. Natural Law Forum, p 5
Plato (360 B.C., 2003) Timaeus (trans: Benjamin J). Dover Publication, New York, p 11
Polanayi K (1944, 2001) The great transformation: the political and economic origins of our time. Beacon Press, Boston, pp 79, 117
Radhakrishnan S (1927, 1940) Indian Philosophy, Vol 1. George Allen & Unwin, London, p 109
Rich J (2007) An introduction to critical theory. Humanities-Ebooks, Tirril, p 66
Sarkar BK (1920) The theory of property, law, and social order in Hindu Political Philosophy. Int J Ethics 30(3):311–325. Available at: http://www.jstor.org/stable/2377667. Accessed 25 Jun 2020

Sechter D (2010) The critique of instrumental reason from Weber to Habermas. The Continuum International Publishing, New York & London, p 187

Shakespeare W (1599, 2000) Hamlet. In: Sidney L (ed). Hungry Minds, New York, p 85

Smith A (1776, 1977) An inquiry into the nature and causes of the wealth of nations. In: Cannan Edwin (ed). ElecBook Classics, London, p 30

Spivak GC (1998) Preface to the English Edition. In: Jacques Derrida's Of grammatology (trans: Chakravorty SG). The John Hopkins University Press, Baltimore & London, p XVI

Strong TB (1922, 2005). Introduction to the English Edition of Carl Schmitt's political theology: four chapters on the concept of Sovereignty. In: George S (ed). The University of Chicago Press, Chicago, p XVI

Sugirtharajah S (2004) Imagining Hinduism: a postcolonial perspective. Routledge, London & New York, p 55

West R (1997) Caring for justice. New York University Press, New York & London, p 69

Chapter 3
Individual and Community Interests: A Critical Analysis with the Help of Gandhian Philosophy

N. Manoharan, Akshat Agrawal, and Yashwardhan Bansal

1 Introduction

In this crony-capitalistic world, where people aim for self-enrichment and proclaiming power over the others, this chapter intends to remind people of their duties towards the society. Every human being is considered to be a social animal who cannot endure in absence of a society. The basic foundation of a society rests on the mutual relationships of give and take among the individuals. Individuals driven only by their self-interest can nevertheless make collective decisions existing in a society.[1] When we discuss about interests, the natural tension and conflict between individual and community interests are bound to arise. Every human being is born with certain needs that are essential for its survival.[2] These requirements have an incessant growth during the lifetime of the person. All his needs and wants can be classified as subject of his individual interest. Individual interests refer to the actions of a person that tend to elicit personal benefit. It is the act of considering the advantage to oneself while taking any decision. It is also referred to as 'self-interest'. The humans have subconsciously always thrived towards their individual interests.

[1] Koshal and Koshal (1973).

[2] Mallik (1948).

N. Manoharan
Associate Professor, Department of International Studies and History, CHRIST (Deemed to Be University), Bengaluru, India
e-mail: manoharan.n@christuniversity.in

A. Agrawal (✉) · Y. Bansal
Student, School of Law, CHRIST (Deemed to Be University), Bengaluru, India
e-mail: akshat.agrawal@law.christuniversity.in

Y. Bansal
e-mail: yash.bansal@law.christuniversity.in

R. Mittal and K. K. Singh (eds.), *Relevance of Duties in the Contemporary World*,
https://doi.org/10.1007/978-981-19-1836-0_3

On flipping the pages of our history books, it will be discovered that the reason why humans started for a settlement was to save themselves from each other and the constant fear of being hunted by fellow human being. When these settlements became wide-reaching and people started to become civilised, a sense of community was seen to emerge. The first time when a leader or a group of leaders were chosen to make decisions for others, a bleak origin of community interests was seen to make an appearance.[3] Community interests take into account the larger picture being the welfare of the society giving precedence to it over individuals. It is the action taken for the community in its best interest over that of any particular individual. It is also termed as 'group interest'. The system of democracy in which we live in also spreads its roots to the idea of community development. There are a number of ideologies that talk about these interests, where some of them give importance to one whereas some completely deject the other. The chapter contributes more towards the debate of individual and community interests and provides for a comparative approach of ideas of philosophers in the west and that of Gandhi.

When we discuss about Gandhi and his ideas, it is found that his conception was inclined more towards interests of community at large. He respected the fundamental rights of every individual, though believed that every person has a moral obligation to serve the society for community's interest.[4] An important relationship of 'rights' and 'interests' can be established when we understand that rights which are accompanied by duties are necessary to protect some of the important individual interests. Gandhi has always been seen as a leader of masses, and he worked for the welfare of people across the nation. The core concept of Gandhi's philosophy rests on his idea of duty. The chapter discusses more on the Gandhian idea of duty and also throws light on his conception of an ideal state and a society. There were many tools which Gandhi used which promoted the collective goals and interests in a society. These tools were his ideas of *satyagrah*, *Swaraj* (self-rule), *Sarvodaya* (rise of all) and the *Ekadash Vrat* (11 principles).[5] This chapter highlights the importance of these which played a major role in developing a sense of integration and collectiveness in the society. Emphasis has also been made to bring out a picture where his ideas tend to bridge the gap between conflicts of individual and community interests. The chapter with its concluding remarks will surely induce the readers to ponder over the question of 'why is it even required for existence of a debate for preference between individuality and community when they can go hand in hand?'

---

[3] K. Mashruwala, Gandhi and Marx, 1951, Navajivan Publishing House, India pp 16–22.

[4] Dennis Dalton, Gandhi on Freedom, Rights and Responsibilities, Articles on And by Gandhi, https://www.mkgandhi.org/articles/freedom.htm. (last visited on Jun 28, 2020).

[5] Rothermund Indira, "The Individual and Society in Gandhi's Political Thought", 28 *The Journal of Asian Studies* 2 313–322 (1969).

2 The Western Framework of Ideas

One can trace the origin of various key ideas that are in practice from western nations. These ideas pioneered by western philosophers have contributed immensely to the development of both individual and society. The western philosophers have tried to explain individuals and society as abstract entities. The ideas of ethical and moral problems have not really been part of their writings. When it comes to individual interest, it has many layers, and these layers have been interpreted and explained by different western philosophers. There are certain philosophers that have completely dejected the idea of individual interest, whereas some thrive upon it. An attempt has been made to elaborate the ideas of philosophers of the west to give a comparative analysis with that of Gandhian ideology.

The famous philosopher Jeremy Bentham (1748–1832 A.D.) propagated the idea of utilitarianism which is based upon attaining 'greatest happiness of the greatest number' for an individual.[6] He talked about how it is rational for each individual to fulfil their own interest in the best possible way. On the same note, John Stuart Mill (1806–1873 A.D.) also made an effort to explain the utilitarian theory which was a proponent of individual interest alike Bentham. Though, he did not take a rigid stance as like Bentham but tried to explain the theory with the applicability of morals in his work, *'Theory of Human Nature'* and *'Remarks on Bentham's Philosophy'*. He promoted the idea of being morally satisfied and not pig satisfied. He said that maximising the utility by every individual was really essential and that is what is human nature. Though, the act through which one maximises his utility should be morally right which is paradoxical to Bentham's view. Another prominent philosopher supporting the idea of individual interest was Emmanuel Kant (1724–1804 A.D.) where he stated the importance of autonomy and freedom. In his book *'Grounding for the Metaphysics of Morals'*,[7] he was concerned about the dignity of the 'individual autonomous will'. He even goes forward and talks about individuals being treated as an end and not means to an end. Similarly, Friedrich Hegel (1770–1831 A.D.) in his works tries to bring out a different analysis of individual interest where he includes the care about not just oneself but for family and friends too. *'He explains a cycle in which members are nominated according to common interests of different political parties, and as the deputies elected from the parties to the legislative bodies give voice to those interests within the deliberative processes of legislation, the outcome of this process might give expression to the general interest'*.[8]

Adam Smith (1723–90 A.D.) provides a different lens to examine the interests of individual. He elucidated about various concepts like an 'invisible hand', 'creation of

---

[6] Crimmins E. James, "Jeremy Bentham", *The Stanford Encyclopedia of Philosophy Archive*, Edward N. Zalta (ed.) Summer 2020 Edition. Available at https://plato.stanford.edu/archives/sum2020/entries/bentham/. (Last accessed 28 June, 2020).

[7] Kant Immanuel and Gregor Mary J, "Groundwork of the Metaphysics of Morals", ed. 17, Cambridge University Press, Cambridge, United Kingdom, 1998.

[8] Redding Paul, "Georg Wilhelm Friedrick Hegal", *The Stanford Encyclopedia of Philosophy*, 2020, Available at https://plato.stanford.edu/entries/hegel/ (last accessed 06 May, 2020).

wealth', 'free market' and 'economic liberalism'. All of his ideas carried the concept of individual interest giving an economic perspective to it. He in his work '*Wealth of Nations'* explained self-interest as an action which incentives one's personal benefits. His concept of invisible hand explained the driving force in an economy as different acts are committed by thousands of individuals for their own personal interests. According to him, it is rational for people to forward their individual interest which helps the economy to grow as it resulted in creation of wealth.

There are certain philosophers who have rejected the idea of individual interest and have believed in socialism according to which the aim is to attain an egalitarian society where everyone is equal. There is communism which talks about equal distribution of resources among all the people and philosophers like Karl Marx (1818–1883 A.D.) have propagated it. We have 'social contract' theory proposed by Rousseau, Locke and Hobbes which states that all individuals give up their rights and let the state take care of their welfare and make decisions for common good of the people. The idea of community interest is ages old, and the democracy that we see today is based on it. There are three philosophers that have propagated their own versions of social contract theory inspired by the society and political system around them. In each, the roles of state and the level of sacrifice of rights by individuals vary. John Locke (1632–1704 A.D.) in *'The Second Treatise of Government'* established his take on community interest through the social contact theory. '*He explained political power as the right to make binding laws for all and for the sake of community in its best interest'*.[9] He gave examples of public goods that are owned by state and possess the benefit which can be grabbed by everyone.

Jean Jacques Rousseau (1712–1778 A.D.) also contributed immensely towards the theory. He was not a conservative who expected a complete devotion of individual towards the community. He insisted upon an individual making oneself part of a larger community and contributing towards its good in a necessary condition of personal freedom.[10] Individuals should have their own way of leading life though, whereas it needs to be in contrast with the larger community to achieve a sense of belongingness. John Rawls (1921–2002 A.D.) being a covenant of liberalism propagates his version of community interest by explaining the aim behind having the idea which is to achieve a common good in the society. According to him, common good referred to the sum total of social conditions that answers to the interests attached to the position of equal citizenship.[11] It provided citizens with freedom, liberty of expression and conscience which in sense a democracy provides as well. It even consisted of the legal protection of these key elements and a free choice of profession which ensured people are motivated to do well. When this common good is achieved that is when everyone is satisfied, the interest of whole community is respected. Another perspective on community interest is expressed and explained by Aristotle (385–323 B.C.E) where

---

[9] Rothermund, *supra* note 6.

[10] Bertram Christopher, "Jean Jacques Rousseau", *Stanford Encyclopedia of Philosophy*, 2017 Available at https://plato.stanford.edu/entries/rousseau/ (last accessed 14 June, 2020).

[11] Wenar Leif, "John Rawls", *Standard Encyclopaedia of Philosophy Archive*, Spring 2017 Edition Available at https://plato.stanford.edu/archives/spr2017/entries/rawls/ (last accessed 14 June 2020).

he ultimately helps in reaching out to a structured ordered society. He explains it in the most basic way which is by helping and thinking well and high of fellow beings.[12] This according to him was living the choicest worthy life and simplest way of contributing towards community interest.

3 Magnification Through Gandhian Lens

Gandhi was the leader of masses who was a staunch believer for people changing themselves, the change they wish to bring in the world. With his weapons of truth and non-violence, he led the battle for country's independence and also tried to transform the society in different aspects.[13] Gandhian philosophy is based upon idealism and fairness where community is the cardinal point and individuals playing their roles for its development. The society that he aimed to build and qualities which he wanted to embed in people gets light thorough his conception of ideal state, path of duty and ideas like satyagrah, Swaraj, Sarvodaya, among others. These ideas draw a significant sketch of his ideology and can be seen to contribute immensely towards the friction between the individual and community interests acting as a guiding light.

3.1 The Ideal State and Society

As in line with the western ideas of individual and community interests, there were different conceptions that were brought to understand the 'state' as well. A state is generally understood to be as a definite territory of people that is regulated under a particular system of governance. There were many factors that were responsible for the emergence of idea of state which included things like rule, kinship, wars, political consciousness and economic needs. Gandhi did not approve of the conception of a modern state. He equated the idea of modern state synonymously with the actions of coercion and violence. In his words, *'The State represents violence in a concentrated and organised form. The individual has a soul, but as the State is a soulless machine, it can never be weaned from violence to which it owes its very existence'.*[14] He believed that the western idea instilled great powers with the states which reduced exploitation, but it did much greater harm by destroying the individuality which was required for progress.

When we look down through the Gandhian lens, the picture of an ideal society comes out to be one that is of non-violence and democratic social order. He stressed on

[12] Yack Bernard (1985), "Community and Conflict in Aristotle's Political Philosophy", *The Review of Politics* 92–112 Available at https://www.jstor.org/stable/1406724?seq=1.

[13] Mathur J. S. (eds), "Non-Violence and Social Change", Navajivan Mudranalaya, India, 1977.

[14] Guest Author (2015), "Peace, Liberty, and Gandhi" Available at https://spontaneousorder.in/peace-liberty-and-gandhi/ (last visited June 14, 2020).

the idea of *Swaraj* (self-rule) in a society which has equilibrium of individual freedom and social responsibilities.[15] According to him, every individual is responsible for performance of his duties which leads to peace in the society. He believed for an existence of a society that is free from all kinds of exploitation where every individual is protected and is able to exercise his basic fundamental rights. Gandhi believed that existence of man in the society has a purpose and a social order that has to be fulfilled. A society which is filled with a regime of chaos never struck his thoughts. Gandhi's idea of an ideal state is composed with diverse areas which give a well-formed structure in every field. He primarily laid emphasis on the concept of 'enlightened anarchy' where there is a state which has no ruler, subject and government. What he primarily called it was as a *Ram Rajya* (divine rule) which was constituted by ultimate values of non-violence, truth, equality and freedom.[16] In this conception of him, Gandhi is seen to merge the substance of ethics, principles and morality with politics and coming out with a structure for an ideal state.

Gandhi also believed in decentralisation of powers in the state as according to him if the powers are concentrated in hands of one it leads to absolutism, and there were possibilities for them to be misused. Moreover discussing on individuals, Gandhi made an attempt to bring a sense of selflessness among people, and he propagated that no person should run to collect and maximise wealth because this would bring a situation of poverty in the state. If we analyse this idea, it works to prevent the scenario of the 'rich getting richer and the poor getting poorer'. In his conception of the ideal state, Gandhi also promoted the use of *swadeshi* (self-produced) goods by all the people in the country.[17] Talking about the law enforcement agencies such as police, Gandhi's ideal state had a minimal role for them. According to him, crime was a disease for the society and had to be prevented, but he believed in punishing and correcting the conscience of the individual rather than the individual himself. Police brutality was never a fruitful option according to him.

As we saw Emanuel Kant discussing the relationship where he mentioned about means to the end, Gandhi also believed that the state was not just the end but a means to the end where it was responsible for the collective good of its citizens and was always working to promote and improve the conditions of its subjects. It had a responsibility for the greatest good of greatest number of people. We now have an idea about Gandhi's conception of his ideal state and society which was primarily constituted with the ideas of democracy, non-violence, equality, freedom and truth. It aimed to be constituted by citizens who were public spirited and would voluntarily contribute in living a harmonious life.

---

[15] M. K. Gandhi, "Hind Swaraj or Indian Home Rule", Navajivan Publishing House, India, 1938.

[16] Tendulkar Dinanath Gopal, "Mahatma: Life of Mohandas Karamchand Gandhi", vol. 7, The Publication Division, Ministry of Information & Broadcasting, GOI, Patiala House (1950).

[17] Anjaneyulu B.S.R. (2003), "Gandhi's 'Hind Swaraj'—Swaraj, The Swadeshi Way", *The Indian Journal of Political Science* 33–44 Available at https://www.jstor.org/stable/41855768?seq=1.

3.2 The Path of Duty

In today's world, every person is running a constant race for making oneself superior to others. It is often seen that individuals tend to neglect and miss out on their basic obligations and responsibilities in course of this scuttle. Every individual has some basic rights which can be exercised by him. Every person is born with rights, but duty falls in line as a human grows and becomes more and more prudent. Rights and duties are two sides of a coin which go hand in hand. With the existence of every right, there is a duty attached to it. Individuals are more concerned for the enforcement of their rights and are often ignorant for the duties that they need to fulfil. Rights and duties can be defined in a number of ways. In the general sense, a right is understood as some standard of permitted action within a certain sphere. It can constitute of actions that can be moral or legally enforceable. On the other hand, duty can be understood as an obligatory act that has to be discharged, opposite of which would constitute a wrong. The commission of a wrong is the breach of duty, and performance of a duty is avoidance of wrong.[18] Duty can also be classified into 'legal duty' and 'moral duty'. A legal duty is something where breach of it would be subject to penalty, whereas a moral duty is some natural and moral wrong which does not attract any sanction on its breach.

Gandhi also had his idea of duty which he emphasised upon. In fact, it was one of the core ideas of his philosophy. He did not support the idea of imposing rights and letting duties follow through. He even criticised the idea that duties originate from rights. Unlike others, he always gave priority to duties over rights and believed in community good over self-interests. He believed that if a human complies with his duties towards family, friends and society, then his own rights will just follow through. According to him, duty was the expression and explanation of the concept of *dharm*—the binding force of the universe.[19] Gandhi propagated that '*let each do his duty, if I do my duty, that is, serve myself, I shall be able to serve others*'.[20] As per his idea, the path of duty could be classified and understood in twofold perspective where every individual has (i) an obligation towards oneself and (ii) an obligation towards the community. Every individual should fulfil and stand committed on performing these two obligations which result in a harmonious and peaceful society. In Gandhi's own words '… *One has to lose oneself in continuous and continuing service to all life. Realization of truth is impossible without a complete merging of oneself in, and identification with, the limitless ocean of life*'.[21]

---

[18] P.J. Fitzgerald, "Salmond on jurisprudence", 12th edn. Universal Law Publishing, New Delhi, India, p. 271 (2016).

[19] Sethy Satya Sundar, "Reinterpreting Gandhi's notion of "Dharma": An Entanglement of Duty, Religion and Ethics", Articles-On and By Gandhi (2015) Available at https://www.mkgandhi.org/articles/reinterpreting-gandhis-notion-of-dharma.html (last accessed 29 June, 2020).

[20] Dennis, *supra* note 5.

[21] Radhakrishnan S. and Muirhead John H., "Contemporary Indian Philosophy", George G Harrap, London (1936).

It gets very clear that he emphasised promoting people to lend themselves for the service of others and the society without expecting anything in return. He believed that self-realisation which is based on moral and ethical principles need to be imparted among each individual instead of self-interest. This made more conscious of their duties. Gandhi even expressed his opinion upon the importance of self-discipline and self-control, which assisted people in fulfilling their duty. According to him, various acts like fasting helped in self-discipline and brahmacharya (practising celibacy) helped in self-control.[22] Gandhi explicitly emphasises upon the knowledge of duty with individuals. He believed that society and traditions are the most promising sources for one to acquire knowledge of duty. He believed that traditions and traditional institutions played an important role in imparting or making an individual realise his duties. It can thus be seen that Gandhi laid much focus on his idea of duty where he made people realise the importance of community interests and welfare of people giving precedence to it over rights and self-interests.

3.3 Satyagrah

According to Gandhi, everything that has existence in reality is nothing but 'truth'. His idea of *satyagrah* is also based on it. 'Satyagrah' is formed out of two Sanskrit words, 'satya' meaning 'truth' and 'agrah' means to 'insist' which resorts to 'holding of truth'. It is nothing but compliance to non-violence, truth and self-suffering. According to Gandhi, 'truth' was moral and unchanging where one could reach by following the methods which are 'non-violence' *(ahimsa)*. These non-violent routes made an individual go through 'self-suffering' which was voluntarily agreed by him. Some of the non-violent methods which were introduced by Gandhi were non-cooperation, civil disobedience and fasting.

It is essential to note that through his idea of *satyagrah*, Gandhi brought forward that role of individual. He asserted that there is no power on the earth that could make a man/women do anything against his/her will. It is necessary to preserve the freedom and integrity of the individual.[23] *Satyagrah* is a dynamic concept which essentially was in place for holding up to truth, but it was also used by Gandhi as a means to an end for achieving social and political goals. This gave a picture of *satyagrah* where it united people from different backgrounds towards achieving one common objective. Gandhi envisaged *satyagrah* as a universal solvent for injustice and harm which was equally applicable to a large-scale political struggle and interpersonal conflicts.[24] It

[22] M.K. Gandhi, "Self Restraint versus Self Indulgence", Navajivan Publishing House, Ahmedabad, India (1947).

[23] Akella Devi, "Satyagraha: The Gandhian Philosophy of Conflict Management", 14 *Journal of Workplace Rights* (2009) 503–523.

[24] Kumar Ugresh and Panwar Dharam Raj, "An Analysis Upon Participation of Mahatma Gandhi in Indian Freedom Struggle", *Journal of Advances and Scholarly Researches in Allied Education* 83–90 (2019) Available at http://www.ignited.in/I/a/140427.

can be understood that the tool and idea of *satyagrah* by Gandhi highlighted and joined the links of individual as well as community interests in a society.

3.4 Swaraj

As like Gandhi's idea of *satyagrah*, his idea of *Swaraj* was also of much prominence among his political and social ideologies. *Swaraj* could be understood as two words, 'swa' meaning 'self' and 'raj' meaning 'rule' together making up as 'self-rule'.[25] According to him, 'The word Swaraj is a sacred word, a Vedic word, meaning self-rule and self-restraint'.[26] His conception of *Swaraj* can be unfurled in two dimensions where he discusses (i) *Swaraj* in case of individual, where self-control comes in and (ii) *Swaraj* in case of community or country, where there is freedom of village gram panchayat and freedom of country from colonial rule.

On one hand where we see *Swaraj* developing and catering to the needs of masses of people and making them independent, we also see that it carried individuals on their way to make themselves self-sustaining and contained units on the other. *Swaraj* as self-rule also gave as sense of inner freedom or positive freedom where an individual could rule over his passions of aggression and greed. It was seen as one of the most essential tools used by Gandhi towards fulfilling the political objective and unifying the people of the country, irrespective of their case, creed, background and gender towards a common objective of ending the colonial rule in India and leading the battle of freedom. It acted as a strong unifying factor for the people of the country.

3.5 Sarvodaya

During the oppressive colonial rule when the entire country suffered, Gandhi ignited the fire of being free in the hearts of millions of people living in British India. He used various tools to break free from the clutches of the British rule. He always aimed at achieving an ideal society that he dreamed of where everyone was equal, even when economic differences existed. This particular idea of attaining good for all is 'Sarvodaya' which means 'universal uplift' or 'progress of all'.[27] This idea is based on the basic principles like a good for an individual is hidden in the good of all, the different kinds of work have the same value as the aim is to earn a livelihood and everyone's life is of equal worth.

---

[25] Metta Center, "Swaraj, Metta Centre for Non Violence" (2010) Available at https://mettacenter.org/definitions/gloss-concepts/swaraj/ (last accessed 10 June, 2020).

[26] M.K. Gandhi and H.M. Vyas, Village Swaraj, Navajivan Publishing House, India (1963).

[27] Dr. Shubhangi Rathi, Gandhian Philosophy of Sarvodaya & Its Principles, Articles – On and By Gandhi MkGandhi, https://www.mkgandhi.org/articles/gandhi_sarvodaya.html (last visited June 15, 2020).

According to this idea of Gandhi, every member of the society would be free from greed and the race to acquire more and more resources.[28] Everyone would be satisfied with the ample of opportunity to produce with honesty and dignity. The primary objective was to achieve a state in which the villages are self-sufficient. People living would treat each other with respect and no discrimination practiced. It is an idea that is based on socialist principles that tries to bring out the best for the community's interest and not just an individual. It rejected utilitarian principle vehemently which revolved around an individual's greatest good of greatest number. The *Sarvodaya* society is based on principles of equality and liberty, and there exists no place for competition and exploitation.[29] When every individual does his part and follows the idea of not possessing or holding property, then only all will be able to work together in a promising way. Through this particular movement, Gandhi established a strong foundation for the ideal society he wanted to achieve.

3.6 Inner Voice

Gandhi was a leader who believed in bringing change with the support of each individual in the society and for each individual in the society. The idea of the 'inner voice' tends to be one exception as it focuses on individualism. The inner voice what Gandhi talks about is one's conscience which he explains as one's truth force or soul force, which had a divine side to it. During the time of crisis, when the normal course of action or plan does not help one to attain the goal, it is the inner voice that helps an individual to choose the right course of action. It acts as a guiding torch for a person and helps him to take a decision.

The perception of inner voice is a beautiful description of situation which describes the thought process of an individual during the time of crisis. According to Gandhi, '*it's a mystic communication between purified soul and transcendent soul*'.[30] The link between the two is established by silence and focus. When Gandhi talks about two levels of duty, the second is about inner voice when it talks about the others relating to an individual's conscience. This idea is individualistic though a prudent person would use his inner voice to guide and benefit the society.

3.7 The Eleven Vows (Ekadash Vrat)

Gandhi always believed in bringing change from the very ground level. He rejected the idea of trickle-down effect which explains how the ways of bringing change are

[28] Ibid.

[29] N. K. Bose, Selections from Gandhi, Navajivan Mudranalaya, India (1948).

[30] G.N. Sharma, "Gandhi's Concept of Duty", *The Indian Journal of Political Science* 219:214–231 (1980) Available at https://www.jstor.org/stable/41855023?seq=1.

from top to bottom. He always believed that to change the society and for its overall development, each individual had to change and understand their duty towards their family.

Gandhi gave eleven vows for the moral and spiritual uplift of the inmates of Sabarmati Ashram, but these eleven vows were not just confined to that place but acts as principles that give encouragement to individuals in a society who can follow. His eleven principles were satya (truth), ahimsa (non-violence), brahmacharya (celibacy), asteya (non-stealing), aparigrah (non-possession), sharir shram (physical labour), asvada (control of palate), abhaya (fearlessness), sarv dharm samanatva (equal respect for all religions), swadeshi (locally made goods) and sparshabhavan (non untouchability).[31] These eleven principles of Gandhi attempt to provide steps for individual development by aiming for higher attainment and realisation. It provided a holistic approach for the betterment of the society by triggering the fundamental aspects like truthfulness, integrity, fearlessness, global peace and prosperity which tend to the growth of every being. These principles still hold value in present times serving as indicative for well-being and solidarity of the society.

4 Bridging the Conflict Gap

Individuals are born and grown, but it is the community that gives them the reason to live. A community is a mammoth family which consists of people from different walks of life. It is a group of those small families which consists of individuals that belong to different beliefs and convictions. After examining and understanding the intricacies about the conflict that exist for the debate between individuality and community interests and also understanding the standpoint through Gandhian lens, it is now essential to put those upshots in line and analyse whether they do help in finding an answer for the problem or not?

Gandhi in his lifetime was always seen as an inspiration for the masses whose ideology and way of leading life was always looked upon and followed by the people. His thoughts and perception on various fields were towards achieving a peaceful and harmonious society. He always worked for the welfare of the people at large. Gandhi was an individual and an iconoclast who devoted himself to a cause and community. He was an idealist who dreamed of a society in which economic inequality existed though everyone is in a position to avail basic needs like food, shelter, clothes, education and health care. He believed in self-subsistence and each village being able to sustain within the framework and resources available locally. He believed that to achieve this dream, each individual played an important role and was supposed to contribute towards production in their way and make sure they support oneself and family.

[31] Chaturvedi Pushpa, Mahatma Gandhi's Eleven Vows (2013) Available at https://www.speakingtree.in/blog/mahatma-gandhis-eleven-vows (last accessed 16 Jun, 2020).

When we discuss about the preference between individual and community interests for a society, it is essential to understand that if every individual in the society is only to consider towards fulfilling his self-interest, the state of affair gets perplexing. It is of utmost importance to give reasonable and equal attention and to make a balance between the two. The current trend of capitalism mostly dominated in the western countries has played a major role in encouraging and giving more emphasis towards fulfilling self-interests of the individuals. The Gandhian philosophy on the other hand inspires individuals to take a different stance. Across the length and breadth of his ideas, we came over many of his important ideologies and perceptions of seeing things which could be viewed keeping in the account of interests of the society.

According to him, achieving an idealist society depended upon bridging the gap between an individual and community. He believed that each individual is part of a bigger thing which is the community and their interests are catered when the community's interest is forwarded. He emphasised upon attributes like self-realisation, truthfulness, ahimsa, practice of celibacy, devotion towards a cause, loyalty, temperance, etc. which made each individual worthy of living and building an idealist society.[32] He further explains the trickle-up effect through which the interest of both individual and community could be amalgamated. He explained how each individual has the moral obligation to contribute towards the development of society, and in that process, the interest of community and individuals is catered and bridged. Through his ideas, Gandhi amalgamated the interest of individual and community during the time of the nationalist movement. He believed that if social and economic inequality is not levelled, the interests of individuals and the community cannot be bridged. He tried to break the social stigmas which existed in the society which were immoral and disrespectful to an individual. He also analysed the brahmanical system in detail and tried to limelight the false beliefs propagated by the elitist, which was a major barrier between the interests of the community and an individual.

5 Conclusion

It is well said that '*The greatness of a community is most accurately measured by the compassionate actions of its members*'. A sense of a holistic and integrated approach in all the dimensions always reaps fruitful results. 'Interest' is something which is interpreted distinctly by different individuals belonging to divergent backgrounds. The chapter has depicted an analysis primarily focusing upon the concept of interest from the perspective of an individual and society. It has explained what individual interest and community interest truly means in the most generic sense yet highlighting on the small and important nuances to it. It is now evident that Gandhi believed in constructing a harmonious community out of the individual perspectives. He prioritised keeping the welfare of society prior to the fulfilment of self-interests which could be extracted from most of his ideas. The Gandhian philosophy has always

[32] Mathur, *supra* note 14.

been a guiding light which has showed the path of basic principles of truth, equality and non-violence to the people.[33] The aspect of duty propagated by him during the great struggle for independence has been discussed with its relation to both individual and community interest. Giving it a broader perspective, the philosophies of the west which tend to focus essentially on self-interests have been elaborated upon with an analysis over their prejudices towards interest of an individual above anything else.

Gandhi's life was no ordinary, and it was a message for generations to come. The message included qualities like celibacy, non-violence, truthfulness and sacrifice which are necessary for leading a worthy life. The relationship between these qualities and importance of it for furthering community interest has been elucidated in the chapter. Keeping the foundation intact where a society is a homogenous entity where individuals are segments of it, the development of community is ultimately the development of individuals. Every member of this unified entity has a moral as well as legal obligation for its enrichment to which the individual is responsible for. The chapter has broadly outlined the dimensions of individual and community interest with the perspective of Gandhian lens which magnifies his ideas of *satyagrah, Swaraj, Sarvodaya* and *eleven principles*. It has sketched the key developments that have already been made and the take of authors on the subject. It would be no wrong to state that for individuals to thrive to their optimal potential, it is important for the society to develop parallelly with fulfilment of community interests which was highlighted in most of Gandhi's ideas. The Gandhian philosophy has always acted as a guiding light which still holds a significant place in present scenario and will invariably be unfading and timeless.

References

Anjaneyulu BSR (2003) Gandhi's 'Hind Swaraj'—Swaraj, The Swadeshi Way. The Indian J Polit Sci 33–44 https://www.jstor.org/stable/41855768?seq=1

Bose NK (1948) Selections from Gandhi. Navajivan Mudranalaya, India

Christopher B (2017) Jean Jacques Rousseau. Stanford Encyclopedia of Philosophy. https://plato.stanford.edu/entries/rousseau/ Accessed 14 June 2020

Devi A (2009) Satyagraha: the Gandhian philosophy of conflict management. J Work Rights 14:503–523

Fitzgerald PJ (2016) Salmond on jurisprudence, 12th edn. Universal Law Publishing, New Delhi, India, p 271

Gandhi MK (1938) Hind Swaraj or Indian Home Rule. Navajivan Publishing House, India

Gandhi MK (1947) Self restraint versus self indulgence. Navajivan Publishing House, Ahmedabad, India

Gandhi MK, Vyas HM (1963) Village Swaraj. Navajivan Publishing House, India

Gandhi MK (1951) Towards non violent socialism. Navajivan Publishing House India, pp 21–22

Immanuel K, Gregor Mary J (1998) Groundwork of the metaphysics of morals ed. 17, Cambridge University Press, Cambridge, United Kingdom

[33] Gandhi (1951)

James CE (2019) Jeremy Bentham. The Stanford Encyclopedia of Philosophy Archive, Summer 2020 Edition. In: Zalta EN (ed). https://plato.stanford.edu/archives/sum2020/entries/bentham/. Accessed 28 June 2020
Kumar U, Panwar DR (2019) An analysis upon participation of Mahatma Gandhi in Indian freedom struggle. J Adv Sch Res n Allied Educ 83–90 http://www.ignited.in/I/a/140427
Mallik BK (1948) Gandhi—a Prophecy, vol 34, D.K. Print World Ltd., India
Mashruwala K (1951) Gandhi and Marx, Navajivan Publishing House, India, pp 16–22
Mathur JS (ed) (1977) Non-violence and social change. Navajivan Mudranalaya, India
Metta Center (2010) Swaraj, Metta Centre for Non Violence. https://mettacenter.org/definitions/gloss-concepts/swaraj/ Accessed 10 June 2020
Pushpa C (2013) Mahatma Gandhi's Eleven Vows. https://www.speakingtree.in/blog/mahatma-gandhis-eleven-vows. Accessed 16 Jun 2020
Radhakrishnan S, Muirhead JH (1936) Contemporary Indian philosophy. George G Harrap, London
Rajindar KK, Manjulika K (1973) Gandhian economic philosophy. The Am J Econ Sociol 32
Redding P (2020) Georg Wilhelm Friedrick Hegal. The Stanford Encyclopedia of Philosophy. https://plato.stanford.edu/entries/hegel/ Accessed 06 May 2020
Sethy SS (2015) Reinterpreting Gandhi's notion of "Dharma": an entanglement of duty, religion and ethics, articles-on and by Gandhi, https://www.mkgandhi.org/articles/reinterpreting-gandhis-notion-of-dharma.html Accessed 29 June 2020
Sharma GN (1980) Gandhi's concept of duty. The Indian J Polit Sci 219:214–231 https://www.jstor.org/stable/41855023?seq=1
Tendulkar DG (1950) Mahatma: life of Mohandas Karamchand Gandhi, vol 7, The Publication Division, Ministry of Information & Broadcasting, GOI, Patiala House
Wenar L (2017) John Rawls, Standard Encyclopaedia of Philosophy Archive, Spring 2017 Edition https://plato.stanford.edu/archives/spr2017/entries/rawls/ Accessed 14 June 2020
Yack B (1985) Community and conflict in Aristotle's political philosophy. The Rev Polit 92–112 https://www.jstor.org/stable/1406724?seq=1

Chapter 4
Duties—The Building Blocks of Right

Simi Varghese Tharakan, Serafina Illyas, and Saji Sivan

1 Introduction

"People tend to forget their duties but remember their rights"—Indira Gandhi

While one is born into this world with rights, it is a reminder that neither the constitutions of the world nor the governments across the globe are granting any rights rather they are de facto protectors of those rights.

These so-claimed rights have been absolute or conditional, alienable or inalienable, human or divine, *in rem* or *in personam*, inherent and acquired, legal or equitable, moral and jural, natural or artificial, perfect or inchoate, present or future, primary or secondary, and vested or contingent.[1] However, one shall not forget that there exists a correlation between rights and duties. Duties are those that are expected of an individual and when neglected are sanctioned by law. Irrespective of nation, colour, caste, creed, religion and gender, every individual is expected to abide by their duties both expressed and implied.

2 A General Perspective

Various constitutions throughout the world speak of duties their people need to be responsible of to utilize it for the welfare of the public. Japan, German Democratic

[1] Corbin (1924).

S. V. Tharakan (✉) · S. Illyas
Student, B.A. LL.B., Mar Gregorios College of Law, Affiliated with University of Kerala, Thiruvananthapuram, India
e-mail: simi.tharakan@yahoo.com

S. Sivan
Assistant Professor, Mar Gregorios College of Law, Trivandrum, India

R. Mittal and K. K. Singh (eds.), *Relevance of Duties in the Contemporary World*,
https://doi.org/10.1007/978-981-19-1836-0_4

Republic, Yugoslavia, Poland, Netherland, Vietnam, People's Republic of China, Venezuela, Italy, Czechoslovakia, Senegal, Thailand, Mongolia, Philippines, Guinea, Mexico, Cyprus and Egypt are amongst the nations whose constitutions speaks of duties that every man needs to abide by. So does the Constitution of India speak of duties of that every citizen is expected to abide by. The world can be segregated into three: one where greater emphasis is given on duties than on rights and freedom, another where more or less equal emphasis is given to rights and duties, and yet another one where entire emphasis is given to rights and hardly any duty is emphasized upon.[2] Human rights and obligations are carefully designed and enshrined on a global scale in the constitutions of the world, as that in the Universal Declaration of Human Rights.[3] However, unless they are alive in the hearts and minds of men and women, there will be little or no room for human order and justice.[4] Thus, there is a need to stress the significance on striking a balance between the rights and duties. Citizens constitute the state, and hence, this in turn becomes the duty of the state to protect its own citizen. 'Duty' and 'Right' are correlative terms. When a right is invaded, a duty is violated.[5] Both rights and duties are mutually complementary and equally fundamental.

3 The Positive Versus the Negative

Differentiation between the negative and the positive duties reflects the distinction between civil and political rights. Both civil and socio-economic rights give rise to a cluster of obligations.[6] In the course of acknowledging positive duties as the central aspect of human rights, the nature of duty is still questionable as to whom it would be attributed to and also as to how focussing on duties would affect the perception of rights and rights bearer.[7] A shift of responsibility can be noticed, beyond the bipolar relationship of state and individual, while placing the individual within the community. This generates mutual obligation of support which includes the interaction between an individual and society. Hence, the state not only has the duty to not interfere with an individual's activity but also have to protect individual against individual.[8] Numerous authors agreed that the incontrovertible duty that we have is the negative duty to refrain from interfering directly with the others' achievement of their own subsistence needs.[9] However, if one's action results in

[2] Saxena (1988).

[3] Ibid.

[4] Ibid.

[5] *Lake Shore & M.S. Ry. v Kurtz* 37 N.E. 303, 304, 10 Ind. App. 6 e.

[6] Shue (1996).

[7] Fredman (2006).

[8] Ibid.

[9] Boot (2017).

harming another, then one incurs positive obligations to remedy that loss caused.[10] If it is in our capacity to curb some mishap that might happen, that we are aware of then in such instances, we can do so without giving up anything that is of comparable moral importance.[11]

4 Legal Versus Social Duties

Duties are a balanced mix of legal responsibilities and of social responsibilities, that are not sanctioned though. Each of these need to be analysed to understand the difference and the importance of duties over rights in this contemporary world. The concept of duty is employed in two ways, at the transcendental level and the duty that can be evidenced.[12] Examples of transcendental duty would be like: Whether or not a mother owes a duty to care for her children? Whether or not neighbour A owes a duty towards his neighbour B and vice versa for the peaceful use of the public street that runs in front of their homes? The same in ways of proclamation would be that 'the child is owed a duty', as upheld by our Constitution and other statutes, by the mother. Similarly, 'both A and B as users of the public road' owe a duty to each other. To be more specific, we can ask whether driver A of a car must drive in such a way that he must avoid a car driven by B is bound to crash into him at the same time when he averts that accident should he not take care such that an onlooker on the road is not hit? We can thus classify duty as that one which is 'role related', the other being 'duties generated by promise' or 'duties of reciprocation' and yet another being 'duties of respect' or 'duties of beneficence' as addressed by Kant.[13]

4.1 Duty of the State

The League of Nations in the 1920s focussed on the codification of international law, during the conception of the project 'state responsibility'. However, the conference failed to produce any result. Later, the United Nations General Assembly, in the year 1948, had established the International Law Commission to fulfil the Charter mandate of 'encouraging the progressive development of international law and its codification'.[14] And 'state responsibility' was one of the fourteen topics that were selected. Every state has a responsibility on the international level as well as on the domestic level. While the duties on the international level expect a state to conform

[10] Ibid.

[11] Singer (1972).

[12] "Understanding Duty in Tort Law", available at https://tort.laws.com/duty. (visited on May 30, 2020).

[13] Campbell and Lustig (1994).

[14] Art. 13(a) of the United Nations Charter (1965); *See* also H.W. Briggs (1965)

to the laws set out in the matters of peace and war, providing aid to oppressed nations, ensuring that its citizens do not bring harm to a citizen of another nation, keeping a tab on the trade and ventures, on the domestic level it is expected to conform to the duties towards its citizens or even an alien residing within like investigating into grave violations of human rights and the prosecution of the same.

4.2 Duty of the Judiciary

Every nation has its own legal system and these legal systems contain their own obligations imposing laws without any decisive linguistic marker determining which these are. It was argued by Bentham, the advocate of the great Utilitarian Theory, and by Hans Kelsen that every legal system must be represented in the form of duty-imposing or expecting laws.[15] One may wonder what are legal, social and moral duties and is there a necessity for such distinction. Legal duties are those legal requirements with which citizens are bound to conform with.[16] The duty of common law judges is to decide in accordance with the law that is enshrined by the legal system or in accordance with the law of the land. And since Constitution is considered to be above all, it is the duty of the judiciary to uphold the Constitution and to hold any unlawful customs or legislative provisions as void.

4.3 Duty of the Subject

A subject is a citizen in this context and as we are aware a citizen belongs to a nation, a territory and definitely to an entity of people. However, sometime these facts are overlooked by a citizen. The relationship between a democratic polity and that of its citizens cannot be one-sided rather it must be reciprocal where rights and duties must go hand in hand.

In 1947, Gandhi wrote a letter to Julian Huxley and in it he wrote:

> The very right to live accrues to us only when we do the duty of citizenship of the world. From this one fundamental statement perhaps, it is easy enough to define the duties of man and woman and correlate every right to some corresponding duty to be first performed. Every other right can be shown to be usurpation hardly worth fighting for.[17]

---

[15] Green Leslie, "Legal Obligation and Authority", The Stanford Encyclopedia of Philosophy (Winter 2012 Edition),

Edward N Zalta (ed.), available at https://plato.stanford.edu/archives/win2012/entries/legal-obligation/. (visited on May 30, 2020).

[16] Ibid.

[17] Douglas (2008).

5 Indian Perspective

In today's era, we speak and fight for our fundamental rights and seldom do we uphold that we have a duty or as is called more commonly as a responsibility towards our society.

5.1 *'Dharm' as 'Duty'*

In India, religions hold 'dharm' meaning 'duty' as prime element of an individual's life. For example, Hinduism speaks highly of duty which, according to it, upholds the universe and society. It is all about virtue and morality. However, here acting virtuously or morally is a subjective matter. The moral or social duty of an individual differs in different contexts. It is executed on the basis of their age, gender, relationship, religion and even social status or position that they hold. Dharm has been vastly translated as ordinance, duty, right, justice, morality, law, virtue, religion, ethics, good works, code of conduct and so on. Hence, in a nutshell, dharm has its legal, moral and social shades that it embraced in the course of development both traditionally and historically. Accordingly, man is expected to conduct himself in conformity with the higher order of universal dharm in order to preserve himself and his society. These dharmsastras once served as the four legs of law and made the fundamental principle of jurisprudence. With the passing of time, various scholars interpreted dharm in different manner. According to A.K. Sen, it is 'an admixture of socio-ethical religious ideas and not a religious concept alone. Gradually it became codified with the advent of British rule, the only difference being that it became more of a right based one unlike a duty based legal system'.[18]

5.2 *Legal Duties in the Indian Context*

The Constitution of India upholds the rights of each and every citizen or individual under part III. Alongside in it is penned a reminder under Article 51-A that every citizen is duty bound. The duties listed thereunder are the prime duties though not exhaustive in nature. Gandhi once remarked 'a duty well performed creates a corresponding right'. As there exists moral and legal rights so exists moral and legal duties. It is the action of every individual or citizen that he must take care of in order to protect the correlative right of another. When one is ignorant of one's duties, then there is an implied relinquishment of one's own rights since, which means that when one commits a wrong or indulges in a crime, he curbs his rights to the freedom he enjoyed otherwise.

---

[18] Shantanu Rathore, "Dharma and Law", available at https://www.lawctopus.com/academike/dharma-and-law/ (visited on June 1, 2020).

5.3 *Our Constitution on Duties*

The preamble of the Indian Constitution opens to a beautifully crafted promise by the people to self and each other, 'We the people of india, having solemnly resolved to constitute india into a sovereign, democratic, republic and to secure to all its citizens justice ….; liberty….; equality….; fraternity…'. A meticulous perceptivity of this pledge implies that each individual or citizen had a duty to provide his fellow being the same prerogative as he is entitled to. Further, the Constitution has enhanced upon these lines under part III and subsequently in part IV which speaks of rights and duties, respectively. This chapter will present the reader with clarity on how duty is the reciprocal building blocks to one's rights.

The ever-dynamic policies have posed a challenge to the community as a whole. We should revisit the traditional concepts of individual duties that is integral to the origin of human rights that are on the international covenants or treaties which have been ratified by us. Duty here is not confined to the limits of sanctions; however, it encompasses those non-binding responsibilities which amount to the ethical and social functioning of a community.

Gandhi constantly repeated throughout 'Let each do his duty, if I do my duty, that is, serve myself, I shall be able to serve others. Before I leave you, I will take the liberty of repeating: Real Swaraj is self-rule or self-control; the way to satyagraha: that is, soul force or love force; in order to exert this force, Swadeshi in every sense is necessary. What we want to do should be done, not because we object to the English or because we want to retaliate but because it is our duty to do so'.[19]

In a wholesome manner, Gandhi equated freedom with self-rule since it was his desire to embed freedom with the notion of obligation to others as well as to oneself.[20] And he also felt that a right that was not correlated to a preceding duty was a usurpation not worth fighting for.[21] The Constitution encompassed these into its fabric and thus emerged Articles 48-A and 51-A during the 42nd Amendment of the Constitution in 1976.

The fundamental duties under Article 51-A are laid down in its most general terms which calls upon the citizens to inculcate certain values or to cultivate certain temperament. These duties have a want of being specific which makes it non-triable and not prosecutable offences.[22] In fact, the idea of laying down those fundamental duties under Article 51-A within the Constitution is not to penalize a citizen through legal sanctions or otherwise but because it serves as a humble reminder of his fundamental duties.[23] They are more of moral assurances from citizen to citizen.[24] It also

[19] Hind (1909).

[20] Iyer (1973).

[21] See *supra* note 5 at 229.

[22] Corbin, *supra* note 1 at 12.

[23] Ibid.

[24] Ibid.

acts as a social audit of the commission and omissions of executive and gives locus standi to a concerned citizen in relation to the fundamental duties.[25]

A three-Judge Bench of the Supreme Court had made it clear that fundamental duties, though not enforceable by writ of the Court, yet provide valuable guidance and aid to interpretation and resolution of constitutional and legal issues. In case of doubt, peoples' wish as expressed through Article 51-A can serve as a guide not only for resolving the issue but also for constructing or moulding the relief to be given by the courts. The court further held that the state is, in a sense, 'all the citizens placed together', and therefore, though Article 51-A does not expressly cast any fundamental duty on the state, the fact remains that the duty of every citizen of India is, collectively speaking, the duty of the State.[26]

The Supreme Court had stated that it is clear as day that the duty of a citizen has been extended to the collective duty of the state. To elaborate, it becomes the duty of the state to provide for opportunities and not to curtail the opportunities.[27] However, one needs to understand that though the rights are enforceable in court of law the same is not the case with duties because those cannot be enforceable through courts. Simultaneously, the court of law has to take into consideration the fundamental duties and also the directive principles, in the event of interpretation of the fundamental rights or the restrictions imposed upon it.

It has been held, by the Supreme Court, in ***Javed* v. *State of Haryana***[28] that fundamental rights are not to be read in isolation but they have to be read along with the chapter on directive principles of state policy and the fundamental duties enshrined in Article 51-A.

6 Gandhi's Deontology of Duty

Gandhi had rejected the theory of utilitarianism rather he emphasized on the importance of personal autonomy. Gandhi never saw a contrast in the principle of swadeshi, interpreted in terms of neighbourhood and that of rendering service to all humanity. According to him, a man could provide service to his neighbour provided that the service is not exploitative of others. And this service would in turn become a chain of service when each neighbour thought of rendering service to their neighbour.[29] Gandhi had also believed that we had the right to civil disobedience and he derived this from the duty of civil disobedience. Hence, it was a right that was duty based and not rights based.[30] He always preferred duty-based morality over a goal-based

---

[25] Ibid. at 13.

[26] *AIIMS Students' Union v. AIIMS & Ors.*, (2002) 1 SCC 428.

[27] *Charu Khurana v. Union of India*, (2015) 1 SCC 192.

[28] *Javed v. State of Haryana*, (2003) 8 SCC 369.

[29] Dasgupta (1996).

[30] Briggs, *supra* note 14.

one. He used to constantly remind his fellow beings that the noblest goals could be achieved only through earnest performance of one's duties.[31]

Gandhi had made explicit use of the concept of corresponding duties and rights of which a few are mentioned here.

In August 1909, in a letter that he wrote to Arthur Russell, the Baron of Ampthill, he wrote:

> I know that under the British Constitution, British subjects, no matter to what race they belong. They have never got and never can get their rights until they have performed their corresponding duties and until they are willing to fight for them. The fight takes the form either of physical violence, as in the case of the extremists in India, or of personal suffering by the fighters, as in the case of our passive resisters in the Transvaal.[32]

Subsequently, Gandhi wrote of 'Brute Force' in Hind Swaraj:

> The English in 1833 obtained greater voting power by violence. Did they by using brute force better appreciate their duty? They wanted the right of voting, which they obtained by using physical force. But real rights are a result of performance of duty; these rights they have not obtained.... I do not wish to imply that they do no duties. They do not perform the duties corresponding to those rights; and as they do not perform that particular duty, namely, to acquire fitness, their rights have proved a burden to them.[33]

Then in 1921, he delivered a 45-min speech to labourers on strike in Madras:

> It is your right to be advised by whomsoever you may choose and the company cannot dictate to you that you may not be advised by outsiders. You must insist upon your inherent right of selecting any Chairman or President you like of your Union whether out of your own ranks or anybody else.... You have a right to demand such wages as will enable you to sustain life, to educate your children and live a decent life. You are entitled to the same fresh water and fresh air as your employers. You are entitled to insist upon having leisure and recreation from day to day. But you also have corresponding duties to perform. You must render diligent and faithful service to your employers. You have to look after the property of your employers as if it was your own.... These simple rights and duties once being understood must always be insisted upon and fulfilled as the case may be.[34]

In 1924, he wrote a chapter on 'After the War' in Satyagraha in South Africa:

'The Indian question cannot be resolved into one of trade jealousy or race hatred. The problem is simply one of enjoying the supreme right of self-preservation and discharging the corresponding duty'.[35]

In 1931, in an issue of Young India he wrote:

> Every man has an equal right to the necessaries of life even as birds and beasts have. And since every right carry with it a corresponding duty and the corresponding remedy for resisting any attack upon it, it is merely a matter of finding out the corresponding duties and remedies to vindicate the elementary fundamental equality. The corresponding duty is to labour with

---

[31] Corbin, *supra* note 22 at 83.

[32] Mark Lindley, "Gandhi on Corresponding Duties/Rights", available at https://d1wqtxts1xzle7.cloudfront.net/ (visited on 15 June, 2020).

[33] Ibid.

[34] Corbin, *supra* Note 22.

[35] Ibid.

my limbs and the corresponding remedy is to non-cooperate with him who deprives me of the fruit of my labour.[36]

In 1934, he wrote:

I welcome the rise of the Socialist Party in Congress. But I can't say that I like the programme as it appears in the printed pamphlet. It seems to me to ignore Indian conditions and I do not like the assumption underlying many of its propositions which go to sow that there is necessarily antagonism between the classes and the masses or between the labourers and the capitalists, such that they can never work for mutual good. My own experience covering a fairly long period is to the contrary. What is necessary is that labourers or workers should know their rights and should also know how to assert them. And since there never has been any right without a corresponding duty, in my opinion a manifesto is complete without emphasizing the necessity of duty and showing what that duty is.[37]

In 1946, in an issue of Harijan, he wrote:

I have received letters from Harijan friends and some have been to see me too. They feel that now that power is in the hands of people, there should be more than one Harijan minister. According to the population ratio, the number should be at least three, and they should be similarly represented in every department.... I am not ready to admit the correctness of all they say. My ideas in this regard are different.... Rights spring only from duties done well. Such rights alone are becoming and lasting.... I shall therefore advise the Harijan brethren that they should think only of their duties. They may be sure that rights will follow fast on the heels of duties done.[38]

From these, we can understand that Gandhi was never tired of saying that duty came before rights. According to him, modern legal positivism corrupted the notion of law wherein the obedience to positive law and a political and a moral duty independent of the question whether such law is in harmony with dharm or not.

7 Conclusion

In order to save the Indian society from the evils and erosion of values, it is very important that emphasis is laid upon both the fundamental duties laid down by the Constitution as well as the socio-economical duties. An awareness must be created such as to awaken the realization that our basic obligations as a citizen and as a human being is inalienable and that is the one fact that inspired our great legacy to freedom struggle. Irrespective of the conflicting interests and warring ideologies, it is necessary for each and every individual to understand that they cannot walk from their responsibilities rather the execution of the duties owed by them ensures that their rights are protected in due manner.

[36] Ibid.

[37] Corbin, *supra* Note 22.

[38] Ibid.

References

Boot ER (2017) Human duties and the limits of human rights discourse. Springer International Publishing AG, p 111

Briggs HW (1965) The international law commission. Cornell University Press 129:141

Campbell CS, Andrew LB (1994) Duties to others. Kluwer Academic Publishers, pp vii–xvii

Corbin AL (1924) Rights and duties, 33. The Yale Law J 5:501:527

Dasgupta AK (1996) Gandhi's economic thought. Routledge, p 22

Douglas A (2008) The philosophy of Mahatma Gandhi for the twenty-first century. Lexington Book, p 80

Fredman S (2006) human rights transformed: positive duties and positive rights, Paper No 38/2006, August, Legal Research Paper Series, University of Oxford

Green, L (2012) Legal obligation and authority. The Stanford Encyclopedia of Philosophy (Winter 2012 Edition). In: Zalta EN (ed) Available at https://plato.stanford.edu/archives/win2012/entries/legal-obligation/. Accessed 30 May 2021

Iyer (1973) The moral and political thought of Mahatma Gandhi, p 349

Rathore S (2015) Dharma and law https://www.lawctopus.com/academike/dharma-and-law/ Accessed 1 June 2020

Saxena DN (1988) Citizenship development and fundamental duties. Abhinav Publications, p 28

Shue H (1996) Basic rights: subsistence, affluence and US Foreign Policy, 2nd edn. Princeton University Press, Princeton

Singer P (1972) Famine, affluence, and morality, 1 philosophy and public affairs 3, Black Well Publishing p 231

Swaraj H (1909) Collected Works of Mahatma Gandhi (CWMG), vol 10 p 64

Understanding Duty in Tort Law, available at https://tort.laws.com/duty. Accessed 30 May 2020

Chapter 5
Securing Rights by Following Duties: A Substantial Conceptualization Reinforcing Gandhian Credence

Ritika Sharma and Arvind Jasrotia

1 Introduction

Rights that do not flow from duty well performed are not worth having.
—Mahatma Gandhi.

The Gandhian perspective upon the rights and duties clearly suggests that it is entirely a social responsibility to glance into the activities of performing one's duties so that it will lead to the fulfillment of the duty of serving others. The proposition of the notion of *Swaraj* depicted the intention of promotion of the very performance of duties on the part of the citizens of the country. Rights and duties are two sides of the same coin. They are so closely intertwined that it is extremely difficult to even think of separating them as they go hand in hand with each other. It was once said by Mahatma Gandhi that rights can never be divorced from duties.[1] In general sense, rights refer to the common claims of people which each and every civilized society recognizes as essential claims for development. According to Laski, rights are those conditions of social life without which no man can be himself at his best which he can be otherwise.[2] On the contrary, duties refer to obligations or responsibilities in simple terms. It is an obligatory act which a citizen of a country is required to

[1] Ravi Shankar Prasad, *Need to Remember Our Fundamental Duties As We Remember Our Fundamental Rights*, The Indian Express, November 26, 2019.
[2] Nitisha, *Theory of Rights: Laski, Barker and Marxist's Theory*, Political Science Available at https://www.politicalsciencenotes.com/theory-of-rights/theory-of-rights-laski-barker-and-marxists-theories/781. Last visited June 1, 2020.

R. Sharma (✉)
Student, B.A. LL.B. (Hons.) Vivekananda Institute of Professional Studies (VIPS), New Delhi, India
e-mail: sharma.ritika5061@gmail.com

A. Jasrotia
Dean and Professor, Faculty of Law, University of Jammu, Jammu, India

R. Mittal and K. K. Singh (eds.), *Relevance of Duties in the Contemporary World*,
https://doi.org/10.1007/978-981-19-1836-0_5

perform. While rights can be termed as privileges, duties are known as obligations. On the one hand, rights provide privilege; on the other hand, duties provide certain reasonable restrictions on rights at large. Since the aim is to analyze the core aspect of securing right by following duties, it is important to understand that no right exists in isolation and it becomes even more important to understand that duties always accompany them.

2 Historical Background

The ancient texts of Hinduism depict the aspects of 'duty', wherein it has been defined as 'virtue', or even 'morality' for that matter. It refers to the power which tends to nurture the universe and society. The concept of duty has been highly propagated in the Ancient literature not only on the part of the society, but also on the part of the individuals. The duties have always been kept in an upper footing as compared to the rights. The word *dharm* has been derived from the root word *dhri* which means to bear or to support; thus, it has been defined as duty through *dharmshastras*. In Vedas, which are known as literary texts, *dharm* has often been used as an alternate term for the 'universal law' or 'righteousness' which is required to be followed throughout. According to a particular authoritative book tilled *History of Dharmasastra*,[3] the hymns of the Rigveda pronounced the term *dharm* for at least fifty-six times, as an adjective or a noun. According to Paul Horsch,[4] the word *dharm* has its origin in the myths of Vedic Hinduism. Even in *Shrimad Bhagavad Gita*, lord *Krishn*, the charioteer of *Arjun*, has always advised him that the great battle being fought against his own relatives was righteous and it was his duty that he must fight as a warrior and fulfill the call of his *dharm*.[5] Thus, *Arjun* had to fight in order to establish justice with the concurrence of fulfilling his duty. The term *karm* or *kartavya* denotes the action or duty which is the foremost paradigm of the existence of a human being. Toward the end of the Mahabharat (Shantiparvan 12.167), there persisted the quandary discussion pertaining to the comparative importance of the three goals of *dharm*, profit, and pleasure among the *Pandavs* and the wise sage *Vidur*. There are in total ten duties which have been clearly provided in the *dharmashastras,* defining not only the duties toward self but also toward the society as well as the nation per se. Therefore, the ancient Vedic texts have always encouraged individual to live by the principles of *dharm,* thereby following the duties bestowed upon him or her through it. Moreover, in the history of India, Ashok, Chandragupta Maurya, Samudragupt, and other ancient Kings of India have always made it explicit that the follow-up of duties is extremely crucial and the duties over rights have been of major importance. With the advent of British rule, Gandhi, along with other leaders, ensured that each

[3] Commentary by Swami Mukundananda (2020), *Chapter 3: Karm Yog, the Yog of Action*, BHAGVAD GITA Available at https://www.holy-bhagavad-gita.org/chapter/3.

[4] Paul Hacker, "Dharma in Hinduism", *34 Journal of Indian Philosophy 479* (1965).

[5] *Supra* 3.

and every person stays dutiful toward the nation. The framing of Constitution ensured that with assurance of fundamental rights, the citizens must abide by the fundamental duties as well, since the framers of the Constitution knew that the situation imposed otherwise might lead to the arbitrariness with non-compliance of the responsibility toward the nation. The concept of fundamental duties has been adopted from the Constitution of Union of Soviet Socialist Republic (USSR). The fundamental duties have been seen in association with Article 29(1) of the Universal Declaration of Human Rights. Thus, the relation of the citizens with the nation should be of give and take.

3 Jurisprudential Perspective

All legally permitted actions are rights whereas duty refers to no wrong. The rights and duties are explicitly defined in the Indian Constitution, and innumerable judgments have been pronounced by the Privy Council at that point of time and later, by the Hon'ble Supreme Court of India to recognize the significance of the same. The jurisprudential perspective of rights and duties has been provided by various jurists too. It is the basic principle in jurisprudence that every right has a correlative duty and every duty has a correlative right.[6] According to Bhagavad Gita, whatever duty you are engaged in or required to do, that duty must be performed dutifully, to the best of your ability and without any motives attached to it.[7] The jurisprudence of the west and *dharm* of east is the science of law. Even, the Romans have understood the concept of duties; therefore, the principle of *ubi societas ibi ius* was being propounded, upholding the principle that where there is society, there is a law. No wonder that the concept of right postulates the need for recognition of some compulsions or duties on the part of people. As J. S. Mill has pointed out that the freedom which actually deserves the name is that of pursuing one's own good in one's own way as long as that individual does not attempt to deprive others of theirs or impede their efforts to obtain it.[8] According to Salmond, a right is an interest recognized and protected by a rule of right, it is an interest and respect for which is duty, and disregard of which is a wrong.[9] According to Duguit, no one has any other right than always to do his duty; hence, law is only an embodiment of duties which an individual is supposed to perform as a part and parcel of the social organization for furtherance of social solidarity.[10] According to John Austin, rights and duties are interdependent and not correlative that had always stood in complete contradiction to Salmond's

[6] Richa Goel, *Concept of Rights and Duties under Jurisprudence*, iPleaders, Available at https://blog.ipleaders.in/concept-of-rights-and-duties-under-jurisprudence/ (last visited June 4, 2020).

[7] Bhagavatgita, Chapter 2, verse 47.

[8] Vicente Berdyas, Neoliberalism, Economic Radicalism and the Normalization of Violence, (John F. Murphy, Springer International Publishing Switzerland 2016).

[9] P. J. Fizgetald, Salmond on Jurisprudence, (12 ed. London, Sweet & Maxwell ltd. 1966).

[10] Duguit Leon, "the Law & State", *31 Harvard Law Review* (1917).

view. However, it is widely accepted by almost every jurist that rights cannot exist without the fulfillment of duty; thus, it is important to note that citizens must follow their duty in order to claim their rights successfully. The notion of fundamental duty is also exceedingly akin to ancient concept of *sadharn dharm* referring to the duties which are common to everybody and everything for that matter.

4 The Gandhian Deontology and Philosophy

The conception of duties has been the core fundamental of the teachings of Gandhi. The idea of duty that is *dharm,* non-violence that is *satyagrah* and self-reliance that is *swadeshi* have always been purported by Gandhi. The notion of *swaraj* possesses the meaning way different from that of the absence of restraint, dependence, and regulation. It was the notion of self-restraint, self-regulation, and self-dependence which was being propagated throughout. The spirit of social duty flows directly from the belief of the unity which should stay in existence. This has been the vital ingredient of the concept of self as well as of individual and is not separated from each other, thereby said to be the synonyms. The problem of reconciliation of the individual freedom with that of the social responsibility has been an ongoing conflict among various thinkers and Gandhi has always preached the ideology of keeping community interest at the utmost importance than that of an individual interest. Swami Vivekanand anticipated Mahatma Gandhi that only selflessness can solve every problem and selfishness can only lead to destruction of the world. The ideology of right is in itself a limitation as there is no aspect of 'mine' and 'theirs' attached to it as all we have is 'responsibility' and not mere 'rights'. It was reiterated by Aurobindo that the idea of rights and duties in the context of Indian philosophy and deontology is the remarkable feature of the mind of Indians. It is usually expected that the sanctions of the meanings pertaining to the religion and the spiritual sense is often given in most external way of social and political circumstances of life itself. The onus of proof of such impositions on all sections and the classes of the society can be termed as an ideal situation while the rights and the powers being conferred upon the citizens can be questioned upon; however, the duties in consonance of the *dharm* have the spiritual significance.

5 Rights and Duties in Indian Constitution

The Constitution of India was adopted on 26 November 1949 and was enforced on 26 January 1950. The fundamental rights and the fundamental duties are expressly enshrined in the Indian Constitution. There are six fundamental rights in part III from Article 12 to 35 and eleven fundamental duties in part IV-A of the Constitution. The fundamental duties are defined as the moral obligations of each and every citizen in order to promote spirit of patriotism and unity of India.[11] Since the concept of fundamental duties has been taken from the USSR, it was incorporated in the Indian Constitution in 1976 on the recommendation of Swaran Singh Committee. Initially, there were ten fundamental duties, and by virtue of 86th Amendment, the eleventh duty was added in 2002.[12] Among fundamental duties enumerated in Article 51 A of the Constitution, there are six positive duties and five negative duties and clauses (b),[13] (d),[14] (f),[15] (h),[16] (j),[17] and (k)[18] require citizens to perform these duties actively.[19] The Justice Verma Committee provided certain recommendations and provisions. There are certain legal provisions and statutes for the strict and rigid enforcement of duties such as certain sections of Indian Penal Code, 1860, Unlawful Activities (Prevention) Act, 1967, Prevention of Insults to National Honor Act, 1971, and so on. Fundamental duties are not legally enforceable, yet, as conscious and responsible citizens, these duties must be abided by. The Preamble of the Constitution is explicit about the co-existence of rights and duties. These are inseparable notions, and these must be followed in its entirety. Since fundamental duties are just directory which cannot be enforced by the writ of mandamus, it is important to note that these duties are often seen in a haywire situation wherein people tend to ignore following their duties while fighting for their rights.

The Amendments made under the Constitution have been the pivotal ones. The 42nd Amendment, 1976, provided for the enlistment of ten fundamental duties. The 42nd Amendment has a famous history behind it. It was popularly known as 'mini constitution' or the 'Constitution of Indira'. The need of fundamental duties was being strongly felt during the time of emergency in 1975. The 86th Amendment, 2002, made an addition of the duty that every parent and guardian must ensure that their child must be provided with the opportunities of education falling between the age of six and fourteen years which turned out to be the eleventh duty. In the case of ***Unni Krishnan* v. *State of Andhra Pradesh***,[20] it was held that all children who are below the age of 14 years have a right to free and compulsory education. Since it is widely known that the fundamental duties are those statutory duties which are not enforceable by law, yet, the court can make these duties to be a matter of adjudication while taking them into account for this particular aspect. The idea which

---

[11] The Fundamental Duties, Available at https://delhi.gov.in/duties.html.

[12] Saumendra Das, N. Saibabu, "Indian Constitution: An Analysis of Fundamental Rights and the Directive Principles", *1 Journal of Applied Research and Social Sciences* (2014).

[13] To cherish and follow the noble ideals which inspired our national struggle for freedom.

[14] To defend the country and render national service when called upon to do so.

[15] To value and preserve the rich heritage of our composite culture.

[16] To develop the scientific temper, humanism and the spirit of inquiry and reform.

[17] To strive toward excellence in all spheres of individual and collective activity so that the nation constantly rises to higher levels of Endeavour and achievement.

[18] It refers to parent or guardian to provide opportunities for education to his child or, as the case may be, ward between the age of six and fourteen years.

[19] Judith Lichtenberg, "Negative Duties, Positive Duties, and the "New Harms"", 557 *The University of Chicago Press Journal* (2010).

[20] *Unni Krishnan* v. *State of Andhra Pradesh*, AIR 1973 SC 1461.

has been behind the incorporation of fundamental duties was to emphasize upon the responsibilities and the obligations of the citizen with an aim of direct exchange for the fundamental rights that the citizen of the country enjoys to the fullest. The Swaran Committee which was set up in order to incorporate several landmark changes in the Constitution, after a rigorous consideration, but a few of the recommendations stood unaccepted. However, in accordance with the recommendations made, some of them were also accepted, thereby creating a distinct and separate chapter of fundamental duties in the Constitution of India.

6 The Landmark Judgments

There have been innumerable judgments pertaining to the importance of inseparability of fundamental rights and fundamental duties. The case of *Bijoe Emmanuel* v. *State of Kerala*[21] gave an insight of a major duty to respect the National Anthem of India, wherein three children of Jehovah community were expelled from the school as they refused to sing the Nation Anthem while they stood up for the same. It was held that they did not violate their duty and no offense was committed under the Prevention of Insult to National Honors Act, 1971, as they actually stood up for the anthem out of respect. In the case of *State of Gujarat* v. *Mirzapur Moti Qureshi Kassab Jamat*,[22] the question of fundamental duties arose, wherein it was provided that although Article 51A (g) is non-justiciable duty like all the other fundamental duties, yet, it makes it important for the citizens to protect, preserve, and improve the natural environment which includes wildlife, lakes, river, and forests and have compassion for every living being. In *Chandra Bhawan Boarding* v. *State of Mysore*,[23] it was held that it would be a fallacy to think that in our Constitution there are only rights and no duties. In *Ram Prasad* v. *State of Uttar Pradesh*,[24] the Allahabad High Court observed that the Constitutional law demands that the citizens of the nation shall perform their duties in an excellent way rather than performing them half-heartedly. Hence, the performance of these duties falls within Constitutional law and they can be promoted by constitutional methods which include law making.[25]

In *M. C. Mehta* v. *Union of India*,[26] it was held by the Supreme Court that it should be compulsory for each and every educational institution to teach the children about the protection and improvement of the environment in accordance with Article 51A (g) as well as the books pertaining to the same should be distributed free of cost in education institutions. In *AIIMS Student's Union* v. *AIIMS*,[27] it was held by

[21] Bijoe Emmanuel v. State of Kerala, AIR 1987 SC 748.

[22] State of Gujarat v. Mirzapur Moti Qureshi Kassab Jamat, AIR1986 SC 12.

[23] *Chandra Bhawan Boarding* v. *State of Mysore*, AIR 1969 ILLJ 97.

[24] *Ram Prasad* v. *State of Uttar Pradesh*, AIR 1988 All 309.

[25] *Mumbai Kamgar Sabha* v. *Abdulbhai*, AIR 1976 Sc 1455.

[26] *M. C. Mehta* v. *Union of India*, AIR 1987 SC 965.

[27] *AIIMS Student's Union* v. *AIIMS*, AIR 2001 SC 3262.

the Hon'ble Supreme Court that fundamental duties enshrined in Article 51A are equally important like the fundamental rights. In *Mohan Kumar Singhania* v. *Union of India*,[28] the decision of the government to give utmost importance to provide training to the selectees of Indian administrative service was upheld by the court, holding that it was in complete consonance with the fundamental duties enshrined in the Constitution. In *Aruna Roy* v. *Union of India*,[29] the validity of the National Curriculum Framework of School education was upheld by the court which was being challenged because of the violation of Article 28 of the Constitution of India. It was also deemed to be anti-secular because of the nature of anti-secularism as it provided for the development pertaining to value education with relation to the foundation of each and every religion. It was said by the court that the NCFSF has not made a mention of anything which is directly related to instructions which are needed to be imparted by the religious institution which has been strictly prohibited under the Article 28 of the Constitution of India. Moreover, such education pertaining to religion in the institutions which are state funded has been prohibited under the Article 28 of the Constitution, thereby promoting secularism.

In order to create the appropriate equilibrium among fundamental duties and fundamental rights, a letter was written to the President by the petitioner in the landmark case of *Hon'ble Shri Rangnath Mishra* v. *Union of India*,[30] to give directions to the state pertaining to the issue of educating the citizens with regard to the fundamental duties enshrined in the Constitution of India. The court treated this letter like a writ petition. However, this matter turned out to be the one in which the report was submitted to the government of India to be heard by the National Commission which was reviewing the Constitution at that time. In the case of *Government of India* v. *George Philip*,[31] the respondent challenged the issue of compulsory retirement from the service. In this case, a leave of two years was granted to the petitioner which was granted by the department with regard to the pursuance of the advanced research training and even after continuous reminders, the petitioner kept on staying in the foreign country; thus, institution of an inquiry against the petitioner took place. Thus, the high court provided the remedy pertaining to joining the service once again upon a particular clause that there is a concept of no back wages that can be provided. However, the order was set aside by the Supreme Court. The Supreme Court held that in accordance with Article 51A(j), an individual should always strive for excellence in each and every sphere of his or her life and it was also held by the court that such orders which destroy the very essence of Article 51A should never be passed by any court for that matter.

In the case of *Ramlila Maidan* v. *Home Secretary and Ors*,[32] it was held that the term fundamental has been used in two separate senses in which the rights are strictly enforceable and the use of the term fundamental with duties is in normative sense. In

---

[28] *Mohan Kumar Singhania* v. *Union of India*, AIR 1991 SC 1150.

[29] *Aruna Roy v. Union of India*, AIR 2002 SC 3176.

[30] *Hon'ble Shri Rangnath Mishra* v. *Union of India*, AIR 2003 SC 133.

[31] *Government of India* v. *George Philip*, AIR 2012 SC 1.

[32] *Ramlila Maidan* v. *Home Secretary and ors*, AIR 2007 SC 705.

the case of *Dr. Dasarathi* v. *State of Andhra Pradesh*,[33] the judgment of *Government of India v. George Philip* was reiterated by the court that according to Article 51(j) each and every citizen should abide by the duty to always strive towards excellence and the state must provide with the ways and the processes to achieve this excellence as prescribed by the Indian Constitution. In *Charu Khurana* v. *Union of India*,[34] it was held by the Supreme Court that the state is required to provide opportunities to the citizens to excel rather than curtailing the same.

7 Quest of Duties over Rights

It is an accepted fact that there can be no existence of the civilized and just society without legal order as well as there cannot be legal order without legal duties. Many nations across the world have transformed into developed economies by embodying the principles of 'responsible citizenship' while all of the responsibilities and duties that citizens of a nation should exercise and respect is clearly stated.[35] Hence, it becomes essential to understand the interrelationship between rights and duties.

- Rights and the duties are closely related to each other. If right to life and liberty is provided to citizens by the state, there exists the obligation on the part of the citizen as well to respect the life of others and exercise the right within certain limitations.
- The right of one is the duty of others as when the citizens fail to discharge their duties in a proper manner, the rights become completely worthless. With rights come corresponding duties.
- Rights should not be misunderstood to be the monopoly of a single individual. The right of a particular citizen implies duty as well. According to Laski, the right of a man is his duty as well.
- It is the duty of the citizens to use their rights for the betterment of the society rather than creating chaos in it. The social interest should be promoted while exercising the rights and welfare should be elevated.
- Each and every citizen should perform the duty toward the state as it is the state only which protects and enforces rights. However, in the Indian context, it is the Constitution which is supreme, yet, the state is entitled with the task of promoting welfare by protecting the rights in return. It is the duty of the citizens to become a helping hand of the state than creating a havoc like situation.

---

[33] *Dr. Dasarathi* vs. *State of Andhra Pradesh*, AIR 1990 SC 434.

[34] *Charu Khurana* v. *Union of India*, AIR 2015 SC 839.

[35] *Supra* 2.

8 Conclusion

It has been observed with precision that rights can be secured only by performing duties. It has been rightly put across by Shri M. Venkaiah Naidu in his recent speech on 26 November 2019 that while it is absolutely necessary to defend fundamental rights relating to life, liberty, equality and freedom of expression etc., it is the time when one has to realize that we, as citizens, get hold of our duties toward the nation in a serious manner since the entitlements which are provided, come with duties and responsibilities as well.[36] The interrelationship between rights and duties is unquestionable, since it is a well-established fact that if duties are not performed by the citizen, the rights become counterproductive. It is not only the Constitutional obligation of a citizen but also a moral duty to keep an eye towards his or her conduct to the fullest. Hence, it is imperative to note that the task of preserving the rights is to follow the duties with greater fervor. Rights and duties are inevitable components present in any country. Therefore, in order to reach at the heights of progress, it becomes extremely important to perform duties and hence every citizen must abide by the same.

References

Berdyas V (2016) Neoliberalism, economic radicalism and the normalization of violence. Springer International Publishing, Switzerland

Bhagvadgita, Chapter 2, verse 47

Fizgetald PJ (1966) Salmond on jurisprudence. London Sweet & Maxwell ltd, London

Judith L (2010) Negative duties, positive duties and the "new harms". University of Chicago Press Journal, pp 557–578

Leon D (1917) The law & state. Harvard Law Rev. https://www.jstor.org/publisher/harvardlaw?refreqid=excelsior%3A0d45c6b431d599ef3f7567c8121cd338

Naidu VP (2019) Time citizens take duties seriously. Available via Press Trust of India. https://www.business-standard.com/article/pti-stories/time-citizens-take-duties-seriously-vp-naidu-119112600587_1.html

Nitisha (2020) Theory of rights: Laski, Barker and the Marxist's Theory. Available via Political Science. https://www.politicalsciencenotes.com/theory-of-rights/theory-of-rights-laski-barker-and-marxists-theories/781

Paul H (1965) Dharma in Hinduism. J Indian Philos 34:479–555

Saumendra D, Saibabu N (2014) Indian constitution: an analysis of the fundamental rights and the directive principles. J Appl Sci Soc Sci 1(17):55–76

Singh DR (2009) Fundamental rights enshrined in constitution: provisions and practices. Indian J Polit Sci 70(3):779–786

Swami Mukundnanda (2020) Karm Yog, the Yog of Action. Available via Bhagvad Gita. https://www.holy-bhagavad-gita.org/chapter/3

The Fundamental Duties (2019) Available via https://delhi.gov.in/duties.html

Verma S (2020) Fundamental duties. Available via IPLEADERS. https://blog.ipleaders.in/fundamental-duties-2/

[36] Press Trust of India, *Time citizens take duties seriously: VP Naidu*, Business Standard, November 26, 2019.

Chapter 6
Locating Gandhi's Idea of 'Real Rights as a Result of Performance of Duty' in Legal Philosophy

Bhawna

1 Introduction

In today's time, the Indian society is emphasising more on its rights and while doing the same it has forgotten duties which are correlative of rights. The society has ignored the other side of the coin which is indispensable in maintaining the equilibrium. As a result, the society has exposed itself to such circumstances which cannot be considered to be favourable for its own good. Whenever there is any matter pertaining to the Indian society, the name of the father of the nation cannot be overlooked. Therefore, this chapter examines the idea of Gandhi that real rights are the result of performance of duties. The same idea is found in jurisprudence as well. The chapter hence discusses the concept of duties and rights as conceptualised by various jurists. It also includes the relevance of revisiting the earlier theories while dealing with the present problems as faced by the society.

Gandhi believed that duties are more fundamental than rights because the latter springs from the former and ensure its better implementation. He pointed that there should be a charter of the duties of man and the rights will follow it automatically. Gandhi's idea of Swaraj emanates from the performance of duties by citizens without having strong reservations for their rights. He conceptualised India as a society which is guided by dharm which in turn is a duty-based concept. Though the present laws focus on rights as compared to duties, Indian constitution has a specific and dedicated chapter (Chap. IV-A) on fundamental duties; however, its implementation is still a challenge.

As mentioned above, the laws, presently, focus on rights and not duties; at the same time, it is worth highlighting that jurisprudence is full of various jurists' views advocating the contrary. The major concern of every civilised legal system today is

Bhawna (✉)
Research Scholar (Ph.D.), Dr. Ram Manohar Lohiya National Law University, Lucknow, Uttar Pradesh, India
e-mail: bstevatia@gmail.com

R. Mittal and K. K. Singh (eds.), *Relevance of Duties in the Contemporary World*,
https://doi.org/10.1007/978-981-19-1836-0_6

that legal rights must be protected as they will eventually lead to justice. According to Holland, 'It is one man's capacity of influencing the acts of another, by means, not of his strength, but of the opinion or the force of society',[1] He says, 'Jurisprudence is specifically concerned only with such rights as are recognized by law and enforced by the power of State, we may therefore define a legal right' ... as a capacity, residing in one man of controlling, with the assent and assistance of the State, the actions of others'.[2] Salmond defines, 'A legal right is an interest recognized and protected by a rule of law-an interest the violation of which would be a legal wrong done to him whose interest it is and respect for which is a legal duty'.[3]

This implies that a right cannot exist in isolation, and therefore, every right has a corresponding duty. According to Holland, if there is a right, it can be a moral or legal one, which involves the active or passive furtherance on behalf of other persons of the desires of those who possess the right. If this happens, the desire of the one, in possession of the right, is the corresponding duty. The fact that that duty is a legal or moral one can be ascertained by the manner in which that duty can be enforced. If the state is in capacity to enforce the same, it will render it to be a legal one. And if it is only an expectation from the side of the people in a given society, it will be taken as a moral duty.

The relationship is established between two persons whenever there is a question of right. These persons can be natural or legal. In such relationship, the one will be the person who is in possession of the right and the other person will be the one who is under an obligation with regard to the possessor and shall have to perform a duty in this respect. Generally, it can be said that legal right is in a way an advantage or privilege bestowed upon the possessor of right by the law and can be categorised in four different types. These are (l) rights (in the strict sense), (2) liberties, (3) power and (4) immunities. Each of these has its correlative, namely (1) duties, (2) no-rights, (3) liabilities and (4) disabilities.

The purpose of the chapter is to reflect on the significance of the idea that duties are the reason behind rights. The chapter seeks to advocate the point that this idea, if realised, can help in creating a cohesive, responsible and value-based society in the present right-dominated world. It can also provide a viable solution to the current real-world problems.

2 Gandhi's Idea

Gandhi prioritised duties over rights and was of the opinion that rights should be deserved and preserved from duties which are performed well. For him, duty emerges as a result of dispassionate action as has been propagated in Bhagavad Gita. He was of the view that one would always be the slave of anxiety with regard to the result of

---

[1] T. E. Holland, The Element of Jurisprudence, p. 82.

[2] Ibid. p. 82.

[3] P. J. Fitz Gerald, Salmond on Jurisprudence, p. 218.

his/her actions till that action was done with a degree of detachment. Also, when it is said that one must not be attached, it does not imply that he has absence of the clear picture with regard to what one wants to accomplish. The significant point, which is being made here, is that persons should indulge in actions with no inducement, threat or any theological sanctions.

Gandhi believed that the idea behind human rights merely by virtue of being born as humans is flawed and so he rejected the rationale behind 1948 Declaration which provides for human rights to human beings simply by virtue of their humanity. He was of the opinion that 'a duty well performed creates a *corresponding* right'.

Gandhi had reiterated his opinion regarding duties at numerous occasions including one when he delivered a speech on September 16, 1921, to a gathering of labourers on strike in Madras. He remarked that the labourers have all the right to be advised by anyone of their choice and even by any outsider and the right to demand wages which they require to lead life, to provide education to their children and lead life decently. At the same time, they must perform their duties and be sincere and loyal towards their employers. They must take care of the belongings of their employers as if it were their own. Another such incident was when he wrote in a brief essay, titled 'Can you avoid Class War?', in the March 26, 1931, issue of *Young India*, that all have right to the necessaries of life. But what is required to be done is finding the corresponding duty and remedy to resist any attack on the right. In words of Gandhi, 'The corresponding duty is to labour with my limbs and the corresponding remedy is to non-cooperate with him who deprives me of the fruit of my labour'.

One more incident worth mentioning is when in a letter of May 25, 1947, to Julian Huxley, Gandhi wrote[4]: '[T]he very right to live accrues to us only when we do the duty of citizenship of the world. From this one fundamental statement, perhaps it is easy enough to define the duties of man and woman, and correlate every right to some corresponding duty to be first performed. Every other right can be shown to be usurpation hardly worth fighting for'.[5]

From the above-mentioned incidents, it can be deduced that Gandhi put duties on priority whenever the issue of right and duty came up. He believed that before one can claim his right, he must come up with performed duties on his part. This may imply that performance of duty will confer the right to claim right. In the absence of the performance of duties, one does not get the right to demand his right. Also, even a situation where the enjoyment of right without performing the duty is not worth as the enjoyment will not be a deserved one.

3 Resonance of the Idea in Jurisprudence

Many jurists have explained various legal concepts as what is the meaning of law, right, duty, property, possession, etc. As far the concept of duty vis-à-vis right is

[4] Later the same passage was published in the June 8 issue of *Harijan*.

[5] Anasakti Darshan Vol. 2, No. 2, July–December 2006.

concerned, there are numerous jurists who have opined in a similar manner as have been expressed by Gandhi. The jurists who possess similar views as that of Gandhi belong to various schools of thought. Legal right can mean to understand an augmentation, or possibly some assurance, of personal desire of any act or of enjoyment; whereas legal duty, on the contrary, shall indicate a limitation, required due to some other person's interest over interest of one's self.

Rights and duties are not dissociable from each other. While knowing one, one cannot ignore the other one. Both are counterparts of each other and studied together. Sir Frederick Pollock considers law as a system of duties as he believes that rules of law are 'the duties of subjects under the common authority of the State'.[6] Debating and identifying whether right should be given priority over duty or vice versa will be a futile exercise as this shall in no case lead to an answer which is capable of applying universally. It must be mentioned here that this chapter advocates the idea that duties are followed by rights.

Auguste Comte enunciated a principle, according to which a person has only one right that is to do his duty. This principle influenced M. Duguit so much that he mentioned about the same in many of his writings. He agreed to the opinion that rights have a negative function and do exhibit anti-social character. He arrives at this conclusion by the reasons including that law does not always originate from state. He, in fact, rejected the idea of state as a person and considered that the basis of government is the de facto power of the stronger persons of society over the weaker. Origin of law can be attributed to society only. Rights in isolation cannot mean anything as the society comprises human beings who share certain relationships with each other. As per Duguit, these relationships can never be of rights but must be of duties. Duguit believes that there is social law that, in reality, governs the individual. He gave the principle of social solidarity which contains the two indispensable elements, first that humans have some social needs which can be fulfilled by common efforts only and the second element, humans have some different needs which can be fulfilled only by way of exchange and division of labour. This principle of social solidarity is prevalent in society and governs all human beings. One must do acts that help in facilitating and realising this principle. Duguit holds the view that law consists of only duties and not rights, i.e. even the right which exists for human beings is the right to perform his/her duty and none else.

On the same lines, as per Harold Laski, a person's right is also his duty. As if a person has the right to life, in addition he will have an obligation to not expose his life to dangers. At the same time, an obligation to respect others' life is also upon him.

Hohfeld acknowledged the relevance of the concept of rights and duties in comprehending various legal problems. He identified that the source of confusion is due to the meaning attributed to the term 'right' so as to include a privilege, power or immunity. To clarify this confusion, Hohfeld come up with certain fine distinctions and similarities between various legal concepts, thereby limiting the meaning of the word 'right' to depict a definite and proper meaning. He referred to right as a concept

[6] Pollock, First book of jurisprudence (6th ed. 1929) 57.

for which there certainly exists a correlative duty as whosoever shall use the term 'right' will without any efforts think about a duty corresponding to it. Right is such a term that is treated as a generic term which has privilege, power and immunity as its various forms, for this reason Hohfeld tried to come up with a term that shall strictly mean to something which can be defined in a manner as to impose a duty corresponding to it in others. For this, he described the right in terms of 'claim'. He also described that whenever a right is attacked, a duty is breached. This is evident in an example as if X has a right against Y that he shall not indulge in trespass on the former's property; the correlative duty shall be that Y is under a duty (an obligation) towards X to remain away from property.

Hart recognised that every legal system involves creation, variation and enforcement of certain obligations. Understanding of authority of law and its nature will demand the knowledge about the role of obligations. At the same time, one cannot overlook that as there are obligations in the law, there are also obligations to the law. Hart advocated that law is in the form of rules which are normative in nature. And those rules are meant to be conformed to by the society. In cases where people do not conform to obligation-imposing rules, there will be sanctions followed. These obligation-imposing rules can be distinguished by looking into the following three features: firstly, the rules must be backed by serious consequences to make people conform to those rules; secondly, people must think that those rules possess an important role in social life; and thirdly, that the requirements of these rules may be in conflict with the interests and goals of the subject. Legal duties are the creation of legal rules, and likewise, moral duties are the creation of moral rules. For a legal duty to be morally valid, there must be good moral reasons available urging its compliance. Whenever a legal duty is morally valid, it will automatically instil in the subjects of the state to comply with it irrespective of the sanction attached to it. The reason attributable to this is that if a rule has a minimum threshold to qualify it to serve the purpose of justice, the obligation to follow the rule will be internalised. Though in practice, the legal rules are followed as they are not seen from the lens of their substance and content but are qualified because of their form, i.e. the fact of their coming from the state. That is the reason that sanctions attached to duties has a role in obliging the subjects to obey the legal rules. Hart emphasised that rules must be internalised in order to have protection from state, thereby putting weight on the subjects to perform their part in identifying the sense of obligation from within.

Austin, a positivist, also talked about duties. In fact, he classified duties into relative and absolute ones. Relative duties are self-explanatory as they refer to specific right-claims. Absolute duties, on the contrary, were further classified into four kinds:

- Self-regarding duties—e.g. the duty imposed by the prohibition of suicide.
- Duties towards persons indefinitely—e.g. 'towards the members generally of the given independent society; or towards mankind at large'.
- Duties not regarding persons—e.g. duties towards the lower animals or inanimate objects (it may mean to include the duty imposed by a prohibition of defacing some object of aesthetic, sacred or sentimental sanctity).
- 'Where the duty is merely to be observed towards the sovereign imposing it'.

The above mentioned are absolute duties, and these are necessary for purposes that will be beneficial for all. From the point of view of the state, the duty is absolute and it is enforced not in order to implement any specific right, but to maintain order and security.

The emphasis given to the performance of duties is visible in views of the American legal realists such as Robert Hale and Karl Llewellyn as in the twentieth century, they pursued deconstruction of rights. This has happened for the reason that the over-emphasis on rights and overlooking of duties will not result in attaining the equilibrium in society. If people can have rights by virtue of being born as humans, why cannot they possess inherent duties in them? Also, if everybody keeps on asserting their rights, there will emerge chaos in the society as a result of the conflicting social and individual interests.

These aforementioned views and opinions given by some jurists resonate with the idea propounded by Gandhi. In order to enjoy one's rights, one must perform his/her duty as only then it can be considered that the right is well deserved and will consequently bring a sense of happiness not only in the subjects of the state but also the individuals of the whole world. As far as the logic behind sanctions attached to duties or obligations is concerned, it is proposed that it is not the only reason for subjects to follow the rules and perform their duties, though it can be considered as one. In fact, sanctions' aim is to reinforce duties and not to form a constituent part of them.

4 Connection with Present Issues

The whole discussion about claiming rights and ignoring duties has become a burning issue these days. With everyone making efforts to enforce their rights, and over-looking of duties have resulted in various problems being faced by the society as whole. Non-performance of duties is resulting in damage to the environment and to public property, and disharmony among the people. Persons are not budging from the enjoyment of special occasions, festivals in a manner that adversely affects the environment by burning fire crackers, etc. All of this is done as a claim to right to celebrate festivals and follow customs. The result is a society where the environment is not clean and the whole society is being affected by damage to environment. Many people do not even think for a second that their actions might result in destruction of environment, and they owe a duty towards fellow beings as well as the future generations. Incidents involving riots and lynching have been reported more often these days. People do not think before participating in riots which cause damage to public property and persons are becoming part of mob which sometimes lynch people. Also, women and children–related crimes have increased. It can be deduced that today persons are becoming selfish and remain ungrateful who are not reluctant to enjoy the products of civilisation, but will hesitate in doing their part.

It must be noted that as citizens of a country, persons are imposed with a huge bundle of duties. The duties imposed are obligations towards the state and to fellow citizens. For example, there exists a legal duty with regard to the payment of taxes, to abstain from committing any offence against other citizens and to follow the laws that the legislature has enacted. Disobedience to these duties will attract sanctions in the form of punishments provided in statutes. Indian Constitution provides for its citizens with the fundamental duties in Chap. IV-A to be followed. These duties if followed in true sense will provide for solutions to the problems being faced by the country in the present times.

It must also be mentioned here that sometimes state imposes such duties on its subjects which consequently infringe the rights of the marginalised sections of society. There must not be any room left while providing for duties to be abused as a tool to force the ill will of the state or the social majority on weaker groups. Every duty that is imposed on the people must be in accordance with 'due process of law'. The concept of 'due process of law' refers to that no one shall be denied life, liberty or property unless the same is done as per the express legal provisions and with due regard to the person's rights. The absence of this concept in the legal system will render it to adverse results. Another view relevant in this regard is the concern of Dr. B. R. Ambedkar who once indicated through his words before the Constituent Assembly that the fundamental unit of the Constitution remains the individual. While interpreting the duties, duties of those persons must be incorporated who are powerful. The powerful ought not to utilise it to abuse those from whom they wield it. It is only possible after assurance to every person of humanity, dignity, equality and freedom as envisioned in the Constitution, that one can expect, from them, the performance of their duties.

5 Conclusion

The fact which is very familiar is that persons anywhere on Earth possess rights. At the same time, the less popular notion is that the rights possessed by humans are protected by the fulfilment of duties. Philosopher Onora O'Neill once commented that even there is an acknowledgement of existence of corresponding duties, there exist no instrument as Universal Declaration of Human Duties, and not even an international Human Obligations Movements. Rights, strictly, can be held to be benefits, which emerge from duties imposed on others. This idea of him resonates with that of Gandhi's, i.e. real rights are a result of performance of duties. Hart believed that the centre of every legal system is the union of primary and secondary rules. Whoever breaks the rules does something wrong according to those rules. Therefore, the rules generate certain obligations for people in a society. These obligations in order to be followed in true sense should be internalised by the people. This implies that persons who internalise the legal rules of their society will be more inclined towards them and shall show obedience. They will think that rest should obey them too and will wilfully undergo the sanctions imposed on them for the breach of the legal rules. This thought has a glimpse of Gandhi's point of view regarding role of duties in instilling the persons with the quality with which they shall have an ethical existence and consequently to benefit the whole society. An individual can be considered as one who is accomplished only when he shares a relationship with the rest, which is based on mutual respect and cooperation between them.

He believed that a guardian or parent shall invite contempt from his children if he fails in performing the duty due towards the children. And if children are such who flout their parent, who are ever ready to perform their duty then they would be viewed as thankless and would hurt themselves more than their parent. Similar is the situation with spouses. Gandhi considers duties as primary and considers the duty to act morally regardless of the consequences as the highest value.

If persons fulfil their fundamental duties, all the rights can be taken care of consequently. While addressing the inauguration ceremony of International Judicial Conference—2020, Justice SA Bobde highlighted the chapter on fundamental duties in the Constitution and emphasised that every citizen must perform his duties. Chapter IV-A expresses what in law is often implicit—that legal rights have correlatives of legal duties. He also referred Gandhi's book, Hind Swaraj, and observed that real rights are a result of the performance of duties.

In the end, it must be reiterated that peaceful cohabitation requires a degree of self-sacrifice, and if required, this must be followed by a group of sanctions till it is internalised. Gandhi's idea of duties, if imbibed, would give positive results not merely at the level of community or a country but at the global level.

References

Holland T E (1896) The elements of jurisprudence. Oxford: Clarendon Press
Fitzgerald PJ (1966) Salmond on Jurisprudence. Sweet & Maxwell
Pollock F (1929) A first book of jurisprudence for students of the common law. London: Macmillan and Co., Limited

Chapter 7
Dialectics of Individualism and Communitarianism in Gandhian Thought

Surbhi Arora, Sahil Agrawal, and Mritunjay Kumar

1 Introduction

The term individuality refers to differentiating one particular individual based on his unique characteristics and qualities from others. But individualism means a group of individuals who have a common set of beliefs and assumptions that they have a separate existence from society. Individuality originates in the anxious existence of collective identity. The etymological meaning of the word individual comes by adding two Latin words; "in" signifies "not" and "divisible" originated from "dividuus", which means "divisible".[1] Individualism, however, as a political doctrine, or a school, propagates the idea of self-governance and the independence of individuals.[2]

Collectivism, on the other hand, unlike individualism, emphasises on the idea of a collective identity. It believes in the supremacy of the collective identity and the subordination of the individual. In the process to achieve collectivism, the interests of an individual are subordinated under the collective identity of a society of individuals, a group, a particular nation, race, caste, and state. It has the effect of emphasizing over

[1] Oxford English and Spanish Dictionary Available at https://www.lexico.com/definition/individual. Last accessed 13 Feb, 2021.

[2] To explore the theme of individualism *see* John Stuart Mill, *On Liberty* 33 (John W. Parker and Son, London, 2nd edition, 1859); ("If all mankind minus one, were of one opinion, and only one person were of the contrary opinion, mankind would be no more justified in silencing that one person, than he, if he had the power, would be justified in silencing mankind").

S. Arora (✉) · S. Agrawal
Student, LL.B., Campus Law Centre, Faculty of Law, University of Delhi, Delhi, India
e-mail: surbhi0296@gmail.com

S. Agrawal
e-mail: agrawalsahil31@gmail.com

M. Kumar
Assistant Professor, Himanchal Pradesh National Law University, Shimla, India
e-mail: mritunjaykumar@hpnlu.ac.in; mritunjaykumbhi@gmail.com

R. Mittal and K. K. Singh (eds.), *Relevance of Duties in the Contemporary World*,
https://doi.org/10.1007/978-981-19-1836-0_7

collective coping,[3] which makes it easier for the individual to cope with unpleasant life events. This concept is embedded deeply in the political, economic, or cultural systems. It is based upon the principle of common good or utility which aims at efficiency or to provide, in the language of utilitarian ethics, the maximum benefits to the maximum numbers of the people in the society. Communitarian ideals prioritize the collective identities, cohesiveness, and loyalty over the individual's interests, primarily based upon the collective decision-making process to fulfil the common objectives. In order to explain a dichotomy between individualism and communitarianism, Confucius wrote, "By nature, men are alike; by practise, they get to be wide apart".[4] In the eighteenth century, John Locke described the mind as a "tabula rasa"—a blank slate on which experience inscribes a personality.[5]

Thomas Hobbes argued that the human nature is nasty, selfish, brutish, and short.[6] On the contrary, many scientists believe that "genes load the gun, but environment pulls the trigger",[7] meaning that by nature each person has universal consciousness. Due to culture, conditioning, and environment, each and every individual appears to be distinct from each other.[8] But, the problem does not lie in the distinctive traits of the individuals per se in a biological sense; instead, it is about the wider acceptability of the term individuality in the so-called moral and political societies in different nations. It a socio-political issue than a scientific problem.

According to Aristotle, "man by nature is a social animal and that one who does not partake of society is either a beast or a god".[9] The very idea of socialization and involvement in society is essential for human experience and lays the foundation for collectivism across various disciplines. Collectivism is the ethos that emphasizes the priority of the community as a whole or the group as against the individual. Markus and Kitayama in their essay have compared the independent-self with the individualism on the one hand and interdependent self to collectivism on the other.[10] According to them, "the independent derives its identity only from the inner attributes

[3] Kashima and Triandis (1986).

[4] USC-US China Institute Available at https://china.usc.edu/confucius-analects-17. Last accessed 13 Feb. 2021.

[5] Ruth W. Grant, "Locke's Political Anthropology and Lockean Individualism", 50 *The Journal of Politics* 1, (1988), pp. 42–63.

[6] Internet Encyclopedia of Philosophy Available at https://iep.utm.edu/hobmeth/. Last accessed 13 Feb, 2021.

[7] Benn, Thomas (2013a) What's individuality and where does it comes from? Available at https://blogs.scientificamerican.com/mind-guest-blog/whats-individuality-and-where-does-it-come-from/. Last accessed 13 Feb. 2021.

[8] Ibid.

[9] Phil Stevens, Man Is By Nature A Social Animal: Social Integration Following Lower-Limb Amputation (2018). Available at https://opedge.com/Articles/ViewArticle/2018-10-01/man-is-by-nature-a-social-animal-social-integration-following-lower-limb-amputation#:~:text=Aristotle%20asserted%20long%20ago%20that,interruption%20such%20as%20an%20amputation. Last accessed 13 Feb. 2021.

[10] Shinobu Kitayama, Hazel Markus and Masaru Kurokawa, "Culture, Emotion, and Well-Being: Good Feelings in Japan and the United States", *Cognition & Emotion* 14 (2010). https://doi.org/10.1080/026999300379003

of the individual".[11] However, "the interdependent self, in contrast, derives its identity essentially from relations with others".[12] Therefore, in order to understand the concept of being, it is imperative to develop the understanding of the collective identity. Individual is not a separate entity from the collective identity. One's conduct in the society is determined and shaped from the performance of his role and reaction to his actions. His actions are correlative to his interdependent self.

Human beings have unique characteristics, unconventional choices, and different priorities that make each of us a distinct individual. E. Jordan in his essay explains that the "individuality has been one of the strongest influences in human life since man attained the first degree of self-consciousness".[13] The theory of the free individual and the independent entity were a driving force to make humans aware of their need to show recognition for their individuality and self-interest. But a republic-nation is required to achieve a balance between individualism and collectivism by inculcating a principle of self-disciplined collectivism among its members through teaching the value of empathy and compassion.

2 Evolution of Individualism and Collectivism

Our understanding of individuality and collectivism goes back to antiquity when the eighteenth-century political writers and theologists started writing about it. According to them, the cornerstone of individuality lies in the freedom of decision-making by an individual for himself.[14] The underlying assumption behind this conviction is that every person or individual has a better idea about himself, and his interests and choices help in building his character and determines his role in the society. A society therefore consists of individuals, each of whom is capable of making their own decisions keeping in mind the welfare of the society. They can be treated as autonomous and complete entities.

The term "individualism" was first used in France. Akhtar Khan classified the concept of individualism under three categories, "designating the rights of an individual, laissez-faire, and the aristocratic cult of individuality, known as political liberalism, economic liberalism, and romantic individualism".[15] While individuality refers to all the characteristics which make a person unique—a distinct individual from others, it refers only to one person.[16]

[11] Yuriy Gorodnichenko and Gérard Roland, "Understanding the Individualism-Collectivism Cleavage and its Effects: Lessons from Cultural Psychology" (2013).

[12] E. Jordan, "The Definition of Individuality", 30 *The Philosophical Review* 6, 566–584 (1921).

[13] Ibid.

[14] For example, freedom of choice was considered as an important principle or inherent necessity for moral progress. Kantian moral reasoning preferred autonomy as a means to develop moral laws for an individual being.

[15] Akhtar Khan, "Individualism: Origin and Evolution", 48 *The Indian Journal of Political Science* 1, (1987), 126–132.

[16] S. Lukes, The Meanings of "Individualism", 32 *Journal of the History of Ideas* 1, (1971), 45–66.

The historical traces of the individualism could be deciphered in the early eighteenth century, when the western idea of individualism was flourishing. During this development, the communist and socialist groups of the individual criticized the foundation of individualism, based upon the division of labour and egotism. They considered that the individualism is a wicked and dangerous ideology for the mankind. The most famous amongst those critics was Saint Simmons, who openly criticized the concept of individualism and supported the community interests of the society. He stated that individualism promotes anarchy, egotism, and self-interests. It negates the fundamental idea of a progressive society, but a spiritual and enlightened individual should work towards achieving harmony and growth of the society by sacrificing his right and personal interest in devising a sovereign state.[17]

Jean-Jacques Rousseau argued that the state of society or commonwealth became possible under the agreement of "general will and particular will".[18] In the state of nature, according to Rousseau, individuals lived like a "noble savage"[19] In spite of being born free, the human beings remained in chain.[20] The state of lawlessness varies from society to society.[21] Gradually, with time, they exercised control and reason and employed a contract among themselves leading to the formation of a society.[22]

The primary objective behind promoting community interests is the preference for a social order in society. Socialists and communists of the eighteenth century felt that the society can provide both means and ends for an individual without compromising the social harmony. They questioned the idea of individual, expounded a necessary connection between selfishness and self-interest with the fragmentation of the social imagination. The thinkers of modernity propagated the interest of the individuals and its protection through constitution. The raison d'être behind this support lies with the self-interested attitudes among the individuals and the mere existence of separate and distinct individuals create a need for a right to protect and work for his personal interest. Thomas Hobbes wrote, "people in a state of nature ceded their individual rights to create sovereignty, retained by the state, in return for their protection and a more functional society, so social contract evolves out of pragmatic self-interest".[23]

---

[17] Tr. G. Iggers, "The Doctrine of Saint-Simon: An Exposition", First Year 1828–9 (1830) 28, 70, 247 (Boston, 1958).

[18] Dana Villa, "Hegel, Tocqueville, and Individualism", 67 *The Review of Politics* 4, (2005a), pp. 659–686 Available at www.jstor.org/stable/25046471. Last accessed 13 Feb. 2021.

[19] Wasserman, Renata R. Mautner (London, 1994), "Jean-Jacques Rousseau and the Discourse of the Exotic", *In Exotic Nations: Literature and Cultural Identity in the United States and Brazil*, 1830–1930, 69–100, (Cornell University Press, 1994). Available at http://www.jstor.org/stable/10.7591/j.ctt207g5v4.6.

[20] William T Bluhm, "Freedom in 'The Social Contract': Rousseau's 'Legitimate Chains'", 16 *Polity* 3, (1984), pp. 359–383 Available at www.jstor.org/stable/3234555.

[21] The Editors of Encyclopaedia Britannica, Social contract, Encyclopædia Britannica, August 06, 2019, Available at https://www.britannica.com/topic/social-contract.

[22] The History of Western Ethics 67 (1st Ed. Duignan, Brian, 2011).

[23] Ruwantissa Abeyratne, Air Navigation Law 14 (2012).

Unlike Hobbes, John Locke believed that every individual has certain inalienable rights, which cannot be taken away by any authority including state. He was against the idea of absolute monarchy and was of the view that the people had the inherent natural rights to liberty and property. People entered into a social contract, as he believed, to establish a state so as to protect these inherent rights of each individual. For government is required, and if necessary, it may be changed through common-will.[24] He further argued that the protection guaranteed under the social contract was not limited to the liberty of the person alone but also it was extended to the right to have private property.[25] In process of democratization, the rights of human beings were secured through normative progress of constitutionalism. The concept of natural law played an important role in defining the natural rights of the human beings as species. The diverse philosophies behind natural law theories proposed to have universal moral principles, transcending the limited and conventional understanding of moral laws.[26] In natural law theories, the rights of human being were projected as the bundle of properties, meant to be monetized in the symbolic gesture of commercial being. While many western thinkers, like Thomas Paine or Robert Nozick, explained that the individual rights are significant in upholding the human dignity, unlike traditional attitude, craving for security in belonging to a group identity. On the contrary, many thinkers preferred to accept the communitarian ideals as the chief goal to achieve for each and every individual. Fraternity, after all, was one of the significant principles that emerged during and after the French revolution. The collective identity was accepted as the final goal in the Hegelian idealism for he accepted nation-state as the true and highest symbol of social morality, and it is only when an individual truly surrenders to the laws and institutions that he realises his actual worth and experiences liberty.[27] From a sociological perspective, Durkheim enunciated the importance of "collective consciousness"[28] in the development of individual as well as society. He believed that this concept was instrumental for the origin and development of communities and functional societies.

Apart from being associated with the ideologies of socialism, collectivism has found its relevance in the ideologies of Marxism, Communism, Fascism, Democratic Socialism, and Utopian Socialism in the twentieth century. The motto of "all for each and each for all"[29] is regarded by the socialist thinkers as the chief goal to realize. They suspect the concept of individualism, which is primarily based upon the principle of "Each for himself, and each against all".[30] The Socialist thoughts, on the contrary,

---

[24] Volume 1, Global Encyclopaedia of Political Science 1578 (1st Ed. H. P. Chattopadhyay and S. K. Sarkar, 2006).

[25] John Locke, Second Treatise of Government, IV, 22, (1980), p. 17.

[26] John Ruskin, Unto This Last.

[27] Internet Encyclopedia of Philosophy, https://iep.utm.edu/hegelsoc/. Last accessed 13 Feb. 2021.

[28] Barnes, Grace M. "Emile Durkheim's Contribution to the Sociology of Education". *The Journal of Educational Thought (JET)/Revue De La Pensée Éducative,* vol. 11, no. 3, 1977, pp. 213–223. JSTOR, www.jstor.org/stable/23768661. Accessed 13 Feb. 2021.

[29] S. Lukes, Individualism 24 ECPR: Colchester (2006).

[30] Ibid. at 26.

are labelled as utopian, idealist, against the possible practicality of routinized life and transactions. For the language of love and compassion is eclipsed for a new economic being, self-interested, and self-centred. The language of practicality or expediency is employed to diminish the utopian dreams to love and care. Individualism triumphs as an ideology, based on fear and hope, against the spiritual quest of fraternity. Karl Marx, a humanist scientist of utopia, laid the foundation of egalitarian socialism so as to relinquish the production mentality, a chief mover and shaker for the ideas and practices of commodified individualism. His dialectical imagination revolves around the idea of communism, primarily based upon the idea to maintain economic equality and public ownership, governed by the collective interest of the people. On the contrary, American political writer, Alexis de Tocqueville described individuality as a natural product of democracy that always threatens to develop where the conditions are equal for the individuals.[31] According to Tocqueville, "Democracy not only makes each man forget his forefathers, but it conceals from him his descendants and separates him from his contemporaries, it throws him back on himself alone and threatens to confess him in the solitude of his own heart".[32] John Stuart Mill believed that the individuality is the foundation of human life, primarily based upon the principle of production and re-partition of all the material products pursued by all in a vicious and anti-social form.[33] Gandhi was influenced by many thinkers and spiritual leaders in developing his theory of "spiritual individuality" that aimed at securing the best interest of the community at large by suggesting a stateless but self-ruled society.

In India, the spread of Western education aroused a new spirit of individualism among the intelligentsia. This prepared the ground for the emergence of modernization in India. The *Brahmo-Samaj*, originated in Bengal, led by Rammohan Roy, was instrumental in bringing the individualist spirit to question the long-followed customs and traditions. He pleaded for the theological, social, and political reconstruction of the society. In western India, it was Mahadev Govind Ranade who founded the Indian Social Conference. The conference worked on an assumption that there could be no social progress without the prior uplift of the individual.[34] Ranade preferred to have state intervention against the customary practices, for the sake of equity and justice for each and every human being.[35] Similarly, Gopal Krishna Gokhale conceived the idea of individual as a repository of rights, not as a creature driven by pre-determined cosmic forces, but as someone having the power to shape his own life and its destiny.

---

[31] R. Boesche, "The Strange Liberalism of Alexis De Tocqueville", 2 *History of Political Thought* 3, 495–524 (1981).

[32] Alexis de Tocqueville, "De la Democratie en Amerique (1835) bk. II, pt. II, Ch. II, Oeuvres Completes", ed. J. P. Mayer (Paris, 1951), I, II.

[33] J. S. Mill, "Chapters on Socialism" (1879), ibid., 715.

[34] M. A. Buch, Rise and Growth of Indian Liberalism, Atmaram, Baroda, (1938), p. 82.

[35] Ibid., p. 132.

Belonging to the moderate group, he insisted on incorporating the principles of democracy in the country's administration.[36]

3 Dialogical Interface Between Individual and Society

Individualism, a political doctrine, is the *arche-type* of modernity. In ancient time, the conflict between social and individual interests were, though, prevalent, but it was not so predominant characteristic in comparison to the modern psyche of the individuals. Ancient Greek was primarily a society based upon city-states. Individualism was not a dominant characteristic of the ancient societies of Greece. The quest to question each and everything was the first step in the development of critical philosophy. Socratic dialogues were instrumental, as portrayed in the Platonic literatures, in the development of individualistic quest to know and philosophize. However, city-states remained as the basic framework for justice and governance. The ancient societies of Greece were not free from the conflicting interests of aristocratic and democratic attitudes, prevalent among the various members of the society. Plato was a philosopher in the zone of aristocratic attitude,[37] who believed in the idea that only a few are capable to become guardians to govern, assisted by iron class. Socrates, on the contrary, allowed every individual to flourish imaginatively to develop and inquire a sense of critical imagination for knowledge. The origin of science, not necessarily a mechanical one developed after the European Renaissance, could be attributed to the critical methods of inquiry, developed long time ago in Greece, especially their imagination to question and experiment the ideas before practising and propagating it. Aristotelian quest to test the transcendental beliefs in accordance with empirical methodology proved to be instrumental in the individualistic quest for the freedom of inquiry.

In Roman Civilization, on the one hand, stoicism, as an individualistic philosophy, was developed so as to cope up against the suffering, on the other hand, family as a unit of governance was accepted. The *Pater Familias* was the autocratic head of the family, who had power over his family members to govern them. He was considered as the father figure of the family and had legal authority over the members of the family as well as their property. In words of Giorgio Agamben:

> This power is absolute and is understood to be neither the sanction of a crime nor the expression of the more general power that lies within the competence of the pater insofar as he is the head of the domus: this power follows immediately and solely from the father-son relation (in the instant in which the father recognizes the son in raising him from the ground, he acquires the power of life and death over him).[38]

[36] Akhtar Khan, "Individualism: Origin and Evolution", 48 *The Indian Journal of Political Science* 1, 126–132 (1987).

[37] Karl Popper, *The Open Society and Its Enemies* 15–16, Routledge Classics, London, 1945, (2012).

[38] Giorgio Agamben, *Homo Sacer: Sovereign Power and Bare Life* 87–88, Daniel Heller-Roazen (trans.), Stanford University Press, California, 1995, (1998).

Family as a self-sufficient unit for the governance may be understood as the first step towards the imagination of society in the Roman civilization. In ancient India, the people had dialectical imagination regarding individual autonomy and collective identity, whereas the spiritual quest of individual was as important as the common welfare of the society. The tribal cultures since its inception have been organized, even in modern periods, as per "mechanical solidarity",[39] a term coined by Emile Durkheim in which the group solidarity is predominant; especially, such societies are based upon the reciprocal relationship between the members of the society. Their mode of production is based upon need-based rather than greed-based economy, in which the principles of reciprocity and re-distribution are maintained as per the needs of its members.[40]

The European Renaissance brought a new outlook to conceive the society. The emergence of Protestant Ethics, as explained by Max Weber,[41] was instrumental in bringing a new economy into order, in which the spiritual quest to gain, and profit was transformed into calling and vocation, primarily developed a commercial ethics to gain and profit in monetary sense so as to forget a cyclic justification of life and otherworldly achievements, and to ensure a realm of worldly economy, grounded in the psyche of modern man. To prosper or flourish, in modern sense, means to amass resources for the pleasurable possibility of life. The industrial revolution and mass urbanization displaced the sentiments cultivated in the group life of the villages. The economic man had no other alternative but to transfer their life into monetary symbols, leaving behind the memory of interdependence between human to human, human to society, and human to nature.

Modernity as an ameliorative epoch brought a false dichotomy between man versus nature and man versus society. The one-sided discourse is often propagated without developing the proper understanding of truth and its multiple colours. One may find refuge in the collective identity to deny the autonomy of the individual. Another one may rely on the principles of enlightened individualism to rob the traditional knowledge and its values in shaping the discourse vis-a-vis modernity. One appears to be too romantically blind to perceive the limitation of collectivism, and another one is apparently too unreal to ignore the social nature of human being. Any such dichotomy is the by-product of microscopic view, usually accepted as the paradigm of mechanical science and its dissecting methodological rigors.[42]

The human's species is already in the world. Human being is an essential part of the historical process of evolution and societal imagination. The dialectical process of life cycle reflects the transformative relationship between human being and nature, spiritual quest and material satisfaction, consciousness and its projection over the

---

[39] *See* Johannes Lenhard, *A Critical Account of Durkheim's Concept of Organic Solidarity* 2–4 (GRIN Verlag, Norderstedt, 2011).

[40] *See* Karl Polanyi, *The Great Transformation* 49–50, Beacon Press, Massachusetts, 1944, (2001).

[41] Max Weber, *The Protestant Ethic and the Spirit of Capitalism* 102- 125, Talcott Parsons (trans.), Routledge Classics, 1930, (2005).

[42] Fritjof Capra and Pier Luigi Luisi, *The System View of Life* 65, Cambridge University Press, New York, (2014).

external world around him. Human's nature is as natural as nature's humanism[43]; their conflicts and co-operations are dialectically connected. Among the various forms of life, human species is one of the constituents of it, bound by the law of nature, and the possibility of suffering is as real as the want of self-preservation. Likewise, individual as the basic unit of life encompasses the language of society, its cultural riches, taboos, and biases. The religious and ethical standard of every society fulfils the aspirations of individuals in their quest to search the meaning of suffering, which is bound to happen without any exception whatsoever. The moment of happiness or the realization of beauty is hardly possible in an isolated desert. Without sharing the feelings in the moment of suffering, one may feel life as a burden to carry on, and without care and compassion, suffering is too unbearable to ameliorate. However, to totalize the social imagination so as to displace the quest of autonomy is the antithesis for the freedom of humanity as a whole. The human's history is the great witness of the human's scientific and artistic imagination, which transcend the tradition to allow freedom to navigate for progress. Every paradigm shift of science or artistic freedom changes the traditional pattern of society and allows new sets of institutions to flourish as per the necessity of the community. The dialectics between institutions and individual or nature and human species creates an integrated reality, devoid of egotistic selfishness or totalitarian blindness. No answer seems to be perfect for a question, which was wrongly formulated. Society and individual are the two sides of same coin, and to perceive them as isolated silos is merely an arbitrary projection of speculative thought. Can there be freedom without restraint? Can there be right without duty? Likewise, it is impossible to conceive individual and society as two separate realities.

4 Dialectics of Individual and Community in Gandhian Thought

Gandhi never explicitly entered into a dialogic landscape between individualism and collectivism but implicitly developed dialectics through actions and thoughts. His approach to economics and politics and his theories of tolerance, solidarity, and ownership indicate his commitment towards much sincere and integrated life.

The oriental wisdom in nature of "spiritual individualism", ingrained and developed through life and actions of many religious leaders like Ram Krishna Paramahamsa and his disciple Vivekananda, transmitted the spiritual values with all its splendours, which were received and enriched by the leaders, such as Bal Gangadhar Tilak, Bipin Chandra, Rabindranath Tagore, and Mahatma Gandhi, who had belief in the civilizational values of spirituality, emphasized upon those values, as the ultimate end of an individual. One may derive the political connotation of Gandhi from

[43] Karl Marx and Friedrich Engels, *The Economic and Philosophic Manuscripts of 1844 and the Communist Manifesto* 104, Martin Milligan (trans.) Prometheus Books, New York, (2009).

the western liberal thinkers, such as John Stuart Mill, and his spiritual quest developed from the various religious principles, including his own faith in the principles of *Santan Dharm.*[44] The primary theme of Gandhi's spiritual individualism is not against an individual merger with the larger social aggregation and neglecting the socialist aspects of individualism but the self-reformation of an individual so as to sacrifice one's individual interests for the mutual benefits of all. The Gandhian ideology was directed towards the human's progress in ethical sense as well as socio-economic and political development. He emphasized on the holistic development of the individual and society.[45] The ideal society visualized by Gandhi, therefore, was not materialistically driven but a society that could take care of the welfare and happiness of all its members. The imagination was channelized in the Gandhian thought towards "Sarvodaya" or "Antyoday".[46]

Sarvodaya may be defined as "the welfare of all"[47] and Antyoday signifies "the welfare of the last human being".[48] The concept of Sarvodaya epitomizes the entire socio-political and economic movement of Gandhi, which defines his principles or practices of justice.[49] Sinha considered Sarvodaya as the driving force for generating movements for changes, outward or inward, and culminated in a socio-economic condition to "strive for an egalitarian social order based on truth, nonviolence, and purity of means".[50] However, accentuating on the principle of "welfare of all", it did not conform to a utilitarian position of "the greatest good of the greatest number".[51] Moreover, The Gandhian ideology, thus, provides an apt solution to counter the majoritarian tendency of utilitarianism. He had intention to prioritize the welfare of "the last man-the most depraved and the weakest".[52] He was not an advocate of the centralized statehood rather believed in the oceanic circle of the decentralized institutions for just and humane society.

Satyagrah was the cornerstone in Gandhian philosophy. He used it as a means to change the mind and heart of oppressor. He emphasised upon the people's participation in every political or social programme. The means of Satyagrah is associated to Dharm and Swaraj in the Gandhian thought. Anthony J. Parel uses the following words to give us an insight about the Gandhian idea of Dharm. For him, "Dharm is not dogma; it is a quality of the soul through which we know our duty in human

[44] Sanatana Dharma, An Advanced Text Book, Madras, Theosophical Publishing House, p. 311.

[45] Usha Thakker, "Gandhian Perspective of Development, Relevance of Gandhi (2011)". Available at https://www.mkgandhi.org/articles/gandhian-perspective-of-development.html.

[46] M.K. Gandhi, Conquest of Self (Bombay), Ed. R.K., (1943), pp. 27–28.

[47] N.K. Bose, Selections from Gandhi (Ahmedabad, 1948), pp 43–47.

[48] Gandhi, *supra* Note 46.

[49] Shubhangi Rathi, Gandhian Philosophy of Sarvodaya & Its Principles, Gandhi's Views Available at https://www.mkgandhi.org/articles/gandhi_sarvodaya.html.

[50] Ashis Sinha, Gandhian perception of Socio-economic Development, The Researchers – March (2020), 6(1):24–30, https://doi.org/10.21276/tr.2020.6.1.AN3.

[51] I. Rothermund, "The Individual and Society in Gandhi's Political Thought", 28 *The Journal of Asian Studies* 2, pp 313-320 (1969).

[52] James Fieser, The Social Contract (10 Jan., 2017), Available at https://www.utm.edu/staff/jfieser/class/300/socialcont.htm. Last accessed 13 Feb. 2021.

life and our relation with other selves".[53] We cannot know this duty, as he believed, unless we know the self in us. Hence, dharm is how we can know ourselves. This interpretation of dharm places in perspective the primary role of the self in fulfilling social or political responsibility.[54]

Gandhi stressed upon following the "dharm" by each individual. As it will help him understand the value of sacrificing his own right in the good of all. The idea behind freedom was to make an individual free to exercise his own will, vis-à-vis developing his "will" to reduce mass exploitation. Gandhi tried to achieve individual independence by "service to his fellow-creatures".[55] He expressed his services in the form of Sarvodaya. He asserted in *Hind Swaraj* that "western civilization diseases man's mind and heart and imprisons man in clothes, house, and factory".[56] Every human being, resourceful and intelligent, should not forget his duties towards the society. Theoretically, freedom can be regarded as "an absence of restraints", irrespective of who imposes the restraint. Thus, there exists a direct relationship between freedom and restraints where one is inversely proportional to the other.[57] Hence, less the restraints will result into more freedom became the new underlining principle of individualism, resulting into an interface between the state and individual. Gandhi, however, opposed the Western definition of the state and individual liberty. He believed in self-restraint rather than institutional restraints to be a predominant factor, advocated to restrict the role of state action to the minimum.[58]

His idea of Swaraj was to learn to rule oneself.[59] It deals with the concept of self-realization and perpetuation of that realization in every aspect of life. Gandhi visualized a society of ethical creatures, where humans are the higher individuals, who rise within the moral order. The idea behind moral order is for the individuals to grow and cater to develop both: individuals and community in a dialectical sense. Gandhi perceived the limitations of legal language and the possibility of just and fair conduct of the individuals. It is often argued by many thinkers, including Gandhi and Immanuel Kant, that morality or self-consciousness cannot be enforced by use of force. *One can enforce someone to love or hate.* ??? These moral values are cultivated through a dialectical relationship between consciousness and the external world. The primary requirements to achieve a just and peaceful life begins with self-initiative, self-realization, and self-reformation. However, he did not completely negate the idea of social restraint. For him, the social restraint was a critical element required

[53] S. L. Goel and Shalini Rajneesh, Management Techniques: Principle and Practices 333 (2nd Ed. 2007).

[54] Parel, The Doctrine of Swaraj, p. 65; quoted from CWMG 32:11.

[55] Johani Xaxa, and B. K. Mahakul, "Contemporary Relevance of Gandhism", 70 *The Indian Journal of Political Science* 1, 2009, pp. 41–54. Available at www.jstor.org/stable/41856494. Last accessed 13 Feb. 2021.

[56] Ibid., pp. 41–54.

[57] Deshpande, *supra* note 24.

[58] Deshpande, *supra* note 24.

[59] Nageshwar Prasad, Hind Swaraj, a Fresh Look 91 (1985).

to mould the individuals into "response-able" and responsible citizens of the state, who care about duties before claiming or enforcing the rights.

Gandhian vision was ameliorative for restraining both: individuals and the collective behaviour of the community. It was an essential condition, as he believed, for personal or collective liberty.[60] Gandhi was concerned about the spiritual quest of human beings as well as ethical progress of the society. Gandhi expressed through his writings that "an individual is one supreme consideration".[61] Individuality is the firm pillar which supports the progress and development of modern societies. This same individuality is increasingly diminished by the "increase in state power".[62] He was inspired from the ancient Indian tradition, which was community-oriented. Gandhi's individualism is less political and social than ethical and religious.[63] He never accepted the view of freedom as arbitrariness or an act to damage community interest. Gandhi's devotion for individual's emancipation made him a fighter for democratic freedom. This theory is contrary to moderates like Gopal Krishna Gokhale, who focused on creating a state by adopting a constitutional mandate and establishing fundamental rights for individuals inspired by the American jurisprudence.[64] The term "Swaraj Government", which means "Self-Government",[65] works on an assumption that individuals governing themselves must work with an idea of achieving social harmony. The assumption leads into a direction that in an ideal society all individuals would contribute to a self-governing society.[66]

Gandhi explained the need for an individual to learn and practise self-control. Freedom from the feelings of anger, hatred, and selfishness may help him to experience the joy that is attained with the practise of self-control. Gandhi described self-reliance as one of the essential ingredients of the individual's character. The "Charkha" or the spinning wheel became the symbol of self-reliance for Gandhi. He used it to disseminate the idea of economic independence and regeneration by motivating the people to use it to produce Khadi.[67] "Self-sufficiency" and "decentralization" formed the pillars on which villages were rebuilt.[68] As a result, it paved the way for the idea of Swadeshi to seep in. The concept of Swadeshi propagated this very idea of self-reliance of Gandhi extending its ambit to include the society as a whole. It prohibited the use of imported goods and material and relied on the use of goods and materials made in one's own country. Swaraj, thus, was a collective goal of the Indians as well as their individual goal; and it did not necessarily mean

---

[60] Deshpande, *supra* note 28.

[61] Young India, 13 November 1924, p. 378.

[62] N K Bose: Selections from Gandhi (Ahmedabad, Navajivan), p. 26.

[63] Tahtinen, C.F.U.: "The Core of Gandhi's Philosophy", New Delhi, Abhinav, (1970), p. 42.

[64] Gokhale, Oxford University Press, (1977), p. 466.

[65] Akhtar Khan, Individualism: Origin and Evolution, 48 *The Indian Journal of Political Science* 1, 126–132 (1987).

[66] A. Appadorai, "Gandhi's Contribution to Social Theory", 31 *The Review of Politics* 3, 312–328 (1969).

[67] Thakker, *supra* note 20.

[68] Ibid.

an alternative state that is some kind of a reformed structure against the structure of the modern State. Gandhi believed that an individual's actions and behaviour are the result of society's reaction and conditioning. This principle may be better understood by looking at the relationship between crimes and criminals in Gandhian thought. For him, there are only crimes and not criminals. He was of the view that criminality was not an inherent disposition, and the decision to commit an act of crime itself is dependent on plenty of external factors and is hardly related to the character of an individual. This can be compared to Durkheim's study of suicide where he talks about suicide being a social phenomenon. It is imperative to note that law and state are like two sides of a same coin where law cannot be considered and judged alone without looking at the character and role of the state. It is imperative that we pay attention to both the aspects together even while dealing with one of them. The "collective consciousness" of the people forms an intrinsic factor in determining the cause of suicide.[69]

Gandhi had clarity about his vision that it is the cooperation of the people, whether active or passive, which plays an instrumental role in the development of just and peaceful society. It is hardly possible to have a consent or will among the people with invariable status, knowledge, and experience. Therefore, a legal model to create a society, based upon the principle of social contract is bound to be efficient but not necessarily socially and culturally responsive to the need and welfare of each and every person. Gandhi believed in spiritual individualism, based on duty-based relationship among the members of the society. The existence of a duty, for him, is not conditional on the existence of rights. Duties, in few cases, may exist independently of rights and even in the absence of rights. The existence of rights reciprocates the need for duties in the realization of such rights for the individuals. In that sense, rights and duties, as per Gandhi, are complementary to each other. The concept of right is meaningful in a society, because no individual interest has any meaning whatsoever without having common interest for the community. Gandhi expressed in favour of self-realization so as to promote social goods. In his views, the principle of self-assertion needs replacement in favour of mutual trust and welfare. In that sense, Gandhi visualized the necessity to advance the social cause over enlightened self-interest. At the level of consciousness, being is universally connected. Thus, harming others implies the harm for the self and vice versa. Rights start with self-assertion while duty starts with self-discipline. Discipline sometimes is demanded to achieve the total subordination of self to the dictates of a higher authority.

Gandhian ideology always prioritized the societal interests over the state's and individual's interest. He was of the opinion that a person can reap the benefits of freedom "only to a certain extent, and it has to be curtailed at every step".[70] Gandhi believed that, "society cannot be sacrificed for the sake of an individual or a group of individuals or even a nation".[71] Moreover, the key to ensure smooth functioning of the

---

[69] Robert Alun Jones, *Emile Durkheim: An Introduction to Four Major Works*, 82–114, Beverly Hills, CA: Sage Publications, Inc., (1986).

[70] Indira Rothermund, 28 *The Journal of Asian Studies* 2, (Feb., 1969), pp. 313–320.

[71] Ibid.

state was the cooperation from all its citizens. For him, the concept of individualism is not absolute rather relative. With individualism being a relative concept for him, he emphasised on collectivism and not on individual wants and avarice when it came to economic and political stability. According to him, "wealth has to be created collectively and enjoyed collectively".[72]

In the economic sphere, the values of determining the role of an individual are "Aparigrah" (Non-possession) and "Asteya" (Non-stealing).[73] To address the question of inequalities in the society, Gandhi propagated the idea to use wealth prudently and in accordance with the principle of "each according to his need".[74] He considered all material properties as the "social trust" and prohibited the accumulation of wealth in the absence of a valid cause. For him, such unnecessary hoarding of wealth was equivalent to the offence of "theft".[75] The greed and desire to obtain wealth beyond one's need often deviates an individual from his path to "discover truth" and leads him into temptation, making him susceptible to violence, anger, and exploitation. Gandhi promulgated the idea of joint ownership of material property where all the members along with the owners of that society were collectively responsible for the maintenance, management, and welfare of the society. To counter the model of rampant industrialism and capitalism, Gandhi advocated for the principle of trusteeship. Under the Gandhian economic order, "the character of production was determined by social necessity and not by personal greed".[76] Gandhi explained that his idea behind balancing individuality with community interests in a stateless society will bring in financial stability to keep the individuals serving in the interests of society. The "concept of bread and labour" comes into play along with the "principle of occupational equality".[77] A man must earn his own bread, the society must function with components of ideals and practicality. He followed that intellect must not be used to exploit the larger masses; instead, it should apply in the service of mankind. Similarly, if all rich and poor work for their bread, it would obliterate distinctions of rank. His concept of trusteeship was thus aimed to bridge the gap between the rich and the poor by relying on the principle of "bread for all before cakes for some".[78]

---

[72] Jeyaraj Dasan, "History of Science and Technology in India". *Academia,* https://www.academia.edu/30971454/History_of_Science_and_Technology_in_India. Accessed 13 Feb. 2021.

[73] M.K. Gandhi, "Yeravda Mandir", Chapters 5, 6.

[74] Xaxa, Johani, and B. K. Mahakul, "Contemporary Relevance of Gandhism", 70 *The Indian Journal of Political Science* 1, 2009, pp. 41–54. Available at www.jstor.org/stable/41856494. Last accessed 13 Feb. 2021.

[75] Harijan, 11 August 1946.

[76] M. K. Gandhi: Young India, 16 December 1939.

[77] Rajindar K. Koshal, and Manjulika Koshal, "Gandhian Economic Philosophy", 32 *The American Journal of Economics and Sociology* 2, (1973), pp. 191–209. www.jstor.org/stable/3485726. Accessed 13 Feb. 2021.

[78] Subratesh Ghosh, "Trusteeship in Industry: Gandhiji's Dream and Contemporary Reality", 25 *Indian Journal of Industrial Relations* 1, (1989), pp. 35–44 Available at www.jstor.org/stable/27767077. Last accessed 13 Feb. 2021.

Gandhi was not a socialist per se, he fought for the basic individual right to freedom, but he wanted to instil a sense of responsibility in the members of the society to use their properties and resources for the welfare of all and not resort to an egoistic approach of creating a state. Gandhi wanted to prevent the accumulation of political and economic power among a few people. He was strictly against the idea of creating a "monopoly capital".[79] He preferred Satyagrah as means or tools to achieve truth or justice. He developed the art of persuasion, so as to ask the propertied class to share their property and wealth with the have-nots of the society. Gandhi rejected the proposal of enforcing rights by the violence of the law enforcement".[80] Rather, Gandhi relied upon the healing of the heart and mind of the rich and appealing to their moral consciousness to achieve a socialistic quality. The "theory of trusteeship" was thus his idea of "socialism".

5 Conclusion

There has been a drastic change in the political ecosystem all through the world, as things change with the progression of time so does the human mindset. The desirable goals of ancient and mediaeval time is discarded in modern period. For example, communitarianism was once admired as the basic principle to live has been overshadowed by the importance of individual interests. After the emergence of concept, such as rights, the language of duty lost its relevance. No popular government can absolutely guarantee the protection of rights of each of its citizens, but a socialist society can put family and community over the individuals to ensure equal welfare to all. The idea behind the origin and progress of such a community was to ensure collaborative and cooperative approach between society and individuals. In this way, the Gandhian principle of the basic human rights to all and trusteeship obligations of rich over poor were conceived to ensure fair opportunities for the enrichment of everyone. Besides, the minimum intervention of state in a socialist society is the best way to protect the basic freedoms of each individual. The cause cèlébre of democratic issues between majority and minority may always remain unsolved in an enforcement set up, designed to follow the utilitarian logic of maximum benefits to the maximum numbers of the people. The only plausible solution to ensure freedom and good governance is to strive for a common consensual society based on the principle of simple living and wilful sacrifice in the welfare of all members of the society. It may be said that rights without realization are as good as rhetoric. Duties are synonyms to the positive legislation of being, which are instrumental in the development of just and peaceful society. Duty based upon social solidarity can ameliorate suffering and may be instrumental in the enhancement of freedom. To substantiate this statement,

[79] Indira Rothermund, *The Journal of Asian Studies,* Vol. 28, No. 2 (1969), pp. 313-320.

[80] Trusteeship, The Gandhian Model of Development-An Outline and A Critique of The Policy Regime, Including The New Economic Policy, p. 17. Available at https://shodhganga.inflibnet.ac.in/bitstream/10603/604/12/12_chapter6.pdf.

one may investigate the case of Tulsa in the USA, where African-American Blacks were tortured for a considerable length of time, they were genuinely broken by the ground-breaking powers of white Americans for years. Being a piece of the world's most powerful democracy has not guaranteed the protection of Tulsa blacks from state viciousness and abominations. However, a self-created network advanced to facilitate monetary and social offices for the individuals in their locale has helped to accomplish freedom while as yet being a part of their country. Currently, there has been an ongoing outbreak of a deadly pandemic pan-world, making it a threat on humanity, during this period developed nations were not able to contain the outbreak, while community efforts in protecting individuals proved to be an efficient remedy at a stage when no individual or state can cure a threat to entire humanity.

Freedom ought not to come as a political declaration; rather, an individual ought to be liberated from injustice and violence. Gandhi was not completely opposed to making a state; yet, he propounded that such a demonstration would disregard the prime target of peacefulness among the general public. This would degenerate the ethical idea of pioneers in the organization of state. The Gandhian standards in a populist society may be a leading light for those who accept inertia as their fates. Gandhi emphasized over action and self-reformation. In his words, "We but mirror the world. All the tendencies present in the outer world are to be found in the world of our body. If we could change ourselves, the tendencies in the world would also change. As a man changes his own nature, so does the attitude of the world change towards him. This is the divine mystery supreme. A wonderful thing it is and the source of our happiness. We need not wait to see what others do".[81] This change might be effectuated by spreading mindfulness among the people of the need to forfeit individual interests for the advantages of the general public. It is only through progressive education and developing edification, one may achieve truth and peacefulness in his life. The possibility of truth does not lie in isolated realm of individualism or collectivism rather harmony in two inter-dependent realities.

References

Abeyratne R (2012) Air Navigation Law 14

Agamben G (1995, 1998), Homo Sacer: Sovereign power and bare life (Daniel Heller-Roazen (trans.)). Stanford University Press, California, pp 87–88

Appadorai A (1969) Gandhi's contribution to social theory. Rev Politics 31(3):312–328

Ashish S (2020) Gandhian perception of socio-economic development. The Researchers 6(1):24–30. https://doi.org/10.21276/tr.2020.6.1.AN3

Barnes GM (1977) Emile Durkheim's contribution to the sociology of education. J Educ Thought (JET)/Revue Pensée Educative 11(3):213–223

Benn T (2013a) What's individuality and where does it comes from? https://blogs.scientificamerican.com/mind-guest-blog/whats-individuality-and-where-does-it-come-from/. Accessed 13 Feb 2021

Benn T (2013b) What's individuality and where does it comes from? Sci Am 100–180

[81] The Collected Works of Mahatma Gandhi, vol. 13, chapter 153, p. 241.

Bluhm WT (1984) Freedom in 'the social contract': Rousseau's 'legitimate chains.' Polity 16(3):359–383. JSTOR www.jstor.org/stable/3234555

Boesche R (1981) The strange liberalism of Alexis De Tocqueville. History Political Thought 2(3):495–524

Bose NK (1948) Selections from Gandhi, pp 26–47

Buch MA (1938) Rise and growth of Indian liberalism. Atmaram, Baroda, p 82

Chattopadhyay HP, Sarkar SK (2006) Global encyclopaedia of political science, 1578, 1st edn, vol 1

Dasan J. History of science and technology in India. Academia https://www.academia.edu/30971454/History_of_Science_and_Technology_in_India. Accessed 13 Feb 2021

de Tocqueville A (1951) De la Democratie en Amerique (1835) bk. II, pt. II, Ch. II. *Oeuvres Completes*, ed. J. P. Mayer I, II.

Dharma S. An advanced text book. Theosophical Publishing House, Madras, p 311

The Editors of Encyclopaedia Britannica (2019) Social contract. Encyclopædia Britannica, August 06, 2019. https://www.britannica.com/topic/social-contract

Fieser J (2017) The social contract. https://www.utm.edu/staff/jfieser/class/300/socialcont.htm

Fritj of Capra and Pier Luigi Luisi (2014) The system view of life. Cambridge University Press, New York, pp 65–70

Gandhi MK (1939) Young India, December 16, 1939

Gandhi MK (1943) Conquest of self (Bombay), Ed. R.K., pp 27–28

Gandhi MK Yeravda Mandir, Chapters 5, 6.

Goel SL, Rajneesh S (2007) Management techniques: principle and practices, 2nd edn, p 333

Gokhale (1977) (Oxford University Press), p 466

Gorodnichenko Y, Roland G (2013) Understanding the individualism-collectivism cleavage and its effects: lessons from cultural psychology, pp 25–80

Grant RW (1988) Locke's political anthropology and Lockean individualism. J Politics 50(1):42–63

Harijan, August 11, 1946.

https://www.mkgandhi.org/articles/gandhian-perspective-of-development.html.

Iggers TG (1958) The doctrine of Saint-Simon: an exposition. First Year 1828–9 (1830) 28, 70, 247

John Ruskin, Unto this last

Jordan E (1921) The definition of individuality. Philos Rev 30(6):566–584

Kashima Y, Triandis HC (1986) The self-serving bias in attributions as a coping strategy: a cross-cultural study. J Cross Cult Psychol 17(1):83–97

Khan A (1987) Individualism: origin and evolution. Indian J Polit Sci 48(1):126–132

Kitayama S, Markus H, Kurokawa M (2010) Culture, emotion, and well-being: good feelings in Japan and the United States. Cogn Emotion 14. https://doi.org/10.1080/026999300379003

Koshal RK, Koshal M (1973) Gandhian economic philosophy. Am J Econ Sociol 32(2):191–209

Lenhard J (2011) A critical account of Durkheim's concept of organic solidarity. GRIN Verlag, pp 2–4

Locke J (1980) Second treatise of government, IV, 22, p 17

Lukes S (1971) The meanings of individualism. J Hist Ideas 32(1):45–66

Lukes S (2006) Individualism 24 ECPR: Colchester

Marx K, Engels F (2009) The economic and philosophic manuscripts of 1844 and the communist manifesto. Prometheus Books, New York, pp 102–105

Mill JS (1859) On liberty, vol 33, 2nd edn. John W. Parker and Son, London

Mill JS (1879) Chapters on socialism, p 715

Oxford English and Spanish Dictionary. https://www.lexico.com/definition/individual. Accessed 13 Feb 2021

Parel. The Doctrine of Swaraj, p 65; quoted from CWMG 32:11

Internet Encyclopaedia of Philosophy. https://iep.utm.edu/hegelsoc/. Accessed 13 Feb 2021

Internet Encyclopaedia of Philosophy. https://iep.utm.edu/hobmeth/. Accessed 13 Feb 2021

Polanyi K (1944) The Great Transformation. Beacon Press, Massachusetts, pp 49–50

Popper K (2012) The open society and its enemies. Routledge Classics, London, pp 15–16

Prasad N (1985) Hind Swaraj, a fresh look 91
Rathi S. Gandhian philosophy of Sarvodaya & its principles. Gandhi's Views. https://www.mkgandhi.org/articles/gandhi_sarvodaya.html
Jones RA (1986) Emile Durkheim: an introduction to four major works. Sage Publications, Inc., Beverly Hills, CA, pp 82–114
Rothermund I (1969) The individual and society in Gandhi's political thought. J Asian Stud 28(2):313–320
Stevens P (2018) Man is by nature a social animal: social integration following lower-limb amputation. https://opedge.com/Articles/ViewArticle/2018-10-01/man-is-by-nature-a-social-animal-social-integration-following-lower-limbamputation#:~:text=Aristotle%20asserted%20long%20ago%20that,interruption%20such%20as%20an%20amputation. Accessed 13 Feb 2021
Subratesh G (1989) Trusteeship in industry: Gandhiji's dream and contemporary reality. Indian J Ind Relations 25(1):35–44
Tahtinen CFU (1970) The Core of Gandhi's Philosophy. Abhinav 42
Thakker U (2011) Gandhian perspective of development, relevance of Gandhi
The Collected Works of Mahatma Gandhi, vol. 13, chapter 153, p 241
The History of Western Ethics 67, 1st edn. Duignan, Brian (2011)
Trusteeship, The Gandhian model of development-an outline and a critique of the policy regime (including the new economic policy), p 17. https://shodhganga.inflibnet.ac.in/bitstream/10603/604/12/12_chapter6.pdf
USC-US China Institute. https://china.usc.edu/confucius-analects-17. Accessed 13 Feb 2021
Villa D (2005a) Hegel, tocqueville, and 'individualism.' Rev Politics, 67(4):659–686. JSTOR, www.jstor.org/stable/25046471. Accessed 13 Feb 2021
Villa D (2005b) Hegel, tocqueville, and 'individualism.' Rev Politics 67(4):659–686
Wasserman R, Mautner R (1994) Jean-Jacques Rousseau and the discourse of the exotic. In: Exotic nations: literature and cultural identity in the United States and Brazil, 1830–1930. Cornell University Press, pp 69–100. http://www.jstor.org/stable/10.7591/j.ctt207g5v4.6
Weber M (2005) The protestant ethic and the spirit of capitalism, pp 102–125
Xaxa J, Mahakul BK (2009) Contemporary relevance of Gandhism. Indian J Polit Sci 70(1):41–54
Young India (1924) 13th November 1924, p 378

Part II
Duties in the Contemporary World

Chapter 8
A Pandemic, Racial Tensions and Civil Unrest, and Democracy in Turmoil: Rights V. Duties in 2020 America

Edward C. Harris

Every person in a well-ordered state is fully conscious of both his responsibilities and his rights.

—Mahatma Gandhi

The year 2020 has witnessed perhaps the greatest turmoil in American society since the Great Depression and the Second World War. Understandably, much of the social and legal discourse taking place through this tumultuous year has centered on rights—rights of citizens to be kept safe by their government from a virulent and dangerous virus, rights of racial minorities to be treated the same as members of the racial majority at the hands of law enforcement and the criminal justice system, and rights of citizens in a modern democracy to expect free and fair elections.

Notwithstanding the intense focus given to the subject of legal rights in the context of the seismic events of 2020, viewing these events through the lens of legal duties or responsibilities casts a critical light on the arguments and efforts required to advance such rights. The Western literature on rights and responsibilities is, to be sure, anything but coherent and consistent. Indeed, it is evident that Western philosophers and legal thinkers have gone to great lengths to maintain separation between rights and duties, as if they were wholly independent of one another. In her 1991 book, *Rights Talk: The Impoverishment of Political Discourse*, Mary Ann Glendon argues that American society is dominated by an obsession with individual rights to such an extent that little else has the opportunity to be discussed , including individual

E. C. Harris (✉)
Associate Professor, Chicago-Kent College of Law, Illinois Institute of Technology, Chicago, IL, USA
e-mail: eharris@kentlaw.iit.edu

R. Mittal and K. K. Singh (eds.), *Relevance of Duties in the Contemporary World*,
https://doi.org/10.1007/978-981-19-1836-0_8

responsibility and civic duty.[1] In addition, the separation of rights and duties was likely exacerbated beyond the influences of Locke, Mill, and Blackstone in Western legal theory by Professor Hohfeld's classifications of rights in the early twentieth century.[2] And, as recognized by Glendon and others, the separation of legal rights from legal duties in Western legal thought has continued down to the present and has given rise to a culture of a constant clamor for rights and a dearth of discourse on responsibilities (save, perhaps, in the law school classroom).

Therefore, the events that unfolded during 2020, particularly in the United States with its global reputation as a model of modern democracy and a (mostly) well-functioning legal system, create a particularly auspicious opportunity to reexamine rights from a different and perhaps more instructive perspective: that of the Eastern tradition from the moral and political philosophy of Mahatma Gandhi. But first, a brief summary of the three sea-changing events of 2020 in the U.S. that are subject to this examination and the outcry for rights that were born of each:

1 The SARS-CoV-2 Pandemic

The pandemic caused by the SARS-CoV-2 virus hit U.S. shores with the first confirmed case on January 21, 2020, after it had already been rapidly spreading throughout large cities in China and had arrived in several other countries. The rapid spread and the measures taken or not taken by the U.S. federal and state authorities are well documented and thus do not need to be recounted here. For purposes of this discussion, however, a few salient points are worth noting. First, in the first few weeks and months of the pandemic, President Donald Trump downplayed the impact the virus would have on U.S. society and its economy for the ostensible reason that damage to the economy and U.S. citizens' inability to work, attend schools, attend places of worship, and engage in all manner of social interaction threatened President Trump's political prospects in the national election later that year.[3] Second, once it became impossible to ignore the virus' threat to the public health of U.S. citizens

---

[1] See, *Rights Talk: The Impoverishment of Political Discourse*, Mary Ann Glendon, (Free Press 1991). Mary Ann Glendon is Learned Hand Professor of Law, Emeritus, at Harvard Law School and former U.S. Ambassador to the Holy See. She is the author of numerous books and articles on topics in human rights, comparative law, and political theory. In *Rights Talk*, Glendon adeptly argues in part that, from influences beginning with Locke, Mill, and Blackstone, American society's near fanatical obsession with individual rights has eviscerated any potential discussion of individual responsibility and communitarian duties, notwithstanding the important correlative relationship between rights and duties.

[2] *Fundamental Legal Concepts as Applied in Judicial Reasoning*, W. N. Hohfeld, 26 *Yale Law Journal* 710 (1917).

[3] See, *The President vs. the Experts: How Trump Played Down the Coronavirus*, The New York Times, March 18, (2020), Linda Qiu, Bill March, John Huang, accessed January 26, 2021 at https://www.nytimes.com/interactive/2020/03/18/us/trump-coronavirus-statements-timeline.html; see also, "'*It will disappear': The Disinformation Trump Spread About the Coronavirus—Timeline*," The Guardian, April 14, (2020a), Tom McCarthy, accessed January

and the impact on the lives and livelihoods of citizens, the Trump Administration engaged in several forms of conduct, which at times appeared contradictory. The Administration began to excise itself and the federal government as a whole from its role in dealing with the pandemic and placed that responsibility squarely on state and local governments.[4] In addition, the Trump Administration also did little to provide support to the states in the form of funding and releasing essential equipment and supplies from federal stockpiles. Also, the Administration continued to downplay the pandemic generally and added steam to this strategy by attempting to discredit the views and recommendations of reputable expert members of the scientific community,[5] and, indeed, it sought to discredit entire expert organizations such as the World Health Organization and, at times, the U.S. Centers for Disease Control (CDC). Further, the Administration overtly sought to fan the flames of nascent protests by citizens in various states who were upset by state ordered shutdowns of much economic and social activity. The Administration's conduct relative to the pandemic was not all bad, however. A particularly positive step taken by the administration was its "Operation Warp Speed" and partnership with the private sector to move the development and production of effective vaccines against the virus forward at a pace never before witnessed in human history. The first two effective vaccines against SARS-CoV-2 cleared the Federal Food and Drug Administration's emergency regulatory process by November 2020 and began distribution of the vaccines in early December 2020. Another positive step taken by President Trump was his invocation of the Defense Production Act in early April 2020 which permits federal authorities to order private industry to produce certain equipment or materials essential to combatting a national crisis. The Trump Administration used its power under the Act to order several large-scale manufacturing companies to produce ventilators needed by hospitals to keep alive the sickest victims of the COVID-19 disease.

Amidst this backdrop, several veins of argument over rights have emerged. The most obvious argument raised by a large portion of the American public is their right to expect the federal government to protect the public from a national emergency like the current pandemic. This argument encompasses the expectation that the federal government will marshal all of its resources in fighting the pandemic in terms of supplying essential equipment and medical supplies, ensuring that citizens have financial resources to sustain themselves and their families while being unable

26, 2021 at https://www.theguardian.com/us-news/2020/apr/14/trump-coronavirus-alerts-disinformation-timeline.

[4] See, *How Trump Sowed Covid Supply Chaos. 'Try Getting It Yourselves.'* The Wall Street Journal, August 31, (2020), Michael C. Bender and Rebecca Ballhaus, accessed February 5, 2021 at https://www.wsj.com/articles/how-trump-sowed-covid-supply-chaos-try-getting-it-yourselves-11598893051.

[5] See, *Health Experts, Democrats Rally to Fauci's Defense After White House Criticism*, The Wall Street Journal, July 13, (2020), Stephanie Armour and Andrew Restuccia, accessed February 5, 2021at https://www.wsj.com/articles/health-experts-democrats-rally-to-fauci-defense-after-white-house-criticism-11594667308; see also, Why exactly is Trump lashing out at the World Health Organization?, The Washington Post, April 8, (2020), Amber Phillips, accessed February, 10, 2021 at https://www.washingtonpost.com/politics/2020/04/08/why-exactly-is-president-trump-lashing-out-world-health-organization/.

to work, and taking national (rather than state and local) measures to combat and control the spread of the virus. Another line of argument centered on rights has been citizens' freedom to make personal choices regarding whether to abide by specific recommendations of public health authorities to protect themselves and others from the virus such as practicing social distancing and wearing face coverings.

2 Racial Injustice and Civil Unrest

The death of African-American citizen George Floyd at the hands of four Minneapolis, Minnesota police officers during a police-citizen confrontation on May 25, 2020, was reported widely around the globe and sparked a massive wave of civil unrest in the United States and in some other countries.[6] The tensions surrounding widespread racial injustice against black citizens perpetrated by police (largely white officers but not exclusively so) and other players in the criminal justice system has been simmering for decades in the United States, but the murder of George Floyd represented an inflection point in terms of public outrage and the level of attention given to the issue by not only members of black American community and those sympathetic to their struggle for justice, but also by the law enforcement and criminal justice communities, as well as political actors and every-day Americans who previously had not paid a great deal of attention to the matter. Massive protests, which in some instances, involved violence, looting, and destruction of property, spread across major U.S. cities during late May and into June 2020 before the unrest temporarily eased. A second wave of protests and civil unrest erupted later in the summer months and into the early autumn in response to further deadly encounters involving black citizens and police. Although much of the protest activities from late May into September 2020 were organized by the Black Lives Matter movement, there were some far-right groups which staged counter protests and in some instances perpetrated violence and destruction either to voice their opinions against the citizens protesting for equal justice or simply to take advantage of the chaos and advance their own objectives. In addition, some far-left organizations had participated in the protests and riots, with some perpetrating violence, looting, and property destruction.

Although not much legislative or political activity has thus far resulted from this recent wave of civil unrest, the election of President Biden and Vice President Harris suggests that reform measures for law enforcement and the criminal justice system are a high legal and political priority for the new presidential administration. The private sector has also taken note, and various actors, from large national and multinational corporations and universities to small businesses, have released official

[6] See, *George Floyd Protests: A Timeline*, The New York Times, January 6, (2021), Derrick Bryson Taylor, accessed February 11, 2021 at https://www.nytimes.com/article/george-floyd-protests-timeline.html, see also, In (2020), The Black Lives Matter Movement Shook the World, Al Jazeera, December 31, 2020, Laurin-Whitney Gottbrath, accessed January 26, 2021 at https://www.aljazeera.com/features/2020/12/31/2020-the-year-black-lives-matter-shook-the-world.

statements and implemented measures purportedly to root-out racism within their organizations.[7]

While much of the rights-centered discourse throughout 2020 civil unrest has understandably been expressed in broad terms, on the side of those arguing against racial injustice, much of the discourse is rooted in the Fourth and Fourteenth Amendments to the U.S. Constitution. The Fourth Amendment protects U.S. citizens from unreasonable searches and seizures by government actors, e.g., police.[8] This constitutional guarantee to citizens and the abundance of U.S. Supreme Court precedent interpreting the Fourth Amendment is central to police encounters with citizens when police are investigating potential crime or engaged in crime prevention measures. The Fourteenth Amendment's Due Process and Equal Protection Clauses are also at the foundation of the rights over which ignited the 2020 civil unrest.[9] The Fourteenth Amendment's Due Process Clause guarantees the right of citizens not to be deprived of their life, liberty, or property without due process of law. The Fourteenth Amendment's Equal Protection Clause guarantees all citizens the right to equal protection of the laws, which, in the context of race and the criminal justice system, essentially means that the Constitution commands that all citizens are to be treated equally with respect to enforcement of the law and without regard to their race, and that law in the United States is to be applied equally without regard to race.

---

[7] Here's What Companies Are Promising to Do to Fight Racism, The New York Times, August 23, (2020), Gillian Friedman, accessed January 4, 2021 at https://www.nytimes.com/article/companies-racism-george-floyd-protests.html.

[8] United States Const. Amend. IV (1791). The Fourth Amendment reads: "The right of the people to be secure in their persons, houses, papers, and effects, against unreasonable searches and seizures, shall not be violated, and no Warrants shall issue, but upon probably cause, supported by Oath of affirmation, and particularly describing the place to be searched, and the persons or things to be seized." The Fourth Amendment is relevant to the rights at issue for the protesting citizens since a great many of the incidents involving black citizens harmed or killed in the context of a confrontation with police relate to traffic stops and vehicle searches, or so-called stop and frisk encounters or police attempts to search private property.

[9] United States Const. Amend. XIV sec.1 (1868). The Fourteenth Amendment's Due Process and Equal Protection Clauses were ratified in the immediate post-Civil War period and were particularly intended to guaranty basic American constitutional civil rights to black citizens who lacked any civil rights prior to the end of slavery. The relevant portions of the Amendment read: "No State… shall… deprive any person of life, liberty, or property, without due process of law; nor deny to any person within its jurisdiction the equal protection of the laws." While the Due Process Clause has relevance to citizen encounters with police, it is particularly relevant to issues of criminal prosecution and sentencing. The Equal Protection Clause is highly relevant to citizen encounters with police since, the gross disparities between the death or serious injury of black citizens versus the death or serious injury of white citizens occurring in the context of police encounters would not be what they currently are if laws regulating police conduct were applied and observed equally without regard to race of the citizen.

3 A National Election Never Before Witnessed

President Trump began 2020 touting a strong economy and continuing his controversial policies in areas such as immigration, foreign affairs, and the dismantling of the "administrative state." He also faced his first impeachment trial in the U.S. Senate based on a phone call with a newly elected president in Ukraine in July 2019 wherein Trump indicated that he would withhold foreign aid allocated by Congress to Ukraine unless the new Ukrainian president agreed to announce or initiate investigations into the son of his political rival, former Vice President, Joe Biden. Although President Trump's impeachment trial ended in February 2020 with his acquittal on the charges and leaving him in a somewhat stronger position for the national election later in 2020, the pandemic soon began to create more significant threats to his prospects for reelection. By mid-March 2020, former Vice President Joe Biden had emerged from the Democratic Party primary elections as that party's candidate to run against Republican Party incumbent, President Donald Trump.

Amidst the spring and early summer lockdowns, social distancing, and other strict measures ordered by state and local governments to combat the pandemic, the Trump campaign, facing increasingly grim reelection prospects due to Trump's handling of the pandemic and a slumping economy, embarked on a coordinated effort of disseminating claims that the upcoming election will be ripe for fraud and irregularities making the results unreliable and the antithesis of a free and fair election. These claims were largely based on the prediction that, due to the pandemic, the number of voters casting ballots in-person would be significantly lower than in previous elections and the number of mail-in ballots would dramatically increase compared to all previous national elections in modern times.[10] Over the summer months of 2020 and into the autumn, as each state prepared and implemented its election procedures to carry-out the November 2020 national election during a deadly pandemic, the claims of a potentially fraudulent and unreliable election spread, expanded, and morphed into various strands of conjecture to provably false stories in the news to "deep state" conspiracy theories. Certain conservative-leaning news outlets such as Fox News and the New York Post played a key role in spreading the false and misleading claims of the Trump campaign and its allies by editorializing on these claims and thereby lending credibility to them.[11] Social media also played a critical role in giving users a platform to disseminate the falsehoods and unfounded conspiracy theories about the election. It was clear to many astute observers in the months prior to the election that the Trump campaign's claims of likely widespread election fraud and an ultimately

[10] Voting by mail favored the Democratic candidate for two primary reasons: Democratic voters generally outnumber Republican voters, so if the overall turnout of Democratic voters in a given election is high, the Democratic candidate is more likely to win, and, with the pandemic still ongoing, the states' relaxing of requirements for mail-in or absentee voting, the pandemic itself would not be a deterrent to Democratic voter turnout.

[11] See, *How Conservative Media Stoked Baseless Election-Fraud Claims that Motivated D.C. Rioters*, USA Today, January 11, (2021), Bill Keveney and Maria Puente, accessed January 13, 2021 at https://www.usatoday.com/story/entertainment/tv/2021/01/11/dc-riots-how-newsmax-oan-conservative-outlets-fueled-mob/6589298002/

unreliable election result were President Trump's attempt to sow doubt in the minds of the public of the trustworthiness of the election results, even before the election had taken place.

Most major news networks called the results of the November 3 election in favor of Joe Biden by November 7 but that did not cause President Trump to concede the victory to Biden. He, his campaign, and his supporters continued their effort to spread false claims and misinformation by every means possible including statements to the media, posts on social media, making public demands of state legislators and election officials to recount votes or declare the election results in their states as invalid, and filing lawsuits to challenge election results in numerous states. As of January 5, 2021, just one day ahead of the constitutionally required official counting and certification of the Electoral College votes by a joint session of Congress, the Trump campaign and Trump allies had filed a breathtaking 62 lawsuits in state and federal courts (including the U.S. Supreme Court) challenging the results of the election, and by January 5, 2021, Trump had lost an astonishing 61 of the 62 lawsuits, with only one minor and inconsequential victory in a Pennsylvania appellate court.[12] The near universal failure of these lawsuits was by the decisions of both Democratic and Republican judges and even some who are Trump's own judicial appointees. While some of the suits were dismissed on procedural grounds, many were dismissed as meritless and for lack of any credible evidence to support the claims of massive widespread fraud and irregularities in the election. Notwithstanding these very public and humiliating losses in a wide range of courts across the country, Trump and his allies continued trumpeting claims that the election was "stolen" from him by Biden and the Democrats.

The claims of a fraudulent and stolen election by President Trump, Rudy Giuliani, Trump's personal attorney, and other prominent Trump allies and Republicans culminated in the storming of the U.S. Capitol building by a violent mob of hundreds of Trump supporters on January 6, 2021, as the joint session of Congress to certify the election results was underway. The storming of the U.S. Capitol resulted in five deaths, including the death of a Capitol police officer, numerous injuries to police officers and members of the violent mob and others, and destruction of federal property. A faction within the mob were captured on video calling for the public execution of various congressional officials as they stormed and invaded the Capitol building. In the days following the storming of the Capitol, the FBI and other law enforcement agencies made hundreds of arrests of citizens alleged to have taken part in the insurrection, and Congress passed an Article of Impeachment against President Trump

[12] *By the Numbers: President Donald Trump's Failed Efforts to Overturn the Election*, USA TODAY, January 5, (2021), William Cummings, Joey Garrison, and Jim Sergent, accessed on February 4, 2021 at: https://www.usatoday.com/in-depth/news/politics/elections/2021/01/06/trumps-failed-efforts-overturn-election-numbers/4130307001/. (The article provides a detailed chronical of President Trump's and his allies' efforts to overturn the November 2020 national election results, before, during, and after the election. The article notes that the one minor victory among the 62 lawsuits involved a Pennsylvania state court's decision that a small and inconsequential number of votes are to be thrown out since the voters had not supplied proper personal identifying information by the state's required deadline).

for fomenting insurrection, giving President Trump the dubious distinction of the only president in United States history to be impeached twice.

The events surrounding the 2020 national election in the U.S., beginning with the Trump campaign's barrage of misinformation and unsupported claims of massive widespread fraud both prior to and after the election and which finally resulted in insurrection at the U.S. Capitol, are steeped in the rights-based arguments of citizens' rights to rely on a free and fair electoral process absent fraud or malfeasance and a citizen's right to have her vote counted and to not have her vote or right to vote suppressed. Each of these rights-based arguments takes on an entirely different appearance, in the context of the 2020 U.S. election, depending on whether the proponent is a Trump supporter or a Biden (or any other sort of non-Trump) supporter. Trump supporters argue for free and fair elections because they do not believe that the 2020 election would be, or eventually was, free and fair, they argue that they are the victims of a stolen and fraudulent election and voter suppression tactics, and thus, that they have been disenfranchised. The non-Trump supporters, on the other hand, argue that the sowing of doubt in the reliability of the election undermines the free and fair election which in fact took place and that any action that is or would be taken by officials on the basis of the claims of fraud would essentially be voter suppression and disenfranchisement of Democrat voters. An additional rights-based argument circulated among the non-Trump supporters has been the right to rely on the veracity of statements made by elected officials, or at the very least that such statements are not made as knowingly false statements of fact. This argument further extends to the right to rely on the veracity of news reports in the mainstream media regarding these sorts of false or misleading claims by a political candidate and his or her supporters. The extension of this argument to the news media, however, becomes murky due to the increasing blurry lines between factual reporting and editorial and opinion segments that have become a standard feature of most mainstream news outlets in recent decades.

On the Trump supporter side, in light of all such claims of election fraud and malfeasance having been determined to be categorically baseless by nearly every Republican and Democrat state election official and nearly every impartial judge in both state and federal courts asked to consider such claims, it is clear that these rights-based arguments are founded on an entirely false premise, notwithstanding the validity and sanctity of these rights under American law in the abstract. The fact that the Trump supporting side of these arguments bases them on a false foundation, makes their consideration from the perspective of a duty even more illuminating and important, even if the specific duty is not the precise corollary to the right claimed.

4 Application of the Gandhian Conception of Responsibility

The short quote from Gandhi at the outset of this chapter is revealing of Gandhi's conception of the position "rights" should occupy with individuals and in society. In the quoted passage, Gandhi conspicuously placed the word "responsibilities" before the word "rights" which essentially defines his view of rights. "The true source of rights is duty. If we all discharge our duties, rights will not be far to seek. If leaving duties unperformed we run after rights, they will escape us like a will-o'-the-wisp. The more we pursue them, the farther will they fly."[13] The crux of Gandhi's view on rights is, simply put, individual rights flow directly from the individual's and the community's observance of his/its responsibilities toward others and toward the community as a whole. As Dalton recognizes, modern political thought is often tied to the unique historical context, and it is no different in the case of modern Indian political and legal thinkers such as Gandhi.[14] Notwithstanding that the context of the development of Gandhi's views on rights and responsibilities was India's independence from Great Britain, his conceptualization of individual rights and responsibilities is framed in such a way to be broadly applicable to virtually any claim of individual rights in a modern industrialized society. Dalton provides a detailed survey of the most influential Western liberal political theorists which led to an over-emphasis of individual rights and eventually generated the critiques of Glendon and others who note the singular focus on individual rights at the expense of individual or civic responsibility.[15] Dalton goes on to explain the arguments of prominent modern Indian thinkers, with particular emphasis on Gandhi, on freedom, rights, and responsibility and concludes that Western political discourse would be better served to include these voices as "resources for better conceptualizing a strong social conscience and commitment to a higher quality of civic life."[16] Dalton's analysis, however, was in the context of the political, whereas the present analysis attempts to view the rights versus duties discussion from a legal perspective.

The Gandhian conception of rights as a product of the observance of duties to one's self, to others, and to the community, in the context of the current clamor for rights from the societal elements outlined above, reveals that the law itself is replete with responsibilities placed on elected and appointed officials, many of which, if observed, would obviate the need for individuals or groups to demand rights.

[13] *Selections from Gandhi*, Nirmal Kumar Bose, p.48 (Published by Desai & Mudranalaya in Ahmedabad, India) accessed January 20, 2021 at https://www.gandhiashramsevagram.org/pdf-books/selections-from-gandhi.pdf.

[14] *Gandhi on Freedom, Rights, and Responsibility*, Dennis Dalton, International Seminar on Gandhi and the Twenty-First Century, Jan. (1998), accessed on January 5, 2021 at https://www.mkgandhi.org/articles/freedom.htm (Dalton explains that much of Gandhi's view of rights and responsibility is taken in the context of India's struggle for independence from British rule.).

[15] Ibid.

[16] Ibid.

With respect to the rights-based arguments raised in the context of the pandemic, i.e., the right to expect that the national government takes action to protect citizens' lives and livelihoods, the starting point is Article II of the U.S. Constitution's description of the power of the executive branch of the federal government.[17] Article II, Sect. 1, Clause 1, states that "[t]he executive Power shall be vested in a President of the United States of America."[18] Under Article II, the President assumes broad powers and responsibilities over certain spheres, such as the power and duty to serve as Commander in Chief of the armed forces,[19] the power and duty to appoint ambassadors, judges to the Supreme Court, and other ministers, the duty to periodically provide information to the Congress on the State of the Union and make recommendations to the Congress,[20] and "[the President] shall take Care that the Laws be faithfully executed…"[21] Whether phrased as powers or as imperative duties, the framing of the executive branch within the Constitution explicitly places significant legal responsibilities on the shoulders of the President and consequently all federal executive branch officials functioning under the authority of the President.[22]

When considered in their totality, the executive responsibilities outlined in Article II, without question, place an overall responsibility on the President and other executive branch officials to protect the interests of the nation, to protect its citizens, and to protect the institutions of American democracy, e.g., faithfully executing the laws made by the co-equal legislative branch. In fact, virtually every U.S. President in modern times, including President Trump, has proclaimed that his primary duty as President is to protect the American people.[23] Therefore, if our President and all subordinate federal executive branch officials had in fact observed their responsibilities to protect the interests of the country and its citizens, the struggle against the pandemic would likely have looked quite different. Vast federal resources would have been unleased, state and local governments would have received as much support as was possible from the federal government, the President would have made stronger efforts to unify members of his political party (the majority party in the Senate) to provide more financial relief to individuals, families, and business significantly impacted by the pandemic, the President would have worked tirelessly to keep the public and Congress informed, he would have consistently acted on the advice of

[17] United States Constitution, Article II (1789a).

[18] Ibid. at Sec. 1. Cl. 1.

[19] Ibid. at Sec. 2, Cl. 1.

[20] Ibid. at Sec. 3.

[21] Ibid.

[22] The powers and responsibilities conferred on the President under Article II have been the subject of numerous Supreme Court cases since the ratification of the Constitution in 1789; given the great number of cases and variation in subject matter, they are beyond the scope of this analysis.

[23] In his 2015 acceptance speech of the Republican Party nomination as the Republican candidate for president, then-candidate Trump said, "The most basic duty of government is to defend the lives of its own citizens." Fact-Check: Donald Trump's Republican Convention Speech, Annotated, National Public Radio, accessed February 2, 2021, at https://www.npr.org/2016/07/21/486883610/fact-check-donald-trumps-republican-convention-speech-annotated. Numerous presidential candidates and Presidents in modern history have made similar statements.

experts in the scientific and medical communities, and he would have sought to foster a moral obligation among citizens to take the recommended personal measures to protect themselves and others from infection of the virus. In many instances, President Trump and the officials in his administration did precisely the opposite of the requirements of their constitutional duties.

Of particular note in the context of the pandemic is the notion that it is a citizen's individual right to choose to wear or not to wear a face covering and to observe proper social distancing and proper hygiene. In the face of overwhelming scientific evidence that shows that face masks, proper social distancing, and habitual hand-washing help significantly to control the spread of the virus, President Trump repeatedly encouraged a sentiment among his supporters that taking these steps is a personal choice and to force any such measures on the American people would be an abridgment of their personal liberty. Fostering this sentiment among his supporters dovetailed well with Trump's strategy of downplaying the pandemic and its seriousness as a threat to public health in the U.S. However, aside from the Trump Administration and others who were closely aligned with Trump, officials at every level of government, both Democrat and Republican, decried mask-wearing, social distancing, and proper hygiene as every American's individual duty owed to his or her fellow Americans, the community and the country, even if it is not a defined legal duty. A useful analogy to test whether mask-wearing and social distancing ought to be considered a personal choice or a civic responsibility is to consider conscription into the armed services during wartime. Certainly, in the U.S., military service during wartime to defend the country against its enemies is considered a legal, civic, and moral responsibility. Why then should mask-wearing and maintenance of proper social distancing and habitual hand-washing to defend the country against a destructive pathogen be any less of a moral or civic responsibility of every American citizen, even if it is not a legally mandated obligation? The Trump Administration's encouragement of the personal choice argument, therefore, is an abrogation of the Chief Executive's duties to protect the country, which then results in the failure of millions of Americans to observe this moral and civic duty.

To be clear, the above is not to suggest that, had the Trump Administration observed its legal duties under the Constitution in handling the response to the pandemic, the U.S. would not have suffered the devastating human and economic costs of the pandemic (although it seems likely that the impacts would have been to some extent less than they in fact have been). Instead, the argument is that the Chief Executive's and his administration's dereliction of their legal duties to the country has predictably spawned the demand for rights by citizens. Citizens would not be reasonable in their demands to be kept safe by their national government, to be provided with financial and medical assistance, to be informed about the state of the pandemic and about measures taken by the government upon the recommendations of scientific experts, etc., if the federal executive branch had used every means at its disposal to handle the crisis, even if such means and measures were to ultimately fail. In other words, it is not reasonable to blame the pandemic on the government, but it is reasonable to blame the government for the lack of a meaningful response under its legal duties owed to the people, irrespective of the outcome of the response.

In addition, Gandhi's conceptualization of one's rights flowing from observance of one's duties to self, to others, and to the community is clearly borne from his belief in democratic institutions and how they should function. In a modern representative democracy, the officials elected and appointed to serve the people and the nation are in fact "us," and as they observe the legal duties attached to their offices, they fulfill those responsibilities toward individual citizens, the community and the country as a whole, and to themselves. Thus, citizens, communities, and the representatives themselves are each and all the beneficiaries of the rights in question. There is no clearer meaning to be a "government by the people and for the people."

Turning to the issue of racial injustice and the civil unrest, Gandhian concepts of rights resulting from the observance of responsibilities would suggest a rather obvious answer: If those charged with enforcing the law (e.g., police and prosecutors) were vigilant in observance of their constitutional duties to guarantee due process of law and equal protection of the laws, the rights of black Americans would not be offended as frequently and their outrage and protest would not be necessary. That overly simplistic view, however, ignores the complexities of a multiracial society and the importance of the historical persecution and discrimination suffered by black Americans, first by subjugation and slavery, and then by institutionalized discrimination in the post-Civil War era through the 1960s, into the civil rights movement of the 1960s, down to the present day. The history of black discrimination in America is in large part responsible for the continued disparate treatment by black citizens by law enforcement and the criminal justice system. Most commentators over the most recent two decades describe the situation of black Americans vis a vis law enforcement and the criminal justice system as "systemic racism,"[24] meaning that the inequality of treatment of black Americans is not so much the product of some percentage of police and others in the system bringing racist ideology to their jobs, but that racism is baked into the criminal justice system as a structural element which is produced by the history of discrimination against black Americans, and the implicit and explicit biases toward black citizens that exist in the law enforcement community which result largely from policing strategies and training and how social science data is interpreted and used for law enforcement purposes. Therefore, it is too simplistic to argue that if police and prosecutors did a better job at fulfilling their responsibilities under the Fourth and Fourteenth Amendments to the U.S. Constitution, all would be well.

Instead, given these constitutional commands to ensure respect for the rights of citizens to be free from *unreasonable* searches and seizures in police-citizen encounters, to ensure respect of every citizen's right not to be deprived of life, liberty, or property without due process of law and every citizen's right to enjoy equal protection of the law, a further responsibility on law enforcement and criminal justice personnel appears to be necessary: to ensure that their organizational cultures, policies, and trainings target the systemic racism in their organizations to guarantee that

---

[24] See, e.g., Jeffrey A. Fagan & Alexis D., "Campbell, Race and Reasonableness in Police Killings", 100 *Bos. U. L. Rev.* 951, 1006 (2020); *An Empirical Analysis of Racial Differences in Police Use of Force*, Ronald G. Fryer, J. of Pol. Econ. (2017) at 34.

their personnel are able to meet their constitutional responsibilities. This is not merely to be suggestive of ways to reform the criminal justice system in order to realize the individual rights for black Americans, but rather, it is to demonstrate a legal obligation on the part of the criminal justice community to identify and implement any and all reforms which are necessary for black Americans to fully realize their Fourth and Fourteenth Amendment rights. Therefore, the civil unrest during the summer of 2020 in the U.S. has its origins in the failure of the law enforcement community to meet its responsibility to reform its cultures and systems if it is (ever) to meet its constitutional responsibilities to all citizens. The Gandhian concept of observance of civic responsibility which will inevitably result in the provision of individual rights is therefore at the core of any solution to this complex problem of race and the criminal justice system in America.

Of the rights-based arguments raised in the context of the 2020 U.S. national election, Gandhi's conceptualization of responsibility is particularly illuminating. The arguments for a free and fair electoral process devoid of widespread fraud and malfeasance and arguments against voter suppression and disenfranchisement, regardless of which side is making them, rather poignantly reveal two important responsibilities of public officials: (1) to abide by the commands of the Constitution and of statutory law in regards to voting, and (2) to adhere to ethical and honest standards of conduct, and specifically to avoid knowingly making false or misleading statements and claims which lack any underlying factual basis.

The Constitution contains several important provisions regarding the conduct of elections, and notably, Article I, Section 4, leaves the responsibility of the conduct of Congressional elections to the state legislatures.[25] Article II, Section 1, Clause 2, leaves the responsibility to the state legislatures to select "Electors" for the election of President and Vice President.[26] Numerous other federal and state statutes apply to the right to vote. Even the most cursory survey of the federal and state constitutions and the plethora of state and federal legislation demonstrates that the right to exercise the franchise in the United States is sacrosanct. Various struggles over suffrage in American history chronicle the importance with which Americans regard this particular right. From the early debates about qualification based on property ownership, to the post-Civil War period and the initial franchising of newly freed black American slaves, to the women's suffrage movement of the early twentieth century, to the passage of the Voting Rights Act of 1965 designed to finally eliminate voting discrimination against black American citizens, the law itself is saturated with legal duties designed to ensure every citizen's right to vote and to eliminate any attempt to disenfranchise particular groups or individuals who meet the most basic qualifications of being an adult (18 years or older) and a U.S. citizen. Viewed in their totality, the duties on public officials found in the abundance of constitutional and statutory law, as well as the judicial interpretation of the enacted law, at a minimum demonstrate a duty to not engage in conduct intended to disenfranchise the American voter. Yet, this is much of what President Trump's campaign during the 2020

[25] U.S. Constitution, Art. I, Sec. 4 (1789b).

[26] U.S. Constitution, Art. II, Sec. 1, Cl. 2. (1789a).

election and afterward attempted to do. Beginning with the sowing of doubt about the reliability of the election and continuing with the dissemination of false claims about voter and election fraud after the election and then fomenting an insurrection, these actions betray not merely the abrogation of the public legal duty to ensure the franchise to every American, but an active and concerted attempt to thwart the franchise of millions of American voters. Therefore, the argument demanding a free and fair election would not have been necessary (by either side), but for the actions by the incumbent candidate and his team which run counter to the over-abundance of constitutional and statutory duties of elected officials in aiding the conduct of elections.

It is also worth noting that all government officials who hold a license to practice law (which a significant number of those holding public office in the U.S. do) are bound by the rules of ethics in the legal profession, and these rules include a "duty of candor."[27] Members of Congress are also bound by ethical rules which require honesty.[28]

While it is perhaps plausible, *prior to* the election, for the Trump reelection campaign and Trump supporters to say that they believed at that time that the sharp increase in vote-by-mail and absentee voting due to the pandemic creates an environment ripe for widespread fraud to occur, and proponents of these sorts of statements could still be perceived as having observed their responsibility to be ethical and honest. This could constitute mere opinion in the months and weeks prior to the election, and it is their prerogative to convey such opinions. Such arguments could even be considered "opinion" after the election, but before the great weight of the conclusions reached on the integrity of the election shows the claims of fraud to be entirely false.

But, once the election has occurred and all of the procedures and safeguards used to tally and verify the results have been done, the misinformation, falsehoods, and baseless claims take on greater significance as an abrogated responsibility in light of the knowledge that the claims are, in fact, false. As more state and federal officials from both sides of the political spectrum in the U.S. announced the results of the election in their respective jurisdictions, including in many cases, mandatory verification procedures such as recounting (and even multiple recounts), and as more Democrat and Republican appointed and elected judges from state and federal courts dismissed as meritless claims filed by the Trump campaign and other supporters to challenge the results, it becomes clear that false information and baseless claims are no longer in the realm of opinion, but are knowingly made to deceive and thus an abrogation of the responsibility to act ethically and honestly is evident. It follows then

[27] See, Rule 3.3 of the *Model Rules of Professional Conduct, "Candor toward the Tribunal"* American Bar Association (2020). The Model Rules have been widely adopted in jurisdictions across the United States.

[28] See, *Congressional Standards*, promulgated by the House Ethics Committee, *Advisory Opinion No. 1*, accessed on February 15, 2021 at https://ethics.house.gov/casework/congressional-standards. (Describing House Member's ethical obligation to assert as fact only that which he or she knows to be true in the context of communications on behalf of a constituent with other agencies or departments of government).

that the responsibility of public officials to adhere to standards of ethics and honesty in the conduct of an election, especially concerning claims of potential wrong-doing, are significant factors in guaranteeing rights to free and fair elections absent fraud and malfeasance and the right to every citizen to exercise the franchise. To be certain, numerous public officials, Democrat and Republican alike, took extremely seriously and observed their public responsibility to be ethical and honest in their work to report and verify election results and to respond to the claims made by Trump and his supporters. It is indeed the specific observance of this public duty by the officials who performed it that has, in fact and in hindsight, *guaranteed* that a free and fair election did take place.

The responsibility to be ethical and honest in the context of elections also filters down from public officials to private actors with disproportionate influence, such as mainstream news networks and social media platforms, and then down to the individual citizen, who may participate in the spread of false information. Although there certainly are ethical standards of honest reporting in journalism which apply to news networks, the blurring of the lines between factual reporting and editorializing creates difficulties in enforcing these standards within the news media. Social media platforms, up to this point, have not been highly regulated and are largely self-policed. Individual citizens, who mostly rely on news networks and social media to obtain information, are to some extent at the mercy of the former in determining facts from fiction. Nevertheless, the civic duty is on each of these constituent actors to, at the very least refrain from disseminating false or misleading information, and perhaps to research and investigate the veracity of information. The events that have taken place prior to, during, and after the 2020 national election in the United States plainly demonstrate the ill effect on society as a whole when misinformation is permitted to spread as truth. Interestingly, some social media platforms such as Facebook and Twitter have instituted their own policies with regard to posting false or misleading information, particularly in regard to matters of public concern, or information intended to incite violence.[29]

5 Conclusion

Although some Western political and legal theorists have considered responsibilities as the necessary corollary of individual rights, this has not always worked in the Western tradition, given the conception of certain rights as inalienable and natural, and therefore, such rights would not necessarily require a concomitant responsibility to be observed for the right to attach. For American society to overcome its modern obsession with individual rights so as to allow for discourse on other necessary and valuable topics, we would do well to incorporate Gandhi's critical points in regard

[29] See, *Trump Threatens Social Media After Twitter Puts Warning on His False Claims*, The Guardian, Tom McCarthy, May 27, (2020b); See also, *Twitter Says Trump Ban is Permanent—Even if He Runs for Office Again*, The Guardian, Guardian Staff Report, February 10, 2021.

to observance of duty as the source of rights as essential to the proper functioning of a democratic system where the rule of law is paramount. Indeed, the law in the U.S. tells us a great deal about precisely what these duties are.

Acknowledgements The author thanks his dear friend and colleague, Dr. Kshitij Kumar Singh, at the University of Delhi, Campus Law Centre, for the invitation to contribute, and thanks Sara Rusnak for her able research assistance.

References

American Bar Association (2020) Rule 3.3 of the model rules of professional conduct. Candor toward the tribunal

Armour S, Restuccia A (2020) Health experts, democrats rally to Fauci's defense after white house criticism. Wall Street J. Accessed 5 Feb 2021at https://www.wsj.com/articles/health-experts-democrats-rally-to-faucis-defense-after-white-house-criticism-11594667308

Bender MC, Ballhaus R (2020) How Trump sowed covid supply chaos. 'Try getting it yourselves.' Wall Street J. Accessed 5 Feb 2021 at https://www.wsj.com/articles/how-trump-sowed-covid-supply-chaos-try-getting-it-yourselves-11598893051

Bose NK. Selections from Gandhi. Desai & Mudranalaya, in Ahmedabad, India, p 48. Accessed 20 Jan 2021 at https://www.gandhiashramsevagram.org/pdf-books/selections-from-gandhi.pdf

Cummings W, Garrison J, Sergent J (2021) By the numbers: President Donald Trump's failed efforts to overturn the election. USA Today. Accessed 4 Feb 2021 at: https://www.usatoday.com/in-depth/news/politics/elections/2021/01/06/trumps-failed-efforts-overturn-election-numbers/4130307001/

Dalton D (1998) Gandhi on freedom, rights, and responsibility. In: International seminar on Gandhi and the twenty-first century, January 1998. Accessed 5 Jan 2021 at https://www.mkgandhi.org/articles/freedom.htm

Fagan JA, Campbell AD (2020) Race and reasonableness in police killings, 100 Bos. U. L. Rev. 951:1006

Friedman G (2020) Here's what companies are promising to do to fight racism. The New York Times. Accessed 4 Jan 2021 at https://www.nytimes.com/article/companies-racism-george-floyd-protests.html

Fryer RG (2017) An empirical analysis of racial differences in police use of force. J Pol Econ 34

Glendon MA (1991) Rights talk: the impoverishment of political discourse. Free Press

Gottbrath L-W (2020) In 2020, The Black Lives matter movement shook the world. Al Jazeera. Accessed 26 Jan 2021 at https://www.aljazeera.com/features/2020/12/31/2020-the-year-black-lives-matter-shook-the-world

Guardian Staff Report (2021) Twitter says Trump ban is permanent—even if he runs for office again. The Guardian

Hohfeld WN (1917) Fundamental legal concepts as applied in judicial reasoning. Yale Law J 26:710

House Ethics Committee. Congressional standards, advisory opinion No. 1. Accessed 15 Feb 2021 at https://ethics.house.gov/casework/congressional-standards

Keveney B, Puente M (2021) How conservative media stoked baseless election-fraud claims that motivated D.C. rioters. USA Today. Accessed 13 Jan 2021 at https://www.usatoday.com/story/entertainment/tv/2021/01/11/dc-riots-how-newsmax-oan-conservative-outlets-fueled-mob/6589298002/

McCarthy T (2020a) 'It will disappear': The Disinformation Trump spread about the coronavirus—timeline. The Guardian. Accessed 26 Jan 2021 at https://www.theguardian.com/us-news/2020a/apr/14/trump-coronavirus-alerts-disinformation-timeline

McCarthy T (2020b) Trump threatens social media after Twitter puts warning on his false claims. The Guardian

National Public Radio. Fact-check: Donald Trump's Republican convention speech. Annotated, Accessed 2 Feb 2021 at https://www.npr.org/2016/07/21/486883610/fact-check-donald-trumps-republican-convention-speech-annotated

Phillips A (2020) Why exactly is Trump lashing out at the World Health Organization? The Washington Post. Accessed 10 Feb 2021 at https://www.washingtonpost.com/politics/2020/04/08/why-exactly-is-president-trump-lashing-out-world-health-organization/

Qiu L, March B, Huang J (2020) The President vs. the Experts: How Trump played down the coronavirus. The New York Times. Accessed 26 Jan 2021 at https://www.nytimes.com/interactive/2020/03/18/us/trump-coronavirus-statements-timeline.html

Taylor DB (2021) George Floyd protests: a timeline. The New York Times. Accessed 11 Feb 2021, at https://www.nytimes.com/article/george-floyd-protests-timeline.html

United States Constitution (1789a), Article II, Sec. 1, et seq

United States Constitution (1789b) Article I, Sec. 4

United States Constitution (1791) Amendment IV

United States Constitution (1868) Amendment XIV Sec. 1

Chapter 9
Immortality of the Vision: How Gandhi Can Guide the Future of India's Refugee Policy

Anita Yadav and Nausheen Khan

1 Introduction

The concept of asylum has been in existence for at least 3500 years and is found, in one form or another, in the text and tradition of most ancient societies.[1] A person seeking asylum or refuge in another country is often pushed out of his own country due to armed conflict, persecution and various other reasons. Persons given such asylum are termed as refugees.

The current legal framework in India does not recognise refugees and treats them as foreigners or illegal entrants. In the absence of a law specifically dealing with refugee rights and protection, the Indian approach so far has been to pass temporary, problem-specific laws to deal with any influx of refugees whenever the need arises. This creates uncertainty, especially considering the large number of refugees that reside in India.[2] Therefore, India needs a uniform, codified refugee policy.

While codification is important, any discussion on human rights-based legislation, such as the present one on refugee law, remains incomplete without mentioning Gandhi, who was the greatest Indian proponent of human rights. His ideas on morality

[1] Nazeem Goolam, "The changing face of German asylum law-a critical reappraisal", 34 *The Comparative and International Law Journal of Southern Africa* 51 (March 2001).

[2] India was home to 1,98,665 refugees as of June 2014 and had 4,718 pending cases of asylum seekers, bringing the total population of concern to 2,03,383, available at https://www.thehindu.com/news/national/india-home-to-200000-refugees-in-first-half-of-2014-unhcr/article6771040.ece (last visited on June 25, 2020).

A. Yadav (✉)
Assistant Professor, Campus Law Centre, Faculty of Law, University of Delhi, Delhi, India
e-mail: ayadav@clc.du.ac.in

N. Khan
Student, LL.B., Campus Law Centre, Faculty of Law, University of Delhi, Delhi, India
e-mail: khannausheen1998@gmail.com

R. Mittal and K. K. Singh (eds.), *Relevance of Duties in the Contemporary World*,
https://doi.org/10.1007/978-981-19-1836-0_9

and non-violence were revolutionary at the time; they remain the greatest yardstick for Indian policies today.

However, this intersection between refugee rights and Gandhian ideals has little to no literature and remains largely unexplored. To fill this gap, we proceed to analyse the history of India's refugees and the Gandhian philosophy, suggesting ways in which the intersection between the two can guide India in formulating a refugee policy.

This chapter is divided into three parts. Part 1 on 'Refugees in India' deals with who refugees are, traces the history of refugees in India, gives an account of the current legal framework relating to refugees and makes a case for the codification of a refugee policy in India. Part 2 on 'Gandhi' follows his experience with refugees during the partition of India and provides an insight into the Gandhian ideals of sarvodaya, satyagrah and dharm, linking it with the question of how Gandhi's life and work can guide the refugee policy, which finally, leads to part 3 on 'The Interface between Refugee Rights and Gandhi's Life and Works' which interprets the ideals discussed in part two to suggest original solutions and address concerns regarding the protection of refugee rights. The chapter is an attempt to provide a persuasive moral foundation to the argument in favour of codification of the refugee policy in India, based on Gandhian ideals.

2 Refugees in India

2.1 Modern India Took Birth in the Midst of a Refugee Crisis

India's history with refugees has been long. It has been involved in dealing with refugee problems ever since the mass migration triggered by its partition.[3] When tracing India's history with refugees, one is reminded of Nehru's famous words from a speech made on 14th August, 1947, just hours before India officially became an independent state, *"At the* stroke *of the* midnight *hour, when the world sleeps, India will awake to life and freedom"*. While the spirit of independence must surely have been intoxicating, not everyone was rejoicing at the midnight hour; some were mourning the loss of their loved ones, their homes and their former lives.

The partition of the Indian subcontinent triggered a mass migration on both side of the newly created border. With an estimated 14 million persons displaced and reduced to the status of refugees, it has been termed as the largest refugee crisis since World War II. Since then, millions from Bangladesh,[4] Tibet, Nepal, Afghanistan,

---

[3] Arun Sagar and Farrah Ahmed, "The Model Law for Refugees: An Important Step Forward?", 17 *Student Bar Review* 74 (2005).

[4] On 29 March 1971, it is reported that nearly a million refugees had entered India, fleeing the military repression in East Pakistan. By the end of 1971, figures provided by the Indian government to the United Nations indicate that this total had reached 10 million, available at: https://www.unhcr.org/3ebf9bab0.pdf (last visited on June 24, 2020).

Sri Lanka and Burma (now Myanmar) have sought peace and freedom within the borders of India.[5] But before we delve into India's refugee situation, it is necessary to develop a basic understanding of the term 'refugee' itself.

2.2 *Who is a Refugee?*

In popular understanding, any person who has left his or her home fearing for his life and liberty or due to lack of subsistence is regarded as a refugee.[6] To address refugee issues in International Law, the global community has shown due concern by adopting International Convention Relating to the Status of Refugees, 1951 (henceforth, the 1951 Convention).[7] According to Article 1(A)(2) of the 1951 Convention, a 'refugee' is a person who "owing to well-founded fear of being persecuted for reason of their race, religion, nationality, membership of a particular social group or political opinion is outside the country of his nationality and is unable or, owing to such fear, is unwilling to return to his country".[8]

Even though the definition seems very comprehensive, the 1951 Convention was enacted mainly to address the East European refugee situation created in the aftermath of World War II, which makes its application to modern refugee situations somewhat difficult.[9] While the convention is universally applicable, its definition of refugees has never been amended. At the same time, the nature of refugee-creating events has changed over time.[10] Consequently, the gaps in the 1951 definition grew wider with time.

In the meanwhile, political changes in the world since the second half of the twentieth century have aided the recognition of new types of refugees, which has led to the adoption of various regional conventions to protect and deal with them. In 1969, OAU Convention governing the specific aspect of refugee problem in Africa was adopted. It extended the definition of refugees to include those refugees who left their place of habitual residence due to external aggression, occupation, foreign

[5] Omar Chaudhary, "Turning Back: An Assessment of Non-Refoulement under Indian Law", 39 *Economic and Political Weekly* 3257 (July-2004).

[6] Tapan K Bose, Protection of Refugees in South Asia: Need for Legal Framework, 27 (South Asia Forum for Human Rights, Kathmandu, 2000).

[7] International Convention Relating to the Status of Refugees, which entered into force on 22 April, 1954, is the most important document on international refugee protection.

[8] Convention Relating to the Status of Refugees, 1951, has been subject to only one amendment in the form of a 1967 Protocol, which removed the geographic and temporal limits of the 1951 Convention. The 1951 Convention consolidates previous international instruments relating to refugees and provides the most comprehensive codification of the rights of refugees at the international level *available at:* https://www.unhcr.org/3b66c2aa10 (last visited on July 30, 2020).

[9] J.N, Saxena, "Problems of refugees in Developing Countries and Need for International Burden-sharing" in K.P. Saksena, (ed.), Human Rights: Perspective and Challenges 356 (Lancers Books, New Delhi 1994).

[10] Taylor H. Garrett, "Refugee Protection In International Law: UNHCR's Global Consultations on International Protection", 25 *Michigan Journal of International Law* 751 (2004).

domination or events seriously disturbing public order in either part or the whole of his country.[11] This definition covers many more types of refugees than the 1951 definition does. Further, with the experience gained from the massive flows of refugees in the Central American area, the Cartagena Declaration on Refugees adopted in 1984 extended the definition to cover persons fleeing their country because their life, safety and/or their liberty were threatened by massive violation of human rights.[12]

The various definitions, however, have one thing in common. They all define the basic human rights of a person who is in distress due to circumstances which are not under his control. A person when he becomes a refugee loses all his possessions and in most cases even his family. The protection of rights of such persons is our essential duty as humans towards humankind. The spirit of humanity and brotherhood should be prime considerations in dealing with refugee issues.

2.3 *India's Refugees*

India's multi-ethnic, multilingual and relatively stable society has often made it an attractive destination for refugees.[13] It has seen many refugee influxes, beginning since the partition in 1946–47. In more recent history, large numbers of Tibetans and Sri Lankans fleeing their homes have sought refuge in India. There have also been smaller refugee movements and individual refugees such as Afghans, Bhutanese, Iranians, Somalis, Burmese and Sudanese.[14]

2.3.1 What is the Legal Framework Regulating Refugees?

Despite an estimated 2,00,000 refugees residing in India,[15] it does not have a codified legislation or a uniform policy dealing specifically with refugees. Indian law has no definition of refugees, treating them under the category of foreigners or illegal immigrants under the existing laws. Moreover, India has signed neither the Convention

---

[11] Article 1 (2) OAU Convention on Refugee defines the term "refugee" available at: https://www.unhcr.org/about-us/background/45dc1a682/oau-convention-governing-specific-aspects-refugee-problems-africa-adopted.html (last visited on June 15, 2020).

[12] Cartagena Declaration on Refugees, adopted by the Colloquium on the International Protection of Refugees in Central America, Mexico and Panama, Cartagena de Indias, Colombia, 22 November 1984 available at: https://www.unhcr.org/about-us/background/45dc19084/cartagena-declaration-refugees-adopted-colloquium-international-protection.html (last visited on July 2, 2020).

[13] Ravi Nair, "Refugee Protection in South Asia" 51 *Journal of International Affairs* 201 (Summer 1997).

[14] Sagar and Ahmed, *supra* note 4.

[15] India was home to 1,98,665 refugees as of June 2014 and had 4718 pending cases of asylum seekers, bringing the total population of concern to 2,03,383 available at: https://www.thehindu.com/news/national/india-home-to-200000-refugees-in-first-half-of-2014-unhcr/article6771040.ece (last visited on June 5, 2020).

Relating to the Status of Refugees, 1951, nor its 1967 Protocol. However, the Indian government continues to grant asylum and refugee status based on its existing colonial legislation or by enacting temporary legislation applying to the specific situation whenever a new group of refugees needs recognition.

At present, refugees in India are dealt under general laws such as the Foreigners Act, 1946, the Registration of Foreigners Act, 1939, and the Foreigners Order, 1948.[16] Occasionally, refugees are also dealt with under the Passport Act, 1967 for illegally crossing the border without a valid passport. In conjunction, all these laws give ample power to government to restrain, deport or even imprison refugees, since their status as refugees is not determinable under Indian law.[17]

2.3.2 What is the Jurisprudence on Refugee Protection?

The Indian Constitution provides certain fundamental rights to all persons (including foreigners). Therefore, a person seeking refuge in India also has these rights under the Indian Constitution.[18] The jurisprudence evolved by Indian courts while interpreting these constitutional rights in the context of protection of refugees has been ridden with conflicting trends. On the one hand, the judiciary has adopted a very liberal interpretation of the rights of refugees in specific cases,[19] whereas in a few cases, it has strictly interpreted legislation against foreigners by refusing to interfere with the powers of the government.[20]

The inconsistency in the judicial approach to the refugee problem has given rise to ambiguity and uncertainty which can only be resolved through codification of a refugee law in India.

---

[16] Rule 5 of Foreigners Order, 1948 provides that foreigners may be detained when permission to enter is refused.

[17] Section 3 (1) of the Foreigners Act provides "the Central Government may by order make provision, either generally or with respect to all foreigners or with respect to any particular foreigner or any prescribed class or description of foreigner, for prohibiting, regulating or restricting the entry of foreigners into India or their departure therefrom or their presence or continued presence therein.." available at: http://legislative.gov.in/sites/default/files/A1946-31.pdf (last visited on June 5, 2020).

[18] Article 14 of the Constitution of India provides "the state shall not deny to any person equality before the law or the equal protection of the laws within the territory of India." Article 21 provides "no person shall be deprived of his life or personal liberty except according to procedure established by law".

[19] In *National Human Rights Commission* v. *State of Arunachal Pradesh* 1996 SCC, Supreme Court of India upheld that Chakma refugees cannot be forcibly sent back to Bangladesh because their life is under threat and sending them back against their will be violation of Article 21 of the Constitution of India. In *Ktaer Abbas* case, 1999 CriLJ 919, the Gujarat High Court declared that principle of non-refoulement is enshrined in Article 21 of the Indian Constitution, as long as presence of refugee does not create threat to national security of India. Principle of non-refoulement further recognised on *Dongh Lian Kham* v. *Union of India,* 2015 SCC as a part of Article 21 of Indian Constitution.

[20] In *Hans Muller* v. *Superintendent Presidency Jail, Calcutta,* AIR 1955 SC, the Supreme Court of India gave "absolute and unfettered" discretion to the government to expel foreigners. Further, in case of *Mohd. Sediq* v. *Union of India,* 1998 SCC court granted permission Central Government to deport foreigners from India keeping in mind paramount interest of government.

2.4 Why Does India Need a Refugee Policy?

The Indian government has been inconsistent in dealing with refugees, changing its official policy from time to time on the number and origin of refugees to be allowed.[21] Despite the fact India receives a large number of refugees, the Indian government is yet to adopt a domestic refugee law.[22] While it has certain obligations under International Customary Law,[23] which have usually been fulfilled in past practice, there remains uncertainty on whether the treatment of refugees will be equally fair in the future. Additionally, Article 51 (c) of the Constitution of India[24] imposes only a non-justiciable direction to "respect" international law, and in cases of conflict with domestic law, the latter prevails.[25]

Omar Chaudhary[26] argues that, "while refugee-friendly practices may constitute an ultimate goal of reformers, laws remain important as safeguards against rash decision-making in the future". Change in the political regime and emergence of leaders who propound conservative views are factors that affect policies regarding refugees. To secure rights, there is need to codify them. The political dynamics of a nation should not be allowed to easily interfere in the sphere of larger human rights regime. The presence of a minimum threshold for refugee protection is necessary, even if it is disregarded by the government in actual practice. This is because the presence of this minimum standard defined in law ensures that even though the practice differs, there is a basic understanding that it is in derogation of the rule of law.

The inadequate statutory framework, the inconsistency in refugee policy over time, threat of change treatment of refugees with change in political regimes, the contradictory jurisprudence and the large estimated number of refugees residing in India create a grey area where the state rules by executive decree rather than by the

[21] India's track record in the treatment of Chakmas has not been particularly great as compared to that of the Sri Lankan Tamil refugees and the Tibetan refugees. In an answer to a question in Parliament, Minister of State for Home Affairs Mr. Hansraj Gangaram Ahir explained various welfare schemes run by Indian government specifically for Sri Lankan and Tibetan refugees available at: http://164.100.47.194/Loksabha/Questions/QResult15.aspx?qref=56854&lsno=16 (last visited on June 16, 2020).

[22] Nair, *supra* note 14.

[23] Article 33 of the 1951 Convention provides that "No Contracting State shall expel or return ("refouler") a refugee in any manner whatsoever to the frontiers of territories where his life or freedom would be threatened on account of his race, religion, nationality, membership of a particular social group or political opinion.".

[24] Article 51(c) Constitution of India has been incorporated as a Directive Principles of State Policy (DPSP) in Part IV of the Constitution. It obligates the state to foster the respect for international law and treaty obligations.

[25] In *Jolly George Varghese and another* v. *The Bank of Cochin* AIR (1980) SC Justice Krishna Iyer upheld that "until the municipal Law is changed to accommodate the treaty, what binds the courts is the former not the latter". See Prabhash Ranjan, Anmolan and Farheen Ahmad, "Is the Supreme Court Confused About the Application of International Law?" available at: https://thewire.in/law/supreme-court-international-law (last visited on June 16, 2020).

[26] *Supra* note at 3263.

democratic process of legislation, resulting in injustices which are not visible due to lack of status determination. In the face of these compelling reasons, one can only raise so many arguments against the codification of refugee law. In this context, Gandhi's ideas and thoughts can be looked at as the guiding source to the formulation of India's future policy on refugees.

3 Gandhi and India's Future Policy on Refugees

Mohandas Karamchand Gandhi, better known as The Father of the Indian Nation, was the leader of the anti-colonial movement in India. His ideas were instrumental in bringing freedom to and the creation of the world's largest democracy. His life's work was dedicated to the cause of independence and freedom from oppression, working in Africa for anti-apartheid and then in India for independence from colonial rule, or as he put it—*swaraj*.

3.1 Gandhi's Experience with Refugees During Partition

To Gandhi, independence came at a great cost to humanity. He had dedicated his life to the unity of Indians under a national banner divorced from narrow religious, linguistic or caste-based identities. The partition of India was unacceptable to him as it went against his vision of communal unity. He campaigned for months in areas where communal hatred was rampant and his last years were marked by the struggle to convince religious groups to maintain peace.[27] His death came at a time when India was reeling under communal tension.

Gandhi's personal diaries and the public speeches[28] made during the period of partition and the ensuing refugee crisis provide a deep insight into his views on the issue of refugee rights. The major theme in all his speeches and writings at the time is that of communal harmony and brotherhood. He appealed to the Congress party in India to treat Muslims fairly so as to garner a similar response from Pakistan in their treatment of Hindus who chose to remain there, the aim being minimisation of movement of refugees and loss of lives.

Delhi became a major destination for refugees coming from the other side of the border. In his diary on 10th September, 1947, while questioning the government of Pakistan as to why the refugee influx continued despite promises of fair and equal treatment for all made by both countries, Gandhi wrote, *"Is it not our shame as a nation that there should be any refugee problem at all?"*[29]

[27] First in Calcutta, then in Delhi in 1947–48.

[28] Gandhi's selected works, available at: https://www.mkgandhi.org/ (last visited on June 16, 2020).

[29] *Ibid*.

His deep empathy for the suffering of refugees is reflected in his diary entry on 15th September, 1947, where he expressed his thoughts in a melancholy tone, saying,

> During the night as I heard what should have been the soothing sound of gentle life-giving rain, my mind went out to the thousands of refugees lying about in the open camps in Delhi. I was sleeping snugly in a veranda protecting me on all sides. But for the cruel hand of man against his brother, these thousands of men, women and children would not be shelter-less and in many cases foodless… was it all inevitable? The answer from within is an emphatic No. Was this the first fruit of freedom, just a month-old baby?... Let the Hindus and Sikhs take the right step and invite the Muslims who have been driven out of their homes to return. If they can take this courageous step worthy from every point of view, they immediately reduce the refugee problem to its simplest terms… For me the transfer of millions of Hindus and Sikhs and Muslims is unthinkable. It is wrong. The wrong of Pakistan (in not controlling the outflow of Hindus and Sikhs to India) will be undone by the right of a resolute non-transfer of population.

Gandhi was deeply troubled by the violent tendencies of the common people and called for an immediate stop to the violence. After successfully convincing hostile parties to stop killing in Calcutta, he arrived in Delhi in September, 1947, on hearing the violence and the abhorrent condition of the refugees at the camp in Purana Qila. His final fast "unto death" in January, 1948, was meant to restore peace between Hindus and Muslims of Delhi. The fast lasted a mere 6 days, as leaders of major groups and political parties agreed to a peaceful resolution. At his final prayer meeting on the evening of 30th January, 1948, Gandhi was assassinated and the light went out of our lives.[30] The man may have died, but his ideas live on.

Gandhi's entire life was his "experiment with truth",[31] as reflected in his fearless embrace of new ideas which emerged in his search for truth, even if they detracted from his own earlier stance. *Satyagrah* or "truth force" was Gandhi's approach to life. His strong moral appeal and his successful attempts at revolution through non-violence gave him the label of the "moral initiator of the global peace and justice movement".[32]

For a subject such as that of refugee law and policy which draws form the moral duty of man towards man in the humanitarian spirit, it is only natural to use Gandhian ideals as a yardstick against which to measure arguments for and against the codification of refugee rights. A discussion on these lines follows evaluating Gandhi's ideas of *satyagrah, sarvodaya* and *dharm* in order to inform our understanding of refugee rights. It will be seen that these ideas provide a strong moral persuasion for the adoption of a refugee law to ensure the fair treatment of refugees.

---

[30] "The light has gone out of our lives" were Jawaharlal Nehru's words in the radio address announcing M.K. Gandhi's assassination on 30th January, 1948.

[31] "The Story of My Experiments with Truth" is Gandhi's autobiography.

[32] Abraham Joseph, "Gandhism and International Criminal Law," in Morten Bergsmo and Emiliano J. Buis (eds.), *Philosophical Foundations of International Criminal Law: Correlating Thinkers* 545 (Torkel Opsahl Academic E publisher, Brussels, 2018).

3.2 Sarvodaya

> "Sarvodaya", literally meaning "uplift of all", views society as a body of individuals knit together by a bond of love and fraternity striving after ideal moral life and fullest upliftment of all. In *sarvodaya* society people are not guided merely by the utilitarian formula of the greatest good to the greatest number but the greatest good for all, on the principle "each for all and all for each.[33]

The idea of *sarvodaya* is central to Gandhi's philosophy. It is inspired by several religious and social traditions of the East and the West and the writings of great thinkers, like Ruskin, Tolstoy, Emerson, Thoreau, Carlyle, Mazzini, Gandhi, Bhave and Narayan.[34] The concept is based on the assumption of the inherent goodness of man, which is considered instrumental in bringing about a 'moral reconstruction' in the collective consciousness of mankind. This 'moral reconstruction' is the pathway to the ultimate aim of a establishing a peaceful and just society guided by the ideals of *sarvodaya.* Such a society would reach the highest moral ground where no individual would be left out and where all forms of discrimination and ill-will would disappear.

Sarvodaya is a broad visualisation of a society guided not by authority of law, but by morality. Gandhi visualised it as a blueprint for a desirable societal structure, and so naturally it holistically addresses multiple aspects of day-to-day socio-economic behaviour of individuals. However, five basic features, apart from the obvious emphasis on 'equality', underlie all the arguments.

1. **Revolution through Moral Appeal**: *Sarvodaya* puts great emphasis on the moral appeal to human nature in creating a society without political, social and economic exploitation where no person will feed off the labour of another. Satish Sharma (1989)[35] explains that the true spirit of a Gandhian society lies in simultaneous emphasis on social and moral reconstruction by character building and social, political and moral revitalisation. *Sarvodaya* postulates that the root of evil is the lack of moral values, which can be cured through self-introspection and practicing acts of selflessness (anasakti).
2. **Individuality**: The emphasis on individuality is central to Gandhi's philosophy. In *sarvodaya,* people would not be guided merely by the formula of "the greatest good to the greatest" number but by the "greatest good for all", implying that no individual's interest will be sacrificed and society would operate on the principle "each for all and all for each".[36]Sarvodaya espouses individual freedom and the decentralisation of economic, social and political power, so that people and communities can become self-determining, self-dependent and free from the

[33] A. K. Ghosal, "Sarvodaya Gandhian philosophy and way of life", 20 *The Indian Journal of Political Science* 24 (1959).

[34] Satish Sharma, "Problem Resolution Through Social Reconstruction: An Exposition of the Sarvodaya Principles", 21 Peace Research, Canadian Mennonite University 30 (August 1989).

[35] *Ibid.*

[36] *Supra* note at 24.

demands of larger social and political bureaucracies.[37] Further, Gandhi did not believe that the interest of the state could justify the sacrifice of individual rights. He called this aggressive nationalism. He was against such nationalism and looked upon it "*with the greatest fear, because although while apparently doing good while minimising exploitation, it does the greatest harm to mankind by destroying individuality, which lies at the root of all progress*".[38,39]

3. **Manual Labour**: *Sarvodaya* insists on every man doing some manual labour. Ghosal (1959) states, 'to Gandhi, to eat without some manual work is morally degrading. He refers to the principle preached in the third chapter of the "Gita" that he who eats without sacrifice (and sacrifice he interprets as bread labour), eats stolen food.'[40] Gandhi is known to espouse manual labour and encouraged developing skills like spinning, believing that it is essential for the well-being and development of the individual as well as the society. Manual labour serves a twin purpose, firstly it contributes to the economy at the lowest levels of the society, and secondly, it connects man to his basal instinct of working with his hands.
4. **Inclusivity**: *'Sarvodaya'* believes that the welfare of the individual in society is inextricably bound up with the all-round welfare of all including the lowliest and cannot be realised in the absence of that of the last.[41] The establishment of a *sarvodaya* society requires simple, utilitarian, people-oriented institutions which will promote communal harmony.[42] Local consensus among the members of a community is the preferred mode of problem resolution in such a society, with decisions ideally being unanimous. The spirit of non-discrimination and equal treatment underlies each and every idea that Gandhi has developed.
5. **Lack of Subjugation and Exploitation**: Gandhi's idea of self-governance and self-sufficiency explains that in a *sarvodaya*-based society, people will not need an authority to control their behaviour. The society will be advanced enough to morally delineate the limits of its own actions and thus govern itself. Additionally, *sarvodaya* applies the same standards to the conduct of the state as it does to the conduct of an individual. It states that the subjection of one people by another is unnatural and immoral. Gandhi was absolutely opposed to the idea of aggressive nationalism (as discussed above) which he described as the greatest threat to individuality, which is the basis of all development. An act that is wrong when done by an individual is also wrong when done by the state, albeit at a larger level in the guise of state interest.

---

[37] Sharma, *supra* note at 35.

[38] A. Parel, "Gandhi and the state" in Judith Brown and Anthony Parel (eds.) The Cambridge Companion to Gandhi (Cambridge Companions to Religion) (Cambridge University Press, 2011).

[39] M.K. Gandhi, "The Collected Works of Mahatma Gandhi" Publications Division, Ministry of Information and Broadcasting, Government of India (New Delhi 1958–94).

[40] Jolly George Varghes case, *supra* note at 26.

[41] *Ibid.*

[42] B.N. Ganguli, Gandhi's Social Philosophy (New York: John Wiley & Sons, 1973).

3.3 Satyagrah

Satyagrah is perhaps Gandhi's most popular idea. According to him, *satyagrah* means 'holding on to truth' or 'truth force', and discovery of truth through non-violence (ahimsa).[43] He believed that truth and non-violence are the cardinal principles of *satyagrah*. These principles are derived from the value of *dharm*.[44]

Gandhi identifies three main characteristics of *satyagrah* which include the following:

(1) Personal suffering oriented towards converting the views of one's opponents[45];
(2) Consistency between means and ends; and
(3) Non-cooperation as a response to an 'unjust political, social and economic system'.[46]

In his political vision of *satyagrah*, he "*imagined a world in which each and every person would feel that he or she is not afraid of anyone, nor would they do anything to make anyone else afraid of them*".[47]

The focus of *satyagrah* on the force of truth was the central theme of Gandhi's life and work. His political strategy in bringing independence to India depended heavily on non-violence and the search for the ultimate truth. The unflinching adherence of Gandhi and his followers to these ideals remains the most remarkable feature in India's anti-colonial struggle, making the entire experience wholly unique as an example of change through peace, persistence and tolerance. However, despite Gandhi's strong commitment to truth and non-violence[48] as a means for realisation of

[43] Michael Emin Salla, "Satyagraha in Mahatma Gandhi's political philosophy" 25 *Peace Research Canadian Mennonite University* 55 (February 1993).

[44] 'There was no dharma higher than truth' and 'no dharma higher than the supreme duty of non-violence'. available at: https://www.mkgandhi.org/articles/freedom.htm (last visited on June 16, 2020).

[45] "*Gandhi believed that the suffering a Satyagrahi (one who practices Satyagrah) would voluntarily undergo to convert an opponent was consistent with the pursuit of Truth, and was certain to 'melt the hearts of even the most implacable of opponents*" (see *Supra* note 44).

[46] "I believe, and everybody must grant, that no Government can exist for a single moment without the cooperation of the people, willing or forced, and if people suddenly withdraw their co-operation in every detail, the Government will come to a stand-still".

available at: https://www.gandhiheritageportal.org/ghp_booksection_detail/Ny0yMjYtMg%3D%3D (last visited on June 22, 2020).

[47] Devi Prasad, "Satyagraha: The Way", 32 *India International Centre Quarterly* 46 (Summer 2005).

[48] "*This ahimsa is the basis of the search for truth. I am realising every day that the search is vain unless it is founded on ahimsa as the basis… Ahimsa is the means; Truth is the end. Means to be means must always be within our reach, and so ahimsa is our supreme duty…*" (*see* Gandhi, Selected Works *available at:* https://www.mkgandhi.org/ebks/SWMGandhi.pdf (last visited on June 29, 2020).

sarvodaya through *satyagrah*,[49] unfortunately, in modern India very little attention has been paid towards this political philosophy.

3.4 Duty

The discourse on rights and duties has permeated all spheres of modern political, social and economic life. In its ordinary sense, the term 'duty' can be described as an obligation to perform a certain activity or task due to some moral, ethical, cultural, legal or other obligation. Further, a duty can create positive or negative obligations depending upon the corresponding right. Various theories on rights and duties have been propounded by political philosophers in their writings over centuries. However, their understandings are often divergent.[50]

Political philosophers such as Rawls and Dworkin advocated the concept of rights-based liberalism. John Rawls in his celebrated book 'A Theory of Justice' published in 1971 discussed the idea of modern liberalism based on rights. His work on the theory of justice sets out to discover what rights we have against one another.[51] However, unlike Rawls, Gandhi spoke of rights in context of duties. His philosophy is centred on the basic tenet that "*a duty well performed creates a corresponding right*".[52]His teachings and philosophy emphasise that duty is the source of right and thus give priority to duties over rights.

Gandhi's idea of duty is derived from the teachings of *Bhagavad Gita,* which states that the 'idea of dispassionate action' means doing action (duty) without attachment.[53] His teachings of selfless service emphasise on helping the other without discrimination. According to him, performing selfless service is the spirit of sacrifice, which means exerting oneself for the benefit of others. Gandhi believed that through selfless service, one serves all of life with devotion.[54] In the conduct of one's duties, one must be selfless and must not expect any return. The very essence of duty is selflessness, and any rights that accrue are based on duty done selflessly. This idea of duty advocates two kinds of obligations—first, it can be an obligation towards oneself, towards the community or society in terms defined by social

---

[49] "Satyagrah was described by Gandhi as the path to sarvodaya; in other words, the search for truth is the path leading to the uplift of all".

[50] "Austin's idea of "absolute duties" and denial of "rights and duties are co-relatives" is criticised by Salmond stating that, "there can be no duty without the existence of right" available at: https://shodhganga.inflibnet.ac.in/bitstream/10603/71969/3/03_chapter%201.pdf (last visited on June 29, 2020).

[51] Ryan (2012).

[52] Mark Lindley, "Gandhi on corresponding duties—rights" available at: https://www.mkgandhi.org/articles/gondutiesrights.htm (last visited on July 2, 2020).

[53] Rights and Duties, available at: http://egyankosh.ac.in/bitstream/123456789/63124/2/Unit-5.pdf (last visited on July 2, 2020).

[54] Selfless Service Available at: http://www.gandhimemorialcenter.org/selfless-service (last visited on June 27, 2020).

tradition, social institutions and custom. Second, it can be an obligation to individual conscience or the inner voice.[55] Gandhi believed that 'rights' start with self-assertion and 'duty' starts with the idea of self-discipline.[56]

3.5 How Can Gandhi Guide the Refugee Policy in India?

Laws which stem out of an inherently moral-ethical sense of duty towards humanity, such as refugee laws, should not ignore Gandhi. Martin Luther King once said, *"If humanity is to progress, Gandhi is inescapable. He lived, thought, and acted, inspired by the vision of humanity evolving toward a world of peace and harmony. We may ignore him at our own risk"*.[57]

The concept of a *sarvodaya* can be looked at as a solution to the refugee problem in India. As *sarvodaya* posits that the solution to all social problems lies in moral reconstruction, we can examine the refugee problem as a social issue as the starting point of this discussion. The influx of refugees creates significant impacts on various aspects of the social life of the destination state such as demographic changes and increasing pressure on existing resources. However, concern for human life and dignity trumps all other social concerns, which are secondary issues.

Satyagrah provides the pathway to creating a framework where refugee-status determination becomes an undeniable right of all those seeking protection under refugee law. The concept of status determination is essentially a process of seeking out the truth, which in this case would answer the question of whether a person is or is not a refugee.

In the absence of specific domestic legislation in India on refugees, the idea of duty explained by Gandhi's teaching and philosophy can be a guiding source to understand individuals' duties towards the refugees. There is a close link in the underlying philosophy of Gandhi's concept of duty and that of the basic, internationally recognised rights of refugees.

Additionally, Gandhi holds the state responsible on the same level as an individual, and thus, the idea of duty of a state towards others takes on a meaning that transcends geographical boundaries. The duty extends to the whole of humanity as a community. The idea of duty towards community imposes an obligation to everyone be it state or individual to give shelter and protection against forcible return to those refugees who have fled from their homes and are unable to return.

The time is ripe to rethink ways to imbibe Gandhian principles of *sarvodaya, satyagrah* and *dharm* in India's laws, especially in the context of the present discussion on refugee rights.

[55] G. N. Sarma, "Gandhi's Concept of Duty", 42 *The Indian Journal of Political Science* 228 (June 1980).

[56] *Ibid*.

[57] Quotations by Dr. Martin Luther King Jr. available at: https://www.mkgandhi.org/Associates%20&%20Disciples/quote_king.htm (last visited July 2, 2020).

4 The Interface Between Refugee Rights and Gandhi's Life and Works

In the preceding discussion on refugees, we saw that in the absence of a definite policy on refugees, the government has wide discretion in dealing with them and that obligations under international law are not legally enforceable in court.

We interpret Gandhi's ideas to give various suggestions on how they can be brought to life in the formulation of a new refugee law. Then, we proceed to debunk two popular arguments against protection of refugee rights and suggest ways to reconcile them with refugee protection based on Gandhi's ideals. Analysing *sarvodaya, satyagrah* and *dharm*, one can trace a solution to each argument raised against guaranteeing protection to refugees.

4.1 Interpreting Gandhi to Protect Refugee Rights

The intersection between Gandhi's ideals and refugee protection is a vast unexplored territory. Here, we attempt to give a list of rights that can be granted in the spirit of Gandhi's love for humanity. This is by no means an exhaustive list, but it does serve as the starting point for a discussion on a refugee policy measured on the Gandhian touchstone.

4.1.1 Issue of Work Permits

To Gandhi, to eat without some manual work was morally degrading. The Gandhian solution to the increasing pressure on resources is to grant refugees work permits. In his last speech at the prayer meeting on 29th January, 1948, in New Delhi, Gandhi said:

> .. if the refugees want to end their sufferings, if they want to convert suffering into happiness and serve India and serve themselves, they must not shirk work. A refugee has no right to live comfortably without working. The Gita says: "Eat only after you have performed yajna." Eat what remains after the yajn. This has not been said only for me but also for you and all others. It applies also to the refugees.

In modern India, refugees are not allowed to work unless they are issued work permits. Therefore, work permits, short term and long term, must be issued to all those able to work as an interim measure while their status is being determined. This will not only reduce the economic burden of consumption without labour, but will also provide moral uplift of the refugee who will not be rendered destitute due to his sufferings.

4.1.2 Non-Discrimination

Sarvodaya believes in equality and egalitarianism, and hence, there is no place in a refugee policy for differential treatment based on identities of caste, class, religion, sex, political affiliation, etc. This idea of equality is enshrined in Article 14 of the Indian Constitution, and the debate on "reasonable" discrimination ends at the altar of Gandhi, who unconditionally believed in the inherent goodness of mankind and the fair and equal treatment of all, free from conceptions of 'otherness'. The *sarvodaya* feature of 'inclusivity' cannot be reconciled with laws that discriminate on the basis of narrow social constructs.

4.1.3 Status Determination and Non-Refoulement

Status determination means the process by which an authority determines whether a person seeking asylum is a refugee under international law or not. Currently in India, refugees are not a separate category and are treated as foreigners who have illegally entered India and are punishable under the law.

However, the international law principle of non-refoulement[58] contradicts with Indian law in this regard. In ***Ktaer Abbas Habib Al Qutaifi* v. *Union of India,***[59] Gujarat High Court declared that the principle of non-refoulement is 'encompassed in Article 21 of the Constitution of India', so long as the presence of the refugee is not prejudicial to the law and order and security of India. Status determination of refugees is a necessary precondition to them not being forcefully deported as illegal entrants. This creates a fundamental problem as genuine refugees are refused asylum.

Gandhi's ideal of *satyagrah* applied to status determination would mean the search for the truth of whether or not a person is a refugee. Additionally, one can also look at the spirit of individuality espoused by Gandhi to give due consideration to refugees. By grouping refugees along with foreigners and illegal entrants, their individuality is ignored. As long as the refugees' status remains undetermined, they will be deported along with other illegal entrants in India, and the actions of the state will continue to be objectively un-Gandhian.

4.1.4 Resettlement and Repatriation Through Burden Sharing

Once refugees enter the borders of India, it becomes the duty of the state to ensure they are treated without discrimination. *Sarvodaya* discourages temporary solutions. The repatriation of refugees might serve the state's interest, but humanity suffers.

---

[58] 'The principle of Non-refoulement' i.e. the principle of international law which requires that no state shall return a refugee in any manner to a country where his or her life or freedom may be in danger is also embodied in Article 33(1) of the United Nations Convention on the Status of Refugees, 1951.

[59] *Ktaer Abbas Habib Al Qutaifi v. Union of India* 1999 CriLJ 919.

Sarvodaya philosophy urges the formulation of welfare goals based on universal needs and not some situational, locational or regional considerations.[60]

Further, the doctrine of trusteeship states that resources held by the rich are not for their personal enjoyment only, but are held in trust by the for them benefit of the society at large. Their proprietary instinct must not come in the way of public service, as wealth is not a personal asset but a tool for social welfare. Since Gandhian thought holds the state to the same standards as that of the individual, the state's resources must also be used for the welfare of the larger society, and not just for its own citizens.

4.1.5 Removal of the Root Cause of Conflict Through Moral Appeal

Satyagrah involves a moral resistance to inequality, discrimination and injustice. It must not be confused with passive resistance. It is an active moral resistance and moral appeal to parties in conflict to bring about peace. Gandhi's instrument of choice in this matter was fasting in order to create pressure to give up violent means, which was highly successful. However, we do not suggest that the Government of India should start fasting in order to convince its neighbours to stop their violent conflicts, but we do suggest resolution through peaceful means such as mediation and peace talks.

With its rich and diverse culture and deep historic connection with its neighbours, India commands respect in South Asia much like Gandhi did among his compatriots. Drawing parallels from the Gandhian approach, India can morally appeal to refugee-sending countries to resolve their issues. Additionally, India must not hesitate to offer its own resources to aid the alleviation of conflict between warring parties.

4.2 Addressing Concerns Against the Protection of Refugees' Rights

4.2.1 National Security

The dominant argument against refugee-friendly policies is the potential threat they pose to the receiving country. While this is a legitimate concern, it is often used merely as an instrument to shrug off humanitarian obligations. However, without attempting to discredit all national security concerns, we suggest that a *sarvodaya*-based society will be able to minimise threats by creating a morally just society without violence or exploitation.

Gandhi was completely opposed to a soulless state machinery which would operate without moral legitimacy. The theory of "reason of state", which holds that a state can make the claim that its interests are morally superior to any human interest,

---

[60] Sharma, *supra* note 35.

was completely unacceptable to Gandhi.[61] He stated, *"The means may be likened to a seed, the end to a tree; and there is just the same inviolable connection between the means and the end as there is between the seed and the tree"*.[62] In simpler, more Gandhian terms, the theory of reason of state entitles the state to justify the means, even if exploitative or violent, for the end of state security. Therefore, the justification of national interest in not formulating a refugee law does not hold ground when measured on the Gandhian yardstick. As long as humans (refugees) suffer due to the absence of such a law, the state's position is not reconcilable with Gandhian ideals.

4.2.2 Resource Scarcity and Economic Burden

The argument that the influx of refugees will lead to increased burden on the economy is easily resolved through the Gandhian idea of duty or *dharm*. If each able refugee is provided work and employment, there will never be an economic burden so large that it trumps humanitarian concerns. Gandhi considered it an act of theft to eat without doing some work. We suggest the grant of short- and long-term work permits to refugees, as it is not available in the present law where they are treated as foreigners without any special status.

It is thus seen that Gandhi's vision for the future continues to be relevant in modern times, serving as the moral saviour of mankind through providing practical, people-oriented policy suggestions. It is up to the present generation to keep up his legacy by using his ideas as justifications for arguments in the present times. Perhaps the greatest political philosopher of India, Gandhi continues to be the guiding source for current policy debates.

5 Conclusion

Gandhi's ideas are based on the premise of universal brotherhood and peace. Modern Indian legislation can greatly benefit from drawing ideals from Gandhi's philosophy. In the specific issue of protection of refugee rights, his ideas provide a moral argument in favour of fair treatment for all, irrespective of national identity. The concepts of *sarvodaya*, *satyagrah* and the spirit of *dharm* give the philosophical foundation to refugee protection. Moreover, Gandhi's own experience during the partition of India in the largest refugee crisis since World War II provides a practical guide to the way the refugee issues should be approached.

Gandhi's ideals when applied to the refugee problem give solutions such as the issue of work permits, which would fulfil *dharm* and reduce economic burden, resettlement and repatriation through resource sharing through the doctrine of trusteeship,

[61] Parel, *supra* note 39.

[62] R. P. Mishra, Hind Swaraj: Gandhi's vision and ground realities available at: https://www.mkgandhi.org/articles/gandhi_vision.htm (last visited on June 27, 2020).

status determination and non-refoulement through *satyagrah* and lead up to a larger solution, suggesting the resolution of conflicts through peaceful means by mediation between conflicting parties and extending economic support when needed.

The absence of a law relating to the peculiar situation of refugees, who are currently understood in Indian law as foreigners or illegal entrants, is against the Gandhian spirit, and the codification of a refugee policy is an absolute requirement in current times. In Gandhi's own words, it will be "our shame as a nation", if the refugee problem persists in India.

It is undeniable that political disturbances will continue in India's neighbourhood in the foreseeable future. In fact, there is never surety of stability in any political system in the world. Refugees are the by-product, the collateral damage in such conflicts. This chapter suggests certain ways in which the interaction between Gandhian ideals and refugee rights can guide India's future policy to provide protection to refugees. This is an unexplored correlation, and there is a vast scope for future research in the field of Gandhi's potential contribution to humanitarian legislation.

References

Bose TK (2000) Protection of refugees in South Asia: need for legal framework, 27. South Asia Forum for Human Rights, Kathmandu

Chaudhary O (2004) Turning back: an assessment of non-refoulement under Indian Law. Econ Polit Weekly 39:3257

Ganguli BN (1973) Gandhi's social philosophy. Wiley, New York

Garrett TH (2004) Refugee protection in international law: UNHCR's global consultations on international protection. Michigan J Int Law 25:751

Ghosal AK (1959) Sarvodaya Gandhian philosophy and way of life 20 Indian J Polit Sci 24

Goolam N (2001) The changing face of German asylum law-a critical reappraisal. Comp Int Law J Southern Africa 34:51

Joseph A (2018) Gandhism and international criminal law. In: Bergsmo M, Buis EJ (eds) Philosophical foundations of international criminal law: correlating thinkers 545, Torkel Opsahl Academic E publisher, Brussels

Kivistö HM (2014) Rights of non-citizens: asylum as an individual right in the 1949 West German. Contributions to the History of Concepts, 9:61

Nair R (1997) Refugee protection in South Asia. J Int Affairs 51:201

Parel A (2011) Gandhi and the state. In: Brown J, Parel A (eds) The cambridge companion to Gandhi (Cambridge Companions to Religion), Cambridge University Press

Prasad D (2005) Satyagraha: the way, 32 India International Centre Quarterly 46

Ryan A (2012) The making of modern liberalism: John Rawls 508, Princeton University Press

Sagar A, Ahmed F (2005) The model law for refugees: an important step forward? Student Bar Rev 17:74

Salla ME (1993) Satyagraha in Mahatma Gandhi's political philosophy. Peace Res Canadian Mennonite Univ 25:55

Sarma GN (1980) Gandhi's concept of duty. Indian J Polit Sci 42:228

Saxena JN (1994) Problems of refugees in developing countries and need for international burden-sharing. In: Saksena KP (ed) Human rights: perspective and challenges, vol 356. Lancers Books, New Delhi

Sharma S (1989) Problem resolution through social reconstruction: an exposition of the Sarvodaya Principles. Peace Res Canadian Mennonite University 21:30

Chapter 10
Individual as the Supreme Consideration: Analysing the Gandhian Philosophy On Rights and Duties

Puja Raghavan and Sujith Koonan

1 Introduction

To situate Mohandas Karamchand Gandhi's philosophy of rights and duties in twenty-first-century India, it is crucial to understand his philosophy in greater detail. While Gandhi concentrated his political philosophy on the word *'swaraj'* which means one's own *(swa)* rule *(raj),* swaraj for Gandhi was a 'state of being' of individuals and nations and an important aspect of this concept was the political freedom of the individual.[1] Gandhi did not posit duties and rights as being in diametrical opposition and argued that *dharm (duty)* was necessary for sealing political well-being. Rights needed to be complimented by duties. Gandhi did not buy into the assumption of the western theory of rights that placed duties and rights in opposition to one another, this is discussed in detail in subsequent sections. The Gandhian ideas of rights and duties open new possibilities to imagine both in contrast to the dominant understanding of the concepts that is rooted in liberalism. They provide an interesting epistemology to even challenge the mainstream individualised notion of 'rights'.[2]

This chapter in the first part deals briefly with the western theories on rights and duties before discussing Gandhi's approach in the second part. The third part discusses the individual, state intervention in the development of fundamental rights and duties and the philosophical familiarity with Gandhian *swaraj*.

[1] Anthony Parel, Gandhi, Freedom, and Self Rule, Vistaar, New Delhi (2002).

[2] John Finnis, Natural Law, New York University Press, Reference Collection, New York (1991).

P. Raghavan (✉)
Student, Campus Law Centre, Faculty of Law, University of Delhi, Delhi, India
e-mail: pujaraghavan@gmail.com

S. Koonan
Assistant Professor, Campus Law Centre, Faculty of Law, University of Delhi, Delhi, India

R. Mittal and K. K. Singh (eds.), *Relevance of Duties in the Contemporary World*,
https://doi.org/10.1007/978-981-19-1836-0_10

2 Western Theories on Rights and Duties

Before exploring Gandhi's perspective on *swaraj* as political freedom of the individual and his idea of rights, it is important to discuss the theories of rights as conceptualised by the 'global north' because the 'global north' version of rights is the dominant understanding prevalent among legal scholars and practitioners. This goes with a broader criticism of the Constitution of India which has little resemblance to the 'Indian way of thinking about law' and for jettisoning the political theory of Gandhi.[3] The epistemological world of 'rights' is dominated by western philosophical assumptions, the background of which was the emergence of nation states and sociopolitical struggles of seizing power from small groups who were embedded in power.[4] This is, for instance, reflected in the natural rights theory of Hobbes and Locke. Before Locke's theory, Thomas Hobbes expounded a natural rights theory based upon the 'state of nature'. According to Hobbes, the right of nature or 'jus naturale',

> is the liberty each man hath to use his power as he will himself for the preservation of his own nature, i.e. to say his own life, and consequently of doing anything which in his own judgment and reason he shall conceive to be the aptest means.[5]

Hobbes believed that the state of nature is a condition of war and concluded that the natural right of a man must be surrendered to the sovereign as a necessary precondition for the establishment of a government in order to end the anarchy of the state of nature. The right to life according to Hobbes, however, is the only natural right that one can retain. The Hobbesian premise of state of nature and the consequent justification of absolute power were informed by the chaos in seventeenth-century Britain. It is doubtful how, and to what extent, this premise can be generalised because societies survived and prospered in the history of humankind without the protection of absolute rulers.[6]

John Locke in *Second Treatise on Civil Government* also looks at the state of nature as the condition of human beings in the absence of a government but unlike Hobbes, he does not believe that it is a state of war. In his opinion, '*Men live together according to reason, without a common superior on earth with authority to judge between them, is properly the state of nature*'. The state of nature has a law of nature to govern it and all individuals are equal '*wherein all the power and jurisdiction is reciprocal, no one having more than the other*'.[7]

---

[3] Choudhary, Khosla & Mehta, 2016: 5.

[4] Brown 2000.

[5] Thomas Hobbes, Leviathan, Basil Blackwell, Oxford (1946).

[6] Ratnapala, 2009: 29.

[7] John Locke, "Second Treatise of Civil Government" (1690) available at https://www.marxists.org/reference/subject/politics/locke/ch03.htm. (last accessed 02 April, 2020).

Isiah Berlin argues that there exists a binary conception of liberty: ‘positive’[8] and ‘negative’.[9] The latter involves the satisfaction of individual wants by withdrawal from interference while the former involves the collective goals through interference and social engineering.

The meaning of rights underwent changes, and according to John Finnis, there was a ‘choice’ theory of rights and a ‘benefit’ theory of rights. The former saw rights as the freedom to choose what one wants, and the latter looked upon rights as something beneficial an individual has (Finnis 1991). The theory of rights began to expand post the development of the natural theory of rights and the utilitarian theory of rights and saw the development of other strands like the libertarian theory of rights, John Rawls’ idea of rights and human rights theories.

The dominant conception of rights, therefore, has two main characteristics. First, it is centred around the conception of individual who needs to be protected from the state as well as other individuals, and second, it strengthens the idea of state as the most appropriate and legitimate institution to exercise the monopoly of legislation through which rights are to be recognised or granted and the violation of rights are to be dealt with. The conceptions of state and right apparently grew in tandem, and both acquired immense legitimacy to the extent that ‘even the most basic human needs do not generate an appropriate moral response unless those involved are shown to have a right to their satisfaction’.[10] The dominance of rights has made duties contingent upon the existence of rights, and not the other way around. At the same time, it needs to be underlined that the emergence of communitarianism in political theory has raised an unease concerning the extent to which liberal theories neglect the interests of the community, civic virtue and social solidarity.[11]

3 Gandhian Swaraj and the Philosophy on Duty

In conceptualising Gandhi’s concept of Swaraj, it has to be understood that the notion is twofold because it involved the inner and outer liberation, i.e. of the self and the country. The development of this concept must be traced in its context of writing and is compiled in his work *Hind Swaraj* written in 1909. Gandhi’s ideas of swaraj were written in the ten days between 13 and 22 November, 1909, when he was travelling

[8] Berlin in *Four Essays on Liberty* argues that positive liberty is the idea that there each self has a higher and lower self. The higher self was the rational self that needed to attain mastery over the lower self in order for people to be liberated. Positive liberty in Berlin’s conception includes self-mastery of the higher self over the lower self. (Berlin, 1969).

[9] Berlin states that negative liberty has two axioms, the first is that each one knows their own interests, and based on this, the individual is a rational agent with the capacity to make an informed choice; the second axiom is that the state has a limited role to play and therefore cannot decide ends and purpose for the individual. Berlin says ‘Over what area am I a master?’ is the answer to the question on the scope of negative liberty. (Berlin, 1969).

[10] Parekh, 1987.

[11] Raymond Wacks, 3rd ed., 2012:241.

via ship from London to South Africa. His writings can therefore be said to have grown out of his context of being situated in a racially segregated South Africa and the experiences being discriminated against on the basis of skin colour.

Gandhi used the term '*swaraj*' in the context of varied freedoms, two of which include the ***political freedom*** of the individual from oppression by other individuals, state or groups and ***spiritual freedom*** of the individual or self-rule, an aspirational state of being to be achieved by politically and economically free individuals. The other components of swaraj include external autonomy or freedom from alien rule.[12]

This section concerns itself with the aspects of political freedom, spiritual freedom and external autonomy.

Gandhi held the freedom of the individual as a hallmark of an independent India, and it is vital that the Gandhian concept of rights of the individual or political freedom be understood in the context in which Gandhi wrote. Anthony Parel argues that India's multiethnic, multi-caste and multi-linguistic society shaped ideas of freedom in his recognition of the individual manifestation of freedom for the cherishment of it, regardless of their differences.[13]

Gandhi argued that life worthy of a human being was impossible sans the benefits of rights and in South Africa realised that 'more correctly, I discovered that I had no rights as a man because I was an Indian'.[14] Gandhi's major political philosophical contribution of *satyagrah* was a means to defend rights, he defined *satyagrah* as '*passive resistance [satyagrah] is a method of securing rights by personal suffering; it is the reverse of resistance by arms*'.[15] This signifies two aspects—substantive and methodological elements. From a substantive point of view, it underlines the recognition of rights as a political goal in Gandhian thoughts, and it also emphasises non-violence and voluntary self-suffering as a mode of struggle to achieve rights. However, as is discussed later, Gandhi puts rights in its relational context with duties and society.

Gandhi co-drafted the 'Resolution on Fundamental Rights and Economic Changes' along with Jawaharlal Nehru, that was passed in the 1931 session of the Indian National Congress.[16] This is a hallmark moment in the defence of individual freedom and rights. One of the aims of the Resolution was 'to enable to the masses what swaraj…will mean to them'.[17]

It is interesting to evaluate that Gandhi's defence of rights deviates from the modern western theory's underlying epistemology and premises. Anthony Parel in *Gandhi, Freedom and Self-Rule* argues 'that the modern western theory of human

---

[12] M.K. Gandhi, Hind Swaraj or Indian Home Rule, Navajivan Publishing House, Ahmedabad (1909).

[13] Parel 2002.

[14] CWMG 23.

[15] Gandhi 1909, *supra* note 12.

[16] Mentioned in Collected Works of Mahatma Gandhi ('CWMG') volume 45 in pages 370 to 372 as well as in *An Autobiography* by J.Nehru in pages 267-68 where he speaks of his time co-drafting the Resolution with M. K. Gandhi.

[17] CWMG 45.

nature on which rights are based presupposes that humans are bodily creatures led by their imagination, appetites, aversions, and instrumental reason'. He further states that in this theory, humans are looked upon as individualists who distrust one another and rights are the means they use to protect their individual interests from others. In terms of western theory's epistemology he says that '…much of modern western theory of rights is based on dogmatic empiricism' which he explains as 'that which cannot be empirically verified or demonstrated has no cognitive status'. In Parel's opinion, there is no space for spiritual insights and the theory of the soul.[18]

Gandhi on the other hand based his defence of rights and freedom on his perspective on human nature that seems to be drawn from sources like the Bhagavad Gita. In the *Hind Swaraj*, he states that 'Man is not born to live in isolation but is essentially a social animal independent and interdependent'.[19] Gandhi explains the bodily existence as a justification for rights and the dimensions of spiritual powers as allowing rights to be pursued within the boundaries of natural ethics.

On the argument of epistemology, Parel puts forth that Gandhi assumes 'that humans live by truth established by empiricism, reason and spiritual insights'. Gandhi relies on the Bhagavad Gita's hierarchy of powers in the human: body, sense, the mind, intelligence *(buddhi)* and immortal spirit (*atman*). Based on these differences, Gandhi puts forth his understanding of the theory of rights on duty (*dharm*) and *satyagrah*.

Judith Brown in her chapter titled *Gandhi and Human Rights: In Search of True Humanity* interestingly argues that though Gandhi often defends freedom in the 'rights' context, he is not a 'rights theorist' as understood in western political thought. There are many aspects of the theory of rights as seen in the western political thought that differ from Gandhi's understanding. The rights theory was protective of the individual *vis-a-vis* the state and was additionally sceptical about society and humanity. This acted as a guard for the individuals against the threatening forces in society and groups of humans.[20] Gandhi's understanding of rights was based on *dharm* or duty. *Dharm* meant not only the religious duty of an individual but included duties towards the group with the aim of creating a society that would be in conformation with the order and balance in the universe *(rta)*. Brown states that 'this led to a stress on duties rather than on rights and on the mutual interdependence of individuals and groups if the whole was to function morally'. Thus, Gandhi's notion of rights seems closer to a communitarian perspective and a qualitative deviation from the individualistic notion of rights.

In a paper published in *Harijan* in July 1947 titled *Rights or Duties?,* Gandhi argued that 'if all simply insist on rights and no duties there will be utter confusion and chaos'. He further said 'if instead of insisting on rights everyone does his duty, there will immediately be the rule of order established among mankind…I venture to suggest that rights that do not flow directly from duty well performed are not worth

[18] Parel 2000, *supra* note 13.

[19] Gandhi 1909, *supra* note 12.

[20] Brown 2000, *supra* note 4.

having. They will be usurpations sooner discarded the better'.[21] In the October 6, 1946, issue of *Harijan* Gandhi wrote '...Rights only spring from duties well done. Such rights alone are becoming and lasting'. He further stated 'I shall therefore advise Harijan brethren that they should think only of their duties done'. Gandhi in *Young India* said that,

> The true source of rights is duty. If we all discharge our duties, right will not be far to seek. if leaving duties unperformed we run after rights, they escape us like a will-o'-the-wisp. The more we pursue them, the farther they fly. The same teaching has been embodied by Krishna in the immortal words; 'Action alone is thine. Leave thou the fruit severely alone.' Action is duty: fruit is the right.[22]

Gandhian political philosophy appears to attribute a differential moral and political weightage to rights and duties. Thus, according to Gandhi, duties must be given priority in individuals' moral and political choices. As a result, Gandhi believes that 'rule of order' will be established among mankind if everyone pursues duties as a priority moral obligation. Rights that are not flowing from or deriving from duties, according to Gandhi, are 'not worth having', and such rights are unlikely to last. Thus, Gandhi makes the moral strength and normative sustainability of rights contingent upon the duties as a source of rights.

While it is clear from these observations of Gandhi that rights were insufficient for a political being sans duty and duties complimented rights and therefore there was no opposition between the two, it becomes important to raise questions on Gandhi's understanding of the 'duties of harijans' and if he was implying a caste-based occupational divide for a holistic understanding of his theories. Gandhi indeed condemned the social ostracism and exploitation faced by the so-called untouchables from caste Hindus. At the same time, he seems to have believed in caste-based occupation in India. Thus, while emphasising the role of 'duties' in Gandhian thoughts, one needs to be cautious in understanding its generalities and abstractness on the one hand and its operational dimensions and relation with the prevailing social institutions (caste and gender) on the other.

Modern Western theory of rights posited that rights and duties opposed one another, and this can be traced back to the two arguments of Parel on their anthropological and epistemological presuppositions of individualism where there was distrust between human beings. Gandhi deviated from this understanding and built his vision on the explanation of *dharm* that he described as,

> Dharm does not mean any particular creed or dogma nor does it mean reading or learning by rote books known as Shastrs or even believing all that they say. Dharm is a quality of soul and its present, visibility or invisibly, in every human being.[23]

It is evident from this explanation that Gandhi believed that there were two sorts of dharm, the first being one that is derived from books or sociolegal codes that are products of society, for instance those that govern the political and social relations

---

[21] M. K. Gandhi, "Rights or Duties", Harijan (1947).

[22] M. K. Gandhi, Young India 08.01.1925.

[23] CWMG 32.

and the second that derives itself from the 'quality of soul'. The latter form of dharm would only have an effect on society and impose upon its people a moral duty if it is compatible with the first kind of dharm, that of the soul. By extension, in Gandhi's opinion, if this sociolegal code was inconsistent with the *dharm* of the soul, then it would have to be abandoned or changed so that it becomes compatible. An example of this can be seen in Gandhi's understanding of the sati system in India. The understanding of the compatibility of 'dharm of the soul' and dharm derived from sociolegal codes is one of the reasons behind the relational nature of duties and rights, according to Gandhi. Gandhi also famously stated 'No one will have any right but what are inherent in the willing performance of one's duties'.[24] He vehemently opposed the idea that rights were superior to duties, and this can be drawn from his opposition to H.G. Wells's *Charter of Rights of Man*[25] when he said that time should have been spent on drafting *Duties of Man* instead. When the Universal Declaration of Human Rights was being drafted by the United Nations in 1948, Gandhi responded to it by saying that,

> All rights to be deserved and preserved come from duty well done. Thus the very right to live accrues to us only when we do the duty of citizenship of the world. From this fundamental statement perhaps it is easy enough to define the duties of man and woman and correlate every right to some corresponding duty to be first performed. Every other right can be shown to be a usurpation hardly worth fighting for.[26]

Gandhi's ideas of rights and duties deviated from the discourse plaguing rights at the time, and the contribution developed a political praxis that also draws attention to the importance of contexts and assumptions in understanding a philosophy or theory because Gandhi challenged the assumptions of the western theory of rights. Even though Part III of the Indian Constitution on Fundamental Rights covers rights that are prevalent in the Universal Declaration of Human Rights and even the *Resolution of Rights* co-drafted by Gandhi and Nehru reflect similar principles and guarantees, the important point of discussion is the philosophical justification to the right. Jacques Maritain in *Man and the State* said 'Yes, we agree about the rights, but on condition no one asks why'.[27]

Dallmayr and Sudarshan argue that Gandhi's *swaraj* is at a distance from Berlin's argument of a binary conception of positive and negative liberty because negative liberty has streaks of self-centredness and positive liberty ignores self-restraint and the fruits of action; Gandhi's idea 'squarely faced' the dilemma between the opposition of positive and negative liberty as the negative strand could not negotiate between spiritual self and led to 'chaos of conflicting claims' where the will of the strongest trumped while the positive strand stepped aside from self-transcendence for collective goals.[28] *Swaraj's* emphasis on self-rule and liberty in the sense of 'freedom of self-actualisation' helped in overcoming the gap between the higher and lower self

---

[24] CWMG 73.

[25] H.G Wells wrote the 'Rights of Man' in 1940 during World War II.

[26] CWMG 88.

[27] Jacques Maritain, "Man, and the State", The Catholic University of America, Washington (1998).

[28] Ramashray Roy, "Self and Society", *Sage*, New Delhi (1985).

in the sense of the world.[29] Self-rule, an important component of Gandhian Swaraj, is based on the process of removing internal obstacles to freedom where the practice of self-rule cannot be done in the absence of virtue and was a self-transformative activity. Self-rule according to Gandhi required 'self-restraint' or 'rule from within'. Independence according to Gandhi was a modern concept and meant the 'licence to do as you like' which was negative freedom as understood by Berlin while *swaraj* or 'self-rule' was drawn from Vedic words and was sacred in nature. He wanted Indians to embrace Independence but interlink it with swaraj.[30]

Gandhi argued that independence should mean not only replacing British rule with Indian rule but must mean *swaraj* that linked independence and self-rule. For Gandhi, independence in the absence of self-rule would lead to a situation of the rule of the strong over the weak, where the strong is politically and economically stronger and the fact that they are of the same nationality would not make it acceptable because it was not the rule of equals by equals. In the *Constructive Programme* in 1941, Gandhi argued that sans a strong civil society only the upper castes and class would benefit. He argued for the requirement of a strong civil society that needed to create peace between Hindus and other religious minorities, remove the caste system and untouchability and ensure village sanitation, adult literacy and the emancipation of women, and it was only through the strengthening of this civil society would India attain 'poorn swaraj' or complete independence by truthful and nonviolent means.

Gandhi in *The Declaration of Independence* in 1930 wrote that it was the inalienable right of Indian people to have freedom and enjoy the fruits of their toil so that they had opportunities for growth and any government that would deprive people of these rights and oppress them had a right to be abolished or altered. What is striking in Gandhi's observations is that he did not believe in subordinating political freedom of the individual for the interest of any national myth. This can be understood from his words in 'Mere withdrawal of the English is not independence. It means the consciousness in the average villager that he is the maker of his own destiny, he is his own legislator through his chosen representatives'.[31] Therefore, *swaraj* for Gandhi did not mean the replacement of the oppressor but the replacement of any coercive power with equality. He made self-rule compatible with modern ideas of freedom and got rid of the assumption that there existed a dichotomy between rights and duties, albeit by approaching the idea of rights from a communitarian perspective.

The concepts of dharm, duty and *swaraj*, in Gandhian thoughts, seem to maintain intimacy; however, it is difficult to say if Gandhi meant these concepts to be primarily secular or religious. If the 'quality of the soul' is to be the Gandhian 'grundnorm', the religious texts are to be treated at the most as a subsidiary source of the rules of conduct whose validity may be questioned on the basis of the 'grundnorm'. At the same time, the very expression 'quality of the soul' seems to be religiously motivated that the secular coating that one may try to put on it will, in fact, strengthen the religious nature of it.

---

[29] Dallmayr and Sudarshan 2000.

[30] CWMG 45.

[31] CWMG 42.

4 Twenty-First-Century India and Gandhi's Idea of Self-Rule [Swaraj and Contemporary State of Human Rights in India]

In order to evaluate the influence of Gandhi's ideas of individualism and his understanding of rights and duties within the Constitution of India and in the present-day legal context, it is important to discuss the notion of state intervention in Gandhi's writings as well as other western political philosophers before delving in the present-day ecosystem.

Aristotle's distinction of the private and public sphere is interesting in order to understand the implementation of fundamental rights and the role of political power. The former is associated with family and domestic life while the latter with political activity.[32] Mill in his essay '*On liberty*' argues that the public realm is that of governmental authority as opposed to the private realm for self-regulation. John Locke in *The Second Treatise of Government* argued that lives, liberties and estates of individuals were private reserves that acted as a barrier from external interference.[33] William Blackstone in *Commentaries on the Laws of England* referred to 'natural liberty' as absolute rights vested in individuals by nature. The absolute rights included the rights of personal security, personal liberty and property. Personal security was explained as the legal and uninterrupted enjoyment of life, limbs, body, health and reputation by an individual.[34] Justice Louis Brandeis and Samuel D. Warren's article titled *'The Right to Privacy'* argued that the rights of individuals must be recognised in order for the protection of society to occur.[35]

Gandhi's writings warned of the dangers in the existence of any human institution and the scope of abuse within them. He argued that a democratic structure was therefore susceptible to misuse and the remedy to this problem lays in finding ways for the reduction of this possibility.[36] He argued vociferously for the evolving of democratic structures with the individual at its core, and he stated that 'the spirit of democracy is not a mechanical thing to be adjusted by abolition of forms. It requires a change of heart'.[37] While discussing the responsibility of individuals within a state structure, he argued that if individuals took the law in their hands, a state would not exist and the absence of the social law or state would lead to the destruction of liberty. Therefore, Gandhi, while a proponent of self-rule, cautioned against the individual securing justice through illegitimate means sans state intervention.[38] He argued that political power was a means for a better condition and only when national life became

---

32 Aristotle used the term *polis to refer to politics and political activity and oikos to refer to private life.*

33 Locke, *supra* above note 7.

34 William Blackstone and David Lemmings, Commentaries on The Laws of England (1765).

35 Warren and Brandeis 1890.

36 Gandhi 1919a, b, c.

37 Gandhi 1920.

38 Gandhi 1947, *supra* note 21.

perfect there was room for no representatives, a state he called 'enlightened anarchy'. He is also known to invoke Thoreau's understanding of governments being the best that govern the least.[39] Gandhi therefore, while being a proponent of democratic setup in the absence of the state of 'enlightened anarchy', believed that minimal state intervention was the requirement for a truly democratic country, and it was only in a nation that saw the minimal interference of the freedoms of the people that the form of government was democratic in all senses. The tussle between state intervention for the giving of freedoms and in the taking away of freedoms is vital in the discussion of fundamental rights guaranteed within Part III of the Constitution of India and Gandhian influence in the present-day ecosystem.

Gandhi identified decentralised power as a building block for a successful nation and argued for the self-reliant and autonomous communities that saw people's participation at its fullest. He propounded that the vehicle for political and economic democracy lays in village panchayats, and he looked at villages as decentralised as a vital unit of the devolution of power from the hands of one. While Gandhi was not a member of the drafting committee of the Indian Constitution, the influence of his ideas and vision can perhaps be seen in the Seventh Schedule of the Constitution that lays down the responsibilities between the Union and the State government. The 73rd and 74th amendment gave constitutional recognition of Panchayati Raj Institutions in 1992 and gave meaning to democracy at the grassroots level. While this was brought about through an amendment decades after the drafting phase, it can be argued that the Gandhian idea of democracy finds itself here.

On the 24th of August 2017, the Supreme Court of India in *KS Puttaswamy* v. *Union of India*[40] declared that the right to privacy was a fundamental right protected under Part III of the Constitution on Fundamental Rights and was to be read in Article 19 (freedom of expression, association, residence and occupation) and Article 21 (right to life and personal liberty) therefore including it as a part of the fundamental rights discourse in Part III of the Indian Constitution. The landmark judgement was pronounced in the context of the Aadhar, India's national identity project, and the cases of *MP Sharma* v. *Satish Chandra*[41] in 1954 and *Kharak Singh* v. *State of Uttar Pradesh*[42] in 1962 became important. The Supreme Court's nine judge bench overruled these two cases to the extent of those cases that held that the right to privacy was not a fundamental right. The SC also overruled the *ADM Jabalpur* case[43] that allowed fundamental rights to be suspended in a state of declared emergency and further raised questions on the judicial justification in *Naz Foundation* case[44] that held that 'minuscule minority' like the LGBTQ community was not entitled to the right to privacy.

[39] Gandhi 1937.

[40] 2017 SCC OnLine SC 996.

[41] 1954 SCR 1077.

[42] AIR 1963 SC 1295.

[43] (1976) 2 SCC 521.

[44] (2016) 7 SCC 485.

These judgements invoke the flavour of Gandhi in his understanding of self-rule. Ananya Vajpeyi argues that the term 'privacy' in Hindi means 'nijata' that means 'mineness'; therefore, from the terminology, the philosophical similarity to *swaraj* can be drawn as both *swa* and *nija* 'encompass the self'. Vajpeyi says that etymology unveils the closeness of the language of freedom and privacy.[45]

The world has witnessed several epochs in history that have involved wars and health emergencies that have gone on to contextually sculpt the social, economic and political landscape. In light of the coronavirus health emergency, debates surrounding state intervention and 'surveillance' have gripped the imagination of the populace especially in the context of data collection, data protection and the frameworks for regulating artificial intelligence.

The discussion plaguing data privacy found itself in the forefront in light of the usage of the data collection app—Aarogya Setu. Michel Foucault's discussion on power herein is an important one. Foucault argued that through the mechanism of 'governmentality',[46] individuals are produced as subjects of governance subjected to the different forms of classification and surveillance like identity cards, passports in short, through documents used for tracking that in the modern age we can see its reflection in the data collection of health apps. Foucault argues that governmentality operates via *normalisation* where the individual conforms to norms. These norms are often created by surveillance mechanisms of the state because individuals begin to question identities based on the data asked and are judged by the information provided. This can be better understood by the example of the usage of data collection applications like the usage of the Aarogya Setu app that enables the government in identifying individuals who show symptoms of the COVID-19 virus. Under the Epidemics Diseases Act, 1897, disobedience to regulations by the state is criminal offence under Sect. 3 and individuals can be charged under Sect. 188 of the Indian Penal Code. Section 270 of the IPC further states that, '*Malignant act likely to spread infection of disease dangerous to life.—Whoever malignantly does any act which is, and which he knows or has reason to believe to be, likely to spread the infection of any disease dangerous to life, shall be punished with imprisonment of either description for a term which may extend to two years, or with fine, or with both.*'. Therefore, the criminalisation of the spread of the virus in this context is important while understanding the psychological and sociological impacts of judgement making of individuals on the basis of information provided while using mechanisms of surveillance by the state.

It is of vital importance here to remember Gandhi and his ideas expounded on *swaraj.* Gandhi emphasised in his writings that the British coloniser must not be replaced by a same nationality coloniser and also that the individual's interest must not be subordinated to the 'national myth'. Gandhi warned against the rule of one man over many and argued that 'Government of the people, by the people and for

[45] Ananya Vajpeyi, "Privacy Is the Swaraj Of Our Times" (2017) available at https://www.thehindu.com/opinion/op-ed/privacy-is-the-swaraj-of-our-times/article19781516.ece (last accessed 20 July, 2020).

[46] Refers to the increased organisation of society by state bureaucratic machinery.

the people cannot be conducted at the bidding of one man, however great he may be'.[47] The risk of turning into a dictatorship from a democracy was one that Gandhi constantly cautioned against while arguing for a participative, decentralised democracy. Foucault's idea of governmentality as a means of surveillance by the state and the example of health collection apps like the Aarogya Setu bring the discourse in Gandhi's conception of *swaraj* to the front because questions regarding the scope of state intervention in the right to privacy become important. The proportionality and legitimacy test established in *Puttaswamy* case state that a fourfold test needs to be fulfilled before state intervention in the right to privacy:

i. The state action must be sanctioned by law.
ii. In a democratic society there must be a legitimate aim for action.
iii. Action must be proportionate to the need for such interference.
iv. And it must be subject to procedural guarantees against abuse of the power to interfere.

This test of proportionality is of vital importance in determining the legitimacy of action by the state; however, several instances of the test not being fulfilled can be seen even in the example of the Aarogya Setu app because the need for the interference is linked to an assumption that it is an effective interference. The Brookings paper titled *'Contact-tracing apps are not a solution to the COVID-19 crisis'* argues that contact tracing is effective where there exists large-scale testing capacity and less spread and that the app is not effective where there is a high risk of false positives and false negatives, something that gets worse as the population size increases. Further, the absence of complete smartphone penetration can defeat the purpose of such an app.[48] Therefore, the Aarogya Setu app seems to falter upon the test set out.

Gandhi's arguments are more relevant than ever in light of this, and the principles of *swaraj* need to be invoked. The cornerstone of policy making and judicial pronouncement must be guided by the philosophical basis of Gandhi's notion of self-rule. Duty as the precondition to a right is crucial in understanding that Gandhi never argued that rights are absolute in nature sans any responsibility of individual duty that includes complying with restrictions imposed on individual rights by the state for the well-being of the larger populace.

Gandhi's arguments regarding the replacement of the coloniser became important in the context of severe civil society backlash often seen when the state threatens fundamental rights, that is also in sync with the Gandhian idea of doctrines harmonising themselves with morality of the time. However, Gandhi's argument of morality must not be misconstrued to think that his leaning to morality would mean mainstream understanding of morality at the time because that would further invert the power structure in favour of the upper caste and class who would insubordinate the others. Gandhi's philosophical commitment to equality in all his writings must be

[47] Gandhi 1947, *supra* note 21.

[48] A Soltani, R Calo and C Bergstrom, "Contact-Tracing Apps Are Not A Solution to the COVID-19 Crisis" (2020) Available at https://www.brookings.edu/techstream/inaccurate-and-insecure-why-contact-tracing-apps-could-be-a-disaster/ (last accessed 19 May, 2020).

kept in mind while drawing links between the harmony of morality and doctrines, documents and sociolegal texts.

While some of the ideas and vision of Gandhi managed to find its way into the Constitution of India, they seem to have received far less attention than they should. At a time when issues of self-autonomy and self-identification of individuals and groups as reflected in the *Puttaswamy* case, Gandhian ideas of dharm, rights, duties and Swaraj seem relevant to project a perspective towards issues related to human rights and the nature of the post-colonial Indian state.

5 Conclusion

Despite *swaraj* being criticised for being utopia in nature by Aurobindo and Tagore arguing that the idolisation of the leader leads to an 'unthinking acceptance of dogma' therefore putting at risk Gandhi's *swaraj* from being unquestionable, it opens up the possibility of alternative imaginations.

Gandhi's ideas of dharm, duties, rights and swaraj provide important conceptual tools to have a critical understanding of the contemporary conception of rights and the nature of the modern state. The Gandhian concept of *swaraj* is reflected in the understanding of a democracy in terms of individual liberty, rights and duties and in the present day and is an effective tool in evaluating the state interference with the rights of individuals. While the idea of swaraj has been discussed in the context of decolonization, it also has the potential to understand the sites of exploitation and oppression in post-colonial societies, including the authoritarianism of the modern states.

References

2017 SCC OnLine SC 996
Berlin I (1969) Four essays on liberty. Oxford University Press, London
Blackstone W, Lemmings D (1765) Commentaries on the laws of England
Bhargava A (2008) Political theory. Pearson Education India, New Delhi
Bloombergquint, Right to privacy: surveillance in the post-Puttaswamy era". https://www.bloombergquint.com/law-and-policy/right-to-privacy-surveillance-in-the-post-puttaswamy-era. Accessed 1 July 2020
CWMG, 45
CWMG,23
CWMG,32
CWMG,42
CWMG,73
CWMG,88.
Dallmayr F (2000) What is Swaraj? Lessons from Gandhi. In: Parel A (ed) Gandhi, freedom and self rule. Lexington, New York, pp 103–118

Foucault M (1980) Power/knowledge: selected interviews and other writings 1972–1997. Pantheon Books, New York
Finnis J (1991) Natural law. New York University Press, Reference Collection, New York
Gandhi MK (2010) Constructive Programme. Navajivan Press, Ahmedabad
Gandhi MK (1919a) Young India 02 Jan 1937
Gandhi MK (1919b) Young India 07 May 1931
Gandhi MK (1919c) Young India 08 Dec 1920
Gandhi MK (1925) Young India 08 Jan 1925
Gandhi MK (1946a) *Harijan*
Gandhi MK (1946b) Harijan 14 Sept 1947
Gandhi MK (1946c) Harijan 28 Sept 1947
Gandhi MK (1947) Rights or Duties. Harijan
Gandhi MK (1909) Hind Swaraj or Indian home rule. Navajivan Publishing House, Ahmedabad
Hobbes T (1946) Leviathan. Basil Blackwell, Oxford
Hohfeld W (1920) Fundamental legal conceptions as applied in judicial reasoning and other legal essays. Yale University Press
Locke J (1690) Second treatise of civil government. Available via Marxists.Org. https://www.marxists.org/reference/subject/politics/locke/ch03.htm. Accessed 02 Apr 2020
Maritain J (1998) Man. The Catholic University of America, Washington, And the State
Mill JS, Lindsay AD (1998) On liberty and other essays. Oxford University Press, London
Mkgandhi.Org "Declaration of complete independence|Mahatma Gandhi pictorial biography. https://www.mkgandhi.org/biography/declratn.html. Accessed 1 July 2020
Mohan S, Dwivedi D (2019) How Gandhi's writings justify a security state using notions of "cleanliness". Available via Caravan. https://caravanmagazine.in/security/gandhi-justify-security-state-cleanliness. Accessed 02 May 2020
Prasanna S (2018) One year of India's right to privacy: no step forward and two steps backAvailable via *The Wire*. https://thewire.in/law/india-right-to-privacy-aadhaar-srikrishna-committee. Accessed 18 May 2020
Parel A (2002) Gandhi, freedom, and self rule. Vistaar, New Delhi
Roy R (1985) Self and society. Sage, New Delhi
Soltani A, Calo R, Bergstrom C (2020) Contact-tracing apps are not a solution to the covid-19 crisis. Available at Brookings. https://www.brookings.edu/techstream/inaccurate-and-insecure-why-contact-tracing-apps-could-be-a-disaster/. Accessed 19 May 2020
The Epidemic Diseases Act
The Indian Penal Code
US 438 (1928)
Vajpeyi A (2017) Privacy is the swaraj of our times. Available on The Hindu. https://www.thehindu.com/opinion/op-ed/privacy-is-the-swaraj-of-our-times/article19781516.ece. Accessed 20 July 2020
Warren SD, Louis DB (1890) The right to privacy. Harv Law Rev 4(5):193. https://doi.org/10.2307/1321160

Chapter 11
Priority to Duties Over Rights: Towards a Better World

Deepak Joshi and Rupali Prashar

1 Introduction

When we think about priorities to duties over rights, we recollect an interesting incident wherein Julian Huxley, an English evolutionary theorist and director-general of UNESCO, wrote to Mahatma Gandhi to contribute an essay to a collection of philosophical reflections on human rights. Gandhi declined to contribute and replied, 'I learned from my illiterate but wise mother that all rights to be deserved and preserved came from duty well done'.[1] In another instance wherein HG Wells solicited Gandhi's support for his bill of rights defining war aims, Gandhi recommended Wells to write a cosmopolitan charter of duties, a statement of what citizens of the world owe to each other.[2]

For thousands of years, duties were the main commitment of religious ethics. When there were no governments or charters of rights, the men's conduct was governed by their sense of duties and responsibilities toward each other and the society. Even the most celebrated shloka from Bhagwat Gita 'कर्मण्येवाधिकारस्ते मा फलेषु कदाचन। मा कर्मफलहेतुर्भूर्मा ते संगोऽस्त्वकर्मणि॥' means 'You have a right to perform your prescribed duty, but you have no right over the fruits of your actions.

[1] "Hindustani The collected works of Mahatama Gandhi", available at https://www.gandhiashramsevagram.org/gandhi-literature/mahatma-gandhi-collected-works-volume-97.pdf. (last accessed on November 25, 2021).

[2] David C. Smith and William F. Stone, Peace and Human Rights: H.G. Wells and the Universal Declaration, Canadian Mennonite University, (1989) available at https://www.jstor.org/stable/23609935 (last accessed on October 26, 2021).

D. Joshi (✉)
Research Scholar (Ph.D.), Faculty of Law, University of Delhi, Delhi, India
e-mail: Deepakjoshi1392@gmail.com

R. Prashar
Student, LL.B., Campus Law Centre, Faculty of Law, University of Delhi, Delhi, India

R. Mittal and K. K. Singh (eds.), *Relevance of Duties in the Contemporary World*,
https://doi.org/10.1007/978-981-19-1836-0_11

Never consider yourself to be the cause of the results of your activities, and never be attached to not doing your duty'.[3]

In the present era, on one side, a particular set of intellectuals vehemently talk about just rights; on the other side, they want full enjoyment of their right to freedom of speech and expression, including the right to protest freely without any fulfillment to the correlated duties. Now it becomes pertinent to understand and set a narrative on the importance and priority of duties over rights in a civilized society.

2 The Evolution of Rights

The history of rights covers thousands of years and draws upon religious, cultural, philosophical, and legal developments. It is believed that the concept of rights is as old as human civilization. This belief is based on the premise that at all stages of mankind there have been human rights documents in one form or the other in existence. Several ancient texts included a variety of concepts that may be considered to be human rights.

In ancient times, people acquired rights and responsibilities through their membership in a group—a family, indigenous nation, religion, class, community, or state. Most societies have had traditions similar to the 'golden rule' of 'Do unto others as you would have them do unto you'.[4] The Hindu Vedas, the Babylonian Code of Hammurabi, the Bible, the Quran, and the Analects of Confucius are the oldest written sources which address questions of people's duties and rights.

Rights are considered as entitlements as compared to duties which are treated as obligations. Rights are common claims, essential for people's development, and are enforced by the state. It may be considered as the standard of permitted action within a certain sphere. The action which is permitted by the law is called a legal right. Whereas moral or natural right means an interest recognized and protected by the rules of natural justice, an interest the violation of which would be a moral wrong, and respect for which is a moral duty.

John Austin distinguished between legal rights and other types of rights such as natural rights or moral rights. According to Austin, 'A party has a right when another or others are bound or obliged by law to do or forbear toward or in regard of him'.[5] He was of the opinion that other kinds of rights are not armed with legal sanction and cannot be enforced judicially. On the contrary, Gray defines legal rights as that power which the man has to make a person or persons do or restrain

[3] Shlok 47, Chap. 2, Bhagwad Gita available at https://www.gitasupersite.iitk.ac.in/srimad?htrskd=1&httyn=1&htshg=1&scsh=1&choos=&&language=dv&field_chapter_value=2&field_nsutra_value=47 (last accessed on November 25, 2021).

[4] Matthew, "Bible", 7:12 available at https://biblehub.com/matthew/7-12.htm (last accessed on October 26, 2021).

[5] Available at http://www.smmpalwal.com/SILR_PALWAL/pdf/2ndsem/ballb6/ballb6thsem2.pdf (last accessed on November 25, 2021).

from doing a certain act or acts so far as the power arises from society imposing a legal duty upon the person or persons.[6] He states that the 'right is not the interest itself; it is the means to enjoy the interest secured'.[7]

The discourse on rights is linked with the rise of liberal individualism. The language of rights permeates and dominates all walks of modern political, social, and economic life. In defining the proper relationship between the individual and the state, the philosophical defense of rights has assumed unparalleled importance in modern political discourse. The idea for the protection of rights grew on a global level only after the tragic experiences of the two world wars. Earlier, there was not much codification done at the international levels to protect and implement human rights.

'A Declaration of Rights is in reciprocity, a declaration of duties also. Whatever is my right as a man is also the right of another, and it becomes my duty to guarantee as well as to possess'.[8] It is ironical that written precursors to many of today's human rights documents asserting individual rights, such the Magna Carta (1215), the English Bill of Rights (1689), the French Declaration on the Rights of Man and Citizen (1789), and the US Constitution and Bill of Rights (1791), when originally translated into policy, excluded women, people of color, and members of certain social, religious, economic, and political groups.

The belief that everyone, by virtue of her/his humanity, is entitled to certain rights is fairly new. Salmond also believed that no right can exist without a corresponding duty.[9] Every right or duty involves a bond of legal obligation by which two or more persons are bound together. Thus, there can be no duty unless there is someone to whom it is due and there can be no right unless there is someone from whom it is claimed.

3 The Evolution of Duties

It is aptly stated in the Ramayan, 'As birds are made to fly and rivers to run, so the soul follows duty'.[10] Contrary to popular belief, duty is an obligation to perform an act by which an individual shows his respect to the right holder. Salmond defines duty as an act which one ought to do, an act the disregard of which would be

[6] *Ibid.*

[7] *Ibid.*

[8] Thomas Paine, The Rights of Man 1791.

[9] Anamika Singh and Shriya Badgaiyan, "Legal Rights", 2 *International Journal of Law and Legal Jurisprudence Studies* 6, 176–186. http://ijlljs.in/wp-content/uploads/2015/10/13.pdf (last accessed Oct. 29, 2021).

[10] "Notion Press' Latest is a new retelling of Valmiki's Ancient Epic; The Ramayana", available at https://notionpress.com/blog/valmikiya-ramayan-hindi-kavyanuwad/. (last accessed on November 25, 2021).

wrong.[11] The commission of a wrong is the breach of duty, and the performance of duty is avoidance of wrong. There can be no right without a corresponding duty and no duty without a corresponding right. Duguit totally rejects the idea of rights.[12] He says that man is a social animal and has many social relationships, and these relationships are always duties and never rights and that is why law contains only duties without any corresponding rights and the only right a person has is always to do his duty.[13]

In a community, all individuals are interlinked and interdependent. What one does or omits to do has a direct or indirect impact on others. Thus, one man's right is another man's duty and these rights can only be enjoyed when duties are performed well and effectively. Like, one's right to drive her/his car also brings along with it a correlative duty and responsibility to drive safely and without harming others and follow all traffic rules. To protect and safeguard the interest of others, everyone must obey their duties rightfully. Duties and rights are correlative, which implies that there can be no duty unless there is someone to whom it is due. Similarly, there can exist no right if there is not someone from whom it can be claimed.

Types of Duties

- Moral Duty—If a man is drowning in water and you jump in the water to save him, that is your moral duty. Even if you do not save him, you are under no obligation by law. It is merely by choice or conscience.
- Legal Duty—Paying tax to the government is a legal duty and is obligatory under law. If one tries to avoid it, then it is an offense and the person is liable for punishment.

Concept of Duty in Bhagavad Gita

Dharm is the first word and the central theme of Bhagavad Gita which forms the basis for karm. Though the word dharm has no precise equivalent English translation, it has been used interchangeably with the words 'duty' and 'virtue'. It has been defined as 'right action' or 'the path of righteousness' and is said to play a pivotal role in an individual's social, psychological, and spiritual life. It is highlighted during the war between the Kauravs and the Pandavs when the Pandav warrior, Arjun, faces a moral dilemma and is reluctant to fight. He adjures his charioteer, the God incarnate Krishn, to relieve him of his duty saying 'I will not fight'.[14] To this, Krishn responds that 'the duty of a soldier is to fight—and fight

---

[11] Anamika Singh & Shriya Badgaiyan, *supra* note 9.

[12] Srinivasan, "The Juristic and Political Ideas of Duguit", 1 *The Indian Journal of Political Science* 1, 1–22 (July—September, 1939) https://www.jstor.org/stable/42742907 (last accessed Oct. 28, 2021).

[13] *Ibid*.

[14] Shlok 9, Chap. 2, Bhagwad Gita available at https://www.gitasupersite.iitk.ac.in/srimad?language=dv&field_chapter_value=2&field_nsutra_value=9&ecsiva=1&etsiva=1&etpurohit=1&etgb=1&setgb=1&etssa=1&etassa=1&etradi=1&etadi=1. (last accessed on October 26, 2021).

well', urging the prince to fight the war and fulfill his duty as a warrior explaining that it is both his 'karm' and 'dharm' to fight. It is further said that it is far better to discharge one's duties faultily (as a Kshatriy) than to discharge another's duties perfectly (as a Brahman).

Duties in the Gandhian Perspective

According to M.K. Gandhi, the very performance of a duty secures us our right.[15] Rights cannot be divorced from duties. He highly emphasized in his writings on duties and identification of dharm as the path of duty. In pursuit of swaraj, i.e., self-rule, he dwells into the duty of self-discipline and argues that swaraj enables one to pursue arth and kam within the bounds of dharm. He upheld the path of dharm and considered the varnashram dharm as the appropriate path of duty. He states that 'varn is nothing more than an indication of a duty that has been handed down to each one of us by our forefathers'.[16] He vehemently believed in setting oneself free toward self-realization and self-rule through non-attachment to material possessions and belongings. He further held that 'Satyagrah was born, for I was always striving to decide what my duty was'.[17]

Gandhi's ideas and thoughts on one's duty are increasingly relevant today. Any movement he started or any discourse he took was under the influence of his dharm or duty. He considered his duty as supreme, and it guided him throughout. Even in his fight for the nation and his fellow beings, he never emphasized on rights. He believed that if one follows one's duty properly, then other's rights follow and the same goes for others.

Today, the scope of rights that the citizens demand and claim from the state is ever expanding. These rights include the right to decent and equal wages, right to education, right to work, right to healthcare, and right to a safe and good environment, to name a few. The state seeks to guarantee these rights to its citizens but it would have to incur colossal amounts of money to meet these obligations in the process. This would become all the more difficult for the state if citizens do not pay their taxes properly and on time. Therefore, every able-bodied individual must pay taxes on time and contribute to the wealth of the society and then the state will effectively and efficiently be able to meet its obligations and provide maximum rights and comforts to its citizens. Thus, an individual's rights are the duties of the state and, similarly, the duties of the individual are the rights of the state. Recently, Indian Prime Minister Narendra Modi has emphasized on the importance of

---

[15] "Quotes by Founding Fathers and Others on Citizens' Duties", available at https://doj.gov.in/sites/default/files/Quotes%20by%20founding%20fathers.pdf. (last accessed on November 26, 2021).

[16] G. N. Sarma, "Gandhi's Concept of Duty", 41 *The Indian Journal of Political Science* 2, 214–231 (1980).

[17] "Gandhi on Freedom, Rights and Responsibility", International Seminar on Gandhi and the Twenty First Century, available at https://www.gandhiashramsevagram.org/gandhi-articles/gandhi-on-freedom-rights-and-responsibility.php.) last accessed on October 26, 2021.

sensitizing children about the role of duties in the Constitution of India.[18] The Supreme Court has also said that since duties are obligatory for citizens, the state should make citizens aware of the same and strive to achieve the said goal.[19]

4 Rights Through the Glasses of Duties

Scholars debate whether rights and duties are two separate principles or they are connected in some ways. Salmond believed that no right can exist without a corresponding duty.[20] Every right or duty involves a bond of legal obligation by which two or more persons are bound together. Thus, there can be no duty unless there is someone to whom it is due and there can be no right unless there is someone from whom it is claimed. Further, there can be no wrong unless there is someone who is wronged, that is to say, someone whose right has been violated.

Gandhian emphasis on duties well performed than rights won is a great example for twenty-first century protestors indulged in violent protests for claiming their rights. Gandhi's first satyagrah in India was against the Indigo planters who, in nexus with the state apparatus, pauperized the peasants with impunity by forcing them to grow indigo. He made the authorities realized that the satyagrah was not to challenge the legitimacy of the state but against an illegitimate practice and the satyagrah was not in demand of a claimed right but a conscious performance of duty, he famously said in his trial.[21]

> I venture to make this statement not in any way in extenuation of the penalty to be awarded against me, but to show that I have disregarded the order served upon me not for want of respect for lawful authority, but in obedience to the higher law of our being, the voice of conscience.

When Gandhi faced racism in South Africa, he, instead of claiming his rights, focused on his duties. He took the task of rooting out the disease of racism as his responsibility. In his autobiography[22], he mentions the famous Pietermaritzburg train incident and his reactionary thought process on that[23]:

---

[18] "Modi's new love: Fundamental duties Indira Gandhi inserted in Constitution during Emergency", available at https://theprint.in/opinion/modis-new-love-fundamental-duties-indira-gandhi-inserted-in-constitution-during-emergency/326258/. (last accessed on November 28, 2021).

[19] Durga Das Basu, Introduction to the Constitution of India (Prentice Hall of India, New Delhi, 1993).

[20] Anamika Singh & Shriya Badgaiyan, *supra* note 9.

[21] Mahadev Desai, The Story of My Experiments with Truth (Navjivan, Ahmedabad, 1927).

[22] *Ibid*.

[23] *Ibid*.

> I began to think of my duty. Should I fight for my rights or go back to India, or should I go on to Pretoria without minding the insults, and return to India after finishing the case? It would be cowardice to run back to India without fulfilling my obligation. The hardship to which I was subjected was superficial—only a symptom of the deep disease of colour prejudice. I should try, if possible, to root out the disease and suffer hardships in the process. Redress for wrongs I should seek only to the extent that would be necessary for the removal of the colour prejudice.

As a lawyer, Gandhi held that his duty was not to prove the guilty innocent but to help the court to arrive at the truth.[24] He insisted that his clients tell him the whole truth; he dropped many cases when he discovered that he had been deceived. One of his friends, Parsi Rustomji, involved in smuggling, repentant enough, and came to Gandhi for help. He was advised to confess the truth to authorities and be prepared for both fine and punishment. Gandhi persuaded the authorities for compromise, and eventually, his friend was fined twice the amount smuggled. Gandhi wrote,[25] '*I felt that my duty was to befriend both parties and bring them together. I strained every nerve to bring about a compromise.*' This is in direct contrast with the present trend among lawyers, who advise their clients to snatch away their rights irrespective of the fact that the client had never ever performed his duty, leave apart the fact of being guilty.

It is unbelievable how Gandhi had devoted his life for the welfare and rights of the poor, weak, and downtrodden people. In the authors' view, the thing which makes him unique and different is his approach and philosophy toward such people and handling such situations. His journey was inspired and guided by a basic sense of regard for others and a sense of duty and responsibility toward his fellow mate, toward the society. His struggle seems not just a furious demand for rights but in a peaceful attempt to make the authorities realize what is right. So, in the twenty-first century we must learn a very important lesson from the life of Gandhi—it is better to see rights as responsibilities to fulfill not freebees to keep and chill.

5 Duties: The Tool for Social Change

The French Declaration of the Rights of Man and Citizen of 1789, and its even more liberal update of 1793, were answered by the conservative 1795 Declaration of the Rights and Duties of Man and Citizen which declares that 'The maintenance of society requires that those who compose it should both know and fulfill their duties'.[26] Rights start with self-assertion, whereas duties start with goodwill toward the society backed by a sense of responsibility and service. Performance of duties instead of demanding implementation of rights is an instant tool for bringing social

---

[24] Fischer Louis, Mahatma Gandhi His Life and Times (Bhartiya Vidya Bhawan, Mumbai, 1951).

[25] *Ibid.*

[26] "Declaration of Rights and Duties of Man and Citizen, Constitution of the Year III (1795)", available at https://chnm.gmu.edu/revolution/d/298. (last accessed on November 25, 2021).

change. Thus, it is right that demands or protests for rights may work as a great tool of changing governments but the only effective tool to bring about social change is performing duties.

Let us take one simple example of environmental pollution. The struggle of many environmentalists and social and political workers has resulted in the Supreme Court adjudging that the Constitution of India encompasses the right to clean environment under Article 21 of the Constitution.[27] Consequently, we have witnessed huge numbers of protests and even stronger voices demanding the implementation of the right to clean the environment. The irony of fate with us is that the environment is deteriorating day by day and we are unable to understand the simple fact that to bring social change we need to perform our duties rather than demanding performance of those by governments in the name of our rights.

Gandhi's famous remark that the 'earth has enough for man's needs but not for his greed' is most widely used in the sustainable development discourse throughout the world. He led a carbon-neutral life at a time when there was no concept of it. He was against conspicuous consumption and his simple living high thinking bodes well for today. In this climate-sensitive discourse, his ideas, especially on vegetarianism, help in reducing carbon footprint,[28] generating resource efficiency and circular economy. Gandhi speaks of rights in the context of duties and that is his distinctiveness; he considers 'real rights as a result of the performance of duty'.[29] Rights cannot be divorced from duties and that rights have to be exercised in the interests of all. For him, the concept of duty is derived from the idea of dispassionate action, advocated by Bhagavad Gita.

Vasudhaiv Kutumbakam is one of the lofty concepts that is representative of the unmatchable ideological stature of Hinduism. 'The whole world is a single family' or 'this whole earth is our family'—this statement enjoins humans to exhibit the highest sense of responsibility toward each other and the earth as they do in their respective families. Let us take a simple example of cleanliness, everybody feels they deserve cleanliness in their surroundings but is everybody willing to serve for the cause? In the 1901 annual session of Indian National Congress in Calcutta, Gandhi picked up a broom and cleaned the night soil from the venue of the session himself—a task which the high-born loathed as they believed it was reserved for lower class people. The Swachh Bharat Abhiyan (SBA) launched in 2014 is the modern reiteration of ancient vedic ideals. This is an appreciable step to make people realize their responsibility toward their Home (India) and their duties toward their extended family.

---

[27] *Subhash Kumar v. State of Bihar* (1991) 1 SCC 598.

[28] "Going vegan can help reduce greenhouse-gas emissions", Koduri Chaitanya, available at https://www.downtoearth.org.in/blog/going-vegan-can-help-reduce-greenhousegas-emissions-49341 (last accessed on November 25, 2021).

[29] "Gandhi", Hind Swaraj, available at https://www.mkgandhi.org/ebks/hind_swaraj.pdf. (last accessed on October 26, 2021).

At the time of independence, many harijans had written to Gandhi demanding that there be more than one harijan minister in the government of India. Explaining the importance of duties over demands Gandhi wrote on October 6, 1946[30]:

> I have received letters from Harijan friends and some have been to see me too. They feel that now that power is in the hands of the people, there should be more than one Harijan minister [in the cabinet of the government of the Republic of India]. According to the population ratio, the number should be at least three, and they should be similarly represented in every department….I am not ready to admit the correctness of all they say. My ideas in this regard are different….Rights spring only from duties well done. Such rights alone are becoming and lasting….Holding the views I do, and having acted on them and made others act on them over the last fifty years, I have no interest left in fighting for personal rights. I shall, therefore, advise Harijan brethren that they should think only of their duties. They may be sure that rights will follow fast on the heels of duties done.

The greater the powers you have greater is your responsibility, this principle does not only apply to superheroes in reel life but it applies equally in real life. The people with higher power and bigger stature in society hold greater responsibilities to fulfill their duties toward the nation and its people. Gandhi borrowed the idea of 'trusteeship' from John Ruskin's work 'Unto the Last'.[31] According to it, the rich hold the wealth as a trustee of the poor, and thus, the wealth earned must be spent on the welfare of the less privileged. This is essentially the philosophy behind the modern Corporate Social Responsibility (CSR) adopted by companies and mandated by law. In a letter of June 14, 1934, Gandhi wrote[32]:

> I welcome the rise of the Socialist Party in Congress. But I can't say that I like the program as it appears in the printed pamphlet. It seems to me to ignore Indian conditions and I do not like the assumption underlying many of its propositions which go to show that there is necessarily antagonism between the classes and the masses or between the labourers and the capitalist, such that they can never work for mutual good. My own experience covering a fairly long period is to the contrary. What is necessary is that labourers or workers should know their rights and should also know how to assert them. And since there never has been any right without a corresponding duty, in my opinion, a manifesto is incomplete without emphasizing the necessity of performance of duty and showing what duty is.

[30] "Compensation for Murder the collected works of Mahatma Gandhi", available at https://www.gandhiashramsevagram.org/gandhi-literature/mahatma-gandhi-collected-works-volume-92.pdf. (last accessed on November 25,2021).

[31] "Universal Benefit: Gandhi's Doctrine of Trusteeship", Bidyut Chakrabarty, available at https://doi.org/10.1017/S0026749X13000383 (last accessed on October 26,2021).

[32] "Gandhi On Corresponding Duties/Rights", Mark Lindley, available at https://www.gandhiashramsevagram.org/gandhi-articles/gandhi-on-corresponding-duties-rights.php. (last accessed on November 25, 2021).

6 Conclusion

Over two hundred years of colonial rule had made Indian masses mere subjects, who felt alienated and distant from state processes and thus lacked both a sense of rights as well as that of duties. Duties inherently bring restraint and a society which just got freedom after more the colonial rule might desist from it. The question that arises is whether restraint is helpful for societies? It has to be conceded that no human civilization with unfettered freedom has ever existed in the history of mankind. Further, the ethos of Indian civilization since long back put more emphasis on duties rather than rights.

Gandhi's individualism is less political and social than being ethical and religious which makes stronger appeal as it directly speaks to inner conscience. Gandhi did not fight for rights only but he had fought with the duty begotten state and reminded them time and again their duties. According to Gandhi, every man has an equal right to the necessaries of life even as birds and beasts have and since every right carries with it a corresponding duty and a corresponding remedy for resisting any attack upon it, and it is merely a matter of finding out the corresponding duties and remedies to vindicate the elementary fundamental equality.[33]

Gandhi speaks of rights in the context of duties and that is his distinctiveness; he considers 'real rights as a result of the performance of duty' meaning thereby that all rights (for them to be preserved as rights) are derived from duties which are performed well. Rights cannot be divorced from duties, and that rights have to be exercised in the interests of all. The concept of duty, for him, is derived from the idea of dispassionate action, which the Bhagavad Gita advocates.

Duty presupposes a twofold obligation—one is towards oneself and the other one towards the society while rights starts with self-assertion, duties start with discipline, self-discipline in particular, even to the extent of subordination to a higher authority or alternatively, to individual conscience as Gandhi called it the 'inner-voice'. This is one reason that while fighting for rights you might not bring change by yourself as the outcome is dependent on performance of duties by the authorities but performing your own duties is an instant tool for bringing the change within yourself as well as in the society.

References

Basu DD (1993) Introduction to the constitution of India, Prentice Hall of India, New Delhi
Bible, Matthew 7:12 available at https://biblehub.com/matthew/7-12.htm. Last visite on 26 Oct 2021

[33] "The Collected works of Mahatma Gandhi", available at https://www.gandhiashramsevagram.org/gandhi-literature/mahatma-gandhi-collected-works-volume-51.pdf. (last accessed on November 25, 2021).

Compensation for Murder the collected works of Mahatma Gandhi, Available at https://www.gandhiashramsevagram.org/gandhi-literature/mahatma-gandhi-collected-works-volume-92.pdf. Last visited on 25 Nov 2021

David C, Smith, William F, Stone (1989) Peace and human rights: H.G. Wells and the universal declaration. Canadian Mennonite University https://www.jstor.org/stable/23609935. Accessed 26 Oct 2021

Declaration of Rights and Duties of Man and Citizen, Constitution of the Year III (1795) available at https://chnm.gmu.edu/revolution/d/298. Last visited on 25 Nov 2021

Desai M (1927) The story of my experiments with truth, Navjivan, Ahmedabad

Fischer L (1951) Mahatma Gandhi his life and times (Bhartiya Vidya Bhawan, Mumbai

Gandhi on Corresponding Duties/Rights, Mark Lindley, available at https://www.gandhiashramsevagram.org/gandhi-articles/gandhi-on-corresponding-duties-rights.php. Last visited on 25 Nov 2021

Gandhi on Freedom, Rights and Responsibility, International seminar on Gandhi and the twenty first century, available at https://www.gandhiashramsevagram.org/gandhi-articles/gandhi-on-freedom-rights-and-responsibility.php. Last visited on 26 Oct 2021

"Gandhi", Hind Swaraj, available at https://www.mkgandhi.org/ebks/hind_swaraj.pdf. Last visited on 26 Oct 2021

Going vegan can help reduce greenhouse-gas emissions, Koduri Chaitanya, available at https://www.downtoearth.org.in/blog/going-vegan-can-help-reduce-greenhousegas-emissions-49341. Last visited on 25 Nov 2021

Hindustani The collected works of Mahatama Gandhi https://www.gandhiashramsevagram.org/gandhi-literature/mahatma-gandhi-collected-works-volume-97.pdf. Last visited on 25 Nov 2021

Kumar S (1991) v. State of Bihar 1 SCC 598

Modi's new love: fundamental duties Indira Gandhi inserted in Constitution during Emergency, available at https://theprint.in/opinion/modis-new-love-fundamental-duties-indira-gandhi-inserted-in-constitution-during-emergency/326258/. Last visited on 28 Nov 2021

Notion Press' Latest is a new retelling of Valmiki's Ancient Epic; The Ramayana, available at https://notionpress.com/blog/valmikiya-ramayan-hindi-kavyanuwad/. Last visited on Nov 25 2021

Paine T (1791) The rights of man

Quotes by Founding Fathers and Others on Citizens' Duties, available at https://doj.gov.in/sites/default/files/Quotes%20by%20founding%20fathers.pdf. Last visted on 26 Nov 2021

Sarma GN (1980) Gandhi's concept of duty. Indian J Polit Sci 41(2):214–231

Shlok 47, Chapter 2, Bhagwad Gita available at https://www.gitasupersite.iitk.ac.in/srimad?htrskd=1&httyn=1&htshg=1&scsh=1&choos=&&language=dv&field_chapter_value=2&field_nsutra_value=47. Last visited on 25 Nov 2021

Shlok 9, Chapter 2, Bhagwad Gita available at https://www.gitasupersite.iitk.ac.in/srimad?language=dv&field_chapter_value=2&field_nsutra_value=9&ecsiva=1&etsiva=1&etpurohit=1&etgb=1&setgb=1&etssa=1&etassa=1&etradi=1&etadi=1. Last visited on 26 Oct 2021

Singh A, Badgaiyan S (2021) Legal rights. Int J Law Legal Jurisprudence Stud 2(6):176–186. http://ijlljs.in/wp-content/uploads/2015/10/13.pdf. Accessed 29 Oct 2021

Srinivasan N (1939) The juristic and political ideas of Duguit. Indian J Polit Sci 1(1), 1–22 https://www.jstor.org/stable/42742907 Accessed 28 Oct 2021

The Collected works of Mahatma Gandhi, available at https://www.gandhiashramsevagram.org/gandhi-literature/mahatma-gandhi-collected-works-volume-51.pdf. Last visited on 25 Nov 2021

Universal Benefit: Gandhi's Doctrine of Trusteeship, Bidyut Chakrabarty, available at https://doi.org/10.1017/S0026749X13000383. Last visited on 26 Oct 2021. Available at http://www.smmpalwal.com/SILR_PALWAL/pdf/2ndsem/ballb6/ballb6thsem2.pdf. Last visited on 25 Nov 2021

Chapter 12
Liberal Individualism and Public Health: Case Study of Coronavirus Pandemic in Gandhian Duties' Context

Rajesh Ganesh Parthsarthi

1 COVID-19 Pandemic: The Public Health Emergency

A novel coronavirus, SARS-CoV-2, is the pathological entity that has caused the coronavirus disease 2019 (COVID-19) pandemic.[1] This respiratory ailment originated in Wuhan city of China[2] and subsequently has engulfed the entire globe.[3] With no pre-existing immunity in humans and mutating strains of the virus characterized by high infectivity and low case fatality rate, all 222 countries, territories, and geographical areas[4] have been affected by the presence of viruses, which have been reported in animals too.[5] Severe disease or death is caused only in a small proportion of the infected population, those having other comorbidities. A big proportion of the infected population remains healthy and asymptomatic carriers and keeps spreading the disease. Infected droplets harbouring the virus come out of the infected persons, and they either remain airborne or subsist on various surfaces where a new person gets the infection and carries it forward. The second, third, and incumbent subsequent

---

[1] World Health Organisation 2019.

[2] *Ibid.*

[3] WHO Coronavirus disease (COVID-19) pandemic situation, 2021, Confirmed cases-82 579 768, Confirmed deaths-1 818 849, Countries, areas or territories with cases-222.

[4] *Ibid.*

[5] Chapple A, 'Up Close with the enemy: The Coronavirus in stunning detail' available at https://www.rferl.org/a/microscope-photos-capture-coronavirus-in-stunning-detail/30518135.html (last accessed 27 May, 2020).

R. G. Parthsarthi (✉)
MBBS, Medical Director at Janaki Healthcare and Diagnostic Centre, New Delhi, India
e-mail: rajesh.parthsarthi@gmail.com

LL.B. Campus Law Centre, Faculty of University of Delhi, Delhi, India

LL.M. Indian Law Institute, New Delhi, Delhi, India

R. Mittal and K. K. Singh (eds.), *Relevance of Duties in the Contemporary World*,
https://doi.org/10.1007/978-981-19-1836-0_12

waves have caused real uncertainties and concerns especially for the developing world.

1.1 *Public Health Crises as an Eye-Opener for the Global Health Systems*

Working in unknown territory with reactive countermeasures, the pandemic preparedness and virus containment strategies of countries have used a sizable amount of State's resources, in order to save the unexposed populations and carry out the core functions of the public health law. The rapidity of global spread has been a fallout of globalization with increased trade and economic activities among international communities necessitating people travelling far and wide. Such disease outbreaks are mostly zoonotic infections that result from close interactions between humans and animals (mostly wild) as people are more inclined to experience alien things that they come across in a globalized village. Industrialization and urbanization with urban conglomerates having dense populations with unsafe and unhygienic conditions of housing and living further contributed to the outbreak having increased intensity and spread. India saw large-scale internal and external migrations letting the virus reach every nook and corner quickly and affect the hitherto untouched parts. The development of effective vaccines stipulated to have a neutralizing effect on viruses and providing pre-existing immunity takes its own time. There has been a dearth of evidence-based effective medical treatment modalities that can stop the virus from multiplying in the human body. Safety, efficacy, and adverse effect issues have been further put into question in respect of newer vaccines and therapeutic armamentarium hastily developed. As the humans harbour the virus which goes on multiplying unchecked, it leads to debilitating physical and mental conditions in vulnerable populations pre-laced with comorbid conditions, with the use of steroids resulting in severe post-COVID effects. Quarantines, lockdowns, social and physical distancing, personal hygiene including hand hygiene, contact tracing, testing, and treating have been the measures resorted to, which in the absence of effective remedies have resulted in a colossal cumulative loss of persons and properties. Severe shortages of supplies of social consumption of health and healthcare facilities in face of huge demands for health resources such as personal protective kits, health workforce, essential medicines, beds, oxygen, intensive care units, and ventilators have put severe resource constraints on health infrastructure. All geographies have eagerly waited to see R-naught becoming less than one, signifying the peak intensity with receding infections gradually reaching the last of pandemic phases.[6] States have

[6] Ramirez (2020), R naught is a mathematical term indicating how contagious and infectious the disease is. Also referred to as the reproduction number, R0 for COVID-19 is a median of 5.7 meaning one infected person can transmit coronavirus to 5-6 people. $R0 < 1$, decreasing epidemic situation. Also, it is deduced that 82 percent of the population needs to be immune through vaccination or herd immunity before transmission stops.

struggled in the face of economic recession, joblessness, hunger, and civil unrest with enormous safety concerns affecting peace and justice for significant proportions of the population. The unanswered question remains whether this public health emergency could have been avoided for one, or if there were ways to manage it better, but 'how' is the million dollar question.

1.2 Public Health Crises and Human Rights to Health

Public health crises test the endurance of the functioning of the multiple organs of governance as well as the collective conscience of individuals. Pandemic management requires international coordination among State Parties responding to the emergencies with a show of cooperation and solidarity for mitigating damaging effects on the human rights of peoples as mandated by Article 1.3 of the United Nations Charter.[7] Measures intended for preventing the spread of infection leading to the earliest possible recovery of health and safety requires respect of human rights in its entirety which is in contrast to piecemeal or *en bloc* derogation which has taken place in many situations and in many territories affected with the pandemic. Such aggravated nature of public health emergencies is known for its short-term and long-term consequences and requires a timely and planned address for the restoration of health, economy, and rights of people. Context-based appropriate and adequate access to healthcare justice is required in a non-discriminatory manner for all ailing, especially the deprived, vulnerable, and marginalized sections. Pre-existing barriers of gender, sexual orientation, age, and other disabilities as well as for people in detention require to be addressed with their own specific needs. Containment efforts need clubbing of education and information measures for the subjects, with the issuance of necessary guidelines through proper channels of national and international agencies. Amendments and implementations of laws are focused on keeping people safe. International instruments dealing with the right to health guarantees are found in Article 12 of the International Covenant on Economic, Social and Cultural Rights[8]

---

[7] The United Nations Charter, Article1.3 states the purpose of UN as 'To achieve international co-operation in solving international problems of an economic, social, cultural, or humanitarian character, and in promoting and encouraging respect for human rights and for fundamental freedoms for all without distinction as to race, sex, language, or religion'.

[8] The International Covenant on Economic Social and Cultural Rights ('ICESCR'), Article 12.

1The States Parties to the present Covenant recognize the right of everyone to the enjoyment of the highest attainable standard of physical and mental health.

2. The steps to be taken by the States Parties to the present Covenant to achieve the full realization of this right shall include those necessary for:

(a) The provision for the reduction of the stillbirth-rate and of infant mortality and for the healthy development of the child;

(b) The improvement of all aspects of environmental and industrial hygiene;

(c) The prevention, treatment and control of epidemic, endemic, occupational and other diseases;

(d) The creation of conditions which would assure all medical service and medical attention in the event of sickness.

which mandate State Parties for ensuring the realization of rights through legislative measures and international assistance.[9] The Committee on Economic, Social and Cultural Rights (a body comprising independent experts for the monitoring of state implementations) in its General Comments 14 offers an interpretation of the content as an explanatory note and guides with clarification of the treaty obligations for the best use of the instrument by the State Parties. As per the instrument, the right to health is a fundamental human right and is indispensable in order to exercise other human rights. All human beings are entitled to enjoying the highest attainable standard of health which is conducive to a life with dignity. Availability, accessibility, and affordability of health care are of prime importance which the State must ensure with quality and safety for its inhabitants, including lawful citizens as well as asylum seekers, refugees, and immigrants. The international instrument, International Health Regulations 2005, pertains to health and safety and emphasizes on the right to prevention, treatment, and control of outbreaks with education in respect of health related behaviours. Further, treatment in accidents, outbreaks, and disaster relief requires the creation of urgent medical care systems to overcome emergencies. International soft laws prescribe supranational and transnational obligations explicitly and encourage State Parties to build capacities especially for providing health facilities in low-income states, thus ensuring the right to high-quality affordable health services.

1.3 Public Health Cosmopolitanism and Global Distributive Health Justice

When there is a rise of considerable dissatisfaction for the functioning of democratic institutions in many nations, equally there is strong public support to be found for democratic ideals. Democracy is an idea, and more than that it has been practiced at work. Liberal constitutional democracies have been growing in numbers as compared to the growth of other systems of governance.[10] As stated by Rawls, among the five kinds of identified societies, liberal states have been responsibilized with duties to assist burdened states which find it daunting to form just domestic institutions lacking enough resources in its territories.[11] There is a justification in armed aggression which liberal and civilized states may carry out against outlawed

[9] *Ibid.*, ICESCR, Article 2.

Each State Party to the present Covenant undertakes to take steps, individually and through international assistance and cooperation, especially economic and technical, to the maximum of its available resources, with a view to achieving progressively the full realization of the rights recognized in the present Covenant by all appropriate means, including particularly the adoption of legislative measures.

[10] Desilver D, 'Despite global concerns about democracy, more than half of countries are democratic' (2019) available at https://www.pewresearch.org/fact-tank/2019/05/14/more-than-half-of-countries-are-democratic/. (last accessed 5 June, 2020).

[11] Rawls J, The Law of the People, Harvard University Press (1999).

states for the protection of human rights, Rawls opines. Kantian cosmopolitanism is founded on the basis of liberal democratic governments recognizing the human rights of both citizens as well as foreigners.[12] Kant and Grotius have a concurrence with respect to independent nations having moral obligations to all three constituencies consisting of fellow citizens, wider societies of states, and the universal community of humankind. Thomas Pogge posits the word 'cosmopolitan' to have acquired a secondary meaning. The theory as a person's commitment to cosmopolitanism deals equally in normative aspects of how things ought to be in a global context than how they currently exist.[13] Pogge's cosmopolitan assessment and prescription takes into account the interests of all human beings in an equitable manner. Rawls' social justice is Pogge's social justice cosmopolitanism and is the most promising conception in the normative and moralistic sense for global distributive justice. In contrast, legal cosmopolitanism has its emphasis on institutional designs for founding universal legal society, providing for a single power with one rule for the whole world which is feared to turn despotic and tyrannical while social justice cosmopolitanism is based on human conduct improving the social fabric. Legal cosmopolitanism recognizes original positions to be different, for people born in affluence and those into poverty, which creates an injustice primarily to be redressed. The corresponding diagnosis of social justice conception is based on institutional order, giving rise to the unequal starting position as unjust.[14] While the former focuses on the States of the world for its assessment and improving the positions of States per se, later tries to reform the institutions like patriarchy, racial, and caste-based discriminating agencies, which give rise to unequal positions in society. In societies based on justice, political institutions seek equal opportunities for people, whereas societies having social justice have social institutions designed in such a fashion that they automatically have equal positions for people. Kantian cosmopolitanism has a plurality of independent states merging voluntarily and peacefully for a common goal, a state which is preferable to universal monarchy achieved by conquest.[15] Perpetual world peace possibilities in a Kantian sense are likely to result in healthcare access justice for global citizens. All efforts for legal cosmopolitanism without reforming social institutions result in global injustice as is reflected in the Oxfam report. It is reported that the world's 2153 billionaires have more wealth than 4.6 billion human people on the earth (60% of the world's population).[16] The report observes that the rich–poor divide has deepened and the number of billionaires has doubled in the last decade. Seldom a government seems to be ready for any inequality busting policy, rather on the contrary government itself is responsible for an inequality crisis in many situations as exemplified by

[12] Kant I, Perpetual Peace: A Philosophical Essay (1795), Cosimo Classics, NY (2010).

[13] Pogge TW, World Poverty and Human Rights: Cosmopolitan Responsibilities and Reforms, Polity Press, Cambridge (2002).

[14] Pogge TW, Cosmopolitanism: A Path to Peace and Justice, In: Goodin RE, Pogge T (ed.), Cosmopolitanism, A Companion to Contemporary Political Philosophy, Blackwell, London (2001).

[15] Kant I, Groundwork of the Metaphysics of Morals (1785), In trans: Wood AW (2002), Yale University Press, New Haven.

[16] Oxfam, 'World's billionaires have more wealth than 4.6 billion people: Fight Inequality, Beat poverty', World Economic Forum, Davos, Switzerland.

Zimbabwe, by providing access to safe drinking water for its women citizens, it can save four hours per woman per day, which may be utilized in other productive works than in commuting and carrying water. The human rights crisis is often resulting from deliberate man-made designs giving rise to social and economic inequalities. Original position in the 'veil of ignorance' experiment of Rawls, by doing away with race, religion, life status, and hierarchy is able to recreate a just society.[17] Rawls sensitizes humanity to man-made developmental errors which have seen countries rich in natural resources as being kept in sustained poverty by bankers, rulers, and foreign nations for their own vested interests.[18]

1.4 International and the Municipal Bodies' Response to the Situation

This study, having introduced discourses on public health crises and rights aligned with cosmopolitanism and global distributive justice, seeks to address relevant issues in two parts. Part I surveys the concept of individual liberty if it is a boon or bane for global public health justice and right to health guarantees for global citizens in a consequentialist manner. Part II put forth an analysis of Gandhian deontology in the current context of supranational legislation by international institutions. These international instruments are used to read the rights and the duties of the State Parties and translate the same for each individual, if it is successful in preventing and mitigating the health crisis. The paper emphasizes on rights being correlative to duties. Day-to-day tackling of public health situations as they evolve, with all the organs of governance reading the crisis in concurrence, and adapting their tools and techniques combating the contagion, is part of the study. Resource allocation and sharing in the present situation with an eye on future impacts on the life of a common man is seen in the context of the Gandhian prescription on duties (dharm). How far international instruments in its normative framework and municipal legislations dealing with crises are aligned with the duty focussed approach, and what amounts of such measures are likely to continue in the future public health research.

2 Liberal Individualism: Boon or Bane for Public Health

Liberty does not descend upon a people
A people must raise themselves to liberty.
It is a blessing that must be earned before it is enjoyed.

---

[17] Rawls J, A Theory of Justice, Harvard University Press (1971).

[18] Wenar L, Property Rights and the Resource Curse, 36 *Philosophy and Public Affairs*, Blackwell Publishing Inc. (2008).

Charles Caleb Colton

2.1 *Individual Autonomy and Public Health*

Individualism as a political philosophy, ideology, or moral stance emphasizes the moral worth of the individual. This is one of the most criticized and least understood ideas among social scientists and political philosophers of the day. General queries pertaining to this ideology are (1) Does this define an individual's ability to act independently amid multiplicities of social forces? and, (2) Whether by its nature, it is to unify individuals with the communities, or does it work as a force keeping them apart? Individualists value their independence and based on their self-reliance seem to promote their goals and desires. Mostly, it advocates individual interests to have precedence over the interests of other social groups or the State as an entity.

2.1.1 Dangers of Extreme Individualism

In contrast to collectivism and totalitarianism, individualist tradition began with a negative connotation of intentional avoidance of social groups, echoing that human life can be lived away from larger communities and happily too. Sometimes it amounts to the unilateral imposition of individualistic and private ideas on larger social groups which possibly affects others' lives adversely. Thus, selfish individuals may pose a threat of destruction of common goods, and individualism thus gets exposed thoroughly as an ideology of advancement of humankind. In the same vein, serial killers or serial rapists exemplify extreme individualism.[19] American culture has seen abandoning family ties and breeding of hostile loners with a fascination for serial offenses which often get glamorized in the media.[20] Contrast to this, Asian culture protects older people within the cocoon of loving extended family.[21] There is an increased vulnerability of elderly in the Western societies when exposed to extreme forms of dangers of individualism there. Several scholars concur with the opinion of individualism being divorced from moral prescription and assessment being detrimental to the interests of humankind.

[19] Wiest JB, Casting Cultural Monsters, representations of Serial Killers in US and UK News Media, Howard J Communication 27:327-346 (2016).

[20] Robinson L and Shultz J, Role of Mass Media and New Media Cultures, Communication and Information Technology Annual, Emerald GroupPublishers (2016).

[21] Shared 'care' and reciprocal relationship of carer and care recipient augurs well for 'value living' of the entire older section in Japan where elderlies are looked upon with respect, and families and societies are of utmost concern for their safety and well-being.

2.1.2 Proponents' Views

Individualism as per Maccall is the reason for the accumulation of property and wealth, thus resulting in increased happiness.[22] As per Jung, the process of individuation is central to human development.[23] Mill has dealt with a continuous struggle between liberty and authority with liberty as the means of protecting against tyrannical power.[24] His discourse projects rulers or authorities as antagonistic to the subjects of their rule. Those ruled, in turn, instead of being subjects to innumerable vultures give the ruler the power to rule in a social contract for protecting them from other powers. The power of the ruler thus is kept subject to limitations which is the foundational element of a democratic government and recognized as the rule of law, constitutionalism, separation of powers, protection of human rights, etc. The social contract establishing modern governments is based on the pretext of limiting governmental powers and giving liberty to individuals.

2.1.3 Media Freedom: A Case Study

Mill's free speech theory has three-fold roles of free speech and press: (1) it leads to the evolution of truth, (2) it has functions of shaping good governance, and (3) it functions as a bedrock for individual autonomy.[25] Mill has extended the liberal idea of Milton and Locke, to read with freedom of the press. Press is a profit-making concern and run by a group of individuals and with time develops its own interests of doing business and making a profit.[26]

The aftermath of the Second World War has seen the advent of the supranational roles of international institutions. The International Bill of Rights being held as *jus cogens* is regarded premptory norm. The Universal Declaration of Human Rights (UDHR) states[27]:

> Everyone has the right to freedom of opinion and expression; this right includes freedom to hold opinions without interference, and to seek, receive and impart information and ideas through any media, and regardless of frontiers.

---

[22] Maccall W, Elements of Individualism, A Series of Lectures, John Chapman, London (1847).

[23] Jung C, 'Analytical Psychology' (1962) available at https://www.carl-jung.net/individuation_steps.html. (last accessed 7 June, 2020). In Analytical Psychology, Jung states that through individuation process, an individual self develops with an undifferentiated unconsciousness as a part of developmental psychic process. Individuation is an innate element of personality, and it helps identify a person as an individual that is not someone else.

[24] Mill J S, On Liberty, John W. Parker and Sons, West Strand, London (1859) in Chapter I, Introduction.

[25] *Ibid*.

[26] Sivakumar S, Press Law and Journalists: Watchdog to Guidedog, Universal Law Publishing, New Delhi (2015).

[27] The Universal Declaration of Human Rights (1948), Shaping our future together, The United Nations.

The Press and Media function as the fourth pillar in a democracy with its specific role as a watchdog. For this, it requires special powers of speech and expression for the function of watching the other three organs, *viz.* legislative, executive, and judiciary. It may have varied interests of business, region, and religion, but all-inclusive, its functional role remains watching only and not biting. While watchdog media has a check and balance function in a democracy, the guide-dog media functions as a social necessity by keeping the citizens informed and updated about government functions. On the contrary, the guard dog media guards one-sided interests of business or politics and is increasingly seen as a social reality in modern times. The fourth kind, the lap-dog media, functions as a governments' mouthpiece.

2.1.4 The Balancing Act

As the fourth estate in democracy, the media is mandated to carry out the functions of communication, dissemination, propagation, education, and information. The development of four different kinds of media persona relates to unregulated freedom which paves way for lack of professionalism and moralism. With a similar analogy drawn, it may be put forth that in a plural society, excessive emphasis on individual autonomy without correlating it with duty and morality leads to the development of certain guard dog personalities who are focussed on serving their own interests even at the cost of harming others.

2.2 Individual Autonomy and Freedom

Isaiah Berlin deliberates on negative and positive liberties. A person is unfree if his liberty is restricted or interfered with.[28] If the restriction exceeds a certain minimum, it will lead to coercion or enslavement. While negative liberties mean free from interference, this allows an individual mature and develop, positive liberties instead mean freedom to do an act and necessarily represent the Kantian self-governance of human beings. The author finds it relevant to discuss the social contract theory of Hobbes, Locke, Rousseau at this juncture, with its later developments, with focus on individualism and socialism. Man's beginning in the state of nature saw no government or law regulating them. Hardships and oppressions from different sections of society led them to enter into agreements of *pactum unionis* and *pactum subjectionis.* First, they undertook to respect each other living in peace and harmony, and secondly, people united together with a pledge to obey an authority to whom they surrendered part or whole of their freedom and rights. This authority in turn guaranteed for protection of their life and property, which in later times assumed the name of the sovereign, government, or State. In *Leviathan*, man's life in the state

[28] Berlin I, Two Concepts of Liberty in Four Essays on Liberty, Oxford University Press (1969).

of nature was filled with fear and selfishness, and it was solitary, short, and poor.[29] Hobbes has echoed absolutism in the transformation from the state of nature to the authority of a ruler with people surrendering all their rights and vesting all liberties in the sovereign. This arrangement or social contract was based on 'might is right' principle with the bargain of peace and prosperity for the subjects. This mechanistic prescription of Hobbes categorizes human beings as self-interested entities who work for their personal best. Though Hobbesian theory has recognition of human capacities in fulfilling their desire efficiently and maximally, it is founded on the principles of materialism, utilitarianism, and individualism. Locke emphasized life in the state of nature necessarily being good, with a major concern of lacking security of the property. Lockeans recognize the 'state of nature' as the golden age where a sense of goodwill and mutual assistance prevailed with peaceful coexistence among people. This phase found all human beings as independent and equal and hence was perfect with men exercising their liberties. For Locke, this pre-political state was not necessarily pre-moral as it focused on peaceful pursuance of human endeavours. The Lockean social contract is primarily concerned with the protection of private property as people mixing their labour with raw material increasingly created and developed private interests. Locke, thus, provides for established laws, impartial tribunals, and regulatory bodies, for protecting man's interests and properties.[30] Lockean treatises held people surrendering rights as not absolute but only extending to the preservation of, and enforcement of a law of nature. Rest all the rights, as the right to life, liberty, and estate remained with people as part of natural and inalienable rights. Law has no validity in case of government failure in the performance of its assigned tasks, and in such a situation, it can be legitimately thrown out. Locke disregards Hobbesenian principles in unlimited sovereignty being contrary to natural law and advocates a state of liberty as not being the state of license. The Lockean government is a constitutionally limited government and is for the general good of the people. His social contract theory proved to be the foundation for the Declaration of American Independence, securing him the place of the father of liberalism. Rousseau found the invention of private property as the single most factor responsible for humanity's fall from grace. His 'General Will' was the will of the community where an individual surrendered his rights, and this 'general will' being the creator of the State as well as the state's laws. The government not functioning in accordance with the general will of the people can be discarded. This modern conception of social contract provides for people's rights and liberties. Individual capitalism founded on unregulated industrial and scientific development, is not fully subscribing to the general will, and it serves only the minority capital interest, thus giving rise to inequalities in society. Such rising inequality and poverty level is the biggest polluter of humankind and its natural habitat.

---

[29] Hobbes T, The Matter (1651), Forme and Power of a Common-Wealth Ecclesiastical And Civil Commonly referred to as Leviathan (Penguin Classic, 1982).

[30] Locke J, Two Treatises of Government, A. Churchill, London (1690).

2.2.1 Individual Autonomy and Rise of Capitalism

General assembly resolution for decolonization has been the factor responsible for the world being divided into two powerful blocs.[31] Communism receding in influence, and the communist bloc dissolution following the fall of the Berlin wall, had their own internal factors to blame. This event furthered the debates on constitutionalism, rule of law, democracy as all these ideologies are nearer to capitalism than socialism. The capitalist monopoly with no counterbalancing force propelled the supranational agencies like the United Nations in assisting countries for their Constitution-making in the post-cold war era. The increasing clout of capitalist forces through the establishment of democracy and rule of law in most territories is re-invention of exploitative relations between haves and have-nots in a newer context.[32] In terms of patents and innovations, the situation favours rights holders' interests and keeps a larger section of the world population away from the benefits of inventions. Modernity comes at a price and all are not supposed to afford it. Thus, we find that evolution of laws has lacked the moral content, focus being on exploiting humans rather than being a force in service of it. Such a modernist approach could lead to the Nazi holocaust, and henceforth postmodernists and critical legal thinkers have pointed to interrogating such developments. Codified laws are often the constitution of societies' biased approach towards depriving marginalized segments, thus helping only the interests of those making the laws.[33] Powerful and rich find the law as a tool of exploitation, which helps maintain their place in the hierarchy. If a law is to sub-serve the masses, hierarchical systems need to be done away with, is the opinion of critical legal scholars.

2.2.2 Liberal Individualism and Free-Market Capitalism

Liber refers to free men who are neither serfs nor slaves. Liberalism as an ideology is deeply permeated in the western socioeconomic culture and in life as being part of individualism, tolerance, and progress. It prevailed in ancient Greece and Rome as an intellectual tradition and political current. Liberal outlook also finds expression in the philosophical thinking of Hobbes and Locke. In general, it relates to ideas of generosity, open-mindedness, choice, and freedom. Andrew Heywood states:

> The central theme of liberal ideology is a commitment to the individual and the desire to construct a society in which people can satisfy their interests and achieve fulfillment.

Liberals find human beings to be endowed with reasons. Spencer emphasizes individual rights for equal freedoms, self-interests of people as a cause of prosperity, and

[31] UNGA resolution, Declaration on the Granting of Independence to Colonial Countries and Peoples, A/RES/1514 (XV) of 14 Dec. 1960.

[32] Sripati V, The United Nations Role in Post-Conflict Constitution-Making Process: TWAIL Insights, 10 *International Community Law Review* 411-420 (2008).

[33] Critical Legal Theory, Legal Information Institute (2020) Available at https://www.law.cornell.edu/wex/critical_legal_theory. (last accessed 5 June, 2020).

life improvements in numerous ways.[34] Men have the freedom to act as long as they do not infringe on somebody else's equal freedom.[35] He advocates people having the right to ignore the State and drop connection with the State by relinquishing protection provided by it and refusing to pay towards its support. Acting in this manner with his passive actions he is not trenching the liberty of others as he is not an aggressor. Spencer focused on extraordinary human progress as a result of people being free. Individual human efforts when working freely without any government facilities or hindrances have resulted in food production, town buildings, communication networks, scientific progress, and increased productivity in many fields. Spencer is in concurrence with F. A. Hayek holds spontaneous market actions responsible for the most stunning human achievements without any help from central planning. Hayek advocates individuals to participate freely with the market as liberating forces without being subject to excessive controls.[36] Thus, individuals are left free to decide their own ethical compass with the state as protector of their private properties as Hayek renders libertarian justification for free-market capitalism.[37]

2.2.3 Liberty and Freedom

Three bundles of freedom denote individual liberty. The first bundle is legal or political freedom, which has negative connotations, and comprises (i) limited government, (ii) rule of law, (iii) speech freedom, (iv) freedom to associate and move, (v) freedom to profess and propagate a faith or religion, and (vi) freedom to change a government. The second bundle is the seat of economic freedom consisting *of laissez-faire* in relation to a domestic free-market economy and international free trade. The third bundle as social freedom is equality before law and equal protection guaranteed in the form of toleration of dissenting behaviour and consenting adults' acts.

Liberty as a normative conception is open to a multitude of interpretations, and its central concerns are its constitutive elements. Libertarian conception necessarily means 'certain conditions must be met,' as more than the opportunities of being free, this means to use the opportunities in such a manner to realize oneself fully. A discussion pertaining to freedom and its concerns of autonomy and morality has all the contextual relevance in the present public health crisis. The current situation warrants for the re-exploration of the categorical imperative of Kant and the moral man of Gandhi, for the basic health guarantees at the global level. State's obsession with military and economic power and economic man's materialistic quests has left social goods and social expenditure in health at dearth and lurch. Individuals' free choices are pitted against coercive laws of the state which stand for curbing

[34] Spencer H, Social Statics: Or, the Conditions Essential to Human Happiness Specified John Chapman, London (1851).

[35] *Ibid.*

[36] Hayek F A, The Constitution of Liberty and Law, University of Chicago Press (1960). As a pioneer in monetary theory and leading proponent of classical liberalism.

[37] Hayek FA, The Fatal Conceit: The Errors of Socialism, University of Chicago Press (1988).

freedom in liberal societies. Allowing individuals to make choices without excessive curbs and without the State's interference is the prerequisite of being a free society. Individual rationality and freedom for making free and fair choices are foundational in developing societies. The Kantian notion of freedom is based on self-legislation and self-governance of individuals, with self-reasonings and self-directed actions. Kantian philosophy weaves freedom, autonomy, and morality together with a categorical imperative, or a *priori maxim*. Its universal appeal is to individuals following only those laws and actions which they want others to imbibe unconditionally in the same conditions. Kant emphasizes an individual's maturity on the enlightenment path once the person explores the best ways to develop himself without the aid of external assistance and without being interfered with by outside forces. Kantian ethical understanding is grounded on free will and autonomy in the absence of guidance by religion or faith. The moral normative influence makes Kantian categorical imperative good in itself and does not need any external approval or justifications. Kant finds real happiness, not in hypothetical imperative or dictates of consequentialism, but deontology provides moral foundations to all actions precluding the requirement of approval by any agency. In the same breadth, Misesian praxeology rejects 'economic man' as a very narrow conception. Economics has logical implications for all human actions and not necessarily for the economic actions only, when in the pursuit of goals.[38] Mises has drawn profusely from Max Weber's version of *Verstehen*, a tool used by historians for having an understanding of historical actions founded on the basis of an individual human's motive. The father of the free-market economy, Adam Smith, interrogated the flip side of economic self-interest and made a statement for the greater good in his treatise *The Theory of Moral Sentiments* with philosophical, ethical, psychological, and methodical underpinnings for the growth of later literature. His writings accept the ideology of man being capable of forming moral judgements and which in turn are centred on his own self-interest. For Smith, universal happiness of all people is the concern of almighty god, men's immediate concern remains caring for their own happiness and that of their family, friends, and country. The famous 'invisible hand' theorization provides for the distribution of life's necessities with the interests of society being advanced as a result of 'the rich' dividing the produce of their improvements with other thousands in their employments. The two different sets of people as the 'person principally concerned' and the 'spectator' are imbibed with different virtues. The persons principally concerned demonstrate self-denial and self-government, while spectators with candid condescension and indulgent humanity enter into the emotional environment of the persons principally concerned.

[38] Mises L, Human Action: A Treatise on Economics. Indianapolis, In: Liberty Fund (2007).

3 Human Rights Violations in Public Health Crises

Public health crisis situations such as the coronavirus pandemic demand solidarity of human efforts in all societies, communities, and governments. It needs measures with unity of approach in order to mitigate the deadly effects of the virus and halting its spread in unexposed geographies. Respecting human rights and liberties of people in all the endeavours the state undertakes and functioning of supranational and international authorities on similar lines remain instrumental for fighting crisis situations.

X.3.1 ***Access to health care*** for all human beings without discriminations of age, sex, religion, race, disability, mental illness, and for those most vulnerable and marginalized is the first requirement in events of healthcare crisis. Such pre-existing barriers need to be identified and addressed to ensure no one remains without medical treatment because of physical, social, or economic factors impeding access. Civil societies, local communities, and human rights commissions help identify weaker sections needing special and additional care, who may be missed or be excluded, and give feedback to authorities about the impact of measures taken for such marginalized communities. States with shortages of health infrastructures are unable to meet the mounting requirements for each section of society. Prioritization of available resources for the select section is bound to result in human rights violation for those left out.

X.3.2 ***Housing*** is one of the basic needs of human living, and safe habitable conditions for all human beings are one of the goals all governments aspire to provide. Lockdown and isolation measures required people to remain home bound with social and physical distance. For people without adequate housing facilities and living in overcrowded places, it has created a lot of hardships. Providing emergency housing facilities to homeless people, people in transit, and people in shanty towns becomes vital in protecting their interests. Measures are also taken to isolate those carrying infection, for keeping them under vigil for signs of deterioration, and protecting others from getting infected. Authorities also target and take steps for preventing additional people from getting homeless as they face evictions due to loss of income and resulting inability to pay rents. Emergency arrangements of housing have been found devoid of hygienic and habitable conditions, many times making inmates flee and further endangering their health and life.

X.3.3 ***Emergency measures*** do allow for significant derogation of human rights, but care must be taken that such derogations are proportionate to risk assessed and applied in non-discriminatory ways. State Parties to UN covenants are to notify any such declaration of emergency affecting human rights. Emergency powers are required to be used only for public health causes and not for silencing dissents. Some rights remain non-derogable even in the state of emergencies, as right against torture and right to life, and the state authorities are to inform all people about actions taken for containing the damage caused by health emergency situations. Emergency powers are not to be used for controlling the day-to-day life, and sooner return to normalcy is warranted. Allocation of scarce medical resources such as ventilators, intensive care facilities, and costly life-saving medicines should not have medical bias but strict allocation as per needs has to be assured, especially poor, marginalized and disabled being taken care of.

X.3.4 ***Older People*** saw increased vulnerabilities to aged, infirm, and those suffering from other health conditions. Old people have the same human rights as any other. Age-based discrimination has been noted in availability and accessibility to health care and other services for elderly who were asked not to come out of their homes, and in the face of rampant scarcity, they were left unattended and fending for themselves. Age and disability *per se* should not be a guiding factor deciding treatment modalities, and it has to be only and only medical needs based on clinical assessment and scientific evidence for each human being. The risks to elderly heightened in an already entrenched epidemic of ageism, and devaluing of older lives and many of them were made to believe that humankind can do without them, with hospitals and disaster management employing triage systems deprioritizing anyone aged 65 or older.

X.3.5 ***People in prisons***, pre-trial detentions, drug rehabilitation centres, and reformatories are at increased risks of infections in case of outbreak, because of overcrowding and poor hygienic conditions. Option of release remains with the state for those convicted for minor and non-violent crimes and persons in administrative detention and at rehabilitation centres. People with disabilities and older persons are likely to face further neglect in such cases, and therefore, community-based support is desirable.

X.3.6 ***Free flow of Information*** should be readily available and accessible for all populations, including those with special needs, in all languages for people to be able to understand, and for both the populations of internet users as well as non-users. This helps people in measures they need to take to keep themselves non exposed to the infection, and also in case of emergencies the support system they need to avail for getting access to all required resources. Medical and other experts should be able to freely disseminate their opinions and advice for the larger public. Media persons should be allowed to be critical of government measures and freely report on pandemics without any gag or censorship.

X.3.7 ***Racial and religious discriminations***

State should act as a powerful authority to allay all fears of discriminations on the grounds of race, religion, gender, and other polarizing factors. Where Muslims were called 'corona bombs' and labelled with anti-national tags, it led to communalization of COVID-19, affecting the secular nature of polity and undermining the collective strength of 'we the people'.

X.3.8 ***Migrants*** in this crisis were left without jobs and without any hope of income in the near future to sustain their own and family lives, with looming fear of hunger. With no transport facilities in the lockdown period, many had to walk and cycle miles, with children and luggage, to reach their native places, where again they were discriminated against, as carriers of viruses. People who built cities, economies, and industries were left helpless and suffered the worst human rights violations, and few lost lives too.

X.3.9 ***International assistance*** to support host nations for stepping up its services for including all its subjects in national plans for tackling public health crises is required for many developing nations. Failure in getting assistance endangers health for all, risking the health of each global citizen, and also increasing the chances of stigmatizations and hostilities. Collectivism in the healthcare ecosystem should be the buzzword for making the health of world citizens safe and secured.

X.3.10 ***Right to Education***: Children in the 0–14 years age group account for 25.797% of the global population in 216 countries. With the regulations for social and physical distancing, lockdowns and travel restrictions, and several other measures in place for preventing the spread of coronavirus infection, schools and educational institutions were closed all over as a preventive measure. These restrictions are likely to have short and longer-term consequences. Girl's right to education is to be affected significantly because of their involvement in increased care work at home. Balancing caregiving responsibilities with education have long-term impacts, and State authorities need special care and attention for addressing girls' need for health, education, and economic opportunities. Governments globally are trying to compensate for their losses via the use of online media, specialized television, and radio broadcasts. Limited access to the Internet makes non-digital savvy students more at loss which further gets deepened by the effects of poverty and the digital divide. With schooling being hampered, nutritional services such as mid-day meals are also negatively affecting physical, intellectual and emotional development, especially of girls, which is likely to have far reaching effects. Children confined to home increasingly are victims of maltreatment including physical and sexual abuse. Support systems and care homes are to be thought of addressing these issues.

X.3.11 ***Occupational hazards*** of working in health crises situations at workplaces without proper safety and hygiene measures increase workers' chance of getting infected. No worker should be forced to work endangering health and life for the reasons of loss of job or pay-check reduction. Universal basic income can prove to be handy for everyone fighting pandemic events and should be a food for thought for the future.

X.3.12 ***Privacy issues*** tracking behaviour and movement of people, by administrative authorities using contact tracing apps (Arogya setu app. in India), have given rise to privacy issues. Such surveillance and monitoring has to be limited for the desired health outcome and limited in duration and scope. Such data and confidential information should not be used by authorities for any other purposes except for managing public health concerns.

4 Gandhian Philosophy and Concept of Duty

Gandhi believed that the state was an instrument of coercion, having the immense power of undermining cherished human rights and fundamental freedoms of individuals. Taking cue from *Civil Disobedience*, a treatise of Thoreau which uses the term 'human rights' for the first time, Gandhi developed his ideas on non-violent resistance to unethical government. Gandhi was one of the few leaders and thinkers of modern India who accepted Hinduism as a way of life. His religious humanism and attitude of 'orthodox sanatani hindu' as he self-described himself, reflected when H G Wells sent the Charter of Human Rights for Gandhi to subscribe and approve, and his revert was for the preparation of a charter of human duties instead, and he said:

> The True Source of Right is Duty. If we all discharge our duties, rights will not be far to seek. Rights accrue automatically to those who perform their duties. In fact, the right to perform one's duty is the only right worth living and dying for. It covers all legitimate rights.[39]

Harold Lasky, the great political philosopher opines, 'Rights are related to functions and are given only in return for some duties to be performed.'[40] Rights and duties are correlative and therefore no right can exist without a correlative duty, which is also held by Gita, Gandhi, and most other religious and social leaders. Modern scholar Henry Shue has proposed triple duties, doing away with the negative–positive rights dichotomy. As per him, there is a fine distinction between merely having a right and its actual enjoyment. Three duties are interlinked, with basic rights, and are important to be performed to protect any right.[41] Norwegian scholar Asbjorn Eide has used this framework in the Food and Agricultural Organization for Right to food guarantees for global citizens towards fulfilment of SDG-2. To Gandhi, every illness was but a breach of some unknown law of nature. As against the doctrine of majoritarian democracy, every issue to him needed to be judged from the touchstone of morality rather than in terms of numbers. Though Gandhi appeared very frail, he was a man of extraordinary courage, determination, and perseverance in the face of adversity. He had an original mind which probed into the matrix of human problems. His magnetic personality could command the loyalty of men and women of diverse temperaments and differing intellectual endowment and incorporation of Gandhian principles in the Indian Constitutional texts is ample testimony to that. Was Gandhi a libertarian? Ideally, a least-governed state has to be an ordered anarchy and least violent. Any man who submits his will to the state, in fact surrenders his liberty. Gandhi was in anarchist tradition, and his anarchism was highly individualistic. Gandhi believed that no society can possibly be built by denying individual freedom. As a man cannot grow a tail, so his existence is not possible if he does not use his own mind. Even those people who do not believe in the liberty of individuals, believe in their own. Gandhi was the most revolutionary of individualists and most individualistic of revolutionaries. His focus was on decentralized village republics ordered on social sanctions and being free of state control. He was against the idea of war, imperialism, or any kind of state intrusions. Anarchism believes that men need neither a political system nor a government. Men should be free to do anything they are pleased to do in respect of other men. Gandhi's individual 'Man' is not the 'Economic Man' who has emerged from modern western civilization. Gandhi's man

---

[39] Dasgupta A K, Gandhi's Economic Thought, Routledge (1996).

[40] Laski H, A Grammar of Politics George Allen & Unwin Ltd., London (1925).

[41] Shue H, Basic Rights, Princeton University Press, New Jersey (1996).

is quintessentially a moral and ethical man, a self-regulated individual, and according to Gandhi, such men only can contribute the best to the formation of a humane and harmonious society, because then there would be the least opportunity to govern. For this, he mentions seven sins if taken care of can lead to real sustainable developments, in peace and happiness.[42] Gandhi believed in a minimum state. This is possible in his scheme only when individuals are liberated, with a high degree of self-regulation, and are thus self-disciplined. Rather, the authorities in recent times have adopted Bentham's panopticon approach[43] creating thus a surveillance state, which is a thing of worry and needs to be addressed as per the general will of the people. Recent developments in social contract as visualized by Muldoon are a multi-perspective bargain benefiting each participant with some advantage, though need not be strictly egalitarian in allocation of rights as per liberal political conception of justice. He uses diversity to increase opportunities as each one in diverse and plural conditions specializes in production. A more diverse society is inclined to have more social surplus creating opportunities for newer innovations which in turn foster more diversity and still higher levels of production. Though Rawlsian models in the wake of public reason do not support this. Public reason cannot accommodate diverse perspectives for the determination of a regulative ideal. In the same vein, regulative ideals have difficulty responding to social change. In Ryan Muldoon's bargaining model, 'The View from Everywhere,' agents cooperate despite facing different perspectives without arguing for an ideal principle of justice.[44] This revision of social contract rules expands Mill's experiments in living, having a foundational principle and counters Rawls for his common reason in a pluralistic society of all citizens, who identified it as a basic element of political liberalism.[45] Rawls' public reason is deliberative of shared beliefs, constitution of democratic polity, public goods concerns, and matters of basic justice. Thus, Rawls to Muldoon is a move from an end state of conception of justice to a trajectory of conception of justice which emphasizes movement from consequentialism to deontology.

4.1 Way Forward

5A. ***International Arena***

5A.1. Gandhi described the state as a soulless machine based on the premise that no society can be built on a denial of individual freedom. A swaraj, from all types of exploitations, and socioeconomic freedom for poor and downtrodden masses, is

[42] The Collected Works of Mahatma Gandhi.

[43] Panopticon being a disciplinary conception with the central observation tower having guards watching every cell and inmates, while inmates not being able to see into the tower or not knowing whether they are being watched.

[44] Muldoon R, Diversity and Disagreement are the Solution, Not the Problem, 2017, Niskanen Center available at: http://tinyurl.com/j9oq324 (last accessed 31 May, 2021).

[45] Rawls J, Political Liberalism, Columbia University Press (1993).

needed which is individual-centric, communitarian in approach with a flexible broad social justice cosmopolitan normative framework as the guiding force for all State Parties.

5A.2. All human beings are born equal in dignity and rights, no discrimination should be allowed to be tolerated either on national landscape or international arena, and all UN member countries having signed and ratified ICCPR and ICESCR should follow the legal framework in letter and spirit. Progress in a society is to be judged as to how much it cares for the people at the edges, be it elderly, women, children, migrants, persons with disabilities (PWDs), mentally ill, people in detention, or aboriginal populations.

5A.3. Jacobsons for compulsory vaccination as public health measures have mandated that in conflicting interests of individual autonomy and health of the public at large, the latter interest will prevail and has guided the jurisprudence in this area for long. Lockdown, isolation, quarantine, cluster and contact tracing, sealing of hotspots, compulsory wearing of masks, testing with hastily prepared kits, drugs and vaccines being tried on human subjects without properly having been assured of their safety, curbs on news in the guise of this being fake, closure of religious and educational institutions, provide multitudes of human rights derogation. States can derogate such rights but only through proper accountability, and such derogation must be in good faith. Targeting minorities and playing state-craft with the lives of people should justify national and international legal and normative framework.

5A.4. Care seekers and care providers in a healthcare ecosystem have gone through transformations in the slow-motion revolution encompassing the history of 'care'. Need-based, welfare-based, rights-based, and participation-based approaches of care have required all stakeholders to come together for access to healthcare justice for all. The healthcare system must consider the care-seeker as a partner in care delivery, and there should be informed consent for all issues which come up for care as a guiding norm for primary rule making.

5A.5. Though public health crises and pandemics affect populations as per their herd immunity, climatic conditions, and level of development, few countries such as Japan, South Korea, Singapore, South Africa, and Germany provided successful models for early containment and resulting in less casualties while dealing with the coronavirus crisis. Highest standard of health and medical care is available to Japanese people, as 'for-profit corporations' are not allowed to own or operate hospitals. Government strictly regulates prices of care to keep it affordable for the masses. South Africa has an agency for its citizens to choose quality health care. Norway spends much more on social sectors like health and education. The emergency has an inbuilt learning of what is needed for a good human development index. Human capital is the biggest asset, and maximum investment of all countries should be earmarked for it to enable humanity to prevent, mitigate, and treat such public health crises.

5B. ***Indian Context***

5B.1. In Indian context, there is a multiplicity of legislation without any proper authority for coordinating in times of such crisis. Epidemic Diseases Act 1897 (Act

3 of 1897), National Disaster Management Act 2005 (Act 53 of 2005), National Security Act 1980 (Act 65 of 1980), Aircraft (Public Health) Rules, 1954, provisions have been invoked to curb people's freedom in the interest of public safety, health, and welfare. Laws should be updated and should have certainty and clarity to have prior-informed citizenry. A change of stance every now and then creates more confusion.

5B.2. Health is a subject where experts have more roles to play. In most situations, experts are side-lined by bureaucrats, and without proper teamwork among epidemiologists, clinicians, scientists and other stakeholders, a step is taken in the wrong direction. Emergencies do not give a second chance. Let us learn from this pandemic and be prepared for such emergencies, making our health systems robust.

5B.3. A policy is only as good as its implementation. Hence, this paper finds wisdom in holding health as a continuum from disease to absolute health. An integrated approach to holistic health inclusive of indigenous health systems and participatory decentralizing approach will reduce overall healthcare cost and will make health delivery more acceptable to the masses as per local and cultural needs. There should be an approach of 'task shifting' as provision of 'Community Health Worker (CHP)' in recent legislation of the National Medical Commission Act provides. CHPs are to be one third of the number of doctors and will be trained for having the prescriptive power and manning the health and wellness centres as provided in Ayushman Bharat, the flagship scheme of the Government of India, for healthcare delivery being close to the community.

5B.4. With the private health sector lacking the trust of a large part of Indian population and public sector not having been able to fulfil the expectation of masses, time seems ripe for improved healthcare budgeting, a well-managed public healthcare system with nationalization of healthcare services, an Indian Medical Service on the lines of the Central Services, and all Indian citizens insured for its healthcare needs. A healthy Indian workforce will be more productive and happy, transforming India as per the dreams of Indians and not as per foreign expectations.

5 Conclusion

Among the three limbs of civilization, first, science has its own share of uncertainties in fighting emerging newer infections, second, law is outpaced by developments and is reactive to change, while third, politics tends to be status quoist. That leaves human beings only with the moral courage and with physical, mental, and socioeconomic health, making them geared up to tackle unprecedented issues like COVID-19 pandemic. World wars saw the United Nations and Gandhi both vying for world peace for all global citizens on the path of development. It seems we focussed more on a consequentialist mode that a well-developed economy will take care of the rest of humanity's requirements and developed nations ultimately will pass on the benefits to the developing world through trickle down mechanisms under the aegis of supranational institutions. The present model of development led to more inequalities in income, wealth and distribution of primary social goods by the way of capitalists being interested in only profit making even at the cost of suffering for the rest of humanity. All economic and trade laws, investment treaties, and intellectual laws developed nations are advocating a protectionist system for their own interest and are disadvantageous to the southern world. Hobbesian absolutism, Adam Smith's wealth, and Kant's enlightenment all have emphasized morality. Development divorced from morality has developed into a lop-sided civilization and is prone to developing infirmities. Karl Loewenstein talks of authoritarian government as an emotional government, enacting positive laws being measured not in terms of constitutional legality but as unchallengeable commands. National enthusiasm and permanent psychic coercion being common elements in authoritarian rules, many saw them in times of emergency, and many are inclined to read the same in today's situations worldwide. The de-globalization with sanctions and trade barriers leads to more conflicts and moving away from peace, looks to develop a new ecosystem requiring utmost attention now.

References

Berlin I (1969) Two concepts of liberty in four essays on liberty. Oxford University Press

Chapple A (2020) Up close with the enemy: the coronavirus in stunning detail. https://www.rferl.org/a/microscope-photos-capture-coronavirus-in-stunning-detail/30518135.html. Accessed 27 May 2020

Critical Legal Theory (2020). Legal information institute. https://www.law.cornell.edu/wex/critical_legal_theory. Accessed 5 June 2020

Dasgupta AK (1996) Gandhi's economic thought. Routledge

Desilver D (2019). Despite global concerns about democracy, more than half of countries are democratic. https://www.pewresearch.org/fact-tank/2019/05/14/more-than-half-of-countries-are-democratic/. Accessed 5 Jun 2020

Hayek FA (1960) The constitution of liberty and law. University of Chicago Press

Hayek FA (1988) The fatal conceit: the errors of socialism. University of Chicago Press

Hobbes T (1651) The matter, forme and power of a common-wealth ecclesiastical and civil
Commonly referred to as Leviathan Penguin Classic, 1982)

Jung C (1962) Analytical psychology. https://www.carl-jung.net/individuation_steps.html. Accessed 7 Jun 2020

Kant I (1785) Groundwork of the Metaphysics of Morals. In trans: Wood AW (2002) Yale University Press, New Haven

Kant I (1795) Perpetual peace: a philosophical essay. Cosimo Classics, NY (2010)

Laski H (1925) A grammar of politics. George Allen & Unwin Ltd., London

Locke J (1690). Two Treatises of Government. A. Churchill, London

Maccall W (1847). Elements of Individualism. A series of lectures. John Chapman, London.

Mill J S (1859) On liberty. John W. Parker and Sons. West Strand, London

Mises L (2007). Human action: a treatise on economics. Indianapolis, In: Liberty Fund

Muldoon R (2017) Diversity and disagreement are the solution, not the problem, (Niskanen Center available at: http://tinyurl.com/j9oq324 Accessed 31 May 2021)

Oxfam (2020). World's billionaires have more wealth than 4.6 billion people. Fight Inequality, beat poverty, World Economic Forum, Davos, Switzerland

Pogge TW (2001) Cosmopolitanism: A Path To Peace And Justice. In: Goodin RE, Pogge T (eds) Cosmopolitanism, a companion to contemporary political philosophy, Blackwell, London

Pogge TW (2002) World poverty and human rights: cosmopolitan responsibilities and reforms. Polity Press, Cambridge

Ramirez VB (2020) What is R0? gauging contagious infections. Healthline. https://www.healthline.com/health/r-nought-reproduction-number. Accessed 31 May 2020

Rawls J (1971) A theory of justice. Harvard University Press

Rawls J (1993) Political Liberalism. Columbia University Press

Rawls J (1999) The law of the people. Harvard University Press

Robinson L, Shultz J (2016) Role of mass media and new media cultures. Emerald Group Publishers, Communication and Information Technology Annual

Shue H (1996) Basic rights. Princeton University Press, New Jersey

Sivakumar S (2015) Press law and journalists: watchdog to guidedog. Universal Law Publishing, New Delhi

Spencer H (1851) Social statics: or, the conditions essential to human happiness specified, John Chapman, London

Sripati V (2008) The United Nations role in post-conflict constitution-making process: TWAIL insights. Int Community Law Rev 10:411–420

The Collected Works of Mahatma Gandhi (electronic edition), Vol. 33, pp. 133–134. ISBN 8123007353, ISBN 9788123007359OCLC 655798065, wealth without work, pleasure without conscience, knowledge without character, commerce (business) without morality (ethics), science without humanity, religion without sacrifice, politics without principle, see also, available at: https://www.mkgandhi.org/mgmnt.htm Accessed 21 Jan 2021

The Universal Declaration of Human Rights (1948). Shaping our future together. The United Nations

Wenar L (2008) Property rights and the resource curse. 36 Philosophy & Public Affairs. Blackwell Publishing Inc

Wiest JB (2016) Casting cultural monsters, representations of serial killers in US and UK news media. Howard J Commun 27:327–346

World Health Organisation (2019) https://www.who.int/emergencies/diseases/novel-coronavirus-2019/events-as-they-happen Accessed 29 May 2020

WHO Coronavirus disease (COVID-19) pandemic situation (2021) https://www.who.int/emergencies/diseases/novel-coronavirus-2019 Accessed 2 Jan 2021

Part III
Duties Under the Indian Constitution

Chapter 13
Facilitating the Convergence of Directive Principles of State Policy and Fundamental Duties Through the Gandhian Interpretation of '*Dharm*'

Sanjeeb K. Panigrahi and Siddharth Anand Panda

1 Gandhian Interpretation of 'Dharm' vis-à-vis Governance

The word '*dharm*' has different connotations; similar to the English word 'law'. It is believed that *dharm* regulates the behaviour of an object and upholds its existence.[1] In Indian jurisprudence, *dharm* is invariably equated with the notion of justice. The interpretation of *dharm* in Smritis, Dharmshastras and Arthashastra has explicated that justice and law are strictly interlinked such that 'justice is considered as a distinct segment of morality to which law must conform'.[2] This segment has been implicated as the 'rule of law' in contemporary society. According to Dr S. Radhakrishnan, '*dharm* denotes righteousness. It is the ruler of both the people and the ruler themselves. It is the sovereignty of the law'.[3] Similarly, in the context of the governance of the state, *dharm* has been stressed as a unique blend of law and morality, a pillar that safeguards the sovereign state.[4] K. M. Panikkar believed that: 'The king's coronation ceremony is a *diksha* devoting his life to the cause of *dharm* (service of the

---

[1] Persaud SN, "Eternal law: the underpinnings of Dharma and Karma in the justice system", 13 *Rich JL & Pub Int* 1, pp. 49–90 (2009).

[2] Sarda M, "Concept of dharma, justice and law: a study", 8 *Supreme Court Review* 50, pp. 179–183 Available at https://ssrn.com/abstract=2792042 (2010).

[3] Sheikh T, Ethics of rajdharma, 40 *Studies in Indian Place Names* 68, pp. 801–7 (2020).

[4] Sihag BS, "Kautilya on law, economics and ethics", 25 *Humanomics* 1, pp. 75–94 (2009).

S. K. Panigrahi (✉)
Judge, High Court of Orissa, Cuttack, India

S. A. Panda
Student, National Law University Odisha, Cuttack, India
e-mail: 16ba099@nluo.ac.in

R. Mittal and K. K. Singh (eds.), *Relevance of Duties in the Contemporary World*,
https://doi.org/10.1007/978-981-19-1836-0_13

people)'.[5] Therefore, *dharm* was given the connotation of both faith and duty. Ergo, this notion was responsible for keeping the society together.

Gandhi's description of a righteous world is called '*Ramrajya*' (meaning 'kingdom of Lord Ram').[6] The Hindu scriptures have emphasized the fact that the king or the head of the state will have to wield the gauntlet of *dharm* while making decisions because *dharm* encircles every sphere of activity and also embraces governance of the nation.[7] Gandhi's ideology revolved around the philosophy of *satya* ('truth') and *ahimsa* ('non-violence') in addition to *dharm*. Gandhi agreed to Kant's notion of 'kingdom of ends'[8] and claimed that '*the fruits of action were irrelevant to the righteous act, and that no person should be treated as a means*'.[9] However, unlike Kant's notion where the society was guided by a rule of principles which set obligations for individuals in the society, Gandhi's *Ramarajya* was based on the truth that was experienced by each individual, and this conviction was comparatively personal.[10] Gandhi's emphasis on *dharm* as complimentary to rights is what separates him from other scholars of 'rights' discourse. According to him, rights do not make sense in solidarity unless they are connected with *dharm* or duties. *Dharm* is therefore a certain instinctive code of conduct.[11] He further explained:

> *Dharm* does not mean any particular creed or dogma. Nor does it mean reading or learning by rote books known as *Shastras* [traditional scriptures] or even believing all that they say. Dharm is a quality of the soul and is present, visibly or invisibly, in every human being. Through it, we know our duty in human life and our true relations with other souls. We cannot do so till we have known the self in us. Hence dharm is the means by which we can know ourselves.[12]

The concept of *dharm* during the historical times strongly emphasized on the significance of fulfilling duties and obligations, but it was also tied to the preservation of status.[13] However, there was no emphasis laid on the importance of democratic citizenship which drew Mahatma Gandhi's attention. In his book *Hind Swaraj*, he, therefore, attempted to redefine *dharm* as a new vision that every Indian should have

---

[5] Sarda, *supra* note 2 at 182.

[6] Lal V, The Gandhi everyone loves to hate, 43 *Economic and Political Weekly* 40, pp. 55–64 Available at http://www.jstor.org/stable/40278027 (2008).

[7] Gill NK, "Good governance in India: The concept and the practice", 7 *Asian Journal of Multidimensional Research* 3, pp. 199–206 (2018).

[8] Bilimoria P, Protestant Ethic and Hindu Dharma: With Reference to the Kant and Gandhi, In: Sinha BM (ed.) The Contemporary Essays on the Bhagavad Gītā, Siddharth Publications, New Delhi, pp. 69–101 (1995).

[9] Bilgrami A, "Gandhi's religion and its relation to his politics", In: Brown JM, Parel A (eds.), Cambridge companion to Gandhi, Cambridge University Press, Cambridge, pp. 93–116 (2011).

[10] Ibid. at 97.

[11] Creel AB, "The re-examination of 'dharma' in Hindu ethics", 25 *Philosophy East and West* 2, pp. 161–173 Available at https://doi.org/10.2307/1397937 (1975).

[12] Chakrabarty B, Social and political thought of Mahatma Gandhi, Routledge, London, p. 38 Chakrabarty (2006).

[13] Mandelbaum DG, "The study of life history: Gandhi", 14 *Current Anthropology* 3, pp. 177–206 http:// Available at www.jstor.org/stable/2740760 (1973).

in the form of 'Gandhian civic humanism'.[14] He perceived that the foundation of *dharm* should include the concepts of citizenship, liberty, equality, fraternity and mutual assistance.[15] This was articulated to be something which the Hindu epics of Ramayana and Mahabharata had always contained *in potentia*, but was not realized to the fullest by the people yet.[16] In a world where there has been a continuous expansion of the public sphere characterized by homogeneity, universality and impersonality, the central values rest around self-interest, national self-rule and *realpolitik*, it attempts to use modern vanguard as the pacesetter when it comes to social change.[17] The pace is exercised through a moral foundation as well as a rational approach towards political decision-making by the state.[18] However, there has to be an achievement of equilibrium of duties by the corresponding notion of *swadharm*. *Swadharm* is when the citizens participate in the initiatives of state but at the same time abide by their own duty which has been mandated for them.

The author shall elucidate the interplay of *rajdharm* and *swadharm* with the corresponding constitutional ideals of the directive principle of state policy and fundamental duties, respectively.

2 Directive Principles of State Policy as an Extension of the Notion of '*Rajdharm*'

Gandhi always articulated and championed the notion of '*rajdharm*' which is an epitome of intelligence in the sphere of assertive political leadership.[19]

Rajdharm revolves around the concept of how the king should exercise his political power towards his subjects and aims at maximizing the welfare of the people.[20] Therefore, the kings as well as the Kingship are significantly concerned for the *prajapalanah*.[21] Even in the *saptang* theory of Kautilya, the concept of *rajdharm* has been assigned importance in the welfare of the state.[22] If the king performs the duties

---

[14] Parel AJ (ed.), Gandhi: 'hind swaraj' and other writings, Cambridge University Press, Cambridge, p. xvi (2009).

[15] Ibid., p. xvii.

[16] Gokhale BG, "Gandhi and history", 11 *History and Theory* 2, pp. 214–225 (1972).

[17] Nandy A, "Culture, state and the rediscovery of Indian politics", 49 *Economic and Political Weekly* 19, pp. 2078–2083 (1984).

[18] Ibid.

[19] Juergensmeyer M, "Doing ethics in a plural world", In: Shelp EE (ed.), Theology and Bioethics, Springer, Dordrecht, pp. 187–201 (1985).

[20] Duncan M Derrett, Rajadharma, 35 *The Journal of Asian Studies* 4, pp. 597–609 (1976).

[21] Singh SP, Concept of rajdharma in adi-kavya: Ramayana and Mahabharata, 61 *Indian Journal of Public Administration* 1, pp. 132–138. Prajapalanah means Protection and welfare of the state people (2015).

[22] Menon P, Kajari K (2020), "Viewing contemporary India through the kautilyan lens" (2020) Available at https://thewire.in/politics/viewing-contemporary-india-through-the-kautilyan-lens (last accessed 29 June 2020).

most desirably and righteously practising *dharm* with an open mind and impartial decision-making, a *Dharmarajya* or *Ramrajya can be achieved.*[23] *Rajdharm* talks about the achievement of a decent standard of living for the society through values that allow an individual to live a life of order, peace and prosperity governed by good ethical conduct in the polity.[24] Even though there has been a significant change in society, the concept of *Rajdharm* still holds prime importance when it comes to the governance of society. In order to regulate government affairs and practice of justice, it is very common to regard unethical and unprincipled politics as reality in the contemporary society. This is the reason why it is essential to observe the concept of *rajdharm.*

In the classical Indian texts, *rajdharm* embraced the principles of peace, equality, liberty and justice. However, it is more concerned with how the king discharges his duties. The king had to perform his duties according to the laws prescribed in the *dharmasastras.*[25] Any kind of deviation from the principles of *dharm* would lead to the people feeling that the king is unfit for the rule. Therefore, to be respected, the king had to be true to his duties. Also, the rules of *dharm* could not be altered according to what the king's conveniences, and this led to a strict form of discipline. Therefore, there has to be conformity in power which mirrors the contemporary 'rule of law'.[26] Kautilya's *Arthashastra* also succinctly puts that the authority of a ruler should not be arbitrary even if he is a representative of God. The king had to strictly follow the ethical code of conduct prescribed for the rulers.[27] Similar principles can also be observed in Chinese legal tradition; the word for law in classical mandarin is *Fǎ w*hich also means fair, straight or just. It also carries the sense of a 'standard or a model'.[28] The notion of *Fǎ* is often associated with 'Yi' which means 'social righteousness'.[29]

---

[23] Tewari D, Finding swadhinta, swaraj and dharmarajya, 1 *Indian JL & Pub. Pol'y* 2, pp. 58–79 (2014).

[24] Parekh B, "Nehru and the national philosophy of India", 26 *Economic and Political Weekly* 1/2, pp. 35–48 Available at http://www.jstor.org/stable/4397189 (1991).

[25] Singh SP, "Concept of rajdharma in adi-kavya: Ramayana and Mahabharata", 61 *Indian Journal of Public Administration* 1, pp. 132–138 Available at https://doi.org/10.1177/0019556120150109 (2015).

[26] Ibid. at 132.

[27] Ibid. at 137.

[28] Tripathi V, Misri IV (2020) How history shapes the march towards rule of law: lessons from India and china. Institute of Chinese Studies 47:20.

[29] Deborah C, "Desperately Seeking 'Justice' in Classical Chinese: On the Meanings of Yi", *International Journal for the Semiotics of Law* 32, pp. 13–28 Available at https://doi.org/10.1007/s11196-018-9566-9 (2019).

Gandhi realized that the administrative and legal system of any state is directly or indirectly linked to its customs and traditions which are influenced by the historical norms. Ergo, one would find the influence of the preaching of Ram and Krishn from Ramayan and Mahabharat, respectively, in the Gandhian interpretation of *rajdharm*.[30]

According to Valmiki, 'a King guards mankind from scathe and wrong, and lends his aid and ne'er in vain, the cause of justice to maintain'.[31] Furthermore, Ramayan encapsulates the point that the divine origin of the king does not authorize him to act against his dharm. He can be disobeyed, killed or deposed if he does not follow his dharm.[32] We learn from the epic that if a king should astray from the path of dharm, he will be damned of unforgivable fortunes.[33] In Ayodhyakand, a brahman, whose son was mistakenly killed by Dashrath (Ram's father) openly accused him and cursed him of having committed the unrighteous deed.[34]

Mahabharata's *Shantiparv* (parvs are the chapters of Mahabharata) is the most relevant to this study. This parva discusses *rajdharm* and gives a hypothesis of a state which is momentous for the age as it manages such crucial inquiries as to the significance of the state and study of legislative issues, the elements of good governance, a welfare state and so forth.

In the 27th shloka of 64th adhayay in Mahabharat's Shantiparv, Bhism edifies Yudhistir[35]:

> Sarve Dharm rajyadharmpradhnah, sarve varnah palyaman bharvanti
> Sarvstayago rajdharmeshu rajasyatyagandharmechaurgr ayapuranam

This means the ruler is vested with the power and authority of administration, but 'true sovereignty' belongs to *dharm*, not to the ruler. The epic of Mahabharat recurringly states that in every exercise of power and governance, the objective of the ruler or the state is to promote the welfare of the individuals and protect them. This notion of welfarism underpins good governance under which individuals flourish, and by flourishing, they enrich the state in return. It is emphasized that the ruler must aim and advance the welfare of its subjects. The ruler must be benevolent to the people of all segments of society without any discrimination and focus on their individual and collective development.[36]

---

[30] Paranjape MR, The "Persistent" Mahatma: re-reading Gandhi post-hindutva. In: Paranjape MR (ed.) Making India: Colonialism, National Culture, and the Afterlife of Indian English Authority, Springer, Dordrecht, pp. 237–251 (2013).

[31] Gritffith, Ramayan of Valmiki, Devoted Publishing, Ontario, p. 9 (2008).

[32] Narayan J, "Relevance of rajadharma of ancient India", 65 *The Indian Journal of Political Science* 1, pp. 21–28. Available at http://www.jstor.org/stable/41855794 (2004).

[33] Brockington J, The concept of "dharma" in the Ramayana, 32 *Journal of Indian Philosophy* 5/6, pp. 655–670 Available at http://www.jstor.org/stable/23497156 (2004).

[34] Gritffith, *supra* note 31, at 168.

[35] Garg S, "Political ideas of shanti parva", 65 *The Indian Journal of Political Science* 1, pp. 77–86 Available at https://www.jstor.org/stable/41855798 (2004).

[36] Ibid.

Rajdharm, as elucidated above, recapitulates certain ubiquitous standards and principles of governance which includes ensuring security and wellbeing of the stakeholders, dislodging the law of wilderness (*matsyanyay*) by the equitable notion of law, justice and morality. *Rajdharm* is not restricted to the protection and wellbeing alone.[37] Rather, it is stretched out to ensure harmony and material prosperity for the populace. Kautilya in his magnum opus *Arthashastra* (Book 1, 18th Adhyay) has opined that:

prajah kite hetangrajyah, praja sukhe sukah rajyah

It means the joy of the ruler of the state lies in the joy of his kin and its welfare lies in the welfare of the people. This appropriately mirrors the beliefs of *rajdharm*.[38]

The notions propounded in the Ramayan, the Mahabharat and in the Arthshastra have not at all lost its relevance even today. It manages to highlight an essential element of *dharm*: the importance of governance and the art of welfare politics. All these writings centred on the welfare of the individuals and characterize the commitments of the ruler towards his subjects. However, an improved notion of *rajdharm* must be conceptualized which would suit the contemporary state of political and social affair.

The directive principles of state policy enshrined in Part IV of the Constitution of India which enumerates the aims and objects for the better governance of the state could be understood as the contemporary expansion of *rajdharm*. The mandate is best comprehended as a framework of principles which buttress and structure the construction and interpretation of fundamental rights.[39] The possibility of 'welfare state' as envisaged by our forefathers through our constitution could be achieved if the state endeavours to actualize these standards. The principal object underlying these provisions is to set a certain standard of achievement for the legislature and executive to comply.[40]

The policy principles set out in this part are planned for the guidance and direction of the state. While these standards will not be cognizable by any court, they are nonetheless substantial in the administration of the nation, and their application shall be the obligation of the state. Courts cannot dismiss them entirely regardless of their non-justiciability. Fundamental rights are comprehended and interpreted relying on the vision formulated in the DPSP.[41]

Directive principles of state policy have been given special importance by the Supreme Court of India through various pronouncements. In *Minerva Mills*, the

---

[37] Narayan, *supra* note 32, at p. 26.

[38] Joshi A, "Strategic wisdom from the orient: evaluating the contemporary relevance of Kautilya's arthashastra and Sun Tzu's art of war", 43 *Strategic Analysis* 1, pp. 54–74 (2019).

[39] Narain J, "Judicial law making and the place of Directive Principles in Indian constitution", 27 *Journal of the Indian Law Institute* 2, pp. 198–222 (1985).

[40] Ibid.

[41] Gautam Bhatia, Directive principles of state policy: theory and practice, In: Mehta BP, Choudhry S, Khosla M (eds.), Oxford Handbook for Indian Constitution, Oxford University Press, Oxford, pp. 644–661 (2015).

Indian Apex Court held that '*The DPSP are an arrangement of legitimately unenforceable objectives which are basic to the administration of the nation and which put positive obligations on the state*'.[42] The fundamental rights of the citizens have a social, monetary, social and instructive character.[43] In *Ranjan Dwivedi*, Justice AP Sen declared that the DPSP provide a structure inside which the fundamental rights could be fully realized and exercised. The fundamental rights are intrinsically 'negative' in nature and are 'mark of a world in which the administration has no jurisdiction', but these directives mandate 'positive' activity by the state with a reasonable political and legal outcome.[44] While DPSP are non-justiciable in nature,[45] it is nonetheless fundamental in the governance of the country. BR Ambedkar while elaborating the utility of DPSP said: 'The biggest moral force is public opinion which can enforce the directive principles and ensure government's accountability at the time of elections'.[46] It was figured that without a far-reaching socio-political underpinning for the country, the constitution would become 'useless and obsolete' for without duties being committed against the state, the constitution would be no superior to a dead paper. The courts have subsequently allowed different administrative limitations on fundamental rights with the ultimate objective of the fulfilment of the DPSP.

DPSP, when looked through the lens of '*rajdharm*', signify that the constitutional instruments of governance, i.e. the legislature, the executive and the judiciary must hold fast to righteousness and do justice to people. It has an indistinguishable link to the ultimate goal of creation of welfare state of *Ramrajya*. All the conspicuous and latent deficiencies in society could be attributed to the compromise of the principles of governance in more than one way which burglarizes the populace of their social and economic rights. Good governance means fundamental boundaries, for example rule of law, inclusive policy-making, participatory decision-making, accountability, responsiveness, value and comprehensiveness. A nation's state organizations need to run on these standards. This requires a reorientation in the viewpoint of the common administration of the country.

3 The Corresponding Notion of '*Swadharm*' in Constitutional Fundamental Duties

The notion of 'duty' has consistently been a subject of conversation and discussion among the sages, thinkers, philosophers and scholars since days of yore. It has been

[42] *Minerva Mills v. Union of India* AIR 1980 SC 1789.

[43] *State of Kerala v. Thomas* AIR 1976 SC 516.

[44] *Ranjan Dwivedi v. Union of India* 1983 SCR (2) 982.

[45] Constitution of India 1950, Article 37.

[46] Constituent Assembly Debates (December 13, 1946) Speech by BR Ambedkar Available at https://www.constitutionofindia.net/constitution_assembly_debates/volume/7/1948-11-04.

consistently emphasized that everyone ought to discharge their 'duty'.[47] It is in the idea of personhood to act or to stay engaged with multifarious exercises of body and psyche. All the living beings in this world are pre-occupied in some sort of action or other. Among these actions, the fulfilment of one's 'duty' can be viewed as the most elevated and the most flawless one.[48] Each man must seek after the orders of his profound morality. Ergo, the notion of 'duty' is about an action dependent on values.

Dharm established the ubiquitous feeling of 'duty' that held society together; however, there is a contrapuntal notion of *swadharm* as well, which was bestowed upon every person in the society. *Swadharm* comprises two words—*swa* and *dharm*. *Swa* can allude to self, and *dharm* can be alluded to lawful conduct or righteousness.[49] Together, it may be interpreted as the legitimate direction of oneself. An understanding of self is made up of gradual comprehension of one's *swadharm* and living by it; not living its life onto one's own whims and fancies. Subsequently, the term gets immersed in the formula for 'the lawful art of being'.[50] The notion of *swadharm* limits any activity which endeavours to infringe the dharm of another person.[51]

Shri Krishn pronounces the substance of *swadharm* in Gita, Chapter 3 verse 35:

śhreyānswa-dharmoviguṇaḥ para-dharmātsv-anuṣhṭhitāt
swa-dharmenidhanaṁśhreyaḥ para-dharmobhayāvahaḥ

It implies that it is better to perform one's own prescribed duties imperfectly rather than perform another's duty perfectly for executing the duties which is directionless and fraught with uncertainty.

Swadharm has been clarified as the lawful direction of self, based on the realization of one's own ability.[52] A person in the realization of his *swadharm* is aware of his own qualities, shortcomings and potential. Their acknowledgement of self-capacity drives them to acknowledge others as they may be. The comprehension of the structure of *dharm* motivates them to fulfil their rightful duty in any unique situation. Consequentially, when one is aware of his *swadharm*, it gradually pushes him to the understanding of the common cause.[53]

---

[47] Jahanbegloo R, The Gandhian Moment, Harvard University Press, Cambridge, Massachusetts; London, England, pp. 23–52 (2013).

[48] Enoch D, "A right to violate one's duty", *Law and Philosophy* 21, pp. 355–384 (2002) Available at https://doi.org/10.2307/3505056.

[49] Rastogi K, "Exploring Swadharma: an overview", 6 *The International Journal of Indian Psychology* 3, pp. 2348–5396 (2007) Available at https://doi.org/10.25215/0603.023.

[50] Rothermund I, "The individual and society in Gandhi's political thought", 28 *The Journal of Asian Studies* 2, pp. 313–20 (1969).

[51] Ibid.

[52] Tomalin E, Religion and a rights-based approach to development, 6 *Progress in Development Studies* 2, pp. 93–108 Available at https://doi.org/10.1191/1464993406ps130oa (2006).

[53] Mohanty PK, "The "Mahabharata": a reading in political structuring", 49 *Indian Literature* (1 (225)), pp. 146–151. Available at http://www.jstor.org/stable/23346584 (2005).

The concept of *swadharm* was only a profoundly individualized case for Gandhi to disregard shallow human aspirations wherein one envisions that one can essentially topple what was given to him, for his selfish demands.[54] One ought not to disregard another's dharm unless the self-reflection inside mandates one to do so in a rightful circumstance.[55] On similar lines, Gandhi says that the character of a society can be assistance or an obstruction in the way of national and individual reintegration, contingent upon its moral direction. The uplift of society is dependent on its subjects who perform the duties bestowed on them with zeal and zest. A civilization or nation, where the kin does not perform its duty, could not evolve past a specific stage and ultimately, loses all sense of direction in the history. Gandhi apprehended that Indian civilization in its present immature self is an obstruction to the establishment of *Ramrajya*. He penned down his apprehensions in a letter dated 24 January 1922[56]:

> We should remember that immediately on the attainment of freedom, our people are not going to secure happiness. As we become independent, all the defects inherent in the system of election, injustice, the tyranny of the richer class as also the burden of running administration, are bound to come upon us. People would begin to feel as to why they should have at all invited these troubles? They would remember the pre-independence days and feel that during those days, there was more justice, there was better administration, there was peace, there was honesty to a very great extent amongst administrators, compared to the days after independence. But there is hope if education spread throughout the country. …Swaraj would give us happiness only when we attain success in that task. Otherwise, India would become the abode of grave injustice and tyranny of rulers.

Gandhi goes a step forward to say that only an evolved and informed Indian civilization can assist India with accomplishing the much sought after *Ramrajya*.[57] Such a civilization would contribute towards the decline of political brutality and corporate greed, the expansion of societal sympathy, the financial wellbeing and spiritual reconciliation of the person in it.[58]

Gandhi strongly advocated that performance of one's duty is imperative for the preservation of social, political and economic wellbeing of the nation.[59] Maybe those were the reasons which motivated the legislators to cherish the idea of *swadharm* through Part IV-A in Article 51-A of the Constitution of India which enumerated general duties which shall not be disregarded by the citizens of India.

So far as fundamental duties are concerned, these provisions cannot be enforced by the courts, but in *Chandra Bhavan*,[60] Supreme Court emphasized the need of various duties of a citizen in building a welfare society. Justice K. S. Hegde said: '*It*

---

[54] Rao KR, Gandhi's dharma, Oxford University Press, New Delhi (2017).

[55] Ibid.

[56] Rajput JS, Seven social sins: the contemporary relevance, Allied Publishers, New Delhi, p. 2 (2012).

[57] Chimni BS, "The self, modern civilization, and international law: learning from Mohandas Karamchand Gandhi's Hind Swaraj or Indian home rule", 23 *European Journal of International Law* 4, pp. 1159–1173 Available at https://doi.org/10.1093/ejil/chs075 (2012).

[58] Parel, *supra* note 14 at 34.

[59] Ibid.

[60] *Chandra Bhavan Boarding and Lodging v. State of Mysore* 1970 SCR (2) 600.

is fallacy to think that under our Constitution, there are only rights and no duties. The provisions of Part IV enable the Legislature to impose various duties on the citizens. The mandate of our Constitution is to build a welfare society and that object may be to the extent the Directive Principles are implemented by legislation'. Later in *Mohan Kumar Singhania*,[61] Supreme Court has held that '*courts can uphold the constitutionality of a statute, the object of which is in consonance with a provision in Article 51A of the Constitution*'. Justice Lahoti has further extended its scope by asserting that Article 51-A is the yardstick against which the actions of the state may be assessed.[62]

Even though Part IV-A is not enforceable, the authors observe that key obligations enumerated in it are firmly identified along with Part III and Part IV of the Indian Constitution. Part III of the Constitution of India which bestows fundamental rights on citizens can only be granted in its totality if that they play out their principal obligations and, in this way, oblige the state to work.[63] If citizens are not playing out their obligations, they do not ethically or morally deserve to enjoy these rights. Comparably, if the citizens are endeavouring towards the improvement and well-being of their nation, they need to do justice to the founding principles enshrined in the preamble of the constitution as well as the corresponding DPSP.[64] In this way, fundamental duties are firmly associated with the fundamental rights and directive principles of state policy. While fundamental rights cast a duty upon the state to look after its citizens, fundamental duties are commitments of the person towards the state to guarantee that the country moves towards advancement.[65] Essentially, DPSP assist the state in its policy decisions; fundamental duties manage the citizens' conduct while conducting themselves as citizens of the state. Even though the two arrangements of obligations cannot be upheld, they go about as core values and guide the state and its citizens to accomplish the guarantee we have made ourselves in the preamble. Even though these 'fundamental duties' are so explicitly mentioned in the constitution, they will be reduced to dead letters if the citizens do not assimilate and actualize these principles into real practice.

---

[61] *Mohan Kumar Singhania v. Union of India* 1991 SCR Supl. (1) 46.

[62] *AIIMS Student Union v. AIIMS* AIR 2001 SC 3262.

[63] Sethi D, Fundamental duties under the constitution of India: their role and importance, Dissertation, National Law University Delhi (2019).

[64] Duhan R, Fundamental rights and directive principles: an analytical approach towards social justice. *Journal of Advance Research in Social Science and Humanities* 2(5), pp. 1-5 (2016) Available at https://doi.org/10.53555/nnssh.v2i5.196.

[65] Sethi, *supra* note 63.

4 Governance on the Convergence of '*Swadharm*' and '*Rajdharm*'

Governance could be elucidated as the administration of every single aspect that characterizes a state of affairs which allows and empowers people to raise their level of their ability, also providing chances to discover their latent capacity and enlarge the forums of available opportunities. This arrangement covers the social, political and economic aspects of life at each level of the human venture. It covers the state, common society and the market, every one of which is basic for continuing human state of affairs. The market is relied upon to open doors of opportunities for individuals. In summary, the essential factors of good governance are the exercise of timely action detailing and execution of policy decisions and projects that are impartial, unambiguous, non-prejudicial, non-discriminatory, participatory or more all answerable to the individuals it affects.[66]

The customary perspective on good governance observes that a legislature must safeguard the rule of law, improve social and physical infrastructure, provide thriving conditions for development projects and guarantee common and political opportunities.[67] However, in the evolution of the 'state', the definition of good governance has started to acknowledge the importance of duties which accompany rights for the advancement of a new social conscience and order that widens into the promotion of human dignity and pride, the essence of equity and various elements that go to make life rich and all the more satisfying for every person.

It is a perceived rule of ethics and social relations as well as that of legislative prudence which dictates that rights and duties go hand-in-hand, that rights originate from obligations performed and that if an individuals' right is to be steady with another individual's right, that can only happen through acknowledgement of comparing obligations by both the men. Rights are basically social ideas that spring from human convention, customs, tradition and legal thought-process, and these are constantly accompanied by comparing duties and commitments. Ergo, rights cannot be separated from duties. It is the non-recognition of duties that makes the enforcement of (state and individual) rights unreasonable and coercive. Ergo, it is the mandatory prerogative of the citizen of the state to complement the duties of the state with his own. Fulfilment of individual duty is the right way to channel rights flowing from the state's duty.

Each privilege compares with a corresponding 'duty'. The reciprocity of both rights and duties is vital for the development of the citizens which eventually comes full circle buttressing development of a country. The preamble of the Indian Constitution adumbrates rights just as duties. The best possible approach to comprehend the constitution is to sympathize with its foundational notion. Consequently, one would

---

[66] Harriss J, "Antinomies of empowerment: observations on civil society, politics and urban governance in India", 42 *Economic and Political Weekly* 26, pp. 2716–2724 (2007).

[67] M Johnston, Good governance: rule of law, transparency, and accountability, New York: United Nations Public Administration Network (2006) Available at https://etico.iiep.unesco.org/sites/default/files/unpan010193.pdf.

realize that fundamental rights ought not to be worshipped alone. In the society, the privileges given to an individual are offset in it with the duties bestowed upon it. On the same note, it is imperative to judge a model of governance by way of a state by the action of the state and its citizens alike. In Gandhian terms, *rajdharm* and *swadharm* are the two paddles of good governance of the welfare state. They are reciprocal terms; the duties of the state and the citizens balance the factors of power and rights for the state and the citizens, respectively. The state does not hold absolute power, and the citizens are not to disregard the rightful mandate of the state. The utopian dream of an Indian welfare state is possible only with the convergence of the directive principle of state policy along with the fundamental duties of citizen. It is only with such holy convergence, the 'circle of *dharm*' shall then be complete.

In conclusion, it is imperative to highlight the Rig Vedic percepts of '*Atmano mokshartham jagat hitayacha*', i.e. the dual motivation behind the notion of life is the liberation of the spirit and welfare of the world.[68] The purpose of overall public good lies in the welfare of the world; or as it were, self-advancement or private wellbeing ought to be compliant to the greater good. In fact, it is the highest duty of the state and an individual at the same time to take care of the welfare of the society and the collective good.

References

Bilgrami A (2011) Gandhi's religion and its relation to his politics. In: Brown JM, Parel A (eds) Cambridge companion to Gandhi. Cambridge University Press, Cambridge, pp 93–116

Bilimoria P (1995) Protestant ethic and Hindu dharma: with reference to the Kant and Gandhi. In: Sinha BM (ed) The Contemporary Essays on the Bhagavad Gītā. Siddharth Publications, New Delhi, pp 69–101

Brockington J (2004) The concept of "dharma" in the Ramayana. J Ind Philos 32(5/6):655–670. http://www.jstor.org/stable/23497156

Chakrabarty B (2006) Social and political thought of Mahatma Gandhi. Routledge, London, p 38

Chimni BS (2012) The self, modern civilization, and international law: learning from Mohandas Karamchand Gandhi's Hind Swaraj or Indian home rule. Eur J Int Law 23(4):1159–1173. https://doi.org/10.1093/ejil/chs075

Creel AB (1975) The re-examination of 'dharma' in Hindu ethics. Philos East West 25(2):161–173. https://doi.org/10.2307/1397937

Deborah C (2019) Desperately seeking 'Justice' in classical Chinese: on the meanings of Yi. Int J Semiot Law 32:13–28. https://doi.org/10.1007/s11196-018-9566-9

Derrett DM (1976) Rajadharma. J Asian Stud 35(4):597–609. https://doi.org/10.2307/2053673

Duhan R (2016) Fundamental rights and directive principles: an analytical approach towards social justice. J Adv Res Soc Sci Humanit 2(5):1–5. https://doi.org/10.53555/nnssh.v2i5.196

Enoch D (2002) A right to violate one's duty. Law Philos 21:355–384. https://doi.org/10.2307/3505056

Gandhi M (1983) Autobiography: the story of my experiments with truth. Courier Corporation

Garg S (2004) Political ideas of shanti parva. Ind J Polit Sci 65(1):77–86. https://www.jstor.org/stable/41855798

[68] Mathur KM, Vedantic wisdom and contemporary management, 45 *Indian Journal of Public Administration* 1, pp. 5–16 (1999).

Gautam B (2015) Directive principles of state policy: theory and practice. In: Mehta BP, Choudhry S, Khosla M (eds) Oxford handbook for Indian constitution. Oxford University Press, Oxford, pp 644–661

Gill NK (2018) Good governance in India: the concept and the practice. Asian J Multidimens Res 7(3):199–206

Gokhale BG (1972) Gandhi and history. History Theory 11(2):214–225. https://doi.org/10.2307/2504587

Gritffith (2008) Ramayan of Valmiki. Devoted Publishing, Ontario, p 9

Harriss J (2007) Antinomies of empowerment: observations on civil society, politics and urban governance in India. Econ Pol Wkly 42(26):2716–2724

Jahanbegloo R (2013) The Gandhian moment. Harvard University Press, Cambridge, Massachusetts; London, England, pp 23–52

Johnston M (2006) Good governance: rule of law, transparency, and accountability. United Nations Public Administration Network, New York. https://etico.iiep.unesco.org/sites/default/files/unpan010193.pdf

Joshi A (2019) Strategic wisdom from the orient: evaluating the contemporary relevance of Kautilya's arthashastra and Sun Tzu's art of war. Strateg Anal 43(1):54–74

Juergensmeyer M (1985) Doing ethics in a plural world. In: Shelp EE (ed) Theology and bioethics. Springer, Dordrecht, pp 187–201

Lal V (2008) The Gandhi everyone loves to hate. Econ Polit Wkly 43(40):55–64. http://www.jstor.org/stable/40278027

Lindley M (2006) Gandhi on corresponding duties/rights. Anasakti Darshan 2(2). https://www.mkgandhi.org/articles/gondutiesrights.htm

Mandelbaum DG (1973) The study of life history: Gandhi. Curr Anthropol 14(3):177–206. http://www.jstor.org/stable/2740760

Mathur KM (1999) Vedantic wisdom and contemporary management. Ind J Public Admin 45(1):5–16

Menon P, Kajari K (2020) Viewing contemporary India through the kautilyan lens. https://thewire.in/politics/viewing-contemporary-india-through-the-kautilyan-lens. Accessed 29 June 2020

Mohanty PK (2005). The "Mahabharata": a reading in political structuring. Ind Literature 49(1(225)):146–151. http://www.jstor.org/stable/23346584

Nandy A (1984) Culture, state and the rediscovery of Indian politics. Econ Pol Wkly 49(19):2078–2083

Narain J (1985) Judicial law making and the place of Directive Principles in Indian constitution. J Ind Law Inst 27(2):198–222

Narayan J (2004) Relevance of rajadharma of ancient India. Ind J Polit Sci 65(1):21–28. http://www.jstor.org/stable/41855794

Panda SA, Mohanty S (2017) Uniform civil code: unified laws and divergent ways. NLS J Law Public Policy 4(Special Edition):215–230

Paranjape MR (2013) The "Persistent" Mahatma: re-reading Gandhi post-hindutva. In: Paranjape MR (ed) Making India: colonialism, national culture, and the afterlife of Indian English authority. Springer, Dordrecht, pp 237–251

Parekh B (1991) Nehru and the national philosophy of India. Econ Polit Wkly 26(1/2):35–48. http://www.jstor.org/stable/4397189

Parel AJ (ed) (2009) Gandhi: 'hind swaraj' and other writings. Cambridge University Press, Cambridge, p xvi

Persaud SN (2009) Eternal law: the underpinnings of Dharma and Karma in the justice system. Rich JL Pub Int 13(1):49–90

Rajput JS (2012) Seven social sins: the contemporary relevance. Allied Publishers, New Delhi, p 2

Rao KR (2017) Gandhi's dharma. Oxford University Press, New Delhi

Rao VK, Singh SS (1976) Fundamental duties and directive principles under the proposed amendments to the constitution [with concluding remarks by the Chairman Sardar Swaran Singh]. India Int Centre Quarterly 3(4):266–284

Rastogi K (2007) Exploring Swadharma: an overview. Int J Indian Psychol 6(3):2348–5396. https://doi.org/10.25215/0603.023
Richards G (2005) The philosophy of Gandhi: a study of his basic ideas. Routledge
Rothermund I (1969) The individual and society in Gandhi's political thought. J Asian Stud 28(2):313–320
Sarda M (2010) Concept of dharma, justice and law: a study. Supreme Court Rev 8(50):179–183. https://ssrn.com/abstract=2792042
Sarma GN (1980) Gandhi's concept of duty. Ind J Polit Sci 41(2):214–231
Sethi D (2019) Fundamental duties under the constitution of India: their role and importance. Dissertation, National Law University Delhi
Sheikh T (2020) Ethics of rajdharma. Stud Ind Place Names 40(68):801–807
Sihag BS (2009) Kautilya on law, economics and ethics. Humanomics 25(1):75–94
Singh SP (2015) Concept of rajdharma in adi-kavya: Ramayana and Mahabharata. Ind J Publ Admin 61(1):132–138. https://doi.org/10.1177/0019556120150109
Tewari D (2014) Finding swadhinta, swaraj and dharmarajya. Indian JL Pub Pol'y 1(2):58–79
Tomalin E (2006) Religion and a rights-based approach to development. Prog Dev Stud 6(2):93–108. https://doi.org/10.1191/1464993406ps130oa
Tripathi V, Misri IV (2020) How history shapes the march towards rule of law: lessons from India and China. Inst Chin Stud 47:20
Wolpert S (2002) Gandhi's passion: the life and legacy of Mahatma Gandhi. Oxford University Press

Chapter 14
Jurisprudence of Duty, Fundamental Duties and Gandhian Philosophy

Chandra Sen Pratap Singh

> The true source of right is duty. If we all discharge our duties, right will not be far to seek. If leaving duties unperformed, we run after rights, they will escape us like a will-o'-the-wisp. The more we pursue them, the farther they will fly.
>
> —Mahatma Gandhi

1 Introduction

Four revolutions of the world, namely the American Revolution, the French Revolution, the Russian Revolution and the Gandhian Revolution, have had a deep impact on Indian Constitution. For example, similar to the preamble of the U.S. Constitution, which begins with "We the people of the United states", the preamble of the Constitution of India also starts with the initial lines "We the people of India". Both French and American revolutions raised the issue of "liberty" as a core issue influencing the legal systems around the world. The drafters of the Constitution of India too were influenced by the concept of liberty, and consequently, they gave more importance to rights as compared to duties. The Indian Constitution being the supreme law of the land provides the fundamental rights under Part III running through Article 12 to Article 35. In order to provide remedy to enforce these fundamental rights, the constitution itself provides provisions under Articles 32 and 226 of the Constitution of India. Thus, the most important aspect of fundamental rights is that "they are judicially enforceable". These fundamental rights are not only enforceable against the state but also against the different agencies of the state. Further, directive principles of state policy, which have been enshrined in Part IV of Indian Constitution, are non-justiciable.[1] When we look at the original text of the Constitution of India,

[1] Article 37, The Constitution of India.

C. S. P. Singh (✉)
Assistant Professor, Faculty of Law, University of Lucknow, Lucknow, India
e-mail: pyarechandu@gmail.com

R. Mittal and K. K. Singh (eds.), *Relevance of Duties in the Contemporary World*,
https://doi.org/10.1007/978-981-19-1836-0_14

which came into force on January 26, 1950, we find that, at that time, there was no provision regarding fundamental duties for the citizens. Rights and duties are two sides of the same coin. Keeping in view the equal importance of duties along with rights, later on, fundamental duties have been incorporated in Indian Constitution. India had witnessed internal emergency from 1975 to 1977. Sardar Swaran Singh Committee was constituted which recommended the incorporation of a separate chapter on fundamental duties in the Indian Constitution.

Thus, we see that in the trilogy of fundamental rights, directive principles of state policy and fundamental duties, the Gandhian emphasis on duties was largely overlooked at the initial stage and has been accepted as creed of our multi-religious society on the basis of the post-constitution experiences. The significance of Gandhian concept of duty may be well appreciated in the context of the current world scenario of right duty orientation. Against this backdrop, the present chapter seeks to analyze the jurisprudential basis of duty, the position of fundamental duties under the Constitution of India and Gandhian philosophy on duties and its reflection in the Constitution of India.

2 Jurisprudence of Rights and Duties

Rights represent a particular way of talking about law and politics. Historically, rights were associated with revolution: for example, the 1789 French Declaration of the Rights of Man, in defiance of the old aristocratic order, asserted that "men are born and remain free and equal in rights".[2] Natural Law doctrine plays a very important role in the origin and development of rights. In fact, it has deep impact on the legal and political philosophy of John Locke. Locke suggested that "humans originally lived in a state of nature in which they were free and equal, and possessed certain natural rights, particularly the right to property".[3] Locke acknowledged the supremacy of natural law and clarified that "natural law is the eternal law for all the people- the law makers and others alike".[4]

According to John Salmond, legal right is "an interest recognized and protected by a rule of legal justice".[5] Therefore, in the view of Salmond, both "legal protection" as well as "recognition" are necessary for an interest to be regarded as a legal right. Rudolf Von Ihering in the "Spirit of Roman Law" has declared rights as "legally protected interests". Human interests are protected through law by compelling individuals to do or forbear from doing particular things. Prof. Gray has explained the concept of duty in the following words: "The acts or forbearances, which an organized society commands in order to protect legal rights or the legal duties of the

[2] Scott Veitch, Emilios Christodoulidis & Lindsay Farmer: *Jurisprudence: Themes and Concepts* (II Edition, 2012) p. 26.

[3] Ibid. at p. 27.

[4] John Locke, "*Of Civil Government*", Book II, chap. XI, S.135.

[5] Salmond, *Jurisprudence*, p. 278.

persons to whom those commands are directed".[6] Hibbert, however, points out that "duty" does not mean the "act" or "forbearance" which the law commands for these are the objects of the duty. Legal duty may be defined as the predicament of a person whose acts are liable to be controlled by another with the assent and assistance of the state.[7]

Generally, it is said that rights and duties are correlative, and they are the two sides of the same coin. Every right has a corresponding obligation or duty. Salmond says that there can be no right without a corresponding duty or duty without a corresponding right, as there can be no husband without a wife or a father without a child. According to Salmond: "A duty is an obligatory act. It is an act, the opposite of which would be wrong. Duties and wrongs are correlative. The commission of a wrong is the breach of a duty and the performance of a duty is the avoidance of a wrong".[8] Austin contrasted with the Salmond's view. Austin observed that there can be duties even without a corresponding right. He termed it as "absolute duties". Austin mentions four classes of duties, which are absolute, i.e., which do not correlate with any right.

1. Self-regarding duties (e.g., no one is allowed to end his life or remain in the stage of intoxication. He has duty toward self).
2. Duties to the public or persons, (e.g., duty not to commit nuisance).
3. Duties to one not a human being (e.g., duties owed to God or the lower animals).
4. Duties to the sovereign or state.[9]

On the other hand, Duguit says that "no one has any other right than always to do his duty. Law is only an embodiment of duties which an individual is supposed to perform as a part and parcel of the social organization for furtherance of social solidarity".[10] But, C. K. Allen opines that "Duguit's theory is incomplete as we have duties towards the society at large, we have also rights for the exercise of certain interests. It is erroneous to say that man only has the duty and nothing but duty. No legal system except perhaps those of the totalitarian state have accepted or incorporated the view of Duguit".[11]

The term "right" has been defined in numerous ways by numerous jurists and philosophers. "Right" is perhaps the most significant and contentious concepts for the jurists and philosophers to understand and define it. In legal parlance, "legal right" means the "standard of permitted action by law". Generally, rights and duties are correlated to each other, and one cannot be conceived without the other. But, there are certain rights which do not have corresponding duties. Salmond defined

[6] Gray, *Nature and sources of the Law*, p. 18.

[7] Prof. G.C. Venkata Subbarao, *Jurisprudence and Legal Theory*, p. 136.

[8] Salmond, *supra* above note 5.

[9] G.C. Venkata Subbarao: *Jurisprudence and Legal Theory*. 9th Edition, Lucknow: Eastern Book Company, 1975, p. 137.

[10] Duguit, "Law & State", 31 *Harvard Law Review* (1917).

[11] Nomita Aggarwal: *Jurisprudence (Legal Theory)*, 4th Edition (Allahabad: Central Law Publications, 2003) p. 145.

legal right in its generic sense as "any advantage or benefit which in any manner conferred upon a person by a rule of law".[12] In this sense, "rights" can be divided into following four kinds: (i) right, (ii) liberty, (iii) power and (iv) immunity. This broad view has been accepted and applied by Indian Apex Court in *State of Rajasthan* v. *Union of India*[13] and *State of Karnataka* v. *Union of India*[14] while expressing the expression "legal right" under Article 131 of the Constitution of India.

Hohfeld has discussed the concept of right in the form of *jural relations* and sets out his table of jural relations and jural opposites as follows:

Jural Correlatives:	Right	Privilege	Power	Immunity
	Duty	No right	Liability	Disability

Jural opposites:	Right	Privilege	Power	Immunity
	No right	Duty	Disability	Liability

Hohfeld analyzed it with greater accuracy in *Fundamental Legal Conceptions as Applied in Judicial Reasoning*.[15]

Hohfeld says that if "X has a right against Y to do R", then it has following four meanings:

1. Y's duty with regard to X is to allow X to do R. It means that X has a claim against Y and this claim in strict sense means "right".
2. X has a freedom to do something or refrain from doing something in relation to Y. Hohfeld calls this as "liberty" or "privilege".
3. X has ability to alter the legal position of Y. Hohfeld termed this as "power".
4. X's legal position cannot be altered by Y. Hohfeld expressed this as "immunity".

Thus, many jurists are of the opinion that every legal system is made up of both rights and duties and both are reciprocal and interdependent. For a legal system, both are exactly the same as the two sides of a coin. But, jurist like Duguit does not believe that rights and duties are concurrent. On the other hand, he says that law is constituted only by duties. Meaning thereby, Duguit completely rejects the notion of right. He repeatedly repeats Comte's statement that, "The only right which a man can possess is the right always to do his duty".[16]

The question to be considered is whether jurisprudence should be right-oriented or duty-oriented. Both have their own risks. If jurisprudence is rights-oriented, then in law, rights will have importance or prominence. This can have serious consequences. If the duties are ignored, then social development will stop, the needs of the society

---

[12] Salmond, *op. cit.*, p. 224.

[13] 1977 AIR 1361, 1978 SCR (1) 1.

[14] AIR 1978 SC 68 para 53, (1977) 4 SCC 608.

[15] *Lloyd;s Introduction to Jurisprudence*. 9th Edition, London: Sweet & Maxwell, 2014, pp. 454–60, 569–74.

[16] Friedman, *Legal Theory*, 5th Edition, p. 232.

will not be fulfilled. There will be lack of "work ethics" or "work culture" in the society. Lack of "work culture" in society will one day destroy the rights. That is why Gandhi used to say that "the true source of right is duty".

3 Fundamental Duties

Fundamental duties represent "duty-oriented jurisprudence". There are two approaches in the jurisprudential thinking: (i) the western philosophy that gives main emphasis on "right" and (ii) the Indian Philosophy which is "duty-oriented". It is somewhat like Duguit who said that "everybody has only right to perform his duties properly". The message of "Gita" is the same. In "*Bhagavad Gita*", Lord Krishn has beautifully explained the concept of "right" and "duty" to Arjun in the following popular verses: "Your right is to work only, but never to the fruit thereof. Let not the fruit of action be your object, nor let your attachment be to inaction".[17]

In the above extremely popular verse of "*Bhagavad Gita*", Lord Krishn says that "we have the right to do our duty". We should not be concerned about the results because various other factors such as—(1) our efforts, (2) destiny which is dependent upon our past karms, (3) the will of God and lastly (4) the destiny and efforts of others are also responsible in deciding our fate. The next to this popular verse of "*Bhagavad Gita*" clearly talks about duty in the following beautiful way: "Arjun, perform your duties dwelling Yog, relinquishing attachment, and indifferent to success and failure; equanimity is called Yog".[18]

"Dharm" has a very wide meaning in Indian perspective. There is no other word found similar to "Dharm" in different parts of the world/western literature that can substitute it in the true sense. Law should be based on "Dharm". "Dharm" is the cumulative result of rights, duties, conduct/ virtues of human being and their right way of living.

A popular Sanskrit verse of "Manusmriti" gives a deep insight regarding the true meaning of "dharm" in the following words:

Dharm eva hato hanti dharmo rakshati rakshitah.

Tasmad dharmo na hantavyo ma no dharmo hato'vadhit.[19]

The gist of the phrase "***dharmo rakshati rakshitah***" in above verse is that "dharm protects those who uphold or protect dharm".

Dharm in essence means "performance of one's duty" honestly. Each and every person has to perform his duties properly. Even the King is no exception. The King has also to perform his duties in the name of "Raj Dharm". The basic difference between "eastern jurisprudence" and "western jurisprudence" is that "in eastern jurisprudence

[17] Bhagwad Gita: Chapter 2, Verse 47.

[18] Ibid., Verse 48.

[19] Manusmriti: Verse 8.15.

duty occupies a very pivotal position", whereas "in western jurisprudence right is predominant". Fundamental duties are generally found in the "socialist constitutions" but not in "western liberal traditions". The inclusion of cultural traditions of societies (like Asian and African societies) in the constitution itself is the reason behind giving more emphasis to duties in comparison to western societies.[20]

At the time of the framing of the constitution having had the sad experiences of the violation of rights of Indians at the hands of the foreign rulers, the framers gave main emphasis on the fundamental rights. But, the experiences of more than two decades compelled the parliamentarians to rethink about the importance of duty as preferred by Gandhi in comparison to rights. It resulted in the inclusion of fundamental duties in the Constitution of India. It goes without saying that duties spread social cohesion, love, affection and a sense of "otherness" among the citizens in comparison to fundamental rights which are divisive and conflict creating.

The concept of fundamental duties has been borrowed from the erstwhile USSR. On the recommendation of Swaran Singh Committee, it had been incorporated in the Indian Constitution in the year 1976. Initially, the total number of fundamental duties was ten in number, but later on by 86th Constitutional Amendment Act, one more fundamental duty relating to "education of child" has been added in the year 2002. Now, there are Eleven Fundamental Duties for Indian Citizens. These fundamental duties are based on certain "code of conduct", viz., cultural, ethical, moral, etc. which has to be followed by all the citizens of India.

It is true that "there is no provision in the constitution for direct enforcement of any of these duties".[21] Further, it also does not contain any sanction for the prevention of the violation of any of these duties. But the court while determining the constitutionality of any law can give effect to any of these fundamental duties by considering such law to be reasonable and in accordance with Article 14 or 19. In this way, any law relating to fundamental duties can be saved from becoming unconstitutional.[22] Further, any citizen who have been engaged in any anti-social activities such as destroying public property, burning the constitution will be punished by courts by interpreting the constitution in a broader way and giving effect to sanctions in case of the violation of fundamental duties.[23] For instance, a person who burns the constitution, in violation of the duty in Article 51A(a), cannot assert that the meeting or assembly at which it was burnt by way of demonstration against the government should be protected by the freedom of expression or assembly guaranteed by Article 19.[24]

The Supreme Court has held that "since the Duties are obligatory for a citizen, it would follow that the State should also strive to achieve the same goal. The court

---

[20] *See*, W.D. O'Flaherty and J.D.M. Derrett, *The Concept of Duty in Asia; The Concept of Duty in Asia; African Charter on Human and People's Right of 1981.*

[21] *Ramsharan v. Union of India*, AIR 1989 SC 549 (para 14).

[22] Durga Das Basu *Constitutional Law of India*, 6th Ed., 1991, pp. 134–35.

[23] For example, Article 51A(a) and Article 51A(i) of the Constitution of India.

[24] Durga Das Basu *Shorter Constitution of India*, 13th Ed. Reprint 2006, pp. 134–35.

may, therefore, issue suitable *directions* in these matters, in appropriate cases".[25] Similar to the fundamental duties, the Directive Principles of State Policy under the Constitution of India are not enforceable by courts. The Supreme Court in order to give effect to some of the fundamental duties and Directive Principles of State Policy correlate it with other fundamental rights. For giving effect to the provisions of Article 51-A (g), regarding protection and improvement of the natural environment, the Supreme Court clubbed it with Article 21, 47, 48A and accepted the principles of "sustainable development". The essential features of "sustainable development" are the "precautionary principle" and "polluter pays principle".[26] The Supreme Court has accepted these principles in deciding the cases and making fundamental duties as well as Directive Principles of State Policy enforceable along with fundamental rights. The Supreme Court further held that "the rules of the customary international law which are not contrary to the municipal law shall be deemed to have been incorporated in the domestic law and shall be followed by the courts of law".[27]

Different articles of Indian Constitution refer either only to the citizens of India or only to the "all persons". Person includes citizens as well as non-citizens. Some of the fundamental rights such as Articles 14 and 21 are available to every person, but fundamental duties under Article 51-A are addressed to the Indian citizens only.

In a democratic set-up, people must realize that they also owe some responsibilities and duties toward the nation as well as to the others. They cannot claim that they have only rights. Gandhi defined right as "duty well performed". Fundamental duties enshrined in Article 51-A of the constitution can be considered as a "code of conduct" for citizens. Though the fundamental duties are not enforceable by the courts as fundamental rights, yet it can be effectively used as a tool for the interpretation of the constitution. Furthermore, even in the absence of sanction for the enforcement of the fundamental duties, it can be self-imposed, realized and performed by the citizens of India. Further, since the duties incorporated in the constitution are constitutional duties, so it can be made enforceable by law through the parliament. The parliament can also make provisions regarding penalties to be imposed in case of failure of fulfillment of certain duties and obligations. There are certain statute(s) like the Environment Protection Act, 1986; Indian Penal Code, 1860; Emblem and Names (Prevention of Improper Use) Act, 1950 read with the Prevention of Insult to National Honour Act, 1971, etc., which already contain provisions regarding providing remedy in case of the breach of the constitutional duties. A number of fundamental duties such as clauses (a), (c) and (d) of Article 51A which deals with national flag, national anthem, territorial integrity and sovereignty of India are already enforceable today through specific laws. With respect to the duty enshrined in clause (a) of Article 51-A, it has been held that "proper respect is shown to the national anthem by standing

[25] *Rural Litigation v. State of U.P.,* AIR 1987 SC 359 (para 20).
Vellore Citizen's Welfare Forum v. Union of India & Ors., (1996) 5 SCC 647.

[26] *Indian Council for Enviro-Legal Action v. Union of India,* 2011 (8) SCC 161; *Vellore Citizen's Welfare Forum v. Union of India,* AIR 1996 SC 2715; *M.C. Mehta v. Kamal Nath* (1997) 1 SCC 388; *M.C. Mehta v. Union of India,* AIR 1987 SC 965; *M.C. Mehta v. Union of India* (1997) 2 SCC 411; *Narmada Bachao Andolan v. Union of India,* AIR 2000 SC 3751.

[27] *Vellore Citizen's Welfare Forum v. Union of India & Ors.,*(1996) 5 SCC 647.

up when the national anthem is sung. It will not be right to say that disrespect is shown by not joining in the singing".[28] Similarly, "flying of national flag freely with respect and dignity is consistent with the duty in clause (a)".[29]

Article 51A-k was introduced as a fundamental duty in 2002 along with Article 21A as a fundamental right. A composite reading of Article 21-A along with Article 51-A(k) makes it clear that it is the obligation of the state to provide free and compulsory education to all children of the age of six to fourteen years, and it is also the fundamental duty of parent or guardian to provide opportunities for education to his child or ward for the above mentioned said period of age, i.e., 6–14 years.

It is clear that with the passage of time, there has been an increasing reference to Article 51-A and its various clauses giving them content and a kind of enforceability.

4 Gandhian Philosophy

> Let each do his duty, If I do my duty, that is, serve myself, I shall be able to serve others. Before I leave you, I will take the liberty of repeating:
>
> 1. Real Swaraj is self-rule or self-control.
> 2. The way to it is satyagrah: that is, soul force or love-force
> 3. In order to exert this force, Swadeshi in every sense is necessary.
> 4. What we want to do should be done, not because we object to the English or because we want to retaliate but because it is our duty to do so.[30]

India has given many political and spiritual leaders to the world, but Gandhi's message of "non-violence" can be considered as the greatest contribution of India to the global world in order to maintain global peace. The ideal of "ahimsa paramo dharmah" was the key philosophy of Gandhi's life. He not only formulated it but also practiced it throughout his life. He has been considered as the "Man of the Millennium". Truth or satya, ahimsa or non-violence constitute the core of Gandhian philosophy.

Gandhi was one of the greatest leaders and freedom fighter of India who fought against the colonial rule for the independence of the country through peaceful means. Gandhi was not only a political leader but also a great social reformer. He was the person who fought simultaneously not only on political front but also on economic, social and religious fronts. He was a visionary man and had a great vision in these diversified fields. He was of the firm belief that the working of the courts should be done in regional languages. He advocated and favored the alternative dispute resolution (ADR) system. Although the government should run according to the will

---

[28] *Bijoe Emmanuel v. State of Kerala*, (1986) 3 SCC 615; AIR 1987 SC 748, 752.

[29] *Union of India v. Naveen Jindal*, (2004) 2 SCC 510; AIR 2004 SC 1559.

[30] Hind Swaraj, 1909: *Collected Works of Mahatma Gandhi*-hereafter referred to as CWMG, Vol. 10, p. 64.

of the people, still any kind of injustice should not be allowed in the name of majority. In the eyes of Gandhi, the "charter of rights" is less important in comparison to the "charter of duties". He always asked people to perform their duties and follow the ideals of truth and non-violence. He opined: "I do not believe in the doctrine of the greatest good of the greatest number. The only real, dignified, human doctrine is the greatest good of all".[31]

Some of the Gandhian principles are incorporated in the Constitution of India, particularly in the form of Directive Principles of State Policy, which have been enshrined in Part IV of the constitution mentioned from Articles 36–51. These are similar to the socio-economic program enunciated by Gandhi during the long-drawn freedom struggle. The following important articles of Indian Constitution have direct connection with Gandhian principles:

1. Organization of Village Panchayats[32]: The 73rd Constitution Amendment Act gives effect to Article 40 of the Indian Constitution.
2. Promotion of Cottage Industries[33]: Article 43 of the Indian Constitution states that the state shall frame its policy to promote cottage industries in rural areas. Gandhi had already advocated it.
3. Promotion and protection of interests of educational and economic interests of SCs, STs and other weaker sections of the society and to protect them from social injustice and exploitation.[34]
4. Prohibition of consumption of intoxicating drinks and drugs which are injurious to health[35]: Prohibition of intoxicating drinks and drugs was an important element in Gandhi's view, and accordingly, it has been incorporated in Article 47 of the Indian Constitution.

Explaining the Gandhian concept of self-rule, Raghavan Iyer observed:

> Gandhi equated freedom with self-rule because he wished to build into the concept of freedom the notion of obligation to others as well as to oneself, while retaining the element of voluntariness that is the very basis of freedom. The notion of self-rule implies the voluntary internalization of our obligation to others which will be obstructed by our placing ourselves at the mercy of our selfish desires.[36]

Thinkers like Vivekanand, before Gandhi, explicitly raised the issue of rights by connecting it to the basic problem of reconciling individual freedom with social responsibility. Vivekanand anticipates Gandhi: "Selflessness only, not selfishness, can solve the question. The idea of 'right' is a limitation: there is really no 'mine' and 'thine', for I am thou and thou art I. We have 'responsibility' not 'rights'".[37]

---

[31] Mahatma Gandhi Quotable Quotes, 2016.

[32] Article 40, The Constitution of India.

[33] Article 43, The Constitution of India.

[34] Article 46, The Constitution of India.

[35] Article 47, The Constitution of India.

[36] Iyer: *The Moral and Political Thought of Mahatma Gandhi*, 1973, p. 349.

[37] Works, Volume III, p. 23.

Aurobindo beautifully explained this idea with reference to Indian Philosophy in the following way—"It was a marked feature of the Indian mind that it sought to attach a spiritual meaning and a religious sanction to all, even to the most external social political circumstances of its life, imposing on all classes and functions an ideal, not except incidentally of rights and powers, but of duties, a dharm with a spiritual significance".[38]

"Ahimsa paramo dharmah" is the ideal of Gandhi's philosophy. Truth and non-violence are the most important virtues in Gandhi's life. He used "satyagrah" as a tool to protest against injustice. In the views of Gandhi, "truth" and "non-violence" play a very important role in translating dharm as the path of duty or "the royal road of dharm that leads to both earthly and spiritual bliss".[39] Gandhi's philosophy of dharm is based on "truth" and "non-violence". In his view, "dharm" has no existence in the absence of "truth" and "non-violence", and he considers it as "religion in the highest sense of term".[40] He strongly condemned the commission of any type of violence in any form in the name of religion. Violence has no place in Gandhi's philosophy. He strongly opposed violence and said that, "The truth is that all activities in this world are related to dharm or adharm", Gandhi has given a lot of examples from his life through his writings like "My Experiments with Truth" which are concerned with path of "morality" and "immorality". This leads to a pertinent question, "whether dharm is a moral duty or religious duty". Various people might misinterpret it, but Gandhi says that "the true test lies in the intention of pursuing the correct path". Gandhi says, "So long as I do not see my mistakes, I must practice the dharm which I consider to be true".[41]

Gandhi has utilized the above theory of "dharm" in creating his idea toward the concept of rights. In Gandhi's word, "Having a right surely does not mean that I should exercise that right in utter disregard of my sense of proportion…The exercise of rights depends on one's sense of duty. It is my duty to follow dharm… I do what I consider my duty".[42] The above idea has been borrowed by Gandhi from his earlier writing of "Hind Swaraj", where he says that "real rights are a result of performance of duty".[43]

Gandhi in his book "Ethical Religion" explained the concept of "personal morality" and said that morality begins with "our duties towards ourselves". In the words of Gandhi, the following phrases—"I am responsible for this", or "This is my duty" plays a very important role in creating a man's thought regarding their duties. The moral nature of a man itself is responsible for the creation of good and noble thoughts. When a person is ready to perform his duty, it means, according to Gandhi, that some mysterious, resounding voice seems to say, "To thee, individually, O man, is given this task". Gandhi said that it is the prima facie duty of each and every man to have

[38] Aurobindo Ghose: *The spirit and Form of Indian Polity*, 1966. pp. 7-8.

[39] Collected Works of Mahatma Gandhi 72:48.

[40] Collected Works of Mahatma Gandhi 64:191.

[41] Collected Works of Mahatma Gandhi 38:21–2.

[42] Collected Works of Mahatma Gandhi 69:208.

[43] Collected Works of Mahatma Gandhi 10:44.

respect for themselves as they have respect for others before having sympathy and kind regards for others. The most important and foremost duty of every person is to develop the virtue of character and inculcate the habit of social services in themselves. In the words of Gandhi, "Man's highest duty in life is to serve mankind and take his share in bettering its condition. This is true worship- true prayer". Each and every human being is obliged to "contribute to an ideal order of human life". In order to achieve this, according to Gandhi, the individual must through self-examination become "sincere in himself, bear no malice, exploit no one and always act with a pure mind. Such men alone can serve mankind".[44] Strong social conscience and personal integrity are necessary for the formation and recognition of the good relationship between "rights" and "duties", and it is also the gist of Gandhi's individualism. Gandhi says: "So long as one has not developed inner strength, one can never practice the dharm of ahimsa".[45]

India as a nation can flourish only when we follow the Gandhian approach to duties which is based on compassion, respect for all religions, scientific temper and humanism, respect for composite culture, etc. as desired by Gandhi.

In the eyes of Gandhi, if the duty is well performed, then it can only be termed as "right" in the true sense. Every citizen of India is obliged to certain duties along with their corresponding rights. In the view of Gandhi "duty is a debit while the rights belong to a creditor". According to Gandhi, "duties and rights" both are important, but they are somewhat different in certain ways, as he says,

> Rights accrue automatically to him who duly performs his duties. In fact, the right to perform one's duties is the only right that is worth living for and dying for. It covers all legitimate rights[46]

Gandhi represents the Indian ethos of duty orientation which he had learnt from his uneducated but very just thinking mother who had taught him to perform duty. In his words:

> I learnt my duties on my mother's lap. She was an unlettered village woman... She knew my dharm. Thus if from my childhood we learn what our dharm is and try to follow it our rights look after themselves... The beauty of it is that the very performance of a duty secures us our right. Rights cannot be divorced from duties. This is how satyagrah was born, for I was always striving to decide what my duty was.[47]

Ignoring the very notion of fundamental duties in the original Constitution of India was theoretically and practically big deviation from Gandhian thoughts. The forty-second Constitutional Amendment incorporated Article 51-A listing various fundamental duties and tried to bring in Gandhian idea although without making

---

44 Collected Works of Mahatma Gandhi 6: 340–41.

45 Collected Works of Mahatma Gandhi 28: 49.

46 Gandhi, M.K., *India of My Dreams* (1947) Compiled by Prabhu, R.K., Ahmedabad: Navjivan Publishing House.

47 Collected Works of Mahatma Gandhi 88: 230.

them automatically enforceable or pre-requisite for entitlement to fundamental rights as Gandhi had contemplated.[48]

5 Conclusion and Suggestion

Right and duty are two most important concepts of law. Various jurists like Locke, Salmond, Austin, Prof. Gray, Hibbert, Duguit, C. K. Allen, Hohfeld, etc. have explained the concept of right and duty in a systematic way and are of the opinion that every legal system is made up of both rights and duties. Rights and duties are correlative. Both are equally important. But, people are mostly concerned about their rights. They forget that duties are equally important along with rights. If each and every person performs his duty properly, they do not have to demand for their rights. Rights and duties are so interconnected that if the duty will be performed properly, rights will be automatically enforced. But, the harsh reality is that most people are not ready to perform their duties properly, and they only shout for the enforcement of their rights.

As mentioned before, there are two approaches in the jurisprudential thinking: (1) the eastern/Indian approach is "duty-oriented", and (2) the western approach gives main emphasis on right. Despite the fact that Indian approach is "duty-oriented", the non-inclusion of fundamental duties, initially, in the Constitution of India attracted criticism from various thinkers. Before the inclusion of the fundamental duties, P. V. Kane was critical of the Constitution of India that it ignored the Indian tradition of duties and spoke only of rights.[49] Reference to duties, however, finds place even in international instruments such as the Universal Declaration of Human Rights and International Covenant on Civil and Political Rights.[50]

Fundamental duties have now become the part of the Constitution of India, and it contains eleven fundamental duties for Indian Citizens enshrined in Article 51-A. These fundamental duties are based on certain "code of conduct", viz., cultural, ethical, moral, etc. which has to be followed by the citizens of India. Fundamental rights under Part III of Indian Constitution have gained more significance as they are not considered as mere moral declarations. Articles 13 and 32 of the Indian Constitution give them the necessary teeth. Article 32 along with Article 226 is subject of constitutional remedies. Article 32 of the Indian Constitution is so important that Dr. Ambedkar called it as "the heart and soul of the constitution". Unlike fundamental rights, fundamental duties are comparable to the Directive Principles of State Policy.

Wrongs can be broadly classified into "civil wrongs" (i.e., wrongs against the individual) and "criminal wrongs" (i.e., wrongs against the community at large). Breach of duty is also considered as a wrong of "civil misconduct". Any breach of

[48] Shriman Narayan Agarwal, *Gandhian Constitution for Free India* with Foreword by Mahatma Gandhi, Kitabstan, Allahabad, 1946, pp. 80–87.

[49] P.V. Kane, *History of Dharamsastra*, Vol. V, Pt. II, pp. 1664–65 (1962).

[50] *See*, Article 29 of UDHR and the Preamble to the ICCPR.

duty (act includes omission also) is an actionable wrong which is redressable by an action for damages. Further, punishment can also be provided in case of persistent breach of duty/wrong along with wrong of aggravated form. Different statutes have in itself provided the appropriate remedy in case of breach of duty. In Indian Constitution, various writs, viz., Habeas Corpus, Mandamus, Certiorari, Prohibition and Quo Warranto are in themselves self-sufficient for providing adequate remedy in the case of "constitutional wrongs".

Fundamental duties are addressed to the citizens, and it is the expectation of the country that these duties should be performed by the citizens properly. But, it is a common belief that if a citizen does not perform his fundamental duties, there is no provision provided by Indian Constitution for its enforcement as compared with the case of fundamental rights. This is not completely true. Due to lack of enforcement mechanism for fundamental duties as compared to fundamental rights, fundamental duties cannot be directly enforced, but it could be enforced through specific legislations. It becomes necessary to make appropriate arrangements for the effectuation of fundamental duties by providing statutory protection in this regard.

Gandhi was of the firm view that "charter of duties" are more significant in comparison to "charter of rights". Gandhi never believed in only preaching. His autobiography titled "My Experiments with Truth" throws a deep insight into the Gandhi's philosophy and importance of duties in his life. In the words of Gandhi "If a person follows his duty properly, the right of the other will be automatically followed". Therefore, those who are entrusted with the policy making, they must focus on duties and ensure that their policies are "duty-oriented". With the passage of time, the Gandhian concepts of duty, forbearance and otherness are becoming more and more pressing. The present scenario presented by COVID-19 makes abundantly clear that the world can survive only with cohesion, cooperation and duty orientation of the world community.

References

African Charter on Human and People's Right of 1981.
Agarwal SN (1946) Gandhian constitution for free India (with foreword by Mahatma Gandhi). Kitabstan, Allahabad
Aggarwal N (2003) Jurisprudence (legal theory). Central Law Publications, Allahabad
Basu Durga Das (1991) Constitutional Law of India. LexisNexis Butterworths Wadhwa, Nagpur.
Basu DD (2006) Shorter constitution of India. LexisNexis Butterworths Wadhwa, Nagpur
Bhagwad G. Chapter 2, verse 47
Complete works of Swami Vivekanand, vol III. Advaita Ashrama
Duguit L (1917) The law and the state. Harvard Law Rev 31
Fitzgerald PJ (2010) Salmond on jurisprudence. Universal Law Publishing Co. Pvt. Ltd., Delhi
Freeman M (2014) Lloyd's introduction to jurisprudence. Sweet & Maxwell, London
Friedman W (1967) Legal theory. Columbia University Press, New York
Gandhi (1969) Collected works of Mahatma Gandhi. Publications Division, Ministry of Information and Broadcasting, Govt. of India, New Delhi

Gandhi MK (1947) (Compiled by Prabhu RK) India of my dreams. Navjivan Publishing House, Ahmedabad

Gandhi Mahatma, 1869–1948 (1997) Hind Swaraj and other writings. Cambridge University Press, New York

Ghose A (1966) The spirit and form of Indian polity. Arya Publishing House, Calcutta

Hovenkamp H (1997) In: Campbell D, Thomas P (eds) The nature and sources of the law by John Chipman Gray. Routledge, London

Iyer RN (1973) The moral and political thought of Mahatma Gandhi. Oxford University Press, UK

Locke J (1689) Of civil government. Book II, Chap. XI, S.135

Mahatma Gandhi quotable quotes, 2016

Manusmriti: Verse 8.15.

O'Flaherty WD, Derrett JDM (1978) The concept of Duty in South Asia. School of Oriental and African Studies

Subbarao GC, Venkata (1975) Jurisprudence and legal theory. Eastern Book Company, Lucknow

Veitch S, Christodoulidis E, Farmer L (2012) Jurisprudence themes and concepts. Routledge Taylor & Francis Group, London and New York

Chapter 15
Mahatma Gandhi: Duty and Enlightened Anarchy in Constitutional Governance

Ashish Kumar Srivastava

> Generations to come, it may be, will scarce believe that such a one as this ever in flesh and blood walked upon this earth
>
> Albert Einstein About Mahatma Gandhi

1 Swaraj and Swadharm

Mahatma Gandhi also known as 'Father of Nation' in India is an epitome of truthfulness and non-violence. Dharm in India has been a very different notion altogether. Its meaning has been attached with duty, justice, truth, morality, and rights. Though Indian society has traditionally been duty-oriented society, however, in modern times particularly since independence, India has given prominence to rights over duties due to the emergence of rights-based jurisprudence. India as a nation had several models of governance before it at the time of independence. The models of capitalist state and communist state were the most important models. Gandhi was not happy with the concept of 'laissez faire' state. The non-interventionist state in economic activities was not acceptable to him. Mindless profit maximization through manufacturing and industrialization was not acceptable to him. The capitalist state was based on exploitation of weak. The model of communist state was also not acceptable to him as it was based on totalitarian power of state and suppression of freedom of individual. Gandhi unlike these two popular models of state propounded the model of 'Swaraj' and 'Ramraj' which was based on the fact that sovereignty will lie in the people of India on the moral authority of people. In this type of state, people will act like trustees of money and

A. K. Srivastava (✉)
Assistant Professor, Faculty of Law, University of Lucknow, Lucknow, India
e-mail: srivastava_ashisk@lkouniv.ac.in

R. Mittal and K. K. Singh (eds.), *Relevance of Duties in the Contemporary World*,
https://doi.org/10.1007/978-981-19-1836-0_15

resources which ultimately belongs to God. This state was stout enough to provide for everyone's need but not for everyone's greed. He also propounded the concept of 'Swadharma' which was based on the assumption that one must do his duty and that is his supreme obligation and his rights will be naturally taken care of. Gandhi believed that true source of rights is duty. Running behind rights without performing duties is like a will-o-the-wisp. Swadharm is a kind of Yajnya (sacrifice) which is aimed for Sarvodaya, i.e., good for all. Gandhi, due to his idea of Sarvodaya, Swadharm, and sacrifice, is often conceived as against the individualism which people see as conflict between a humanist preaching for a legal state, individualism, independence and equality and a mystic supporting moral hierarchical order, moral state, group civilization, and unity.[1]

Gandhi found capitalist model oppressive as the same being a right-oriented model talked much about ideas founded on the basis of Charles Darwin and Adam Smith wherein the 'survival of the fittest' was to be secured in the economic order. Gandhi being influenced by John Ruskin's 'Unto This Last' propounded the idea of 'Sarvodaya.' Sarvodaya, i.e., welfare of all, is interlinked to Swadharm which is about doing one's duties, self-sacrifice, and non-violence. The moral authority of people laced with dutifulness will govern the society. In Gandhian philosophy, duties are more important than rights. His sense of duty is different from socialist state as duties in such states are coercive and enforced by brute and totalitarian state.[2] In his work, 'Hind Swaraj' Gandhi made a critique of entire western philosophy, history, culture, and civilization and said that real and genuine civilization can be traced in villages of India where through common morality each member performs his duty.[3]

Gandhi was greatly influenced with John Ruskin's work 'Unto This Last.' He was opposed to the sheer madness of capitalism, based on utilitarian and majoritarian model which justified the sacrifice of minority for happiness of majority. He even did not want sacrifice of the happiness of minority. Gandhi is of the view that work must be steered not by pay but by morality which is beneficial to rich and poor both. He says that 'if one man lives in idleness and another has to put in a double amount of work…it brings about a diminution in the national capital and is not beneficial to the worker himself. The rich oppress the poor by misuse of riches. Employers and employees are at daggers drawn with one another and men are reduced to the level of beasts (Gandhi 2007).'[4]

Swaraj and Sarvodaya can be secured by swadharm. Swaraj is not self-rule only. Gandhi says that, 'Swaraj really means self-control. Only he is capable of self-control who observes the rules of morality, does not cheat or give up truth, and

---

[1] B. K. Mallik, Gandhi-A Prophecy, Oxford, p. 34 (1948).

[2] S.N. Dhyani, Jurisprudence, Central Law Agency, Third Edition, Allahabad, p. 240 (1999).

[3] Rudrangshu Mukherjee, "Gandhi's Swaraj", 44 *Economic and Political Weekly* 50, December 12–18, pp. 34–39 at 35 (2009).

[4] M.K. Gandhi, Ruskin Unto This Last A Paraphrase, Navjivan Publishing House, Second Edition, Ahmedabad, p. 42 (2007).

does his duty to his parents, wife and children, servants and neighbours. Such a man is in enjoyment of swaraj, no matter where he lives. A state enjoys swaraj if it can boast of a large number of such good citizens.'[5] His idea of swaraj is not limited to governance or rule. His idea of swaraj is about truthfulness and morality of people. He says that, "India must indeed have swaraj but she must have it by righteous methods. Our swaraj must be real swaraj, which cannot be attained by either violence or industrialization. He was of the opinion that it can be attained if every Indian stick to truth, and in that case, Swaraj will come to us of its own accord." He talked of 'Ramraj' where the 'moral authority' is the basic foundation of the sovereignty of the people. He, therefore, suggests that the content of the democratic state is expressed by the term 'Ramraj' which he explains as follows: 'Ramraj is the kingdom of righteousness. By Ramraj, I do not mean Hindu raj. I mean by Ramraj, divine raj, the kingdom of God... the ancient ideal of Ramraj is undoubtedly one of true democracy.'[6]

2 Trusteeship

Gandhi again propounded the idea of trusteeship. He was of the view that taking more than one's need is thieving. We are trustee of resources and riches. In his idea of trusteeship, he is not envisaging a totalitarian socialist state which removes the private property as the same would be a violent act of state to deprive and dispossess someone of his worldly possession. He was believer of the mantra 'तेन त्यक्तेन भुन्जथिा:', i.e., enjoy thy wealth by renouncing it. Trusteeship simply means that take what you require for your legitimate needs and use the remaining for society. One who appropriates more than the minimum that is really necessary for him is guilty of theft. He believed that trusteeship is practically possible. Gandhi believed that when one has more than his proportionate portion, he became a trustee of that portion for God's people. Gandhi says, "As for the present owners of wealth, they would have to make their choice between class war and voluntarily converting themselves into trustees of their wealth. They would be allowed to retain the stewardship of their possessions and to use their talent to increase the wealth, not for their own sakes, but for the sake of the nation and therefore without exploitation. The state would regulate the rate of commission which they would get commensurate with the service rendered and its value to society. Their children would inherit the stewardship only if they proved their fitness for it (Gandhi 2009)."[7] Gandhi truly believed in the idea of trusteeship and regarded it practical and possible to achieve. His idea of trusteeship is not based on dispossession by

[5] *Ibid.* at p. 42.

[6] Indira Rothermund, "The Individual and Society in Gandhi's Political Thought", 28 *The Journal of Asian Studies* 2, Feb., pp. 313–320 at 315 (1969).

[7] M. K. Gandhi, Trusteeship, Navijivan Publishing House, Ahmedabad, p. 7 (2009).

annihilation of private property by brute state. It also does not exclude the regulation of private property by legislation and ownership in private property up to one's need is identified, and for remaining, the owner acts like a trustee. His idea of trusteeship was based on 'Aparigrah' (non-possession) and 'Asteya' (non-stealing) of Gita. He says that, "I understand the Gita teaching of non-possession to mean that those who desire salvation should act like trustees who thought having control over great possession regard not an iota of them as his own."[8]

3 State, Individual, Swadeshi, and Satyagrah

Gandhi considers state as snake which is omnipresent, and he wishes to wrestle with the snake. He was against the comprehensiveness of state. He believed that Swaraj and Ramraj were governed by moral authority of people under self-rule and self-restraint. He said that if national life becomes so perfect as to become self-regulated, no representation becomes necessary and this will be a state of '*Enlightened Anarchy'* where everyone shall be ruler.[9] His idea about state is 'enlightened anarchy.'[10] Gandhi gave due regard to individual and his good will???. His freedom was important to him. The relationship between the state and individual must be good. He considered democracy as a way of life. He asked individual to create a balance in his freedom with social restraint. He says, "Willing submission to social restraint for the sake of well-being of the whole society enriches both the individual and the society of which one is member (Kachroo 1992)."[11] Gandhi believed that brute state cannot face the morality of individual as Rabindranath Tagore speaking about Gandhi observed that "We honour Mahatma Gandhi because he has brought this ideal into sphere of politics and under his lead India is proving every day how aggressive power pitifully fails when human nature in its wakeful majesty bears insult and pain without retaliating."[12]

Gandhi believed in village republic. Panchayat Raj System is an idea of Gandhi which was added in Indian Constitution. Local self-governance plays an important role in social, political, and economic life of an individual as the local interests are better represented. Self-sufficient village founded on swadeshi economic model shall be autonomous and will have legislative, executive, and judicial authority which shall vest in 'Panchayats.' Swadeshi economic model shall be executed by harvesting crops and cotton. Crops of opium, tobacco, and ganja shall be excluded. Sanitation and compulsory education to all and non-discrimination shall be practiced in village.

[8] J.L. Kachroo, Gandhi, Tagore & Nehru: Contribution and Thought, Cosmos Bookhive Pvt. Ltd., New Delhi, p. 35 (1992).

[9] Rudranghu Mukherjee (ed.), The Penguin Gandhi Reader, p. 79 (2010).

[10] Kachroo, *supra* note 8 at 31.

[11] *Ibid.* at 32.

[12] Tagore, Rabindranath, Tagore on Gandhi, Rupa & Co., New Delhi, p. 56 (2008).

Gandhi believed in Varnashram Dharm but he was against 'untouchability' and 'casteism.' He propounded the idea of 'harijan', and he wanted the all-round development of harijan. He wanted untouchability to be abolished from the country. He was a firm believer of equality of men and women. He advocated for education of women, monogamy, and widow remarriage.

His idea about economy is based on 'Sarvodaya,' swadeshi, and trusteeship. He said that economy should be instilled with the moral authority. The industrialist should be trustees of riches for the welfare of people. He propounded the idea of 'daridranarayan.' He said, "There cannot be Ramraj in the existing unequitous?? inequalities in which a few role in riches and masses do not get enough to eat."[13] Gandhi was not against capital, and he said if the true worth of capital is to be seen, then it must save the poorest from hunger and starvation. Gandhi was not against industrialization and machinery. He was against the craze for machinery, and if the machinery served the public interests of all, then it was required for society.

He was a staunch supporter of swadeshi. His idea of swadeshi is about being self-reliant. He is not narrow minded swadeshi to refuse all foreign things. He says, "any article is swadeshi if it subserves the interests of the million, even though the capital and talent are foreign but under effective Indian control."[14] Gandhi said that charka and khadi will earn bread to poor and make him self-reliant. He saw charkha and khadi as means of economic freedom of people from poverty and hunger. He believed in bread labor. He said that one who without offering sacrifice eats, he eats stolen food.

His idea of 'satyagrah' speaks about moral authority. Satyagraha means holding on truth. It renounces any kind of violence and includes love, faith, and sacrifice. The satyagrahi has to make realize the opponent about his wrong and induce him to change his course of conduct. Satyagrahi must be non-violent, brahmchari (disciplined in sexual matters) unlike bramcharya in popular sense, fearless, should not hold surplus, follower of swadeshi, must be respectful to all religions, and believe in humanism. Satyagrah can be individual and corporate. Non-co-operation, civil disobedience, fasting, hartal, social boycott, picketing, and hijrat were used by him throughout national struggle.

4 Constitutional Governance, Duties, and Gandhi

Rights and duties are norms in society. Society speaks much about right and less about duty. What we must accept is that the term 'right' in fact stands for a rich set of normative categories found in most normative systems.[15]

---

[13] Mukherjee, *supra* note 9 at 33.

[14] *Ibid*. at 35.

[15] Ori J. Herstein, A Legal Right to Do Legal Wrong, 34 *Oxford Journal of Legal Studies* 1, Spring, pp. 21–45, p. 23 (2014).

Salmond sees duty as a jural co-relative of rights. Salmond defines duty in these terms. "A duty is roughly speaking an act which one ought to do, an act the opposite of which would be a wrong." Salmond classifies duty into moral duty and legal duty. He is concerned with legal duty only. He says that in legal duty, recognition is important than enforcement (Fitzgerald).[16] Right has no meaning without duty. Duty if breached results in wrong and harm which is remedied by law. The positive school of jurisprudence sees the idea of duty as imperative duty, breach of which will attract sanction of sovereign. Wesley Newcomb Hohfeld in his explanation of rights in wider sense explains jural co-relatives and jural opposites, and Glanville Williams adds in it this idea the jural contradictories.[17] These jurists are trying to give a wider meaning of right and its relationship with duty, liability, power, immunity, disability, and liberty.

Duty in India has been very firmly rooted in its cultural and plural diversity. Hence, in ancient time dharm denotes the idea of duty. In Constitution, we had a vision that India being a nation in the making will concentrate on duties of state and citizens will remain duty oriented but things changed swiftly.

The difference between legal and moral duty becomes more important in Gandhian idea which believed in moral duty. Macbeath a philosopher identifies duty in moral sense. He says that, 'Duty in the full sense of the term seems to me to minimum response to a situation that is required from I do not say it is all that is required of a moral agent response of a moral agent) because, according to a common sense of the term duty, it is my duty, e.g., to be just generous.'[18] Gandhi believed in moral duty. Ronald Dworkin in his work *'Taking Rights Seriously'* criticized Hart's 'rule of recognition' for the idea of legal duty and considers moral authority more relevant than rule of recognition (Coleman 1980).[19] Gandhi moral idea of duty becomes clear when he is charged under section 124A, and during his trial, he records his statement. He says, "In fact, I believe that I have rendered a service to India and England by showing in non co-operation– the way out of the unnatural state in which both are living. In my humble opinion, *non-co-operation with evil is as much a duty as is co-operation with good.* But in the past, non-co-operation has been deliberately expressed in violence to the evil doer. I am endeavouring to show to my countrymen that violent non-co-operation only multiplies evil and that as evil can only be sustained by violence, withdrawal of support of evil requires complete abstention from violence. Non-violence implies voluntary submission to the penalty for non-co-operation with the evil… I am here, therefore, to invite and submit cheerfully to the highest penalty that can be inflicted upon me for what in law is a deliberate crime and what appears to me to be the highest duty

[16] PJ Fitzgerald, Salmond on Jurisprudence, Sweet & Maxwell, 12th Edition, New Delhi, pp. 216–217.

[17] Wesley Newcomb Hohfeld, "Some Fundamental Legal Conceptions as Applied in Judicial Reasoning", 23 *The Yale Law Journal* 1, Nov., pp. 16–59 Hohfeld (1913).

[18] A. Macbeath, 23 *Duty Philosophy* 85, Apr., pp. 99–115 at p. 102 (1948).

[19] Jules L. Coleman, "Legal Duty and Moral Argument" Social Theory and Practice, 5 *Taking Dworkin Seriously* 3/4, A Special Issue, pp. 377–407 at p. 377 (1980).

of a citizen."[20] Gandhi was supportive of moral duty not legal duty which jurisprudence identifies as unenforceable duties. R.W.M. Dias has made a wonderful analysis of unenforceable duties. If we go by definition of duty, we can conclude that legal duty is sanction oriented but, in many societies, various unenforceable or non-sanctioned duties are found. These duties often go unrecognized due to faulty definition of duty as such.[21]

Part IV of the Constitution provides for Directive Principles of State Policy (DPSP) enshrined in Articles 36–51 which is also a reflection of the ideas of Gandhi. Article 37 says that DPSP are non-justiciable but still are fundamental in governance of the country. They provide for equal distribution of resources, equal justice and free legal aid, village panchayats, right to work, humane working conditions and maternity benefit, living wages for workers, participation of workers in management, uniform civil code, child education, promotion of educational and economic interests of Scheduled Castes, Scheduled Tribes, and other weaker section, improving public health, nutrition, and standard of living, agriculture and animal husbandry, protection of environment, wildlife and forests, protection of national monuments and places, separation of judiciary from executive, and promotion of international peace and security.

If one gives a bare reading of these provisions, he will conclude that most of these are originating from the idea of Gandhi. DPSP are duties of state, and in the initial stage from Gopalan[22] to Keshvanad Bharti,[23] we have witnessed the odyssey of Indian democracy and tussle between executive and judiciary in giving prominence to fundamental rights over DPSP. The dust settled in Keshvanand[24] by having an ameliorative approach between DPSP and fundamental rights.

In 1976, by Forty Second Amendment in the Constitution on the recommendation of Swaran Singh Committee, Article 51A was added in Part IVA of the Constitution. It is non-justifiable like Directive Principles of State Policy but gradually it is gaining color and momentum in political life of the country. The state is enforcing it gradually. A strong argument is made that talking about duty is withdrawal of state. It shows the helplessness of state as it fails in realization of rights with resources disposal at its end; hence, it shrinks its liability by promoting more duties than rights.

Indian society has always been duty oriented and believed in Gita 'कर्मण्ये वाधिकारस्ते मा फलेषु कदाचन' which means do your duty and do not worry for result. One must work being detached to result. Article 51A casts a duty on Indian citizens only. These duties include abiding by constitution and respecting national flag and national anthem, and cherishing national freedom struggle, on this particular duty, we can see Gandhi submitted his whole life for the cause of national

[20] M.K. Gandhi, Young India (1923).

[21] R.W.M. Dias, "Unenforceable Duty", 33 *Tul. L. Rev.*, pp. 473–490 at p. 489 (1958–1959).

[22] A.K. Gopalan v. State of Madras AIR 1950 SC 27.

[23] Kesavananda Bharati v. State of Kerala (1973) 4 SCC 225.

[24] Kesavananda Bharati v. State of Kerala (1973) 4 SCC 225.

freedom struggle. His desire for freedom of his country reflects in all his important movements, i.e., Champaran satyagraha, civil disobedience, non-co-operation, and quit India are some of the biggest movements led by him in pure peaceful and non-violent manner. When he was convicted under section 124A of Indian Penal Code,[25] he thanked the judge by saying that he kept him in the category of great freedom fighter like Tilak.

The second duty in Article 51 is to defend the county. Gandhi was though against the use of violence but he did not believe in cowardice as practice of non-violence by a weak is an act of cowardice and helplessness. As an example, he asked Indian soldiers to help British Army in world wars.

The third duty is promotion of harmony and common brotherhood in spite of religious, linguistic, and regional diversities. We know Gandhi as a religious man who believed in Varnasharam but he was against the untouchability and he submitted himself to cause of promotion of harijans. His idea of 'sarv dharm sambhav' is deep rooted in the concept of secular state. Unity of countrymen was possible by swadeshi, swadharm, and trusteeship which he not only preached but practiced all his life. The next duty is about renouncing derogatory practices to women. He was a staunch supporter of equality of men and women. He promoted women education, disciplined sex life, monogamous relationship, and widow remarriage of young widows.

The next duty is about valuing composite culture of India. Gandhi knew that unless India will be united, the freedom shall be meaningless. He advocated for real and genuine culture based upon Indian values which has constituents from all types of faiths and religions. The next duty speaks about developing scientific temper, humanism, and spirit of inquiry and reform. He has been the biggest humanist born on earth. Reform, inquisitiveness, and scientific temper reflect in his whole life at micro- and macro-level.

The duty about protecting public property and abjuring violence is again based upon his teachings of trusteeship and non-violence. The duty about striving for excellence individually and collectively so that nation rises to higher level of achievements and endeavor again speaks about his nationalism. The duty about providing opportunity of education to wards and children between the age of six and fourteen years is again a reflection of Gandhian thought as he always advocated that basic education should always be free. He also advocated for basic education

[25] Section 124A. Sedition.—Whoever by words, either spoken or written, or by signs, or by visible representation, or otherwise, brings or attempts to bring into hatred or contempt, or excites or attempts to excite disaffection towards, the Government established by law in India, shall be punished with imprisonment for life, to which fine may be added, or with imprisonment which may extend to three years, to which fine may be added, or with fine. Explanation 1.—The expression "disaffection" includes disloyalty and all feelings of enmity. Explanation 2.—Comments expressing disapprobation of the measures of the Government with a view to obtain their alteration by lawful means, without exciting or attempting to excite hatred, contempt or disaffection, do not constitute an offence under this section. Explanation 3.—Comments expressing disapprobation of the administrative or other action of the Government without exciting or attempting to excite hatred, contempt or disaffection, do not constitute an offence under this section.

including vocational education, higher education, religious education, languages like Sanskrit, and literature.

If we give a cursory look on these duties, we will find the Gandhian influence upon them. These duties are only epitomizing the Gandhian thought which has always been duty oriented. His idea of swadharm is better reflected in these duties. If we analyze certain judgments of the Supreme Court, we can see that our judiciary is incessantly trying to enforce duties in constitutional governance. Supreme Court in *AIIMS Students' Union* v. *AIIMS* held that though Article 51A does not expressly caste any fundamental duty on state, the duty of every citizen of India is a collective duty of state. Its de facto enforceability in the sense that Article 51A is a yardstick against which the action of state may be assessed.[26] Again, in *Ashok Kumar Thakur* v. *Union of India,* Supreme Court held that state is all the citizens placed together, and hence, though Article 51A does not expressly cast any fundamental duty on the state, the fact remains that the duty of every citizen of India is collective duty of state.[27] In *Union of India* v. *Naveen Jindal,* Supreme Court held that right to fly national flag is a qualified right under Article 19(1)(a) and must be seen in the view of Article 51A but court did not speak about enforceability of fundamental duties.[28] In *Charu Khurana* v. *Union of India* on an issue of gender discrimination, apex court while clubbing Article 39A(d) and 51A(e) and (j) held that dignity of women, gender equality, and justice are duties of every citizen and collective duty of the state.[29] The practice of Jallikattu was declared unconstitutional but political fate of the judgment was otherwise. The judgment heavily relied on fundamental duties and DPSP.[30] The apex court emphasized on the need of green energy in Article 51A (g).[31] The court did not allow exodus of doctors from government medical services on the basis of Articles 47, 51A(g) and (h). Voluntary retirement of government doctors may be decided by the state.[32] Supreme Court held that obligation to provide education cannot be offloaded on nonstate actors.[33] The court held that construction in pursuance of a government order to hotels and eateries on the banks of Periyar river is violative of Article 51A(g). Government is the trustee of public property and resources.[34] The Supreme Court reiterated the value of protection of public property and all life forms and abjuring violence in public speaking during campaign by Baba Ramdev in Ramlila Maidan.[35]

---

[26] *AIIMS Students' Union* v. *AIIMS* (2002) 1 SCC 428.

[27] *Ashok Kumar Thakur* v. *Union of India* (2008) 6 SCC 1.

[28] *Union of India* v. *Naveen Jindal* (2004) 2 SCC 510.

[29] *Charu Khurana* v. *Union of India* (2015) 1 SCC 192.

[30] *Animal Welfare Board of India* v. *A. Nagaraj & Others* (2014) 7 SCC 547; *Compassion Unlimited Plus Action* v. *Union of India* (2016) 3 SCC 85.

[31] *Hindustan Zinc Ltd.* v. *Rajasthan Electric Regulatory Commission* (2015)12 SCC 611.

[32] *State of U.P.* v. *Achal Singh* (2018) 17 SCC 578.

[33] *Society for Unaided Private Schools of Rajasthan* v. *Union of India* (2012) 6 SCC 1.

[34] *Association for Environment Protection* v. *State of Kerala & Others* (2013) 7 SCC 226.

[35] *Ramlila Maidan Incident in Re* (2012) 5 SCC 1.

5 Conclusion

If we see the idea of Gandhi on politics, economics, and governance, one can conclude that his idea is not only abstraction but it can be practiced in ground realities. His idea of sanitation, abolition of untouchability, elevation of village panchayats, development of cottage industries, sarvodaya, and swadharm are still very relevant in Indian ethos. Gandhi is very firmly rooted in Indian political governance. His satyagraha, swadeshi, and swadharma are still scattered in the constitutional fabric of the country. His idea of duty is instilled with the value of moral authority of people. He is an advocate of 'enlightened anarchy' where one is concerned with the duty of one's and rights are taken care of automatically in the process. If we analyze each moral duty enshrined in our Constitution, we can see the reflections of Gandhian values and thoughts in the same.

In a gentle way you can shake the world.

Gandhi

References

Coleman JL (1980) Legal duty and moral argument. In: Social theory and practice, vol 5, no 3/4, A special issue: taking Dworkin seriously pp 377–407

Dhyani SN (1999) Jurisprudence, central law agency, 3rd edn. Allahabad, p 240

Dias RWM (1958–1959) Unenforceable duty. 33 Tul L Rev 473–490

Fitzgerald PJ. Salmond on jurisprudence, 12th edn. Sweet & Maxwell, New Delhi, pp 216–217

Gandhi MK (1923) Young India

Gandhi MK (2007) Ruskin unto this last a paraphrase, 2nd edn. Navjivan Publishing House, Ahmedabad, p 42

Gandhi MK (2009) Trusteeship. Navijivan Publishing House, Ahmedabad, p 7

Herstein OJ (2014) A legal right to do legal wrong. Oxford J Legal Stud 34(1):21–45 (Spring)

Hohfeld WN (1913) Some fundamental legal conceptions as applied in judicial reasoning. Yale Law J 23(1):16–59

Kachroo JL (1992) Gandhi, Tagore & Nehru contribution and thought. Cosmos Bookhive Pvt. Ltd., New Delhi, p 35

Macbeath A (1948) Duty philosophy, vol 23, no 85, pp. 99–115

Mallik BK (1948) Gandhi—A prophecy. Oxford, p 34

Mukherjee R (2010) (ed) The Penguin Gandhi reader, p 33

Mukherjee R (2009) Gandhi's Swaraj. Econ Polit Wkly 44(50):34–39

Rothermund I (1969) The individual and society in Gandhi's political thought. J Asian Stud 28 (2):313–320

Tagore R (2008) Tagore on Gandhi. Rupa & Co., New Delhi, p 56

Chapter 16
Secularism and Secularisation of the State: Decoding Gandhian Philosophy in Contemporary India

Narender Nagarwal

1 Introduction

Contemporary thought on secularism appears as an embattled ideology considering the sustained attempts being made to construct a narrative smearing the terms like secularism, multiculturalism and tolerance in India. The present analysis on secularism has legitimate basis as it would be unfair to ignore the rising graph of chauvinistic conflicts and duty of the state. It must also be said that this is not the first time that secularism is being questioned, nor will it be the last.[1] Notably, those questioned the secularism have also questioned its celebrated epitomes, viz. tolerance, non-violence and multiculturalism propounded by Mahatma Gandhi. In "*Discovery of Truth*", Gandhi made a strong defence of tolerance, non-violence and multiculturalism and termed these principles as essential components of secularism.[2] A section of intellectuals and political class wittingly or unwittingly consider Gandhi a spiritual politician and not as a principled politician who defined the secularism as an altogether different equilibrium. This contradiction arises from what appears to be ambivalence in Gandhi's ideas towards the secularism philosophy. The classical interpretation of secular state implies separation of state and religion but Gandhi insists on close connection between the duo.[3]At that moment, Gandhi asserts that politics must be infused with spirituality or religion. Additionally, Gandhi also holds profound mawkishness that state and religion should always maintain a respectful

[1] Panikkar Raimundo, Myth, faith and hermeneutic: cross-cultural studies, Asian Trading Corp., Bangalore (1983).

[2] M. K. Gandhi, What is truth. Navjeevan Publication, Ahmedabad, p. 474 (1984).

[3] The Publication Division (1903–1905), The collected works of Mahatma Gandhi, vol. 4, The Publication Division, Ministry of Information and Broadcasting, Government of India, p. 202.

N. Nagarwal (✉)
Assistant Professor, Campus Law Centre, Faculty of Law, University of Delhi, Delhi, India
e-mail: nnagarwal@clc.du.ac.in

R. Mittal and K. K. Singh (eds.), *Relevance of Duties in the Contemporary World*,
https://doi.org/10.1007/978-981-19-1836-0_16

distance. Gandhi firmly believes that the state should avoid unnecessary interference in the personal affairs of individual particularly in his /her domain of faith and belief.[4] It is pertinent to examine how social scientists and secular theorist elucidate this inconsistency in Gandhian thought of secularism. It may be noted that secularism as an accepted philosophy in the Western political system is alien to the Indian context and differs significantly from Gandhi's viewpoint over the same. The chief reason is that all prominent religions of the world had been considered not merely a religion but a way of life. Besides, the political history of India does not mention any reference of conflict between state and religion. Thus, Gandhi believes that Western thought of secularism has no relevance in India.[5]

Gandhi's exceptional view on secularism put him in the category of *imperfecto* secular politician, but this is also a fact that he stalwartly fought a battle for non-violence, tolerance, multiculturalism as well as religious and cultural rights of minorities which are considered as essential components of secularism.[6] Gandhi's multi-faceted understanding of secularism and his view on religion challenges the conceptual distinction between "private" and "public" as understood in Western discourses on secularism. In doing so, he both offered an idiosyncratic understanding of religious freedom and challenged traditional Western secularist understandings of the relationship between individuals and communities. The individual as a member of a political society has a fundamental freedom to subscribe to any religious belief, or to be an atheist or agnostic. The state has no role to play in determining what religious faith or practice any particular member or individual should subscribe.[7] The primary postulation of this conception is very simple as state and religion function under the two different domains of individual behaviour. The primary role and duty of the state are to ensure happiness of the society and work for the welfare of the people through legislation and governance. The duty of the state is not to endorse directly or indirectly or regulate or interfere in the religious affairs of citizens. The greatest safeguard for the religious minorities in a multi-religious country lies in a secular polity. The main thrust of this chapter is to identify the dynamic and contested trajectory of "secularism" through Gandhian lens and how his secular thought differs from classical interpretation of secularism. A significant section of social scientists from India has attempted to engross Gandhian understandings of secularism to link minorities rights and religious freedom, thus delinked Gandhian thought on religion. A few scholars have characterised Gandhian thought on secularism as half-baked since he focused on how prophetic his opposition was basically on west-centric secularism and he was more focused on India-centric secularism. This chapter discusses the

---

[4] Iyengar AS, All through the Gandhian era, Hind Kitab House, Bombay, p. 223 (1950).

[5] K. N. Tiwari, World religious and Gandhi, Classical Publishing Company, New Delhi, p. 76 (1988).

[6] SN Balagangadhara, Jakob De Roover, "The secular state and religious conflict: liberal neutrality and the Indian case of pluralism", 15 *Journal of Political Philosophy* 1: 73–74 (2007).

[7] Moin Shakir, Gandhi's concept of secularism, In: Secular democracy, Monthly, New Delhi, p. 17 (1969).

varied trajectories of secularism propounded by Gandhi, and attempt has been made to investigate whether Indian state activated the secular philosophy efficaciously or not.[8]

2 Classical Secularism vis-à-vis Gandhian Secularism

The term secularism basically connotes non-religious in primitive sense. To illustrate what constitutes non-religious it stands for, non-interference and individual liberty of faith and role of the state is to define and confine religion. Western secularism defines religion as domain of personal faith. A few countries of the west like France confine the space for individuals to engage in religion to the private sphere. But the countries like USA embrace public religion but keep it separate from state institutions.[9] The secularism concept is a peculiarly modern concept, and it denotes critical engagement with ideas, system of thought, faith and belief.[10] The term secular, secularism and secularisation are generally regarded in same sense or used interchangeably. But the meaning of these terms is different and distinctive, yet often overlapping. We need to distinguish secularisation as a social process, which involves the relegation of religious beliefs and upholds the tradition of community accommodation and secularism as a principle duty of state. In most discussions, the two meanings are conflated. This has given rise to the expectation that secularisation of society is a necessary precondition for secularism as a political norm.[11] Looking at the debates on secularism and the question whether India has achieved secularisation two related but equally distinctive conceptions of secularism developed in India since independence. Firstly, the Western-centric classical model of secularism which is largely accepted in Europe and other Western nations, and secondly, the model based on some principles, viz. religious and cultural freedom, peaceful coexistence, tolerance and communal harmony, mainly attributed to Mahatma Gandhi.[12] To comprehend the Gandhian model of secularism, it would be desirable to examine what actually constitute the classical model of secularism, how it developed and what are its essential attributions. The classical theorist asserts that a secular state implies separation of state and

[8] The Publication Division, The collected works of Mahatma Gandhi, vol. 55 (April 23–Sept 15 1933), The Publication Division, Ministry of Information and Broadcasting, Government of India, p. 443.

[9] Friedrichs Jorg, Hindu-Muslim Relations: What Europe Might Learn From India, Routledge Pub, India, South Asia Edition, pp. 62–64 (2019).

[10] Dipankar Gupta, Secularisation and Minoritization: the limits of heroic thought, In: Sheth DL and Mahajan Gurpreet (ed.), Minority identities and the nation-state, Oxford University Press, New Delhi, pp. 38–44 (1999).

[11] Chandhoke Neera, "Rethinking pluralism secularism and tolerance", Sage Publication, New Delhi, pp. 156–160 (2019a).

[12] Rajeev Bhargava, "What we owe to Gandhi" The Hindu (2019) Available at https://www.thehindu.com/opinion/op-ed/what-we-owe-to-themahatma/article29955342.ece (last accessed 10 May 2020).

religion through an infallible wall. The classical thought on secularism asserts that there is no state religion, and yet, there are community-specific provisions in the Constitution. Religious freedom of the minorities is simultaneously protected, and it can be possible when state adopts secularism as its core policy of governance. A theocratic state cannot protect the interest of religious minorities as it is committed to one particular religion, whereas a secular country acts as the guardian of religious minorities.[13]

The underlining principle of classical thought of secularism basically envisioned to protect the minorities and other oppressed groups who are vulnerable and to ensure equality amongst religious communities. It is not the job of secularism to re-order unequal gender or caste relations that within the provinces of democracy. It is the job of secularism or rather secularist to ensure that the state is not aligned to any particular religion when society is highly diversified, and multiculturalism is its prime feature. The secularism principle treats all religious communities with equal care and consideration that no concept of special privileges to any particular community or class just because of its numerical strength and that no religion is discriminated against just because its numbers are smaller than the majority communities.[14] Principally, there are two models of secularism: firstly; non-establishment secularism or the separation of religion from the state, secondly; the state-owned model of secularism as adopted by the USA and France. But Indian model of secularism has its own niche; it has been traced back to the idea of "composite culture" which is closely associated with ancient Hindu philosophy, *vasudeva kutumbkam*. Scholars agreed that India has inherited secularism from the British when imperial administration used "religion" to sort colonial subjects, presenting themselves as neutral from, but friendly towards, religious events. Basically, Indian secularism stands for community accommodation and most social scientist lean towards more progressive values like positive discrimination, affirmative action and protection of minorities rights.[15] Under the separation of religion model of secularism, it is expected that state and religion to be nonaligned to each other, but in state-owned model of secularism, the state and religion coexist, and therefore, it is possible to have a secular state plus a particular religion will get privileged position by the state.

It should be remembered while recapitulating Gandhi's position on secularism and his idea of secular state that Gandhi was deeply influenced by the Hindu philosophical traditions, especially of the *Upanishada*, the *Gita* and the *Vedas*. Gandhi's religious political understanding can be seen in the following statement he made,

---

[13] Kumar Arun, Cultural and educational rights of minorities under Indian constitution, Deep & Deep, New Delhi, p. 28 (1985).

[14] Mustafa Faizan, Minorities, too, are fed up with this facade of secularism, The Indian Express (2020a) Available at https://indianexpress.com/article/opinion/columns/narendra-modi-govt-6324468/ (last accessed 15 June 2020).

[15] Chandhoke Neera, "Secularism is caught in a crisis", The Indian Express (2019b) Available at https://indianexpress.com/article/opinion/columns/discrimination-hindutva-muslims-rss-alls-not-well-with-secularism-6147422/ (last accessed 05 April 2020).

'every activity' governed by what I consider my religion, 'for "me" Gandhi maintained, "I can't conceive of politics divorced from religion".[16] Gandhi illustrated this explicitly: "religion should pervade our every action and he made no distinction between morality and spirituality and treat both under the realms as identical with seeking truth". It is fascinating to learn that while describing secularism Gandhi insists on significance of religious philosophy and ancient Hindu scriptures.[17] Hence, when Gandhi claims that he cannot see politics without the significant contribution of religion, spirituality and morals, he simply asserts that politics is the medium of governance and this governance should be directed from the quest for truth. Gandhi illustrates the ultimate purpose of truth is to achieve eternal truth, i.e. supreme God, and "the quest for truth" is synonymous with "*dharm*" or "*rajdharm*" for the state, since state's paramount objective is to secure welfare and remove the misery and other social ills.[18] Those who understand secularism with a notion of absolute separation of politics from spirituality, Gandhi's thought thus seems anti-secular. Strikingly, at another occasion, Gandhi expresses a profound and enduring assurance to what he calls secularism. Gandhi said that, "suppose If I were a tyrant ruler, religion and state would be separate in my ruled state, I swear by my religion, I will sacrifice my life for my religion but only in personal capacity." Gandhi further observed that the state has no relation with my private affairs including what is my religious belief; rather, the state has duty to take care of your personal religious freedom and also ensure secular welfare without interfering with your and my religion. On another occasion, Gandhi maintained that state "should undoubtedly be secular and everyone in it should be entitled to profess his religion without any hindrance".[19] To put it more concretely, Gandhi also asserts the significance of synthesising non-secular world with secular state and endorses the words like peaceful coexistence, harmony, fraternity, inter-religious peace and mutual learning.[20] However, Gandhi differs with Westernised theory of secular state and believed that instead of blindly endorsing Westernised secularism we should insightfully develop our own secular policy based on India's rich social experience and past heritage.[21] Hence, Gandhian secular philosophy reminds us to learn the tenets of various religions.

The interesting spectrum of Gandhi's secularism perspective, the integration of spirituality, religion and politics, seems impossible to be made comprehensible through the elucidations given by various scholars and thinkers. Rajmohan Gandhi writes, despite much ado Gandhi's view of secularism can be appreciated easily from the fact that how he stresses for minorities even during holocaust of partition.

[16] Pyarelal, Weekly letter, Harijan 10(33):321, 22 September 1946 (1946) Available at https://www.gandhiheritageportal.org/journals-by-gandhiji/harijan (last accessed 26 Apr 2020).

[17] The Publication Division, *supra* note 8.

[18] Raghavan N Iyer, The moral and political thought of Mahatma Gandhi, Concord Grove Press, Santa Barbara, California, p. 83 (1983).

[19] The Publication Division, *supra* note 8.

[20] Arun Kumar Patnaik, Transgressing secularism, 47 *Economic and Political Weekly* 12 at 78 (2012).

[21] Pantham Thomas, Indian secularism and its critics: some reflections, 59 *The Review of Politics* 3: 523–540 (1997).

Unquestionably, Gandhi wanted Pakistan to protect its minorities, and at the same time, he was committed towards the minorities of India. After partition carnage, Gandhi even had a dream that Indian Muslims who went to Pakistan may return to their home in near future.[22] Gandhi's own work on state, spirituality and secularism is a kind of jumbling but not complex work. However, any work exploring these experiments in relation to his public political statements on secularism has surfaced yet. Gandhi wrote numerous works on varied subjects and statecraft, but very little can be traced about secularism. His ideas of secularism and reasoning can be understood only through certain events, political speeches and statements that helped us to understand Gandhi's contribution to secularism and his viewpoint on polity of a secular state. It may be noted that India's multiculturalism and diverse society made an impressive impact on Gandhi's personality and his political thought.

Gandhi was deeply fascinated about the heterogenous character of Indian society that enthralled him to realise and evolve a social and political philosophy which could accommodate different cultures and religions with his intense personality. It is impracticable for a religious man to confine himself only to the certain tenets of the truth discovered in his own religion. While remaining attached to his own religion, the individual should be advised to expand his understanding about the true philosophy of religion by a reverential understanding of the perennial truth preached in others religions.[23] Hence, the words like "secular" and the "religious" then do not stand in two distinguished categories but beautifully combined. It may be noted that Gandhi supported the Khilafat Movement,[24] during nationalist movement. Gandhi found an opportunity to examine the worth of his religious ideology when Khilafat question arose in Indian nationalist movement. Gandhi wanted to expand the nationalist movement and was passionately working to draw more people from all sections to join the movement and fight unitedly to achieve *Swaraj*. Gandhi believed that communal problem was essentially a religious issue; therefore, the unity in the country could be brought about only through strengthening the inter-religious comity and promoting fraternity in the country. Hence, Gandhi chose to support the Khilafat Movement which was launched by the Muslims, though the movement was based on pan-Islamism ideology but with anti-imperialism contour. Amazingly, the hardliners like B. C. Pal too supported the movement with Gandhi. However, liberals disapproved the Khilafat movement as they considered it is unfair to mix politics with religion.[25]

---

[22] Gandhi Rajmohan, "CAA does not carry mahatma Gandhi wishes, it brazenly defies them", The Indian Express (2020) Available at https://indianexpress.com/article/opinion/columns/caa-secular-nrc-minorities-pakistan-narendra-modi-amit-shah-rajmohan-gandhi-6236881/ (last accessed 22 April 2020).

[23] Bharatan Kumarappa (ed.), M K Gandhi: my religion, Navajivan Publishing House, Ahmedabad, p. 29 (1955).

[24] Encyclopaedia Britannica, Khilafat movement: Indian Muslim movement, Britannica Available at https://www.britannica.com/khilafat/movement (last accessed 22 September 2020) (1919–1924).

[25] DG Tendulkar, Mahatma, vol 3 (1930–34), Publication Division, Ministry of Information and Broadcasting, Govt of India, Patiala House, New Delhi, p. 244 (1951).

Critics also pointed that though Gandhi's passionate belief and his repeated assertion of Ram Rajya in his numerous political addresses sharply contradict his secular ideology, but in reality, Gandhi never dreamt of establishing Hindu raj under the guise of Ram Rajya in India. In 1924, Gandhi said that it was unpatriotic even to nurture a dream of Hindu Raj; a true Ram Rajya according to him was to establish a moral government based upon the principles of truth and non-violence and free from all social ills, equal distribution of economic resources, where all communities live peacefully with brotherhood and thus promoting rich composite culture.[26] Gandhi was not a protagonist of religious nationalism; rather, he portrays the exclusive picture of how different religions can play crucial role to unite India. In 1930, Gandhi's secular views flashed again in the following explanation—Gandhi came to realise that the communal problem was not religious but political and economic one.[27] This was Gandhi's pure secular thought to understand the enmity between the two communities. This episode should be emphasised because this led his critics to describe him as crypto-secular. He asserted that religion is a personal matter which should have no place in politics. It is in the unnatural condition that we have unnatural division according to religion. These historical facts have scarcely been investigated in previous scholarships.[28]

Gandhi believed that to ensure communal harmony amongst the communities is largely a responsibility that lies with communities themselves. If there is a situation when communal harmony is disturbed or harmed by someone, the state must step in to restore the communal harmony and punish the perpetrators. To ensure inter-religious communal harmony and peaceful coexistence, state has to play a neutral role and should not be aligned with any particular religion, rather maintain a respectful distance from all religious affiliations.[29] In such circumstances, secularism marks a certain compartment of the state whereby it makes it more compatible with progressive values like equal distances from all religions and denominations perspectives aiming to ensure state neutrality in religious affairs, elimination of all form of discrimination and socio-economic progress of minorities. This new argument of secularism propounded by Gandhi makes his secular philosophy distinctive. In fact, there is no comparison between Western standardised secularism and Gandhian brand of secularism, since Western thinkers strongly pitched for the strict wall between church and state for the sake of individual freedom and more focus being put on religious and cultural freedom. While Gandhi characterised secularism as the duty of state to remain secular so as to maintain better relation with all religions within the state,

[26] Gandhi, *supra* note 2.

[27] Radhakrishna S, Muirhead JH (eds.), Contemporary Indian philosophy, 2nd Revised edn., Allen and Unwin, London, p. 21 (1952).

[28] Gupta Charu, "Gandhi on cow, Ram Rajya and Hinduism", National Herald (2019) Available at https://www.nationalheraldindia.com/opinion/gandhi-on-cow-ramrajya-and-hinduism (last accessed 15 May 2020).

[29] M. K. Gandhi, Dharma and self-purification, Navjeevan Publication, Ahmedabad, p. 81 (1986).

especially if there are some instances of hostility between the religious communities in the past. The Gandhian thought on secularism is immensely vital in the period of religious disharmony.[30]

3 Crisis of Secularism and Relevance of Gandhian Thought

Any discussion about secularism cannot be complete without analysing communalism. Secularism and communalism seem to be opposed to each other; if secularism is going to be weakened, it is a clear manifestation that communalism is on the rise. Herein, it is useful to begin with the recognition that secularism philosophy has conceptual connection with well-established notions in the literature on democracy, equality and liberty. Recognition of secularism means embracing tolerance, acceptance of other convictions and believes as worthy of respect. Unfortunately, current debate on secularism has been confined to "minorities appeasement" and sole reason of this state of affairs is immense confusion about secularism amongst the political class. Another reason of crisis of secularism is rampant confusion about the essential components of secularism and why secularism is significant for modern democracies like India.[31] Despite the onset of a rich and textual debate on secularism in India, the academics and thinkers do not really seem to universally share the understanding of what constitutes secularism. This unfortunate uncertainty amongst the scholars and the political class dogs secularism and also breeds unfortunate consequences. Romila Thapar has drawn pointed attention in the following words, "though ambiguity of secularism can be considered its strength but its vagueness and poor foundation is a clear indictment of India's weak secularism and it is not a good sign for public policies".[32] It is a recognised fact that there is a great deal of confusion about secularism in India, especially in the political class and civil society. It is true that people are sometime scolded for their misunderstanding about secularism, and this chiding is unreasonable. It is odd because secularism in India has been growing under the clouds of colonial rule and civil society has not developed its understanding why and how secularism denotes progressiveness or modernity.[33]

---

[30] Godrej Farah, Nonviolence and Gandhi's truth: A method for moral and political arbitration, 68 *Review of Politics* (2): 287–317 (2006); Raghavan Iyer, The moral and political thought of Mahatma Gandhi, Oxford University Press, London, p. 160 (1973); Chatterjee Margaret, Gandhi's religious thought, University of Notre Dame Press, Notre Dame, p. 67 (1983).

[31] Bipan Chandra, Communalism in modern India, Vikas Publishing House, New Delhi, p. 1 (1984).

[32] Romila Thapar and Neeladri Bhattacharya, "Romila Thapar on the secular view of Indian history (and its differences with the communal one)", Scroll.in (2019) Available at https://scroll.in/article/936085/romila-thapar-on-the-secular-view-of-indian-history-and-its-differences-with-the-communal-one (last accessed 18 August 2020).

[33] Mukul Kesavan, "India's embattled secularism", 27 *Wilson Quarterly* 1: 61–67 (2003).

Secularism in India is largely credited to the nationalist leaders who fought a long battle against the British administration. Motilal Nehru Committee Report (1928)[34] is worth mentioning in how it substantially emphasised on religious and cultural freedom of minorities and depressed class. The Nehru Committee Report considered as the first significant political document of Indian National Congress that manifested its affirmation on secularism and minorities rights. The report was principally motivated by three main considerations; firstly, minorities should not fear in an independent India; secondly, cultures are important for individuals for many reasons, and if cultures are diminished, individuals are harmed; thirdly, one should not be harmed only because he belongs to a group that has been vilified and subjected to disrespect by a majority group.[35]

After independence, Congress designed secularism succeeded to keep Muslims on board despite the fact that Muslim League won Pakistan in 1947. Even after partition, a substantive population of Muslims decided to remain in India, thereby rejected the two-nation theory and poisonous environment of communalism. The constitution of new independent India was remarkably secular, though the words were inserted by way of 42nd Amendment only in 1976. But in the famous *Keshavanand Bharti*[36] case, the Supreme Court of India affirmed that secularism though was not a part of preamble in the initial drafting, is a part of essential feature of Constitution of India and shall remain unaltered. There are many religions, religious sects and denominations in India, and almost all are getting protection through the Constitution of India. The framers of the Constitution of India were well aware of the religious sentiments of the people of India, and religion plays a pivotal role in social and cultural life of the citizens. So, in the Preamble itself, they secured people's liberty of faith, belief and worship. These liberties can be maintained only when there is unity and integrity of the nation. Secularism in India is unique to the Indian settings, and it is well reflected in the provisions of the Constitution.[37] An undercurrent of anxious concern seems to run through the provisions dealing with religious freedom to protect minorities' rights alongside individual freedom. In this way, probably, it may be explained why secularism in India seems to defy any of the traditionally or historically accepted definitions of the term.

The larger consensus amongst the liberal societies and modern civilised nations about secularism is that it demonstrates modernity and is the best option for any progressive state. India's growth, progress and countless accomplishments in the field of science, technology and social science area attributes to the idea of secularism and India's heterogenous society. India became a global power because of secularism

[34] Nehru Committee Report (1928). The committee consisted of Motilal Nehru, Chairman, Sir Ali Imam, Tej Bahadur Sapru, Subhash Chandra Bose, Annie Besant, M R Jaykar and Jawaharlal Nehru was the secretary of the committee. The committee was given the charge to consider and determine the principles of the Constitution of India along with problem of communalism and issue of dominion status.

[35] Chandhoke, *supra* note 14 at p. 209.

[36] AIR 1973, SCC.

[37] Mahmood Tahir, Minorities commission: minor role in major affairs, Pharos Media, New Delhi, p. 12 (2001).

and neighbouring state Pakistan a failed state because it had not realised the merits of the secular state. South Asia's two important states Nepal and Bangladesh have now moved towards the idea of secularism.[38]

The thoughtful arguments of tolerance, peaceful coexistence, non-violence propounded by Gandhi are immensely significant. The most striking feature of Gandhi's secularism was his profound concern for minorities. Gandhi once said that the claim of a country to be civilised or not depends upon how the country treats its minorities.[39] Gandhi fought a big battle for preserving tolerance, non-violence and protection of minorities through the principle of *Vasudev Kutumbkam* and his efforts should be seen through the lense of his commitment for saving the very idea of India. Gandhi's approach towards secularism is essentially based on truth, and according to him, the discovery of truth is nothing but attaining the highest values of humanism. His thoughts on secularism differed from Western-centric model of secularism that signifies strict disestablishment of religion from the state or the exclusion of state from religion.[40] Gandhi's thoughts on secularism are closely associated with Nehruvian secularism. According to Nehru, "the western-centric model of state and religion separation is quite unsuitable in Indian context, but here secularism means "equal respect for all religion" and "protection of all religion by the state".[41] This precise definition of secularism coined by Nehru received a big applause from Gandhi. Additionally, Nehru was also concerned about the socio-economic plight of minorities and their poor representation in education and employment sector.

Gandhian thought on secularism rarely comes up in academic discourse, but often manifested as religious tolerance, *Sarv Dharm Sambhav* and principle of non-intervention. Gandhi's assertion on secularism based on respect for others religion, therefore, is based on mutual recognition of dependence. Gandhi's whole life can be characterised for the cause of brotherhood and solidarity amongst different religious communities. He was convinced that without communal harmony and unity amongst fellow Indians, it would not be possible to fight against the British government. He often used to say, "if you could dissect my heart, you would find that prayer and spiritual striving for the attainment of Hindu-Muslim unity goes on there unceasingly, all the twenty-four hours without even a moment of interruption, whether I am awake or asleep, I want Hindu-Muslim unity because I know that without it there can be no Swaraj.[42] Gandhi traced the roots of the Hindu–Muslim estrangement not in the material life process of Indian society but in the ethical structure of the

---

[38] Mustafa, *supra* note 14.

[39] Mustafa, *supra* note 14.

[40] Akeel Bilgrami, "Gandhi the philosopher", 38 *Economic and Political Weekly* 39, 2003, pp. 4159–4165 and Uday Singh Mehta, "Gandhi on democracy, politics and the ethics of everyday life", 7 *Modern Intellectual History* 2, 2010, pp. 355–371.

[41] Bhargava Rajeev, Indian secularism: an alternative, trans-cultural ideal, In: Mehta VR, Pantham Thomas (eds.), Political ideas in modern India: thematic explorations, Sage Publications, India (2006) and Davison Andrew, Secularism and revivalism in Turkey: a hermeneutic reconsideration, Yale University Press, New Heavan (1998).

[42] Pyarelal, "Gandhiji's abbottabad speech", 7 *Harijan* 26, 1939, pp. 227–228, Dt 05 August 1939 https://www.gandhiheritageportal.org/journals-by-gandhiji/harijan (last accessed 26 May, 2020).

people. Gandhi pleaded for the generosity on the part of majority community.[43] In the words of Nehru, Mahatma Gandhi had laid down his formula for solving the communal problem. According to the Gandhian understanding—the communalism problem could only be solved by goodwill and the generosity of the majority group and so he was prepared to agree to everything that Muslims might demand".[44]

Gandhi firmly believed that in an independent India, for the electoral purpose there would be a political minority and political majority, but the state will be governed by the social justice formula as enshrined under the Constitution of India. The religious and cultural interests of minorities will be protected. Gandhi once stated that, "no charter of independence will be workable which lacks measures of civil and political rights for the minorities as for the majority". Gandhi further stated that "any party which captures power and formed the government will consist of people representing each and every section of the society, there must be a mixed majority of all groups, sections and communities".[45] This was the sole ground Gandhi was staunchly against the creation of Pakistan on religious line. He emphasised that state should not do anything which create misgiving in the minds of minorities and that was the reason Gandhi strongly advocated for the religious and cultural rights of minorities.

The latest efforts of smearing secularism and constructing its illogical interpretation are basically an attempt to ridicule the actual meaning of secularism, coined by Gandhi. Contemporary development and attempt of re-theorising Gandhian and Nehruvian secularism has posed the question of whether the liberal–democrat–secular politics will survive or not.[46] Looking at the emergence of religious and caste-based identity politics and construction of a narrative with the help of comprador corporate media that puts liberal, democratic and secular in the negative shade while giving room for misgivings about whether secularism in India survived or not.

4 Secularisation of the State: Whether India Succeeded?

The term "secularisation" first appeared in social science in John Locke's work; in his essay on toleration, he exemplified the conceptual twin of secularism, the contested issue of that period. Locke's concern about the religious fanaticism displays in his celebrated work "*A letter concerning toleration*" published in 1667. In this work, Locke arguably demonstrated his deep concern with religious strife and discrimination and persecution against minorities. Locke's main argument was the origin of political conflict is discontent, and he suggested that the dispute lies in the fusion of the state and the religious power. This resulted in official disregard of

[43] M.K. Gandhi, "Unity v. justice", 7 *Harijan* 51, 1940, p. 429, Dt 27 January 1940. Available at https://www.gandhiheritageportal.org/journals-by-gandhiji/harijan (last accessed 26 April 2020).

[44] Nehru Jawaharlal, An autobiography, Allied Publication, New Delhi, 1962, p. 136.

[45] Moin, *supra* note 8.

[46] Kaviraj Sudipta, Languages of secularity, 48 *Economic and Political Weekly* 50, 2013, pp. 93–102.

other religions and intimidation of minorities.[47] In post-renaissance period, gradually the political understanding took shape and developed the area of "secularism" and "secularisation" through further research. In the advanced period of academics' enlightenment, the concept of secularism and secularisation was broadened by the academics like Berger (1969), Wilson (1967) and their chief concern was to decipher the concept of secular and secularisation, assuming that both words are engendering the modern world by replacing religion.[48] Theoretically, the term "secularisation" signifies strengthening the secularism by replacing people's cultural and religious thought with non-religious values as more emphasis on scientific outlook, cherishing the rich composite culture, focusing on science and technology instead of religious scriptures and texts. In order to illuminate this position, it is essential to re-examine secularism. Undoubtedly, in a secular state there is a disestablishment between state and religion or complete neutrality between the duo is a precondition. Hence, when state adopts secularism as its constitutional objective, the secularisation cannot be deferred as both have concomitant effect. A state cannot be secular merely by inserting the word "secularism" in its Constitution. The state shall be judged whether secular or not depending on what efforts it has made for secularisation of the society. In this transition, the religious symbols, authorities and sectarian leaders lose their prominence and authority over society. The term secularisation is a hotly debated topic in the USA, as it has been considered as a state which achieved the highest degree of secularisation. In the USA, there have been many social movements to denounce the religion in public spaces and social life such as school prayer, prohibition of mass religious congregation and social acceptance of same sex marriages; these are the few evidences of secularisation of the American civil society. Although many Christian values are still considered the guiding principles of American policies and laws, yet in the last few decades, with the development of other religions as well as atheism, the nation has achieved the standard secularisation.[49]

In a country like India, secularisation is immensely significant because the individual religious freedom is paramount and undisputed, but at the same time, religious freedom of other communities, especially religious, ethnic and linguistic minorities, is equally important. Any individual can practice any religion, and his decision in his spiritual matter is personal, but his religion does not make any impact on society, and he should not feel privileged by assuming the fact that he belonged to majority community religious group.[50] It may be noted that secularisation does not imply that people should become atheists or agnostics. Nor do they have to abjure religion and replace the empty space in their psyche with rational and scientific modes of thinking. Human beings are rational and self-evaluating. They can believe, or chose

---

[47] Milton JR and Milton Philip (eds.), John lock: an essay concerning toleration, Oxford University Press, 2010, p. 140.

[48] Bhatia Mohita, "Secularism and secularization—a bibliographical essay", 48 *Economic and Political Weekly* 50, 2013, pp. 103–110.

[49] Crossman Ashley, What is secularization, Thought Co, 2019 Available at https://www.thoughtco.com/secularization-definition-3026575 (last accessed 22 April 2020).

[50] Chandra Bipan, "Gandhiji, secularism and communalism", 32 *Social Scientist* 1/2, 2004, pp. 3–29.

not to believe, faintly or intensely in the power of Almighty. The choice is theirs alone.

India ought to defend and promote secularism as it is significant in progressive civilised society as it means universality and ensures modernity, progress and development of the nation. If a democratic state openly supports or adopts a religion, the foundations of democracy, especially justice, undermine before power. Democracy is sadly compromised in such a scenario where state declares its theocratic policies and openly supports a particular religion. We should rather think of secularism as a concept that is closely linked with democracy by reasons of shared commitments to basic values such as freedom, equality and justice. In sum, democracy ensures equality between individual citizens, whereas secularism upholds equality between religious communities. It stands on its own ground, located in democracy, but relatively autonomous of the latter. Notably, we find democracy without secularism in countries that have an official church, even if governments grant and protect the right to religious freedom. But we cannot have secularism without democracy, because the concept is justified by references to the precepts of democracy, and in particular that of equality.

5 Concluding Remarks

In Indian context, there are complexities about secularism as the social scientist and theorist suffer from a dilemma. On the one hand, they are the guardians of the Constitution that look favourably towards religious minorities and cherished India's rich composite culture; on the other hand, political class had a history of distorting the idealistic framework of Gandhi's secularism. In academic arena too, the study of secularism was not given persuasive efforts, and hence, decoding Gandhi's doctrine of secularism has been a challenging task for theorists and social scientists. In contrast to established thoughts on secularism, Gandhi made an attempt to reinterpret the idea of secularism that suits a country like India. Gandhi was aware about India's multicultural character and that it could bridge the empirical proposition that our society is multicultural. Further, the normative proposition that pluralism and unity in the diversity is a progressive thought for a new democracy. Gandhi's secular credentials can be evidenced when he stood against gravest ailment of inter-religious animosity between the communities and his firm stand against post-partition communal riots. Hence, any attempt of learning Gandhian secularism is an attempt to study Indianisation of secularism that is purely different from Western conception. Apart from that, Indian secularism thoughts hardly match with the celebrated "theory of disestablishment" that was firmly established in the USA and also illustrate an optimum example of a secular state.

With the above analysis, it can be stated that Gandhi's view on secularism differ with Western conception since Gandhi's stand on secularism can be better known as "religious freedom" and his apparent desire for politics and religion to be complimentary, rather separate. It is important to emphasise that Gandhi's stand on secularism cannot be seen as standalone concept but he was a firm believer in *anekatavad* (pluralism) that contains epistemic humility that leaves him skittish about claiming to have reached the absolute truth. In addition, we must not disregard enormous importance of commitment of Gandhi towards truth seeking, *sarv dharm sambhav* (inter-religious harmony), religious freedom and minorities' rights which are essential components of his conception of secularism. Gandhi's notion of truth seeking is basically a novel epistemological argument to defend all religions, especially the faith of vulnerable groups from all sorts of pointless violence and religious conflicts. The theory of *sarv dharm sambhav* is another doctrine evolved by Gandhi as how to assimilate all vulnerable groups, sections and communities in a heterogenous society; hence, policy of tolerance was expounded through *sarv dharm sambhav*. The nature of Gandhian thoughts on secularism might prove relevant for today's scenario, because the urgent political task is to bring individuals closer and remove all suspicions amongst each other. Gandhian thought is also significant to understand the vulnerability of minorities as to why they deserve special attention from the state and emphasise the duty of the state in this regard.

References

Ansari I (1999) Minorities and the politics of constitution making in india. In: Sheth DL, Gurpreet M (eds) Minority identities and the nation state. Oxford University Press, New Delhi, pp 113–117

Balagangadhara SN, De Roover J (2007) The secular state and religious conflict: liberal neutrality and the indian case of pluralism. J Polit Philos 15(1):73–74

Bhargava R (2006) Indian secularism: an alternative, trans-cultural ideal. In: Mehta VR, Pantham Thomas (eds) Political ideas in modern India: thematic explorations. Sage Publications, India and Davison Andrew (1998) Secularism and revivalism in turkey: a hermeneutic reconsideration. Yale University Press, New Heavan

Bhargava R (2013) Reimaging secularism - respect, domination and principled distance. Econ Pol Wkly 48(50):79–92

Bhargava R (2019) What we owe to Gandhi. The Hindu. https://www.thehindu.com/opinion/op-ed/what-we-owe-to-themahatma/article29955342.ece. Accessed 10 May 2020

Bhatia M (2013) Secularism and secularization—A bibliographical essay. Econ Pol Wkly 48(50):103–110

Bilgrami A (2003) Gandhi the philosopher. Econ Polit Weekly 38(39):4159–4165. Mehta US (2010) Gandhi on democracy, politics and the ethics of everyday life. Mod Intellect History 7(2):355–371

Chandhoke N (2019a) Rethinking pluralism secularism and tolerance. Sage Publication, New Delhi, pp 156–160

Chandhoke N (2019b) Secularism is caught in a crisis. The Indian Express. https://indianexpress.com/article/opinion/columns/discrimination-hindutva-muslims-rss-alls-not-well-with-secularism-6147422/. Accessed 05 Apr 2020

Chandra B (1984) Communalism in modern india. Vikas Publishing House, New Delhi, p 1

Chandra B (2004) Gandhiji, secularism and communalism. Soc Sci 32(1/2):3–29

Crossman A (2019) What is secularization. ThoughtCo. https://www.thoughtco.com/secularization-definition-3026575. Accessed 22 Apr 2020

Encyclopaedia Britannica (1919–1924) Khilafat movement: Indian Muslim movement. Britannica. https://www.Britannica.com/khilafat/movement. Accessed 22 Sept. 2020
Friedrichs J (2019) Hindu-Muslim relations: what Europe might learn from India. Routledge Pub. India, South Asia Edition, pp 62–64
Gandhi MK (1984) What is truth. Navjeevan Publication, Ahmedabad, p 474
Gandhi MK (1986) Dharma and self-purification. Navjeevan Publication, Ahmedabad, p 81
Gandhi MK (1940) Unity v. justice. Harijan 7(51):429. https://www.gandhiheritageportal.org/journals-by-gandhiji/harijan. Accessed 26 Apr 2020
Gandhi R (2020) CAA does not carry mahatma Gandhi wishes, it brazenly defies them. The Indian Express. https://indianexpress.com/article/opinion/columns/caa-secular-nrc-minorities-pakistan-narendra-modi-amit-shah-rajmohan-gandhi-6236881/. Accessed 22 Apr 2020
Godrej F (2006) Nonviolence and Gandhi's truth: A method for moral and political arbitration. Rev Polit 68(2):287–317. Iyer (1973) The moral and political thought of mahatma Gandhi. Oxford University Press, London, p 160. Chatterjee M (1983) Gandhi's religious thought. University of Notre Dame Press, Notre Dame, p 67
Gupta C (2019) Gandhi on cow, ram Rajya and Hinduism. National Herald. https://www.nationalheraldindia.com/opinion/gandhi-on-cow-ramrajya-and-hinduism. Accessed 15 May 2020
Gupta D (1999) Secularisation and minoritization: the limits of heroic thought. In: Sheth DL, Mahajan G (eds) Minority identities and the nation-state. Oxford University Press, New Delhi, pp 38–44
Iyengar AS (1950) All through the Gandhian era. Hind Kitab House, Bombay, p 223
Iyer Raghavan N (1983) The moral and political thought of Mahatma Gandhi. Concord Grove Press, Santa Barbara, California, p 83
Kaviraj S (2013) Languages of secularity. Econ Pol Wkly 48(50):93–102
Kesavan M (2003) India's embattled secularism. Wilson Quarterly 1976 27(1):61–67
Kumar A (1985) Cultural and educational rights of minorities under Indian constitution. Deep & Deep, New Delhi, p 28
Kumar R, Sharada PHY (1999) Selected works of Jawaharlal Nehru, second series, vol 25. Jawaharlal Nehru Memorial Fund, Oxford University Press, p 226
Kumarappa B (ed) (1955) M K Gandhi: my religion. Navajivan Publishing House, Ahmedabad, p 29
Lok Sabha (1947) constitutional assembly debates (1947) vol 5, 27–28 Aug 1947. In: Lok Sabha (2014) Constituent assembly debates book 1 vol 1–6. Lok Sabha Secretariate, Government of India, pp 211–272
Mahmood T (2001) Minorities commission: minor role in major affairs. Pharos Media, New Delhi, p 12
Milton JR, Milton P (eds) (2010) John lock: an essay concerning toleration. Oxford University Press, p 140
Moin S (1969) Gandhi's concept of secularism. In: Secular democracy, Monthly, New Delhi, p 17
Mustafa F (2020a) Minorities, too, are fed up with this facade of secularism.The Indian Express. https://indianexpress.com/article/opinion/columns/narendra-modi-govt-6324468/. Accessed 15 June 2020a
Mustafa F (2020b) The supreme court has overlooked the gravity of Delhi violence. The Indian Express. https://indianexpress.com/article/opinion/columns/dishonouring-a-pledge-delhi-violence-northeast-judiciary-centre-6290083/. Accessed 21 May 2020b
Needham AD, Rajan RS (eds) (2007) The crisis of secularism in India. Duke University Press, pp 277–289
Nehru Committee Report (1928) The committee was consisting of Motilal Nehru, Chairman, Sir Ali Imam, Tej Bahadur Sapru, Subhash Chandra Bose, Annie Besant, M R Jaykar and Jawaharlal Nehru was the secretary of the committee. The committee was given the charge to consider and determine the principles of the Constitution of India along with problem of communalism and issue of dominion status.
Nehru J (1962) An autobiography. Allied Publication, New Delhi, p 136

Panikkar R (1983) Myth, faith and hermeneutic: cross cultural studies. Asian Trading Corp., Bangalore

Pantham T (1997) Indian secularism and its critics: some reflections. Rev Polit 59(3):523–540

Patnaik AK (2012) Transgressing secularism. Econ Pol Wkly 47(12):78

Pyarelal (1939) Gandhiji's abbottabad speech. Harijan 7(26):227–228. https://www.gandhiheritageportal.org/journals-by-gandhiji/harijan. Accessed 26 May 2020

Pyarelal (1946) Weekly letter. Harijan 10(33):321. https://www.gandhiheritageportal.org/journals-by-gandhiji/harijan. Accessed 26 Apr 2020

Radhakrishna S, Muirhead JH (eds) (1952) Contemporary indian philosophy, 2nd revised. Allen and Unwin, London, p 21

Sen A (1993) The threat to the secular India. The Soc Sci 21(3/4):5–23

ShivaRao B (ed) (1984) The framing of Indian constitution, vol 2. Universal Law Publishing—An imprint of LexisNexis, New Delhi, p 200

Tendulkar DG (1951) Mahatma, vol 3(1930–34). Publication Division, Ministry of Information and Broadcasting, Govt of India, Patiala House, New Delhi, p 244

Thapar Karan (2020) Colloquially speaking, BJP is fascist': Karan Thapar interviews Pratap Bhanu Mehta. The wire. https://thewire.in/video/karan-thapar-pratap-bhanu-mehta-interview. Accessed 25 Apr 2020

Thapar R, Bhattacharya N (2019) Romila Thapar on the secular view of Indian history (and its differences with the communal one). Scroll.in. https://scroll.in/article/936085/romila-thapar-on-the-secular-view-of-indian-history-and-its-differences-with-the-communal-one. Accessed 18 Aug 2020

The Congress-Muslim League Pact 1916 (The Lucknow Pact 1916) It's a reunion of moderate and radical wings of Congress and secularism was adopted as key policy of nationalist movement. http://www.Thebritanica.com/lucknowpact/1916. Accessed 12 June 2020

The Publication Division (1903–1905) The collected works of mahatma Gandhi, vol 4. The Publication Division, Ministry of Information and Broadcasting, Government of India, p 202

The Publication Division (1933) The collected works of Mahatma Gandhi, vol 55 (April 23–Sept 15, 1933). The Publication Division, Ministry of Information and Broadcasting, Government of India, p 443

Tiwari KN (1988) World religious and Gandhi. Classical Publishing Company, New Delhi, pp76

Wilson BR (1967) Religion in secular society fifty years on. Oxford University Press 2016, pp xii–xv

Chapter 17
Mahatma Gandhi's Views on Education and the Indian Education System—Some Insights

Amit Raj Agrawal and Narender Kumar Bishnoi

1 Prologue

Mohandas Karamchand Gandhi was a great politician, lawyer, freedom fighter, social activist, educationist and philosopher ***sui-generis*** of modern day India. Gandhi with his visionary leadership skills and reformist attitude laid the concrete foundation for freedom struggle and indeed realized the dreams of *swaraj* through participative peaceful and firm audacity of the common men.

Gandhi considers education as one of the most important aspects of human existence and estimates education as a vital tool for change, apart from making a man self-dependent and able to earn his livelihood.[1] On this, V. N. Rajashekharan Pillai while deliberating upon the views of Gandhi submits[2]:

> To bring about a change in society, which is really a stupendous task, especially in a country where considerable disparities in income persist and ignorance and illiteracy widen the gulf between the elite and the masses. In a developing society like India, each one adopted a planned approach towards development, ***where education becomes a key agent of socio-economic reform.***

[1] Young India (Young India, 1-6-1921) 'I have never been able to make a fetish of literary training. My experience has proved to my satisfaction that literary training by itself adds not an inch to one's moral height and that character-building is independent of literary training. I am firmly of opinion that the Government schools have unmanned us, rendered us helpless and godless. They have filled us with discontent, and providing no remedy for the discontent, have made us despondent. They have made us what we were intended to become, clerks and interpreters'.

[2] V. N. Rajashekharan Pillai.

A. R. Agrawal (✉)
Assistant Professor, School of Law, G D Goenka University, Sohna, India
e-mail: amitraj.agarwal4@gmail.com

N. K. Bishnoi
Assistant Professor, Campus Law Centre, Faculty of Law, University of Delhi, Delhi, India

R. Mittal and K. K. Singh (eds.), *Relevance of Duties in the Contemporary World*,
https://doi.org/10.1007/978-981-19-1836-0_17

The observations of learned scholar succinctly summarize the need of education in developing countries like India as a key aspect of socioeconomic reform for sustaining the momentum of planned development in order to mitigate the rigours of inequality in income and standard of living among the masses on account of *inter alia* ignorance and illiteracy.

On this note, Gandhi aptly summarizes the value of education and submits:

> That man I think has had a liberal education who has been so trained in youth that his body is the ready servant of his will and does with ease and pleasure all the work that as a mechanism it is capable of; whose intellect is a clear, cold, logic engine with all its parts of equal strength and in smooth working order... whose mind is stored with a knowledge of the fundamental truths of nature... Whose passions are trained to come to heel by a vigorous will, the servant of a tender conscience... who has learnt to have all vileness and to respect others as himself. Such a one and no other, I conceive, has had a liberal education, for he is in harmony with Nature. He will make the best of her and she of him[3]

Gandhi always believes in holistic development of the individual personality. He convincingly practiced and preached the real essence of education as to draw out the best from the boys and girls to be educated. Recently, the Government of India has announced the National Education Policy, 2020,[4] (NEP) which indeed reflects some of the core Gandhian philosophy on education. On this a very significant observation is made in the following terms[5]:

> The National Education Policy 2020 envisions an India centered education system by considering its tradition, culture, values and ethos to contribute directly to transform the country into an equitable, sustainable, and vibrant knowledge society. By drawing inputs from its vast and long historical heritage and considering the contributions from many scholars to the world in diverse fields such as mathematics, astronomy, metallurgy, medical science and surgery, civil engineering and architecture, shipbuilding and navigation, yoga, fine arts, chess, etc., the entire Indian education system is founded and built.

Further, the National Education Policy, 2020, the Government of India, Ministry of Human Resource Development has rightly remarked that,[6] with the quickly changing employment landscape and global ecosystem, it is becoming increasingly critical that children not only learn, but more importantly learn how to learn. Education, thus, must move towards less content and more towards learning about how to think critically and solve problems, how to be creative and multidisciplinary, and how to innovate, adapt, and absorb new material in novel and changing fields. Pedagogy must evolve to make education more experiential, holistic, integrated, inquiry-driven,

---

[3] Bharatan Kumarappa (ed.), Towards New Education, by M. K. Gandhi https://www.gandhiashramsevagram.org/pdf-books/towards-new-education.pdf. Last accessed 12 January 2021.

[4] The National Education Policy, 2020 available at: https://pib.gov.in/PressReleasePage.aspx?PRID=1642061 (visited on 10 January 2021).

[5] P. S. Aithal, & Shubhrajyotsna Aithal, 'Analysis of the Indian National Education Policy 2020 towards Achieving its Objectives', 5 *International Journal of Management, Technology, and Social Sciences (IJMTS)* 2, 2020, pp. 19–41, http://doi.org/10.5281/zenodo.3988767. Accessed 12 January 2021.

[6] Government of India, 'National Education Policy 2020', Ministry of Human Resource Development, 2020.

discovery-oriented, learner-centred, discussion-based, flexible and, of course, enjoyable. However, despite the fact that education is indispensable for meaningful human existence and progressive growth and also India being the signatory to many international human rights declarations and treaties, where right to education has been given due recognition,[7] surprisingly, at the time, when the Constitution of India was put into effect, the subject of education under the provisions of the Constitution was made non-justiciable.[8] However, with the passage of time, some significant steps were taken by the government in this direction,[9] but a major breakthrough was achieved only in the year 1992, when the apex court expressly recognized the importance of education while extending its scope to constitutional provisions of fundamental rights in *Mohini Jain* v. *State of Karnataka.*[10]

It is also important to note that, at the time, when the Constitution did not expressly recognize education as the subject of fundamental rights, however, it did recognize the rights in favour of the citizens to practice any profession or to carry on any

---

[7] The right to education is codified in the Universal Declaration of Human Rights ('UDHR'), International Covenant on Civil and Political Rights ('ICCPR'), International Covenant on Economic, Social and Cultural Rights ('ICESCR'), the Convention on the Elimination of All Forms of Discrimination against Women ('CEDAW') and Convention on the Rights of the Child ('CRC').

[8] M P Jain, *Indian Constitutional Law* 1227 (Lexis Nexis, Gurgaon, seventh edn, 2014). Right to education was initially not included in the chapter of fundamental right in the Constitution, and it was included as directive principles in Art 45 which required the State to endeavour to provide within a period of 10 years from the commencement of the Constitution, for free and compulsory education for all children until they complete the age of 14 years.

[9] Niranjan Aradhya (Dr.) and Aruna Kashyap, *The 'Fundamentals' Right to education in India, available at*: https://unesdoc.unesco.org/ark:/48223/pf0000151010 (last visited on October 27 2020). The Kothari Commission was appointed by the Government of India to have complete scrutiny of education sector in 1964. The Commission submitted its report in 1966 with the recommendations *inter alia* to have a comprehensive National Policy on Education. On the recommendations of Kothari Commission, National Education Policy was enacted by the Government in 1968, which *inter alia* provides for free and compulsory education, though within the existing scheme of the Directive Principles of the State Policy. It is also important to note that ***'The 1968 Policy was the first official document evidencing the Indian Government's commitment towards elementary education'*** A second round of studies was conducted by the Ministry of Education in conjunction with the National Institute of Educational Planning and Administration, and this process contributed to the formation of the National Policy on Education, 1986. This policy, while re-affirming the goal of universalization of elementary education, did not recognize the 'right to education'.

[10] AIR 1992 SC 1858. The matter pertains to charging of capitation fees by the private medical institution as a consideration for admission. The Court observed that "When the State Government grants recognition to private educational institutions it creates an agency to fulfil its obligation under the Constitution". The students are given admission to the educational institutions whether state owned or state recognized—in recognition of their right to education under the Constitution. Charging capitation fee in consideration of admission to educational institution is a patent denial of a citizen's right to education under the Constitution. Restricting admission to non-meritorious candidates belonging to the richer section of the society and denying the same to poor meritorious is wholly arbitrary against the constitutional scheme and as such cannot be legally permitted. In the same case the court has also reiterated that the directive principles and the fundamental rights are not isolated, but are supplementary to each other. The Court authoritatively observed that the State is under a constitutional mandate to create conditions in which the fundamental rights guaranteed to the individuals could be enjoyed by all.

occupation, trade or business and rights of the minorities' to establish and administer educational institutions of their choices in terms of Article 19(1)(g)[11] and Article 30(1),[12] respectively, of the Constitution of India. However, with the passage of time, the Parliament of India in 2002 added a new fundamental right, article 21A[13] which provides for the right to free and compulsory education to all the children in between the age group of 6–14 years in such manner as the State may by law determine. Changes were also introduced in the provisions of directive principles of the state policy[14] and fundamental duties.[15] Thus, initially through judicial decisions and subsequently through legislative measures 'right to education' has finally occupied a definite place under part III of the Constitution of India.

Interestingly, it took almost eight years for the Government to get it fully functional. It is only in the year 2010, when the Parliament of India enacted a comprehensive legislation on the subject of education, thereby giving effect to Article 21A of the Constitution of India in its true sense over the subject of education.[16]

2 Gandhi's Views on Education

Before discussing the views of Gandhi, it becomes pertinent to articulate on the concept of education in general. In general parlance education can be explained as an instrument which provides knowledge, skill, technique, information to the individuals and make them aware about their rights and duties towards society and the nation. It develops vision and the capabilities to fight against injustice, violence, corruption and maladministration in the society. Education is the central element in the evolution of a nation. Education is an important aspect of human peaceful coexistence existence and well-being that plays a huge role in the modern, technology-driven

---

[11] *Supra* note 7 at 1070.

[12] *T.M.A. Pai Foundation* v. *State of Karnataka*, AIR 2003 SC 355.

[13] Inserted by the Constitution (Eighty-sixth Amendment) Act, 2002, sec. 2 (w.e.f. 1-4-2010).

[14] Article 45—Provision for free and compulsory education for children—The State shall endeavour to provide, within a period of ten years from the commencement of this Constitution, for free and compulsory education for all children until they complete the age of fourteen years. However, the original text of Art 45 as mentioned above is replaced with the following text 'The State shall endeavour to provide early childhood care and education for all children until they complete the age of six years' by the Constitution (Eighty-sixth Amendment) Act, 2002, sec. 3 (w.e.f. 1-4-2010).

[15] The Constitution (Eighty-sixth Amendment) Act, 2002, sec. 4 (w.e.f. 1-4-2010). Inserted clause (k) in Article 51A—'who is a parent or guardian to provide opportunities for education to his child or, as the case may be, ward between the age of six and fourteen years.'

[16] The Right of Children to Free and Compulsory Education Act, 2009 (Hereinafter REA) came into stature book with the objective to strengthen the social fabric of democracy through provision of equal opportunities to all, where universal elementary education plays a key role, to address the challenges of drop out ratios, particularly from disadvantaged groups and weaker sections, to ensure satisfactory quality of learning achievement and to achieve the dutiful mandate of article 21A of the Constitution of India.

world. Convincingly, it can be submitted that people need good education to be able to survive in this competitive world.

In this context, it is very important to bring forth the observations from the writings published in ***The Pall Mall Gazette***, a well-known journal in England, where the author has attempted to explain the true nature of real education in following terms[17]:

> We hold that real education does not consist merely in acquainting oneself with ancient or modern books. It consists in the habits which one knowingly or unknowingly imbibes from the atmosphere, one's surroundings and the company one keeps and above all in work. ***It is all very well to acquire a stock of knowledge from good books or from other sources. But the more important thing is to learn humanity***. The primary function of teachers is, therefore, not to teach the alphabet, but to inculcate humanity. Aristotle said that virtue is not learnt by reading big volumes. It is by doing good deeds that we learn virtue. Another great writer also says that it is well for one to know what is good, but one will be considered a happy person only if one acts upon that knowledge.

Further, S. P. Pani and N. R. Dash while deliberating upon the views of ***Swami Vivekanand***, a great educational thinker and humanists, submitted that[18]:

> education is a process in which the young minds will receive strength, energy and vigorous character. Under this process they will mould themselves in such a way in which weakness has no part to play. Thus the larger and nobler aim of education would be ***'life-building, man-making, character-making, assimilation of ideas'***. The entire educational method and programme should keep this high objective in view.

And again while contemplating on the views of a great Nobel laureate, Rabindra Nath Tagore, the learned authors write:

> 'Harmony with all things' is the basic principle of Tagore's philosophy. He interprets this harmony in three contexts-with nature, with human surroundings and with international relations. To him the real education is that which teaches one to live in harmony with all that exists around him...... According to Tagore the primary object of an educational institution should be to being the educated in perfect tune with the symphony of response between life and world. ....We find four fundamentals in Tagore's educational philosophy: ***Naturalism, Humanism***, ***Internationalism*** and ***Idealism***.

Considering the views of the learned scholars, it would be obvious to submit that education does not only mean acquisition of information or knowledge; rather it is a process which includes ***inter alia***, the holistic development of a human personality, empowering them to face the intricate problems of life, develop them with necessary strength and teach them the importance and need of harmonic existence with nature, human surroundings and outside world.

Further, the learned scholars in their wisdom and rich experiences have rightly pointed out the true aim of education as to inculcate the attitude of humanity and a sense of service coupled with new ideas, a strong character and peaceful coexistence.

---

[17] Gandhi on education, National Council for Teachers' Training.

[18] S.P Pani and N.R Dash, Modern Educational Thinkers Part XI, Director Directorate of Distance & Continuing Education Utkal university, Bhubaneswar, 2014 Available at https://ddceutkal.ac.in/Syllabus/MA_Education/Paper_11.pdf (last accessed 15 January 2021).

Wittingly, they emphasize more upon the habits and deeds in the process of receiving education and not just literacy.

Gandhi on similar terms, though in different phraseology, beautifully explained the philosophy of education by stating that a scheme of education should necessarily be based upon the essential values of Indian culture and civilization.[19] He further emphasized that 'by education, I mean an overall all around drawing out of the best in child and man, in body, mind, and spirit.'[20]

He considered education as a birth right of a man. Perhaps this may be the reason, he emphasized upon providing compulsory and free general education for all children up to a certain age.[21] According to him, the aim of education is emancipation of human body mind and soul. He considered the concept of emancipation in a very wide sense as to include physical, mental, economic and political emancipation in the first stage and then spiritual emancipation at a later stage.[22]

Gandhi was never in favour of colonial education system,[23] which was prevailing at that point of time. On this, while deliberating upon the Gandhian conception on education, Devi Prasad writes,[24] for Gandhi, 'the first task was to get rid of the colonial educational system, which was totally unrelated to the life of the people and tended to wean the educated away from their own culture. The second task was to construct a system, which would give the people a sense of self respect and the skills to be able to educate themselves in a way that would make them responsible for their own lives, individually as well as collectively.' Accordingly, as the learned writers observe,[25] Gandhi presented his philosophy of education as a harmonious blending of idealism, naturalism and pragmatism.

For Gandhi, literacy is neither the beginning nor the end of education, it can only be served as a means through which a man or woman can be educated. Gandhi convincingly asseverated that the aim of education should not only be the growth and development of individual personality, but at the same time, it should promote a balanced and harmonious society.[26] He talked about every minute aspects associated

---

[19] A Selvan (Dr.) and P. Paul Devanesan (Dr.), Gandhi's Contribution To Education (last visited on 12 January 2021).

[20] *Supra* note 2 at 74.

[21] Raman Bihari Lal and Neetu Sabbarwal, Philosophical Perspectives of Education 177 (R Lall Book Depot, Meerut, 2013 edn.).

[22] *Ibid.* at 178. He reasoned that until a man is free from physical weakness, mental pressures, economic deficiencies and political slavery, he cannot attain spiritual emancipation.

[23] *Infra* 24 at 241. Colonial rule destroyed the earlier Indian system of education. The East India Company created a distinct class among Indians, which was to be educated in the Western mode. The purpose of this class was to fill the minor positions in the administration, which were considered neither sufficiently dignified nor sufficiently lucrative for Englishmen.

[24] Joy A Palmer, Liora Bresler, (2001).

[25] Sr. Jincy Joseph, Gandhian Philosophy on Education, St. Thomas College of Teacher Education, Pala Available at http://assisiaruvithura.blogspot.com/2013/06/mk-gandhi.html?m=1 (last accessed January 13, 2021).

[26] Ibid.

with the societal well-being, which a man should aspire to pursue in his vogue for the realization of the fruits of true education.

Schematically, Gandhi presented the following[27]:

(a) Adult education of the whole community, including the parents of the newborn babies;
(b) Pre-basic schooling from 2 to 7 years;
(c) Basic schooling from 7 to 14 years;
(d) Post-basic education from 14 to 18 years and
(e) University and teacher training institute education.

In addition to it, he also identified two types of educational aims[28]:

1. Immediate aim
2. Ultimate aim.

In immediate aim, he accentuated upon a wide range of activities, which an individual must aspire to purse as an important essential and inseparable entity of the society as a whole. It includes character building,[29] vocational training,[30] value of culture,[31] perfect development,[32] leadership,[33] freedom[34] and dignity.[35]

In deliberating upon the ultimate aim, Gandhi accentuated on the kernel of self-realization. He strongly believes that all other aims are subservient to this supreme

---

[27] *Supra* note 24 at 242.

[28] *Supra* note 25 at 5.

[29] In defining the concept of 'character building', he emphasized upon of moral values such as truthfulness, non-violence, courage, strength of mind, righteousness, self-restraint and service of humanity. He believes that education will automatically develop an ability in the child to distinguish between good and bad.

[30] He emphasized upon the need of a man for self-reliance and capacity to earn one's livelihood. He wished that each child should earn while engaged in learning and gain some learning as he is busy with earning. In his own words, 'Education ought to be for them (children) a kind of insurance against unemployment. He included education of handicraft or industry in it.'

[31] Gandhi considered cultural aspect of education more important and essential than academic aspects. In the words of Gandhi 'I attach more importance to cultural factor of education than its literary factor. Culture is primary and basic thing which the girls should receive from school.'

[32] According to Gandhi, the real education should bring real change in human personality, and he advocates for complete development of human body mind and soul. According to him, 'Man is neither mere intellect, nor the gross animals' body, nor heart or soul alone. A proper and harmonious contribution of all the three is required for the making of the whole man and constitutes the true economics of education.'

[33] For the survival of democracy, a good leader is sine qua non, and he believed the education should imbibe the qualities of leadership. Cooperation, coordination and taking lead in subject should be taught and practiced.

[34] One should be free from all kinds of social, economic, political and mental slavery.

[35] One should not feel shy from doing any kind of work. The education should enable a person to earn his own livelihood. He should stand up on his own feet. The students must learn the dignity of labour.

aim. On this, a learned scholar has rightly submitted while deliberating upon the observation of Gandhi[36]:

> Development of the moral character, development of the whole- all were directed towards the realization of the ultimate reality- ***the merger of the finite being into the infinite.*** It is realizing Godliness in his self.

Indeed M.K Gandhi's deep ken on education and its realization unfurls many social, economic, cultural and political dimensions of the heterogeneous human society which necessarily called for consistent, planned and inclusive reforms in the education sector. Accordingly, he proposed a systematic road map to ensure meaningful sustainable and progressive edification or education which ***inert alia*** includes curriculum design, importance of craftsmanship, teaching methodology, character and roles of a teacher and importance of discipline and spirituality in human life.

Researchers shall try to present the observations of Gandhi on each of the following elements.

(1) **Curriculum Design**—It is often said about Gandhi that he was a practical idealist[37] and the same is reflected in his writings, when he proposed activity-based curriculum. In the basic education (Classes 1–8), he emphasized upon the prominent place of handicraft and cottage industry. Apart from it, he talked about the importance of mother tongue, practical mathematics, social subjects, general science, music drawing and hygiene including moral education.[38]

Gandhian edification on curriculum includes[39]

- Craftsmanship—Agriculture, spinning weaving, etc.
- Mother tongue[40]
- Practical Mathematics
- Social studies—Social and economic life of the community
- Culture centric education.

(2) **Importance of craftsmanship**—Gandhi laid emphasis on village craft and the need for the development of necessary skills among the villagers as to make them self-dependent. He convincingly argued for the introduction of productive handicrafts in the school education. On this, the learned writer, Mr. Jincy Joseph submits[41]:

---

[36] *Supra* note 25 at 5.

[37] Sarvepalli Radhakrishnan (Dr.) '*Gandhi – The Practical Idealist*', *available at*: https://www.mkgandhi.org/articles/idealist.htm (last visited on 20 January 2021).

[38] *Supra* note 21 at 179.

[39] *Supra* note 25 at 8.

[40] Alladi Veerabhdra Rao, 'Mahatma Gandhi views on Philosophy of Education', 3 *International Journal of Academic Research* 96 (2016).

[41] *Supra* note 25 at 8.

> The idea was not simply to introduce handicrafts as a compulsory school subject, but to make the learning of a craft the centre piece of the entire teaching programme. Knowledge of the production processes involved in crafts, such as spinning, weaving, leatherwork, pottery, metal-work, basket-making and bookbinding had been the monopoly of specific caste groups in the lowest stratum of the traditional social hierarchy.

Gandhi strongly believed that the craftsmanship will ensure the fulfilment of three purposes.[42]

(a) It will help to make education self-supporting, train the bodies of the children as well as their minds.
(b) It will pave the way for a complete boycott of foreign yarn and cloth.
(c) It will make the children self-reliant and independent.

(3) **Teaching Methodology**—Gandhi considered man as the sum total of body mind and spirit, and he asseverated that the development of all these faculties is essential for the all-round development of a human personality. Therefore, he reasoned that teaching must aim at the activities of body, mind and soul. He often emphasized upon the concept of learning by doing and learning by self-activity as an effective way. However, at the same time, he outlines the importance and significance of descriptions, namely narrations, explanation and question–answer methods. Consistent with the philosophy outlined in Vedant, he also advocated for thinking, listening and practice methods.

Some of the important Gandhian Teaching methods are discussed here in brief.[43]

(a) **Emulation Techniques**—Gandhi believed that imitation is the natural tendency of a child, and therefore, a child should be taught by this method. He considered this a good method for training children in good conduct. In his view, good conduct should be inculcated in children during childhood; the qualities developed at this time are permanent in nature. Children generally imitate their elders and parents. Therefore, parents and teachers should behave with children affectionately by which children learn to love. Besides, they should follow truthfulness, non-violence, celibacy, tastelessness, non-stealing, non-hoarding, fearlessness, untouchability removal, physical labour, religious goodwill and politeness in their conduct so that children imitate them to do good conduct.
(b) **Activity Method**—Gandhi strongly believed that activity is the natural tendency of children. They keep doing one or other things at all times, and therefore, education of subject or skills should be imparted by activity. He further emphasized on self-experience techniques in learning and teaching. It includes play-way and experimental method, and according to Gandhi, this activity-based approach shall be a good mode of edification in the field of music, art and handicrafts.

---

[42] Prof. (Dr.) Yogendra Yadav, 'Handicrafts and Mahatma Gandhi', The Gandhi King Community for Global peace with social justice in a sustainable environment available at https://gandhiking.ning.com/profiles/blogs/handicrafts-and-mahatma-gandhi-1 (last accessed 13 January 2021).

[43] *Supra* note 21 at 179–181. Also See, *Supra* note 25 at 8.

(c) **Verbal Mode of edification**—It includes 'Question-Answers', 'Debates' 'Lectures', 'Group Discussions', etc. However, Gandhi permitted these modes of teaching as an auxiliary means of understanding. He clarified that the children are curious, whatever method you employ, they will keep asking questions in between, their questions should be replied immediately, and their doubts should be resolved. At the same time, he emphasized that a care should be taken to keep them physically and mentally alert at all times. They must not be made passive listeners.

(d) **Correlation techniques**—Children must be imparted learning in real sense and in real circumstances, Gandhi observed. The method of connecting all subjects and activities of curriculum with each other is called as correlation techniques. Children's natural environment, social environment or handicraft is taken as the central subject, and all subjects and activities of the curriculum should be integrated with the central subject. This mode of edification exalts natural tendency of learning among the children and prepares them for real-life challenges.

(e) **Integrating listening, thinking and practice**—This is an ancient mode of edification, where a child is made to think upon the observations of the teacher, i.e. oral percepts, learn the same and then practice it. Gandhi strongly preached this ancient technique, and he believed knowledge has no meaning until it becomes the part of our practical life and assist us in our overall growth and development. This technique, as Gandhi wrote, is suitable for religion and philosophy. According to him, during adolescent stage of human life, children should do satsang, listen to precepts, study, contemplate, discover the truth by intellect and reasoning and then practice the same in real life.

(4) **Character and role of a teacher**—Gandhi eloquently presented his edification on the concept of teacher. According to him, a teacher should be an ideal person, a man of wisdom, torch of knowledge and of having good conduct. According to Gandhi, a person who is willing to take up the profession of teaching, must keep one thing in his mind, that it is a social service and not just a mere profession. A teacher is required to discharge several roles, like that of a father, friend, assistant and guide to students, so he should be forbearing, liberal, patient and should exhibit strong moral character:

> ……..A teacher to be a model of behavior an image of society a compendium of virtues……. A teacher to teach by example than by precept. A teacher must be well trained, proficient, man of knowledge, faith action and devotion. Teachers are responsible for carving the statues of their students. A teacher should be the epicene of character, a symbol of values, well disciplined, a unique personality, cultured and having a good mentality. His serenity and magnanimity should be outstanding and shining. He should be polite, pious, and having sea of knowledge. He should be a psychologist, a philosophies, a historian, a technologist in the matters of knowledge and seduction. He should be a guide, mentor, and guru for imparting knowledge to the students – the valuable pearls.

(5) **Importance of Discipline**—Gandhi equated the idea of discipline with self-control. He convincingly believed that self-control promotes inner discipline which eventually leads to self-discipline.[44] However, his idea of self-discipline in ultimate analysis is in tune with social discipline. He argued that every individual should be a productive citizen.

(6) **Importance of Spirituality**—A learned author submits that[45] Gandhi was following an ancient tradition of using spirituality as a basis of social change. He strongly believed that there is something good in every religion, though Hinduism happens to be his core religious philosophy,[46] but at the same time, he emphasized upon the significance and importance of all other religions. He incorporated Christian notions of love, forgiveness and uncomplaining suffering into his philosophy while rejecting the idea that salvation could come only through Christ; he embraced Islam's emphasis on equality. Jainism's anekantavada (the many-sidedness of truth) made him tolerant to all religions.

Gandhi's seminal articulation on the theme of education reflects a calibrated and deft requirement of modern societies' needs for sustainable, progressive inclusive and holistic notion of human civilization, culture, human values, individual autonomy and life of dignity including social economic and political independence. With this, it becomes important to observe how the Constitution incorporates and addresses the edification of the father of the nation.

3 Education and the Constitutional Visions in India

The Constitution of India differentiates between the civil and political rights contained in part III of the Constitution as fundamental rights and social, economic and cultural rights contained in part IV of the Constitution as directive principles of state policy. The distinction between the two is set out in Article 37 of the Constitution, which declares that, while the directive principles are 'fundamental in the governance of the country' and the state is duty-bound to implement them, they 'shall not be enforced in any court.'[47]

---

[44] *Supra* note 25 at 8. See Also, Supra note 21 at 181. Gandhi was never in favour of imposed discipline. He opposed repressionistic method for attainment of discipline. In his view true discipline can be developed by impressionistic method.

[45] Surendra Bhana.

[46] *Ibid.* It offers salvation through karma-yoga (selfless action), raja-yoga (bodily discipline), bhakti-yoga (devotional endeavours) and jnana-yoga (knowledge through mental discipline). He chose to stress the first and adapted it to four fundamental Hindu ideas to suit his philosophy of social activism. Thus, Moksha (individual liberation), Tapasya (penitence), Yoga (mind–body harmonization) and Samadhi (withdrawal to prepare for moksha) all were adapted to suit his commitment for social reform and change in the service of the poor and the needy.

[47] The Constitution of India, part IV, art. 37.

Articles 41 and 45 use the word education,[48] but Article 45 expressly deals with *free and compulsory education* and originally read as follows: '*the State shall endeavor to provide, within a period of ten years from the commencement of this Constitution, for free and compulsory education for all children until they complete the age of fourteen years.*'[49] It is the only provision in part IV of the Constitution that had a fixed time limit, thus signifying the concern of the framers of the Constitution to the implementation of right to education including the Gandhian notion on education.[50]

The right to education passed through various phases.

***Phase 1: Directive Principles and State Legislation* (1951–1992)**

The Constitution of India, 1950, did not guarantee education as a fundamental right. Instead, it was included under part IV as a welfare goal implementable within a time frame of 10 years under Article 45 (erstwhile). The Constitution (42nd Amendment) Act, 1976 altered the basis of executive and legislative competence to permit the Union to exercise concurrent jurisdiction with the States. However, the Union did not enact any law.

***Phase II: Mohini Jain* v. *State of Karnataka and Unnikrishnan* v. *State of Andhra Pradesh* (1992–1993)**

The Supreme Court declared the right to education as a fundamental right in *Mohini Jain* v. *State of Karnataka*[51] and interpreted the directive principle in Article 45 into a right to education under the right to life under Article 21.

In *Unnikrishnan J. P.* v. *State of Andhra Pradesh*[52], the Supreme Court clarified that the right to education is available to all children below the age of 14 years. The Supreme Court by 'harmonious construction' completely transformed the status of Article 45. The Supreme Court ruled that Article 45 has to be read in 'harmonious construction' with Art. 21 (Right to life) as Article 45 loses its import without education and declared that Article 45 has acquired the status of a fundamental right. The right to education continues to exist under Art. 41 even beyond the age of 14 years but is limited by the State's economic capacity and development. The Constitution is clearly directing the State to envisage the entire sector of education from kindergarten to higher and professional education in a holistic manner. Any policy to limit, distort or fragment this vision of education amounts to a violation of the Constitution of India which represents people's aspirations from the freedom struggle against imperialism. So while Unnikrishnan, narrowed the scope of the right to education

---

[48] Article 41, which reads: The State shall, within the limits of its economic capacity and development, make effective provision for securing the right to work, to education and to public assistance in cases of unemployment, old age, sickness and disablement and in other cases of undeserved want.

[49] The Constitution of India, art. 45.

[50] *Supra* note 21 at 177.

[51] 1992 SCR (3) 658.

[52] AIR 1993 SC 2178.

articulated in Mohini Jain to children below the age of fourteen years, with the introduction of Article 21A children below six have now been excluded from the scope of the constitutional right to education. The right to education which is implicit in the right to life and personal liberty guaranteed by Article 21 must be construed in the light of the directive principle in Part IV of the Constitution. Articles 45, 46 and 41 are designed to achieve the said goal among others. The Supreme Court's recognition of the fundamental right to free and compulsory education in *Unnikrishnan* is 'indispensable' to achieving the education goals set forth in the Constitution.

Phase III: The Constitution (Eighty-sixth Amendment) Act 2002

The Ramamurti Committee Report which reviewed the National Policy on Education, 1986 in 1990 observed that the 'continued' failure of the State to realize the goals under Article 45 as a 'teasing reality'[53] and recommended the introduction of a fundamental right to education. The Supreme Court's interventions in 1992 and 1993 realized this recommendation by declaring a right to elementary education. *The Constitution (Eighty-sixth Amendment) Act 2002* added a new fundamental right to education by creating Article 21A[54] to children in the age group of 6 and 14 years. It simultaneously amended Article 45 to retain State's obligation to provide early childhood care and education to all children until the age of six years as a directive principle of the State policy.[55]

Phase IV: The Right of Children to Free and Compulsory Education Act 2009

The fourth phase in the development of the legal environment begins with the enactment of the Right of Children to Free and Compulsory Education Act, 2009 ('RTE Act'). The Act provides free and compulsory education to all children of the age group of six to fourteen years in accordance with the mandate of Article 21 A of the Constitution of India.

Convincingly, on this development the ***Saikia Committee Report*** and ***Unnikrishnan*** ratio played a very significant role. The Act provides that children between the age of 6 and 14 years have the right to free and compulsory education in a neighbourhood school. However, even after the completion of a decade, the progress on the subject of education as envisaged by the REA is not satisfactory.[56] A pertinent

---

[53] Sudhir Krishnaswamy, Securing Universal Education: Directive Principles, Fundamental Rights and Statutory Rights Available at https://azimpremjiuniversity.edu.in/SitePages/pdf/SudhirK.pdf (last accessed 16 January 2021).

[54] Article 21A—Right to Education—The State shall provide free and compulsory education to all children of the age of six to fourteen years in such manner as the State may, by law, determine.

[55] Article 45—provision for early childhood care and education to children below the age of six years—The State shall endeavour to provide early childhood care and education for all children until they complete the age of six years.

[56] Sanchayan Bhattacharjee, (2019). Since its enactment, the RTE Act has achieved success in overall enrolment rates but has faced criticism for administrative and structural lapses. Several provisions have fallen short of achieving their intended effect of significantly improving the quality of learning. While some provisions have failed due to implementation hurdles, others struggle due to a lack of coordination and the paucity of funds or delay in allocation.

question must be asked, how far actually we have succeeded in realizing the objective of Article 21A of the Constitution of India. What are the actual impediments and why there has been a slow progress?[57]

Phase V: The National Educational Policy 2020

The aim of NEP 2020 is to transform India, by providing high-quality education to all and to make India a global knowledge superpower. The curriculum and pedagogy of our institutions must develop among the students a deep sense of respect towards the fundamental duties and belongingness with one's country. It focuses to create a conscious awareness of one's roles and responsibilities in a changing world and also to develop knowledge, skills, values and dispositions that support the character development and assimilations of new ideas.

At this juncture, it would be desirable to observe some of the important characteristics of the National Education Policy 2020 (NEP 2020).[58] The NEP 2020 was approved by the Union Cabinet on 29 July 2020. It is based upon the recommendations of a nine member Committee, constituted under the chairmanship of Dr. K. Kasturirangam, (former ISRO Chief).[59]

A. **Structure**

The Policy is divided into four parts and consists of 27 chapters.

- Part I—School Education
- Part II—Higher Education
- Part III—Professional/adult education and lifelong learning, including promotion of Indian Language Art and Culture
- Part IV—Execution including finance, implementation, etc.

B. **Key Aspects**

- **Change in pattern**—The NEP 2020 has replaced the current pattern of $10 + 2$ with the pattern of $5 + 3 + 3 + 4$ $(5 = 3 + 2)$, it covers age of 3–6 and then 6–8 (foundational), a child's formal education starts at 3, now period of play school will also come into the domain of formal education, and children can participate in school curriculum which is a global practice. Further, 3 (preparatory), it covers

[57] *Ibid*. According to the District Information System of Education, only 13 percent of all schools in India have achieved full compliance with these RTE norms.

[58] *Supra* note 6. Also see Priya Jain, Finology legal, available at: https://m.youtube.com/watch?v=BIJBveGlgo0 (last visited on 26 January 2020).

[59] However, it is important to note that the first education policy was introduced in the year 1968, during the tenure of Smt. Indira Nehru Gandhi, then in 1986 during the reign of Shri. Rajiv Gandhi, Second Education Policy was introduced, which was modified in 1992 under the leadership of Shri. P. V. Narasimha Rao, and finally under the leadership of Shri. Narendra DamodarDass Modi, after the gap of 34 years, we have the first education policy of the twenty-first century.

age from 8 to 11, next 3 (middle), it covers age from 11 to 14, and last 4 years (secondary), it covers the age 14–18. Pattern is as follows—5 Foundational (Class 1 & 2) + 3 Preparatory (Class 3–5) + 3 Middle (Class 6–8) + 4 Secondary (Class 9–12).

- **Education in mother tongue**—Up to 5th standard, an attempt is made under the NEP 2020 to impart education in mother tongue. Unlike the previous policy, there is no requirement to study in Hindi or English. A student is free to choose the medium of instructions, preferably in his/her mother tongue.
- **Multidisciplinary education**—The NEP 2020 permits students to decide the subjects in combination, depending upon the interest of the students, unlike previous policy, under the mandate of Policy, a student can study physics with political science or chemistry with history. Subjects of humanities, commerce and sciences can be studied together.
- **Freedom to opt for another course/Multiple entry and Exit point**—The NEP 2020 permits students to opt for another course or program, if he does not like the current program in which he/she is enrolled. For example, if a student is pursuing B. Tech., he may change his/her course and opt for another program, like LL.B. or BB.A., etc., and depending upon the number of years, he has pursued the course, certificate, diploma and degree will be issued. For example, if he has decided to change his B. Tech. programme after 1 year, he shall be given a certificate, and after 2 years, then diploma, etc.
- **Resumption of course after the gap**—On account of forced circumstances such as family issues or financial crisis, if a student cannot complete his course, he may resume his/her studies at any point of time from the stage at which he left, and for this, the NEP 2020 envisages the creation of Academic Bank of Credit. It means, he should not start over again, and his previous performance shall also be taken into account for his course.
- **Vocational Education**—The NEP 2020 envisages the importance of skills at the early age of human growth, and accordingly, it makes provisions for imparting practical knowledge and skills from class 6 onwards. Along with the regular classes, students shall be encouraged to learn coding, carpentry, gardening, cooking, etc., and focus shall be on overall growth and development of the students.
- **Report Card**—Interestingly, the NEP 2020 envisages the creation of a holistic report card, which does not spell out one's academic performance only but also skills and capabilities. It aims at 360* holistic evaluation. Apart from that, the Policy also makes provisions for self-evaluation and evaluation by peers.
- **Importance of digitalization**—The NEP 2020 envisions the availability of education at grass root level, and for this, it makes provisions for making use of technology in imparting knowledge and education at grass root level. It also enables the beneficiaries to receive education in regional languages.
- **Concept of Lok Vidya**—In order to promote the understanding and importance of Indian languages, customs, traditions and heritage, the NEP 2020 envisions the availability of education on the theme suitable for the purposes. This will facilitate

the knowledge about the working style and modus operandi of ancient people who were engaged in manufacturing, agriculture and other means of livelihood.

- **Single Regulator**—The NEP 2020 envisages for the creation of a single regulator, unlike previous policy, an academic institution requires approval from UGC, AICTE and other bodies, but under the Policy, everything will be taken care of by a single regulator, (The Higher Education Commission of India, hereinafter HECI). However, the Medical and Legal education will not be subjected to the Jurisdiction of this HECI. It means, except Medical and Legal education, every other higher education will be governed by HECI.
- **Expansion of Education**—The NEP 2020 aims at making most of the institution multidisciplinary by 2040. And by 2030, every district of the State should have at least one multidisciplinary institute.
- **Miscellaneous aspects**—The NEP 2020 has the effect of alternating the nomenclature of the Ministry of Human Resource Development as the Ministry of Education. The NEP 2020 aims at increasing the GDP investment in education from 1.6 to 6%. It further aims at increasing the Gross Enrolment Ratio up to 50% by 2035. The Policy aims at creation of Multidisciplinary Education and Research Universities (MERU) and also to establish a national level body to achieve the purpose, i.e. the National Research Foundation.

4 Epilogue

Ominous and sedentary educational affairs in the country, needless to say, require active participation of both the state as well as non-state actors in ameliorating the existing educational atmosphere in the country. On this, Gandhian views on education have much to offer. Clear, unambiguous and honest articulation about the nature scope and importance of education by Gandhi now find place in the ***New National Education Policy 2020*** **(NEP 2020)** but for a long time remain eclipsed from the constitutional visions of democratic socialism and egalitarianism, where Gandhian views on education could have played an important role in developing a just and inclusive sociopolitical order in a heterogeneous society of an unthinkable diversity.

The NEP 2020 aims *inter alia* at the development of the creative potential of each individual. It is based on the principle that education must develop not only cognitive capacities—both the 'foundational capacities' of literacy and numeracy and 'higher-order' cognitive capacities, such as critical thinking and problem solving—but also social, ethical and emotional capacities and dispositions. On this, it echoed an absolute prowess of Gandhian views on education as he also considered man as the sum total of body mind and spirit and asseverated that the development of all these faculties are essential for the all-round development of a human personality. It includes character building, vocational training, value of culture, perfect development, leadership, freedom and dignity and finally the ultimate aim of self-realization.

Convincingly education is viewed as a crucial development tool, the quality of education does not only define and determine the life of an individual citizen, but it also affects the social, cultural, economic, legal and political environment of a nation. It is really surprising that we took around more than seven decades to recognize the Gandhian views on education since independence until some of its edification finds suitable place in NEP 2020.

References

Aithal PS, Aithal S (2020) Analysis of the Indian National Education Policy 2020 towards achieving its objectives. Int J Manage Technol Soc Sci (IJMTS) 5(2):19–41. https://doi.org/10.5281/zenodo.3988767. Accessed 12 Jan 2021

Aradhya N, Kashyap A, The 'Fundamentals' Right to education in India. https://unesdoc.unesco.org/ark:/48223/pf0000151010. Accessed 27 Oct 2020

Bhana S (2021) Gandhi spirituality and social action. https://www.mkgandhi.org/articles/gspiritual&socaction.htm. Accessed 15 Jan 2021

Bhattacharjee S, Ten years of RTE act: revisiting achievements and examining gaps. https://www.orfonline.org/research/ten-years-of-rte-act-revisiting-achievements-and-examining-gaps54066/. Accessed 19 Oct 2020

Gandhi on education, National Council for Teachers' Training. http://www.schoolofeducators.com/wp-content/uploads/2012/02/GANDHI-ON-EDUCATION-BOOK-COMPLETE.pdf. Accessed 12 Jan 2021

Jain MP (2014) Indian Constitutional Law, 7th edn. Lexis Nexis, Gurgaon, p 1227

Jain P, Finology legal. https://m.youtube.com/watch?v=BIJBveGlgo0. Accessed 26 Jan 2020

Joseph J Sr, Gandhian philosophy on education. St. Thomas College of Teacher Education, Pala. http://assisiaruvithura.blogspot.com/2013/06/mk-gandhi.html?m=1. Accessed 13 Jan 2021

Krishnaswamy S, Securing universal education: directive principles, fundamental rights and statutory rights. https://azimpremjiuniversity.edu.in/SitePages/pdf/SudhirK.pdf. Accessed 16 Jan 2021

Kumarappa B (ed), Towards new education, by M. K. Gandhi, https://www.gandhiashramsevagram.org/pdf-books/towards-new-education.pdf. Accessed 12 Jan 2021

Lal RB, Sabbarwal N (2013) Philosophical perspectives of education. R Lall Book Depot, Meerut, p 177

Palmer JA, Bresler L et al (eds) (2001) Fifty major thinkers on education from Confucius to Dewey, 1st edn. Routledge, London and New York, p 241

Pani SP, Dash NR (2014) Modern educational thinkers Part XI, Directorate of Distance & Continuing Education Utkal university, Bhubaneswar. https://ddceutkal.ac.in/Syllabus/MA_Education/Paper_11.pdf. Accessed 15 Jan 2021

Radhakrishnan S, Gandhi—the practical idealist. https://www.mkgandhi.org/articles/idealist.htm. Accessed 20 Jan 2021

Rajashekharan Pillai VN, Gandhi's concept on education and its relevance in the present day. http://www.totetu.org/assets/media/paper/j014_071.pdf. Accessed 20 Jan 2021

Selvan A, Paul Devanesan P, Gandhi's contribution to education. file:///C:/Users/user/Downloads/SSRN-id3599726.pdf. Accessed 12 Jan 2021

The National Education Policy 2020. https://pib.gov.in/PressReleasePage.aspx?PRID=1642061. Accessed 12 Jan 2021

Veerabhdra Rao A (2016) Mahatma Gandhi views on philosophy of education. Int J Acad Res 96

Yadav Y, "Handicrafts and Mahatma Gandhi" The Gandhi King Community for Global peace with social justice in a sustainable environment: https://gandhiking.ning.com/profiles/blogs/handicrafts-and-mahatma-gandhi-1. Accessed 13 Jan 2021

Chapter 18
Relevance of Gandhian Philosophy in Reformation of Prisoners

Anju Sinha and Adyansha Rajpoot

1 Introduction

The existence of inequality, poverty, discrimination, and illiteracy in social structures warrants criminal behaviour in a society. Since, the inequalities in a society and greed of every individual finds no end, crime becomes the mirror of the society reflecting upon the existence of the same. One must address these issues in order to envisage the vision of a crime free society. The development of the idea of *sarvodaya*—"the uplift of all', and the teachings of the fair treatment of every human by Gandhi is one such step towards the achievement of a crime free society or a society with negligible crime. It is a sincere attempt to inculcate the spirit of love, fraternity, truth, non-violence, self-sacrifice and self-denial within the members of the society for the creation of an environment where everyone believes in the welfare of all. It propagates that the progress of an individual lies in the progress of all, that is for the actualisation of one's self, one must strive for the actualisation of his surroundings (nation). Such society will ensure better performance of one's duties (*dharm*), respect of each individual and will have no space for crime in it.

Dharm which is the natural law and is applicable to everyone prescribes a code of living that incorporates the fundamental principles of duties, rights, laws, conduct and virtues. *Dharm* is considered to be eternal and one cannot escape it in one's lifetime and plays an instrumental role in transforming 'human beings' into 'humane beings'[1] It guides one to be righteous and emphasises on the performance of duties in a way

[1] S.S. Sethy, "Reinterpreting Gandhi's Notion of 'Dharma': An Entanglement of Duty, Religion, and Ethics", 37 *Gandhi Marg* 2, pp. 293–312 (2015).

A. Sinha (✉)
Assistant Professor (Senior Scale) Law Centre 1, Faculty of Law, University of Delhi, Delhi, India
e-mail: asinha@lc1.du.ac.in

A. Rajpoot
Student, B.A. Political Science, Miranda House, University of Delhi, Delhi, India

R. Mittal and K. K. Singh (eds.), *Relevance of Duties in the Contemporary World*,
https://doi.org/10.1007/978-981-19-1836-0_18

that must not harm others. In the due process of performance of duties, one will get their rights, bringing universal peace and harmony in the society and transformation within an individual.

Dharm is an ambivalent concept due to which it has been interpreted in multiple ways by various Hindu reformers, including Gandhi. Gandhi reinterprets *dharm* from the spiritual perspective and attempts to associate it with duty, religion and ethics.[2] While associating it with duty, he considers morality as a source of action and implies that performance of duties by an individual helps him to realise his potential and become self-sufficient. This further ensures maintenance of social order by bringing justice and peace to it, as it is a duty based legal system in which every individual owed a duty towards other members of the society. It helps an individual to lead a moral, peaceful, and non-violent life.

When we associate Gandhian ideas with the rehabilitation of prisoners or the concept of open prison system, we come to an understanding that criminals must be given an environment and opportunities to rehabilitate and restart their life in a better way. Gandhi treats criminal as a diseased person, and emphasises that prisons must be no different than reformatories where various activities and trainings must be provided, which will help them to restore their mental health and may also provide them with the understanding of their purpose in life. Gandhi himself describes reading books, and learning different languages while he served in prison as a benefit. He read over 30 books in a span of three months, which provided him a better insight of himself and the world around him. Hence, crime is a disease and is the product of existing social system, it is believed that the punishment should also aim at reformation of the individual along with prevention and deterrence.

2 Crime as a Product of Social Structure

Hunger makes a thief of any man.[3] Poverty, peer pressure, family conditions, politics, unemployment, religion, deprivation, unfair judicial system provides a fertile ground for crime. In such scenarios, there is an everyday struggle to survive, which leads to desperation or hopelessness; in either case this leads to the creation of a criminal mind. Desperate individuals' resort to violent or illicit means to make quick money and get through the daily struggle of survival, while a hopeless individual finds death more appealing than survival, and ends up committing suicide. Poverty stricken household are at constant battle with life and have no means to win it, they want to work for their living, but lack skills for the same. It is a vicious cycle where poverty, trauma and crime go hand in hand; and takes a miracle to get out of it. Society treats poor with utter cruelty, which is why they pay no heed to the performance of duties or *dharm*, and instead of focussing on noble ideals of love, peace, harmony, fraternity,

---

[2] M. K. Gandhi, Collected Works of Mahatma Gandhi (New Delhi: Publications Division), Vol. 59 (1958–1994).

[3] Papaioannou (2017).

self-actualisation, etc. they are more focussed upon starvation and ways to end it. As said by Gandhi that 'no one performs crime for the fun of it' societal pressures leave them with no choice. Hence, overall poverty provides the risk of victimisation and violence.

Further, individual alienation and deliberately not letting a group or community to rise also paves path for violence. Noble prize-winning economist, Garry Becker also explains the stark relationship between income inequalities and crime in his paper 'crime and punishment-an economic approach'. They want to enjoy the comforts of life like the other half of the society, makes an individual do whatever possible to achieve it. In many instances of theft, it is observed that firstly it was done to fulfil the grave need of the hour, but later on individual sees no harm in doing that and makes it an easy way to achieve what he would not have achieved otherwise. Evidently, various research provides that theft, vandalism, murder and assault have strong links with inequalities. In an unequal society the one who is considered to be inferior are victimised by the superiors as the former makes an easy prey to assault. Such incidents frustrate one and drives him to rebel and engage in notorious activities, paving path for violence and crime.

Societal norms and standards are bizarre that an individual fails to demarcate between his needs and wants. As said by Gandhi himself, that there are enough resources to fulfil one's needs but not enough to fulfil one's greed, but due to one's failure to recognise their needs and wants people engage themselves in a rat race of achieving more and more. Such attitude of a society ripens the seed of inequality and further crime. As in this case some individuals may get most of the resources to fulfil every desire, while the others may not have enough even to fulfil his needs, giving rise to inequality. Now, the less privileged one would be compelled to earn more and engage himself in illegal ways to do so.

In various instances, one's religion is also found as a reason behind crime. Staunch religious communities, sometimes instead of promoting respect and love for other communities end up perpetuating hatred paving way to violence and crime, example—the Holocaust.[4] Even though practicing one's own religion is a basic human right, yet many uneducated and illiterate people fail to understand it. In several criminal cases, religious fanatics have been accused of murdering innocent people based on their school of thought.

People who are not served justice or when justice delivery takes time, often lose trust in the judicial system and tends to take law in their own hands. This hostile attitude of individuals towards the system drives them to uproot it and it propogates crime and violence.

The understanding of the causes of crime is necessary to understand why prisons should also be performing the function of reformatories, along with punishing and deterring them, and rather than resorting to violent means of punishing, one must follow the path of non-violence.

[4] "Top 10 reasons of crime by netnewsledger", October 8, 2019. Available at www.netnewsledger.com (last accessed on June 20, 2020).

3 Gandhian Philosophy

Social reformer, spiritual leader, secular saint, philosopher and the reason behind India's freedom- Gandhi continues to fascinate the modern world by his far-sightedness and ideologies. The life and philosophy of Gandhi continues to inspire many and offer a powerful avenue to those who are stuck amidst the challenges or finding the purpose of their life. Gandhi's principles included:

(i) Truth (*saty*),
(ii) Non-violence (*ahimsa*),
(iii) Welfare of all (*sarvodaya*), and
(iv) Peaceful protest (*satyagrah*).

(i) **Truth (*Saty*)**

This was the sovereign principle for Gandhi, he considered truth as god and drew the analogy of truth with a tree saying that the more you nurture a tree, the more fruits it will yield. Similarly the deeper we search for truth, the more we discover about it. Truth endures forever, there is no abandonment of truth and one must have the courage to embrace it however bitter it is. Embracing gives one the power to stand by it, while denial of truth, haunts one for the rest of his life. The search of truth is Gandhi's life was transformative, it gave him the audacity to accept his mistakes and his love for truth helped him to let go off all his misdemeanor. Gandhi mentions that the truth gives him strength and confidence and believes that same shall happen to the fellow-seekers of truth.

(ii) **Non-violence (*Ahimsa*)**

Gandhi said that 'there is no hope for the aching world except through the narrow and straight path of non-violence. He advocated non-violent methods for solving social, economic, political and religious problems. For Gandhi, non-violence was not only a principle but it is the most powerful way of life. Many consider non-violence as a weak or ineffective instrument, but Gandhi preaches that the fiercest battles can be fought and won thorough non-violence, India's freedom movement is the best example to prove that. Gandhi staunchly opposed violence as a principle and pointed out that violence has never done any good, it might seem at times that violence is the effective way in most cases, but it only serves temporary good, as the evil violence brings with itself is permanent. The intentions may be moral, but if it is achieved through violence the end results will always be devastating. It is believed that the values preached by Gandhi are not only relevant to contemporary times, but it will be necessary for future generations too, it will guide the planet earth to a better future of peaceful and harmonious coexistence. Non-violence preaches that the purpose is always to defeat injustice not the people involved, it seeks to win understanding and friendship and chooses love instead of hate. He further adds that violence is a creed of no religion, hence, it is duty of every individual to resist it. Non-violence has not only won battles in India but as a principle it has served its purpose all over the world.

(iii) Welfare of All (*Sarvodaya*)

It is derived from two Sanskrit terms 'sarv' meaning 'all' and 'udaya' meaning 'rise', hence, *sarvodaya* means 'progress of all'. The *sarvodaya* movement is based upon truth and non-violence and aims for creation of self-supported village communities, which represents an equal and liberal society, and leaves no room for exploitation and class- hatred. It is asked that the rich and the poor will provide selfless services, and strive for the common good of all, rather than fall prey to selfishness. His idea of *sarvodaya* gave rise to the principle of corporate social responsibility and doctrine of trusteeship in modern world. CSR and trusteeship doctrine preach that those who are in possession of surplus wealth over their legitimate needs, should consider it their social responsibility and spend the wealth for social causes like, poverty alleviation, education of others, building health infrastructure, etc.

(iv) Peaceful Protest (*Satyagrah*)

It is also derived from two Sanskrit words 'satya' i.e. 'truth' and 'agrah' i.e. holding firmly to, hence, *satyagrah* overall means holding on to truth. His sovereign principle of truth and non-violence gave birth to the philosophy of *satyagrah*. It is a non-violent form of protest or as described by him as 'sadhan', against all sorts of injustice, exploitation and oppression with the belief that the ultimate universe stands on the side of truth.[5] The Gandhian theory of *satyagrah* is a philosophy of life and politics and it contemplates stupendous mass actions for paralyzing the total structure of despotic government.[6]

Gandhi explains *dharm* as the amalgamation of duty, religion and ethics, and treats it as a dynamic force of life. He explains that performance of *dharm* will provide for 'oneness of all' and will give light to an equal society, *dharm* is a moral law and everyone must abide by it. The practice of *dharm* provides for stability and solidarity.[7]

Gandhi preaches non-violence, love and tolerance, and believed that rather than forcing the truth on oppressor, he or she should be persuaded to see the truth. According to him, the application of these principles can take humanity to new heights; otherwise the world could be consumed by vengeance, aggression and violence.

[5] B. Chakrabarthy, "Social and Political Thought of Mahatma Gandhi", London: Routledge, p. 20 (2006); A.J. Parel (ed.), Gandhi, Freedom, and Self-Rule, New Delhi: Vistaar Publication, p. 90 (2000).

[6] R. Choudhari, "Gandhian philosophy of satyagraha on and by Gandhi", 2 *Anasakti Darshan* 2, July-December 2006.

[7] Sethi, *supra* note 1.

4 Application of Gandhian Philosophy in the Reformation of Prisoners

Gandhi considers a criminal as a diseased person and is of the ideology that one should hate crime but, not criminals. Once crime, which is a disease, is treated, the criminal is a person just like all of us; a common man. He proceeds to talk about how no one is born a criminal, or desires to become one, it is the social structure that pushes one to take up the path of crime. At various instances, Gandhi mentions how it is the duty of the prison to restore the mental health of the criminal and ensure that the criminal leaves the prison with better understanding of the world. According to him, everyone must be given a fair chance to restart his life in a way that one wishes to rather than one in which he is pushed by the social norms and standards. Because when we view the journey of an individual being convicted of a crime to being sent to prison for it, the way this process is handled will decide if this process becomes a cycle with the said person turning into a repeat offender.

Gandhi being a strong supporter of non-violence, was deeply disturbed by the extensive use of violence on a daily basis in prisons. He prescribes that everyone must be nurtured with love and jailers rather than imposing force upon the prisoners, must treat them with non-violence, helping them attain the purpose of their life. Gandhi believed in punishment but wanted that it should aim at the reformation of the criminal and must be non-violent. As utilization of violent means on a criminal mind may fume vengeance, and then they will be caught in the vicious cycle of violence forever. Such instance can prove to be more disastrous for the society. Gandhi while explaining the importance of using non-violent means on prisoners' quotes, "Power is of two kinds. One is obtained by the fear of punishment and the other by acts of love. Power based on love is a thousand times more effective and permanent than the one derived from fear of punishment."[8]

There is a wide contradiction between the principles of Gandhi and the current scenario. Gandhi pleads the so-called civilized state to stop inhumane treatment towards its members and find less violent ways to fight crime even if it takes calculated risks the state must take it. Violently treating any individual is a sin itself. Several instances of police brutality in contemporary times even leading to the death of the individuals makes state nothing less than a criminal. Gandhi requests the state to change their attitude towards the inhabitants of prisons and says that prisons must be a place of reforming individuals. Society will become a better place if state takes charge that every prisoner leaves his crime back and steps out as better person.

He prescribes that prisons should provide its inmates with workshops and various constructive and social activities that will help them build their self-respect and a sense of social responsibility. Various programs must be organized to inculcate certain sets of values of honesty and hard work. A criminal mind will be treated well if provided with healthy environment, proper diet and polite relationship with their inmates and wardens. Teaching them certain skills while in jail will help them

---

[8] M.K. Gandhi, Young India, p. 15 (1925).

become self-sufficient, it will also help them in future to sustain a healthy life rather than resorting to criminal ways for earning a living.

It is also widely believed that enlightening prisoners with the noble ideals of Gandhi like truth, satyagrah and performance of *dharm* to achieve peace and harmony will enhance the personality development of inmates and inspire them to lead a peaceful yet great life by serving themselves and humanity at large. His life is also an inspiration for many and serves as a powerful avenue for disillusioned.

His idea of *sarvodaya* if implied efficiently can limit the growing rate of crime to a large extent by ensuring basic rights to all, alleviating poverty, deprivation, unemployment, enhancing family conditions which are the main reason why individual takes up crime.

5 Current Scenario of Prisons in India

There being no possibility to conceive a society without crime and criminals, therefore, the institution of prisons is indispensable for every society. The origin and growth of prison system across the globe corresponded to the changes in society's reaction to crime from time to time.

Prisons have come to occupy the central place in the administration of Justice all over the world. The prison system has come a long way from the concept of jails (which were the dens of lechery, debauchery and moral corruption) to the modern prisons; a place full with all sorts of intramural treatment meant ultimately for rehabilitation of offenders.[9]

The prisons in India are in deep crises and demand immediate betterment. The situation of Indian prison system currently, rather than being a place for reformation, serves more like a predator of human rights. Overcrowding, unhygienic sanitation, extortion, bribery, lack of staff, lack of medical facilities, inequality among prisoners, lack of legal aid, abuse of prisoners by other prisoner or the staff is the reality of prisons in India. Instead of restoring one's mental health the physical and psychological torture one goes through while completing his term in jail is immense and leads to further deterioration of the individuals.

No steps are taken to rehabilitate an inmate and turn them into a better human being. Most prisoners are even not prepared for release, in such cases too, nothing is done by the state to minimize their chances of committing offences, again. Hence, the prisons of India are nothing like Gandhi dreamed of, most of the times the protectors of law are themselves engaged in crime and violence, leaving little hope for humanity for rehabilitation of prisoners.

The Supreme Court of India has given some landmark judgments, which are treated as Magna Carta in the administration of prisons in India.[10] The consciousness

[9] P.J. Fitzgerald, *Criminal Law and Punishment* 79 (1962).

[10] See *Hussainara Khatoon v. State of Bihar* AIR 1360 SC 1979, *Md. Giasuddin v. State of Andhra Pradesh* AIR 1926 SC 1977, *D.B.M. Patnaik v. State of Andhra Pradesh* AIR 2092 SC 1974, *Sheela*

regarding prison reforms is continuously increasing. It has been accepted now that reformation and rehabilitation of prisoners must be part of prison justice. Supreme Court says, "Unfortunately, even though Article 21 of the Constitution requires a life of dignity for all persons, little appears to have changed on the ground as far as prisoners are concerned, we are once again required to deal with issues relating to prisons in the country and their reform".[11] The Supreme Court said that the prisoners are persons and even in custody they are entitled to fundamental rights to certain extent.[12] The Supreme Court identified the following nine issues facing prisons and needing reforms[13]:

(i) Over-crowding;
(ii) Delay in trial;
(iii) Torture and ill-treatment;
(iv) Neglect of health and hygiene;
(v) Insubstantial food and inadequate clothing;
(vi) Prison vices;
(vii) Deficiency in communication;
(viii) Streamlining of jail visits;
(ix) Management of open-air prison

A committee chaired by Justice Amitava Roy was appointed by the Supreme Court in September 2018[14] for analyzing prison problems and suggesting reforms in prison system. Following recommendations were made by the Committee in February, 2020:

(i) Every new prisoner should be allowed a free phone call a day to his family members to see him through his first week in jail.
(ii) Modern cooking facilities, canteens to buy essential items and trial through video-conferencing should be made available.
(iii) Speedy trial remains one of the best ways to remedy the unwarranted phenomenon of over-crowding.
(iv) There should be at least one lawyer for every 30 prisoners, which is not the case at present.
(v) Special fast-track courts should be set up to deal exclusively with petty offences which have been pending for more than five years.[15]

but despite various reforms and recommendations the prison system still has not been able to completely overcome the ill effects of prisonization.

Barse v. State of Maharashtra AIR 378 SC 1983, *Sunil Batra v. Delhi Administration* AIR 1675 SC 1978 and *Prem Shankar v Delhi Administration* AIR 1535 SC 1980.

[11] *Re-Inhuman Conditions In 1382 Prisons*, Writ Petition (Civil) No. 406/2013, decided on 5 February, 2016.

[12] *Sunil Batra v Delhi Administration* (1978) 4 SCC 494.

[13] *Rama Murthy v. State of Karnataka* (1997) 2 SCC 642.

[14] *Re-Inhuman Conditions In 1382 Prisons, supra* note 11.

[15] Abdul, "Supreme Court Panel Recommends Several Prison Reform". Available at https://factly.forumias.com (2020) (last accessed on June 20, 2020).

6 Open Prisons a Step Towards Gandhian Society

For reformation and rehabilitation of prisoners open prisons are been utilized globally as an alternative to imprisonment. Open prison differs from the closed prison in its philosophy of administration, discipline, enforcement of orders, assessment of problems and models of tackling them where the pattern of administration is based on trust, tolerance, truth and totality. The ideas of reformation and rehabilitation of the prisoner is given prime importance. The positive outcomes of this type of penal institution are self-help, constructive work and social usefulness, sense of dignity, positive change in attitudes and behaviour of the prisoners.

Open prisons are known for reducing various known and unknown negative effects of incarceration on the prisoners because of the lack of physical restraints; the degree of the freedom exercised by the prisoners in the open prisons is very close to the freedom exercised by the ordinary citizen; the opportunity to live with the family members and to intermingle with the outside community assist them in their resocialization and reintegration in the society; the prisoners are entrusted with the responsibility to behave in a disciplined manner, system of open institutions, charged with the idea of assuring dignity and respect to prisoners and providing them maximum opportunity for adjusting themselves with the free society.

Since, we can make out that the criminal justice system serves the dual purpose of punishment and rehabilitation, so the all India committee on jail reform which was constituted in 1980, recommended the setting up and development of open prisons in India, with the thought that liberty is necessary for the reformation of the criminal and also for the attainment of his/her fullest potential. In this system individuals are not locked up inside the cell, but are allowed to move freely in prison or outside prison for the purpose of earning a living and becoming self-sufficient. Open prisons are lenient than regular prisons and people who are of low risk to society are kept here. These prisons have negligible security measures against the escape of its inmates. The prisoners have to give their roll call and have to be present in the prison by the time of the next roll call. During, the time between the two roll calls the inmate can move out and do whatever pleases him. Open prison system is a bold experiment to fight crime with non-violent means. It is believed that when the inmates are nurtured with non-violent means and in a friendly manner, they respond to it favorably, and do not tend to betray those who display trust in them. It should be appreciated that even after low security of prisons against the inmates, there is not even a single case of escape.

Moreover, the system of open prison also keeps the psychological state of mind of an individual while deterring oneself. As, the experience inside the prison can be very traumatizing for individuals, so this system ensures gradual cut down of prisoners from society and slowly regaining social ties during the return of life in society. The open prison system focuses more on providing rehabilitative justice along with ensuring the well-being of mental-health of an individual and evaluation of their behavior in normal surroundings.

Hence, open prison system in a way can also serve as a solution to overcrowded and ill-maintained prisons of India. Due to low maintenance of security, low construction cost, and low functional cost and prisoners earning their own living they are economically cheap and pose less financial burden to the state. It can also solve the problem of overcrowding in India. In most of the cases, it is seen that individuals indulge in crime due to the injustice happened to them, such individuals do not really serve as a threat to society. Hence, the concept of open prison holds the potential to revolutionise the entire justice administration not only in India but all over the world.

However, the open prisons in India are underutilized, even when the regular prisons are overcrowded. And, also there has been various instances of deliberate favoring of certain prisoners and sending them to open prisons, promoting inequality and leaving no room for justice.

It is highly recommended that the open prisons in India must be fully utilized in order to serve its purpose in the most efficient way possible. Setting up of ground rules or eligibility criteria to figure out which inmate is capable or holds fair behavior to be moved to open prison system would be helpful in fighting favoritism and discrimination. Further, it will be better if a transparent committee is set up to look upon the behavior of inmates, impartially and provide the list of those who can be moved to the open prison system with fair reasons. These steps will be beneficial in overcoming the shortcomings of open prison system. Open prison system guarantees hope of rehabilitative justice in society.

7 Conclusion

From where we stand right now, there is a gap between society in status quo and the society that Gandhi wanted to establish with his philosophy; and this gap can only be filled by state authorities and how they view sensitive subjects like crime and criminals. Because if we hope to ever create a better society for ourselves or the offenders, we need to stop viewing them as a problem and start thinking in terms of how their resorting to crime is the failure of the system.

States as well as society can employ Gandhian philosophy to ensure that minimum number of people take up crime. When we talk about prisons in particular, the staff at prison must be taught and trained to be non-violent and do not practice violence during the discharge of their duties which will ensure that the inmate isn't subjected to inhumane treatment within the prison. Hence, the promotion of non-violence and truth in the society can contribute to the harmonious and peaceful existence of individuals in a society. In this context, open prison is a very good effort towards the prisoner who is not hard-core criminal. It gives an opportunity of reformation and rehabilitation of prisoner. Traditional prisons have very unhealthy impact on the prisoners because it deprives them from all their inter-social relationships. The long-term imprisonment completely isolates the prisoners from the social framework of free world because, on the one hand, his family members recreate their social life in a manner in which he finds no place after release and on the other hand he gets so used to the daily routine during the stay in prison that he finds it difficult to adjust in a free society. Open prison serves half way homes between the closed institutionalized treatment and free society. Instead of being released suddenly from the closed institution to face responsibilities after a period of more than a decade of imprisonment, the prisoners are sent to open prisons where they stay under minimum security arrangements in the form of a close-knit society exactly on the lines of a free society. This line between isolation and having a connection with the outside world is what ends up defining whether the individual will be able to adjust in the society once he is out, and if he'll make it back in the prison.

References

Abdul (2020) Supreme court panel recommends several prison reform. https://factly.forumias.com. Accessed on 20 June 2020

Chakrabarthy B (2006) Social and political thought of Mahatma Gandhi. Routledge, London, p 20; Parel AJ (ed) (2000) Gandhi, freedom, and self-rule. Vistaar Publication, New Delhi, p 90

Choudharie R (2006) Gandhian philosophy of satyagraha, on and by Gandhi. Anasakti Darshan 2(2), July–December

Fitzgerald PJ (1962) Criminal law and punishment 79

Gandhi MK (1925) Young India, p 15

Gandhi MK (1958–1994) Collected works of Mahatma Gandhi, vol 59. Publications Division, New Delhi

Kostadis KJ (2017) "Hunger makes a thief of any man": poverty and crime in British colonial Asia European Review of Economic History, Volume 21, Issue 1

Sethy SS (2015) Reinterpreting Gandhi's notion of 'dharma': an entanglement of duty, religion, and ethics. Gandhi Marg 37(2):293–312

Top 10 reasons of crime by netnewsledger, October 8, 2019. www.netnewsledger.com. Accessed on 20 June 2020

Chapter 19
The Principle of Restorative Justice Towards the Strengthening of Crime Prevention as Viewed from the Pragmatic Gandhian Lens

Harleen Kaur and Ayushka Sharma

1 Introduction

To "restore" in general parlance means "to bring back", "to return to a former condition, place or position". When a crime is committed, it disrupts the balance in a society. Restorative justice is a novel development in the legal field that seeks to restore this balance, it is a way of seeing crime as more than breaking laws, and it is acknowledging the harms caused by a criminal act and actively responding to the needs thus created, of the victim, the offender, and the community. The literature around restorative justice owes much to the contribution of Western thinkers and jurists, but in Indian jurisprudence, the ideas that dominate the theory of restorative justice are reflected in the philosophy of Mahatma Gandhi, in his teachings of *ahimsa*, often translated as "non-violence"; *swaraj*, the concept of self-rule which encourages both individuals and communities to call upon their best self; and, *satyagrah*, i.e. striving towards truth-telling and truth-seeking. It is through the combined reading of principles of restorative justice and Gandhian principles that we seek to address the challenges faced by the criminal justice system and attempt to arrive at practical solutions.

It is often contended that it is the need for the administration of justice that led to the origin of the state. To uphold the rule of law, to maintain peace and order, to balance the conflicting needs of the society, and to deliver justice in its truest sense, any civilized society relies on a strong and efficient criminal justice system.

Crime is understood as a wrong that is committed against society as a whole, it is understood in the legal framework as a public wrong. Thus, incidentally as and when

H. Kaur (✉)
Assistant Professor (Senior Scale) Campus Law Centre, Faculty of Law, University of Delhi, Delhi, India
e-mail: harleenkauradv@gmail.com

A. Sharma
Student, Campus Law Centre, Faculty of Law, University of Delhi, Delhi, India

R. Mittal and K. K. Singh (eds.), *Relevance of Duties in the Contemporary World*,
https://doi.org/10.1007/978-981-19-1836-0_19

a crime takes place, the state takes up the role of the victim. It is the case of jurists and social scientists across the globe that this invisibilization of the victims is one of the biggest limitations of the current criminal justice system. Along with the needs of the victims, the needs of offenders, the community, and other stakeholders are not being adequately catered to by the state and the criminal justice system. The process of justice is exhaustingly mechanical with little if any consideration of the effect the process has on the stakeholders. Along with the deficiency in addressing the needs of the society at large, theorists have been in recent times, revisiting and analysing the relevancy, efficiency, and rationale behind conventional modes of punishment which are primarily based on the principles of deterrence and retribution. Imprisonment is the norm, and in rare cases, capital punishment is also awarded to the offenders. Studies have shown that these methods have failed to produce the desired deterrent effect. What concerns us, even more, is that there is a disturbing lack of initiative and infrastructure for reformation and reintegration of the offenders by the state. The conventional justice system has significant strengths in its treatment of justice, but there is also a growing concern and acknowledgement of the limitations and fallacies that have surfaced in the system.

The inadequacies of the criminal justice system are aptly captured in the analysis of Author, Ross London in his book Crime, Punishment, and Restorative Justice,

> Despite the efforts of many brilliant minds and the expenditure of vast sums, we have managed to create a criminal justice system that transforms innumerable personal misfortunes into yet other calamities. Victims, who have suffered the trauma of the crime, enter the portals of this system with high expectations of justice, only to find themselves wandering its halls feeling bewildered, unfulfilled, and used. For those accused of a crime, entry into the system portends the beginning of a personal nightmare of dehumanization, ruinous financial losses, and unending suspicion. As a criminal justice professional, I came in contact with hundreds of human beings caught up in this labyrinth. Time and again, I saw the same look of despair on those who emerged from the process, embittered, exhausted, and defeated.[1]

There is an immediate need for the states to address the inefficacies of the criminal justice system and principles of restorative justice offer respite by providing an alternative vision of criminal justice that rightly places the concern of justice as protection of rights and interests of both the victim and offender and aims to repair, restore, reconcile, and reintegrate the offenders and victims to each other and their shared communities.

2 The Concept of Restorative Justice

Restorative justice, as we know it today, is a process that employs active involvement of the victim, the offender specifically, and members of the community generally in responding to each other's justice needs. It is a problem-solving approach to crime that responds to the needs of the stakeholders in the process in all their complexities.

[1] Ross London, Crime, Punishment, and Restorative Justice (2011).

In its typical form, restorative justice involves an encounter of the victim and the offender for decision-making and identifying the harms and needs in the aftermath of crime and then works to restore the trust of the victim in the justice system, restore the offender to a law-abiding citizen, and reintegrate them to their respective communities.

> Restorative justice aims at helping offenders to recognise the harm they have caused and encouraging them to repair the harm, to the extent it is possible. Rather than obsessing about whether offenders get what they deserve, restorative justice focuses on repairing the harm of crime and engaging individuals and community members in the process. (Howard Zehr)

Even though extensive research and contribution to the field of restorative justice only started in the 1970s, the elements of practices, principles, and values that form the basis of restorative justice theories are amply reflected in the indigenous culture and traditions of civilizations across the globe. One distinctive feature of these cultural and traditional practices that got compromised along the way to the modern criminal justice system and has attracted, over the years, the attention of restorative justice theorists is the active involvement of the victims, offenders, and the community in the process of adjudication of justice.

Louk Hulsman, Herman Bianchi, and Nils Christie (abolitionist criminologists) who contributed immensely and directed the development of restorative justice emphasized the lack of and the need for understanding crime as a conflict between "*actual people*". Nils Christie in his article "*Conflicts as Property*" has argued that the criminal justice process steals away the conflicts to which people have a proprietorial right, alienates them, and denies the victims and offenders an active involvement in the resolution of their case.

Along with exponential growth in the research and literature on the subject, the decades post-1970s also saw a rapid rise in the social movements for rights of victims and demand for inclusion of rehabilitative and reformative practices in the criminal justice system which resulted in the adoption of restorative justice practices around the world especially with regard to children in conflict with law.

With its emergence in the United States of America and Canada in an attempt to correct the weaknesses of the Western legal system, restorative justice theories have today cumulated into various practices and programmes being adopted and advanced around the world such as victim–offender conferences, family group conferences, and circles with an aim of restoring equity. New Zealand since 1989 has adopted a functional juvenile justice system based entirely on restorative practices. What is it about the concept of restorative justice that has earned the interest and attention of legal theorists, social scientists, and international organizations?

The concept of restorative justice corrects the restrictive nature of the conventional justice system and responds to and acknowledges the complexities of needs of those involved in the justice process and work to expand the circle of the marked stakeholders beyond the government and offenders to include victims and community members. It recognizes that crime has along with the public, a private dimension, and re-examines the needs and roles implicit in crimes. It is based on relational theory that implicates victims, offenders, and community are all interconnected and have a wider role to play than assigned by the conventional system in each other's restoration.

With its focus on healing and repairing harm, restorative justice seeks to empower the victims by active involvement and responding to their material and non-material needs. It encourages the offenders to understand the consequences of their actions, to empathize with the victim, compensate to the extent possible, and offer them an opportunity to repent and expiate. It also recognizes the impact of crime on the community at large and that they play a significant role in the rehabilitation and reintegration of the victims and offenders. It calls for enhanced responsibility of the state.

3 Restorative Justice and Gandhian Principles

> Restorative Justice is a system of Justice which restores harmony in society; it is a system where everybody lives together and it happens to fit comfortably with Gandhian Philosophy—Albie Sachs

Gandhian principles and theories are often mistaken as being otherworldly, too ideal, and unrealistic where most of his work was ontological and experiential. Throughout his life, Gandhi actively fought and led campaigns against racial discrimination, untouchability, and other unjust practices, powers, and legislation, and it is his collected experience that provides relevance and forms the basis of the principles and theories he advocated.

The ideas of concern for healing, truth, forgiveness, and reconciliation that form the basic underlying values of restorative justice practices are often associated with Gandhian principles of ahimsa, swaraj, and satyagrah.

Ahimsa, often translated as non-violence, was recognized by Gandhi as the greatest of all duties, a vision of how we live together. It is a practice rooted in positive action based on the ideas of respect, responsibility, and recognition of the oneness of all. Gandhi considered non-violence as the greatest weapon at the disposal of mankind, a living source of limitless and immense power.

In the words of Pelton, "*Non-violence means that we do not violate anybody. It means that we do not exploit or oppress anybody. Non-Violence means that we regard life as too sacred to be destroyed for any reason. But, beyond that, it means that we do not tolerate injustice anywhere or to anyone, that we do not turn our backs on the sufferings of others. Non-violence means active goodwill toward all people.*"

In the modern state, as also recognized by Gandhi, Prisons often translate into breeding grounds of violence. Having spent 7 months of incarceration in South Africa and 6 years in India, Gandhi was no stranger to the inherent violence of the modern prison which formed an integral part of the criminal justice system. Restorative justice practitioners have challenged imprisonment as the standard response of the justice system, have called out its inefficiency in deterring crime and furthering the cause of justice and demand, and work for a less violent and more humane way of treating those convicted of a crime to reform them. Modern prison not only dehumanizes and brutalizes the prisoners but also reeks of the state shying away from its responsibility of taking positive action in reformation, restoration, and reintegration of the convict in the society. It provokes the spirit of vengeance on the prisoner and perpetuates the vicious cycle of violence. Moreover, it has failed in containing crimes as can be seen by the constantly rising rates of recidivism. On the contrary, the implementation of restorative justice practices has shown to reduce the rate of recidivism and has increased the sense of accountability in the offenders by allowing them to acknowledge the harm caused by them.

Gandhi detested the manner of treatment of criminals by the state and was of the view that violence begets violence and violence cannot liberate violence. He believed that prisons can be places of reform if the convicts were to be treated with love and respect, as human beings, that real change can be attained if prisons were to work as workshop-cum-educational institutions that encouraged the inmates to engage in constructive and socially useful activities, providing for their moral education and building up their sense of social responsibility. Restorative justice works along similar lines that it is the employment of peaceful means in the administration of the justice system that can bring about an important and meaningful change.

Swaraj is the concept of self-rule that encourages the entire society to bring about best in them. For Gandhi, swaraj was indispensable for the purpose of seeking justice and formed the basis of strong and effective social and political action. Gandhi used swaraj to denote both self-rule and self-government, the freedom of each individual to regulate their own lives without causing harm to anyone else.

Before the formal modern structure of the criminal justice administration was established, every society had its traditional methods of adjudicating justice rooted in their customs, religions, and belief systems, and such institutions were flexible, self-sufficient, and efficient. Due to colonization, especially in most parts of Asia and Africa, such systems were denied their legitimacy in entirety by foreign powers, incidentally hindering the natural process of growth of their legal systems. In most of the traditional justice systems, victim, offenders, their family members, and elders of their community came together for dispute resolution and active involvement ensured that needs, along with the consequent responsibilities, were well placed and looked after.

Restorative justice while acknowledging the limitations of the traditional practices gives space for their adaptation (not replication) in the modern legal framework. Family group conferences, and peacemaking circles, the two most prevalent forms of restorative justice practices, are an adaptation of these traditional practices. For Gandhi, swaraj meant freedom from exploitation, self-rule, and that undeniably involved a just criminal justice system.

For Gandhi, satyagrah was the primary method to attain a just society. **Satyagrah**, "satya" means "truth" and "agrah" means "persistently holding on", satyagrah means persistently holding on to the truth. For Gandhi, satyagrah constitutes two elements, righteousness of cause and purity of weapon which implies that the means to him were as important as ends. Satyagrah is a means of establishing faith in human beings. It is based on the recognition of the inherent goodness of human beings.

For Gandhi, crime was a moral lapse which can be corrected by non-violent means, by adopting peaceful means of conflict resolution and transformation. For him, "*That action alone is just that does not harm either party to a dispute*". *On Crime and Criminals and his vision for Independent India he writes in*, "*The voice of Truth*", "*In Independent India of the non-violent type, there will be Crime but no Criminals. They will not be punished. Crime is a disease like any other malady and is a product of the prevalent social system.*"

Justice, for him, was a quest for restoration and reformation rather than retribution which could be achieved by putting ahimsa and satyagrah in action for true swaraj.

4 Restorative Justice in India

In ancient India, the concepts that came closest to the modern concept of law and punishment were *dharm* and *dand*. *Dharm* represented a moral code of living that embodied principles of law and duties that governed all, and *prayashchit* or atonement was an essential feature of *dand*. Law and punishment are narrower in their connotation. The Sabha (House of elders) and Samiti (assembly of people) in the Vedic times and the Parishads (assemblies of learned men who knew law) in the Sutras age also had elements of restorative justice as dispute settlement was mostly carried out by family and kinship networks and duties were more fundamental than rights.

The criminal justice system in India is predominantly adaptation of the colonial legislations, and even though new legislations have been introduced in the decades post-independence, most of the important legislations have seen only a little change. This is not to say that they have not proved to be effective, they have their strengths, but developments in the field of legal theory call for re-examining the relevancy of practices propounded by the criminal justice system and inculcate new features to add to the efficiency and fill in the gaps that inevitably impetrate any system as time passes by.

There is no one comprehensive legislation in India that relates to the adoption of practices of restorative justice, but it is present within the ambit of major acts like Code of Criminal Procedure (CrPc), 1973, The Protection of Children from Sexual Offences Act, 2012, The Juvenile Justice (Care and Protection of Children) Act, 2015, etc.

Restorative justice manifests itself in Indian legal system majorly in the form of alternate dispute resolution mechanisms in the form of family courts, consumer courts, lok adalats, mediation centres, arbitration, nyaya panchayats, and gram nyayalayas.

In CrPC, elements of restorative justice can be majorly seen in Section 357 and Section 357A which empowers the courts to grant compensation, Section 265 provides for plea bargaining, Section 320 for compounding of offences. Judiciary has also played an important role by laying down grounds and directions for compensation in various cases (*D.K. Basu* v. *State of West Bengal*,[2] *State of Gujrat* v. *High Court of Gujrat*,[3] etc.), and insistence on adoption of state-funded scheme for victim compensation led to the incorporation of Section 357A.

The Juvenile Justice (Care and Protection of Children) Act, 2015, deals with children in conflict with law and children in need of care and protection. Section 8 enumerates the responsibilities of the board which includes ensuring the protection of child's rights throughout the process, the availability of legal aid, and Chapter VII of the Act specifically provides for rehabilitation and social integration. Section 39 provides for the process of rehabilitation and social integration. Section 40 provides for restoration of child in need of care and protection. The Act via Section 44 has introduced the foster system in India which is a positive step in the direction of rehabilitation of children. Section 46 provides for aftercare of children who leave the child care institution. The act, in all, calls upon the state actors to take measures to promote physical and psychological recovery and social integration of child victims and ensure that the environment in which such recovery is to take place promotes the health, self-respect, and dignity of the child. With 41% of Indian population under the age of 18 years,[4] the adoption of restorative practices becomes imperative to keep them outside the clutches of criminal justice system and to provide for their rehabilitation, restoration, and reintegration into their communities.

There has been considerable development in progressive legislations especially with regard to Child Rights and Children in Conflict with Law, but the criminal justice system has failed miserably in identifying and responding to the justice needs of adult victims and offenders.

J, Krishna Iyer *in Rattan Singh* v. *State of Punjab*[5] remarked that "*it is the weakness of our Criminal Justice System that victims of crime do not attract the attention of law*". It was only in 2009 following the report of Malimath Committee and recommendation of Law Commission in its 154 Report[6] and the pressure from the judiciary that definition of victim was added in the Criminal Procedure Code.

5 Gaps Between the Theoretical and Practical Development of Restorative Justice in India

In India, victims suffer stigmatization and often lack the resources to pursue their legal rights and the process for redressal of their grievance. The criminal justice process is expensive and cumbersome, and proceedings are lengthy and draining. Furthermore,

---

[2] 1997 1 SCC 416.

[3] 1983 KLT 512.

[4] Available at https://censusindia.gov.in/ (last visited on 28 June 2020).

[5] 1980 2 SCC 321.

[6] Law Commission of India (1996), Report no. 154, The Code of Criminal Procedure, 1973 (Act 2 of 1974).

there is an alienation of the victims from the dispute resolution process. The justice system has failed to recognize, let alone, respond to the social, psychological, and spiritual needs of victims. Coupled with this, there is a lack of awareness of legal rights in the country and a heavy backlog of cases.

The needs of offenders receive scant attention as well. There is overcrowding of offenders in jails, substantial delay in conclusion of the trial along with lack of infrastructure and initiative to inculcate reformative, rehabilitative practices, dehumanizing treatment of offenders that perpetuate our prison system. There is a clear violation of Gandhian principles in the functioning the machinery of law.

In its 262nd report,[7] a recommendation for absolute abolition of the death penalty for all crimes other than terrorism-related offences and waging war was made by the Law Commission of India and upon being addressed to the commission by the Supreme Court in Santosh Kumar, *Satish Bhushan Bariyar* v. *Maharashtra*[8] *and Shankar Kisanrao Khade* v. *Maharashtra.*[9] The commission questioned the effectiveness of the death penalty for achieving the penological goal of deterrence and noted that the efficacy was not more than that of life imprisonment. Even the doctrine of rarest of the rare case for the administration of the death penalty has been regarded to stand in contradiction with constitutional ethos.

In 268th report,[10] the Law Commission addressed the inefficiencies and inadequacies of bail provisions in the country. 74.18% of the prison population presently constitutes of undertrials.[11] Pre-trial detention beyond the strictly necessary limits and denial of bail puts the legal principle of presumption of innocence in jeopardy and is detrimental to the right of life and personal liberty of the accused. The present system of bail is also highly influenced by the economic status of the accused and thus violates Article 14 (equality before law) of the Constitution of India. Justice Bhagwati in *Hussainara Khatoon* v. *Home Secretary, State of Bihar*[12] observed that *"under-trial prisoners languish in jail because they are downtrodden and poor and not because they are guilty"*. The report admits that the existing system of bail in India is inadequate and inefficient and fails to accomplish the purpose of the provision. The definition of "bail" is yet to be included in the Criminal Procedure Code. In such circumstances, there is an urgent and crucial need for implementation of the recommendations put forward by the Law Commission in the report.

---

[7] Law Commission of India (2015), Report no. 262, The Death Penalty.

[8] (2009) 6 SCC 498.

[9] (2013) 5 SCC 546.

[10] Law Commission of India, Report no. 268, Amendments to Criminal Procedure Code, 1973—Provisions Relating to Bail (2017).

[11] Available at https://nhrc.nic.in/press-release/7418-cent-prison-population-are-undertrials (last visited on 28 June 2020).

[12] 1979 AIR 1369, 1979 SCR (3) 532.

In the 277th report,[13] the Law Commission has pitched for a legal framework to compensate for wrongful prosecution. The report is primarily based on a reference made by Delhi High Court in *Babloo Chauhan @ Dabloo* v. *State of Govt. of NCT of Delhi*[14] where the requirement for an effective legislative framework which could provide relief and rehabilitation to victims of wrongful prosecution was highlighted. Wrongful prosecution refers to the miscarriage of justice caused due to procedural misconducts and resulting in the wrongful conviction of an innocent person who is eventually acquitted by the court. What is pertinent to note is that while recommending amendment to the Criminal Code for grant of compensation to victims of wrongful prosecution, the commission recommended provisions for pecuniary (monetary) as well as non-pecuniary compensation. The reports also provide for setting up of special courts to ensure speedy processing of claim and grant of compensation. The victim can access such courts, irrespective of whether he has been imprisoned or not.

6 Conclusion

In view of the above discussion, it is manifested that restorative justice theory has changed the way we understand crime and justice. It recognizes that crime creates an imbalance in the society that can be remedied by recognizing the needs of various stakeholders. It also, at the same time, expands the circle of these designated stakeholders demarcated by the conventional justice system and attempts to heal and repair the harm caused, to the extent possible. It demands an enhanced role of the state and the community. Gandhian principles offer a deep insight into the desirability of application of non-violent means in the justice delivery system.

Restorative justice and Gandhian principles voice for the need for addressing the root cause of the crime rather than treating it superficially. There is an emphasis on the use of rehabilitative and reformative approaches to restore and reintegrate the victim and the offender into society. Therefore, the in-depth exploration of principles of restorative justice and the application of Gandhian philosophy, in Indian context, not only promises work towards the correction of the many errors that perpetuate the conventional criminal justice system, but it also offers a vision of justice that needs to be pursued.

[13] Law Commission of India (2018), Report no. 277, Wrongful Prosecution (Miscarriage of Justice): Legal Remedies.

[14] 247 (2018) DLT 31.

7 Suggestions and Way Ahead

It is visible that Indian Society and legal theory have evolved manyfold, but the development in law has failed to cope with the growing requirements. The gaps in the theoretical and practical growth of law in India are partly because of the lack of initiative and partly because of improper implementation of policies, but the way ahead lies not only in acknowledging and targeting the limitations in the current system but also in developing on the existing framework and expanding the roles of non-state actors in furthering the cause of justice. Some suggestions, therefore, have been put forward via this research which are as follows:

1. **Implementation of Recommendations of Law Commission of India**

   Law Commission of India in its various reports in the last decade has responded to the concerns that restorative justice practitioners have posed and has substantially employed the principles of restorative justice in dealing with issues subsisting the criminal justice system. In such circumstances, there is an urgent and crucial need for implementation of the recommendations put forward by the Law Commission in those reports.
2. **Prison Reforms**

   Gandhi was of the view that prisons can be institutions of reformation and transformation. His claim that finds support amongst the practitioners of reformative justice was not unfounded and, in fact, has proven to produce real changes. Beena Chintlapuri, a cognitive psychologist has been conducting behavioural training workshops in prisons in Hyderabad, India, since 2016. She works closely with the inmates to reform and transform them, and in one of the prisons, she worked at the rate of recidivism according to the officials went down from 80 to 1%.[15] The reason behind this can be concluded from the statement of one of the inmates she worked with, "*She made us feel like human beings, she gave us respect*." Restorative justice and Gandhian tradition have respect as one of their central values.

   The concept of "open prisons" has also attracted much attention in recent times. In an open prison, there are no armed guards, no confining walls and locks. The inmates are allowed to move freely and maintain self-discipline. They are also provided with an opportunity to make their livelihood employing their labour. Such prisons have proved to respond to the social, economic, and

[15] Chintalapuribeena, https://www.vice.com/en_in/article/vbjn9j/beena-chintalapuri-uses-cognitive-psychology-to-help-prisoners (last Visited, June 28,2020).

moral needs of the prisoners. Currently, there are 77 open prisons in India.[16] Given that these prisons have responded effectively to the justice needs of the offenders, there can be a steady increase in their numbers.

3. **Circles of Support and Accountability and Victim Impact Panels**

   Developing on the models of restorative justice practices from the world, circle of support and accountability and victim impact panels can be inculcated in our justice system. These cater to the justice needs of the victims, offenders, and the community in an efficient manner. Moreover, such models are highly cost efficient. When offenders are released, especially those convicted for sexual offences, they are ostracized by their communities which significantly increases the chance of recidivism. To help them reintegrate into society, circles of support and accountability were developed in Canada. These circles gather a circle of people which includes ex-offenders, community members, and even victims of similar crimes to support and ensure accountability via regular check-ins which are eventually reduced. Victim impact panels again involve a community-based meeting for victims where they share their experiences and offer support to each other. Both of these methods facilitate the healing of victims and offenders.

4. **Need for Extensive Research on the Applicability and Outcomes of the Implementation of Theories of Restorative Justice**

   Even though the theories of restorative justice promise to correct the fallacies of the criminal justice system, the literature on restorative justice is still limited to the theories developed by Western jurists. There is indeed a significant amount of universality in the justice needs of legal systems across the world, but there are also justice needs that are peculiarities that need to be acknowledged. This is one of the greatest limitations that face the adoption of restorative justice in India. There is, thus, a growing need for extensive research on the applicability and outcomes of the implementation of these practices in the specific context of India and its legal system.

5. **Need for Uniform Victim Compensation Fund**

   There is an urgent need to review the current laws governing victim compensation and evolution of an effective system of reparation of victims and setting up of a uniform victim compensation fund.

6. **Re-analysis of the Role and Position of the Victims in the Criminal Justice System.**

   This can be catered to by making special provisions for the protection of women and child victims taking into consideration the nature of the crime committed and their peculiar needs for rehabilitation and reintegration.

---

[16] Available at https://ncrb.gov.in/sites/default/files/Executive-Summary-2018.pdf (last visited on 28 June 2020).

The above suggestions, if properly implemented in their true letter and spirit, would undoubtedly go a long way to address the inefficacies of the criminal justice system via adoption of principles of restorative justice based on Gandhian principles.

References

Chintalapuribeena, https://www.vice.com/en_in/article/vbjn9j/beena-chintalapuri-uses-cognitive-psychology-to-help-prisoners. Last visited 28 June 2020

https://censusindia.gov.in/. Last visited on 28 June 2020

https://nhrc.nic.in/press-release/7418-cent-prison-population-are-undertrials. Last visited on 28 June 2020

Law Commission of India (1996) Report no. 154, The Code of Criminal Procedure, 1973 (Act 2 of 1974)

Law Commission of India (2015) Report no. 262, The Death Penalty

Law Commission of India (2017) Report no. 268, Amendments to Criminal Procedure Code, 1973—Provisions Relating to Bail

Law Commission of India (2018) Report no. 277, Wrongful Prosecution (Miscarriage of Justice): Legal Remedies

Ross London (2011) Crime, Punishment, and Restorative Justice

Chapter 20
Relevance of Duties in Contemporary World with Particular Emphasis on Gandhian Thought with Respect to Respect for Nature and Environment

Kavita Singh

1 Introduction

The Earth has enough resources for our need but not for our greed.

M. K. Gandhi

This frequently used phrase by Gandhi truly shows his concern for nature and environment. Gandhi is generally known for maintenance of peace and state-building. He is not considered as environmentalist per se. However, the present article deals with those beliefs of Gandhian ideology which are concerned with environment in today's times. Gandhi's philosophy is based on ethical behaviour of human beings towards environmental protection. The relevance of Gandhian philosophy can be well perceived in the current times due to the growth in living standards of human beings towards more waste generation and high consumerism. It leads to two major ramifications on nature: first, tremendous increase in rate of consumption of natural resources, and second, increase in air, water and soil pollution. This has a degenerating effect on quality of human life for major sections of the society.

This chapter primarily makes an attempt to appreciate the present pragmatic situation of the environment and to ascertain how to resolve such environmental issues through Gandhian philosophy and practices. It has been noticed by the whole world that environmental concerns have arisen on account of reshaping of lifestyle, high consumerism and massive production which has deteriorated nature at a faster pace. The economic structure and criteria of development are delineated in such a manner that the zenith of production and consumption can be regarded as healthy economy.

K. Singh (✉)
Ph.D. Scholar (Environmental Law), University School of Law and Legal Studies, Guru Gobind Singh Indraprastha University,
New Delhi, India
e-mail: kstevatia@gmail.com

R. Mittal and K. K. Singh (eds.), *Relevance of Duties in the Contemporary World*,
https://doi.org/10.1007/978-981-19-1836-0_20

Hence, the need of the hour is to transform our idea of enjoyable and safe sustenance. This may diminish abundance of riches and realize comfortable, happy and safe livelihood for all.

This sort of inclusive and sustainable development can be attained by improving the utilization of natural resources and waste generation. It is necessary to adopt ethical actions in our economic, social and political life for the same. The global community has even recognized these needs in international documents like Agenda 21, Rio Declaration, etc. Gandhian philosophy teaches about such ethical practices, mentioned in various places. Few ethical practices cast out by Gandhi are of great utility to outline environmental strategies at local, regional and global levels. This chapter has an objective to highlight those ethical principles which can guide the humanity in dealing with current environmental issues like climate change, thereby protecting environment and achieving sustainable development.

2 Non-violence and Conservation of Natural Resources

The notion of non-violence propounded by Gandhi can be beneficial to reduce carbon footprints generated due to wars and missile production. Gandhi had always stressed upon the relevance of utilization and conservation of natural resources. It directly affects interrelationship between man and environment. Gandhian ideology plays an important role in the present times when human beings practise the lifestyle of high consumerism and waste generation.

Gandhi was greatly influenced by Jainism. Jainism spectates nature as a living entity and urges human beings to respect multiple life forms and purify themselves constantly. Gandhian concept of non-violence circumscribed all human beings, and he always incorporated the eternal life principles in his thought and actions. His idea of *Satya* and *Ahimsa* can be of great use in reducing the greed of the individual and hence the society. He reiterated the everlasting sanctity of life which includes a tree, plant or an animal. It is alleged that once the English historian Edward Thomson mentioned to Gandhi that flora and fauna was getting diminished expeditiously in India, to which Gandhi responded ironically, 'Wildlife is decreasing in the jungles, but increasing in the towns'.[1] In his opinion, heedless and unlimited chasing of development by all countries has given rise to significant issues for the very existence of not only human but also for all other living entities on the planet.

The idea of sarvodaya too is akin to that of sustainable development and has become a part of environmental principles. Gandhi's perception of sarvodaya suggests a healthy environment and development that can be developed by man to secure his harmonious existence with nature and other living beings. Gandhi did not admit discrete rules for different realms of life, but identified all realms in consolidated manner, which best epitomizes the human environmental outlook. Whatever he

[1] R. R. Tiwari, 'Gandhi as an Environmentalist', *The Indian Journal of Medical Research 149* (Suppl.), S141–S143 Available at https://doi.org/10.4103/0971-5916.251671 (2019).

sermonized and practised is consistent with what we in present times call eco-friendly actions and living in harmony with nature.

3 Yog and Ecology

The casual study of Gandhi's life also reveals that he was truly a practising yogi, although he never asserted the same. Yog basically means the discipline and rule over one's own body and mind, by physical postures (*Hat Yog*) and moral rules of conduct (*Raj Yog*).[2] In the latter, there are eight ceremonial disciplines, and first two (*yams* and *niyams*) deal with environment and principles of utilization of natural resources. Actually, these were first exercised and then spoken about by Gandhi. The *yams* are moral precepts of human conduct with engender respect to other human beings, living organisms and other non-living resources. Basically, these yamas are a class of prohibited actions. The five yams are: non-violence (ahimsa) towards all living and non-living entities; truth (satya); evading the usage of matter procured by unlawful ways and circumventing demolition and hooliganism (asteya); chastity (brahmacharya) to curb the number of humans; otherwise, it will lead to increase in demand for resources; and lastly, not to desire for or accumulation of materials and wealth beyond the need (aparigrah).

The five niyams are individual-based rules of etiquettes: which prescribe what a man should do, and these are associated with cleanliness (shaucha) of one's body, mind and settings, as human being is fundamentally a filthy animal and produces substantial waste and garbage; in contrast to other animals. Such waste is usually non-biodegradable in characteristics and hence pollutes the environment. Shaucha even comprises of getting rid of excessive libido (kam), rage (krodh), materialism (lobh), inordinate affinity (moh) and egoism and narcissism (ahankar). Rest of the niyams are satisfaction (antosh); self-discipline (tapas); soul-searching (swadhyay); and devotion and contemplation (ishwar pranidhan) for any non-performance of obligations towards yamas and niyams and towards environment consisting of nature to which human beings majorly depend on for their existence.

A yogi can regulate his behaviour by himself, and thus becomes humane. Gandhi never claimed to be a yogi despite practising all yams and niyams regularly. He motivated the traditional capabilities and local self-reliance (swadeshi); self-rule and local self-governance (swaraj) at the rural level; and welfare of the weakest (antyodaya) leading to welfare of all (sarvodaya). Majority of these precepts, although private ethical codes, were converted by Gandhi into a socio-economic and political movement to free India from the British rule. He alone could accomplish this due to his brilliance. In short, he blazed a new trail: non-violent method of conflict resolution, which before him, was seldom, if ever, accomplished.

---

[2] T. N. Khoshoo, 'Gandhian Environmentalism: An Unfinished Task', 16 *IASSI Quarterly* 1 (1997) Available at https://www.gandhiashramsevagram.org/gandhi-articles/gandhian-environmentalism-an-unfinished-task.php (last accessed 28 December 2020).

4 Gandhi and Fundamental Duty of a Citizen to Protect Environment Under the Indian Constitution

The protection and improvement of the environment is a constitutional mandate. It is a commitment for a country wedded to the ideas of a welfare state. The Indian Constitution contains specific provisions for environment protection under the chapters of directive principles of state policy and fundamental duties. Constitutional environmentalism to a certain limit can be evoked under Article 48A[3] of the Constitution of India which is as follows:

> 48A. Protection and improvement of environment and safeguarding of forests and wild life—The State shall endeavour to protect and improve the environment and to safeguard the forests and wild life of the country.

This constitutional provision imposes an obligation on the state to take steps for the protection of environment and to safeguard the wildlife. It is a directive principle of state policy, thus casting a duty upon the state. Article 48A along with Article 21 and Article 51A (g) is the base of environmental jurisprudence in India. The state has a fundamental duty to be pertinent with these provisions while making laws. It is the elucidation of this 'duty' that empowers every citizen to file a matter before the National Green Tribunal in case of any sort of threat to the environment, whether he is individually affected or not. Article 48A provides the citizens with a tool and a structure through which they can approach and question the state and the government regarding environmental issues.

Apart from this provision, a new provision in the form of 'fundamental duties' as Article 51A was also incorporated by the 42nd Constitution amendment. Sub-clause (g) of Article 51A is important:

> 51A. Fundamental duties—It shall be the duty of every citizen of India (g) to protect and improve the natural environment including forests, lakes, rivers and wild life, and to have compassion for living creatures.

The scope of Article 51A (g) was examined by the High Court of Rajasthan in *L. K. Koolwal* v. *State of Rajasthan.*[4] Under the Rajasthan Municipalities Act, 1959, the municipal authority is charged with the primary duty 'to clean public streets, sewers and all spaces and places, not being private property, which are open to the enjoyment of public, removing of noxious vegetation and all public nuisances and to remove fifth, rubbish, night soil, odour or any other noxious or offensive matter'. The petitioner moved a writ petition under Article 226 of the Constitution before the Rajasthan High Court showing that the municipality has failed to discharge it 'primary duty' resulting in the acute sanitation problem in the city of Jaipur which is hazardous to the life of the citizens of Jaipur. The high court while pronouncing as the judgement explained the true scope of Article 51A in the following term:

---

[3] 42nd Amendment to the Constitution of India, 1976.

[4] AIR 1988 Raj. 2. 74.

> We can call Article 51A ordinarily as the duty of the citizens to protect environment.[5] But in fact, it is the right of the citizens as it creates the right in favour of citizens to move to the Court to see that the State performs its duties faithfully and the obligatory and primary duties are performed in accordance with the law of the land. Article 51-A gives a right to the citizens to move the Court for the enforcement of the duty cast on State instrumentalities, agencies, departments, local bodies and statutory authorities created under the peculiar law of the State.

Thus, Article 51A has come as a boon so far as environmental protection is concerned. But its benefit can be availed of only if people are alive to their duties regarding protection of environment. Similarly, in the case of *M. C. Mehta* v. *Union of India*[6], Article 51A-(g) was enforced by the Supreme Court. In this case, 274.50 million litre of sewage water was being discharged into the river Ganga in the city of Kanpur on a daily basis. The petitioner filed a petition in the Supreme Court due to large-scale water pollution. The Apex Court of the country found that municipal bodies like Kanpur Nagar Mahapalika and industries in Kanpur were the main causes for polluting the river and were held liable because it is their responsibility to maintain and protect the environment in the areas of Kanpur. Also, it is one of the fundamental duties in our Constitution which makes a moral obligation on the part of the citizens as well to ensure the protection of the environment. The Supreme Court held that it is the duty of the Central Government to direct all the educational institutions of our country to teach and train citizens about the protection and improvement of the environment for at least one hour a week. Thus, the Supreme Court held that the environmental education must be provided to students from the initial classes itself. It can be inferred that even Indian judiciary has recognized the relevance of individual's duty to protect environment. Replicating constitutions like that of India, and creating and enforcing laws and policy agenda that advance animal rights through vegetarianism with the ultimate objective of obtaining widespread recognition of animal rights, can move us forward along the moral arc toward a truly inclusive society. Through vegetarianism and veganism, we can cultivate mindfulness and compassion, progress morally and, ultimately, approach true democracy and peace. We have the power to give the gift of peace to animals, to our children and, eventually, to ourselves and the world.

5 Invoking Gandhian Philosophy in Environmental Protection

There is no denial to the fact that the environmental problems nowadays are more challenging. Hence, we cannot avoid fighting against the same. While looking for various approaches to deal with environmental issues, Gandhian approach seems to be an apt one. However, in the present times, Gandhian notions, approaches and options for social change and progress are internationally debated. Major works

[5] Dr. H. N. Tiwari., Environmental Law, Third Edition, Allahabad Law Agency (2005).

[6] 1988 AIR 1115, 1988 SCR (2) 530.

authored by Gandhi consist of references relating to protection and conservation of environment despite the fact that he is recognized as an environmentalist only by a few writers. But there is nothing inappropriate in calling him as a champion of environmental protection. Prof. Ram Chander Gupta[7] once quoted, "The life and work of Gandhi have had a considerable influence on the contemporary environmental movements in India. The movement truly began with the 'Chipko Andolan' in April 1973. In one of the first printed accounts of 'Chipko', a breathless journalist announced that Gandhi's spirit had saved the Himalayan trees. Ever since then, Gandhi has been usually acknowledged patron saint of the environmental movement. From the 'Chipko Andolan' to 'Narmada Bachao Andolan', environmental activists have relied heavily on Gandhian techniques of non-violent protest and have drawn abundantly on Gandhi's polemic against heavy industrialization. Again, some of the movement's better-known figures, for example Chandi Prasad Bhatt, underlined their own debt to Gandhi".[8]

Although Gandhi's written work does not discuss the type and gravity of environmental challenges of current times in detail, he always manifested his concern about ways adopted in the Western development causing environmental degradation. On account of this only, probably he made a suggestion about an alternative paradigm of development. This new model was liberated from all sorts of disastrous effects and ill-treatment of man and nature by man himself. Gandhi forewarned against rapid industrialization and urbanization in 1908 itself through his work, 'Hind Swaraj'. He advised the literate Indians who used to reside in cities, to return to the rural areas as they were not polluted by railways or influenced due to modern lifestyles. He advocated preserving all that was best in the ancient Indian society, which did not glorify wealth of power but set a limit to man's indulgences.[9] While criticizing further the modern civilization Gandhi said, 'This modern civilization is that one has to be patient, and it will be self-destroyed'.[10]

Gandhi's falsification of reasoning of industrialization actually provides a basis to understand his philosophy. He wrote, 'Our ancestors dissuaded us from luxuries and pleasures. We have managed with the same kind of cottages that we had in former times… It was not that we did know how to invent machinery, but our forefathers knew that if we pursue such things, we would become slaves and lose our moral fibre. They, therefore, after due deliberation decided that we should only do what we could with our hands and feet… reasoned that large cities were a snake and useless encumbrance and that people would not be happy in them, that there would be gangs of thieves and robbers, prostitution and vice flourishing in them and poor men would be robed by rich men. They were, therefore satisfied with small villages".[11] Thus, it

[7] Ashok A. Desai, Constitutional Accountability Towards Environment, 42 *Journal of the Indian Law Institute* 2/4, Constitutional Law Special Issue (April-December 2000), pp. 160–170 (2000).

[8] R. C. Guha, 'Gandhi the Environmentalist', Seminar, January 1974.

[9] M. K. Gandhi, Hind Swaraj, Madras, pp. 48–50 (1921); Mahatma Gandhi: His Life, Writings and Speeches, Madras, 1918, pp. 95.

[10] M. K. Gandhi, Hind Swaraj of Indian Home Rule, NPH, Ahmedabad, p. 37 (1938).

[11] Gandhi (1921), *supra* note 9.

can be inferred that Gandhi was in opposition to industrialism but not at odds with industrialization.

The industrialism in fact could develop the degraded machine culture, which only benefitted some to play up with millions.[12] He stressed upon production by an individual.[13] The problems of terrorism, environmental damage, domestic and global tension and violence and the existing inequalities are the results of industrial age and high technology. Moreover, industrialization and technological advancement make it almost impossible to get back to rationally ordered society within this modern framework. Gandhi had anticipated this situation in 1908 itself when he wrote Hind Swaraj, in which he characterized 'modern civilization' as a 'disease' and nine days 'wonder'.[14] Gandhi's rigid and tenacious stance about the Western civilization as 'satanic' or 'dark age' was grounded not upon some dissembling objection to the machine use but to tyranny and separation of man in such civilization.

There are two major dimensions to international environmental challenges: first is depletion of resources, and second one is pollution. Both of these are connected with modern agricultural and industrial production and poverty. When the industrial revolution began almost two centuries ago, the world population was under 80 million, and now, it has reached 7.8 billion[15] with further expectations to get doubled in twenty-first century. The expanding urbanization captivated the literate rural people towards it and gave rise to the commitment of such people in non-agricultural occupations which eventually led to fall in food production. Simultaneously, the food production has been suffering from heedless demolition of the forests, which further causes floods, soil erosion, silting up of rivers and desertification of fertile land. This careless handling of natural resources began before the independent era in mostly all colonized countries and kept continuing even after their freedom. The zeal portrayed by developing countries or the third world to gain a dignified place in the world map of 'development world' also added fuel to fire.[16]

The contractual relationship of 'buyers' and 'sellers' between the developed and developing or underdeveloping countries relied upon the exploitation of natural resources under certain unethical terms and conditions. For instance, 'Switzerland' has its own forests, but for coffins, they import wood from Africa. This example is sufficient to expose the ethical failure on part of the developed countries. The way of life which was adopted by Gandhi is indeed a strong message to the entire humanity due the fact that whatever he said he followed practically. He could foresee the problems which might occur pertaining to environment in the present and future times. His principles were always based upon respect for nature and harmony with

[12] Pyarelal, Towards New Horizons, Navjivan Publishing House, Ahmedabad, p. 42 (1959).

[13] *Ibid.*, pp. 28–29.

[14] S. C. Gangal, Value of Gandhian Norms Today, The Times of India, 5 October 1994, p. 10 and Gandhi (1921), *supra* note 9 at p. 89.

[15] World Population Clock 2020, 7.8 People, Worldometer (2020) available at https://www.worldometers.info/world-population/ (last accessed on 28 December 2020).

[16] Claude Meillassoux, 'Past and Future Relevance of Marx and Engels' Works to Anthropology', 9 *Dialectical Anthropology* 1–4 June 1985, p. 365.

the nature. He contemplated the natural treatment as the best method of cure and to get rid of any sort of illness. Gandhi said that man can live without food or water for a week or few hours respectively, but not without pure air even for a few minutes.

We have received all essential things from nature which are necessary for sustenance of life. Nature has provided abundance of material for all living entities that is enough for the needy but always insufficient for the greedy. In this context, the reliance is placed upon the notion of 'swadeshi', the moral law of self-reliance. 'Swadeshi' basically refers to the restrictions upon the people to the use and service of immediate surroundings and excluding the more remote ones. However, it does not include being self-sufficient with narrow-mindedness. 'Be Indian and buy Indian' is the basis of swadeshi and self-reliance. It can also be understood with respect to recent announcement made by the Indian Prime Minister Shri Narendra Modi during corona pandemic to become self-reliant (*Atmanirbhar*) using the phrase 'vocal for local'.[17] Gandhian approach provides solution to all problems whether its economic, social, political and environmental. The means suggested by Gandhi to fulfil the requirements of life were entirely eco-friendly. Hence, it can be said that his ideology is deeply concerned with harmony between man and nature. Gandhi's mantra 'swaraj' did not simply imply a transition in political authority. The objective of 'swaraj' was not an end of foreign rule but self-rule. The final aim of 'swaraj' can be achieved by the ideal of non-violence and non-cooperation. Gandhi also came up with a famous constructive programme to acquire sarvodaya. Moreover, sarvodaya is not only helpful to solve ecological issues but is also related to attain highest level of self-realization in which one can see one's exemplification in all others. Gandhi's notion of non-violence is delineated as completely liberated from antipathy, rage and hate and immense love for all. It is actually a 'love force' or 'soul force' with the objective of acquiring major good human values like love, compassion, teamwork, brotherhood, etc. All these values only teach us an important message of 'live and let live'.

One message found in the Upanishads is that all in this manifested world, comprising of moveable and immoveable, are covered by God. Therefore, these resources must be used with prudence. There are mainly four threats to the present world which are known as four 'Ps'—proliferation (of armaments), pollution (arising from industrialization and urbanization), population (due to self-indulgence) and poverty (because of existing inequalities). Gandhi carried a vision to apprise the world of all these problems along with their origins and to suggest the solutions as early as in 1909 through 'Hind Swaraj'. Gandhi's idea of regeneration of decentralized rural industry (cottage industry and arts and crafts) can be of great help in dealing with contemporary issues of global community. Employment can be provided to numerous people, and thus, poverty can be reduced eventually. The structural change in society

[17] Bijoor Harish, 'Self-reliant India: The bounce of vocal for local', The New Indian Express, 26 May 2020 Available at https://www.newindianexpress.com/opinions/2020/may/26/self-reliant-india-the-bounce-of-vocal-for-local-2147966.html (last accessed on 28 December 2020).

can be easily reshaped in all walks of life by adopting employment-oriented, manual–labour-intensive and minimum capital-intensive approach. Conclusively, the adoption of principle of 'simple living and high thinking' can avoid the unnecessary and excessive use of machine.

6 Conclusion

On the basis of the above discussion, it can easily be concluded that Gandhian way of life is the best remedy to solve environmental problems. However, it does not indicate that Gandhi directly talked about the ecological damage and its solution. His opinion about the western model pertaining to industrialization and dismissal of consumerist culture expresses the relevance of maintaining harmony between man and nature. Gandhi's notion of non-violence can be of great utility in reducing the carbon footprint caused due to wars and missile production, considered in the range from international to local politics. His emphasis on conservation of natural resources has a direct impact on human–ecology relationship. Brundtland Commission's definition of 'sustainable development' is quite similar to Gandhi's idea of greed-need syndrome or the concept of *sarvodaya*. His philosophy of decentralization can be applicable in modern socio-economic model which can further lead to more sustainable inclusive growth. Corporate social responsibility and its philosophy of 'beyond philanthropy' show high degree of similarity with the idea of trusteeship. Hence, it is necessary to look for solutions of environmental problems through Gandhian way. However, it seems a long and strenuous way to follow his ideology. But sooner the better we have to make a beginning with the motto 'think globally, and act locally'.

References

42nd Amendment to the Constitution of India, 1976

Bijoor H (2020) Self-reliant India: the bounce of vocal for local. The New Indian Express, 26 May 2020. https://www.newindianexpress.com/opinions/2020/may/26/self-reliant-india-the-bounce-of-vocal-for-local-2147966.html. Accessed 28 Dec 2020

Claude Meillassoux (1985) Past and future relevance of marx and engels' works to anthropology. Dialect Anthropol 9(1–4):365 June 1985

Desai, AA (2000) Constitutional accountability towards environment. J Indian Law Inst 42(2/4) Constitutional Law Special Issue April–Dec 2000:160–170

Gandhi MK (1918) Mahatma Gandhi: his life, writings and speeches, Madras, pp.95

Gandhi MK (1921) Hindi Swaraj, Madras, pp48–49

Gandhi MK (1938) Hind Swaraj of Indian home rule. NPH, Ahmedabad, p 37

Gangal SC, Value of Gandhian norms today. The Times of India, Oct 5 1994, p 10

Guha RC (1974) Gandhi the Environmentalist. Seminar. Jan 1974

Khoshoo TN (1997) Gandhian environmentalism: an unfinished task. IASSI Quarterly 16(1). https://www.gandhiashramsevagram.org/gandhi-articles/gandhian-environmentalism-an-unfinished-task.php. Accessed 28 Dec 2020

Koolwal v LK (1988) State of Rajasthan AIR Raj. 2. 74
Mehta v MC (1988) Union of India AIR 1115, 1988 SCR 530 (2)
Pyarelal (1959) Towards new horizons. Navjivan Publishing House. Ahmedabad, p 42
Tiwari HN (2005) Environmental law, 3rd edn. Allahabad Law Agency
Tiwari RR (2019) Gandhi as an environmentalist. Indian J Med Res 149(Suppl):S141–S143. https://doi.org/10.4103/0971-5916.251671
World Population Clock 2020, 7.8 People (2020) Worldometer. https://www.worldometers.info/world-population/. Accessed 28 Dec 2020

Chapter 21
Protection of Environment as a Fundamental Duty

Jai Prakash Meena

> *The earth, the air, the land and the water are not an inheritance from our forefathers but on loan from our children. So we have to handover to them at least as it was handed over to us.*
> MK Gandhi

1 Environment as a Biggest Concern Today

Given India's 168th rank globally in environment protection index,[1] the issue of environment protection needs urgent attention of all the stakeholders.[2] Post-independence, the rapid industrialization, ambitions of economic development and a push towards tremendous material prosperity and pleasure have enhanced material well-being but only at the cost of much environment pollution.

Gandhi perhaps never used the word "environment protection" in his writings, but his contributions towards the cause of environment certainly make him an environmentalist. In the early twentieth century, he had warned the mankind against the ill effects of unrestricted industrialization and materialism without considering its effect on environment. The life and work of Gandhi on environment have considerable impact on contemporary environment movement in India. We can see the influence of Gandhi from *Chipko* (1976) Movement to *Narmada Bachao Movement.* In all these environment movements, activists adopted Gandhian principles such as non-violence that made environment movements so popular among Indians.

However, in the lifetime of Gandhi, India never witnessed such type and extent of environment problems which India is facing today. Gandhi always warned mankind

[1] https://www.nationalheraldindia.com/national/india-ranks-168th-on-environmental-performance-index (last visited on 15 December 2021).

[2] Stakeholders include government, corporations, citizens, environment activists, environmental organisations and NGOs.

J. P. Meena (✉)
Assistant Professor, Campus Law Centre, Faculty of Law, University of Delhi, Delhi, India
e-mail: jpnalsar@gmail.com

R. Mittal and K. K. Singh (eds.), *Relevance of Duties in the Contemporary World*,
https://doi.org/10.1007/978-981-19-1836-0_21

about the ill effects of rapid industrialization prevailing at that time. According to him, unregulated Western modal of industrialization was responsible for environment degradation. In 1908, through his writings in *Swaraj*, Gandhi warned the people about it. He suggested educated people who lived in cities to go back to villages as it was free from any kind of pollution as industrialization was not so much in villages, and hence, ancient Indian culture was also preserved there.[3] Furthermore, he had termed modern civilization as a *disease* and *nine days wonder*.[4] He was not against the use of machines but to enslavement of man in industrial civilization.[5] He advocated for systematic use of natural resources to save them for coming generations.

Instead of preaching, Gandhi believed in applying the same in his own life demonstrating his popular saying "my life is my message". Gandhi had trust in all ways of life, which has harmony and sustainability with nature. Gandhi emphasized the need for protecting environment by citing example of food, water and air. He considered these essential for mankind to sustain on the earth. Gandhi said, "Earth provides enough to satisfy every man's needs but not every man's greed".[6]

2 Influence of Mahatma Gandhi on the Environmental Movement in India

The biggest example of influence/significance of Gandhi's messages on environment can be seen as *Chipko Movement* in April 1973 where a breathless journalist had announced that he has seen Gandhi protected Himalayan trees.[7] In the present time, environment activists acknowledge/adopt techniques of Gandhi in environment movements.

We may divide Gandhian philosophy of environment protection in following three broad categories[8]:

1. General concern: environment degradation, pollution, waste, uncleanness and ugliness
2. Biotic concerns: ecological disharmony and its effect on non-human life
3. Social concerns: modern civilization, development (urbanization), agriculture crisis, and mechanization.

---

[3] Gandhi, Mohandas Karamchand, *Hind Swaraj.* Madras, 1921. Pp 48–50 and Mahatma Gandhi: His Life, Writing and Speeches, Madras 1918 pp 95.

[4] Gandhi Mohandas Karamchand, *Hind Swaraj.* Madras, 1921. Pp 89.

[5] Ashraf Ali, "Gandhian View of Sustainable Development", IJPA, Volume 39, No. 8, July–September 1993, p. 270.

[6] Pyarelal, Towards New Horizons, Navjivan Publishing House, Ahmedabad, 1959, p.12.

[7] Ramachandra Guha (1995) Mahatma Gandhi and the environmental movement in India, Capitalism Nature Socialism, 6:3, 47–61, https://doi.org/10.1080/10455759509358641

[8] Haydock & Himanshu Srivastava (2019) Environmental philosophies underlying the teaching of environmental education: a case study in India, Environmental Education Research, 25:7, 1038–1065, https://doi.org/10.1080/13504622.2017.1402170

To address environment problems, all the stakeholders have to understand these concerns first and then need to address them. First and foremost, the suggestion of Gandhi was back to nature as when we go back to nature only then we can truly understand the importance of nature in our lives. With this realization, our inner conscience will not allow polluting the environment and we all will strive for environment protection as we do for ourselves.

3 Ecological Dimension of Gandhi

To understand ecological dimension of the Gandhian thought, first we need to accept relation between ethics, politics and ecology through the Gandhian lens. For example, observance of *maunvrat* has significance place in Hindu religion. But it does not mean by observing *maunvrat, Gandhi is following his religious belief or tradition. It is also a mode of making himself receptive and listening to inner voice (introspection).* Since Gandhi used this during pre-independence, many readings suggest that it was the way in which Gandhi used to negotiate with Britishers for his terms. But if we understand it through ecological perceptive, then we will find this is a mode of conserving energy and to keep away from materialistic prosperity. To understand nature, Gandhi believed that we should not exploit nature and take only minimum from nature as required. Excess use of natural resources should not be allowed. If we are extracting more from nature than required, we are exploiting natural resources. Excess use of nature by us today will deprive upcoming generations from enjoyment. Therefore, Gandhi was in favour of judicious use of natural resources. It is our collective responsibility to preserve and protect environment for upcoming generations. For that we should be sensitive towards natural resources. Preservation and protection of natural resources are essential to maintain food chain as these are inter connected.

Gandhi was a critique of *waste* but he also considered modern industrial civilization responsible for this. As per Western thoughts, indigenous people "*wasted*" their land as they had not made it productive. Gandhi did not agree to this. According to him, whatever is used by humans is bound to turn to waste ultimately. We can understand this with the life instance of Gandhi also. His close associate and disciple Kaka Kalelkar was in the habit of plunking entire twig merely for four or five neem leaves. Gandhi termed it as *violence*. He viewed that Kalelkar should plunk only what he required for use and before that he should offer apology to tree. Because whatever exceeds the requirement would become waste and that is not good for environment.

4 Contribution of Judiciary in Environmental Jurisprudence

Judiciary also played a significant role to develop environmental jurisprudence in India. Several high courts in their judgements have established relationship between fundamental duties and fundamental rights for the protection of environment in India. In the landmark case of *L. K. Koolwal* v. *State of Rajasthan*,[9] Rajasthan High Court established a significant connection between fundamental duties and fundamental rights with special reference to environment protection.

In the opening part of the judgement, it was rightly asserted by the court that rights and duties coexist. Existence of both relies on each other. Through the 42nd Amendment, fundamental duties vide Article 51A have been added to the Constitution of India. After this addition, a citizen has the right to approach to the court for enforcement of duties which is cast on state. It is provided under clause (g) of Article 51A that it is the duty of state through its various agencies to take measures to improve and protect our environment including rivers, forests, wild life and lakes. It also casts a duty to have compassion for living creatures.

Prior to 42nd Amendment, 1976, there was too much discussion on fundamental rights as at that time fundamental duties were not part of the constitution. It is only after 1976, when fundamental duties were inculcated in the Constitution of India with certain objectives. It was also felt necessary as the existence of both rights and duties is interdependent and cannot exist without each other. Now, it is the duty of a citizen that rights which are guaranteed by the constitution are fulfilled.

42nd Constitutional Amendment

At the time of commencement, the Constitution of India did not contain any specific provision with regard to environment. It took almost 25 years to realize that we need to include environment in our Constitution. After Stockholm Conference, India made a significant progress towards environment protection by including environment protection as a fundamental duty. In addition to this, the Directive Principles of State Policy under the Constitution of India embody the following provision:

Article 48A states that:

> The State shall endeavor to protect and improve the environment and to safeguard the forests and wildlife of the country.

But such endeavours have some limitations, and hence, it has not been as effective as expected. Since these are part of the Directive Principles of State Policy, it is undoubtedly a tool for policy makers to guide them; however, it is not binding on them. It is up to the policy makers to creatively employ this principle for addressing environment issues. In this situation, such provisions seem a declaration rather than constitutional determination on environment protection.

Article 51A (g)

---

[9] AIR 1988 Raj. 2.

> It shall be duty of every citizen of India to protect and improve the natural environment including forests, lakes, rivers and wild life and to have compassion for living creatures.

It is a fundamental duty of Indian citizens to protect and preserve environment with all its components. This duty is corresponding to the Directive Principles of State Policy in Article 49. However, there is no mechanism provided in the Constitution to enforce fundamental duties. In that situation, failure to discharge fundamental duties may not have direct adverse consequence on a citizen individually.

Through 42nd Constitutional Amendment, certain entries related to environment were inserted in concurrent list to enable both parliament and state legislature to legislate on such subjects.[10] As a result, many environment legislations were enacted by the parliament as well as state legislature for environment protection.

Environment vis-à-vis the Constitution
The 42nd Constitutional Amendment through which environment was adopted in our Constitution was the result of an appeal of *Stockholm* conference. Though this movement was seen as a mere formality to fulfil international obligations, however, the amendment has initiated accountability towards environment protection. Since fundamental duties are essential feature of Indian constitution in the light of *Keshavanand Bharti*,[11] it is a significant tool to protect environment as well.

5 Global and National Legal Scenario for Environment

Environment protection is something which required collective efforts of all the stakeholders. It will be wrong if we assume that protection of environment is necessary for a specific group of people or a country in particular. Environmental protection in the real sense can be possible only when all the stakeholders come together and become conscious for it. All individuals belonging to different countries, ideologies, political groups, etc., need to be sensitive towards ecological integrity. For this, the role of various non-government organizations trying to influence policies of the government is significant.

Stockholm Declaration, 1972 was the first initiative which laid down foundation of international cooperation for environment protection. It consisted of 26 principles which deal with environment protection initiatives by stakeholders who are primarily responsible for environment degradation. It was a starting point of dialogue between developing and developed/industrialized countries for air, water pollution and well-being of people residing there.

Principle 1 of the **Stockholm Declaration** of 1972 highlights the importance of environment:

[10] Entry 17A in List III.-Concurrent List.

[11] (1973) 4 SCC 225.

> Man is both creature and module of environment which gives him physical sustenance and affords him the opportunity for intellectual, moral, social and spiritual growth.[12]

Therefore, while enjoying all environment creatures, it imposes collective responsibility of humans to *protect* and *improve* environment for enjoyment of present and upcoming generations.[13] The Rio Declaration on Environment and Development 1992 is another significant international initiative to put human being at the centre of environment protection. The Rio Declaration emphasized that for the overall development of human beings, preservation and conservation of environment are essential. In this regard, the role of various laws at international and national levels is crucial. These laws are essential tools to follow the mandate given by Stockholm and Rio declarations. After these declarations, various nations adopted environmental concerns in their constitutional texts. Various laws enacted for the protection of environment incorporated underlined principles of these international declarations related to environments.[14]

Anti-Pollution Laws

The Indian Parliament took significant legislative initiative for environment protection in the last four decades. Through these laws, the Parliament tried to address environment problems by making separate laws for each aspect of environmental challenge.

6 Right Duty Discourse for Environment

India's constitutional commitment towards environment appeared after 42nd Constitutional Amendment. It puts environment protection as part of the Fundamental Duties and Directive Principles of State Policy. So, it was not only direction for policy-makers but also duty of citizens to protect environment. Introduction of the chapter on fundamental duties reflected global initiatives as well. Article 48A and Article 51A (g) contain *protection* and *improvement* which speak a lot about environmentalism and constitutionalism. Constitution appeal citizens to have kindness and compassion for natural creatures. It reflects conscience of the Constitution towards environment.

Right to life under fundamental rights also includes the right to clean environment and that is possible only when we give effect to fundamental duty to protect and improve environment, thereby establishing essential linkages between fundamental

[12] Declaration of the UN Conference on Human Environment, 1972 principle 1.

[13] Rio Declaration On Environment And Development 1992 (available at https://www.jus.uio.no/lm/environmental.development.rio.declaration.1992/portrait.a4.pdf last accessed on 15 December 2021).

[14] Parliament of India passed the Air (Prevention and Control of Pollution) Act, 1981, the Water (Prevention and Control of Pollution) Act, 1974, and the Forest Conservation Act, 1980, to give effect to the Stockholm Declaration.

rights and fundamental duties. In this fashion, the concepts of fundamental rights and fundamental duties converge on a singular objective, i.e. protection and preservation of environment.

While the Constitution enumerates fundamental duties, it is, however, silent about enforceability of these duties. The following observations may be made in this regard:

(1) Fundamental rights are enforceable, while Directive Principles of State Policy cannot be directly enforced. There is nothing mentioned with regard to the enforcement of fundamental duties. Since there is no specific prohibition on enforceability of fundamental duties, it can be inferred that fundamental duties can be enforced by judiciary. In the landmark case of *L.K. Koolwal* v. *State of Rajasthan*,[15] Rajasthan High Court established a significant connection between fundamental duties and fundamental rights with special reference to environment protection. It was held that Article 51A gives right to citizens to approach court to enforce duties through state agencies for environment protection. In case omission or commission bring into notice of court, court can ask state to take necessary stapes for enforcing fundamental duties.

(2) Interrelation of rights and duties cannot be ignored in jurisprudence. For instance, if A has right, then it is obligation/duty for B to not violate the right of A. Similarly, if a citizen fails to perform duties, then it is violation of rights which corresponds to above duty. Hence, it can be asserted that fundamental duties are rights which are not enumerated in Indian Constitution. Non-enumeration of such rights should not make any difference. On the other side by including the chapter of fundamental duty in Indian Constitution, it has accepted the concept of "unremunerated implied rights". In this scenario, it becomes the duty of judiciary to protect these implied rights like other constitutional rights. In Javed v. State of Haryana,[16] the Supreme Court held that fundamental duties, fundamental rights and Directive Principles of State Policy should be interpreted together, not in isolation.

(3) These implied rights should also act as implied limitations over legislature's power to legislate. Legislature cannot violate such implied right. In this manner, fundamental duties get passively implemented by restricting and guiding the power of the legislature. Environmental legislations give teeth to fundamental duties by indirectly imposing specifications, penalties and punishment for violations.

(4) Fundamental duties for every citizen of India implied corresponding rights of Indian citizen. Judiciary will have to take into account the above while interpreting laws. The same has been done in the context of environmental protection. In Vellore Citizens Welfare Forum v. Union of India,[17] while recognizing "Precautionary Principle", Supreme Court held that it is part of environment law while interpreting Article 21 and Article 51A (g) together. Hence, the Supreme Court considered fundamental duties as a rule of law.

[15] AIR 1988 Raj. 2.

[16] (2003) 8 SCC 369.

[17] (1996) 5 SCC 647.

(5) Combined reading of fundamental duties and directive principles of state policy make them more effective. It has exposed the executive to the greater judicial scrutiny. For instance, if one reads Article 48A and Article 51A (g) together, both talk about environment. Article 48A provides that "The State shall endeavor to protect and improve the environment and to safeguard the forests and wildlife of the country".[18] This directive principle places an obligation on the State to protect the environment and wildlife. Separately, it is not judicially enforceable, but it may become enforceable under the light of Article 21 which deals with right to life, whereas Article 51A (g) says "It shall be duty of every citizen of India to protect and improve the natural environment including forests, lakes, rivers and wild life and to have compassion for living creatures".[19] Fundamental duties and fundamental rights should be given equal significance as it was also held by the Supreme Court in AIIMS Students' Union v. AIIMS.[20] In Vellore Citizens Welfare Forum v. Union of India,[21] the Supreme Court expanded scope by including right to have clean environment under Article 21.

(6) How fundamental duties and directive principles of state policy can be helpful in environment protection can be explained by the following instance. Any citizen can move to the High Court under Article 226 against any order of government officer which is inconsistent to Article 48A and Article 51A (g). The citizen cannot be stopped on the ground of *locus standi*. Similarly, if government officer issued no objection certificate for chemical factory construction which might cause air or water pollution as the case may be, such order of government officer would be violative of "implied rights" of citizen and also the concerned officer would be guilty of not performing fundamental duties. Hence, inclusion of fundamental duties through 42nd amendment in constitution opened way for judicial interpretation. It also opened possibility of ensuring "implied right' of Indian citizens. S. Jagannath v. Union of India,[22] the Supreme Court stressed that before granting permission to install commercial, there must be an environmental impact assessment before permission is granted to install commercial shrimp farms and there must be environmental impact assessment done by the officials so that in case someone is aggrieved by that may get compensation.

---

[18] Article 48A.

[19] Article 51A (g).

[20] (2002) 1 SCC 428.

[21] (1996) 5 SCC 647.

[22] AIR 1997 SC 811.

7 The Gandhian Solutions

There is no doubt that environment problems which are persisting today are more challenging than before. To deal with environment problems, we need to adopt Gandhian solutions creatively offered by Gandhi during his life and work. Prof. Ram Chander Guha quoted that "The life and work of Gandhi have had a considerable influence on the contemporary environmental movement…"[23]

Gandhian approach offers solution for almost all kinds of problems which a common man faces in a day-to-day life, i.e. social, economic, ecological, etc. Gandhi suggests that method to fulfil needs of life should be environment-friendly. Hence, Gandhian method and ideology have a deeper concern of harmony between nature and man. His idea of *self-rule (Swaraj)* was not limited to termination of foreign rule in India.[24]

For achieving *Sarvodaya,*[25] Gandhi devised famous constructive programme. As per Gandian solution, *Sarvodaya* will not only be helpful to redress environment problem but will also be helpful in achieving the idea of self-realization.[26] If all stakeholders are serious for environment protection, then it will be a way to achieve objects of *Sarvodaya*. It will be in benefit of all stakeholders. The concept of *Sarvodaya* is very similar to sustainable development and also part of environmental ethics. It can be achieved by harmonious existence with nature and human being.

8 Conclusion

In the current times, when all stakeholders are engaging themselves in discussions to solve environmental problem including pollution, Gandhian approach of life is an ideal method for solving problems related to environment. We should also keep in mind that Gandhi offered solution for environment related problems through adoption of certain changes in human behavior; hence, it is the duty of each individual to adopt these in their lives. Gandhian view with regard to be cautious to Western industrialization model calls for maintaining harmony with mother earth and rejection of consumerism. There is no doubt that economic growth cannot be overlooked, but it should not be at the cost of environmental degradation. The fundamental duties enshrined in Indian Constitution impose obligations on citizens to act for environmental concerns. From time to time, judiciary has interpreted right to life with the help of fundamental duties to preserve and protect environment for a better life. There are some laws which are enacted by legislature after 42nd Constitutional Amendment,

---

[23] Guha, R. C., "Gandhi the Environmentalist", Seminar, January 1974.

[24] Pathak R. P., "Environmental Challenges And Gandhian Solution", The Indian Journal of Political Science, July–Sept., 2004, Vol. 65, No. 3 (July–Sept., 2004), pp. 367–376.

[25] Sarvodaya means "the rise or welfare of all", Gandhi.

[26] Dwivedi O. P., "Global Dharma to the Environments", IJPA, Vol. XXXIX, No. 3, July–September 1993, p. 572.

but still problems related to environment are increasing rapidly. In this situation, it can be concluded that for every problem solution lies in fulfilment and enforcement of duties with respect to environment.

Economic growth without forsaking environment and sustainable development may be achieved by Gandhain way. To some extent, it may be difficult to follow the right path suggested by Gandhi. But for long-term solution, we all have to make a beginning with motto “think globally, and act locally”.

References

AIIMS Students' Union v. AIIMS (2002) 1 SCC 428

Ali A (1993 Jul–Sept) Gandhian view of sustainable development. IJPA 39(8):270

Declaration of the UN Conference on Human Environment (1972)

Dwivedi OP (1993 Jul–Sept) Global dharma to the environments. IJPA XXXIX(3):572

Gandhi M (1918) His life, writing and speeches. Madras:957

Gandhi MK (1921) Hind Swaraj. Madras pp 48–50

Guha RC (1974) Gandhi the environmentalist. Seminar

Guha R (1995) Mahatma Gandhi and the environmental movement in India. Capital Nat Social 6(3):47–61. https://doi.org/10.1080/10455759509358641

Haydock, Srivastava H (2019) Environmental philosophies underlying the teaching of environmental education: a case study in India. Environ Edu Res, 25(7):1038–1065. https://doi.org/10.1080/13504622.2017.1402170

Jagannath v Union of India AIR 1997 SC 811

Javed v. State of Haryana (2003) 8 SCC 369

Keshavanand Bharti v. State of Kerala (1973) 4 SCC 225

L.K. Koolwal v. State of Rajasthan AIR 1988 Raj. 2

Pathak RP (2004 Jul–Sept) Environmental challenges and Gandhian solution. Indian J Polit Sci 65(3), pp 367–376

Pyarelal (1959) Towards new horizons, Navjivan Publishing House, Ahmedabad, p 12

Rio declaration on environment and development 1992. https://www.jus.uio.no/lm/environmental.development.rio.declaration.1992/portrait.a4.pdf. Accessed 15 Dec 2021

Vellore Citizens' Welfare Forum v. Union of India (1996) 5 SCC 647

Chapter 22
Gandhian Perspective on Women's Role in India—With Special Reference to Fundamental Duties

Ankita Srivastava

1 The Idea of Modernism and Post—Modernism: Gandhi's Viewpoint

> And then Gandhi came. He was like a powerful current of fresh air that made us stretch ourselves and take deep breath; like a beam of light that pierced the darkness and removed the scales from our eyes; like a whirlwind that upset many things, but most of all the working of people's mind. He did not descend from the top; he seemed to emerge from the millions of India, speaking their language and incessantly drawing attention to them and their appalling condition.
>
> —Jawaharlal Nehru

To understand Gandhi's perspective on women's role in India, it is important to comprehend his views on modern society. Modern society defines a shift in thinking patterns, value systems, world view, customs, technology, etc. It is a description of the new way the world thinks, lives, and acts.

It was in the wake of the seventeenth century that transition took place from mediaeval to the modern era. It was during this period that modern man emerged in society and led to the development of a democratic state based upon the ideals of life and liberty. This transition also led to the emergence of concepts like secularism. With the advancement of modern society, the man became more focused on his self-interest and the state attained its present status.[1] It was during the period of the Renaissance around the fourteen to sixteenth century that the entire process of reformation began. The period of Renaissance witnessed the steady revival of art, music, and literature. This period was followed by the age of enlightenment which

[1] Ram Chandra Pradhan, Gandhi: A proponent of Pre-Modernity, Modernity or Postmodernity? In: Reading and Re-Appraising Gandhi, Macmillan, India (2011).

A. Srivastava (✉)
International Lawyer, 122, Srestha Vihar, First Floor, Delhi 110092, India
e-mail: ankita_srivastava97@yahoo.co.in

R. Mittal and K. K. Singh (eds.), *Relevance of Duties in the Contemporary World*,
https://doi.org/10.1007/978-981-19-1836-0_22

saw the rise of scientific reason. It further led to the expansion of awareness among the society which turned the way for human progress.

In his book *Hind Swaraj*, Gandhi observed that the source of modern civilisation lies in the basic philosophy of the industrial revolution. It was the industrial revolution that changed the worldview of western society in terms of religion, ethics, and knowledge. He came to believe that in such a new world, the society was managed, manipulated, and mastered for the fulfilment of ever-spiralling human desire and aspirations. The industrial revolution only fastened the process as machines came to dominate human life instead of becoming its allies.[2]

In his book, *Hind Swaraj,* replying to the question whether he was against all machinery, Gandhi said:

> How can I be when I know that even this body is a most delicate piece of machinery? The spinning wheel is a machine; a little toothpick is a machine. What I object to is the craze for machinery, not machinery as such. The craze is for what they call labour-saving machinery. Men go on 'saving labour' till thousands are without work and thrown on the open streets to die of starvation. I want to save time and labour, not for a fraction of mankind but for all. I want the concentration of wealth, not in the hands of a few, but in the hands of all. Today machinery merely helps a few to ride on the backs of millions. The impetus behind it all is not the philanthropy to save labour, but greed. It is against this constitution of things that I am fighting with all my might... The supreme consideration is man. The machine should not tend to atrophy the limbs of man. For instance, I would make intelligent exceptions. Take the case of the Singer's Sewing Machine. It is one of the few useful things ever invented, and there is a romance about the device itself.

He not only rejected the notion of modern civilisation but also provided an alternative culture which he called *Ram Rajya.* Ram Rajya means self-rule by an individual. Gandhi believed that Ram Rajya meant the rule of Dharm, the rule of justice. And for Ram Rajya to be observed, the man has to reduce his needs to a bare minimum. He never talked of Ram as an individual; for him, Ram was a metaphor and an abstract concept, which stood for justice, equity, self-sacrifice, concern for others, etc.[3] More recently, a post-modern world has emphasised the aggressive and destructive march of this 'age of reason'. However, Gandhi would test his faith with reason, but he would not allow his reason to destroy his faith. What makes such technological rationalism even more destructive in Gandhi's view is its flawed materialism. That is the negation of the spiritual, the transcendent, or in other words, the denial of a religious worldview.[4]

Gandhi believed that the claim of modern civilisation to provide physical comfort to masses is nothing but a mirage. Gandhi said in his own words that modern civilisation is a '*mouse gnawing while it keeps on soothing us*'. Gandhi also compared it to the tree which destroys everything it comes in contact with.[5.]

---

[2] Mahatma Gandhi, Hind Swaraj and Other Writings, Cambridge University Press, New York. (1997).

[3] *Ibid.*

[4] Rudolf C Heredia, Interpreting Gandhi's Hind Swaraj, 34 *Economic and Political Weekly* 24, 1497—1502 (1999).

[5] Ram Chandra Pradhan, *supra* note 1.

Since Gandhi's core beliefs included concepts like Ram Rajya, it is entrancing to comprehend his understanding of social progress when it came to women in society.

Bikhu Parekh, a British political theorist in his academic work, *Gandhi's Political Philosophy,* analyses Gandhi's critique of modernity. According to him, Gandhi laid over emphasis on disadvantages of modernism and refused to accept its positive aspect. Even when Gandhi acknowledged the positive aspect, he only referred to it as being incidental.

Another political philosopher, *Ramashray Roy* wrote two books on Gandhi, namely *Self and Society & Gandhi: Sounding in Political Philosophy,* where he says that Gandhi's critique is based on the world view that self-knowledge is the ultimate purpose of human existence. For him, the real progress lied in self-discovery.

Although Gandhi's views on modern civilisation could be faulted on various grounds, it is viable to a certain extent in the present scenario. Whether modernisation changed the world for better is still a question that demands a definitive answer. If we take a closer look at the problems that exist in the modern world like climate change, ecological imbalance, marginalisation of millions of people, increasing cases of violence, intolerance among people, we can see that Gandhi's criticism of modern civilisation cannot be outrightly rejected.

Moreover, gender issues have always been a topic in society as well as in literature, so gender naturally became a major focus of the modernist movement. Women, their intelligence, and their judgement had always been regarded with contempt by a male oriented society, and it is still a question whether Gandhi's idea of a modern woman favoured the notion of equality in its true essence or not.

2 Gandhi's Perspective of Women

Gandhi, as a nationalist leader and husband to his wife, Kasturba, had strong views when it came to women. India has a varn system that divides society into four classes. Contrary to the position of women in ancient India, women in modern times have been treated as lesser than men in society. *Charles Darwin* explains in his book, *The Descent of Man,* that most people at leading positions are men, and he assumed that it was because men were biologically superior to women. He strongly held the belief that men were born superior to women, and since in reality, the majority of professionals including artists, writers, and scientists were all men, it further reinstated his belief.[6] Although, they were protesting voices against such views. One such woman who made history by raising her voice was *Mary Wollstonecraft* whose book called *'Vindication of the Rights of Women'*, where she argued for equal rights for men and women. Another plea for equal rights was raised by *John Stuart Mill* in his book *'The Subjugation of Women'*. He put forward the argument that equal citizens' rights to men and women would bring out a real social transformation, as the society would derive great benefits from proper utilisation of their talents. By the

[6] Angela Saini, Woman's Inferiority to Man, In: Inferiority, Harper Collins, UK (2017).

beginning of the twentieth century, the demands of women's rights started to include equal pay for equal work, women's representation in public institutions, voting, and other political rights for women, etc. It was only after 1882 that married women in the UK were allowed to own and control property in their own name. The ancient Hindu text of the Mahabharat speaks of women being unconfined and independent before marriage was invented.[7]

A milestone was reached when *Shulamith Firestone* published her book, *Dialectic of Sex*, in 1970, where her primary thesis was that the problem of oppression and domination of women was so basic that it could not be made a subordinate part of the struggle against the domination of other dispossessed sections based on class or race. Firestone's work was followed by *Kate Millet*, another prominent woman thinker, who published her work in *Sexual Politics* in 1970. She argued that the chain of domination has to be smashed via social authority and economic power structure. Another landmark was reached by *Sheila Rowbatham* with the publication of her two books, *Women Resistance and Revolution* (1972) and *Hidden from History* (1975), where she tried to prove that there exists a close link between class and gender oppression. It is the long battle with patriarchy that has been held responsible for gender inequality including the denial of property rights to women and right over their bodies. Through years, women have been fighting to receive equal rights to employment and healthcare services. Despite such strong voices emerging in different parts of the world in favour of a more liberal position of women in society, Gandhi had a comparatively different view on the matter.

George Orwell, in his 1949 essay *Reflection of Gandhi*, said that 'saints should always be judged guilty until they are proved innocent'. It is has been argued by Manu that women should live under the protection of her father, husband, or her son at different stages of her life.

Gandhi had a very strong and loving relationship with his mother, Putalibai, whom he extremely adored. In his view, she was an ideal woman as she was described as self-sacrificing, service-oriented, liberal in her social and religious interactions, and on top of it, quite independent-minded. And, it was for these reasons that she left an ever-lasting impact on Gandhi's life and thought process. Another woman who left a remarkable imprint on Gandhi's life was his wife, Kasturba. As early as 1909 in Hind Swaraj, Gandhi explained some of the issues faced by Indian women, viz., child marriage, child—widowhood, incompatible marriages, devadasi, and other direct forms of prostitution, polygamy, and polyandry, etc. He also believed that women were known for qualities like patience, forbearance, self—sacrificing, and serving—nursing nature, and they have the potential to be better *satyagrahis.* He was an admirer of women's qualities but also, he did not consult his wife before becoming a brahmachari (a concept in Hindu religion which means taking the vow of celibacy), which might seem contradictory to his own belief. He adored the life of brahmachari despite being married and did not hesitate to sacrifice his married life. In family life, his view was limited to looking at women as the mistress of the house, the one who looks after the children and other household affairs. He believed that women should

[7] *Ibid.*

primarily look after the household affairs, while men could work to find necessary means for its maintenance. But despite holding such views, he was in favour of gender equality. He believed that such role differentiation could not be used against women to stop them from enjoying their freedom and independence. He rejected the basic idea that women constitute the 'weaker' sex and preferred to call them 'better-half' and female sex. So convinced was he about the prevailing unjust and inequities nature of the man-woman relationship that he went to the extent of saying that if he is ever born as a woman, he would certainly rebel against male pretensions.[8]

The fact that Gandhi believed men and women to be equal has been evident through his writings and the writings of his hagiographers. Gandhi wanted women to be part of the freedom struggle and believed that women have a significant role to play. Although his views on equality have been praiseworthy, but the same cannot be said about his views of the female body. In her book *'Sex and Power'*, Rita Banerjee uses the following words to describe Gandhi's school of thought on women's body, *'he believed menstruation was a manifestation of the distortion of a woman's soul by her sexuality'*.[9]

Gandhi held the view that men and women should cohabitate only for procreation. He was not in favour of any kind of artificial system of birth control.

Gandhi is called 'Bapu' by the world, but it is also a fact that his wife, Kasturba, also called him father, Bapu.

> All of them, including Kasturbai, now called him Father, 'Bapu', or, 'Bapuji', the ji connoting a Hindu mixture of respect and tenderness. He received and gave a great deal of love.[10]

The book written by Louis Fischer on the life of Gandhi narrates that Gandhi was sweet and kind as a young man towards everybody except his wife and sons. Louis Fischer talks about Gandhi and his wife in the following words:

She never behaved like Mrs. Gandhi, never asked privileges for herself, never shirked the hardest work, and never seemed to notice the small group of young or middle-aged female disciples who interposed themselves between her illustrious husband. Being herself and being at the same time a shadow of the Mahatma made her a remarkable woman, and some who observed them for long years wondered whether she had not come nearer the Gita ideal of non-attachment than. He was too passionate to be the perfect yogi.[11]

Gandhi was influenced by Sita's (a female character in Hindu epic, Ramayan) chastity and gave her example on various occasions in his speeches. Gandhi wanted women to do the work of cotton spinning, which according to him could protect the purity of all women.

---

[8] Ram Chandra Pradhan, *supra* note 1.

[9] Michael Connellan, Women suffer from Gandhi's legacy, the Guardian (2010) Available at https://www.theguardian.com/commentisfree/2010/jan/27/mohandas-gandhi-women-india (last accessed 15 June, 2020).

[10] Louis Fischer, Gandhi's Family, In: The Life of Mahatma Gandhi, Harper Collins, India (2010).

[11] *Ibid*.

On 26th November 1947, for instance advising families to rehabilitate the victimised women, he said, '*It is my belief that any woman who has the purity of Sita cannot be touched by anyone*'.

Gandhi laid special emphasis on the character of Sita throughout his writing and significantly appreciated Sita's virtue. According to Gandhi, Sita was the perfect example of a chaste, devoted and silently suffering wife, which is how Gandhi perceived the model Hindu woman.

According to Gandhi, if the victim of any sexual crime resolves to become Sita like pure and chaste in her virtue, then she would naturally repel sexual aggression from men. If women face immoral sexual behaviour, it is because of the moral failure on part of women.[12]

Despite having such views, Gandhi stood for universal education of both girls and boys. He brought out a scheme called *Nai Talim* (1937), where he proposed a system of free and compulsory education for both the sexes till the age of 14 years. The same has also been incorporated in the Indian Constitution under Article 21A which says that '*the State shall provide free and compulsory education to all children of 6–14 years in such manner as the State, may by law determine*'.

As previously stated, Gandhi decided to practise Brahmacharya without consulting his wife, Kasturba. It seems contradictory that on one hand, he was advocating a women's right to independence and rebelling against evil practices like child marriage, dowry system, purdah system, but, on the other hand, he failed to give voice to his wife. Gandhi's life has been prominent throughout history, but the same is not true of his wife who played a huge role in being the support that he required at the time. *Hardiman*, in his book, *Gandhi: In His Time and Ours*, argues that Gandhi was nothing but a true votary of patriarchy. He added in his book that Gandhi took the momentous decision of Brahmacharya in 1906 primarily on his own and consulted Kasturba only after he had made up his mind. Feminists like Madhu Kishwar, Sujata Pateland, and others criticise him on many counts. The main argument that comes up is that Gandhi was extremely insensitive to women's sexuality and sexual desires. He looked at the victims of prostitution in a low manner and did not consider them fit to become members of Congress. Although he wanted to create a society where women were not forced to take up such professions at the same time, he ignored the fact that prostitutes were victims of the social conditions and needed special attention. Another issue that comes up is that women who became part of the women's movement came from a high-class background. He failed to attract lower-class women within his movement. Sujata Patel, another thinker, argued that Gandhi himself suffered from such a high-class and upper-class mindset. On the other side, the fact that various women leaders emerged during the reign of Gandhi's nationalist movement including Indira Gandhi, Sarojini Naidu, Aruna Asaf Ali, and Sucheta Kripalani cannot be ignored.[13]

---

[12] Debali Mookerjea-Leonard, "To be pure or not to be: Gandhi, Women, and the Partition of India", *Sage* Available via https://journals.sagepub.com/doi/full/10.1057/fr.2009.39 (last accessed on 20 June, 2020).

[13] Ram Chandra Pradhan, *supra* note 1.

3 Do Gandhi's Views Stand the Test of Time in Terms of Article 51-A (e) of the Indian Constitution?

The situation of women in present-day India has improved considerably but still, and there is a long way to go as per the research and data available on crimes against women. According to the *National Crime Record Bureau Report*, 2018, the cases of crime reported against women were 378,277 in 2018, which is an increase from 359,849 in 2017. According to this report, '*Cruelty by husband or his relatives* (31.9%) *followed by an assault on women with intent to outrage her modesty* (27.6%) *constituted the major share of crimes against women*'.[14] In the wake of rising crimes against women, our constitution incorporates certain duties to be observed by Indian citizens as part of Article 51-A which were added through the 42nd Amendment Act, 1976. Article 51-A for the very first time specified a code of fundamental duties to be abided by the citizens under Part IV-A of the constitution. The fundamental duties are the other side of the same coin. When the citizens are bestowed with fundamental rights, it becomes imperative for them to perform their duties towards the country.[15] Article 51-A (e) says 'to promote harmony and the spirit of common brotherhood amongst all the people of India transcending religious, linguistic and regional or sectional diversities; to renounce practices derogatory to the dignity of women'. The latter part means that every individual must fight against inequality and injustice against women. That inequality and injustice range from personal to the public sphere. To add, equality which Gandhi talked about included fighting against social evils like Sati Pratha, Purdah System, etc. which existed at the time. In the present scenario, the evil practices against women are not limited to such systems. The number of cases of sexual assault and rape has immensely increased in modern India. Besides, women no longer want to be confined to the walls of the household. Even housewives lookout to work from the arenas of their homes to support the family.

In the case *C. B. Muthamma* v. *Union of India*, the Supreme Court observed that 'the law under Indian Foreign Service Rules which required that a woman member in the service should obtain permission from the government in writing before the solemnisation of marriage and that no married women shall be entitled as of right to be appointed to the service stands invalid'.[16] The court remarked that such a regulation furthered the culture of masculine superiority.

Gandhi failed to consider the issue of male preference in Indian society when he talked about women as the mistress of the house. It is only when women are allowed to be born that the nation can renounce practices derogatory to women. It is a well-known fact that families prefer a male child since a man is said to carry the family name and add income to the household, while the woman is only born to

---

[14] Vijaita Singh, Uttar Pradesh tops the list in crimes against women (2020) Available at https://www.thehindu.com/news/national/uttar-pradesh-tops-in-crimes-against-women/article30526919.ece (last accessed 21 June, 2020).

[15] J. N. Pandey, Constitutional Law of India, Central Law Agency, India (2015).

[16] *C. B. Muthamma v. Union of India* AIR 1979 SC 1868 (India).

be married into another house which is an added burden to the family. According to Gandhi, as the mistress of the house and having the responsibility of looking after young, impressionable, and sensitive minds, women could play a very significant and positive role in the entire process. While his views on women's rights deserve much appreciation but at the same time, he failed to address that seeing women as only the mistress of the house is the root cause of the problem including the offences against women.

In the significant judgement of *Maya Devi* v. *State of Maharashtra*,[17] 'the Hon'ble court observed that the requirement of married women obtaining the husband's consent before applying for employment was held violative of Articles 14,15, and 16'. The Supreme Court emphasised on the importance of financial independence for women and ordered against imposition of any condition which discourages women to engage in her profession.[18] The court emphasised on the importance of economic independence for women and the importance of not creating conditions that discourage such independence. Recently, Article 51-A (e) came up to be discussed in the case *Indian Young Lawyers Association* v *State of Kerala*,[19] also known as 'Sabarimala judgement' wherein a group of lawyers filed the petition in the Supreme Court of India to lift the ban against women aged between 10 and 50 to enter the Sabarimala temple. The argument was that women of menstruating age should not enter the temple since it is an impure act against the deity Ayyapan. It was believed that since he was a celibate deity, the presence of women in the temple would have led to his distraction. The major argument against it was that it is gender discrimination and violative of constitutional provisions. The Supreme Court gave its ruling in 2018 in favour of women in the following words:

> We have no hesitation in saying that such an exclusionary practice violates the right of women to visit and enter a temple to freely practice the Hindu religion and to exhibit her devotion towards Lord Ayyappa. The denial of this right to women significantly denudes them of their right to worship.

In the present scenario, granting equal rights to women does not suffice as justice. It is a scientific fact that both the sexes are biologically different from each other, and men and women are raised in entirely different social conditions. For example maternity leave for a woman is the right that every woman deserved to be granted in light of childbirth and the raising of the child. For example in the above-mentioned case law, the court recognised the injustice suffered by the women against non-allowance of entry into the temple and addressed that biological difference between men and women should not lead to discrimination. Our constitution also allows positive discrimination in favour of women to ensure that they are given equal opportunities. For instance Article 15(3) of the constitution states that 'nothing in this article shall prevent the state from making any special provision for women and children'.

While Gandhi talked about the equality and power of women at great lengths, he failed to undertake the idea of equity. Women can only be given power in the

---

[17] *Maya Devi v. State of Maharashtra* 1986 ISCR 748.

[18] *Ibid.*

[19] *Indian Young Lawyers Association v State of Kerala*, Writ Petition (Civil) No. 373 of 2006.

public sphere when they are treated powerfully within their homes. Only if Gandhi had treated his wife, Kasturba, with more dignity and given her the equal power to take important decisions, then his views on equality of women would have had more credibility.

4 Conclusion

Gandhi's notions about women often contradicted his own beliefs. On one hand, he says that women should be treated equally and educated. On the other hand, he confined women's role to the household and kitchen. Despite such contradiction, his views on women's education deserve much appreciation as in the present scenario, women can be seen serving at various positions including the battlefield. In India and at a global level, women are now working at top positions that exclusively belonged to men in the earlier era ranging from prime ministers, presidents, doctors, lawyers, judges, etc. In the recent historic judgement, the Supreme Court of India allowed women to serve as army commanders. As a result, women will now be able to manage the entire army units. The argument against appointing women as army commanders was that the men who join the army often come from backgrounds where they are not conditioned to accept women at such positions. The Supreme Court blatantly rejected this argument and favoured gender equality. According to the media report, '*women's representation has steadily increased in the Lok Sabha. In the first-ever election, only 5% of the House consisted of women. Now, that has increased to 14%*'.[20]

Gandhi has often emphasised in his speeches that it is the woman who is also at fault if they get raped or sexually assaulted, which is also the view taken by many Indian conservatives.

When we talk about a rudimentary commitment to renounce the practices derogatory to women, it does start from the household and the family. It includes not blaming the women for getting raped. It includes acknowledging the biological, physiological, and mental differences between men and women, and it includes giving women the right to choice. Most importantly, it does not include giving women just symbolic power. While Gandhi may have been seen as a progressive nationalist on the issue of women during the era of the independence struggle, but in the present times, his views can be seen as conservative and contradictory. In light of recent judgements, it is important to note that even the opinions of judges have changed considerably when it comes to women's rights and duties, while the law in the books largely remains the same. Such a revolution in the minds of judges is a clear indication of how the society and jury perceive women is not the same as it was at the time of independence. This also suggests that if Gandhi would have been present in the current world, his

---

[20] Sruthi Radhakrishnan, "New Lok Sabha has the highest number of women MPs", *The Hindu* (2019) Available at https://www.thehindu.com/news/national/new-lok-sabha-has-highest-number-of-women-mps/article27260506.ece (last accessed 22 June, 2020).

opinion on women might not have been the same. Although some of Gandhi's views do stand the test of time, it cannot be said with conviction that his ideas on women would still be relevant in the present times.

References

Connellan M (2010) Women suffer from Gandhi's legacy. The Guardian

Gandhi M (1997) Hind swaraj and other writings. Cambridge University Press, New York

Heredia Rudolf C (1999) Interpreting Gandhi's hind swaraj. Econ Pol Wkly 34(24):1497–1502

https://www.theguardian.com/commentisfree/2010/jan/27/mohandas-gandhi-women-india. Accessed 15 June 2020

Indian Young Lawyers Association v State of Kerala, Writ Petition (CIVIL) No. 373 of 2006

Louis F (2010) The life of Mahatma Gandhi. Harper Collins Publisher, India

Maya Devi v. State of Maharashtra (1986 ISCR 748)

Mookerjea- Leonard D (2010) To be pure or not to be: Gandhi, Women, and the Partition of India. Sage J https://journals.sagepub.com/doi/full/https://doi.org/10.1057/fr.2009.39 Accessed 20 June 2020

Muthamma CB v Union of India AIR 1979 SC 1868 (India)

Pandey JN (2015) Constitutional law of India. Central Law Agency, India

Pradhan Ram Chandra (2011) Reading and reappraising Gandhi. Macmillan, India

Saini A (2017) Inferior. Harper Collins, United Kingdom

Singh V (2020) Uttar Pradesh tops the list in crimes against women. The Hindu https://www.thehindu.com/news/national/uttar-pradesh-tops-in-crimes-against-women/article30526919.ece Accessed 21st June 2020

Part IV
Relevance of Duties in Knowledge Economy: A Special Case of Intellectual Property Duties, Obligations and Responsibilities

Chapter 23
Make Without Take

Shubha Ghosh

> *You have a right to your actions,*
> *but never to your actions' fruits*
> *Act for the action's sake*
> *And do not be attached to inaction.* [Stephen Mitchell, trans., Bhagavad Gita 54 (2000)]

Lord Krishn's admonishment to Arjun has implications beyond the actual battlefield. Assuaging concerns about murdering one's kinsmen in war, these words are reminders against acquisitiveness. In the pedestrian world of the marketplace, we are reminded to act for the sake of action alone without obsession on how our actions aggrandize us. But this distancing from the fruits of what we do does not support complete renunciation. We must act, but we need not take.

As the Mahatma explains: "Your right is to work, and not to expect the fruit." Adopting a troubling metaphor, he elaborates:

> The slave-owner tells the slave: "Mind your work, but beware lest you pluck a fruit from the garden. Your is to take what I give." God has put us under restriction in the same manner. He tells us that we may work if we wish, but that the reward is entirely for him to give.[1]

Invoking the master–slave relationship defines the relationship of human to God. One thinks perhaps of the moral: Man proposes, but God disposes. Yet, the lesson is not so deterministic. One should act; one should work. And presumably this act, this work is a choice, not compelled by a master, even God. The master–slave metaphor is inapposite. More appropriately, one who works only compelled by the acquisition of fruits is the actual slave.

[1] The Bhagavad Gita According to Gandhi 48 (2000).

S. Ghosh (✉)
Crandall Melvin Professor of Law, Syracuse University College of Law, 950 Irving Ave, Syracuse, NY 13244, USA
e-mail: sghosh01@syr.edu

R. Mittal and K. K. Singh (eds.), *Relevance of Duties in the Contemporary World*,
https://doi.org/10.1007/978-981-19-1836-0_23

Mahatma's interpretation rests on a notably different translation of this passage, a translation that is more revealing:

> Action alone is the province, never the fruits thereof. Let not thy motive be the fruit of action, nor shouldst thou desire to avoid action.[2]

The key word here is motive. Mitchell's translation juxtaposes a "right to act" with "no right to the fruits of the actions." The difference is more than subtle. What Gandhi teaches is to not be motivated by fruits. We should act in a detached manner, not focused on the ends. Mitchell's translation speaks in terms of rights, resonant of legal rights, but presented in more abstract, philosophical terms. How motives transform into rights is not completely clear. Rights may emerge from self-interest. What one wants to do may become what one is entitled to do. Rights may define self-interest as entitlements turn into objects of pursuit. Rights and motives may also be completely different categories. Mitchell's translation and Gandhi's offer two contrasting interpretations of this famed passage, leading toward different paths.

Lord Krishn's message to Arjun is to act according to his duty as a warrior. This duty requires him to fight despite his psychological conflict. Such detachment guides how to live one's life. But one must act; one must live. This message is not a matter of rights or motivation. Instead, it is an admonishment to act without the doubts that frustrate Arjun. Fruits of acts and motives for action do not capture this message. Arjun should act without obsession for the consequences of the acts. He has a duty and must fulfill it.

To ignore the consequences of one's actions may suggest immorality. Certainly, acts with bad consequences are to be avoided while those with good ones are to be embraced. But what is at issue is neither immorality nor amorality. Arjun's dilemma stems from his duty as a warrior which now requires him to kill members of his family in a war stemming from greed and self-interest. He struggles to reconcile the duty to his families with what his expected of him as a warrior. Lord Krishn's admonishment is against inaction. To follow his duty as a warrior does not require Arjun to forsake his duty to his family. His duty is to act for inaction too has consequences which Arjun cannot imagine. One cannot know the consequences of one's acts and to think that one does have such certainty is to be beholden to fruits in which no one has a claim. Lord Krishn does not urge Arjun to embrace immorality or amorality. Instead, one should act with humility.

As Gandhi teaches:

> This is the unmistakable teaching of the Gita. He who gives up action falls. He who gives up only the reward rises. But renunciation of the fruit in no way means indifference to the result. In regard to every action, one must know the result that is expected to follow, the means thereto, and the capacity for it. He, who being this equipped, is without desire for the result, and is yet wholly engrossed in the due fulfillment of the task before him, is said to have renounced the fruits of his actions.[3]

---

[2] Id.

[3] Id. at 20.

The lesson is to serve humbly. Lord Krishn's words are not directly solely to Arjun, the warrior, but to Arjun, the person, and hence to all of us. Our duty is to act in the world as we find ourselves in it and to seek not rewards, or fruits, or consequences, but the humility of serving.

Arjun's dilemma can be applied to many contemporary situations. A doctor must decide how and to whom to render care. A judge must decide on the correct punishment, including the ultimate punishment of the death penalty. An attorney must decide which client to serve. For an inventor, action might lead to a new item being created. Such a person may be driven by many passions. The urge might be spiritual; it might also flow from a sense of pleasure or trivial amusement. Acting to create forecloses other options, such as direct service to others through education, provision of personal needs or developing interpersonal relationships. But when the new item is created, the inventor must decide what to do with it. Shall it be given away for free? To the highest bidder? As with Arjun, the critical question is how to decide, not simply what to decide. Arjun's doubts stem from not understanding how to decide to act.

Since Arjun confronts a question of life or death, we can posit an analogous problem for the inventor that illustrates the relevance of Arjun's doubts to intellectual property law. Suppose our hypothetical inventor conceives of a wonder drug that can cure disease and comfort the suffering. Should this person invent the drug? Is there an obligation to invent? Or can the inventor decide that such an invention would not be desirable because of the consequences of overpopulation or the strain on economic resources? If the drug is invented, should it be made available to everyone or should we countenance the death of some who cannot have access because of lack of ability to pay, lack of medical care systems for drug distribution or failure to provide alternatives such as generics? Is there a duty to provide the drug once invented? Or is the provision contingent on other factors, such as ability to pay? These questions ask us to confront deeper choices about how to organize invention and distribution.

With intellectual property, the parallels to Arjun's dilemma point to the ethical underpinnings of technology and its role in social progress. A dominant assumption is that progress and innovation are the primary goals of intellectual property. Such a view echoes the poet T. S. Eliot, who, according to Sen, interprets Krishn's advice to Arjun as follows: "And do not think of the fruit of action. /Fare forward.'… 'Not fare well, /But fare forward, voyagers.'"[4] To Eliot's thinking, people should create and invent without consideration of consequences. The act of creation itself that produces the new thing is what matters. In this way, invention "fares forward" and progresses. The goal is indiscernible and irrelevant.

My characterization of intellectual property in non-consequentialist terms is counterintuitive. After all, creation does not occur randomly. A poet wants to write a specific poem, and a chemist wants to isolate a particular compound. Invention and creation are thus goal-oriented. But the shibboleth is not espousing randomness of

[4] Amartya Sen, The Idea of Justice 23 (2009) (quoting T. S. Eliot, Dry Salvages, in Four Quartets 29–31 (1944)).

any kind; rather, Eliot's poetic rendition of Krishn's encouraging Arjun is in opposition to consequentialist thinking. Dr. J. Robert Oppenheimer quoted Krishn's words during the first detonation of the atomic bomb in the New Mexico desert: "I am become death, the destroyer of worlds."[5] As for technology, Dr. Oppenheimer in his own words stated a version of Krishn's admonition against consequentialism: "When you see something that is technically sweet, you go ahead and do it and you argue about what to do about it only after you have had your technical success."[6] Satirist Tom Lehrer expressed this sentiment in more stark and striking terms in a song about another rocket scientist: "Once the rockets are up, who cares where they come down? That's not my department. (says Wernher von Braun)."[7]

To act as Krishn teaches is not to adopt Dr. Oppenheimer's approach to achieving technical success. Acting without attachment does not mean acting with indifference to results. What Krishn teaches is action without expectation of a result, without attachment to specific consequences, or action solely to an end. When Krishn speaks of duty, he is speaking of the correctness of the act, a correctness that is understood comprehensively. While such teaching guides individuals in spiritual battle, the question is whether Krishn teaches how to build a cathedral, doghouse or any edifice in between. Krishn's principle of action frees us from the threat of inaction and the myopia of means-end rationality. Arjun, with all his doubts and indecision, becomes more appealing by comparison.

But the verbal battle between Arjun and Krishn points to the internal battle of any decision-maker. A judge chooses between following precedent or breaking from it to reach the correct result. An advocate decides how to defend an indefensible client. Consequences matter; right action does not entail indifference to ends. Instead, as Sen puts it, "sensitivity to consequences does not demand insensitivity to agencies and relations in evaluating what is happening in the world."[8] Furthermore, attachment to consequences can cause tunnel vision and deviation from the right action. Arjun's and Krishn's dialogue are the poles of any decision-making process which reaches resolution through deliberation, an understanding of consequences and a keen attention to action and service. Speaking broadly, the ethics of consequentialism can inform all action, especially the acts of creation and innovation that are the subject of intellectual property.

But, one would object, intellectual property is all about rewards and self-interest. The logic of intellectual property law rests on the coupling of motive for rewards with a right in rewards. Patents provide strong rights of exclusion for inventors so that they can commercialize their inventions in as many feasible markets as possible. Copyrights protect the rights of creative persons—writers, musicians, movie makers,

---

[5] Alex Abella, Soldiers of Reason: The RAND Corporation and the Rise of American Empire 41 (2009).

[6] Sen, supra note 5, at 211 (quoting U.S. Atomic Energy Comm'n, In the Matter of J. Robert Oppenheimer: Transcript of Hearing Before Personnel Security Board 81 (1954)).

[7] Tom Lehrer, Werner Von Braun on That Was the Year that Was (Reprise Records, 1965).

[8] Sen, supra note 5, at 221.

designers—so they can commercially exploit their works—books, songs, films, decorations—through many derivative forms as consumers want. Trademarks aid both these efforts by granting exclusive rights in words and shapes that brand the products that embody the patented inventions and copyrighted works. Other intellectual property rights follow suit, offering legal protection for commercial secrets, publicity and attendant matter.

Add to this mismatch between intellectual property and Lord Krishn's pronouncement the attention given to these exclusive rights as avenues for innovation, economic growth and material expansion. The World Bank offers this vision:

> A modern regime for IPR is critical to promoting innovation and facilitating technology commercialization. Intellectual property rights are an important inventive for encouraging greater innovative effort. This is becoming increasingly important now that India has critical mass and greater capacity for creating cutting edge knowledge.[9]

This vision clashes with the Mahatma's vision of civilization and possibilities for India. Not only did he condemn British (and Western) political institutions as riddled with lack of discipline and thought, concerned with entrenching its own power "rather than furthering public welfare,"[10] the Mahatma condemned Western economics as privileging physical comfort and making "bodily welfare the object of life, enslaving men "by temptation of money and of luxuries money can buy."[11] More consistent with the Mahatma's moral, political and economic visions was the plan of economist and sociologist, Radhakamal Mukherjee, who in 1916 critiqued Western industrialization "for its fixation on the division of labor, its difference towards community bonds, and its rejection of transcendentalism."[12] Contra the World Bank's promotion of innovation, Mukherjee advocated for a decentralized system of village economies, along Gandhian principles.

Act without a concern for rewards is in opposition to intellectual property's promotion of "make and take." But there are accommodations and a path to reconciliation. Intellectual property law and policy recognize the role of communal development that does not rest solely on the individualistic pursuit of reward. Sometimes touted in terms of the commons, sometimes in terms of social justice, this alternative understanding of intellectual property rests on the realities of how artists and scientists work—in concert with others, rather than in isolation. Work is often for the pursuit of nobler goals: art for its own sake, knowledge for the pure understanding. Accompanying these social platforms for art and science is economic theories that recognize partial appropriation of gains in promoting innovation. While full appropriation would assert that intellectual property rights holders are entitled to the full economic value of the work they create, meaning all that can be earned in every possible exploitation of the rights, partial appropriation recognizes that sharing the economic rewards from

[9] Carl Dahlman et al., Creating and Commercializing Knowledge in Mark A. Dutz, ed., Unleashing India's Innovation: Towards Sustainable and Inclusive Growth 71 (The World Bank 2007).

[10] Madhav Khosla, India's Founding Moment: The Constitution of a Most Surprising Democracy 75 (2020).

[11] Id. at 75–6.

[12] Id. at 81.

intellectual property can benefit follow-on innovation, creative appropriators and educational uses.[13]

Still one may doubt how an individual, not to mention society, can survive without clinging to rewards as motivation. This challenge is at the heart of what it means to live in the world. One can forsake the world's bounty, or one can seek them rapaciously. One can also seek a balance between the pursuit of rewards and other virtues. Lord Krishn offers Arjun not only an encouragement to act but also to live without over attachment. As a practical course for law and policy, this encouragement may suggest a balance between the simplistic village economies extolled by Dr. Mukherjee in 1916 and the hard-driving industrialization echoing in directives from The World Bank. But Lord Krishn, and Gandhi, does point toward a practical course of action, one whose fruits blossom in specific instances, rather than in big theory. A few examples from intellectual property can illustrate.

The Gita teaches the ethics of decision making. As applied to intellectual property, the ethical theory might pose limitations to the exercise of self-interest by rights owners who seek to maximize their economic returns through strict enforcement of intellectual property rights. I am less concerned with changing behavior—my assumption is that individuals will pursue their narrow self-interest. But over time, how one conceives of one's interest might evolve to include broader constituencies and relationships that extend beyond one's immediate material concerns. That said, I do not expect individuals to change their behavior and certainly not to engage in the soul searching of Arjun. Intellectual property rights holders will not realistically adjust their sights to include the broad consequences of enforcing patents, copyrights or other types of rights on society. Nor do I think the state—through its instrumentalities of the courts and the legislature—can nudge rights holders in a socially beneficial direction. Instead, legal rules should be constituted around ethical norms, such as the nuanced consequentialism I identify in the Gita.

It is more than poetic to compare the debates among legislators and among judges to the back-and-forth of Arjun and Krishn on the battlefield. Some actors agonize over consequences; others point to obligations. But the nuanced consequentialism I discern provides an ethical framework for defining intellectual property rights. While current intellectual property law assumes the primacy of the rights of owners (emphasizing the attachment to legal ownership), nuanced consequentialism would recognize the place of the intellectual property owner in a network of relationships which creates duties and obligations. Sensitivity to the consequences of intellectual property rights is, to quote Professor Sen, sensitive "to agencies and relations in evaluating what is happening in the world."[14]

Three examples illustrate the prescribed "sensitivity." In Mayo v. Prometheus, the Supreme Court addressed the question of whether a medical diagnostic method is

---

[13] See, e.g. Stan Leibowitz, "Copying and Indirect Appropriability: Photocopying of Journals," Journal of Political Economy, October 1985, pp. 945–957.; Brett M. Frischmann, An Economic Theory of Infrastructure and Commons Management, 89 Minn. L. Rev. 917, 919 (2005).

[14] Sen, supra note 5, at 21.

patentable subject matter.[15] The Court ruled against Prometheus, the patent owner, holding that the diagnostic method at issue covered an unpatentable law of nature.[16] In reaching this ruling, the Court looked to the consequences of patenting medical diagnoses and treatment on the decisions and actions of medical professionals.[17] Justice Breyer's opinion, for a unanimous court, illustrates two points from my argument. First, the Court does not emphasize the primacy of the patent owner's interests, which would support a very broad conception of patentable subject matter. Instead, the Court recognizes limits on patent ownership.[18]

The nature of this limitation illustrates my second point. By identifying the consequences of broad patent rights, the Court ruled that these consequences would justify a narrowing of patentable subject matter.[19] Although couched in the legal category of "law of nature," the limitation as reflected in the Court's reasoning builds on specific relations and agencies. In short, the rights of the patent owner hinder the duty of the medical practitioner. To avoid this conflict, the Court created an exception to the rights of the patent owner.

The analysis in Prometheus goes beyond identifying juridical binary relationships of rights and duties. Implicit is a duty not to interfere with the duties of others. But I am less interested in these formal juridical pairings than in the Court's identification of the important consequences of its decision. The Court's reasoning demonstrates a useful style of consequentialism. Many critics of Prometheus' patent on diagnosing and treating Crohn's disease emphasized the harmful effects on patients and medical costs.[20] The Court, however, did not take this tack. Medical practitioners, and not patients, were the immediate focus for the Court. Knowledge of the patent would inhibit the ability of the medical professionals to communicate with patients and carry out their duties to treat and heal. Consequences matter but are cabined by the set of relationships implicated by the invention. The Prometheus case raises a challenge to the position of Krishn the charioteer. Do one's duty, even as an inventor and patentee, but what if one's duty conflicts with the obligations of others? To answer this question, one must turn to Arjun's self-questioning to identify the scope of consequences and limits on duty.

The guiding principle I advocate is one of recognizing the consequences of intellectual property rights for the duties of third parties, such as healthcare providers and medical practitioners. I will present two further examples that illustrate additional third parties that are affected by intellectual property rights. The first example comes from the fair use doctrine in copyright. The second addresses the first sale doctrine,

---

[15] Mayo Collaborative Servs. v. Prometheus Labs., Inc., 132 S. Ct. 1289 (2012).

[16] Id. at 1293.

[17] Id. at 1297–98.

[18] Id. at 1301–02.

[19] Id. at 1304–05 (detailing effects of patents on physician conduct).

[20] See, e.g., Brief for AARP and Public Patent Foundation as Amici Curiae Supporting Petitioners at 2–3, Mayo Collaborative Servs. v. Prometheus Labs., Inc., 132 S. Ct. 1289 (2012) (No. 10–1150) (arguing that allowing patents based merely on medical correlations would increase costs and reduce quality of care).

a limitation on intellectual property rights arising under copyright, patent and trademark laws. Both doctrines are relevant because of the debates they foster about rights. Courts have been very careful in not calling "fair use" a right of users.[21] Instead, judges adopt the formal designation of the fair use "defense." Analogously, courts do not treat first sale as a right to resell or redistribute a copyrighted (or patented or trademarked) work, but as a limitation on intellectual property arising from competition policy. Behind these formal designations is a focus on consequentialism. The nuanced consequentialism espoused in this article can serve as a model for reforming these two controversial areas of law.

Under current application, fair use in copyright suffers for emphasizing the primacy of the copyright owner's rights to commercially exploit the copyrighted work.[22] An unauthorized use of a copyrighted work is fair only if the use does not produce a commercial substitute for the copyrighted work. An exact copying of all the elements of work would rarely be considered fair unless the full scale copying transformed the work in some way or was necessary for communicative value.[23] However, even uses of portions of a work can fall out from fair use if these uses would exploit a market that the copyright owner could enter, as, for example, with university course packs,[24] with the sampling of sound recordings,[25] with the uploading of film clips on social networking sites[26] and with the display of excerpts from books.[27]

In each of these examples, the fair use analysis would be attentive to the copyright law and the interests it serves to promote. Vesting strong rights in the copyright owners interferes with the creative endeavors of educators, musicians, movie documentarians and digitizers of books. Each of these alleged infringers are also creative individuals who have audiences for their works. The challenge for the fair use doctrine is to delineate limitations on copyright that take into consideration the consequences of enforcing the rights of owners. As illustrated in the Prometheus opinion, attention to relations and agencies of other actors is desirable.

---

[21] See, e.g., Golan v. Holder, 132 S. Ct. 873 (2012) (referring to fair use as an accommodation).

[22] See Barton Beebe, An Empirical Study of U.S. Copyright Fair Use Opinions, 1978–2005, 156 U. Pa. L. Rev. 549 (2008) (discussing how case law has minimized the fair use doctrine).

[23] See, e.g., Hustler Magazine v. Moral Majority, Inc., 796 F.2d 1148 (9th Cir. 1986) (holding that a full reproduction of a copyrighted work was fair use because it was used for an activity that plaintiff could not have used for economic gain).

[24] See, e.g., Cambridge Univ. Press v. Becker, 863 F.Supp.2d 1190 (N.D. Ga. 2012) (holding that copyrights in out-of-print textbooks still had economic value because of demand from permissions for excerpts).

[25] See, e.g., Bridgeport Music, Inc. v. Dimension Films, 410 F.3d 792 (6th Cir. 2005) (holding that there is a direct market for samples of sound recordings).

[26] See, e.g., Viacom Int'l., Inc. v. YouTube, Inc., 676 F.3d 19 (2d Cir. 2012) (holding that an entity like YouTube cannot knowingly allow users to post infringing content).

[27] See, e.g., Authors Guild v. Google, Inc., 282 F.R.D. 384 (S.D.N.Y. 2012) (concerning unauthorized duplication and display of copyrighted books on the Internet).

The first sale doctrine, as applied, is perhaps more attuned to the type of consequentialism I am advocating.[28] In a number of cases, courts have confronted the question of when an intellectual property owner can prevent redistribution of a work after an initial dissemination of the protected work. In Kirtsaeng v. Wiley Publishing, the Supreme Court addressed this broad question in the context of reselling imported textbooks.[29] In Bowman v. Monsanto, the issue of reusing genetically modified and patented seeds implicates the first sale doctrine for purchased seeds.[30] Whether the first sale doctrine allows the petitioners in these two cases to make use of the protected items rests on if and how the Court construes the consequences of allowing the reuse. In Kirtsaeng, lower courts (and the Supreme Court in its first consideration of this issue) 62[31] grappled with statutory language to discern the limitations on copyright. The intermediate appellate court in Bowman held that such reuse "eviscerated" the patent owners' rights and therefore concluded that the first sale doctrine would not apply.[32] The Supreme Court rejected this broad approach although finding for the patent owner.[33] I propose that courts need to start with a consideration of consequences to determine whether the first sale doctrine provides a relevant defense. A consequentialist approach was the method in early first sale doctrine cases in the nineteenth and twentieth centuries.[34] The Supreme Court should start with that approach.

The verbal sparring of Arjun and Krishn provides an ethical framework from which to rethink intellectual property law. We can imagine the applications to particular cases from the USA. But particular cases do not by themselves organize a society. How would a society committed to innovation adopt intellectual property rights along Lord Krishn's principles of acting without the pull of rewards, of making without taking? Professor Anil Gupta offers such a vision in his "Grass Roots Innovation," a book that sets forth the principles underlying his Honey Bee Network.[35] Professor Gupta, a renowned professor of management, offers a counter to the "old model of

---

[28] For a full discussion of first sale doctrine within the broader framework of exhaustion of rights, see Shubha Ghosh & Irene Calboli, Exhaustion of Intellectual Property Rights (2018); Péter Mezei, Copyright Exhaustion (2018).

[29] See Kirtsaeng v. John Wiley & Sons, Inc., 133 S. Ct. 1351 (2013).

[30] See Bowman v. Monsanto Co., 133 S. Ct. 1761 (2013).

[31] See Costco Wholesale Corp. v. Omega, S.A., 131 S. Ct. 565 (2010) (mem.).

[32] See Monsanto Co. v. Bowman, 657 F.3d 1341, 1348 (2011).

[33] See Bowman, 133 S. Ct. at 1769.

[34] See, e.g., Bobbs-Merrill Co. v. Straus, 210 U.S. 339 (1908) (holding that the first sale doctrine prevents a copyright holder from dictating the resale price); Adams v. Burke, 84 U.S. 453 (1873) (holding that while patents grant exclusive rights to make and sell goods, they cannot restrict the use of those goods after the first sale); see Kirtsaeng v. John Wiley & Sons, Inc., 133 S. Ct. 1351 (2013) (adopting a broad reading of the first sale doctrine in copyright based on a consideration of common law, statute and consequences).

[35] Anil K. Gupta, Grass Roots Innovation: Minds on the Margin Are Not Marginal Minds (2016). For details of the Honey Bee Network, see http://tcleadership.org/the-honey-bee-network/. I note here in passing the interesting coincidence that Professor Gupta is a graduate of Kurukshetra University in Haryana.

centralized manufacturing and decentralized consumption."[36] Through the Honey Bee Network, he promotes problem solving at the local, village level to address issues of irrigation, sanitation, finance and healthcare delivery. Innovation festivals showcase many inventions from villages throughout India and inventions to address sometimes overlooked needs for the visually impaired and physically disabled. Many of his principles parallel those of start-up culture in the USA and Europe attempt to unleash entrepreneurial energies at the local level, in universities, economically disadvantaged communities and rural areas. Although it would be naïve to equate these initiatives with Gandhian principles or Lord Krishn's directive, the connections are worth considering. One direction that Professor Gupta points to is action, creation for its own benefits and not the accumulation of material rewards.

What I have set forth is a normative argument. One should not confuse it with so-called faith-based approaches to intellectual property (and to legal policy more broadly).[37] The latter base policy and legal decisions on moral authority, rather than facts. Normative arguments are prescriptive and run parallel to analytical and empirical arguments. But action based on a normative argument needs to be supported by facts. To simply act without an understanding of the actual and potential consequences of one's acts is foolish. Mahatma reminds of this: "In regard to every action, one must know the result that is expected to follow, the means thereto, and the capacity for it."[38] But often facts are confused with statistics and data, which are without doubt important for decision making and action. But the appeal to figures should not be an obsession that eclipses experience. In extolling us to act and avoid inaction, Lord Krishn is reminding us to experience the world. Presumably, from that experience one can gain knowledge, even for its own sake, that can lend itself to practical action. Such is the lesson from Kurukshetra.

References

Abella A (2009) Soldiers of reason: The RAND corporation and the rise of American Empire. Houghton Miflin, Boston

Dahlman C et al (2007) Creating and commercializing knowledge. In: Dutz A (ed) Unleashing India's innovation: towards sustainable and inclusive growth 71. The World Bank, Washington, DC

Frischmann BM (2007) An economic theory of infrastructure and commons management. Minn L Rev 89:917

Gandhi M (2000) Bhagavad Gita according to Gandhi. North Atlantic Books, New York City

Gupta AK (2016) Grass roots innovation: minds on the margin are not marginal minds. Penguin Random House, India

Sen A (2000) The idea of justice. Harvard University Press, Cambridge

Mitchell S (2000) (trans) Bhagavad Gita. Harmony Books, New York City

---

[36] Id. at 221.

[37] See, e.g., Mark A. Lemley, Faith-Based Intellectual Property, 62 UCLA L. Rev. 1328 (2015).

[38] See Footnote 4, supra.

Chapter 24
Intellectual Property Duties: Exhumation, Exploration and Examination

Raman Mittal

1 Introduction

While much attention has been given to intellectual property rights, this chapter focuses on the corresponding duties that emanate from the creation, protection and exploitation of intellectual property. It presents an evaluation of the principle of utilitarianism and particularly how it falls short of being all embracive and how it focuses on ends while conveniently forsaking the means. On the contrary, the theory of trusteeship proposed by Gandhi seeks to work towards the welfare of all by postulating that property has to be held by the owner for the benefit of others. The Constitution of India by way of incorporating fundamental duties enjoins all citizens to develop scientific temper; therefore, creativity becomes a responsibility of all of us. An analysis of the theory of exclusivity of rights shows how from the right to exclude follows the duty to include. Once intellectual property is created, its products need to be distributed and the chapter discusses the duties of various stakeholders in such distribution particularly in fair dealing, maintaining quality of products and compulsory licences.

R. Mittal (✉)
Professor, Campus Law Centre, Faculty of Law, University of Delhi, Delhi, India
e-mail: mittalraman@gmail.com

R. Mittal and K. K. Singh (eds.), *Relevance of Duties in the Contemporary World*,
https://doi.org/10.1007/978-981-19-1836-0_24

2 Intellectual Property, Utilitarianism and Gandhi

Eighteenth century British philosopher Jeremy Bentham is known to have first propounded the theory of utilitarianism which was later expanded and refined by John Stuart Mill.[1] Utilitarian philosophers judge an action as to whether it is right or wrong on the basis of the principle of utility. Accordingly, an action will be regarded as good if and only if it promotes maximum happiness to the maximum number of people and minimum pain to the minimum number of people.

Gandhi was not in favour of such utilitarianism, and his opposition to it was based on two reasons. First, a satisfaction with the principle of 'greatest good of greatest number' allows us to forsake some persons. He believed that the principle of utilitarianism would provide insufficient protection for the forsaken minority by treating them as mere numbers as following this principle some persons, even though comprising a minority of the entire population, could conveniently be left out.[2] Gandhi believed that the good of the individual is contained in the good of all.[3] He was thus against of the idea that for the benefit of a majority, a minority of society could have their interests and welfare altogether ignored, not just in practice, but additionally as a matter of principle.[4]

Second, this equation of utilitarianism puts 'ends' as the only objective while conveniently overlooking the 'means'. Gandhi believed in the inseparability of means and ends, and therefore, he disapproved of this theory. It may be the case, where the actions are good, but the means are foul. He said[5]:

> A votary of Ahimsa (non-violence) cannot subscribe to the utilitarian formula (of the greatest good of the greatest number). He will strive for the greatest good of all and die in the attempt to realize the ideal. He will, therefore, be willing to die, so that the others may live.... The greatest good of all inevitably includes the good of the greatest number, and therefore, he and the utilitarian will converge in many points in their career but there does come a time when they must part company, and even work in opposite directions.

Gandhi was greatly influenced by the core idea of John Ruskin's Unto This Last: The good of the individual is contained in the good of all. He was sincerely interested in *sarvodaya*[6] signifying 'universal uplift' or 'progress of all'. He firmly

---

[1] Mill defines utilitarianism as follows: The creed which accepts as the foundation of morals, Utility, or the Greatest Happiness Principle, holds that actions are right in proportion as they tend to promote happiness, wrong as they tend to produce the reverse of happiness. See, Mill, J. S., Utilitarianism, Fraser's Magazine, London, 1879, P-9.

[2] M. K. Gandhi, *Sarvodaya* 4 (1954).

[3] M. K. Gandhi, *The Story of My Experiments With Truth*, Part IV, Chapter xviii.

[4] Shanti S. Gupta, The Economic Philosophy of Mahatma Gandhi 42 (1994). See, Balganesh, Shyamkrishna, "Gandhi and Copyright Pragmatism" (2013). Faculty Scholarship at Penn Law. 445. https://scholarship.law.upenn.edu/faculty_scholarship/445.

[5] M. K. Gandhi, *Young India*, 9 December 1926.

[6] The term was used by Gandhi as the title of his 1908 translation of John Ruskin's tract on political economy, *Unto This Last*, and Gandhi came to use the term for the ideal of his own

believed that the uplift of one cannot be done at the cost of the welfare of another. Therefore, he was not satisfied with utilitarianism and said, 'In comparison with *sarvodaya*, utilitarianism shows a lack of dignity and humanity'.[7] Gandhi rejected utilitarianism as he desired a richer and all embracive theory that could cater to 'all' and not just 'majority'. In the light of facts like these, if one were to judge the issue on purely practical grounds alone, *sarvodaya* would appear to be more dignified and humane doctrine.

Intellectual property law is frequently justified on the basis of utilitarian principle.[8] That means it is justifiable to forsake a minority of individuals from the benefits of intellectual property. In the absence of a better theory of intellectual property, scholars have continued to justify such exclusion. This exclusion becomes soul searching when the discussion centres around copyright, patent and trade secret law especially in the context of availability of educational materials, availability of life saving drugs and access to new technologies. However, if we see and interpret it in the light of duties of the owner of intellectual property, then it can become all inclusive.

3 Duty to Create and Invent

Creativity is seminal to mankind and characterises our species. In the context of intellectual property, creativity manifests itself through human endeavours in the fields of scientific inventions, development of new business models and expression of original literary, dramatic, musical and artistic works. More creativity in these fields of science, arts and commerce will ultimately enrich our society, and the benefits that stem out of creativity will percolate to the masses ameliorating their health while also making their lives more comfortable and culturally vibrant. In today's world, creativity is fundamentally important for our social, economic and cultural well-being. Hence, our lives are increasingly being shaped by the creativity that takes place around us. This call for creativity and the corresponding duty to create stems from Article 51A of the Constitution of India.

The Constitution of India by way of incorporating fundamental duties enjoins all citizens to develop scientific temper.[9] The development of scientific temper will naturally induce creativity in various fields which will not only lead to self-realisation of the creator but also help alleviate hunger, poverty and disease

political philosophy. See, Bondurant, Joan. *Conquest of Violence: The Gandhian Philosophy of Conflict.* (Princeton, 1958) p. 156.

[7] Glyn Richards, The Philosophy of Gandhi, Calcutta: Rupa and Co., 1991, p. 74.

[8] See, Merges, Robert P., Menell, Peter S., Lemley, Mark A. and Jorde, Thomas M., Intellectual Property in the New Technological Age, New York, Aspen Publishers, Inc. (1997). The United States Constitution expressly conditions the grant of power to Congress to create patent and copyright laws upon a utilitarian foundation: 'to Promote the Progress of Science and useful Arts'.

[9] Art. 51A(h), Constitution of India: It shall be the duty of every citizen of India to develop the scientific temper, humanism and the spirit of inquiry and reform.

while making ideal use of abundant natural resources of our country. Development of scientific temper will also offer viable solutions to many of the future maladies that will challenge us in times to come.

The fundamental duty to develop scientific temper, therefore, is not just a pedantic or technical language but is meant to be a response and solution to various challenges that would arise from time to time in our society. This duty to develop scientific temper is supplemented by the fundamental duty to strive towards excellence in all spheres of activity so that we rise to higher levels of achievement.[10] The invention of new medicines, machinery and instruments will indeed permit us to solve our problems and also help others too.

The genesis of scientific temper and its further development is often associated with Charles Darwin, who in a letter to E.B. Aveling wrote, 'freedom of thought is best promoted by the gradual illumination of men's minds, which follows from the advance of science'.[11] The great spiritual master Osho has said, 'Science has great possibilities, just we have not yet been able to use those possibilities'.[12] Indeed, the scientists are the most important people for the survival of humanity. The first Prime Minister Nehru wanted the rationalism of science to spread throughout the length and breadth of our land. To him, this appeared to be the only method of alleviating the suffering of our country. To him, scientific temper was the sword which by its rationalism could fight the darkest forces of superstition. It was also the shield which could protect the people of India from prejudice, ignorance and obscurantism which have kept the people enslaved and degraded all these years. Only by having the scientific temper in every one, India could launch a new adventure into the unknown.[13]

4 Protection of Intellectual Property as Exclusive Rights and Corresponding Duties

Thomas Jefferson, in a letter to Isaac McPherson, had said,[14] 'If nature has made any one thing less susceptible than all others of exclusive property, it is the action of the thinking power called an idea, which an individual may exclusively possess as long as he keeps it to himself; but the moment it is divulged, it forces itself into the

[10] Art. 51A(j), Constitution of India: It shall be the duty of every citizen of India to strive towards excellence in all spheres of individual and collective activity so that the nation constantly rises to higher levels of endeavour and achievement.

[11] Darwin, Charles, *Darwin Correspondence Project, Darwin, C. R. to Aveling, E. B. 13 Oct 1880.* [From a letter written by Charles Darwin to E.B. Aveling October 13th, 1880].

[12] Osho, *The Golden Future,* Ch 36, See, https://www.osho.com/osho-online-library/osho-talks/sexuality-enjoyment-scientists-40fd5290-7ff?p=844cca49a539c1938fe4e1b5b6a99708.

[13] *Hulikal Nataraju* v. *State of Karnataka*, para. 16, W.P.N0. 1750/2008, Karnataka HC, Sept. 13, 2010.

[14] Thomas Jefferson, Letter to Isaac McPherson dated 13 August 1813, available at: https://founders.archives.gov/documents/Jefferson/03-06-02-0322.

possession of everyone, and the receiver cannot dispossess himself of it. Its peculiar character, too, is that no one possesses the less, because every other possesses the whole of it. He who receives an idea from me, receives instruction himself without lessening mine; as he who lights his taper at mine, receives light without darkening me'. The transformation of idea into expression and execution bestows such transformer with exclusive rights which grant the owners of intellectual property the right to exclude others from using these rights without authorization. This part presents an analysis of how from the right to exclude follows the duty to include.

An exclusive right is a non-tangible prerogative guaranteed by law to a person to perform an action or acquire a benefit and to permit or deny all others the right to perform the same action or to acquire the same benefit. Exclusive rights are understood to be a form of monopoly.[15] The rights granted by intellectual property laws are exclusive in nature and exclusivity forms the conceptual basis for the ownership of intellectual property. That means without the permission of intellectual property owner no one is permitted to use his property.

Exclusivity of rights is popularly understood to mean that the owner of intellectual property has the right to restrain all others from the use and enjoyment of that property. However, appreciating the grant of exclusivity only as a right to exclude others covers only half the spectrum of intellectual property; the other half being the possibility or the capacity to include others. The owner of intellectual property being the owner of nonrival rights can invite others to participate in the exploitation or utilisation of the property. This capacity of permitting others in the exploitation and utilisation of intellectual property is the corresponding duty of the owner of intellectual property. Therefore, while one side of the coin of exclusivity represents the right to exclude all others, the other side embodies the duty to include others.

Gandhi considered private property as a necessary evil. Evil, because he felt it was the root cause of many ills in our society and necessary, as it was not possible to do away with the institution of property. Therefore, in his quest for reforming the institution of property he developed the concept of trusteeship which means that private property has to be held by the owner for the benefit of others. Asked, 'how would you in a word describe the rich man's legitimate position?', Gandhi replied, 'That of a trustee'.[16]

Gandhi's trusteeship is not actually a substitute for the institution of private property, rather it is a way of looking at property with a different orientation. In this approach, the owner is not divested of his interest in the property that he either inherited or acquired, albeit the owner acquires and holds it for the benefit of all. Again it does not mean that the owner cannot use his property for his own benefit at

---

[15] Adam Smith described it as desirable monopolies. See, Adam Smith, Lectures on Jurisprudence 83 (R.L. Meek, D.D. Raphael & P.G. Stein eds., Oxford Univ. Press 1978) (1896). Thomas Jefferson viewed both copyrights and patents as dangerous government "monopolies" that should be strictly limited, if they were to be granted at all. See, Letter to James Madison, August 28, 1789, in 7 The Writings of Thomas Jefferson 444, 451 (Andrew A. Lipscomb, ed. 1904).

[16] M. K. Gandhi, Harijan, 1–6-1935, pp. 121–22.

all. The owner is not required to forsake his interests in favour of others as long as his interests and requirements are legitimate and reasonable. Referring to the rights of owners Gandhi said, ‘They would be allowed to retain the stewardship of their possessions and to use their talent to increase the wealth, not for their own sakes, but for the sake of the nation and, therefore, without exploitation’.[17] It seems that Gandhi, while arriving at the concept of trusteeship, drew upon the concept of fiduciary obligations that trust law necessarily binds the trustees with.[18] Gandhi based the doctrine of trusteeship on the first verse[19] of Isopanisad which in essence means, ‘Do not covet, whose, after all is wealth?’.[20]

According to Gandhi, private property was justifiable only when owners perceived themselves as trustees who held their property not in the pursuit of their own selfish interest, but instead for the benefit of society at large. Proprietary ownership thus had to transform into a form of trusteeship, wherein owners would place more emphasis on the obligations that come with it rather than just the pursuit of individual self-interest.

The idea of trusteeship subjects the institution of property to a consequentialist purpose—social welfare. What is clearly rejected in this formulation is the idea of property as an individual’s despotic dominion.[21] To the extent that private ownership was a valid institution to Gandhi, it revolved around the affirmative obligations cast on owners to look out for and act in the interest of those without wealth and assets, the central idea behind trusteeship.[22] Gandhi was, therefore, disdainful of the predominantly rights-oriented approach to property which is gladly oblivious to the correlative duties.[23] In an interview with Nirmal Kumar Bose Gandhi remarked, ‘Love and exclusive possession can never go together’.[24]

Under trusteeship owners of property were thus restricted in pursuing their selfish interest as they were bound by the duties that came along with rights.

---

[17] M. K. Gandhi, Harijan, March 31, 1946, pp. 63–64.

[18] See, Geeta Abrol, “Gandhian Doctrine of Trusteeship and its Relevance to Modern Times”, in J. S. Mathur, Gandhian Thought and Contemporary Society 147 (1974).

[19] ईशावास्यमदिं सर्वं यत्कञ्चि जगत्यां जगत् । तेन त्यक्तेन भुञ्जीथा मा गृधः कस्य स्विद्धनम् ॥ १ ॥ īśāvāsyamidaṃ sarvaṃ yatkiñca jagatyāṃ jagat | tena tyaktena bhuñjīthā mā gṛdhaḥ kasya sviddhanam || 1 ||.

[20] See, Y. Kesavulu, “Gandhian Trusteeship as an ‘Instrument of Human Dignity’” Gandhi Marg, Vol. 25, No. 4, Jan-March, 2004.

[21] Balganesh, Shyamkrishna, “Gandhi and Copyright Pragmatism” (2013). Faculty Scholarship at Penn Law. 445. https://scholarship.law.upenn.edu/faculty_scholarship/445.

[22] Ibid.

[23] Gandhi wrote in Harijan, “Understand that your wealth is not yours; it belongs to the people. Take what you require for your legitimate needs, and use the remainder for society.” See, M. K. Gandhi, *Harijan*, February 1, 1942, p, 20.

[24] M. K. Gandhi, Trusteeship, available at: https://www.mkgandhi.org/articles/gandhis-interview-with-nirmal-kumar-bose.html#:~:text=Love%20and%20exclusive%20possession%20can%20never%20go%20together.&text=So%20a%20man%20can%20only,the%20sake%20of%20human%20service.

According to Gandhi, 'the true source of rights is duty. If we all discharge our duties, rights will not be far to seek. If leaving duties unperformed we run after rights, they will escape us like a will-o'-the-wisp. The more we pursue them, the farther will they fly. The same teaching has been embodied by Krishn in the immortal words: "Action alone is thine. Leave thou the fruit severely alone." Action is duty; fruit is the right'.[25] Exhibiting confidence Gandhi himself said, 'My theory of trusteeship is no make-shift, certainly no camouflage. I am confident that it will survive all other theories. It has the sanction of philosophy and religion behind it.… No other theory is compatible with non-violence'.[26]

Gandhi was alive to the challenges the concept of trusteeship would face when it would be sought to be implemented in the society. On its practicality he said, 'You may say that trusteeship is a legal fiction. But if people meditate over it constantly and try to act up to it, then life on earth would be governed far more by love than it is at present. Absolute trusteeship is an abstraction like Euclid's-definition of a point, and is equally unattainable. But if we strive for it, we shall be able to go further in realizing a state of equality on earth than by any other method'.[27] Gandhi's critics believe that Gandhi's idea of trusteeship is idealistic and too good to be true and practically implemented in its real spirit. But if the society continually harps on it and also takes practical steps for its implementation, then the life on the planet would be free from exploitation and unnecessary domination, thereby avoiding conflict situations. In the case of trusteeship, the social order would be based on cooperation, co-existence and mutual respect.[28] Therefore, in the opinion of Gandhi, trusteeship in its perfect state might be a utopian ideal but still it was an idea worth experimenting with for bringing the desired change in the society.

Gandhi was not in favour of any violent action to bring about artificial equality of wealth amongst the citizens and felt that this could never benefit the society. The Gandhian theory of trusteeship departs significantly from Marxian economic philosophy too. If Marxism is the child of the Industrial Revolution, Gandhian theory can be understood only in the context of certain basic spiritual values.[29] Marxian socialism aims at the annihilation of the class called capitalists, whereas the Gandhian approach is not to destroy the institution, but to look at it in a different perspective where the common man trusts the trustee and the latter is alive to the duties that come with the property he owns.

The theory of trusteeship applies equally to both tangible and intangible property, such as the muscular energy of the labourers and the talents of a Helen

[25] M. K. Gandhi, Young India, January 8, 1925, pp. 15–16.

[26] M. K. Gandhi, Harijan, December 16, 1939, p. 376.

[27] M. K. Gandhi, Trusteeship: Not a Legal Fiction", The Modern Review, October, 1935, p. 412.

[28] See, C. S. Dharmadhikari, "Gandhi's concept of Trusteeship", available at: https://www.mkgandhi.org/trusteeship/chap07.htm.

[29] Y. Kesavulu, "Gandhian Trusteeship as an 'Instrument of Human Dignity'" Gandhi Marg, Vol. 25, No. 4, Jan-March, 2004.

Keller.[30] Gandhi was alive to the importance of creation of wealth in the society, and he recognised the talent of some persons who knew how to create wealth. He said, ‘Society will be the poorer, for it will lose the gifts of a man who knows how to accumulate wealth. The rich man will be left in possession of his wealth, of which he will use what he reasonably requires for his personal needs and will act as a trustee for the remainder to be used for society’.[31] The above statement by Gandhi is significant for intellectual property because the very premise of intellectual property law is that it seeks to incentivise those persons who are talented and permits them to devote themselves in the pursuit of creativity. Gandhi was not against incentives for promotion of scientific inventions. He is known to have organised a competition in 1929, with rupees one lakh as the prize money, calling for entries for an improved design for the charkha. The brief was to create a lightweight, reasonable (costing not more than Rs. 150) version with enhanced productivity.[32]

5 Intellectual Property and the Duty to Distribute

This section narrates the duties of various stakeholders in the distribution of intellectual property products. The idea is to explore laws related to intellectual property and find out the duties that have been prescribed for the owners of intellectual property, their licensees and the state.

5.1 Limitations and Exceptions to Rights: Fair Dealing

Copyright law grants exclusive rights to the owners of copyright. In order to create a balance, while granting these rights, copyright laws around the world have created certain limitations and exceptions to the exclusive rights granted to owners.[33] These limitations and exceptions comprise an enumerated set of defences against an action for infringement of copyright. Such exceptions and limitations allow for the use of a copyrighted work without any requirement of obtaining permission from the owner of copyright.[34] Further, there is no requirement to either pay any fees to the owner

[30] K. G. Mashurwala, *Gandhi and Marx,* Navajivan Trust, Ahmedabad, 1951, p. 79.

[31] M. K. Gandhi, Harijan, August 25, 1940, p. 260-1.

[32] See, http://www.design-theindiastory.com/appliances/floor-charkha.html.

[33] More than forty countries with over one-third of the world’s population have fair use or fair dealing provisions in their copyright laws. These countries are in all regions of the world and at all levels of development. See, Jonathan Band and Jonathan Gerafi, *The Fair Use/Fair Dealing Handbook*, 2015 Policybandwidth, available at: http://infojustice.org/wp-content/uploads/2015/03/fair-use-handbook-march-2015.pdf.

[34] See, S. 52, Copyright Act, 1957.

of copyright or give any notice of usage before or after such use. However, in certain cases there is a requirement of acknowledging such use.[35]

This doctrine of limitations and exceptions has developed over the years as courts have tried to balance the rights of copyright owners with the interests of society in permitting copying in certain limited circumstances. In the absence of these exceptions and limitations, the copyright system would stifle the very creativity that it was meant to foster. The copyright system will be fair only when the exclusive rights granted to the owners are subjected to these exceptions.

Different nomenclatures have been used to refer to such limitations and exceptions. The term 'fair use' is peculiar to the United States.[36] 'Fair dealing' is used in the laws of U.K., Canada, Australia and New Zealand.[37] In India, the expression used is 'Certain acts not to be infringement of copyright'.[38] Some provisions of section 52 of Indian Copyright Act include a specific requirement of fair dealing while the same requirement is conspicuously absent in others. Whatever the statutory nomenclature, these exceptions and limitations have popularly been described either as 'fair use' or 'fair dealing'. Such limitations and exceptions have also been described as 'loophole in copyright law' or 'safety valve of copyright' by publicists.[39] Some scholars have opined that such limitations and exceptions are in fact the 'rights of the public'.[40]

These limitations and exceptions to the exclusive rights of the owners of copyright can also be perceived as correlative duties to such rights. While recognising and protecting the rights of copyright owners, the state has imposed corresponding duties on the owners. What is sought to be achieved by these limitations and exceptions are certain goals with regard to access, convenience, freedom to create, institutional availability, criticism, comment, news reporting, promotion of teaching and learning, research, etc.[41] These are socially laudable purposes.[42]

---

[35] See, S. 52(1)(y)(Proviso), Copyright Act, 1957: "Provided that the provisions of sub-clause (ii) of clause (a), sub-clause (i) of clause (b) and clauses (d), (f), (g), (m) and (p) shall not apply as respects any act unless that act is accompanied by an acknowledgment—(i) identifying the work by its title or other description; and (ii) unless the work is anonymous or the author of the work has previously agreed or required that no acknowledgment of his name should be made, also identifying the author.

[36] The US Copyright law uses the expression "Limitations on exclusive rights: Fair use" in §107.

[37] Chapter III of the UK Copyright Statute uses the expression "Acts Permitted in relation to Copyright Works".

[38] See, S. 52, Copyright Act, 1957.

[39] Timothy Lee Wherry, *The Librarian's Guide to Intellectual Property in the Digital Age: Copyrights, Patents, and Trademarks* at 17, 2002.

[40] See, *The Chancellor, Masters & Scholars of The University of Oxford & Ors* v. *Rameshwari Photocopy Services & Anr.*, 2017 (69) PTC 123 (Del) para. 25.

[41] Deciphering and listing these objectives and purposes and the conditions subject to which these uses can be made is an elaborate exercise which is beyond the scope of this chapter.

[42] See, *Universal City Studios* v. *Sony Corp. of America, 659 F 3d 963 (971–72) (9th Cir 1981) at 479.*

The Berne Convention enjoins the member countries to follow a three-step test for legislating exceptions and limitations in their respective laws. It states, 'It shall be a matter for legislation in the countries of the Union to permit the reproduction of such works in certain special cases, provided that such reproduction does not conflict with a normal exploitation of the work and does not unreasonably prejudice the legitimate interests of the author'.[43] This test in international copyright law examines the legitimacy and fairness of limitations and exceptions under national copyright systems. While the limitations and exceptions keep a check on the scope of rights, the three-step test keeps a check on the limitations and exceptions—trying to maintain the balance between rights and duties under copyright law.

The limitations and exceptions under the Copyright Act, 1957, are listed in a way which makes them specific to work, the use of work, the purpose for which the work is to be used, the person who uses the work, the quantity to be reproduced, the reason for which the work is copied and the medium of reproduction of work. Certain limitations and exceptions mandate that the user does not earn from such use and in some cases the owner of copyright can opt out of them by a notice.[44]

Under the US Copyright Act, determining fair use requires a fact-based analysis that takes into account the purpose and character of the use, the nature of the copyrighted work, the amount and substantiality of the portion used in relation to the copyrighted work as a whole and the effect of the use on the potential market for or value of the copyrighted work.[45] The Delhi High Court in the landmark Delhi University Photocopying case[46] stated that the four-factor test used in the US and other jurisdictions to make a fair use determination does not apply under the Indian law. The court clarified that the fairness is to be determined only by the provisions contained in section 52.[47]

5.2 Duty to Control Quality of Goods or Services Supplied by the Licensee

Quality control by the proprietor of a trade mark over the use of the licenced mark is a duty imposed on the proprietor of trade mark both under common law and statutory law. Under this duty, the licensor of the trade mark is required to regulate

[43] Art. 9.2, Berne Convention, 1886.

[44] See, S. 52, Copyright Act, 1957.

[45] §107, Copyright Act, 1976 (USA).

[46] See, *The Chancellor, Masters & Scholars of The University of Oxford & Ors* v. *Rameshwari Photocopy Services & Anr.*, 2017 (69) PTC 123 (Del).

[47] The Delhi High Court found that preparing academic course packs (namely, compilation of photocopies of parts of books recommended in the syllabus), and distributing them to students does not violate copyright under Copyright Act, 1957.

the quality of the products/services supplied by his licensee. In *Barcamerica International USA Trust* v. *Tyfield Importers, Inc. et al.*,[48] it was stated:

> It is important to keep in mind that 'quality control' does not necessarily mean that the licensed goods or services must be of "high" quality, but merely of equal quality, whether that quality is high, low or middle. The point is that the customers are entitled to assume that the nature and qualify of goods and services sold under the mark at all licensed outlets will be consistent and predictable.

As per general practice of trade, quality control could be achieved in the following manners[49]:

- By specification of the formulae, standards, methods, directions, instructions, etc., to be followed by the licensee;
- By inspection of manufacturing processes, facilities, products, packaging, services, advertising, etc., of the licensee;
- By analysing the samples of the licensee's products.

The consumers have no right to demand goods or services bearing a particular quality from a trade mark proprietor, but they have a right to demand that the goods/services of the proprietor's licensee must match the quality of goods/services supplied by the proprietor himself. Therefore, the corresponding duty lies on the proprietor of the trade mark.

Such duty of quality control by the proprietor of trade mark is mandated by law because without it there is a possibility that the quality of two products sold under the same mark might vary. This may eventually become a source of confusion and deception in the mind of the consumer which is sought to be prevented under the trade mark law by imposing duty on the proprietor of mark. In *SA CNL-Sucal* v. *HAG GF AG*,[50] the European Court of Justice described the essential function of a trade mark as giving to the consumer or ultimate user 'a guarantee of the identity of the origin of the marked product by enabling him to distinguish, without any possible confusion, that product from others of a different provenance'. Apart from duty imposed by law, quality control is exercised by the proprietor of a mark in order to pursue his own interest because if the proprietor fails to enforce quality control, the brand value of the trade mark will decline. Therefore, the necessity of quality control is a function of legal requirements (aimed at protecting public interest) and safeguarding self-interest of the proprietor of the mark.

Merely, the provision for payment of royalty in the licence contract without any clause as to quality control would turn the licence to be a naked licence.[51] Without proper quality control, unscrupulous licensors or licensees could change product

[48] *Barcamerica International USA Trust* v. *Tyfield Importers, Inc. et. al.* 289 F.3d 589, 595-98 (9th Cir.2002).

[49] See, Raman Mittal, "Analysis of the Mysterious Element of Quality Control in Trademark Licensing", JIPR, Vol 15, July 2010, pp 285-292.

[50] *SA CNL-Sucal* v. *HAG GF AG* [1990] 3 CMLR 571, 608.

[51] *Ritz Associates* v. *Ritz-Carlton Co.* 134 USPQ 86 (SDNY 1962).

quality and take advantage of unwary consumers.[52] The absence of quality control could lead to a number of consequences.

First, without a provision as to quality control, the licence contract will not be registered by the Registrar.[53] The grant of registration as 'registered user'[54] is subject to the exercise of proper control by the registered proprietor over the use of the mark by the registered user. The Trade Marks Act requires that the licensor must furnish an affidavit indicating 'the relationship, existing or proposed, between the registered proprietor and the proposed registered user, including particulars showing the *degree of control* by the proprietor over the permitted use which their relationship will confer…'.[55] Second, it is not enough to simply write such terms into the licence and leave it at that. It is incumbent upon the proprietor to *enforce* proper quality control as per the contract over the use of licenced trade mark. If the proprietor fails to perform his duty, the Registrar, either on his on motion or on an application by any person, may cancel the registration of the licence agreement.[56] In pioneer *Hi-Bred International Inc. USA* v. *Pioneer Seed Co. Ltd.*[57], the plaintiff was a US company owning the trade mark 'pioneer' for seeds as it was into research, development, production and marketing of hybrid seeds. The plaintiff had licenced the trade mark to the defendant, an Indian entity, to sell seeds. The plaintiff successfully sought an injunction against the use of the licenced trade mark by the defendant licensee because the defendant had not allowed the licensor to test the quality of seeds produced by the licensee. Third, the absence of quality control could bring into question the very validity of the trade mark. This is because in the absence of quality control the trade mark ceases to perform its essential function as an identifier of the source of goods. The trade mark then could be said to be deceptive, misleading or generic. In these situations, the mark is open to be revoked.[58] Where the character and name 'King Kong' was permitted to be used by multiple licensees for forty five years without subjecting the use to any supervision or control, the court held it to be an abandonment of the trade mark.[59] Fourth, lack of exercise of quality control can be equated with allowing misuse of one's mark. It is the duty of the trade mark proprietor to enforce its mark against misuse, and if he fails to do so, he risks being deemed to have abandoned the mark and thus may lose

---

[52] *Dawn Donut*, 267 F.2d at 367.

[53] See, s. 49(1)(b), Trade Marks Act, 1999.

[54] Licensing of registered trade marks has two aspects—one where the license contract is registered under the Trade Marks Act and the other where the license contract is not so registered. Section 2(1)(r) of the Act defines the expression 'permitted use' which includes use of a trade mark by both registered and unregistered licensees. Where the license contract is registered under the Trade Marks Act, the licensee is known as 'registered user'. Hence, all registered users are licensees but all licensees are not registered users.

[55] See, s. 49(1)(b)(i), Trade Marks Act, 1999.

[56] See, S. 50(1)(d), Trade Marks Act, 1999.

[57] *Hi-Bred International Inc USA* v. *Pioneer Seed Co. Ltd.* 1990 IPLR 17.

[58] S. 57, Trade Marks Act, 1999.

[59] *Universal City Studios Inc.* v. *Nintendo Co. Ltd.* 578 F. Supp. 911 (SDNY 1983).

his rights to the mark. In *Barcamerica International USA Trust* v. *Tyfield Importers, Inc. et. al.*,[60] it was held that: 'Uncontrolled or "naked" licensing may result in the trade mark ceasing to function as a symbol of quality and controlled source.... Consequently, where the licensor fails to exercise adequate quality control over the licensee, a court may find that the trade mark owner has abandoned the trade mark, in which case the owner would be estopped from asserting rights to the trade mark'. Fifth, if the proprietor does not exercise required quality control and allows the quality of products under the licensee's mark to decline, he may be made liable under product liability claims.[61]

5.3 Duty to Grant Compulsory Licence

The owner of intellectual property has the exclusive right to licence it or not; however, this exclusive right is subject to certain limitations. One of these limitations permits the state to grant compulsory licence without the permission of the owner of intellectual property in certain situations.[62] A grant of compulsory licence can be seen as a response mechanism which authorises the state to grant compulsory licence should the owner of intellectual property fail in the performance of his duties which are cast upon him under the relevant intellectual property law. This power of the state to grant compulsory licence can also be perceived as the duty of the state to step in should the owner of intellectual property fail in his duties.

It is the duty of the owner of the patent to work the patented invention in India, make it available and affordable to the public and see to it that the reasonable requirements of public are satisfied. If the patentee fails in performance of these duties,[63] then at any time after the expiration of three years from the date of the grant of a patent, any person interested may make an application to the Controller for grant of compulsory licence of a patent.[64]

---

[60] *Barcamerica International USA Trust* v. *Tyfield Importers, Inc. et. al.* 289 F.3d 589, 595–98 (9th Cir.2002).

[61] Under Product liability a manufacturer, distributor, supplier, retailer, and anyone else who makes a product available to the public could be held responsible for the injuries that product causes. See, Raman Mittal, "Analysis of the Mysterious Element of Quality Control in Trademark Licensing", JIPR, Vol 15, July 2010, pp 285-292.

[62] The provisions for such compulsory licenses exist in Patents At, Copyright Act and Semiconductor Act.

[63] S. 84(1), Patents Act, 1970. The grounds for such an application may be: (a) that the reasonable requirements of the public with respect to the patented invention have not been satisfied, or.

(b) that the patented invention is not available to the public at a reasonably affordable price, or.

(c) that the patented invention is not worked in the territory of India.

[64] S. 92 of the Patents Act authorizes the Controller to grant compulsory licenses suo motu pursuant to a notification issued by the Central Government in cases of "national emergency" or "extreme urgency" or "public non-commercial use". India's first ever compulsory license was granted by the Patent Office on March 9, 2012, to Natco Pharma for the generic production of

In case of copyright, the owner has a duty to make his work available to the public at prices which are affordable and reasonable. There are provisions for grant of compulsory licences in case the copyright owner fails to perform his duties. Therefore, a failure on the part of copyright owner to perform his duties triggers a duty of the state to step in and take over such duties of the copyright owner. These duties command the state to grant compulsory licences in various situations some of which are described below. In these situations, the state becomes a watchdog of public interest—for it is under a duty to grant compulsory licence to a person who would best serve the public interest.

Any person may make a complaint regarding an Indian work, during its term of copyright, which has been published or performed in public and apply for compulsory licence if the work has been withheld from the public.[65] In case of an unpublished Indian work whose author is dead or unknown or untraceable or whose owner cannot be found, any person may apply for issuance of a compulsory licence to publish such work or a translation thereof in any language.[66] In case of an unpublished Indian work whose author is dead, the Central Government may, if it considers that the publication of the work is desirable in the national interest, require the heirs, executors or legal representatives of the author to publish such work.[67] Any person may apply for a licence to produce and publish a translation of a literary or dramatic work in any language after a period of seven years from the first publication of the work.[68] Any person may apply for a licence to produce and publish a translation, in printed or analogous forms of reproduction, of a literary or dramatic work, other than an Indian work, in any language in general use in India if such translation is required for the purposes of teaching, scholarship or research.[69] Any person working for the benefit of persons with disability on a profit basis can obtain a compulsory licence to publish any copyrighted work for the benefit of such disabled persons.[70] The provision is designed to facilitate the issuance of compulsory licence for the conversion of work in any format for the use of the disabled persons.

Bayer Corporation's Nexavar, a life saving medicine used for treating Liver and Kidney Cancer. Bayers sold this drug at exorbitant rates, with one month's worth of dosage costing around Rs. 2.8 Lakh. Natco Pharma offered to sell it around for Rs 9000, making it affordable for people belonging to every stratum. All the 3 conditions of section 84 were fulfilled and the decision was taken for the benefit of general public.

[65] S. 31(1), Copyright Act, 1957.

[66] S. 31A(1), Copyright Act, 1957.

[67] S. 31A(6), Copyright Act, 1957.

[68] S. 32(1), Copyright Act, 1957.

[69] S. 32(1A), Copyright Act, 1957.

[70] S. 31B(1), Copyright Act, 1957. This provision is applicable in cases where S. 52(1)(zb), which grants similar rights under different situations, does not apply.

5.4 *Duty of Licensee to Publish*

It is the duty of an assignee or licensee to exercise the rights transferred to him. If he fails to make sufficient exercise of the rights transferred to him and such failure is not attributable to any act or omission on his part then, on receipt of a complaint from the assignor or licensor the licence or assignment can be revoked.[71]

6 Conclusion—The Delicate Balance

Man was a hunter and when he started to gather
Law and property were then born together
When was it? It's not in my memory's lather
We know it riding only on imagination's feather

When things were available in nature for free
Then they belonged to the marauder's spree
To avoid the disputes being decided by blood
The norm of ownership sprouted like a little bud

From movable to immovable the bud continued to grow
Things then belonged to the sweat of the brow
Man's labour was the subject then to protect
To own more became a matter of respect

Limited were the things created with labour
But man wanted to own more than his neighbour
Intellectual creations were added to the list
Man then wanted to capture whole world in his fist

When 'exclusive' was the genre of all his right
Drunk he became with the wine of his might
Bothered he was not about the people's plight
Who would then give the mighty a fight?

[71] S. 19A(1), Copyright Act, 1957.

To transmute to order from such a chaos
'Public interest' soon came across
Though one is still permitted to own
But of sharing you cannot now be shorn

As the people's lawyer laid bare this plea
It were the masses who shouted out with glee
But wait! Are we not approaching the same old spree?
Where all things were set just for free

Public interest came as a gift to wonder
But even this can verily become a plunder
Is it in man's destiny to go round and round?
And continue eternally with the same old wound?

Owning and sharing must go hand in hand
For expression, for invention and also for that famous brand
Striking this balance is like playing with glass
Delicate it remains even for the men of class[72]

Intellectual property discourse has been focussed on the rights of the owner while paying little attention to the corresponding duties that come along with the rights. In a world where intellectual property has become important in almost all segments of our society, a focus on duties becomes crucial to respond to myriads of challenges like access to medicines, education, technology and quality products. Emphasis on duties along with rights is the only possible solution to resolve the conflicts surrounding the theory and practice of intellectual property and to be able to realise the ancient Sanskrit aphorism 'sarve bhavantu sukhinaḥ'[73] which is also a part of prayer sending out a wish to the universe wishing 'happiness of all'.

[72] Raman Mittal, The Delicate Balance, https://spicyip.com/2013/11/guest-post-the-delicate-balance-a-poem-on-ip-3.html.

[73] The Sanskrit verse 'sarve bhavantu sukhinaḥ' (सर्वे भवन्तु सुखनिः) can be found in ancient Sanskrit texts—Garuḍa Purāṇa (35.51), Aśīrvacanam 2 of itihāsa samuccaya and Mantrabhāṣya of Uvaṭa.

Chapter 25
Gandhian Philosophy and Indian Intellectual Property

Enrico Bonadio, Krishna Ravi Srinivas, Balaji Parthasarathy Iyengar, and Atreya Choudhary

1 Introduction

In this chapter, we discuss how certain aspects of Gandhian philosophy seem to be reflected in some areas of the Indian intellectual property (IP) system. Such reflection can be appreciated even though Mahatma Gandhi died more than 70 years ago. After all, his thoughts still have an evident and lasting impact on many sectors of Indian society.

Curiously enough, Gandhi was not born into a family environment of simple living lifestyle and had his own share of rebellion phase in his early years, which included eating meat and smoking cigarettes. Yet, he was directed towards legal studies by his father and in 1888 finished his law school in London at the Inns of Court School of Law (which much later in the late twentieth century merged into The City Law School, a faculty of City, University of London). In the British capital, he joined the vegetarian movement and devoted himself to a meatless diet. His life changing moment occurred when an event made him question his own existence. In June 1883, Gandhi, who was at that time 23 years old, was travelling to Pretoria, South Africa, in the first-class area of the train and a white man did not

E. Bonadio (✉)
Reader, The City Law School City, University of London, London, UK
e-mail: enrico.bonadio.1@city.ac.uk

K. R. Srinivas
Consultant, Research and Information System for Developing Countries (RIS), New Delhi, India

B. P. Iyengar
Consulting Scientist, Business Liaison & Patent Analyst, Bangalore, India

A. Choudhary
Legal Associate, WebLegal, Trani, Italy

R. Mittal and K. K. Singh (eds.), *Relevance of Duties in the Contemporary World*,
https://doi.org/10.1007/978-981-19-1836-0_25

approve of a brown person being in the same compartment, even though Gandhi had purchased the first-class ticket. His civil disobedience started from there and committed to voluntary simplicity. As a true acolyte of *aparigrah*—the virtue of non-possessiveness—[1]Gandhi relinquished his home and abode. He also evoked some of his votaries to surrender their possessions and join the *ashrams*, which represent the spiritual hermitage in Indian religions. However, he could not set his ideals in full motion because of his pre-engagement and commitment towards the freedom movement for independence in India.

After his death, his 'worldly possessions' included only bare and plain essentials. He propagated the idea of a simple minimalistic and humble living. He famously affirmed that 'what is a *need* to one person can be a *want* to another—and vice versa'.[2] Gandhi believed that encouraging a minimalistic and simple lifestyle is key to maximising economic efficiency and fairness. He channelled his simple way of living and sharing through his ideology of *true brahman*. A *true brahman* is a person who has attained *moksh*. In the *Upanishads*, the philosophical-religious texts of Hinduism, *moksh* is defined as the highest state of self-actualization and perfection. A person who attains *moksh* transcends the 'self' (body, feeling, personality, ego). As Gandhi said, 'one ought always to remember, while dwelling on Him, that one is but a drop, the tiniest of creatures of the ocean that is God'.[3] He believed that the essence to *true brahman* amounts to offering limitless service to others. The Mahatma also stressed that every creature survives because of the sacrifices made by other and that all are linked to this endless cycle of giving.[4] When it came to culture and science, Gandhi's ideals were those of a liberal person who was against the idea of exclusivity. He believed that open, free and sharing minds are helpful for the development of the society and cultures.

Gandhi's theory of trusteeship is relevant for the purposes of this chapter. It is built on the idea of developing a society based on trust for each other and to bestow the wealth for all in the society 'in trust'.[5] Mahatma believed in the idea of a world's shared property and that each property owners shall take the responsibility to carefully possess without exploitation or increase their wealth not for their own selfish sake but for the sake of the nation. His idea of property ownership was based

---

[1] *Aparigraha* stands for the "*concept of 'non-greed', 'non-possessiveness', and 'non-attachment'*. The word 'graha' means to take, to seize, or to grab, 'pari' means 'on all sides', and the prefix 'a' negates the word itself.' See Emma Newlyn, Aparigraha- Practicing Non-Attachment (2020) *Ekhart Yoga*.

[2] Kyle Kowalski, "The Why behind Gandhi's Simple Living Transformation at Age 23", 2020, available at https://www.sloww.co/gandhi-simple-living.

[3] Gandhi, M.K., (s.d.) *Gandhi's experiments with truth: Essential Writings by and About Mahatma Gandhi* (1st ed.) (R.L. Johnson, ed.) (Oct 2005) Lexington Books-Rowman & Littlefield Publishers. Inc.

[4] Ira Chernus, *American Non-Violence: The History of an Idea (7th Ch.),* ORBIS (2004), Chap. 7.

[5] On this theory see, amongst many works, Siby. K. Joseph, et. al., *Trusteeship: A Path less Travelled.* (B. M. Siby K Joseph, ed.) (2016) Wardha, Maharashtra, India: Institute of Gandhian Studies.

on promoting simplicity, sharing and refusal of selfishness. He suggested to strike a balance between the wealth possessed by an individual and the value rendered to the society. The wealth should not outweigh the responsibility borne by, and the benefits that need to be offered to, society. This is not to say that Gandhi was opposed to private property as such. Mahatma certainly did not support states holding total control over the means of production—he accepted property subject to certain duties. From a Gandhian perspective, there can be no rights without duties, and both are linked. As Dasgupta points out:

> Gandhi did not assert only that rights and duties were correlative but also that rights were derived from duties which, therefore, was the more important concept. … Trusteeship, backed up by the sanction of *Satyagrah*,[[6]] seemed to Gandhi to offer the possibility of a way out.[7]

Unlike a devotee of marxist theory, Gandhi accepted property rights and the idea of private ownership, provided that the wealth is possessed by the owners as 'trust' for the public welfare. He believed that the skills and rights of property owners must be protected only if there is a corresponding duty to the public—and that such owners must earn the rights they seek. Thus, exclusive ownership is only justifiable when there is a sense of trusteeship on the part of the owners—meaning that they must not only hold their assets, but they should also hold themselves accountable for the welfare of the society at large. Trusteeship's pursuit begins with self-sacrifice and uplift of the backward sector of the society along with the economy.[8] Gandhi thus addressed those who owned large shares of wealth and resources in the society, stressing that such people should overcome their greed and sense of possession so to understand the struggle of those who earn their bread daily through sweat and labour.

Against this background, we will see in this chapter that some aspects of Gandhi's thoughts—including fairness and refocus of property rights on society's needs—emerge within certain areas of the Indian IP system: a regime which strikes a unique balance between the private interests of creators of culture and technology and the need to protect the public welfare by guaranteeing the dissemination and public use of needed technologies and the promotion of public goods such as human health and environmental protection.[9]

---

[6] *Satyagraha* is the policy of nonviolent protest practiced by Gandhi from about 1919 to oppose British power and rule.

[7] Ajit K.Dasgupta, (1996), Gandhi's Economic Thought London: Routledge, pp. 55 and 131.

[8] Gandhi, M. K., *Constructive Programme: Its Meaning and Place (2nd ed.)* Ahmedabad: Navajivan Publishing House.

[9] Nehal.A. Patel, Mindful Use:Gandhi's Non-Possessive Property Theory (2014) *Journal for Social Justice Article* 5, 13(2).

2 Gandhian Philosophy and IP

Gandhian approach to IP is not something that can be directly deduced or derived from the writings of Gandhi and/or his disciples such as J.C. Kumarappa. While US scholar Shyamkrishna Balganesh has interestingly claimed that Gandhi's approach to copyright has been that of copyright pragmatism,[10] such a view may not be entirely helpful in arriving at what Gandhian philosophy can offer to IP. This is because what Gandhi did or wrote on copyright was more his response that was contextual than based on any coherent analysis or theoretical principles on copyright or on IP more in general. Indeed, there has been no Gandhian philosophy of IP or perspectives on innovation, IP and society. Another issue is that while the political and ethical dimensions of his life and workings have received much attention, not much has been written on his views on science, technology and innovation (STI). Gandhi inspired scientists and economists such as A.K.N. Reddy, C.V. Seshadri and J.C. Kumarappa to think on the relationship between science, technology and society and of alternative approaches. In one way, his ideas and that of Reddy and Seshadri are comparable to the idea of responsible research and innovation.[11] While in the initial years of post-independence India his opinions had great influence in policy making, later they waned and the Nehruvian paradigm gained an upper hand and as a result his followers like Kumarappa found themselves marginalised.[12]

Gandhi always posed a challenge to those who wanted to classify his life and thoughts into neat and fundamentally different categories. His writings collected in about 105 volumes help more understand how his thinking has evolved than to develop a coherent framework or response to many topics that we are confronting today. This is obvious because some issues like the role of IP in society was not a major issue in those times, nor was he an economist or policymaker who dealt with them in theory or practice. Yet, it is still possible to derive an idea on what would be a Gandhian approach to IP based on his socio-economic philosophy and his views on property, science and ethics. But such an approach can give us leads or ideas for further development than straightforward ideas or solutions to issues related to IP.

---

[10] Balganesh, Shyamkrishna, "Gandhi and Copyright Pragmatism" (2013) 101 California Law Review, available at https://scholarship.law.upenn.edu/faculty_scholarship/445/.

[11] See Krishna Ravi Srinivas, Poonam Pandey 2019 Indian Perspectives on Responsible Innovation and Frugal Innovation in Rene Von Schomberg and Jonathan Hankins (ed.) International Handbook on Responsible Innovation: A Global Resource, Edward Elgar.

[12] Sachin Chaturvedi, Krishna Ravi Srinivas, 2015 Science and Technology for Socio-economic Development and Quest for Inclusive Growth: Emerging Evidence from India, in Science and Technology Governance and Ethics: A Global Perspective from Europe, India and China (Eds) Miltos Ladikas, Sachin Chaturvedi, Yandong Zhao, Dirk Stemerding—Springer 2015 ISBN [Chap. 7, pp. 83–98].

Contrary to what has been written,[13] Gandhi was not against science or technology as such. Rather, his opposition had more to do with what he assumed to be the problems with them and also his views on industrialization, use of machinery to displace labour and ethical issues in production and consumption. Gandhi propagated *sarvodaya*, namely welfare of all, but qualified it by stressing the need for *antyodaya*, that is welfare or needs of the marginalised or those left behind. While the opinion on Gandhi's views on science and their relevance for today is divided, a view that is shared by many scientists is that his views are relevant in meeting challenges faced by humanity. An editorial in *Nature* published in 2019 claims that the Mahatma can be considered as a supporter of sustainable science, seeking truth from every-day life experiments. The Mahatma was an:

> enthusiastic inventor and an assiduous innovator, making, discarding and refining snake-catching tools, sandals made from used tyres, and methods for rural sanitation, not to mention the small cotton-spinning wheels that would become his trademark. … Influential figures from history often leave contested legacies. But in one respect at least, the space for debate about Gandhi's life and impact has narrowed. As the world continues to grapple with how to respond to climate change, biodiversity loss, persistent poverty, and poor health and nutrition, Gandhi's commitment to what we now call sustainability is perhaps more relevant today than in his own time.[14]

Similar views are echoed in a 2010 volume on Gandhi edited by Raghunath Mashelkar that has many contributions by scientists and technocrats, industrialists and others, including policy makers.[15] While these opinions can be taken with a pinch of salt as many of them talk in general terms or do not offer any concrete solutions based on his ideas, it is equally true that Gandhi and his views could be sources of inspiration for enhancing contributions from STI for common good. Moreover, Gandhi's views as espoused by Shambu Prasad and Madhav Govind indicate that he had a pragmatic perspective on science and his views could not be categorised as 'anti-science' or as a deep suspicion on role of science. In fact, they point out that Gandhi was not an opponent of innovation. Quite the contrary.[16] According to Prasad, Gandhi's views on science had undergone changes as it is increasingly recognised that he was indeed engaged with science and its utilisation for common good till the end:

---

[13] See Shambu Prasad C (2001a) Towards an Understanding of Gandhi's Views on Science Economic and Political Weekly 2001 Review of Science Studies Sept. 29, pp. 3721–32.

[14] Nature, Gandhi on science: The champion of India's freedom movement was a supporter of sustainable development, 10 October 2019, p. 150.

[15] Raghunath Mashelkar (ed) 2010 The Tireless Inspirator: Reliving Gandhi Pune: Sakar Newspapers Ltd.

[16] Shambu Prasad C (2001b) Towards an Understanding of Gandhi's Views on Science Economic and Political Weekly 2001 Review of Science Studies Sept. 29. 3721–32; Govind (2009). Science, Truth and Gandhi: Divergence and Convergence. Gandhi Marg: Quarterly Journal of the Gandhi Peace Foundation, 31(1).

> Gandhi did not see science as an autonomous search independent of the individual scientist. In Gandhi's scheme, the agency of the scientist was of critical importance. The scientist had to be conscious and self-reflecting. He was not to flinch from the question of 'what should the scientist be working on'? He was clear that the right place of the scientist lay neither with the exploiting market nor with the stifling state, but with the people. All Gandhi's experiments in science attempted to carve out and articulate this domain.[17]

Gandhi had a wider idea on science and society, and his idea was linked with ethics on one hand and with the role of science for common good and for meeting the needs of the downtrodden, on the other. This point can be appreciated in a speech the Mahatma delivered in Trivandrum in 1925: 'in my humble opinion there are limitations even to scientific search, and the limitations that I place upon scientific search are the limitations that humanity imposes upon us'.[18] Govind is also keen to make this point:

> It is the era of globalization and economic liberalization and there is a shift in the cognitive orientation of the scientific community from 'knowing for its own sake' to 'knowing with an eye on patent'. … As a consequence of this trend even essential commodities such as life-saving drugs are becoming out of reach of common people in many countries. In this context Gandhi's call for the democratization of science to bring people's knowledge and techniques in dialogue with the modern science to produce the 'public science' for the welfare of the entire society requires immediate attention of our policy-makers.[19]

Neither Prasad nor Govind have directly addressed the issue of how Gandhi might have viewed IP. One may speculatively argue that in Gandhian terms the pursuit of science for the sake of privatising it or making a monopoly out of scientific advancements solely for private gain and/or control purposes would be sin and hence abominable. The Gandhian view on IP would therefore be that scientific advancement and technological progress should be linked with societal benefit and that the proprietary rights created by IP laws are desirable only if they materialise without giving an absolute and unconstrained private monopoly control over knowledge and its application. Rajam Neethu has actually attempted to link Gandhi's trusteeship to IP:

> Reading Gandhi into an intellectual property law framework, one finds juxtapositions seemingly at every turn. This is particularly evident in matters with a larger social interface like access to invention (including drugs) or creative works (fair use for study) or protection of culture and environment. Recall that the trusteeship philosophy did not completely reject private property, but instead recognized the skills and efforts invested by the one who created the property.
>
> Gandhi's philosophy is compatible with the utilitarian grounds for granting intellectual property rights … As per Gandhian trust philosophy, right holders must place a restriction on self-interest by finding a way to discharge the fiduciary obligation they have … A more concrete application of this approach would suggest that individual right holders should be

[17] Prasad, above fn. 16, p. 3730.

[18] Ramachandra Guha, How Much Should a Person Consume?: Environmentalism in India and the United States (University of California Press 2006), p. 182.

[19] Govind, above fn. 16, p. 78.

> required to limit self-interest in acting as a trustee. In the IP framework, that means less commodification and monopolistic exploitation by the right holder. Thus, the creator must offer society better access to his works or allow usage of his inventions to encourage research and allow creativity to grow in the society. … What would be the role of the state that regulates IP? While individuals and corporations may be required to limit self-interest in acting as a trustee, the state has an obligation to execute the will of the society and hence limit exploitation by individual right holders.[20]

As mentioned, we cannot directly deduce or derive a specific Gandhian approach to IP from the Mahatma's writings and/or those of his disciples. What we can do is to note that certain aspects of Indian IP regimes seem to reflect some elements of Gandhian views. In the next sections, we will exactly try to do that. After all, expanding Mahatma's theories has already been proposed in other areas. In recent years, for example, the idea of trusteeship has been linked with the concept of corporate social responsibility.[21]

3 Copyright

Gandhi's refusal of individualistic and profit-oriented attitudes may lead one to believe that the Mahatma was against copyright laws. Shyamkrishna Balganesh gives a brilliant and insightful analysis of Gandhi's stance towards this IP right.[22] Balganesh first notes that in his early years the Mahatma was sceptical about copyright because of its focus on markets and self-interested behaviours and the artificial restrictions on the flow of information, culture and knowledge. Gandhi indeed affirmed that:

> I have never yet copyright any of my writings. … Writings in the journals which I have the privilege of editing must be common property. Copyright is not a natural thing. It is a modern institution, perhaps *desirable to a certain extent.* But I have no wish to inflate the circulation of Young India or Navjivan by forbidding newspapers to copy the chapters of the autobiography (emphasis added).[23]

---

[20] Rajam Neethu, Gandhi, Trusteeship and Intellectual Property Law, 24 December 2013, at globaltrust.tau.ac.il/gandhi-trusteeship-and-intellectual-property-law (adding that "[t]he state would therefore regulate the rate of commission (the 'exclusivity rights' in an IP regime) which the right holders commensurate to the service rendered and its value to society, and would also contribute to the larger benefits of the trust by utilization of resources in case the right holder did not pitch in to the trust effectively").

[21] Bidyut Chakrabarty (2017) Gandhi's Doctrine of Trusteeship: Spiritualizing Interpersonal Relationship Working Paper No. 67, Nabakrushna Choudhury Centre for Development Studies, Bhubaneswar.

Pulla, Nayak and Walke. *Contribution of Gandhian Thought to Corporate Responsibility Space and Culture, India* 2017, 4:3 Page | 7 https://doi.org/10.20896/saci.v4i3.246; Pulla, Nayak and Walke. *Space and Culture, India* 2017, 4:3 Page | 7 https://doi.org/10.20896/saci.v4i3.246.

[22] Balganesh, above fn. 10.

[23] Idem, p. 24.

Yet, Gandhi's refusal of copyright was not total, as can be inferred from him clarifying that it may be 'perhaps desirable to a certain extent'. His approach is more nuanced. Not all rights offered by copyright laws—he believed—should be rejected. The Mahatma, for example, wanted to reserve to himself the exclusive right to translate his articles from Gujarati to other languages,[24] an approach which broadly reminds of the Creative Commons philosophy ('some rights reserved'). One may even go as far as speculating that such desire to control his own works would have made him a fan of modern moral rights, which give authors a tool to oppose unwanted and prejudicial treatments of their works—and a supporter of the landmark decision of the Delhi High Court in *Amar Nath Sehgal* v. *Union of India*,[25] which gave a broad interpretation of moral rights and term them as the 'soul' of the author's works.[26] Also, it seems that Gandhi wanted to infuse copyright law with principles such as distributive justice and the prevention of commercial exploitation of a work when this is undesirable, thus effectively subverting its core utilitarian structure towards non-utilitarian and community-based goals.[27] This approach is reminiscent of the teachings of the free software movement created in the US (several decades later) by Richard Stallman,[28] which aims at dissecting copyright's bundle of rights, and using them strategically to reach public interest focussed targets, including enhancing access to culture.[29] This model is in line with the Gandhian concept of *aparigrah* and broadly reflects Mahatma's trusteeship principles—with the society rejecting absolute private ownership of knowledge and having enhanced and equal access to information.

That the Indian copyright system needs to be limited and used to promote overarching public interests is confirmed by domestic case law. We mention here a landmark case of 2016, i.e. *DU Photocopying*. In that dispute, the Delhi High Court found that preparing academic course packs (namely compilation of photocopies of parts of books recommended in the syllabus) and distributing them to students through educational establishments do not violate copyright under the 1957 Copyright Act, provided that the photocopying (regardless of how many pages are

---

[24] Idem, pp. 36–37.

[25] *Amar Nath Sehgal vs Union of India* [2005 (30) PTC 253].

[26] See Mira T. Sundara Rajan, Moral Rights and the Protection of Cultural Heritage: Amar Nath Sehgal v. Union of India.

International Journal of Cultural Property, Vol. 10, No. 1, pp. 79–94, 2001, https://papers.ssrn.com/sol3/papers.cfm?abstract_id=1805237.

[27] Balganesh, above fn. 10, pp. 6–8 and 58–59.

[28] Idem, p. 27.

[29] Idem, p. 66. The free software as well as the open source movements are particularly successful in India. They are championed by the Free Software Foundation of India and the Indian Open Source Foundation. Nowadays, an increasing number of Indian government agencies and software companies are dropping proprietary software and opt instead to adopt open source models, leading to "the development of various forms of technological dialogues and the creation of universally accessible resources that are developed by communities for the benefit of society": see Sarma M. (2016) Development and Use of Open Source Software in India. In Dey B., Sorour K., Filieri R. (eds) ICTs in Developing Countries. Palgrave Macmillan, London.

reproduced) is justified on educational grounds.[30] The case was started by Oxford University Press together with Cambridge University Press and Taylor and Francis, against Rameshwari Photocopy Services together with Delhi University as a co-defendant. The court also interestingly noted that:

> Copyright, especially in literary works, is thus not an inevitable, divine, or natural right that confers on authors the absolute ownership of their creations. It is designed rather to stimulate activity and progress in the arts for the intellectual enrichment of the public. Copyright is intended to increase and not to impede the harvest of knowledge.

External factors may also have convinced the court to reach this decision, including the strong reaction of the academic and intellectual community. In an online petition signed in 2012,[31] 1,348 academics and authors vehemently stressed the importance of avoiding a finding of copyright infringement in this case:

> We recognize the fact that in a country like India marked by sharp economic inequalities, it is often not possible for every student to obtain a personal copy of a book. In that situation the next best thing would have been for multiple copies of the book to be available in the library so that students are able to access these books without any difficulty. But given the constraints that libraries in India work with, they may only have a single copy of a book and in many instances, none at all. The reason we make course packs is to ensure that students have access to the most relevant portions of the book without which we would be seriously compromising their education.

Another letter was then signed in March 2013 by more than 309 writers and academics from India and other countries, asking the publishers which had started the legal action to abandon the suit.[32] Curiously enough, some of the signatories had authored works protected by the very copyright which had allegedly been infringed by Delhi University and its photocopier services. Nevertheless, such authors made clear that they were happy for students to copy their works—and that the publishers which started the legal fight were not speaking in their name. They moreover emphasised that their publication activities were significantly subsidised via their university salaries (with many of these institutions being also funded by the state), government funding to libraries to buy books and the free labour of academics in peer reviews.[33]

The decision of the Delhi High Court shows how Indian copyright law does take seriously users' rights and more in general that the education is the foundation on

[30] The court applied Section 52(1)(i) of the Copyright Act which exempts from copyright infringement private or personal use of copyrighted material, including for research purposes.

[31] See the petition at the webpage https://www.change.org/p/academics-appeal-to-publishers-to-withdraw-suit-filed-against-delhi-university.

[32] The letter can be retrieved at https://spicyip.com/docs/DU%20Photocopying%20case/Covering-Letter-to-Publishers.pdf.

[33] See the comment on the *Du Photocopying* decision by Spicy IP blog, at the https://spicyip.com/resources-links/du-photocopy-case webpage.

which a progressive and prosperous society can be built.[34] And the letters signed by academics and authors to support Delhi University and its photocopier services represent a strong endorsement in favour of academic institutions and students who massively use copyrighted works—an endorsement which rarely materialise in other countries. This approach—based on a flexible concept of copyright aimed to meet the interests of larger society than those who produce it or those who own it—seems to fit into Gandhian thought, which puts the interests of society as the main objective. Indeed, a regime that ensures that copyright remains a fair mechanism that balances interest of different stakeholders including that of society, in particular guaranteeing access to information, is very much in line with Gandhian philosophy. The Mahatma propagated the idea of science as public good and not as market good, which meant that substantive and fruitful knowledge is produced only when the scientists also collaborate with the lay man who is going to be directly affected by such knowledge and not only with their fellow scientists and researchers.[35]

The belief that access to, and reciprocity of, knowledge should be maximised is entrenched in Gandhi's principles of trusteeship between the haves and have-nots of society. The Mahatma believed that to bridge the gap between these two different classes of the Indian society, the former must realise the duties towards the latter and make an adequate return for the strength and sustenance they derive instead of just exploiting them. He believed that this system of co-dependence and sharing of skills at the primary stage will eradicate the pure evils of class system in the society and that knowledge and education would help India achieve real freedom. He propagated the idea of सा वद्िया या वमिुक्तये।[36] which means 'the knowledge is one which liberates'.[37]

4 Patents and Plant Varieties

The Indian patent regime also seems to reflect Gandhi's solidarist views. This is so even though in 2005 India changed its 1970 Patents Act with a view to strengthening the rights of patent owners (the 1970 statute was certainly a good example of the way an emerging country could successfully restructure a patent system that had

[34] Graham Dutfield—Uma Suthersanen, Global Intellectual Property Law (Elgar 2020), p. 365.

[35] Govind, above fn. 16.

[36] सा वद्िया या वमिुक्तये। is a Sanskrit slogan which stands for the knowledge is one which liberates; See the translation on Hinduism Beta https://hinduism.stackexchange.com/questions/5335/sanskrit-full-shloka-of-s%C4%81-vidy%C4%81-y%C4%81-vimuktaye-translation-english-online-r.

[37] Gandhi, M. (n.d.). Basic Education and Students. In S. Narayan (Ed.), *The Voice of Truth* (T. f. Desai, Trans.). Gujarat: Navjivan Publishing House. Retrieved February 04, 2021, from https://www.mkgandhi.org/voiceoftruth/basiceducation.htm.

been imposed by a colonising power).[38] Despite these inevitable changes, prompted by the WTO membership and full implementation of TRIPS provisions,[39] Indian patent law still shows features which clearly stress more than any other country the need to reach a fair balance between the private rights of patentees which develop new technologies and the protection of public goods, especially the right of everyone to access medicines.[40] We focus first on two major pharmaceutical patent disputes of the last decade. Then, a quick look at the *Protection of Plant Variety and Farmers' Right Act* of 2001 will show that Indian lawmakers not only aim at incentivizing innovation in the agricultural sector by providing innovators in this field of monopolistic rights, but do also care about environmental protection by explicitly protecting the rights of farmers. In doing that, we will make the point that the solidaristic features of those legal regimes are in line with Gandhian principles. After all, the Mahatma himself believed that science and technology must eventually reach the common man and that the high-end research and development should benefit the society as much as possible. And he reportedly said: 'I would prize every invention of science made for the benefit of all'.[41]

4.1 Compulsory Licences of Patents in the Pharmaceutical Sector: The Natco v Bayer Case of 2012

In March 2012, the Controller of Patents—the principal officer responsible for administering the patent system in India—granted Natco Pharma Ltd, a generic drugs' producer, the first post-TRIPS compulsory licence. Natco was authorised by the government to produce and sell in India Bayer's patented medicine 'sorafenib', a drug useful to treat liver and kidney cancer (the licence had been opposed by Bayer from the very beginning). It should be reminded that via compulsory licences governments or other public bodies permit someone else to manufacture or use a patented product or process without the authorisation of the patentee or plan to use the patented invention themselves. While the TRIPS Agreement allows such

[38] Peter Drahos, The Global Governance of Knowledge—Patent Offices and their Clients (Cambridge University Press 2010), pp. 203–209.

[39] The TRIPS Agreement mandates minimum standards of IP protection at global level, including the obligation to provide the patentability of both products and processes in all fields of technology [Agreement on Trade-Related Aspects of Intellectual Property Rights, Apr. 15, 1994, Marrakesh Agreement Establishing the World Trade Organization, Annex 1C, 1869 U.N.T.S. 299, 33 I.L.M. 1197 (1994)].

[40] India has traditionally been a country where producers of generic drugs have been able to flourish. Before India changed its IP, particularly patent laws, to comply with the TRIPS Agreement, only processes to obtain a medicine could be patented, but not the final product/drug: which allowed Indian generic producers to use alternative ways to manufacture a drug patented by (often Western) competitors.

[41] M.K. Gandhi, Understanding the Mechanic Life with Gandhi, available at https://www.mkgandhi.org/short/ev46.htm.

licences subject to strict conditions,[42] many other countries have often refused to issue them in circumstances similar to those recurring in *Natco v Bayer*. Why then was the licence granted in this case? The main reason is that Bayer did not sell the sorafenib drug at all in India in 2008—and sold just very limited quantities in 2009 and 2010. In other words, the medicine was not within the reach of most of the people who badly needed it. The Controller clarified that Bayer could have avoided the issuance of the compulsory licence if it had adopted a policy based on a differential and country-specific pricing system. Yet, Bayer itself admitted in the proceedings that it had charged the same price rate in any country where it sold the medicines in question, with a minimum variation based on the respective exchange rates. The Controller added that the price of the sorafenib drug was unaffordable to the average Indian consumer. Indeed, Bayer sorafenib-based therapy cost Rs. 280,000 (around US$54,040) per month and Rs. 3,365,136 (around US$64,947) per year. As noted in the decision, an Indian public sector worker would have to work for three and half years to be able to buy a single month's treatment at the above price. As the life expectancy of this category of patients in India is not more than four months, that worker basically would not have time to earn the money to purchase the drug. Also considering that 72% of India's population is below poverty line, the high price charged by Bayer would have pushed many patients suffering from kidney and liver cancer into even deeper poverty.[43]

The decision to grant the compulsory licence was based on Section 83 of the Indian Patents Act. This provision states that patents not only aim at giving monopolistic rights on the import of the patented products. Their goal is broader, i. e. to make sure that the patented technology is worked in India on a commercial scale without undue delay (this is the so-called local working requirement, which however several commentators believe is contrary to Article 27(1) TRIPS).[44] Section 83 of the Indian Patent Act also clarifies that patents should not hamper the protection of public health and nutrition, but rather should be considered tools to promote overriding public interests—which entails that products incorporating patented inventions should be available to the public at reasonably affordable prices.

Compulsory licencing has been occasionally used by other countries, especially in the developing world, and has a long history.[45] Far from being an instrument which some consider as a hateful expropriation of private property, it constitutes a legal tool which governments can use to maximise societal benefits, without jeopardising excessively right holders (as fair compensation must always be

---

[42] See Article 31 TRIPS.

[43] See *Natco/Bayer* decision at p.25.

[44] Article 27 TRIPS states that "patents shall be available and patent rights enjoyable without discrimination as to … whether products are imported or locally produced". On how this finding may infringe Article 27 TRIPS see Enrico Bonadio, Compulsory Licensing of Patents: The Bayer/ Natco Case, European Intellectual Property Review (2012/10), p. 724.

[45] Reto M. Hilty, Kung-Chung Liu (eds.) Compulsory Licensing: Practical Experiences and Ways Forward (Springer 2015).

guaranteed,[46] amongst other strict conditions). This is exactly what India has done in *Natco* v *Bayer*, namely correcting a situation where a patent owner did not make available products which were badly needed by people. In Gandhian terms, such a situation would be called 'commerce without morality', one of the seven sins mentioned by Gandhi,[47] and—it could be provocatively argued—the Mahatma himself would have addressed it the way it was addressed in *Natco* v *Bayer*, i.e. by putting societal interest before the private profit. Indeed, in Gandhi's philosophy 'commerce without morality' is capable of worsening the gap between the rich and the poor in the society[48] and includes the act of fraud and selling cheap products at a higher cost and situations where the profit becomes the sole motivation over morality, ethics and values.[49] Indeed, the Mahatma always felt that business and ethics were inseparable and both had to go hand-in-hand. To facilitate the access to healthcare system, he advocated against its commercial exploitation because he believed that taking care of sick and needy people was not just merely a business transaction, but a mission to provide the masses with affordable access to medicines and relevant facilities without any form of discrimination.[50]

4.2 Pharmaceutical Patents and Evergreening: The Novartis Case of 2013

The 'evergreening' phenomenon can be defined as a set of legal, business and technological strategies which certain pharmaceutical companies pursue to skilfully (and de facto) extend the duration of their patent, to allow them to extract profits out of their extended monopolies. Such outcome may be reached by filing for and obtaining a patent covering a new use of a known substance or a slight modification of a previous invention, once the patent over the upstream invention expires. While these downstream inventions are often patented in countries such as the US, in other jurisdictions, particularly in India, obtaining evergreening patents is way more difficult.

The Novartis case of 2013[51] is a testament to that. In 1998, Swiss pharmaceutical company Novartis filed a patent application at the Indian patent office for a

---

[46] See Article 31(h) TRIPS Agreement.

[47] On this see Stephen Covey, Principle-Centered Leadership (2009) Rosetta Book, Chap. 7 (Seven Deadly Sins), pp. 87–93.

[48] Grover, Vijay, Gandhi's Seven Sins Still Exist, But We Got a New Tool: Knowledge A Panacea (2015) American Research Thoughts. 1. 1394–1402.

[49] Weber, T., Gandhi's moral economics: The sins of wealth without work and commerce without morality. In J. Brown & A. Parel (Eds.), *The Cambridge Companion to Gandhi* (2011), Cambridge University Press, pp. 135–153.

[50] Nicola L. Bragazzi—Mariano Martini, "The Never-Ending Legacy of Mahatma Gandhi in the Field of Medicine 150 Years After His Birth" (2019) (IMAJ) Vol 21, pp. 641–643.

[51] *Novartis AG v. Union of India (UOI) and Ors.*, Civil Appeal No. 2706-2716 of 2013.

variation of a previous patented substance, i.e. beta crystalline form, the final form of Gleevec, which is an oral chemotherapy medication used to treat cancer. After a long proceeding, the Indian Supreme Court found in 2013 that the new form of a drug must shows an improvement in its therapeutic effect or curative property as compared to the old form, in order to secure a patent. But Novartis did not show the enhanced therapeutic efficacy, which is required by section 3(d) of the Indian Patent Act.[52] The Court also noted that India has adopted a standard of pharma patenting that is stricter than that followed by other countries—and that therefore a patent applicant must not only show that a new form of known compound is different than an old form, but that the modification will result in an improvement in the treatment of the patient. The Court added that by passing section 3(d) of the Patent Act, the Indian Parliament had decided that people in India should only pay for expensive patented medicines when those drugs constitute a genuine advance over earlier versions[53] and that India is a very populous developing country and its primary concern is to be able to facilitate the availability of life-saving drugs at affordable price range for all its people.

The Supreme Court decision in this case is based on solid grounds. The problem with evergreening is that it enables a patent holder to make advantage of an undue right without making a really innovative product—an activity which the Supreme Court could not approve of. Higher standards in patentability criteria are ethical in nature as they ensure that the quality of the innovation and patents are commensurate with the rights claimed and granted. In that sense, section 3(d) of the Indian Patent Act is a moral safeguard to protect the interests of society and to promote only innovation in drugs/pharmaceuticals that result in products that meet an acceptable level of efficacy or improvement.

Said that, one may again see here a reflection of Gandhi's beliefs for self-care and enhanced access to healthcare system, and of his rejection of 'commerce without morality'.[54] How could a thinker like the Mahatma consider ethically

---

[52] Section 3(d) of the Indian Patent Act states that "*the mere discovery of a new form of a known substance which does not result in the enhancement of the known efficacy of that substance or the mere discovery of any new property or new use for a known substance or of the mere use of a known process, machine or apparatus unless such known process results in a new product or employs at least one new reactant, is not patentable.*".

[53] Frederick Abbott, The Judgment in Novartis v. India: what the Supreme Court of India said, 4 April 2013, available at https://www.ip-watch.org/2013/04/04/the-judgment-in-novartis-v-india-what-the-supreme-court-of-india-said/.

[54] Gandhi was very passionate about health. Before being discouraged by his elder brother, he also thought about earning a medical degree. In 1909, he strongly criticised the physicians and medical practitioners of his era because he considered that service to marginalised and needy patients was a commitment and ultimate dedication of life and not just a mere job: see Bragazzi—Martini, above fn. 50. See also Rajni Kant—Balram Bhatgava, Medical Legacy of Gandhi, Demystifying Human Diseases, Indian J. Med Res. (2019). Gandhi's ideology of healthy living is also well-documented in his own book *Key to Health*, where the Mahatma noted that he believed in the ancient form of Indian medicine which advocated *food for medicine*. Foods with medicinal properties need to be incorporated in the day-to-day diet to become healthy and stay healthy. Gandhi incorporated health and hygiene education amongst the masses and promoted village sanitisation and healthy living.

acceptable to artificially and unjustifiably extend a monopoly over a needed medicine? Indeed, one may note in Gandhian terms that in these circumstances profit may very well have to bow to ethical or moral concerns, taking into account that patents over drugs inevitably make them less affordable to people. Rajam Neethu has also commented on the Novartis case and made an indirect link with Gandhian trusteeship. She noted that:

> As per Gandhian trust philosophy … [t]he state would therefore regulate the rate of commission (the 'exclusivity rights' in an IP regime) which the right holders get commensurate to the service rendered and its value to society, and would also contribute to the larger benefits of the trust by utilization of resources in case the right holder did not pitch in to the trust effectively. The 2013 *Novartis* v *Union of India* judgement decided by the Indian Supreme Court may be illustrative of this tendency: the state, through the court, restricted the IP protection after carefully balancing the rights of the IP owner against societal needs.[55]

4.3 The Protection of Plant Variety and Farmers' Right Act of 2001

In India, agriculture accounts as a primary source of 80% of rural India's income and as per the data for year 2020 it is estimated that the agricultural sector accounts for 14% of country's economy and 42% of total employment.[56] Since agriculture is considered the backbone of India's economy, the law in India is mainly focussed on providing support and protection to farmers alongside developing and enhancing agri-tech innovations.

In 2001, India passed the *Protection of Plant Variety and Farmers' Right Act* (PVVFRA).[57] This is the piece of law which grants plant variety rights to breeders, i.e. the innovators who develop new plant varieties.[58] All WTO countries must protect plant varieties via proprietary IP rights,[59] with such protection aiming at encouraging agri-tech innovation. While jurisdictions such as the US, EU, Canada

---

See also the webpage at https://www.mkgandhi.org/articles/gandhian_approach_towards_health.htm.

[55] Neethu, above fn. 20.

[56] India GDP from Agriculture (3 October 2020), see Trading Economics webpage at https://tradingeconomics.com/india/gdp-from-agriculture.

[57] *Plant Variety and Farmers' Right Act* of 2001, Act No. 53 of 2001.

[58] On this Act, and in general on the role of intellectual property rights in agriculture, see Krishna Ravi Srinivas (2015) Intellectual Property Rights and Politics of Food in The Oxford Handbook of Food, Politics, and Society Edited by Ronald J. Herring (2015) New York: Oxford University Press, pp. 381–406.

[59] See Article 27(3)(b) TRIPS which provides that: "Members shall provide for the protection of plant varieties either by patents or by an effective sui generis system or by any combination thereof".

and Japan strongly protect the IP rights of breeders and allow farmers to use the registered seeds in a very limited way via mere exceptions, India has adopted a unique *sui generis* system which not only grants breeders a monopoly over new varieties, but also explicitly protects farmers' rights. Farmers are vested with the rights to save, replant, exchange and even sell the protected seeds in some circumstances. This allows and promotes agricultural practices based on traditional seeds exchange and sharing—practices which are environmentally sound and thus beneficial to biodiversity. It is for keeping such a balanced legal regime that India has not become party to 1991 version of the UPOV Convention,[60] and preferred to join the 1978 version of this treaty, instead. The former protects more strongly breeders' rights, denying farmers any freedom to maintain and reuse seeds from the previous cultivar. Obviously, India being an agrarian nation was not inclined to harm the farmers' interests.

Again, this regime is in line with principles inherent in Gandhi's teachings. The policies behind this statute—especially, guaranteeing the well-being of the hard-working farmers and the poor—mirror some of the Gandhian socio-economic philosophies of trusteeship. Indeed, the Mahatma believed that the elements of nature such as earth, fire, water, air and space are God's own gift to humans and in any case these should not come under anyone's total control, be it business, industrial or any centralised form of power. These public resources belong to the general masses, instead. Since the state is just their trustee and not their owner, such resources belong to the people at large, should be decentralised and be brought under local and community-based system.[61] Gandhi also believed that villagers must possess lands in order to cultivate, so as to help their families, and to grow crops and support their cattle from its produce—which would also help renew and retain biodiversity. He believed and preached farmers to treat their lands, i.e. earth, as their own mother.[62] These ideas do not come as a big surprise if we look at the context and society in which Gandhi lived. In his days, the seed industry was limited to local/national markets and business was mostly based on mutual trust.

Moreover, for Gandhi the livelihood of small and marginal farmers was crucial to the idea of *swaraj* (which means 'self-rule' and is usually used to refer to Gandhi's concept for political and economic independence of India from foreign rule and influence). The Mahatma was of the opinion that 'agriculture was the cornerstone of all development'and that it was the only means of complete independence of villages.[63] He believed that every farmer should own a piece of land to toil and earn his/her own daily bread to lead a life of dignity. To him, their

---

[60] International Convention for the Protection of New Plant Varieties of December 2, 1961, as Revised at Geneva on November 10, 1972, on October 23, 1978, and on March 19, 1991.

[61] Krishnaswarup Anandi, Agricultural System, Agricultural Land and Cottage Industry (In the context of Gram Swaraj), October 2006, available at https://www.mkgandhi.org/vinoba/anasakti/gramswaraj.htm.

[62] Idem.

[63] Idem.

livelihood was the crux of the nation's development.[64] After all, in the last decade anti-biotech movements in India have often invoked Gandhi's teachings to claim that genetically modified organisms produce human costs to farmers.[65]

While Indian plant variety regime addresses the need to avoid robust monopoly over seeds which take away farmers' rights to grow, sell and maintain seeds, a lot of ambiguity still looms over what can be protected by breeders and the scope of their rights. The same could be said of biotech patents. And India is certainly not immune from high-profile biotech patent and plant variety litigations brought by western multinationals, as we have seen earlier with the Novartis case. One of these disputes is still pending, i.e. *Monsanto Technology LLC* v. *Nuziveedu & Ors*.[66] The US company Monsanto owned a patent (now expired) protecting the process by which the gene *Cry2Ab* from the bacterium *Bacillus thuringiensis* is introduced in the cotton genome. The insertion of such gene caused the plant to produce proteins that save the crop from bollworm caterpillars. Many, if not most, Indian cotton-seed companies have accepted to pay a trait fee to Monsanto to be able to introduce the gene into their varieties. One of these seed companies, Nuziveedu Seeds, eventually challenged in 2017 the validity of Monsanto's patent, after a row over the fee to be paid.[67] One of the main issues is whether the genetically engineered seed is excluded from the patentable subject matter under section 3(j) of the Indian Patent Act.[68] The issue has inevitably turned political as Monsanto has a record of going after farmers for technology infringement and harassing them with lawsuits or threats thereof.[69] Needless to say, the (still pending) legal suit by the US multinational sparked vivid criticism amongst many sectors of Indian society. What is certain is that the domestic legal activism arisen to support Nuziveedu Seeds in this legal battle will not stop, with insiders hoping to reach a result similar to the one obtained by a coalition of opponents, supported by the Indian government, in the famous *neem tree* biopiracy case at the European Patent Office.[70]

---

[64] Idem.

[65] Siva Vaidhyanathan, Intellectual Property—A Very Short Introduction (Oxford University Press 2017), p. 100.

[66] Monsanto Technology LLC v. Nuziveedu & Ors AIR 2019 SC 55.

[67] Nidisha Garg, Monsanto v Nuziveedu: A Missed Opportunity by the Supreme Court?, Kluwer Patent Blog, 27 January 2020; Karine Peschard-Shalini Randeria, Keeping Seeds in our Hands: The Rise of Seed Activism (2020) *Journal of Peasant Studies* 47:4, pp. 613–647; Gayathri Vaidyanathan, Indian Court's Decision to Uphold GM Cotton Patent Could Boost Industry Research, Nature, 30 January 2019 (also noting that the varieties developed by Monsanto "accounted for 89% of cotton planted in India in 2017–18").

[68] This provision states that "plants and animals in whole or any part thereof other than micro-organisms but including seeds, varieties and species and essentially biological processes for production or propagation of plants and animals" are not patentable.

[69] Prabir Purkayastha, PepsiCo and Monsanto's Bogus Court Cases is a Wat on Indian Farmers, People Democracy, Vol. XLIII No. 185 May 2019.

[70] The background of this case was as follows. In 1994, the US Department of Agriculture and WR Grace obtained a European patent protecting methods of controlling fungal infections in plants using a composition that included extracts from the neem tree (*Azadirachta indica*), which grows

Another high-profile litigation was recently started by PepsiCo, the US multinational food, snack and beverage giant, which owns plant variety rights in India over the FL-2027 potato variety (commercial name FC-5). This variety possesses decreased water content and hence crispier and is also less susceptible to diseases—it is grown exclusively to support a specific PepsiCo's product, i.e. the Lay potato chips. The US company had filed infringement cases against 11 farmers from Gujarat for unauthorised use of the FC-5 seed, claiming hefty compensations. But with the Indian and Gujarat Governments stepping in to resolve the issue amicably, and growing pressure from activists, farmers' unions and grassroots organisations, PepsiCo withdrew the cases in May 2019.[71] But in December 2021 in a different case still focussing on the potato variety in question (i.e. Kavita Kuruganthi v. Pepsico Holdings India Ltd), the Indian Authority which grants plant protection certificates revoked the Certificate of Registration No 59 of 2016 which protected said variety.[72] Specifically, it was contended that the grant of such plant variety right was not in the public interest. Besides noticing discrepancies in the application, the Authority found that the Registrar had erroneously conducted the procedure and mistakenly granted the certificate.[73]

5 Trademarks and Tobacco Packaging

Public interests such as the protection of human health are also pursued by Indian law governing the use of tobacco brands and packaging. As in several countries in the world, the Indian government has in place legislation compelling tobacco manufacturers to introduce pictorial warnings and other information aimed at informing people about the devastating effects of smoking and encouraging them to

throughout India and Nepal. In 2000 the patent was successfully opposed at the European Patent Office by several groups based in India and Europe including the influential India environmental group Research Foundation for Science, Technology and Ecology, on the basis that the fungicidal activity of neem extract had long been known in Indian traditional medicine. WR Grace appealed the decision, and lost that appeal in 2005. On this case see Hellerer, U., Jarayaman, K., Greens persuade Europe to revoke patent on neem tree, *Nature* 405, 266–267 (2000). On the broader issue of biopiracy, see Vandana Shiva, Biopiracy: The Plunder of Nature and Knowledge (South End Press 1997).

[71] Sohini Gosh, Pepsi Vs Gujarat Farmers: Case, Its Withdrawal, The Indian Express, 3 May 2019. The legal suit by Monsanto has been strongly criticised. Indeed, Section 39(1)(iv) of PPVFRA provides that "[n]otwithstanding anything contained in this Act—a farmer shall be deemed to be entitled to save, use, sow, resow, exchange, share or sell his farm produce including seed of a variety protected under this Act in the same manner as he was entitled before the coming into the force of this Act, provided that the farmer shall not be entitled to sell branded seed of a variety protected under this Act".

[72] See the webpage https://www.plantauthority.gov.in/sites/default/files/public-notice-19-2021.pdf .

[73] See the webpage https://theprint.in/theprint-essential/case-against-farmers-poor-documentation-why-pepsico-india-lost-lays-variety-potato-rights/776644/.

stop or not to start consuming such products. Specifically, in 2014 the Indian Government amended the Cigarettes and other Tobacco Products (Packaging and Labelling) Rules and increased the size of the health warning on the principle display area of tobacco packs from 40 to 80%. The assumption is that less exposure to colourful tobacco brands (whose space available on the packaging has accordingly shrunk) do produce a deterrent effect on consumption.

This move has attracted praise.[74] Yet, some commentators have also pushed for a much bolder legislative step, i.e. the plain packaging of cigarettes.[75] This is a tobacco control policy tool which significantly limits manufacturers' ability to use their packaging for marketing purposes and does so more strongly than the obligation to show pictorial warnings and other information on the 80% of the display area.[76] It requires the removal from the packs of *all* colourful and eye-catching elements from the whole pack, such elements being usually registered by tobacco manufacturers as trademarks. The pack becomes therefore almost completely standardised, with just the name of the brand neutrally displayed at its bottom. The aim of this extreme public health measure is again to make the product as unattractive as possible and thus discourage consumption. Despite the strong opposition by tobacco majors (obviously keen in protecting their trademarks) and some international and national legal disputes centred on its lawfulness under different laws (all lost by the opponents of this measure), plain packaging has been adopted so far by several (mostly developed) countries such as Australia, UK and France.

The Indian judiciary agrees on the need to adopt plain packaging of tobacco products. The decision of the Allahabad High Court in 2014 in *Love Care Foundation* v. *Union of India & Anr*[77] is here relevant. The non-governmental organisation Love Care Foundation petitioned the Indian government to introduce the measure in question, claiming that marketing an eye-catching tobacco packaging is capable of promoting the product and noting that rules preventing the use of logos, colours and other fancy elements on tobacco packs would curb their advertising effects. After assessing the evidence supporting the impact of this measure in Australia (the first country to implement plain packaging in 2012), the court voiced the opinion that such a policy tool, together with health warnings, would significantly reduce the ability of attractive tobacco packs to confuse consumers about the harmful effects of smoking—and urged the Indian government to

---

[74] Jaya Prasad Tripathy—Madhur Verma, Impact of health warning labels on cigarettes packs in India: findings from the global adult tobacco survey 2016–17 (2020) Behavioral Medicine.

[75] Yadav A, Nazar GP, Rawal T, et al., Plain packaging of tobacco products: the logical next step for tobacco control policy in India (2018) BMJ Global Health 2018.

[76] On this measure see Mark Davison, The Legitimacy of Plain Packaging Under International Intellectual Property Law: Why There is No Right to Use a Trademark Under Either the Paris Convention or the Trips Agreement, in A. Mitchell, T. Voon and J. Liberman (eds.) Public Health and Plain Packaging of Cigarettes: Legal Issues (Elgar, 2012); Alberto Alemanno-Enrico Bonadio, John Marshall Review of Intellectual Property Law (2011) Vol. 10, No. 3, 2011.

[77] Love Care Foundation v. Union of India and Others, Writ Petition No. 1078 (M/B) of 2013.

consider introducing it as early as possible. The court added that implementing standardised packaging in India would be a duty of the state under Article 47 of the Constitution, which sets the target to raise the level of nutrition and standard of living and to improve public health as amongst its primary duties. It remains to be seen whether this measure will be finally implemented in India. If so, it would position India amongst the few states which have adopted this measure and confirm that public health interests are capable of trumping the interests of IP owners—in this case, tobacco manufacturers—in using brands to promote their products.

6 Conclusion

This chapter has highlighted how certain areas of IP Indian regimes are also based on firm public interest-focussed principles. They not only offer IP owners monopolistic rights to extract economic value out of their inventions, plant varieties, signs or copyrighted works—they also strongly protect the rights of users, competitors and the public at large, who often have conflicting interests. While it is true that many jurisdictions do provide strong limitations and exceptions to IP rights (think of fair use in US copyright law), it cannot be denied that the way the Indian legal system weigh the different interests of all stakeholders is unique—with the balance often tilting in favour of entities or individuals that do need to access and use socially important goods such as medicines, seeds or books. The propensity of specific areas of Indian IP regimes to constantly look at the public interest is clearly visible in the way the Indian government has recently proposed to address the COVID-19 emergency within the WTO. The proposal consists of waiving temporarily IP rights provided under TRIPS for all coronavirus-related medical products, including vaccines.[78] Far from being radical and unjustified, such a proposal seems entirely appropriate and dictated by the unprecedented health emergency the world is facing, with the death toll still increasing and uncertainties growing over whether new COVID variants are more infectious. Not surprisingly, the US, EU, UK, Switzerland and other industrialised nations strongly oppose the proposal, showing determination in not dropping IP maximalist policies even when terrible health emergencies unfold. This is not the first time India has been vocal within the WTO about the need to balance IP and public health. In 2010, India filed a complaint at the WTO claiming that EU custom authorities detained certain lots of Indian generic medicines in transit to non-EU states, in particular Brazil, on grounds of alleged patent infringement. India argued that these measures contradict relevant TRIPS provisions, *inter alia*. The case was later settled but it still spurred a debate on the clash between IP and the promotion of public health.

---

[78] Ann Danaya Usher, 5 December 2020, available at https://www.thelancet.com/journals/lancet/article/PIIS0140-6736(20)32581-2/fulltext.

We have also made the point that certain features of the Indian IP system are broadly in line with Gandhian solidarist thoughts. Obviously, we do not suggest that the lawmakers, judges and in general Indian IP insiders explicitly follow the Mahatma's teachings—yet we believe that the huge impact his views had on many sectors of modern Indian society may have also indirectly affected certain areas of Indian IP regimes. It should not be neglected that Indian society is still marked by sharp economic inequalities, as reminded by many academics and authors in their online petition of 2012 in the *DU Photocopying* case—inequalities which are often addressed by Indian IP systems by protecting overriding interests which are frequently in conflict with those of IP rights' holders. That is a society which is not very far from the one Gandhi found himself in during his life and provided the context where his influential writings and philosophy emerged.

References

Ann Danaya Usher, 5 December 2020. Available at https://www.thelancet.com/journals/lancet/article/PIIS0140-6736(20)32581-2/fulltext

Anandi K (2006, October) Agricultural system, agricultural land and cottage industry (in the context of gram Swaraj). Available at https://www.mkgandhi.org/vinoba/anasakti/gramswaraj.htm

Balganesh S (2013) Gandhi and copyright pragmatism. Calif Law Rev 101. Available at https://scholarship.law.upenn.edu/faculty_scholarship/445/

Bonadio E (2012) Compulsory licensing of patents: the Bayer/Natco case. Eur Intellect Property Rev

Bragazzi NL, Martini M (2019) The never-ending legacy of Mahatma Gandhi in the field of medicine 150 years after his birth. IMAJ 21:641–643

Chakrabarty B (2017) Gandhi's doctrine of trusteeship: spiritualizing interpersonal relationship working paper No. 67, Nabakrushna Choudhury Centre for Development Studies, Bhubaneswar

Chaturvedi S, Srinivas KR (2015) 2015 science and technology for socio-economic development and quest for inclusive growth: emerging evidence from India. In: Ladikas M, Chaturvedi S, Zhao Y, Stemerding D (eds) Science and technology governance and ethics: a global perspective from Europe, India and China. Springer, Berlin. (Chap. 7, pp. 83–98)

Chernus I (2004) American non-violence: the history of an idea (7th Chap.). ORBIS, Chapt. 7

Covey S (2009) Principle-centered leadership (2009) Rosetta book, Chapt. 7. Seven Deadly Sins, pp 87–93

Dasgupta k (1996) Amar Nath Sehgal vs Union of India [2005 (30) PTC 253]

Davison M (2011) The legitimacy of plain packaging under international intellectual property law: why there is no right to use a trademark under either the paris convention or the trips agreement. In Mitchell A, Voon T, Liberman J (eds) Public health and plain packaging of cigarettes: legal issues. Elgar. Rev Intellect Property Law 10(3) [Alemanno A, Bonadio E, Marshall J]

Drahos P (2010) The global governance of knowledge–patent offices and their clients . Cambridge University Press, pp 203–209

Dutfield G, Suthersanen U (2020) Global intellectual property law. Elgar, p 365

Frederick A (2013, April 4) The judgment in Novartis v. India. Available at https://www.ip-watch.org/2013/04/04/the-judgment-in-novartis-v-india-what-the-supreme-court-of-india-said/

Gandhi M (n.d.) Basic education and students. In: Narayan S (ed) The voice of truth (T. f. Desai, Trans.). Navjivan Publishing House, Gujarat. Retrieved 4 Feb 2021 from https://www.mkgandhi.org/voiceoftruth/basiceducation.htm

Gandhi MK (s.d., October 2005) Gandhi's experiments with truth: essential writings by and about Mahatma Gandhi, 1st edn. In: Johnson RL (ed) Lexington Books-Rowman & Littlefield Publishers. Inc.

Gandhi MK Gandhian approach towards health. https://www.mkgandhi.org/articles/gandhian_approach_towards_health.htm

Gandhi MK (2021) Constructive programme: its meaning and place, 2nd edn. Navajivan Publishing House, Ahmedabad

Gandhi MK Understanding the mechanic life with Gandhi. Available at https://www.mkgandhi.org/short/ev46.htm

Garg N, Monsanto v Nuziveedu: a missed opportunity by the supreme court? Kluwer Patent Blog, 27 January 2020

Grover V (2015) Gandhi's seven sins still exist, but we got a new tool: knowledge a panacea. Am Res Thoughts 1:1394–1402.

Govind M (2009) Science, truth and Gandhi: divergence and convergence. Gandhi Marg Quart J Gandhi Peace Found 31(1)

Guha R (2006) How much should a person consume? Environmentalism in India and the United States. University of California Press, p 182

Hellerer U, Jarayaman K (2000) Greens persuade Europe to revoke patent on neem tree. Nature 405:266–267 (2000). On the broader issue of biopiracy

Hilty RM, Liu K-C (eds) Compulsory licensing: practical experiences and ways forward. Springer, Berlin

Hinduism Beta https://hinduism.stackexchange.com/questions/5335/sanskrit-full-shloka-of-s%C4%81-vidy%C4%81-y%C4%81-vimuktaye-translation-english-online-r

India GDP from Agriculture (3 Oct 2020) See trading economics webpage at https://tradingeconomics.com/india/gdp-from-agriculture

International convention for the protection of new plant varieties of December 2, 1961, as Revised at Geneva on November 10, 1972, on October 23, 1978, and on March 19, 1991

Kant R, Bhatgava B (2019) Medical legacy of Gandhi, demystifying human diseases. Indian J Med Res

Kowalski K (2020) The why behind Gandhi's simple living transformation at age 23. Available at https://www.sloww.co/gandhi-simple-living

Letters from academicians at SpicyIP. https://spicyip.com/docs/DU%20Photocopying%20case/Covering-Letter-to-Publishers.pdf.

Love Care Foundation v. Union of India and Others, Writ Petition No. 1078 (M/B) of 2013

Mashelkar R (ed) (2010) The tireless inspirator: reliving Gandhi Pune. Sakar Newspapers Ltd.

Monsanto Technology LLC v. Nuziveedu & Ors AIR 2019 SC 55

Nature, Gandhi on science: the champion of India's freedom movement was a supporter of sustainable development, 10 October 2019, p 150

Patel NA (2014) Mindful use:Gandhi's non-possessive property theory. J Soc Justice Article 5 13(2)

Peschard K, Randeria S (2020) Keeping seeds in our hands: the rise of seed activism. J Peasant Stud 47(4):613–647

Pulla VR, Nayak V, Walke K (2017) Contribution of Gandhian thought to corporate responsibility. Space And Culture, India. http://dx.doi.org/https://doi.org/10.20896/saci.v4i3.246; Pulla VR, Nayak V, Walke NK (2017) Space and Culture, India 4(3). http://dx.doi.org/https://doi.org/10.20896/saci.v4i3.246

Purkayastha P (2019, May) PepsiCo and Monsanto's Bogus court cases is a war on Indian farmers. People Democracy, vol XLIII, No. 185

Rajam N (2013, December 24) Gandhi, Trusteeship and intellectual property law. At globaltrust.tau.ac.il/gandhi-trusteeship-and-intellectual-property-law

Newlyn e (2020) Aparigraha-practicing non-attachment. Ekhart Yoga

Novartis AG v. Union of India (UOI) and Ors., Civil Appeal No. 2706-2716 of 2013

Prasad CS (2001a, September 29) Towards an understanding of Gandhi's views on science economic and political weekly 2001a. Rev Sci Stud 3721–3732
Prasad CS (2001b, September 29) Towards an understanding of Gandhi's views on science economic and political weekly 2001b. Rev Sci Stud 3721–3732
Sarma M (2016) Development and use of open source software in India. In: Dey B, Sorour K, Filieri R (eds) ICTs in developing countries. Palgrave Macmillan, London
Shiva V, Biopiracy (1997) The plunder of nature and knowledge. South End Press
Siby K, Joseph T et al (2016) Trusteeship: a path less travelled. In: Siby BM, Joseph K (ed) Institute of Gandhian studies, Wardha, Maharashtra, India
Shankar B (2021) Why Indian farmers are so angry about the Modi government's agricultural reforms. The Conversation, 2 Feb 2021
Srinivas KR (2015) Intellectual property rights and politics of food in the Oxford handbook of food, politics, and society. Herring RJ (2015) Oxford University Press, New York, pp 381–406
Srinivas KR, Pandey P (2019) Indian perspectives on responsible innovation and frugal innovation. In: Von Schomberg R, Hankins J (ed) International handbook on responsible innovation: a global resource. Edward Elgar
Sundara Rajan T (2001) Moral rights and the protection of cultural Heritage: Amar Nath Sehgal v. Union of India
The comment on the Du Photocopying decision by Spicy IP blog. At the https://spicyip.com/resources-links/du-photocopy-case webpage. https://spicyip.com/resources-links/du-photocopy-case webpage
Tripathy JP, Verma M (2020) Impact of health warning labels on cigarettes packs in India: findings from the global adult tobacco survey 2016–17. Behavioral medicine
Weber T (2011) Gandhi's moral economics: The sins of wealth without work and commerce without morality. In: Brown J, Parel A (eds),The Cambridge companion to Gandhi. Cambridge University Press, pp 135–153
Yadav A, Nazar GP, Rawal T et al (2018) Plain packaging of tobacco products: the logical next step for tobacco control policy in India. BMJ Glob Health
(2001) Int J Cult Prop 10(1):79–94. https://papers.ssrn.com/sol3/papers.cfm?abstract_id=1805237

Chapter 26
Patent and Pandemic: Exploring Duties, Obligations and Responsibilities

Kshitij Kumar Singh

1 Introduction

In the current patent-pandemic discourse, duties become more relevant than rights to ensure manufacturing, accessibility and affordability of therapeutics, diagnostics and vaccines. The patent system reflects a balanced setup with inherent limits and flexibilities and public disclosure as the *quid pro quo* to patents. However, the current patent practices often ignore these limits and the ultimate purpose of patents, i.e. promoting scientific and technological progress and the public good. With the constant focus on exclusivity, these practices emphasise rights rather than duties, obligations and responsibilities. In the clamour of rights, duties have taken a back seat. It is a casualty to duties, which may help achieve the much-needed balance in the patent system. The duties of third parties find due appreciation while enforcing patentee's rights; however, patentee's duties are restricted to the duty to disclosure. Limiting the patentee's duties to public disclosure overshadows her other duties implicit in the patent system. It leads to a debate whether patent fits in the rigid framework of property (exclusivity being its hallmark) or it suits the framework of a social bargain between the state and the inventor, based on the law of contract? The patent system needs to be examined from the perspective of duty and public interest, focussing on the purpose of the patent.

COVID-19 has led us to rethink and redefine the current patent approaches from a global perspective in the light of global obligations, responsibilities and solidarity. It raises a pertinent question: Can a duty-based approach to patents in the COVID-19 period positively affect the manufacturing and distribution of diagnostics, therapeutics and vaccines, recognised as the global public good? Gandhi's views on property and duties find great relevance in the COVID-19 period as his trusteeship concept imposes duties on the right holder to exercise her rights in a way that promotes the

K. K. Singh (✉)
Assistant Professor, Campus Law Centre, Faculty of Law, University of Delhi, Delhi, India
e-mail: ksingh@clc.du.ac.in

R. Mittal and K. K. Singh (eds.), *Relevance of Duties in the Contemporary World*,
https://doi.org/10.1007/978-981-19-1836-0_26

public good. He considered duties as the precursor to rights, where the performance of duties automatically ensures the enforcement of rights. Therefore, a duty-based approach guided by Gandhian philosophy needs analysis in the context of patent and pandemic. Against this backdrop, the chapter analyses the jurisprudential basis of patents from the perspective of duties and public interest. It contains three crucial aspects: firstly, it enquires the nature of patents, analysing its property status, i.e. whether it fits in the rigid framework of property or not, exploring the right-duty construct, scope of exclusivity and the "public interest" integer in it; secondly, it examines the relationship between patents, pandemic and public health from a global perspective. Thirdly, the chapter contextualises the Gandhian perspective on property and duty in the current patent-pandemic discourse.

2 Conceptual Framework of Patents: Patents as Property and Right-Duty Construct

2.1 Is the Patent System Well-Proportioned?

The theoretical premise of patent system reflects a well-balanced system that incentivises patentee with a limited time monopoly in the exchange of public disclosure. Public disclosure as a *quid pro quo* for patents and the limits to patent rights such as research exemptions, compulsory licencing and governmental use seek to achieve this balance between individual incentives and the public good. Moreover, these limits attempt to streamline the patent system to achieve its ultimate goal, i.e. promoting scientific and technological progress and public good. A limited-term monopoly under patent system found appreciation by the famous economist Adam Smith, who was otherwise a great critic of monopolies and exclusive privileges:

> For if the legislature should appoint pecuniary rewards for the inventors of new machines, etc., they would hardly ever be so precisely proportioned to the merit of the invention as this is. For here, if the invention be good and such as is profitable to mankind, he will probably make a fortune by it; but if it be of no value he also will reap no benefit.[1]

Based on the practical consideration, Bentham also justified the exclusive privilege under the patent system and maintained that "an exclusive privilege is 'of all rewards the best proportioned'".[2] However, the current patent practices tilt the exclusivity under the patent system favouring the patent owner against the public good and

[1] A. Smith (1762–3) *Lectures on Jurisprudence*, Glasgow Edition of the Works of Adam Smith (eds.) R. L. eek, D. D. Raphael and P. Stein, Oxford: Oxford University Press, 1978 quoted in Helen Gubby, "Is the Patent stem a Barrier to Inclusive Prosperity? The Biomedical Perspective" 11:1 *Global Policy* 46–55 (2019) Available at https://onlinelibrary.wiley.com/doi/full/10.1111/1758-5899.12730 (last visited October 12, 2021).

[2] J. Bentham (1843) 'The Works of Jeremy Bentham', in J. Bowring (ed.), A Manual of Political Economy, Chap. 3, Vol. 3, Section 23. Edinburgh: Bowring Edition p.71 quoted in Helen Gubby, "Is the Patent System a Barrier to Inclusive Prosperity? The Biomedical Perspective" 11:1 *Global Policy*

ignoring a well-proportioned approach. The companies are using patents as strategic tools to block the competitors, defeating the very purpose of patents. Furthermore, it has raised the tension between the patent owner and the other stakeholders, giving rise to the issues of accessibility and affordability. Given its specific purpose, patents exhibit a distinct form of property guided by the policy levers, and it does not fit in the rigid framework of property. An overemphasis on exclusivity akin to other properties seems to be a wrong approach as it leads to a right-centric tendency to ignore the duties of patentee. Though few studies suggest another way around, a consistent avoidance of exclusivity element under property and non-enforcement of property rights devalue these rights.[3] Therefore, the situation demands a balanced approach to patents, well-aligned to its purpose. In this context, the chapter examines the property status of patents and the exclusivity under the patent system.

2.2 *Property Status of Patents: Patent as a Property Vis-à-Vis Patent as a Social Bargain*

Conventionally, scholars and practitioners treat patents "as property rights 'granted to encourage desirable innovation'". Srividhya Ragavan contends that this treatment cannot accommodate the limits to patent rights and the public benefit goals of the patent system adequately. She suggests that instead of treating it as a property, it should be treated as a contract—"a social bargain between the state and inventor": "By viewing the grant of a patent as a contract with the government in exchange for the patent holder providing a benefit to society, patent owners shall have duties to the society that correspond to their rights under the patent".[4] This approach to patents emphasises a patent holder's duties to society in tune with the public benefit.

Exclusivity under patent law has a well-defined purpose, i.e. promoting the public good. Traces from the sixteenth century reflect the purpose of granting patents "when Queen Elizabeth adopted a policy of granting manufacturing monopolies to industrialists and tradesmen in order to promote the economic development of the realm".[5]

46–55 (2019) Available at https://onlinelibrary.wiley.com/doi/full/10.1111/1758-5899.12730 (last visited October 12, 2021).

[3] See Jonathan M. Barnett, "The Patent System At a Crossroads" *Regulation* 44–47 (Spring, 2018) available at ttps://www.cato.org/sites/cato.org/files/serials/files/regulation/2018/3/regulation-v41n1-2.pdf (last visited October 12, 2021).

[4] Srividhya Ragavan, "Correlative Obligation in Patent Law: The Role of Public Good in Defining the Limits of Patent Exclusivity" 6 *The NYU Journal of Intellectual Property & Entertainment Law* 47 (2016). Available at: https://scholarship.law.tamu.edu/facscholar/806 (last visited October 12, 2021).

[5] Adam Mossoff, "Exclusion and exclusive use in patent law" 22:2 *Harvard Journal of Law & Technology* 321–379 (Spring 2009). Available at http://jolt.law.harvard.edu/articles/pdf/v22/22HarvJLTech321.pdf (last visited October 12, 2021).

Letter patent, a royal legal device of issuing monopoly grants, reflects "the modern convention of labelling the legal protection of an invention as a patent".[6]

Thomas Jefferson, the principal architect of the US patent law, indicates that exclusive rights conferred by patents are not natural rights. He maintained that these rights have a defined purpose of acting as "an encouragement to pursue ideas which may produce utility, but this may or may not be done, according to the will and convenience of the society, without claim or complaint from anybody".[7] It establishes that Jefferson viewed "benefit to society" as the central theme of patents. Echoing the view that public benefit is at the core of patents, the famous Statute of Monopolies also maintained that "monopolies were only tolerated when they resulted in public good".[8] Accordingly, "[t]he grant of a patent represents a 'social bargain' between the state and the inventor, whereby an inventor who discloses new and valuable technological information to the public is rewarded with a state sanctioned monopoly for twenty (20) years".[9] Therefore, a patent does not fit in the strict framework of conventional property; instead, it has all the indicia of a social bargain. This social bargain clearly imposes specific duties, obligations and responsibilities not only on third parties but on the patent holders too.

2.3 *Duties of Patentee and Public Disclosure as the* Quid Pro Quo

Patent duties have been conceptualised from the standpoint of third parties, and the duties of the patentee are limited to the duty to disclosure.[10] Except for public disclosure as the primary duty of patent owner, no other duty is explicitly provided under the patent system, which might ensure that public considerations could be prioritised over private interests Nevertheless, a patent owner owes a duty to respect a state's power of entire domain, which could be seen in the issuance of compulsory licencing. However, the current patent system does not define the obligations in the context of its larger goals and this deficiency creates an imbalance in the patent system.[11]

A patent has also been defined as a privilege, given its roots in royal privileges. Patent as privilege indicates imposition of duties too. Hohfeld specifically define a "privilege" as a positive grant by the government that limits "the ways in which

---

[6] Ibid.

[7] Ragavan, *supra* note 4.

[8] Ibid.

[9] Shamnad Basheer, "Making patents work: of IP duties and deficient disclosure" 7:1 *Queen Mary Journal of Intellectual Property* 3–24 (2017) available at https://www.elgaronline.com/view/journals/qmjip/7-1/qmjip.2017.01.01.xml?pdfVersion=true (last visited October 12, 2021).

[10] Ibid.

[11] Ragavan, *supra* note 4.

the right to exclude could be used by the property owner".[12] This is well reflected in the proposal offered by Peter Drahos about the property-based framework "for protecting the personhood of indigenous knowledge holder":

> [T]he discourse around intellectual property hark back to an earlier era when it was seen as a mere privilege (as opposed to a property right), noting that such framing would then make this set of privileges more amenable to the imposition of definite 'duties'.[13]

By implication, the privilege while imposing a duty indicates a defined purpose for which it is granted. This also puts check on the manner in which the privileges are exercised:

> ... If the purpose in creating the privilege is to fulfill some approved goal, then it should follow that the privilege holder is subject to duties not to exercise the privilege in a way that defeats the purpose for which the privilege was granted in the first place.[14]

In the Indian context, the main policy document that laid the basis of the Patents Act, 1970, the Ayyangar Committee Report noted:

> Patents must be enabled to fulfil their prime purpose, viz., being worked in the country, and as early as possible after they are granted. Where this is incapable of being achieved, the law must enable a patent to be revoked.[15]

Getting back to the royal privileges, which are considered as one of the oldest traces of patents, if we compare it with modern day patents, we register significant differences:

> One of the primary differences between the sixteenth-century royal manufacturing monopolies or letters patents and the modern day eighteenth century patents is that the former imposed on their recipients an affirmative duty to practice the trade. This aim of granting these monopolies to introduce new trades and products in the English territory and this aim could not be achieved unless the newly minted monopolies did not set up shop in England and begin employing apprentices and selling products.[16]

It establishes that "the *quid pro quo* for receiving a manufacturing monopoly in a royal letter patent was the patentee's promise to work the subject matter of the grant. If he did not work the trade, then he lost his patent".[17]

However, in the United States, the *quid pro quo* imposing "an affirmative duty on patentee to work the patent was shifted to a disclosure of the invention in the patent document by the eighteenth century".[18] In the United States, it was well established by 1790, the year in which Congress enacted the first Patent Act, that "there was no legal requirement that a patentee works his invention".[19] Like an owner of the

[12] Mossoff, *supra* note 5.

[13] Basheer, *supra* note 9.

[14] Ibid.

[15] Ibid.

[16] Mossoff, *supra* note 5.

[17] Ibid.

[18] Ibid.

[19] Ibid.

land, "an American patentee was at liberty to do nothing with his invention but sue other people to prevent them from trespassing on his rights".[20] It has become a common phenomenon in other countries too, where the *quid pro quo* of patents has been limited to public disclosure, barring few which demand working of patents as a necessary condition to sustain the patent. For instance, India moved a step further by adding a requirement for working of patents. With regard to the public disclosure, it maintains that "the disclosure even extend to the mode and manner in which patents are being worked for the greater public good".[21] As an important tool, "[t]his information can then be used to trigger compulsory licences and even patent revocations. To this extent, the Indian patent law not only grants exclusive IP rights, but also imposes a set of IP duties".[22] Indian patent law contains provisions under which, "the Controller General of Patents can direct any patentee or licensee to supply patent working information at any time".[23] Notwithstanding this power of the Controller General, "patentees or licensees have to mandatorily submit periodic statements on patent working" (Form 27 specifically requires from the patentees and licensees to furnish statements regarding working of their patent in India).[24]

2.4 Patents as Privileges Vis-à-Vis Patents as Exclusive Rights

In line with the preceding discussion, "modern patent scholars and jurists reject any use rights in patent law as they hear the echoes of the antiquated privileges granted by the English Crown, which entails a positive duty to work or manufacture the invention". Rather, they focus on exclusivity, while stating that patents necessarily secure only the right to exclude. Challenging this position, the American patent scholar, Adam Mossoff argues that "[I]t is time to reconsider whether the exclusion concept of patents is analytically flawed and whether it may have blinded modern patent jurisprudence to important conceptual and normative features of the American patent system".[25] It raises a pertinent question: can we achieve the balance in the patent system by only focussing on the exclusivity, or do we need to focus on other determinants that limit, regulate and better shape this exclusivity well in tune with the purpose of patents? The exclusivity needs to be balanced through other determinants including limits to patent rights, policy considerations governing patent law and public interest. The patent system in its static form on its own cannot do the

[20] Ibid.

[21] Basheer, *supra* note 9.

[22] Ibid.

[23] Ibid. (See Section 146(1) and 146(2) of the Patents Act 1970).

[24] Ibid.

[25] Mossoff, *supra* note 5.

due as "IP is not just but becomes so when it achieves balance".[26] Much depends on patent administrators, policymakers and interpreters to achieve, ensure and sustain this balance.

2.5 *Viability of the Patent System*

The expectation attached with patents is private return, which does not always produce net social benefits, and there is first mover advantage to "those who manage to patent first and reap unusually high rewards by being able to block subsequent innovation by other inventors". Further, barring few industries such as pharmaceuticals, a patent does not necessarily provide strong incentive to the inventive activity. Given the limited and questionable success of patents in recent times, patent opponents took the extreme position to abolish the patent system and explore an alternative to it. Though the viability and functioning of the patent system could be questioned, nevertheless, it would not be wise to abolish it as it is well-tested system for long, and it still offers a great promise for the inventors, innovators and entrepreneurs:

> Abolishing the patent system would not simply remove a tool from the inventors' and entrepreneurs' kit but probably collapse the whole ecology that had developed from and with it. For better or for worse, the patent system falls in the "too big to fail" category.[27]

So where does the real problem lie, whether patent as a system becomes less efficient to the current demands or the non-realisation of public benefit and duty-based approach that creates an imbalance in the system? A constant focus on the purpose of patent system along with duties, obligations and responsibilities is the key. Further, since every industry is different, a techno-specific approach to patent law is important. To strike a balance in the patent system "we need to move towards a more local and individualised approach to the assessment of the pros and cons of patents".[28]

The current trend of treating patent rights in its absoluteness based on exclusivity and a by-product of property ignores the larger public interest goals. Relying on the law of contract framework as the basis of patents, it imposes corresponding obligations and responsibilities on the right holder and better fit for patent law to encourage innovation without undue social cost. Under this framework, the granted rights are balanced against the corresponding obligations of the patent owner in a well-proportioned manner. It may help achieve "the public benefit goals by limiting the scope of patent exclusivity".[29] Srividhya Ragavan emphasises that "patent law needs a more balanced approach to ensure that the rights and obligations inherent to the

[26] Mario Biagioli, "Weighing intellectual property: Can we balance the social costs and benefits of patenting?" 57:1 *History of Science* 140–163 (2019). Available at https://journals.sagepub.com/doi/pdf/10.1177/0073275318797787 (last visited October 12, 2021).

[27] Ibid.

[28] Ibid.

[29] Ragavan, *supra* note 4.

system work to achieve the targeted objectives".[30] This balance can only be possible if the patentee and the public along with the patent administrators, governments and interpreters realise their respective duties, obligations and responsibilities.

3 Patents, Pandemic and Public Health

3.1 Patent Rights and Public Health

Property owners have "a right not to have their property infringed while rest of the others have a duty not to infringe; however, private property may be appropriated by the state against the will of the owner in the public interest".[31] Therefore, the state has this responsibility to look into the cases where its intervention is required to limit the exercise of ownership rights of a property holder. In this context, many countries worldwide contain limits and exceptions in their patent laws to meet the public health requirements and emergent situations such as epidemics and pandemics. Countries, which do not contain the explicit provisions, find the solution through judicially created limitations and administrative orders.[32] On the patent-public health interface, tension persists between the accessibility and affordability of essential medicines and patent incentives. This tension becomes intense with least developed countries that struggle to pay the price of drugs and lack the technological infrastructure to replicate such medicines.[33] Therefore, a duty-based approach to patents becomes more critical in the case of health crises such as epidemics and pandemics. On the international level, the responsibility lies with individual countries and global community.

3.2 Global Patent Regime and Public Health Commitment

The diminishing boundaries of trade and increasing global travel have led to the rapid transmission of novel strain of viruses at an unprecedented scale.[34] COVID-19 is unique because it affects countries worldwide and raises a global concern for all;

---

[30] Ibid.

[31] A. Samuel Oddi, "Plagues, Pandemics, and Patents: Legality and Morality" 51:1 *IDEA-The Intellectual Property Law Review* 1–45 (2011). Available at https://www.ipmall.info/sites/default/files/hosted_resources/IDEA/idea-vol51-no1-oddi.pdf (last visited October 12, 2021).

[32] Dennis D. Crouch, "Nil: The Value of Patents in A Major Crisis Such As an Influenza Pandemic" 39 *Seton Hall Law Review* 1125–1136 (2009) Available at https://scholarship.law.missouri.edu/facpubs/431/ (last visited October 12, 2021).

[33] Oddi, *supra* note 31.

[34] Phoebe Li (2013) "Rights and responsibilities in patents: a precautionary patent framework in WTO law" 35:9 *European Intellectual Property Review* 516–26 (2013). Available at https://papers.ssrn.com/sol3/papers.cfm?abstract_id=2667867 (last visited October 12, 2021).

however, the asymmetry in the structure and paying capacity makes the condition of developing and least developed countries more vulnerable, where availability is restricted to those who can afford it. On the accessibility vis-à-vis economic incentive front, "if the needed invention is denied or restricted by patents, the moral dilemma arises in the vivid form of protecting property at the expense of life and human being".[35] To address the issues of accessibility and availability, the TRIPS Agreement, along with the Doha Declaration, provides certain flexibilities, having a particular focus on public interest and public health.

Article 7 of the TRIPS Agreement describes the purpose of intellectual property rights:

> The protection and enforcement of intellectual property rights should contribute to the promotion of technological innovation and to the transfer and dissemination of technology, to the mutual advantage of producers and users of technological knowledge and in a manner conducive to social and economic welfare, and to a balance of rights and obligations.

The Article aims at balancing the rights and obligations of producers and users. This balance can only be achieved by realising the rights and obligations of IP owners, ensuring the dissemination of technology and promotion of social and economic welfare. Therefore, the Article also regulates the manner of transfer and dissemination of technology and mandates that it should be conducive to social and economic welfare and also to a balance of rights and obligations.

The principles of TRIPS Agreement contained in Article 8 emphasise "the public health and public interest":

> Members may, in formulating or amending their laws and regulations, adopt measures necessary to protect public health and nutrition, and to promote the public interest in sectors of vital importance to their socio-economic and technological development, provided that such measures are consistent with the provisions of this Agreement.

The emphasis on the terms "public health" and "public interest" in the Article indicates that "IP rights are not absolute"; therefore, "they have to be constantly adapted and fine-tuned to best serve the public and right holders in a mutually beneficial fashion".[36] The proviso as to the consistency of measures necessary to protect public health and nutrition with the provisions of the TRIPS Agreement needs a liberal interpretation so that public interest is not pitted against the individual interest. Moreover, health is also an important consideration for excluding an invention from patenting under Article 27.2 of the TRIPS Agreement.[37]

[35] Oddi, *supra* note 31.

[36] Li, *supra* note 34.

[37] See Article 27.2 of the TRIPS Agreement.

3.3 Compulsory Licence Under the TRIPS Agreement

Compulsory licence is considered as a powerful tool for access to medicine, manifested in Article 31 of the TRIPS Agreement and titled as "Other Use Without Authorisation of The Right Holder". The Article includes not only compulsory licence but also use by governments for its purposes. Article 31 runs as "[w]here the law of a member allows for other use of the subject matter of a patent without the authorization of the right holder, including use by the government or third parties authorized by the government the following provisions shall be respected:". The provisions to be respected are enumerated under Article 31, starting from Article 31 (a) to 31 (l). Article 31 (b) specifies that "such use may only be permitted if prior to such use, the proposed user has made efforts to obtain authorization from the right holder on reasonable commercial terms and conditions and that such efforts have not been successful within a reasonable period of time". However, the same provision allows a relaxation to a member "in the case of a national emergency or other circumstances of extreme urgency or in cases of public non-commercial use".[38] The terms "national emergency", "other circumstances of extreme urgency" and "public non-commercial use" are not defined in the TRIPS Agreement, and much depends on how it is interpreted.

To reaffirm "the flexibilities under the TRIPS Agreement to promote public health and access to medicine, the Doha Declaration on the TRIPS Agreement and Public Health, 2001" was introduced. It has prioritised access to essential medicines over patent rights by ensuring that "the TRIPS Agreement does not and should not prevent members from taking measures to protect public health".[39] It affirms that "the Agreement can and should be interpreted and implemented in a manner supportive of WTO members' right to protect public health and, in particular, to promote access to medicines for all".[40] One of the striking features of the Declaration is the freedom and autonomy it provides to the members not only to grant compulsory licence as a matter of right but also "to determine the grounds upon which such licences are granted".[41] The Declaration recognises that "WTO members with insufficient or no manufacturing capacities in the pharmaceutical sector could face difficulties in making effective use of compulsory licencing under the TRIPS Agreement" and called for "finding expeditious solution to this problem".[42] To this end, the Declaration expands the scope of compulsory licencing, enabling member nations to undertake and fulfil the global responsibility of access to medicine. As a result, an amendment was made in the TRIPS Agreement in 2005, allowing a country under the compulsory licencing to export patented drugs to other countries needing the drug. Furthermore, the Amendment relaxed the obligation of countries under Article 31(f) of the TRIPS Agreement, which stipulates that products made under compulsory

[38] See Article 31 of the TRIPS Agreement.

[39] Paragraph 4 of the Doha Declaration on the TRIPS Agreement and Public Health, 2001.

[40] Ibid.

[41] See paragraph 5 (b) of the Doha Declaration on the TRIPS Agreement and Public Health, 2001.

[42] Paragraph 6 of the Doha Declaration on the TRIPS Agreement and Public Health, 2001.

licencing must be "predominantly for the supply of the domestic market".[43] The Amendment of 2005 added Article 31*bis* to the Agreement, which essentially incorporated the Doha Declaration. While permitting the use of compulsory licence in various situations, the TRIPS Agreement also ensures that the remuneration must be paid to the patent holder either by the exporting or importing country.[44]

There are substantial provisions of compulsory licencing in patent laws of many countries. Countries used compulsory licences in the past to facilitate access to medicine such as for treatments for HIV/AIDS, hepatitis and cancer. However, there are potential impediments too in granting the same. Patent owners refuse to market certain products in the market of compulsory licence granting country; they refuse to invest in that country's infrastructure and seek international and domestic sanctions against the grant. Developed countries, particularly the United States, have also not been very supportive to the use of compulsory licencing by developing and least developed countries.[45] Though patent owning pharmaceutical industry has been challenging the grant of compulsory licencing, nevertheless "in the times of threatened emergency, highly developed countries have and may be expected to grant or threaten to grant compulsory licenses or equivalent".[46] As regards to the circumstances in which and the grounds on which a compulsory licencing can be issued, "despite the desire of patent owners to limit compulsory licences to very limited circumstances, the actual TRIPS provision only requires that licences be limited in scope and duration to the stated purpose".[47]

3.4 Patents and the COVID-19 Pandemic

COVID-19 has exposed the limits of patents in encouraging the production and dissemination of medical technologies. Patents fall short of success in the epidemic and pandemic period as a catalyst for investment and innovation in risky and resource-intensive sector. Pandemic does not guarantee a significant return to investment for investors in vaccine manufacturing. Though there is a strong presence of patents in vaccine production, the prospect of granting patent is of limited importance in catalysing investment in pre-outbreak vaccine R&D.[48] Patents are not the only tool of innovation policy in all the situations. It is but obvious that "patent rights will

---

[43] See Article 31(f) and 31*bis* of the TRIPS Agreement; and WTO General Council Amendment of the TRIPS Agreement (Decision of 6 December 2005) WT/L/641 8 DECEMBER 2005 available at https://www.wto.org/english/tratop_e/trips_e/wtl641_e.htm (last visited on October 12, 2021).

[44] See Article 31 of the TRIPS Agreement generally and Article 31(f), 31(h) and 31*bis* specifically.

[45] Oddi, *supra* note 31.

[46] Ibid.

[47] Ibid.

[48] Ana Santos Rutschman, "The Intellectual Property of COVID-19" (September 11, 2020). Forthcoming in Outsmarting Pandemics, Elizabeth Kirley & Deborah Porter (Eds.) (2021), *Saint Louis University Legal Studies Research Paper Series* 2020–28. Available at https://scholarship.law.slu.edu/faculty/533/ (last visited October 12, 2021).

be largely ignored during an epidemic and that any post-crisis compensation would likely be low when compared to traditional patent rewards or settlements entered under threat of injunctive relief".[49] Dennis Crouch maintains that the government will ignore any patent rights during public health crises if "(i) the patented technology will aid in resolving the crises and (ii) a favourable licence is not available".[50]

Health crises such as COVID-19 pandemic warrant expeditious regulatory approval for complex medical products like vaccines and monoclonal antibodies. In this pandemic period, the alternative producer needs immediate access to other IP-protected assets.[51] In this context, the proprietary framework for pharma/[biopharma] innovation in the COVID period may not yield satisfactory results and fails to reconcile the proprietary claims with the public health demands. Ana Santos Rutschman indicates that the siloed models of R&D along with "the nationalistic approaches to the allocation of emerging medical technologies" are prevailing in the COVID-19 period.[52] The transnational companies try to assert their exclusive right even in the said period considering it the time for business as usual. Many countries seem to deviate from their commitment to global solidarity, e.g. "Canada ordered vaccine doses six times the size of its population, the vaccine rollout is going slowly".[53] The situation suggests that the overall vaccine production scale is insufficient "to provide the promised supply to the rich countries even though they had already outbid lower-income countries by putting in large orders via Advance Market Commitment".[54]

Along comes the wave of vaccine nationalism and vaccine passport, disregarding the international guidelines on vaccine priority groups. Here, the national duty to take care goes against the commitment to international or global solidarity.[55] The variance of prices in different production sites and suppliers is another worrying issue that creates global disparity: "Global intellectual property law underpins and enables vaccine nationalism that serves neither the national nor the international publics and tips the already skewed scale of global public–private balance even more towards the interests of few private corporations and 'entrepreneurial' universities".[56] In the context of patents, the major patent offices, United States Patent and Trademark Office

---

[49] Dennis D. Crouch, "Nil: The Value of Patents in A Major Crisis Such As an Influenza Pandemic" 39 *Seton Hall Law Review* 1125–1136 (2009) Available at https://scholarship.law.missouri.edu/facpubs/431/ (last visited October 12, 2021).

[50] Ibid.

[51] MSF Briefing Document, May 2021: Compulsory Licenses, The TRIPS Waiver and Access to COVID-19 Medical Technologies, available at https://msfaccess.org/compulsory-licenses-trips-waiver-and-access-covid-19-medical-technologies (last visited October 12, 2021).

[52] Rutschman, *supra* note 48.

[53] Hyo Yoon Kang, "COVID-19: Who Is the 'Public' in IP Law That Defines Its Public Purpose? Science-The Wire, 07/03/2021 Available at https://science.thewire.in/health/covid-19-who-is-the-public-in-ip-law-that-defines-its-public-purpose/ (last visited October 12, 2021).

[54] Ibid.

[55] Ibid.

[56] Ibid.

(USPTO) and European Patent Office (EPO), have offered "an accelerated examination of patent application related to COVID-19". But the disappointing thing is that "they have not made public the contents of these applications". Here, the pertinent question is why disclosure is not made early in such an exceptional situation? Again, the reason for the non-expedited disclosure is that for many companies, the pandemic made no difference to them as they still consider it business as usual. This approach leads to "the process of capitalisation and unequal distribution of inventions through the legal institutional infrastructure that enacts the transnational patent regime".[57]

To address the COVID-19 led IP challenges, the options available under the patent system need to be analysed. Various approaches, including compulsory licencing, voluntary licencing, patent pledges, patent pools and IP waiver, are in the current discussions. They all have their merit and relevance in a given situation. It is a strategic choice of countries both at the national and international level to read the situation well and adopt the best suited approach/approaches. However, the global nature of pandemic necessitates a sense of global responsibility and solidarity among the nations to curb this menace.

3.4.1 Compulsory Licence in the COVID-19 Period

Countries consider compulsory licence an effective tool to respond to COVID-19 pandemic. Since Article 31 of the TRIPS Agreement stipulates that the government seeking to invoke compulsory licence must have authorisation of the law and procedure of that country, many countries have taken legislative measures to effectuate compulsory licencing. Countries already having laws and procedures have made it more efficient through amendments, e.g. Canada, Chile and Ecuador laid the legal groundwork for the issuance of compulsory licences to address COVID-19.[58] Israel issued a compulsory licence against AbbVie to import the generic versions of lopinavir/ritonavir from India, given the inability of AbbVie to produce a sufficient number of drugs. Pharmaceutical companies often challenge the issuance of compulsory licences against the issuing state through litigation, and this phenomenon has been continued even in the COVID-19 period. As per the Russian media reports, Gilead filed "a lawsuit before the Supreme Court of Russia challenging the compulsory licence granted on Remdesivir by the Russian government".[59]

Compulsory licencing may or may not be necessary for certain situations during the COVID-19 period: "A COVID-19 cure may turn out to be an existing drug that is no longer patented. Even if the discovered cure is patent protected, there may be drug donations, discounts, or the patent holder may offer voluntary licenses at

---

[57] Ibid.

[58] Hilary Wong, "The case for compulsory licensing during COVID-19" 10:1 *Journal of global health* (2020) Available at https://jogh.org/documents/issue202001/jogh-10-010358.pdf (last visited October 12, 2021).

[59] *Supra* note 51.

affordable rates".[60] It is a strategic choice of a government to decide after considering all the options available. For instance, in India, during the second wave of COVID-19, COVID-19-related drugs were scarce and the Supreme Court, and Delhi High Court, strongly advised the government to implement compulsory licencing provision. Though COVID-19 has created the situation where all the emergent provisions including compulsory licencing in Indian patent law could be applicable, the Government of India came up with a surprising response in its submission to the Supreme Court, indicating that "invoking the compulsory licence was not required".[61] Rather, the government maintained that non-availability of raw materials and know-how were the main constraints in making the drugs/vaccines available, which could not be addressed through additional licencing but through other measures such as executive level engagements and diplomacy. However, the government did not rule out the invocation of compulsory licences during COVID-19. It indicated that whenever and wherever the situation warrants for the invocation of compulsory licences, it will look into the matter.[62] COVID-19 has posed different situations, demanding different approaches to promote availability and accessibility of medicines and treatments, and the compulsory licence could be an effective option in a given situation. Therefore, if the situation demands the use of compulsory licence, governments must be proactive to take all the measures necessary for enabling its invocation. At the international level, countries as well as international organisations owe a responsibility to support the efforts to successfully apply compulsory licence.[63]

3.4.2 Collaborative Approaches in the COVID-19 Period

In the COVID-19 period, many strategies such as voluntary patent pledges, patent pools and pledges to procurement strategies are in place. Yet, they are time-consuming and resource-intensive that largely depends on geopolitical consideration.[64] One of the patent pledges, "Open COVID pledge", seems to be successful given the wide adoption of the same by small as well as large organisations holding excess of 250,000 patents worldwide. Japan-based Open COVID-19 declaration attracted 90 signatories who pledged close to one million patents.[65] Yet, the global efforts of patent pledges have not registered the same success. One of such global initiatives is the Costa Rica initiative backed by the WHO, the C-TAP, i.e. COVID-19 technology access pool, "a mechanism through which "knowledge, IP and data

---

[60] Wong, *supra* note 58.

[61] Shukadev Khuraijam, "Positive outlook for India's patent regime in a pandemic age" *Managing IP* 23 September 2021. Available at https://www.managingip.com/article/b1tq527x8x9p4n/positive-outlook-for-indias-patent-regime-in-a-pandemic-age (last visited October 12, 2021).

[62] Ibid.

[63] Wong, *supra* note 58.

[64] Rutschman, *supra* note 48.

[65] Jorge L. Contreras, Michael Eisen, Ariel Ganz et al., "Pledging intellectual property for COVID-19" 38 *Nature Biotechnology* 1114–1149 (2020). Available at https://www.nature.com/articles/s41587-020-0682-1#citeas (last visited October 12, 2021).

could be shared by companies, for example, by pooling existing relevant patents".[66] However, no significant pharma companies have turned up to C-TAP as the standard pharma companies still rely on the patent system and are not open to C-TAP.[67] Companies maintain that the current lot of technologies (adenovirus and mRNA technologies) are pretty new and the patent information will not be sufficient to replicate them since the patent documents are often incomplete recipes. Rather, they consider the sharing of know-how is vital for manufacturing the vaccines. However, when it comes to sharing the know-how, companies always look at what is there for them in sharing the know-how with other companies. They usually chose to keep the information secret.[68]

Another crucial global initiative aimed at equitable access to COVID-19 vaccines, COVAX, has been launched. COVAX (abbreviation of COVID-19 Vaccines Global Access) is a collaborative effort of GAVI, the Global Alliance (formerly known as the Global Alliance for Vaccines and Immunization), the Coalition for Epidemic Preparedness Innovations (CEPI) and the World Health Organization (WHO) along with UNICEF as the key delivery partner.[69] Though COVAX started with an ambitious aim of providing "fair access to COVID-19 vaccines for every country worldwide, and to give them free to the poorest", however, first 18 months have not produced the desired result:

> As richer countries roll out booster shots, 98% of people in low-income countries remain unvaccinated. Covax, described as "naïvely ambitious" by one expert, has contributed just 5% of all vaccines administered globally and recently announced it would miss its 2 billion target for 2021.[70]

The delay in delivery, communication gap/miscommunication between COVAX authorities and stakeholders, non-inclusion of organisations representing the interest of poorer nations in the top tier discussions of COVAX and in general, "insufficient inclusion and meaningful engagement of low- and middle-income countries, civil society organisations and community representatives" in COVAX have created resentment and frustration among the stakeholders.[71] Although it is the "world's first global allocation mechanism based on principles of equity and fairness", it has failed to achieve its promise.[72] The primary reasons for such failure are the

66 Kang, *supra* note 53.

67 Ibid.

68 Ibid. (For example, 'Pfizer/BioNTech have chosen to keep vaccine information secret; BioNTech has previous patents in mRNA technology').

69 World Health Organisation: "COVAX-With a fast-moving pandemic, no one is safe, unless everyone is safe" available at https://www.who.int/initiatives/act-accelerator/covax (last visited October 12, 2021).

70 Rosa Furneaux & Olivia Goldhill, "'Naïvely Ambitious': How COVAX Failed on Its Promise to Vaccinate the World" Science-The Wire 09/10/2021. Available at https://science.thewire.in/health/naively-ambitious-how-covax-failed-on-its-promise-to-vaccinate-the-world/ (last visited October 12, 2021).

71 Ibid.

72 Ibid.

failure of time bound production and delivery of vaccines by manufacturers and an overambitious/non-realistic target set up by COVAX. COVAX lacked the anticipation of contingencies. For instance, India as a contributor of vaccines to COVAX has to ban its export given the overwhelming surge of COVID-19 during second wave and there has been a significant increase in bilateral agreements to effectuate the procurement of vaccines outside of COVAX mechanism. COVAX has developed a new tactic, requesting wealthy countries with excess vaccines to donate them to the needy countries. However, the requested countries were slow to respond to this call rather "they continued to make their own deals": "In total, wealthy countries have pledged to donate roughly 785 million doses to Covax as of 24 September [2021]. But just 18% have arrived, according to data compiled by Our World in Data".[73] Nevertheless, COVAX as a global allocation mechanism for vaccines still creates hope if the lessons are learned from the deficiencies incurred during this period.

During the COVID-19 pandemic, the strategies mentioned above constitute remedial response subject to accelerated timelines and political constraints. Ana Santos Rutschman argues that if the world community has to focus upon the next pandemic, it has to strengthen these strategies on a permanent basis (e.g. translating the COVAX or pandemic patent pools into more permanent structures). All these initiatives are needed to be developed not only to take prompt measures but also to promote the notion of equity.[74] There has been a call for global solidarity. "No one is safe until everyone is safe"[75] is the statement for the global solidarity that pushes the agenda of access to medical tools to everyone at every place. The current IP practices, however, suggest that many corporations "continue to pursue secretive and limited commercial deals that exclude many low- and middle-income countries, even in the midst of the pandemic".[76] These trends go against the global solidarity and responsibility and necessitate a genuine push for the same by the global community.

3.4.3 Desirability of the IP Waiver

India and South Africa moved a proposal for "a waiver from specific provisions of the TRIPS Agreement for the prevention, containment and treatment of COVID-19 (a waiver from the implementation, application and enforcement of Sections 1,

[73] Ibid.

[74] Rutschman, *supra* note 48.

[75] UNICEF Statement: "No-one is safe until everyone is safe—why we need a global response to COVID-19" 24 May 2021 available at https://www.unicef.org/press-releases/no-one-safe-until-everyone-safe-why-we-need-global-response-covid-19 (last visited October 12, 2021).

[76] "Countries obstructing COVID-19 patent waiver must allow negotiations to start" *relief web* 09/03/202. Available at https://reliefweb.int/reportworld/coutries-obstructing-covid-19-patent-waiver-must-allow-negotiations-start (last visited October 12, 2021).

4, 5 and 7 of Part II of the TRIPS Agreement in relation to prevention, containment or treatment of COVID-19)".[77] It highlights that "[t]here are several reports about intellectual property rights hindering or potentially hindering timely provisioning of affordable medical products to the patients".[78] The proposal also refers to the other flexibilities available under the TRIPS Agreement, such as compulsory licence, stressing upon the time-consuming process and complexities attached with it.[79] The IP waiver proposed by India and South Africa includes patents, industrial designs, copyrights and undisclosed information, guarded by the TRIPS Agreement, for at least three years.[80] The proposal attracted the support of more than a hundred countries, including the USA (though its support was limited to vaccines only). However, the call for the IP waiver has not produced the intended result thus far as even "[a] year later, about 77% of the 6.41 billion vaccine doses so far administered globally have gone to people in high- and upper-middle-income countries. But the proposal remains stalled, despite the support of more than 100 countries".[81] The United States though extended its support to the waiver yet has done little to advance it. There is a need to reinstate and realise the call for global solidarity under the proposal: "[i]nternationally, there is an urgent call for global solidarity, and the unhindered global sharing of technology and know-how in order that rapid responses for the handling of COVID-19 can be put in place on a real time basis".[82]

Countries have taken contrasting positions over the IP waiver. European Union suspects that the IP waiver could make any difference in the manufacturing and access of vaccines and other support mechanisms. It considers the sharing of know-how as the major issue, which requires other measures. Countries opposing the waiver feel that IP waiver may set a bad precedent, demanding the dilution of IP rights in other health crises. They also raise the issue of quality compromise in the IP waiver as many countries cannot ensure the quality of vaccine because of the dearth of know-how and other infrastructural deficiencies.

On the other hand, the proponents of the IP waiver see the enormous benefit of the same in the pandemic situation in terms of speeding up manufacturing and taking more autonomous decisions in deciding who can manufacture for whom.[83] They expect that IP waiver would provide more autonomy to countries to produce their own vaccines against the handful of vaccine manufacturing companies. They believe

---

[77] WTO Council for Trade-Related Aspects of Intellectual Property Rights: "Waiver from certain provisions of the trips agreement for the prevention, containment and treatment of Covid-19"-communication from India and South Africa, IP/C/W/669 2 October 2020. Available at https://docs.wto.org/dol2fe/Pages/SS/directdoc.aspx?filename=q:/IP/C/W669.pdf (last visited October 12, 2021).

[78] Ibid.

[79] Ibid.

[80] Andrew Green, "Where are we on COVID-19 after a year of TRIPS waiver negotiations?" *devex* 7 October 2021 Available at https://www.devex.com/news/where-are-we-on-covid-19-after-a-year-of-trips-waiver-negotiations-101795 (last visited October 12, 2021).

[81] Ibid.

[82] *Supra* note 77.

[83] *Supra* note 76.

that the waiver proposal "may remove legal uncertainties and risks for potential producers and governments to quickly start preparing to scale up production and supply of treatments, vaccines, and other essential medical tools".[84] Against the persistent disparities among the countries, "waiving monopolies will help level the playing field in this pandemic and ensure access for all".[85] Leaving the decision of manufacturing to pharmaceutical industries on the belief that they do the right thing to secure global access to COVID-19 medical tools for people who generally need them is not yielding good results. It seems to be a risky affair as the situation demands a change in the strategy or simply, "it is time for change and not charity".[86]

3.4.4 Government's Duty to the Public and Global Public Good

In order to define the government's duty to public, we need to define what constitutes "public good"? Director General of the WHO, in his speech delivered on 12 November, 2020, emphasised that "[a]s global public goods, COVID-19 vaccines, therapeutics and diagnostics must be available on the basis of equitable and affordable access for all, especially for health workers, the elderly and other at-risk groups".[87] However, the behaviour of global pharmaceutical companies has been discouraging as the companies focus more on profit making rather than enabling access to low-income countries. These companies have been selectively delivering the vaccines to high-income countries.[88]

The patent system is supposed to serve the public and the patent owner's interest; however, given the global nature of COVID-19, we need to define who the public is? In the context of the global pandemic, the notion of "public" is not restricted to the public in an individual nation only, but it extends to the "global public". Numerous provisions and strategies are available globally, such as national arrangements of compulsory licencing for public emergency use and a general TRIPS waiver on COVID-19-related know-how and inventions, "reconceiving the public in intellectual property law's narrative as a global public".[89] Governments need to realise which publics they serve during this pandemic. They need to regulate their giant companies to go for open licences, limiting their profit margin. Otherwise, these companies find

---

[84] Ibid.

[85] Ibid.

[86] Ibid.

[87] "WHO Director-General's speech at the Paris Peace Forum Panel: ACT-A: Covid-19 Vaccines, Tests and Therapies, the Global public good Solution- 12 November 2020". Available at https://www.who.int/director-general/speeches/detail/who-director-general-s-speech-at-the-paris-peace-forum-panel-act-a-covid-19-vaccines-tests-and-therapies-the-global-public-good-solution---12-november-2020 (last visited October 12, 2021).

[88] See Rebecca Robbins, "Moderna, Racing for Profits, Keeps Covid Vaccine Out of Reach of Poor" The New York Times 9 October 2021. Available at https://www.nytimes.com/2021/10/09/business/moderna-covid-vaccine.html (last visited October 12, 2021).

[89] Kang, *supra* note 53.

little incentive to serve the global public against the great prospect to dominate the global market through proprietary claims (e.g. Pfizer projects $ 15bn in 2021 vaccine revenues alone).[90]

4 Gandhian Perspective on Property and Duty and Its Relevance in the Pandemic Period

If we consider diagnostic, therapeutic and vaccines, global public goods, as emphasised by the UNESCO[91] and WHO, Gandhi's view on property becomes very relevant. Gandhi viewed that "the resources of the world are held in common, and hence anyone who secures the bridle to control the use of resource needs to be reminded about the 'trusteeship role' that she has in the exploitation and utilization of such resources".[92] Gandhi's view on ownership is not about discrediting the owner of her possession. It does not require the dispossession of the material wealth gained by owners. Gandhi recognises the owner's capability with respect to securing the wealth amassed by her. He believes that "if the state take away the wealth from its owner, society will be the poorer, for it will lose the gifts of the person who knows how to accumulate wealth".[93] Here, Gandhi recognises the skill and talent of the owner to accumulate wealth though he attaches the purpose to the property, for which it is to be used, and the role of the government in regulating it. He emphasised:

> [T]he ideal strategy would be to retain the owners' stewardship over their possessions and to use their talent to increase the wealth, not for their own sakes, but for the sake of the nation and, therefore, without exploitation. The State would regulate the rate of commission which they would get commensurate with the service rendered and its value to society.[94]

Suppose if this could be contextualised in the realm of patents. In that case, Gandhi recognises the efforts of inventor and the ownership of patentee with the caveat that she must use it not for her own sake but for the sake of society. It is in tune with the broader goals of patents, i.e. to promote public good. Though the patent law does not explicitly prescribe how patented invention could be used, it contains limits to regulating the use of patent system to the promotion of public good.

Gandhi's trusteeship concept provides a limited space to private property as "it does not recognise any right of private ownership of property except in so far as it may be permitted by society for its own welfare". It has two distinct features:

---

[90] Ibid.

[91] "UNESCO calls for COVID-19 vaccines to be considered a global public good" 24/02/2021. Available at https://en.unesco.org/news/unesco-calls-covid-19-vaccines-be-considered-global-public-good (last visited October 12, 2021).

[92] S. Neethu, "Gandhi, Trusteeship and Intellectual Property Law" *Global Trust* 24/12/2013. Available at http://globaltrust.tau.ac.il/gandhi-trusteeship-and-intellectual-property-law/ (last visited October 12, 2021).

[93] Ibid.

[94] Ibid. (referring to *Harijan*, 31–3-1946, pp. 63–64).

> …firstly, that the concept of private property is not self-negating so long as it does not become an autocratic tool for exploitation, and secondly, that private property is not a matter of right and in its conception ought not to distance itself from the duty its possession encompasses.[95]

Though Gandhi's view of property may be contentious concerning other properties, yet it seems very relevant in the case of patents. It fits well within its framework as a social bargain, which attaches reciprocity of public good to the exclusivity. Further, regarding the enforceability of Gandhi's view of property, "Gandhi finds the solution to this in the role of the state in ensuring that the profits gained by possessors of material wealth do not outweigh the benefits it may offer to society".[96] It imposes a duty on the state to strike a balance between individual incentives and the public good through various means available to it in compulsory licencing and governmental use.

When it comes to striking a balance between property owner's interest and the interest of society, the aspect of essentialism in Gandhi's view of trusteeship becomes relevant. It demands that "right holders must place a restriction on self-interest by finding a way to discharge the fiduciary obligation they have".[97] The equitable distribution system under trusteeship philosophy emphasises on "what is essential", no more and no less: "[w]hile individuals and corporations may be required to limit self-interest in acting as a trustee; the state has an obligation to execute the will of the society and hence limit exploitation by individual right holders".[98] If we translate it in the IP framework, it indicates "less commodification and monopolistic exploitation by the right holder".[99] Though maximisation of profit is an obvious goal of a company, yet it must not be unregulated, negating obligations to society (such maximisation must not impair the interests of others).

The idea of duty is central to Gandhi's thought; he considers duties as precursor to rights. All the rights, according to Gandhi, emanate from duties only, and right is nothing but a well performed duty. His emphasis on duty as a source of right ensures the enforcement of right with a sense of self-realisation by those who owe a duty. Gandhi's view on the concept of duty creates no dichotomy between public and private duty regarding the enforcement: "Public duty was the extension of duty to oneself, and the discipline required for the performance of both types of duty was identical. From Gandhian point of view, one who had not undergone self-discipline can hardly claim to be a public servant".[100]

In the context of COVID-19, this self-discipline and sense of self-realisation find a connection with the voluntary patent pledges and voluntary licencing commitments made by pharmaceutical companies. Gandhi's concepts of duty and trusteeship can

---

95 Neethu, *supra* note 92.

96 Ibid.

97 Ibid.

98 Ibid.

99 Ibid.

100 G. N. Sarma, "Gandhi's Concept of Duty". 41:2 *The Indian Journal of Political Science*, Indian Political Science Association 214–231 (1980) Available at http://www.jstor.org/stable/41855023 (last visited October 12, 2021).

guide the IP discourse in the pandemic period. More responsible behaviour by patent owning companies, government and the public, guided by Gandhi's philosophy, can promote global solidarity against this pandemic. Though Gandhi's thoughts find relevance in COVID-19 period, yet it is surprising that Gandhi did not mention in his writing about one of the most severe pandemics of the highest magnitude occurred during his lifetime. He paid enough attention on public health instead.[101] Nevertheless, it does not belittle the relevance of his thoughts on property and duty in the current pandemic period. Therefore, Gandhi's view of trusteeship and duty can guide the IP discourse in COVID-19 period in particular and public health in general.

5 Conclusion

A duty-based approach to patents helps achieve the balance in the patent system to further its objectives. It creates a sense of realisation among all the stakeholders, including patentees, third parties and governments, regarding their respective duties, obligations and responsibilities. An overemphasis on exclusivity against the public interest deviates the patent system from its purpose to promote the public good. Based on policy considerations, a patent fits better in the framework of a social bargain than in the rigid property framework. Even if we define it as a property, undoubtedly, it is a property with a well-defined purpose. As mentioned before, "IP is not just but becomes so when it achieves balance", and in this context, the limits to patent rights recognised under the patent law need appreciation to achieve this balance. A right-centric approach cannot do the due as the method and manner of exercising the rights are as vital as the rights. Here, the role of governments, courts and executors becomes crucial to translate these limits from theory to practice and fine-tune the patent system to the broader social goals.

COVID-19 as a global pandemic provides an opportunity to raise the concerns of global responsibilities among the nations to commit themselves to global solidarity. During COVID-19, increasing collaborative agreements, voluntary licences and patent pledges, patent pools and individual commitments by the patent holders not to enforce their rights during the pandemic are encouraging signs. However, the behaviour of many pharma/biopharma companies is still alarming given their constant focus on profit-making alone, considering the pandemic period business as usual. The situation warrants that along with the self-discipline reflected in patent pledges and voluntary licencing arrangements, governments need to read the situation well and take the appropriate measures available in the form of compulsory licences, governmental use and other regulations. The IP waiver enables countries to ensure

[101] Thomas Weber & Dennis Dalton, "Gandhi and the Pandemic" 55:25 *Economic and Political Weekly* (20 June 2020). Available at https://www.epw.in/journal/2020/25/perspectives/gandhi-and-pandemic.html (last visited October 12, 2021). See also Dilip Datta, "Gandhi and an epidemic" *The Statesman* 20/10/2020. Available at https://www.thestatesman.com/opinion/gandhi-and-an-epidemic-1502929764.html (last visited October 12, 2021).

the manufacturing and distribution of vaccines in an autonomous way rather than leaving the decision to a handful of companies regarding the same. Despite WHO's call for considering diagnostics, therapeutics and diagnostics as a global public good, companies, by and large, have not shown a strong commitment regarding the call (though a piecemeal approach is apparent in the form of differential pricing of drugs in different countries). A duty-based approach may trigger a sense of global responsibility among individuals, nations and companies. Gandhi's view of property through the lens of trusteeship reflects the purpose behind the property and obligates the owner of the property to exercise her rights in a way that promotes the public good. In treating diagnostics, therapeutics and vaccines as a global public good, Gandhi's view of treating the world resources as global commons becomes relevant, ensuring equitable distribution. Further, the essentialism ('no more, no less') component of Gandhian philosophy can guide the manufacturing and distribution of vaccines so that countries accumulate them as per their need. Gandhian thought on duty as a precursor to rights may ensure better implementation of patent policies in tune with the health requirements.

References

Barnett JM (2018, Spring) The patent system at a crossroads. Regulation 44–47. Available at https://www.cato.org/sites/cato.org/files/serials/files/regulation/2018/3/regulation-v41n1-2.pdf. Last visited 12 Oct 2021

Basheer S (2017) Making patents work: of IP duties and deficient disclosure. Queen Mary J Intellect Prop 7:3–24. Available at last visited 12 Oct 2021

Biagioli M (2019) Weighing intellectual property: can we balance the social costs and benefits of patenting? History of Science 57:140–163 (2019). Available at https://journals.sagepub.com/doi/pdf/https://doi.org/10.1177/0073275318797787. Last visited 12 Oct 2021

Contreras JL, Eisen M, Ganz A et al (2020) Pledging intellectual property for COVID-19. Nat Biotechnol 38:1114–1149. Available at https://www.nature.com/articles/s41587-020-0682-1#citeas. Last visited 12 Oct 2021

Crouch DD (2009) Nil: the value of patents in a major crisis such as an influenza pandemic Seton Hall Law Rev 39:1125–1136. Available at https://scholarship.law.missouri.edu/facpubs/431/. Last visited 12 Oct 2021

Datta D (2021, October 20) Gandhi and an epidemic. The Statesman. Available at https://www.thestatesman.com/opinion/gandhi-and-an-epidemic-1502929764.html. Last visited 12 Oct 2021

Furneaux R, Goldhill O (2021, October 9) 'Naïvely Ambitious': how COVAX failed on its promise to vaccinate the world. Science-The Wire. Available at https://science.thewire.in/health/naively-ambitious-how-covax-failed-on-its-promise-to-vaccinate-the-world/. Last visited 12 Oct 2021

Green A (2021, October 7) Where are we on COVID-19 after a year of TRIPS waiver negotiations? devex. Available at https://www.devex.com/news/where-are-we-on-covid-19-after-a-year-of-trips-waiver-negotiations-101795. Last visited 12 Oct 2021

Gubby H (2019) Is the patent system a barrier to inclusive prosperity? The biomedical perspective. Glob Policy 11:46–55. Available at https://onlinelibrary.wiley.com/doi/full/https://doi.org/10.1111/1758-5899.12730. Last visited 12 Oct 2021

Kang HY (2021) COVID-19: who Is the 'Public' in IP law that defines its public purpose? Science-the wire 07/03/2021. Available at https://science.thewire.in/health/covid-19-who-is-the-public-in-ip-law-that-defines-its-public-purpose/. Last visited 12 Oct 2021

Khuraijam S (2021) Positive outlook for India's patent regime in a pandemic age. Managing IP 23 September 2021. Available at https://www.managingip.com/article/b1tq527x8x9p4n/positive-outlook-for-indias-patent-regime-in-a-pandemic-age. Last visited 12 Oct 2021

Li P (2013) Rights and responsibilities in patents: a precautionary patent framework in WTO law. Eur Intellect Property Rev 35:516–26. Available at https://papers.ssrn.com/sol3/papers.cfm?abstract_id=2667867. Last visited 12 Oct 2021

Mossof A (2009, Spring) Exclusion and exclusive use in patent law. Harvard J Law Technol 22:321–379. Available at http://jolt.law.harvard.edu/articles/pdf/v22/22HarvJLTech321.pdf. Last visited 12 Oct 2021

Neethu S (2013, December 24) Gandhi, trusteeship and intellectual property law. Glob Trust. Available at http://globaltrust.tau.ac.il/gandhi-trusteeship-and-intellectual-property-law/. Last visited 12 Oct 2021

Oddi SA (2011) Plagues, pandemics, and patents: legality and morality. IDEA Intellect Property Law Rev 51:1–45. Available at https://www.ipmall.info/sites/default/files/hosted_resources/IDEA/idea-vol51-no1-oddi.pdf. Last visited 12 Oct 2021

Ragavan S (2016) Correlative obligation in patent law: the role of public good in defining the limits of patent exclusivity. New York University J Intellect Property Entertain Law 6:47. Available at https://scholarship.law.tamu.edu/facscholar/806. Last visited 12 Oct 2021

Robbins R (2021, October 9) Moderna, racing for profits, keeps Covid vaccine out of reach of poor. The New York Times. Available at https://www.nytimes.com/2021/10/09/business/moderna-covid-vaccine.html. Last visited 12 Oct 2021

Rutschman AS (2020) The intellectual property of COVID-19 (September 11, 2020). Forthcoming in outsmarting pandemics. In: Kirley E, Porter D (eds) Saint Louis University legal studies research paper series 2020–28. Available at https://scholarship.law.slu.edu/faculty/533/. Last visited 12 Oct 2021

Sarma GN (1980) Gandhi's concept of duty. Indian J Polit Sci (Indian Political Science Association) 41:214–231.Available at http://www.jstor.org/stable/41855023. Last visited 2 Oct 2021

Weber T, Dalton D (2020, June) Gandhi and the pandemic. Econ Polit Wkly 55. Available at https://www.epw.in/journal/2020/25/perspectives/gandhi-and-pandemic.html. Last visited 2 Oct 2021

Wong H (2020) The case for compulsory licensing during COVID-19. J Glob Health 10. Available at https://jogh.org/documents/issue202001/jogh-10-010358.pdf. Last visited 12 Oct 2021

The manufacturer's authorised representative in the EU is Springer Nature Customer Service Centre GmbH, Europaplatz 3, 69115 Heidelberg, Germany. If you have any concerns regarding our products, please contact ProductSafety@springernature.com

Printed and bound by CPI Group (UK) Ltd, Croydon, CR0 4YY
30/09/2026
02225237-0013